Fundamentals of
Parallel
MULTICORE
Architecture

Chapman & Hall/CRC
Computational Science Series

SERIES EDITOR

Horst Simon
Deputy Director
Lawrence Berkeley National Laboratory
Berkeley, California, U.S.A.

PUBLISHED TITLES

COMBINATORIAL SCIENTIFIC COMPUTING
Edited by Uwe Naumann and Olaf Schenk

CONTEMPORARY HIGH PERFORMANCE COMPUTING: FROM PETASCALE
TOWARD EXASCALE
Edited by Jeffrey S. Vetter

CONTEMPORARY HIGH PERFORMANCE COMPUTING: FROM PETASCALE
TOWARD EXASCALE, VOLUME TWO
Edited by Jeffrey S. Vetter

DATA-INTENSIVE SCIENCE
Edited by Terence Critchlow and Kerstin Kleese van Dam

THE END OF ERROR: UNUM COMPUTING
John L. Gustafson

FUNDAMENTALS OF MULTICORE SOFTWARE DEVELOPMENT
Edited by Victor Pankratius, Ali-Reza Adl-Tabatabai, and Walter Tichy

FUNDAMENTALS OF PARALLEL MULTICORE ARCHITECTURE
Yan Solihin

THE GREEN COMPUTING BOOK: TACKLING ENERGY EFFICIENCY AT LARGE SCALE
Edited by Wu-chun Feng

GRID COMPUTING: TECHNIQUES AND APPLICATIONS
Barry Wilkinson

HIGH PERFORMANCE COMPUTING: PROGRAMMING AND APPLICATIONS
John Levesque with Gene Wagenbreth

HIGH PERFORMANCE PARALLEL I/O
Prabhat and Quincey Koziol

HIGH PERFORMANCE VISUALIZATION:
ENABLING EXTREME-SCALE SCIENTIFIC INSIGHT
Edited by E. Wes Bethel, Hank Childs, and Charles Hansen

PUBLISHED TITLES CONTINUED

Fundamentals of Parallel
MULTICORE
Architecture

Yan Solihin

Solihin Publishing and Consulting, LLC
Raleigh, North Carolina, USA

CRC Press
Taylor & Francis Group
Boca Raton London New York

CRC Press is an imprint of the
Taylor & Francis Group, an **informa** business
A CHAPMAN & HALL BOOK

CRC Press
Taylor & Francis Group
6000 Broken Sound Parkway NW, Suite 300
Boca Raton, FL 33487-2742

First issued in paperback 2020

© 2016 by Yan Solihin
CRC Press is an imprint of Taylor & Francis Group, an Informa business

No claim to original U.S. Government works

ISBN 13: 978-0-367-57528-1 (pbk)
ISBN 13: 978-1-4822-1118-4 (hbk)

Visit the Taylor & Francis Web site at
http://www.taylorandfrancis.com

and the CRC Press Web site at
http://www.crcpress.com

To my wife, Liehwa Lim, and my two daughters, Tiffany Tang and Megan Tang.

Contents

Preface

Starting roughly 10 years ago, the landscape of processor design changed in a significant way. On the surface, nothing major seems to have changed: transistor density kept growing according to Moore's Law, doubling every 18-24 months. Upon closer inspections, things have changed dramatically. Once growing at the same rate as Moore's law, the growth in processor clock frequency stalled. Processor manufacturers switched their design en masse from a single core on a die, to multiple cores on a die, popularly known as *multicore*. The development of these multicore chips marked an important shift in the processor industry. From the physics side, the switch to multicore was motivated by the intolerable power density growth that came from making a single core processor more powerful (deeper or wider pipeline design). This was the second time processor design bumped into hard physical constraints of power consumption, the first time resulting in a switch from bipolar transistors to the more power-efficient CMOS transistors. This time there was no power-efficient alternative for CMOS transistors, thus the power constraints had to be absorbed by changes to the architecture, from single core to multicore design. While parallel architectures have been present for a long time, with multicore, parallel architectures have become mainstream.

From the processor designers' perspectives, performance growth could in theory be kept going for a long time by first switching to multicore and then by growing the number of cores on a die. From the programmers' perspective, however, the switch to multicore had a very important consequence: the growth in performance is now predicated on the ability of the programmers in making their code parallel, and tuning their parallel code to scale well with the number of cores. Prior to multicore, programmers could focus solely on increasing programmability or the level of programming abstraction at the expense of code complexity and execution inefficiency, knowing that the processor core would become faster and more than negate the increase in complexity and inefficiency. Now, however, programmers have to worry about how to write their programs to take advantage of the parallelism provided by multicore, if they want to overcome the adverse performance impact coming from increasing programmability and the level of abstraction. In other words, parallel programming and tuning have become necessary skills for many programmers.

Despite multicore having become a mainstream architecture, at the time of this book's writing, there are hardly any textbooks that cover parallel multicore architectures. There are many existing textbooks on parallel programming, and there are several textbooks on traditional parallel architectures. There are also several synthesis lectures on specific topics related to multicore architectures. But the author could not find textbooks on multicore architectures. This hole provided the author the motivation to write this book. The author hopes that instructors who currently teach computer architecture will find this book useful in providing materials for covering multicore architectures. The author also hopes this book enables some instructors who are not currently teaching multicore architecture to offer such a course. Finally, the author hopes that professionals dealing with programming on multicore or designing multicore chips will find this book useful as a reference.

There are big challenges that the author faced while writing this book. First, the pace of change in microprocessor technology has been rapid. Some of the topics covered in this book have been a moving target, prompting multiple rewrites by the author. For example, at the start of the writing, a typical multicore had two cores which share the L2 cache, while at the end of the writing, the number of cores on a die has grown to 16, with deeper and more complicated memory hierarchy. It has been challenging to write about a technology that changes so rapidly. Another big challenge is that there are simply a lot more topics to cover than what the author can write within the length of a textbook. Thus, the author has had to make many decisions on what topics to include and what topics to exclude. Regrettably, this book cannot be all things to all readers. Some readers may find their favorite topics missing or not receiving deep coverage. However, what the author has attempted to do is to cover fundamental topics that hopefully act as a springboard for readers to continue reading other materials. The author believes that the textbook prepares readers well to continue reading research papers in the multicore architecture area.

This book is built on the predecessor textbook "Fundamentals of Parallel Computer Architecture: Multichip and Multicore Systems" written by the author and published in 2009. Compared to the predecessor textbook, this book not only has significantly expanded the coverage of the multicore-specific topics, it has also made multicore architectures the center of the discussion.

The book was written with the following philosophies in mind. First, the material is intended for graduate students, senior undergraduate students, or professionals who have had prior computer science or engineering training. Some basic concepts from operating system (processes, threads, virtual memory) and basic computer organization (instruction sets, register files) are discussed in a manner that assumes that readers already know them and only need a refresher.

Second, when introducing a concept, the author has tried to start by building an intuition and understanding of the problem that lead to the need for the concept. As a consequence, while to some the writing may appear a bit verbose, others may appreciate the intuition and clarity.

Third, with a few exceptions, chapters in the book are designed to be relatively short, so that readers do not find it overwhelming to read each chapter in one weekend. The author hopes that students will be encouraged to read the entire book, and even if they skip parts of the book, we hope that they will skip entire chapters rather than parts of a chapter. To reach the short chapter length goal, the author breaks down the content into a larger number of chapters than a typical textbook in the field. For example, the cache coherence coverage is split into three chapters: one that introduces the problem (Chapter 6), one that covers broadcast cache coherence protocols (Chapter 7), and one that covers directory cache coherence protocols and more advanced topics (Chapter 10).

Fourth, the author has made serious attempts to make the book engaging to read. One unique feature is "Did you know?" boxes scattered through the text that present mini case studies, alternative points of view, examples, or other interesting facts or discussion items. Another unique feature is the inclusion of interviews with experts in parallel multicore architectures to capture their perspectives on multicore architectures in the past, at the present, and in the future. These interviews may mention technologies that may be speculative, but may also be promising and thought-provoking. Readers are invited to not accept the positions of the author and interviewees verbatim, but instead use them as a springboard to formulate their own thinking based on the concepts given in the book.

The book will also have supplemental parts online. Programming assignments and solutions that can enhance readers' understanding will be posted online.

Organization of this Book

After the author's perspectives on multicore architectures (Chapter 1), the book is organized into three parts. The first part includes Chapters 2–4. It deals with programming issues in shared memory multiprocessors, such as the programming model, techniques to parallelize regular and irregular applications. The goal of the first part is to give readers perspectives on what software primitives may be important and what hardware support may be needed to support them. The goal of the first part is not to give readers a comprehensive discussion of parallel programming, as there are already many textbooks that cover parallel programming.

The second part includes Chapters 5–11. It is the heart of this textbook. It deals with the architectures for shared memory multiprocessors: introduction to memory hierarchy, basic problems when designing shared memory parallel multiprocessor, cache coherence, memory consistency, synchronization, and interconnection network. The final chapter in this part (Chapter 12) is contributed by the author's colleague Huiyang Zhou. It deals with single-instruction multiple-thread (SIMT) programming model, which is often used in graphics processing unit (GPU) system.

The last part of the book contains a chapter of interviews with experts in the multicore architecture. The author is glad to bring the following experts contributing to the book through an interview:

- Josep Torrellas, contributing his views on parallel multicore architectures

- Li-Shiuan Peh on network on chip design

- Youfeng Wu on compilation for parallel multicore architectures

- Paolo Faraboschi on future memory and storage architectures of data centric systems

Suggested Curriculum

The book contains more materials than what can be covered in a typical three credit hour semester-long course. Consequently, there are different ways of using the materials in this textbook to cover such a course, depending on which topics an instructor chooses to emphasize. The residual materials can be used as significant parts of a separate course, possibly a more advanced graduate course. At North Carolina State University, the author places a stronger emphasis on hardware topics, and the curriculum is as shown in the left column of the following graph. A more software-focused coverage is also possible and is shown in the right column of the following graph. In both columns, the top set of boxes contain materials suitable for an introductory graduate course and is suitable for a three credit hour semester-long course. The bottom set of boxes contain materials suitable for a separate, more advanced, graduate course.

In the author's experience, when the hardware-focused curriculum is used, the parallel programming portion takes up approximately one third of a semester, while the parallel architecture portion takes up the remaining two thirds of a semester.

More HW-focused

Perspective Chapter 1

Parallel Programming Chapter 2 Chapter 3

Parallel Architecture Chapter 5 (5.1 - 5.4, 5.8) Chapter 6 Chapter 7 (7.1 - 7.4) Chapter 8 (8.1 - 8.2) Chapter 9 Chapter 10 (10.1 - 10.3) Chapter 11

↓

Advanced Graduate Topics

Parallel Programming Chapter 4

Parallel Architecture Chapter 5 (5.5 - 5.7) Chapter 7 (7.5) Chapter 8 (8.3) Chapter 10 (10.4 - 10.5) Chapter 11

More SW-focused

Perspective Chapter 1

Parallel Programming Chapter 2 Chapter 3 Chapter 4

Parallel Architecture Chapter 5 (5.1 - 5.4, 5.8) Chapter 6 Chapter 7 (7.1 - 7.4) Chapter 8 Chapter 9

↓

Advanced Graduate Topics

Parallel Architecture Chapter 5 (5.5 - 5.7) Chapter 7 (7.5) Chapter 10 Chapter 11

Acknowledgement

The author thanks the students from the Fall 2006 course CSC/ECE 506 at NCSU for motivating the author to embark on writing the predecessor of this book. The author thanks students from CSC/ECE 506 in subsequent semesters for their feedback and encouragement to write this book. The author also thanks all his past PhD students who have encouraged him to complete the project: Mazen Kharbutli (graduation: 2005), Seongbeom Kim (2007), Fei Guo (2008), Brian Rogers (2009), Xiaowei Jiang (2009), Siddhartha Chhabra (2010), Fang Liu (2011), Ahmad Samih (2012), Anil Krishna (2013), Devesh Tiwari (2013), and Ganesh Balakrishnan (2013). The authors would like to acknowledge the contribution of experimental results from studies by Fang Liu, Ahmad Samih, Brian Rogers, Xiaowei Jiang, Sharad Bade, Asaf Ebgi, and Venkata.

About the Author

 **Yan Solihin** is a Professor of Electrical and Computer Engineering at North Carolina State University. He obtained his B.S. degree in computer science from Institut Teknologi Bandung in 1995, B.S. degree in Mathematics from Universitas Terbuka Indonesia in 1995, M.A.Sc degree in computer engineering from Nanyang Technological University in 1997, and M.S. and Ph.D. degrees in computer science from the University of Illinois at Urbana-Champaign in 1999 and 2002. He is a recipient of 2010 and 2005 IBM Faculty Partnership Award, 2004 NSF Faculty Early Career Award, and 1997 AT&T Leadership Award. He is listed in the HPCA Hall of Fame, tied for the second position (as of 2015). He is a senior member of the IEEE.

He has engaged in teaching of computer architecture since 2002. His research interests include computer architecture, computer system modeling methods, and image processing. He has published more than 50 papers in computer architecture and performance modeling. His past research has been supported by the National Science Foundation, Intel, IBM, Samsung, Tekelec, Sun Microsystems, and HP. He has released several software packages to the public: ACAPP - a cache performance model toolset, HeapServer - a secure heap management library, Scaltool - parallel program scalability pinpointer, and Fodex - a forensic document examination toolset. He has written a graduate-level textbook titled *Fundamentals of Parallel Computer Architecture: Multichip and Multicore Systems*, which is the predecessor of this book.

At North Carolina State University, he founded and leads the Architecture Research for Performance, Reliability, and Security (ARPERS) group. He has graduated 13 Ph.D. students and 8 Master's degree students and is currently advising 5 Ph.D. students.

List of Abbreviations

AAT Average Access Time, referring to a metric that represents the mean of time to access the memory hierarchy.

CCR communication-to-computation ratio, referring to the amount of communication of a thread divided by the amount of computation of the thread. The parameters are the number of processors and the input size.

CISC Complex Instruction Set Computer, referring to an instruction set architecture (ISA) which has relatively complex instructions that can perform several simple operations in one instruction. For example, an instruction in CISC may involve multiple addressing modes, accessing both register and memory operands, etc.

CMP Chip Multi-Processors, referring to multiple processor cores implemented in a single chip. Also referred to as multicore processors.

COMA Cache-Only Memory Architecture, referring to a multiprocessor architecture in which the main memory is organized like a cache, supporting cache-like placement, replication, and eviction.

DMA Direct Memory Access, referring to a device that can transfer data in and out of the memory (main memory or on-chip scratch memory) without involving the processor. The processor is only interrupted at the completion of the transfer.

DRAM Dynamic Random Access Memory, referring to a type of memory that can be accessed randomly but loses its content over time. DRAM cells need to be refreshed periodically to keep its content.

DSM Distributed Shared Memory, referring to a multiprocessor architecture in which nodes have their local memories that abstracted as a single shared memory. Also referred to as NUMA.

FSM Finite State Machine, referring to a machine that has states and transitions from one state to another state. The transition in an FSM depends only on the type of event and the current state.

HTM Hardware Transactional Memory, referring to a hardware mechanism for supporting a transactional memory programming model.

ILP Instruction Level Parallelism, referring to a parallelism that exists at the level of instructions, in which different instructions from a sequential flow are executed in parallel because they are speculated or discovered to be independent from one another.

ITG Iteration-space Traversal Graph, referring to a graphical representation of the order of traversal in the iteration space. ITG shows the order in which an iteration is visited before another.

LDG Loop-carried Dependence Graph, referring to a graph that shows true, anti, and output dependences graphically, in which a node is a point in the iteration space and the directed edge shows the direction of the dependence.

LDS Linked Data Structures, referring to a data structure that consists of nodes that are linked by pointers. Examples include linked lists, hash tables, trees, and graphs.

LINPACK refers to a parallel benchmark containing a library of numerical linear algebra. Linpack is a benchmark used for ranking the performance of top supercomputers in www.top500.org.

LL Load Linked or Load Locked, referring to a load instruction that is linked to a specific address. LL is paired up with a matching store conditional (SC) instruction. LL is used for implementing other basic primitives such as atomic instructions and locks.

LRC Lazy Release Consistency, referring to a relaxed memory consistency model where values written prior to the release synchronization are propagated together with the propagation of the release synchronization itself.

LRU Least Recently Used, referring to a replacement policy in caches in which the cache block that was accessed the farthest back in the past is selected to be evicted to make room for a new block.

MESI refers to a cache coherence protocol that keeps four states for a cache block: Modified, Exclusive, Shared, and Invalid.

MIMD Multiple Instruction Stream Multiple Data Stream, referring to multiple processing elements executing different instruction streams and the instructions execute different data. MIMD is the most flexible machine in the category of machines under the Flynn's taxonomy.

MISD Multiple Instruction Stream Single Data Stream, referring to an architecture in which multiple processing elements execute from a single instruction stream, and data is passed from one processing element to the next. MISD is one category of machines under the Flynn's taxonomy.

MLP Memory Level Parallelism, referring to the overlap between multiple accesses to the main memory.

MOESI refers to a cache coherence protocol that keeps five states for a cache block: Modified, Owned, Exclusive, Shared, and Invalid.

MPI Message Passing Interface, referring to an application programming interface (API) standard for expressing parallelism where processes interact with each other through explicit messages.

MSHR Miss Status Handling Register, referring to a register that tracks the status of a cache miss, in order to facilitate waking up the load instruction that causes the cache miss, or to merge a written value to the block before it is stored in the cache. MSHRs allow multiple cache misses to be serviced simultaneously.

MSI refers to a cache coherence protocol that keeps three states for a cache block: Modified, Shared, and Invalid.

NINE Non-Inclusive Non-Exclusive, referring to a policy on a cache where the cache enforces neither inclusion nor exclusion.

NUMA Non-Uniform Memory Architecture, referring to a multiprocessor architecture in which nodes have their local memories that abstracted as a single shared memory. Also referred to as DSM.

OOO Out of Order, referring to a technique to exploit parallelism among instructions by issuing instructions out of the program order, based on other criteria such as whenever their operands are ready.

OpenMP refers to an application programming interface (API) standard for expressing parallelism at the program source code. OpenMP includes a platform-independent language extension for Fortran/C/C++, a library, and a run-time system.

OS Operating System, a software layer between the hardware and applications. It manages hardware, gives an abstraction of the machine to applications, and protects one application from another.

PARSEC Princeton Application Repository for Shared-memory Computers, a collection of shared memory parallel benchmarks consisting of primarily emerging non-scientific computing applications.

PC Processor Consistency, referring to a memory consistency model that is almost as strict as sequential consistency, but allows a younger load to bypass an older store.

RC Release Consistency, referring to a memory consistency model that allows reordering of memory accesses except at synchronization boundaries, and the synchronization accesses are distinguished between acquire and release accesses.

RISC Reduced Instruction Set Computer, referring to an instruction set architecture (ISA) which has relatively simple instructions that are amenable to pipelining.

SC refers to either Store Conditional instruction, or Sequential Consistency model. Store conditional instruction is matched with a load link (LL) instruction to provide an effect of atomicity in a sequence of instructions. SC fails when the address linked by an earlier load link mismatches the address in SC when the SC is executed.

SC refers to either Store Conditional instruction, or Sequential Consistency model. Sequential consistency model refers to a model of the ordering of memory accesses that corresponds the closest to programmers' expectation.

SIMD Single Instruction Stream Multiple Data Stream, referring to a parallel architecture in which a single instruction operates on multiple data. SIMD is one category of machines under the Flynn's taxonomy.

SISD Single Instruction Stream Single Data Stream, referring to an architecture in which a processing element executes from a single stream of instructions, and each instruction operates on a single data stream. SISD is one category of machines under the Flynn's taxonomy.

SMP Symmetric Multi-Processing, referring to a multiprocessor system in which the latency to access the main memory from any processor is uniform. SMP often refers to a bus-based multiprocessor.

SMT Simultaneous Multi-Threading, referring to a processor architecture in which a single processor core can execute multiple threads simultaneously. Most processor resources can be shared by the thread contexts, with the exception of thread-specific structures such as program counters and stack pointers.

SPEC Standard Performance Evaluation Corporation, a non-profit corporation formed to establish, maintain and endorse benchmark suites for evaluating the performance of computers. One such suite is the SPEC CPU 2006, a collection of benchmarks to evaluate the performance of the processor and cache memories.

SRAM Static Random Access Memory, referring to a type of memory that can be accessed randomly and does not lose its content over time.

STM Software Transactional Memory, referring to a software mechanism for supporting a transactional memory programming model.

TLB Translation Lookaside Buffer, referring to an on-chip storage that keeps most recent virtual-to-physical address translation. TLB is used in conjunction with the OS page table to support OS memory management functions.

TM Transactional Memory, referring to a programming model that allows programmers to specify sections of code that should be executed atomically (i.e., all-or-nothing execution) and in isolation (i.e., the result of executing transactions in parallel is identical to executing them sequentially).

WO Weak Ordering, referring to a consistency model that allows memory accesses to be reordered except at synchronization points.

Chapter 1

Perspectives on Multicore Architectures

Contents

This book is about parallel multicore architectures. What is a multicore architecture? A multicore architecture is an architecture where multiple processor *cores* are integrated on a single die [1]. A processor core is also popularly referred to as a central processing unit (CPU). A processor core or CPU typically refers to a processing element capable of independently fetching and executing instructions from at least one instruction stream. As such, a core typically includes logic such as instruction fetch unit, program counter, instruction scheduler, functional units, register file, etc. Beyond that, what other components a core includes is less clearcut. To many, a small memory closely integrated with the core, the level 1 (L1) cache, is considered a part of the core. To some, the level 2 (L2) cache is considered a part of a core because it is private to the core. The term "processor" is not consistently used. Sometimes it is used to refer to the die where the cores are located. Sometimes it is used to refer to the CPU. To avoid confusion, in this book I will restrict the term "core" to include *only the CPU, without the L1 and L2 caches*, and the term "processor" to refer to *any CPUs without considering any specific cores*. To refer to the die or chip, this book will use the term "processor die" or "processor chip".

An example of a recent multicore die is shown in Figure 1.1. The figure shows 16 cores integrated on a die, sharing eight L3 cache banks interconnected to the cores with a crossbar. Note that the figure implicitly places the L1 and L2 caches as parts of cores.

A parallel architecture refers to an architecture where multiple CPUs are tightly coupled so that they can work together to solve a single problem. Throughout the history of computer systems,

---

[1] Some people distinguish multicore with manycore depending on the number of cores integrated on a die. We will use the term multicore to include both, regardless of how many cores are integrated on a die.

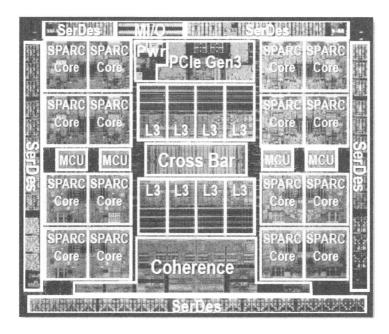

Figure 1.1: Die photo of Oracle T5 multicore, showing 16 cores on a die.

parallel computers have been an important class of computers. A parallel computer, by combining a large number of processing elements (CPUs) into a single system, allows a large computation to be carried out faster by orders of magnitude. Scientists and engineers have relied on parallel computers to solve important scientific questions by running simulations on them. Parallel computers have contributed to the fast pace of scientific discovery and engineering innovations. Over time, parallel computers have found a broader audience. For example, corporations rely on mining data from a large collection of databases, which is a very computation intensive process. Businesses rely on data analytics and transaction processing on parallel computers, while internet search engine providers use parallel computers to rank web pages and evaluate their relevance based on a search criteria. Game players demand games that show more realistic simulation of physical phenomena and realistic rendering of three-dimensional images. In short, there have been needs for parallel computers, and there will be even more needs for them in the future.

A multicore architecture is a relatively recent design, having emerged only in the last decade of four decades of microprocessor history. In the next section, I will discuss what factors prompted microprocessor designers to start designing the multicore architecture.

1.1   The Origin of the Multicore Architecture

The emergence of the multicore architecture marked an important turning point in the evolution of parallel computer architectures. They evolved from the architecture of big, powerful, and expensive computer systems to multicore systems in the mainstream architecture of servers, desktops, and even mobile devices such as cell phones. Prior to 2001, parallel computers were mainly used in servers and supercomputers. Client machines (desktops, laptops, and mobile devices) were single-core systems. For various reasons that will be discussed in more details later, 2001 marked a turning point when the first multicore chip, the IBM Power4, was shipped. The Power4 chip was the first non-embedded microprocessor that combined two cores on a single die, and the cores are integrated tightly to support parallel computation. The three decades prior to 2001 saw a design approach where a single core became more complex and faster, and the decade since 2001 has seen a design approach where multiple processor cores are implemented in a single chip. At the time of the writing of this book, an 8-core IBM Power7 is in the market, while an 8-core Intel Haswell chip is being readied for production. What has caused this transition from a single-core to a multicore design?

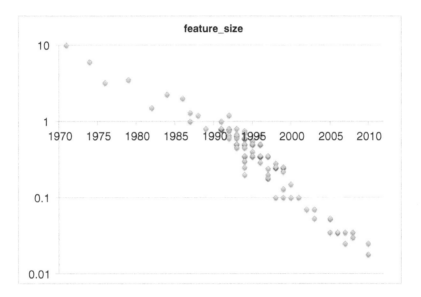

Figure 1.2: Feature size of transistors from 1971 to 2010 in μm.
Source: cpuDB [16].

One of the enabling trends for the move to multicore architectures has been the increasing minia-turization of transistors, through which more and more transistors can be packed in a single die. The pace for this transistor integration has been staggering. For decades, it has followed a prediction made by Intel co-founder Gordon Moore in 1965 that the number of transistors that can be manu-factured inexpensively in a single integrated circuit (IC) would double every two years. Figure 1.2 plots the feature size of microprocessors from 1971 to 2010 in μm on a logarithmic y-axis scale. Note that $1\mu m$ is equivalent to 10^{-6} meters, and is sometimes referred to as micron. The feature size refers to a dimension in photolitography that is closely related with the transistor gate length. The feature size of a transistor needs to shrink by about 30% in order for a constant die area to fit twice as many transistors, because transistors are two dimensional.

The figure shows that indeed, in the last 40 years, there has been an exponential shrinking of the feature size. Interestingly, it was slower in the first two decades than the last two decades. From 1971 to 1992, the feature size decreased by 30% roughly every three years. However, from 1993 to 2010, the feature size has decreased by 30% roughly every 18 months. This staggering growth has resulted in a phenomenal increase in the number of transistors implemented on a single microprocessor die, from 2,300 in 1971 to 2.3 billion in 2012, a phenomenal 1,000,000 × increase.

> ■ *Did you know?*
>
> While feature size scaling is the major reason for the increase in number of tran-
> sistors on a die, there are other factors at play. The number of transistors per die
> has increased far faster than feature size scaling. One factor causing this is the die
> size, which has increased from 103 mm^2 in Intel 386 to up to 296 mm^2 in Intel Core
> i7. The increase in die area size was likely enabled by the increase in manufacturing
> process which has increased yield (number of good dies out of the total dies manu-
> factured) even as the die area increased. A second factor is the increase in transistor
> density from better routing due to the increase in the number of metal layers from 2
> to 10 or more in recent fabrication (IBM Power7+ has 13 metal layers). A third factor
> is more of the die area has been allocated to denser structures such as caches. All
> these three factors contributed to a fourfold increase in transistor density beyond what
> was provided by feature size scaling alone, for the 25 years since the release of Intel
> 386 [17].

For a historical look at how fast transistor integration changes processor architectures, Table 1.1 shows an example of Intel processors developed from 1971 to 2006. Other manufacturers, such as Motorola, AMD, IBM, etc. also showed significant changes in processor architectures during the same time period. During that same time period, the clock frequency of the processor has also grown from 750KHz to 3.5 GHz, representing a $4,667\times$ increase, while the width of the processor has increased from 8 bits to 64 bits. The number of transistors on a die increased by six orders of magnitude, from a few thousand in 1971 to a few billion in 2012. Such increase in the number of transistors on a die has not been wasted: processor designers have increasingly added performance-enhancing features as well as new functionalities to the processor chip. For example, virtual memory and protection, considered some of the key features of modern operating systems, were added to the Intel 80286 (and other processors such as Motorola 68030 and Zilog Z280). Pipelining, floating point unit integration, on-chip caches, dynamic branch prediction, considered as fundamental techniques for enhancing the performance of microprocessors, were introduced in 386, 486, and the Pentium chips. In 2006, Intel Xeon integrated two cores on a die. Most recently, Intel Sandy Bridge chips integrated graphics processing on die, along with sophisticated power management techniques such as the TurboBoost.

> ■ *Did you know?*
>
> From 1971 to 2000 the number of transistors on a chip has increased by a factor
> of 18,260. The clock frequency has increased by a factor of 18,519. This represents
> a phenomenal annual growth rate of approximately 40%.
> Gordon Moore once joked, "If the automobile industry advanced as rapidly as the
> semiconductor industry, a Rolls Royce would get a half million miles per gallon and it
> would be cheaper to throw it away than to park it."

One interesting question with the doubling of the number of transistors on a die every 1.5 to 3 years is: why were some features implemented earlier than others? The question is important to analyze if we want to understand why integrating multiple cores on a die occurred in 2001, three decades after Intel 486, which was much later compared to other types of integration (see Table 1.1). At first, transistor integration was used to move components of a single processor that did not fit on chip into the chip. For example, Intel 486 integrated the floating point unit (FPU)

Table 1.1: Evolution of Intel processors. Other chipmakers also enjoyed a similar transistor integration progress scaling according to Moore's law.

Year	Processor	Specifications	New Features
1971	4004	740 KHz, 2300 transistors, $10\mu m$, 640B addressable memory, 4KB program memory	
1978	8086	16-bit, 5–10MHz, 29,000 transistors at $3\mu m$, 1MB addressable memory	
1982	80286	8–12.5MHz	Virtual memory and protection mode
1985	386	32-bit, 16-33MHz, 275K transistors, 4GB addressable memory	Pipelining
1989	486	25-100MHz, 1.2M transistors	FPU integration
1993	Pentium	60–200MHz	On chip L1 caches, SMP support
1995	Pentium Pro	16KB L1 caches, 5.5M transistors	Out-of-order execution
1997	Pentium MMX	233-450MHz, 32KB L1 cache, 4.5M transistors	Dynamic branch prediction, MMX instruction sets
1999	Pentium III	450-1400MHz, 256KB L2 cache on chip, 28M transistors	SSE instruction sets
2000	Pentium IV	1.4-3GHz, 55M transistors	Hyper-pipelining, SMT
2006	Pentium Dual-Core	64-bit, 2GHz, 167M transistors, 4MB L2 cache on chip	Dual core, virtualization support
2011	Sandy Bridge (i7)	64-bit, up to 3.5GHz, 2.37B transistors, up to 20MB L3 cache	Graphics processor, TurboBoost

on chip. Previously, floating point computation was performed by a co-processor. Then, as more and more transistors could be integrated on a chip, the processor was augmented with features that exploited parallelism at the instruction level, such as pipelining (Intel 386), out-of-order execution (Intel Pentium Pro), and dynamic branch prediction (in the Intel Pentium MMX). Since the speed of main memory was not keeping up with the growth of speed of the processor, it was necessary to introduce memory hierarchy, where a smaller memory was integrated on chip for faster data access. It started with the integration of first level (L1) data and instruction caches in Intel Pentium, a second level (L2) cache in Intel Pentium III, and a third level (L3) cache in Intel Sandy Bridge.

Hence, why is it that integration of multiple cores on a die lose out in utilizing the abundance of transistors for other things discussed above: FPU integration, caches, pipelining, out-of-order execution, and even vector instruction sets? Surely someone in the microprocessor industry had thought of integrating multiple cores on a die ahead of caches or pipelining. In fact, the intensity of parallel computer research in the past demonstrated that researchers did consider placing multiple cores on a die early. In addition, there have been multiple components that were integrated on a die *after* multicore, such as memory controllers, the level 3 cache, accelerators, embedded DRAM, etc. Thus, it seems that there is a good explanation why integration of various components on a die followed the path that they followed.

I believe an appropriate explanation can be made based on the low hanging fruit theory. For a hypothetical fruit tree, the farmer picks up the lowest hanging fruits first because they require the least effort to pick. As the lowest hanging fruits are picked up, higher hanging fruits are picked up next, and so on, until the most difficult to get fruits are finally picked up. If we analyze the components integrated on a die prior to multicore, they were essentially components of a single core. They accelerate the execution of a single thread, with instructions from a single stream. Parallelism within the single instruction stream does not require programmers or the compiler to split the program into different instruction streams, or require programmers to write their code any differently. Thus, performance improvement that could be obtained from instruction level parallelism was for the most part transparent to programmers, even though the hardware implementation may be complex. In contrast, exploiting multicore architecture for performance often demands parallel programming, which usually requires significant programmers' effort. The reason is that most high level programming languages express computation as a sequence of operations, and programmers are already accustomed to them. Thus, specifying multiple instruction streams for a single program require explicit efforts by programmers. Programmers often have to consider issues such as data races, synchronization, and thread communication, to ensure correct execution of parallel programs. Given the difficulty in programming, everything else equal, microprocessor designers would have picked (and indeed picked) architecture techniques for instruction level parallelism rather than multicore.

Gradually, however, the instruction level parallelism low hanging fruits were picked. There started to be a diminishing return on the performance obtained from a single core execution. Two key approaches to increasing the instruction level parallelism exploited by the processor were processing instructions in more pipeline stages so the clock frequency could be run higher (i.e., increasing pipeline depth) and processing more instructions on one pipeline stage (i.e., increasing pipeline width). Increasing the pipeline depth bumped into an efficiency problem when pipeline overheads became significant and critical latencies were unaffected by the depth of the pipeline. Several papers published in 2002 covered and analyzed the inefficiency, for example [23].

A processor capable of processing multiple instructions per cycle on its own is referred to as a *superscalar* processor. Increasing the pipeline width in a superscalar processor also bumped into complexity issues, where the complexity of the logic circuitry needed to process the instructions increases quadratically in complexity (in some cases even worse) as the pipeline width increases, as discussed by Palacharla et al. [44]. Inspecting a die photo of the Intel Pentium 4 Northwood, one can observe that functional units, which perform the actual computation for instructions, only occupy about 5% of the total die area, whereas close to 90% of the die area implement logic that ensures sufficient rates of instruction and data delivery to the functional units. With much of the die already occupied by superscalar logic, increasing the pipeline width requires a near quadratic increase in the amount of logic on die. Thus, it became gradually more difficult to push the degree of instruction level parallelism that could be utilized.

1.1.1 Power Consumption Issue

In the 2000s, another problem surfaced and asserted itself: *power consumption*. In roughly the first three decades since 1971, instruction level parallelism exploitation has led to increasing *power density*, i.e., the power consumed per unit of die area. Keynote speeches and publications in the late 90s showed that if the past trend was extrapolated, the power density of a microprocessor was going to reach that of a nuclear reactor or even the sun. Up until roughly year 2001, the increase in power density could be dealt with by air cooling, or by increasing the size of fan to cool down the processor. However, there is a limit of roughly 75 watts before air cooling is unable to dissipate the heat generated by the high power density chip. Beyond that, designers either had to switch to liquid cooling, which is expensive and cannot fit the form factor acceptable in some computer systems (especially laptops and smart phones), or change the design approach to keep the power density constant even as more and more transistors were packed on a single die.

In order to discuss the problem of power consumption, let us first revisit basic concepts of power consumption. It is important to distinguish between *energy* and *power*. Energy is the ability of a physical system to do work for other physical systems, measured typically in joules. It takes a little over four joules to heat one teaspoon of water by 1 degree Celcius. The law of conservation of energy states that energy can be converted from one form to another but cannot be destroyed or created (except through nuclear reactions). For example, chemical energy in gasoline is converted into kinetic energy and heat when it is burned in an automobile engine. Power is the rate at which energy is consumed in one form (and converted into different forms). Power is measured in watts, where 1 watt is defined as consuming 1 joule in 1 second. The problem with microprocessor design is power density (power per unit area) as heat has to be dissipated at the same rate as it is generated, rather than energy. An exception is for battery-powered devices where the length of time between battery charging is important. For such devices, both power and the total energy used from the battery are important.

For a die, there are two sources of power consumption: static and dynamic. Dynamic power consumption is incurred due to transistor switching activities (from 1 to 0 and from 0 to 1). Static power consumption is not incurred due to transistor switching, but incurred due to a small current leaking through what is ideally an insulator. The current is referred to as *leakage current*. Dynamic power consumption in a die follows the following formula:

$$DynP = ACV^2 f \qquad (1.1)$$

where A is the fraction of transistors that are switching, C is the total capacitance of the transistors, V is the voltage supplied to the transistors (supply voltage), and f is the switching or clock frequency. Thus, dynamic power consumption is affected quadratically by the supply voltage but linearly by the clock frequency. Furthermore, the maximum clock frequency of transistors is affected by the supply voltage:

$$f_{max} = c\frac{(V - V_{thd})^\alpha}{V} \qquad (1.2)$$

where V_{thd} is the threshold voltage, the minimum voltage considered to make a transistor conductive. α and c are constants, with α considered to have a value of roughly 1.3.

If we substitute f_{max} in Equation 1.2 into f in Equation 1.1, then we can see that the dynamic power consumption is affected by at least the cube of the supply voltage or V^3. Thus, perhaps the single most important lever in affecting dynamic power consumption is the supply voltage of the transistors. However, while reducing supply voltage is very effective in reducing power density, it comes at a cost of slower logic circuit and lower maximum clock frequency f_{max}, unless the threshold voltage can be reduced sufficiently to compensate, thereby preserving $\frac{(V - Vthd)^\alpha}{V}$. Can the threshold voltage be reduced proportionally as the supply voltage is reduced? Unfortunately, it is not easy to reduce the threshold voltage, because we may bump into another problem: static power consumption.

The static power consumption of a die is simply the multiplication of the supply voltage and leakage current. The leakage current is related to the threshold voltage in the following way:

$$I_{leak} > f_1(w)e^{-V_{thd}f_2(V,T)} \tag{1.3}$$

where f_1 is a function that depends on the gate width w, f_2 is a function that depends on the supply voltage and temperature. The $>$ sign is there because the right hand side expression only accounts for one type of leakage current caused by subthreshold leakage, which is probably the most dominant source of leakage current. Equation 1.3 shows that the leakage current increases exponentially as the threshold voltage is lowered. While this inequality has held true for a long time, the magnitude of static power consumption was small enough to ignore until the last decade or so. In the past decade, the threshold voltage could not be lowered as quickly as the feature size was scaled in order to cap the static power consumption within an acceptable limit. This problem has become worse today, where some experts offer an opinion that the threshold voltage may even need to be increased. Since Equation 1.2 states that the maximum frequency depends heavily on the difference between supply voltage and threshold voltage, the inability to scale down the threshold voltage would have resulted in an abrupt slowing in the maximum clock frequency of the microprocessors. Figure 1.3 confirms the abrupt slowing of the growth of microprocessor clock frequency starting some time between 2001-2005. This slowdown supports the theory that since 2001-2005, static power consumption could no longer be ignored, and it has become difficult to reduce the threshold voltage as quickly as the feature size scaling down.

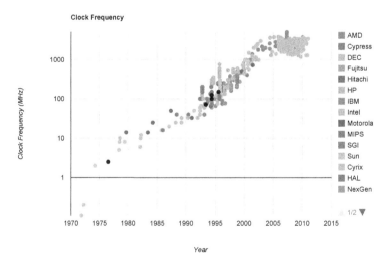

Figure 1.3: Clock frequency of microprocessors over time. Source: [16].

Note that the transition from single core design to multicore design in 2001-2005 coincided with the stagnating clock frequency growth, which eliminates increasing the pipeline depth as an option. In fact, the opposite occurs. Rather than slicing the same work into more and more pipeline stages, since around 2001-2005, architects have crammed the same work into fewer pipeline stages. Figure 1.4 shows the number of "FO4" delays per clock cycle in microprocessors. FO4 delay is the delay of a standard logic gate, defined as the delay of an inverter with a fan-out of 4 (i.e., the inverter that is driving four inverters as its output). The figure shows how many FO4 delays can fit in one clock cycle or one pipeline stage. From 1985 to 2001-2005, architects deepened the pipeline by slicing the processing of instructions in the processor into more and more pipeline stages, resulting in only 20 FO4 delays per pipeline stage. However, that trend reversed in 2001-2005 when in a pipeline stage, higher FO4 delays indicate there is more logic work being done. The total number of pipeline stages, however, may not necessarily experience a proportional reduction, depending on the complexity of instructions and instruction processing.

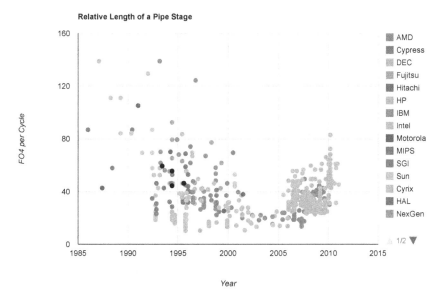

Figure 1.4: The FO4 delay of microprocessors over time. FO4 delay is the delay of an inverter with a fan-out of 4. Source: [16].

We have discussed the impact of power wall on pipeline depth and clock frequency. It is natural to ask how the power wall has impacted the pipeline width and the complexity of the processor in general. Has it also stalled the growth of the processor complexity and its pipeline width? It turns out that they have also slowed or stalled. The pipeline width and depth are related. The total number of instructions that are in flight in the processor core determines the complexity of the processor core. The number of in-flight instructions is proportional to the multiplication of the pipeline depth and pipeline width. With the depth stalling, the processor complexity slows, and increasingly depends on the pipeline width. Increasing pipeline width, however, is also difficult due to the quadratic increase in complexity of the processor core. Hence the pipeline width growth has also slowed or stalled.

Thus, overall, since 2001-2005, the exploitation of instruction level parallelism as the main growth avenue for performance has been largely diminished in favor of a multicore design. This shift suggests that there were no longer many low hanging fruits in exploiting instruction level parallelism: there were no techniques left for increasing performance significantly without also significantly increasing the power consumption of the processor. On the other hand, increasing the performance through multicore design was pursued even when it required additional programming efforts for programs to benefit from it. Thus, it is intuitive to question whether there is a significant power-efficient performance improvement advantage of the multicore design over a single core design.

Suppose that we want to double the performance of a processor system. One way to achieve it is to double the pipeline depth, assuming an ideal case where performance increases linearly with the pipeline depth. However, from Equation 1.2, we know that we will need to approximately double the supply voltage (or approximately halve the threshold voltage). Thus, the processor dynamic power consumption increases by $8\times$ due to the doubling of supply voltage and clock frequency. An alternative to increasing the pipeline depth would be to increase the pipeline width, again assuming an ideal case where the pipeline width increases performance proportionally. However, many structures increase quadratically in complexity (thus power consumption) when the pipeline width increases. This results in a quadrupling of the processor dynamic power consumption. Finally, if we double the number of cores, in an ideal case where the performance increases with the number of cores, the processor dynamic power consumption also doubles. Thus, in a perfect world, the multicore design is the most power-efficient way to scale up performance. Obviously, the above analysis is oversimplified. It assumes linear speedup, where doubling the number of cores translates to doubling the performance. In reality, linear speedup is often achievable for a subset of programs that apply the same computation over a large number of data items (referred to as having *data parallelism*), but hard to achieve for programs without data parallelism or irregular code structures. Second, doubling the number of cores does not *automatically* double the performance, depending on several factors including that it requires programmers to write their programs so that they can run in parallel to exploit the multiple cores. The latter constraint cannot be underestimated.

There are examples of situations in which programmers face two options: spend additional programming efforts and obtain a much better performance vs. obtain substantially lower performance in exchange for lower programming efforts. For example, in many cases programmers may significantly improve the performance of their code if they optimize at the assembly language level, but in many cases they choose not to do that. Another example is choosing conservative compiler flags that ensure correctness versus aggressive compiler flags that may dramatically improve performance but at the same time introduce risks of instability. In many cases, production software developers have chosen more conservative compiler flags. Thus, programmers have not always chosen performance over other concerns such as programming efforts and software stability. From this view, it was a risky decision for processor designers to choose the multicore design approach versus keeping on improving instruction level parallelism. For example, suppose company A chooses a multicore approach while company B finds a way to improve instruction level parallelism to achieve a similar improvement in performance level. Assuming everything else the same, consumers would prefer to shift their preference to the microprocessor produced by company B because they can get the same performance level while expending less programming efforts. As a result, company A loses business to company B. Thus, a microprocessor company will not transition to a multicore design unless it is convinced that instruction level parallelism will no longer provide room for power-efficient performance improvement. This suggests that the transition from instruction level parallelism to multicore occurred because there was no other viable power-efficient alternatives.

The transition to multicore manifested in a hybrid technology for some manufacturers. For example, a technology called *simultaneous multithreading* (SMT) allows parallel execution utilizing largely processor resources designed for exploiting instruction level parallelism. Intel released a processor with 2-way SMT in 2002, allowing two threads to execute simultaneously on one processor core, before introducing a dual-core processor in 2006.

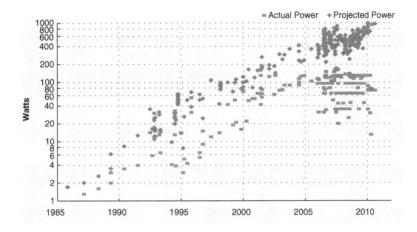

Figure 1.5: Power density of microprocessors: projected based on technology parameters vs. actual. Source: [17].

One interesting question is whether the switch from instruction level parallelism to multicore design has been effective in dealing with the power wall problem. Figure 1.5 shows power density of microprocessors in watts. The figure compares two series of data: the projected power consumption, calculated based on process technology parameters such as the supply voltage, threshold voltage, etc. versus the actual power consumption. The figure shows that the stall in processor clock frequency is capable of slowing down, but not stopping, the growth in power consumption of microprocessors. The projected power consumption kept on increasing from the 2001-2005 period to 2012. However, the actual power consumption stopped growing since 2001-2005 and even declined since. The figure suggests that the clock frequency stagnation by itself is insufficient in containing the dynamic power consumption. However, the addition of other optimizations in circuit and microarchitecture optimizations, such as clock gating, are sufficient to contain the dynamic power consumption [17].

Table 1.2: Examples of recent multicore processors.

Aspects	Intel IvyBridge	Oracle Sparc T5	IBM Power7+
# Cores	6 superscalar 2-way SMT cores	16 2-issue superscalar cores	8 superscalar, 4-way SMT, cores, plus accelerators
Technology	22nm	28nm	32nm, 13 metal layers, 567mm^2, 2.1B transistors
Clock Freq	up to 4.0GHz	3.6GHz	up to 4.4GHz
Caches	64KB L1, 256KB L2 (per core), up to 15MB L3 (shared)	16KB L1 (per core), 128KB L2 (per core), 8MB L3 (shared)	256KB L2 (per core), 80MB eDRAM L3 (shared)

Table 1.2 shows some examples of recent multicore systems at the time of this writing (2012-2013 time frame). The processors shown are for server platforms. They show anywhere between 6 to 12 cores on die, each core is capable of executing between 2-4 thread contexts. IBM Power7+ added several accelerators to aid the cores for specific computation purposes. The technology ranges from 22nm to 32nm. The achieved maximum clock rates are between 3.6GHz to 4.4GHz. They have three cache levels, with the last level cache between 8 to 15 MB, with the Power7+ as an exception, achieving 80MB capacity using the much denser embedded DRAM (the IvyBridge and T5 utilize SRAM for the last level cache).

■ *Did you know?*

  Experts believe that the power consumption problem will likely remain with us far into future microprocessor generations and may get worse over time. They coined a term dark silicon *to indicate a situation where an increasing fraction of the die cannot be powered on due to insufficient power budget. Intel's recent Sandy Bridge chip has a TurboBoost feature which runs eight cores on a die at a normal frequency of 2.5GHz, but if only 1 or 2 cores are active it runs them at 3.5GHz or 3.4GHz, respectively. TurboBoost likely signifies the onset of a mild form of dark silicon where there is not sufficient power budget to run all eight cores at the full 3.5GHz frequency.*

1.2   Perspectives on Parallel Computers

We have discussed the microprocessor transition from single-core to multicore design. Let us now discuss it in the context of parallel computers. Most multicore systems today can be considered a type of parallel computer as the cores are tightly integrated enough to provide a platform for parallel computing. Multicore enables for the first time parallel computing on a chip. Prior to multicore, users had to rely on purchasing an often-expensive system consisting of multiple processors in order to perform parallel computing. Today, virtually all new computer systems, from servers, desktops, laptops, and cell phones, are parallel computers. Thus, it is helpful to consider multicore architecture from the perspective of parallel computer design.

What motivates people to use parallel computers? One reason is the *absolute performance* that a parallel computer provides compared to that provided by a single processor system. Researchers at the cutting edge of science and technology need to run a large number of very large simulations and need cutting edge raw computational power provided by parallel computers. For example, the simulation of a single protein folding may take years on the most advanced processor, but it may only take days to perform on a large and powerful multiprocessor. The pace of scientific discovery lies on how fast a particular computation problem can be solved on the computer. In addition, some applications have a real time constraint, which necessitates the computation to be fast enough to be useful. For example, weather modeling for predicting the precise direction of hurricanes and tornadoes must be performed in a timely manner, otherwise the prediction is not useful.

Another reason to use a parallel computer system such as a multiprocessor or multicore system is that it is more attractive in terms of *cost-adjusted performance* or *power-adjusted performance*. This is especially true today for the multicore chip. For medium-sized machines consisting of between 2 and 8 processor chips, the cost of making such a multiprocessor is relatively small compared to having 2 or 8 independent systems, especially with regard to the cost of software and maintenance of the systems. However, large-scale multiprocessors rarely achieve superior low cost-adjusted or power-adjusted performance because of the high cost of providing a very high scalability. Hence, such systems are either used for niche computation that requires absolute performance or do not get built.

When looking at the history of parallel computers, we should keep in mind how Moore's law has changed processor architectures. Parallel architectures were initially a natural idea because there were not enough transistors on a chip to implement a complete microprocessor. Hence, it was natural to have multiple chips that communicated with each other, either when those chips implemented different components of a processor or when they implemented components of different processors. Initially, all levels of parallelism were considered in parallel computer architectures: instruction level parallelism, data parallelism, etc. What defined parallel architecture was unclear but has solidified over time.

Almasi and Gottlieb [3] defined a parallel computer as:

> "*A parallel computer is a collection of processing elements that communicate and co-operate to solve a large problem fast.*"

While the definition appears straightforward, there is a broad range of architectures that fit the definition. For example, take the phrase "*collection of processing elements*". What constitutes a processing element? A processing element is logic that has an ability to process an instruction. It can be a functional unit, a thread context on a processor, a processor core, a processor chip, or an entire node (processors in a node, local memory, and disk). From this definition, instruction level parallelism can be thought of as parallel processing of instructions on functional units as the processing elements. Does it mean that a superscalar processor can be thought of as a parallel computer? A superscalar processor detects dependences between instructions and executes independent instructions in parallel on different functional units whenever possible. Here the definition seems to include a superscalar processor as a parallel computer. In contrast, today, many people do not consider a superscalar processor as a parallel computer. Such an ambiguity was understandable at the time because the level of parallelism being exploited was still fluid. However, today, it seems that the popular view is that a core defines the boundary of a processing element. In that view, parallelism among cores is considered the domain of a parallel computer, whereas parallelism within a core is not considered the domain of a parallel computer.

While reasonable, the popular view has some flaws. For example, a simultaneous multi-threaded (SMT) core has multiple program counters and can execute instructions from different threads or even programs. Thus, an SMT core provides a platform for parallel programming, so it seems appropriate to refer to it as a parallel computer. Another example is a vector core, where it may fetch instructions from a single program counter, but each instruction processes multiple data items simultaneously. For example, a vector addition instruction fetches elements of an array and elements of another array, and pairwise add elements from the two different arrays and write the results on a third array. Again, it seems appropriate to refer to the vector core as a parallel computer. Thus, it is useful to define a processing element as *logic that fetches instructions from a single program counter and each instruction operates on a single set of data items*. To this end, Flynn provided a useful taxonomy that categorizes parallel computers based on the number of program counters ("instruction streams") and sets of data items ("data streams"), which we will discuss later.

The term *"communicate"* refers to the processing elements sending data to each other. The choice of communication mechanisms determine two important classes of parallel architectures: *shared memory* systems in which parallel tasks that run on the processing elements communicate by reading and writing to a common memory location, or *message passing* systems in which all data is local and parallel tasks must send explicit messages to each other to pass data. The communication medium such as what interconnect network is used to connect the processing elements is also an important issue that determines communication latency, throughput, scalability, and fault tolerance.

The term *"cooperate"* refers to the synchronization of the progress of the execution of a parallel task relative to other tasks. *Synchronization* allows sequencing of operations, for example requiring a task to have completed a certain computation before another task can commence on its computation. Synchronization is required for ensuring correctness. Important issues in synchronization include granularity (when and how often tasks synchronize with each other) and mechanism (the sequence of operations that achieve the synchronization functionality). These issues affect scalability and load balance properties.

The phrase *"solve a large problem fast"* indicates the processing elements work together to deal with a single problem, and that the goal is performance. Interestingly, there is a choice of using a general versus special purpose architecture. A special purpose machine can be designed and tuned for a specific computation in mind, making it fast and scalable for the particular computation, but may be slow for other types of computation.

Parallel computers may also be referred to as *multiprocessors*. In the rest of the book, we will use the term multiprocessors to refer to a collection of processors regardless of whether the processors are implemented in different chips or a single chip, and multicore to refer specifically to multiple processors implemented on a single chip.

In the early stages, different types of parallelism were researched for the parallel computer. Over time, it became clear which types of parallelism were more appropriate for implementation across processor cores or within a core. For example, instruction level parallelism is now implemented in a core because it requires register-level communication among instructions, which can be provided with a low latency on a core.

As transistor integration continued, an entire microprocessor fit into a single chip (e.g., Intel 4004 in 1971). Since then, the performance of a single microprocessor increased rapidly, roughly tracking the speed of transistor integration described by Moore's law. As discussed earlier, such a rapid performance growth was fueled by transistor miniaturization, but primarily enabled by the abundance of low hanging fruits from exploiting the instruction level parallelism and caches. Gains from these architecture techniques were so significant that uniprocessor systems could catch up to the performance of parallel computers in a few years, while costing a tiny fraction of parallel computers. It was hard to justify purchasing expensive parallel computers unless there was an immediate demand for intensive computation, such as in the supercomputer market.

To give an illustration, suppose that a 100-processor system was produced, and it could achieve a perfect speedup of $100\times$ for an application under consideration. That is, if the same application was run on a single processor system, it would be $100\times$ slower. However, when a single processor's speed grew at Moore's law (doubling every 18 months or 60% annual growth), one year later the application was only $\frac{100}{1.6} = 62.5\times$ slower on the latest single processor system, and two years later the application was only $\frac{100}{1.6^2} = 39\times$ slower on the latest single processor system, and so on. Ten years later, running the application on the latest single processor system yielded the same speed as in the 10-year old 100-processor system. It was difficult to justify purchasing a large and highly expensive parallel computer if its performance would be eclipsed by a single processor system in just a few years. Few companies could find economic justification for such a purchase, except a few large companies and national laboratories at the cutting edge of scientific discovery. This example used optimistic assumptions – using pessimistic assumptions would reduce the advantage of parallel computers over a single-processor system. For example, on a 100-processor system, the realizable speedup for most applications is often much less than 100. Second, even for applications that can reach a $100\times$ speedup, it often took weeks to months of highly-manual parallel performance tuning to extract the speedup, while running the application on a single processor system often required simple tuning effort. Third, the market for highly parallel systems was small so it could not benefit from a pricing advantage of high-volume products. As a result, a parallel machine might cost more than $1000\times$ the cost of a single processor machine. Finally, designing parallel computer architectures was a highly complex task and the logic for interconnecting processors to form a tightly-coupled parallel computer was not simple. This caused a significant extra development time that when a parallel computer was launched, the processors it was composed of were often already much slower than the latest single-processor system that was already available. Overall, the combination of all these factors made it hard for parallel computers to be a widespread commercial success, prior to the design of multicore.

Low-cost distributed computers were being developed in the 90s by assembling many uniprocessor systems with an off-the-shelf network. This gave birth to a *network of workstations*, which was later more commonly referred to as *clusters*. Compared to parallel computers, distributed computers were a lot cheaper but had a high communication latency between processors. However, some classes of applications did not have much inter-processor communication and were quite scalable when they ran on clusters.

1.2.1 Flynn's Taxonomy of Parallel Computers

Flynn defined a taxonomy of parallel computers [18] based on the number of *instruction streams* and *data streams*, as shown in Table 1.3, and illustrated in Figure 1.6. An instruction stream is a sequence of instructions followed from a single program counter. A data stream is an address in memory which the instruction operates on. A control unit (CU) fetches instructions from a single program counter, decodes them, and issues them to the data processing unit (DPU). The DPU is assumed to be logic that processes instructions, including functional units. Instruction and data are both supplied from the memory.

Table 1.3: Flynn's taxonomy of parallel computers.

		Number of Data Streams	
		Single	Multiple
Number of Instruction Streams	Single	*SISD*	*SIMD*
	Multiple	*MISD*	*MIMD*

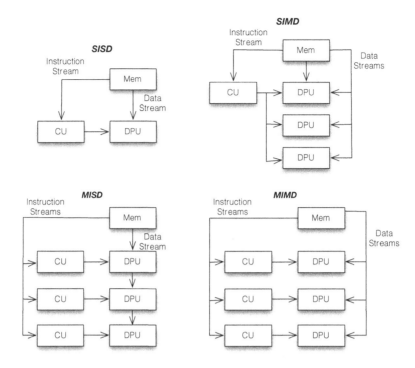

Figure 1.6: Illustration of Flynn's taxonomy of parallel computers.

SISD is not considered a parallel architecture as it only has one instruction and one data stream. However, SISD may exploit parallelism at the instruction level. Even though there is only one stream of instructions, parallelism between the instructions from the stream can be exploited when the instructions are independent from one another. Non-SMT processor cores today are an example of an SISD machine that exploits instruction-level parallelism.

SIMD is a parallel architecture in which a single instruction operates on multiple data. An example of SIMD architectures can be found in vector processors. SIMD-style extension has also been added to many processors. As a simple illustration, consider multiplying a scalar a and an array X. With SISD, we need to execute a loop where in each iteration, we perform a multiplication between a and one element from array X. With SIMD, the entire operation can be performed with one scalar-vector multiply instruction without the use of a loop. SIMD is known for its efficiency in terms of the instruction count needed to perform a computation task. Using a loop to perform a single operation on multiple data is inefficient: one instruction is needed for each data item, and there are loop overheads such as loop index computation and conditional branches.

Today, SIMD architecture can be found in many graphics processing units (GPUs) and in multimedia extension of most instruction set architectures, such as Intel MMX/SSE, AMD 3DNow!, Motorola Altivec, MIPS MIPS-3D, etc. The manner in which a single instruction operates on multiple data items differs across architectures. In some GPUs, cores run threads that execute the same instruction in lockstep, and the instruction operates on different data, hence the cores act similarly to vector lanes in a vector processor. Such an execution model is often referred to as SIMT (single instruction multiple thread) and is discussed in greater detail in Chapter 12. Multimedia extensions are typically not true SIMD because rather than a single instruction operating on many data items, the instructions still operate on a single data that is a packed form of multiple small data items, such as eight 8-bit data items. The most common implementation of parallel computers takes the form of MIMD architectures.

MISD is an architecture in which multiple processing elements execute from different instruction streams, and data is passed from one processing element to the next. An example of this machine is the *systolic arrays*, such as the iWarp [8]. The requirement that data is passed from one processing element to the next means that it is restricted to a certain type of computation but is hard to apply in general.

MIMD is the architecture used in most parallel computers today. It is the most flexible architecture since there is no restriction on the number of instruction streams or data streams, although it is less efficient in terms of the number of instructions it uses to perform a single computation task compared to that used by an SIMD architecture.

1.2.2 Classes of MIMD Parallel Computers

Since MIMD is the most popular form of parallel computers, we will look at how the level processors in an MIMD architecture are physically interconnected. The choices are illustrated in Figure 1.7. Figure 1.7(a) shows an architecture in which the processors share some level of cache (typically the L2 or L3 cache, but a shared L1 cache is also a possibility). Examples of this include many current multicore systems such as Intel Ivy Bridge, IBM Power7+, Oracle T5, etc. Early multicore architectures let cores share the L2 cache, while more recent multicore architectures let cores share the L3 cache. One reason for the cores sharing the last level cache is that the last level cache is a very significant resource, occupying a very large area on die. Cache capacity fragmentation is avoided when all cores share the cache. If some cores are sleeping, a shared cache is still utilized by active cores.

Another alternative is to provide an interconnection between private caches (Figure 1.7(b)). This architecture is commonly referred to as *symmetric multi-processors* (SMP). SMP is an architecture where different processors share the memory and have roughly equal access time to the memory. The interconnection may utilize a bus, ring, crossbar, or point-to-point network. Because all processors can access the memory with approximately the same latency, then this class of MIMD computers are also referred to as *uniform memory access* (UMA) architectures. Today, SMP may be formed with multicore chips as building blocks. Many multicore chips intended for servers already include a router on die to connect a chip to several other chips, in order to create a larger shared memory system consisting of several chips.

Figure 1.7(c) shows an architecture in which each processor has its own caches and local memory, but the hardware provides an interconnect across all local memories to give the abstraction of a single memory. However, the memory access latency varies since remote memory takes longer to access than local memory. Such architectures are referred to as *non-uniform memory access* (NUMA) or as *distributed shared memory* (DSM). They include examples such as SGI Origin and Altix systems, and IBM p690 systems.

Figure 1.7(d) shows an architecture in which each processor is a complete node with its own caches, local memory, and disk; and the interconnection is provided at the level of I/O connection. Since I/O connection latency is very high, the hardware may not provide abstraction of a single memory, although a software layer can accomplish the same abstraction with relatively higher overheads. As a result, they are often referred to as *distributed* computer systems, or more popularly as clusters. In a cluster, each node is its own system, running its own instance of the operating system (OS). Clusters provide parallel computing platforms for certain types of computation that do not require low-latency communication between processes or threads.

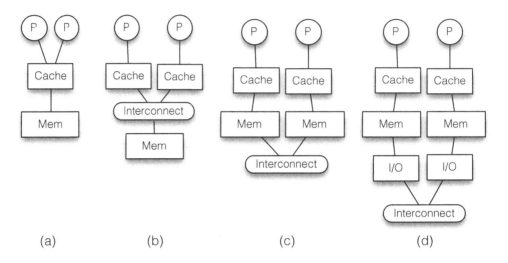

Figure 1.7: Classes of MIMD parallel computers: shared cache (a), uniform memory access (b), non-uniform memory access (c), and distributed system (d).

> ■ *Did you know?*
>
> High-end parallel computers are ranked based on their performance, and the ranking for the fastest 500 parallel computers in the world is published at www.top500.org. The list ranks supercomputing systems based on its Linpack benchmark performance. Linpack is a numerical linear algebra library that is highly parallel and floating point intensive [29]. The top ten of computers in that list can change dramatically from one year to another. For example, in 2004 the top honor went to the Earth Simulator, which was ranked the tenth in just a short two years later!
>
> As recent as June 2013, the top spot goes to Tianhe-2, a parallel computer belonging to the National University of Defense Technology of China. The system was capable of 33.8 tera floating point operations per second (TFlops) with Linpack. The system has 3,120,000 cores, and total memory of 1 petabytes (i.e., 10^{12} bytes). The system is organized as 16,000 nodes, where each node has 195 cores consisting of two Intel Xeon IvyBridge processors and three Xeon Phi processors.

1.3   Future Multicore Architectures

As transistor integration continues as expected in the next several years, an interesting question is what would future multicore architecture be like? We can be sure that whatever the future architecture is, it will be decided quantitatively through a constant assessment of what is the next lowest hanging fruit that can be picked. Such a constant quantitative assessment and reassessment makes it difficult to predict the future accurately.

The simplest way of making a prediction is to predict the continuation of a trend. Such a prediction will be correct most of the time except at transition points. With such an approach, one will predict that in the next decade there will be more and more cores integrated on a die. Several years ago, an expert in computer architecture even predicted that the number of cores would double every 18 months. Would the future of multicore be a doubling of the number of cores every 18 months for the foreseeable future? Unfortunately, I doubt that that will be the case. I will outline several reasons for my thought.

The first reason is the same reason that made designers switch from a single-core design exploiting instruction level parallelism to the multicore design: the gradual disappearance of low hanging fruits. Similarly, I believe that while the transistors to implement more cores will be available, designers may not choose to utilize the transistors that way if there is no compelling reason to do that. There are not likely an unlimited number of low hanging fruits with the multicore design, as with other design approaches. For example, parallel programming has not been shown to be effective for all classes of programs. Parallel programming has been shown to be effective for programs with relatively regular code structures or ones where the algorithm applies an identical (or close to identical) computation over a large amount of data items. Parallel programming has not been shown effective for programs with complex code structures and do not perform the same computation over a large amount of data items. Adding more cores does not help speed up such programs. Second, even for easy-to-parallelize applications, for various reasons their speedups often do not scale linearly past several hundred cores. For many programs, their speedup plateaus before reaching 100 cores and then declines. Essentially, there is a diminishing return from additional cores and even a negative return past a certain point. Thus, as the number of cores increases, there are fewer and fewer programs that can benefit from it. Eventually, when there are very few programs that benefit from additional cores, there is very little marginal utility of having additional cores from the point of view of users.

One caution with the above analysis is that a multicore platform is not necessarily used solely for parallel processing. There may be a large enough number of sequential programs that can run simultaneously creating a multi-programmed environment that can benefit from the multicore architecture. In server consolidation, multiple servers (e.g., web servers, email servers, password servers, etc.) can be hosted on the same multicore platform using different virtual machines. Each server may spawn a large number of threads proportional to the number of users using the provided services. Thus, it seems that servers can still benefit from the increasing number of cores for quite some time, unlike client machines for which the benefit from increasing number of cores may arrive much earlier.

A second reason is that adding more cores requires bulking up the infrastructure components that support them, in a superlinear fashion. Cores, when active, require data to be fetched from the off-die main memory. Doubling the number of cores requires doubling the data bandwidth from/to the main memory. If cores double every 18 months, then the data bandwidth must also double every 18 months for a balanced design. For various reasons such as power consumption and the limitation on scaling the number of chip pins, it is difficult to increase the off-chip bandwidth that quickly. In order to avoid such a fast increase in data bandwidth demand, one may increase the cache capacity on die to filter or reduce the frequency of having to fetch data from off-die memory. As a rule of thumb (which is approximately applicable to an average server workload [49]), one must increase the cache size by $4\times$ to reduce the miss rate by 50%. This strategy requires that an increasing portion of the die be allocated for caches and less for cores. When one die component must grow faster than another, then the latter cannot grow as fast as Moore's law (the speed of transistor integration growth). This in turn restricts the growth of die area for cores.

A third reason for why the growth of cores will slow down in the future is that even if exploiting parallelism in multicore is highly successful, the non-parallel portion of the execution will increasingly become the bottleneck. To illustrate this point, it is helpful to know Amdahl's law. Suppose that the sequential execution of the algorithm or code takes T_1 time units, while parallel execution of the algorithm or code on p processors takes T_p time units. Suppose that out of the entire execution of the program, s fraction of it is not parallelizable while $1 - s$ fraction is parallelizable with a perfect speedup. Then, the overall *speedup* (Amdahl's formula) of the parallel execution compared to the sequential execution is:

$$
\begin{aligned}
speedup_p &= \frac{T_1}{T_p} \\
&= \frac{T_1}{T_1 \times s + T_1 \times \frac{1-s}{p}} \\
&= \frac{1}{s + \frac{1-s}{p}}
\end{aligned}
\tag{1.4}
$$

For a very large number of processors, assuming that the serial fraction s is constant, the speedup of parallel execution becomes:

$$
\begin{aligned}
speedup_\infty &= \lim_{p \to \infty} \frac{1}{s + \frac{1-s}{p}} \\
&= \frac{1}{s}
\end{aligned}
\tag{1.5}
$$

The formula for $speedup_\infty$ expresses the maximum attainable speedup on an unlimited number of processors. While the formula is simple, it has important implications. For example, if the serial fraction s is 5%, then the maximum speedup ratio on an unlimited number of processors would only be 20! However, if the serial fraction s can be reduced to 0.5%, then the maximum speedup ratio on an unlimited number of processors increases to 200. An important observation here is that obtaining a high degree of scalability is hard; it requires all parts of a program to be almost completely parallelizable with a perfect speedup. All other parts that are not parallelized must be very small in order to produce a scalable parallel execution performance. Another observation is that the more successful parallelization becomes, the more the speed of the program depends on the non-parallelized portion of the program.

Note that in practice, s is not the only portion restricting parallel program performance. Other factors, such as load imbalance, and various parallel overheads such as synchronization overheads, communication overheads, and thread management overheads, restrict parallel program performance. s is assumed to be constant as we grow the number of cores, but many components of parallel overheads actually grow with the number of cores. Thus, the reality is worse than what Amdahl's law suggests. Therefore, we can be assured that as parallelization is pursued, the relative importance of the non-parallelized portion of the execution and parallel overheads increases.

Going back to our discussion the scaling of the number of cores, the fourth reason for the limitation on the growth in the number of cores is the power wall problem. We have discussed how the limitation on power consumption prompted designers from moving from a single-core design to a multicore design. How will the same power consumption concern likely change the multicore design in the future?

A useful back-of-envelope calculation based on Dennard's scaling rules may help shed some light on the situation [63]. Suppose one technology generation from now the feature size decreases by 30%, i.e., the feature size scales by $\lambda = 0.7$. Capacitance scales by λ. The transistor area scales down by $\lambda^2 = 0.5$, allowing the same die area to have twice as many transistors. Let us now consider two scenarios. In the first scenario, supply voltage can scale down by a factor λ (and threshold voltage scales down proportionally), allowing the clock frequency to scale up by $\frac{1}{\lambda} = 1.4$. The new die has a new dynamic power of:

$$
\begin{aligned}
DynP' &= A'C'V'^2 f' \\
&= (2A)(0.7C)(0.7V^2)(1.4f) \\
&= ACV^2 f \\
&= DynP
\end{aligned}
$$

Thus in the first scenario, the dynamic power of the new die in the new technology is the same as the original dynamic power of the old technology. In the second scenario, suppose that the threshold voltage cannot be scaled down, hence the supply voltage must be kept the same. In this scenario, $V' = V$, resulting in:

$$
\begin{aligned}
DynP' &= A'C'V'^2 f' \\
&= (2A)(0.7C)V^2(1.4f) \\
&= 2ACV^2 f \\
&= 2DynP
\end{aligned}
$$

meaning that the dynamic power of the processor in the new technology is twice as large compared to the old technology. Since the die area has not changed, the power density doubles along with the doubling of dynamic power. The above back-of-envelope calculation illustrates the difficulty of containing power density when the threshold voltage cannot be scaled down. Such a constraint may eventually lead to dark silicon where some portion of the die cannot be turned on in order to contain power density. Obviously, power density cannot be allowed to double unless there are ways to dissipate the heat. Therefore, techniques must be employed that decrease the power density even as the number of transistors increase. For example, frequency may remain stagnant or reduced instead of increased. The die area may be reduced rather than kept constant. Or voltage reduced instead of constant. While there are many other ways to achieve a reduction in power density, one thing is clear: the amount of power for a given level of performance must be reduced. In other words, energy efficiency must be improved in future microprocessors.

Energy efficiency may be measured as energy consumed divided by work performed. For example, for a given ISA (instruction set architecture), EPI (energy per instruction), measured in joule, is an important metric to optimize. Alternatively, amount of power (watts) divided by performance (instructions per second). Since watts is joule per second, power-performance ratio comes down to joules per instruction, equivalent to EPI.

To summarize, we have discussed several constraints in increasing the number of cores in a traditional multicore design: the gradual disappearance of low hanging fruits for improving performance, increasingly costly infrastructure components needed to support more cores, the increasing importance of non-parallelized portion of the execution time, and worsening power density requiring improved energy efficiency in future architectures. All these point out to a slowdown in the growth of the number of cores coinciding with the deployment of other design approaches. For example, application-specific accelerators may improve performance in a more energy efficient manner compared to simply increasing the number of cores. Thus, accelerators may be increasingly identified and integrated on die. Another possible approach is the use of transistors for integration of other components on die, such as the I/O controllers, graphic engine, and parts of the main memory. Considering the increasing bottleneck contributed by the non-parallel execution, another approach may be introducing heterogeneity in the sense that cores of multiple performance and power characteristics may be added on die. The cores that achieve the best power-performance trade offs may be selected to execute different programs or program phases, while others may be turned off. For example, the large powerful cores may be used for accelerating non-parallel execution. Many small cores may be used for executing highly-scalable programs, while medium-sized cores may be used for executing medium-scalable programs. To support more cores, there may be increasing emphasis on larger, more complex, and more optimized memory hierarchy, network on chip, memory controller architecture, to support the growth of cores. Future multicore architectures are likely going to become significantly more diverse, more complex, and their management more sophisticated.

■ *Did you know?*

To stimulate the discussion on how the power consumption problem may affect future processor design, I asked students in my graduate course in parallel architecture how they would design a house if they have nearly unlimited square footage but very limited power to utilize (light, heat, or cool) it. Their responses were quite innovative and interesting.

Some suggested to turn on only rooms as they are used and turn off others, and route utilities from unutilized rooms to ones being utilized. Some suggested to design rooms that require little or no utilities, such as outdoor decks, sunrooms, porches, etc. Some suggested localizing activities such as integrating the stove into the dining table. Some suggested specialization of rooms, such as the room height: use 9-foot ceiling room for social events, 7-foot ceiling room for dining, and 4-foot ceiling for sleeping.

Besides the power wall, there are other related challenges for designing future multicore architectures. One of them is off-chip bandwidth. In traditional non-multicore multiprocessor systems, adding more processors typically involves adding more nodes, and since a node consists of a processor and its memory, the aggregate bandwidth to main memory increases with more processors. The opposite situation occurs in multicore systems. Adding more cores on a die does not increase the aggregate bandwidth to the main memory. Thus, unless off-chip bandwidth can scale at the same rate as the number of cores in a multicore, the usable off-chip bandwidth per core will decline. Industry projection does not offer much assurance that the problem will be abated. The projected rate of growth in the number of transistors that can fit on a chip (hence the number of cores) in general is much higher than the projected rate of growth of bandwidth to off-chip memory, roughly 50–70% versus 10–15% per year [28]. This potentially causes the performance of a multicore architecture to be increasingly limited by the amount of off-chip bandwidth that a core can use. This problem is referred to as the *bandwidth wall* problem.

In general, doubling the number of cores and the amount of cache in a CMP to utilize the growing transistor counts results in a corresponding doubling of off-chip memory traffic. This implies that the rate at which memory requests must be serviced also needs to double to maintain a balanced design. If the provided off-chip memory bandwidth cannot sustain the rate at which memory requests are generated, then the extra queuing delay for memory requests will force the performance of the cores to decline until the rate of memory requests matches the available off-chip bandwidth. At that point, adding more cores to the chip no longer yields any additional throughput or performance. This means that system performance and throughput are increasingly limited by the amount available off-chip bandwidth.

There are several factors affecting the severity of the bandwidth wall problem in the future. One factor is that providing higher off-chip bandwidth is expensive: one may need to allocate more interconnect pins, run the off-chip interface at a higher clock frequency, or both. Any of them will result in higher power consumption for off-chip communication. This worsens the power wall that was discussed earlier, with a potential consequence of slowing the growth in the number of cores on a die. Another factor is that if performance can be improved in future multicore architectures substantially, then the bandwidth wall problem will become worse. Thus, there is an interplay between the power wall and the bandwidth wall problems, where addressing one of them may worsen the other. A study projecting how severe the bandwidth wall problem may become in the future and what technologies may help address it can be found in [49]. One of the promising technologies is the integration of die-stacked DRAM. By stacking DRAM and logic together (in a 3D chip) or nearly together (in the same module), bandwidth to the stacked DRAM will be much higher than to the off-chip memory. This produces a substantial but temporal relief in the bandwidth wall problem. If the number of multicore keeps growing at the same speed as in the past, the bandwidth wall problem will become pressing again.

Note, however, that the bandwidth wall issue is somewhat less serious than power wall. Under an unmitigated bandwidth wall situation, the number of cores on a die can still keep growing, however at a rate that is smaller than the growth in transistor density. The reason for this is that by slowing the growth in the number of cores, more of the die can be used for caches which act to filter out data communication to off-chip memory. Thus, sufficiently slowing down the growth of the number of cores mitigates the bandwidth wall problem. The power wall, on the other hand, has to be mitigated in future multicore designs for performance to improve.

1.4   Exercises

Worked Problems

1. **Technoloy scaling**. Suppose that instead of progressing at a shrinking of feature size by 30% ($\alpha = 0.7$) every process generation, suppose that feature scaling declines to only 20% every process generation. Find the dynamic power consumption under (a) a scenario where the threshold voltage can scale down by 20% every process generation, and (b) a scenario where the threshold voltage remains constant every process generation. Assume a constant die area, capacitance decreases by 20%, supply voltage decreases by 20%, and clock frequency increases by 25% every process generation.

   Answer: (a) Gate length scales by $S = 0.8$, capacitance scales by $S = 0.8$, transistor area scales by S^2, allowing the number of transistors to scale by $\frac{1}{S^2} = 1.56$. Supply voltage scales by $S = 0.8$. Frequency scales by $\frac{1}{S} = 1.25$. Thus, dynamic power of the chip is unchanged vs. before scaling: $DynP' = A'C'V'^2f' = (1.56A)(0.8C)(0.8V)^2(1.25f) = ACV^2f = DynP$

   Under leakage-limited scaling, gate length scales by $S = 0.8$, capacitance scales by $S = 0.8$, transistor area scales by S^2, allowing the number of transistors to scale by $\frac{1}{S^2} = 1.56$. Supply voltage is unchanged. Frequency scales by $\frac{1}{S} = 1.25$. Thus, dynamic power of the chip increases by 56% each generation: $DynP' = A'C'V'2f' = (1.56A)(0.8C)(V)2(1.25f) = 1.56ACV^2f = 1.56DynP$.

Homework Problems

1. **Technology scaling**. With a scenario where the threshold voltage, supply voltage, and clock frequency unchanged in future process technology generations, if we want to keep the power consumption of the die constant, how much should we reduce the die area to achieve that? Assume that feature size decreases by 30% in each future process generation.

2. **Design trade-offs**. Suppose that we deal with design decision for the current process generation, where we want to choose a design that optimizes for power-performance ratio. More specifically, we are dealing with three designs:

   - Design A: Single core with supply voltage and frequency increased by 20%
   - Design B: Dual core with unchanged supply voltage and frequency
   - Design C: Quad core with voltage and frequency decreased by 20%

   Suppose that performance is proportional to the number of cores and with clock frequency. Also ignore static power consumption and focus only on dynamic power consumption. Which of the designs is most attractive in terms of power-to-performance ratio?

3. **Power management**. Suppose that there are two identical processors that employ different power management: processor A employs dynamic frequency scaling (DFS), while processor B employs dynamic voltage and frequency scaling (DVFS). Processor A can reduce frequency by up to 30%, while processor B can reduce voltage and frequency by up to 10%. Which one

of them has a better ability to reduce dynamic power consumption? Assuming the performance scales with clock frequency proportionally, which one of the processors produces the lowest power-to-performance ratio, in their respective low power mode? Show your computation.

4. **Amdahl's law**. If 5% of the original computation is sequential, what is the maximum speedup of the program on 10, 100, 1000, and nearly unlimited processors?

5. **Amdahl's law**. Suppose that you want to achieve an Amdahl's speedup of 15 when the number of processors is 16. What fraction of the original computation can be sequential?

Chapter 2

Perspectives on Parallel Programming

Contents

In the previous chapter, we mentioned how parallel architectures require programmers' effort in writing a parallel program. Writing a parallel program involves breaking down the program into tasks that can be correctly executed independently from one another, and these tasks need to communicate and cooperate in order to produce the same output as the original sequential program. Given the prevalence of multicore architectures, even desktop and mobile platforms require parallel programming to make use of multiple cores.

In the next three chapters, this book will cover parallel programming, starting from discussing various parallel programming models (this chapter), steps in creating shared memory parallel programs (Chapter 3), and how to write parallel programs for applications with linked data structures (Chapter 4). The purpose of these chapters is to give readers sufficient background knowledge so that they get a perspective on programming abstractions and primitives that a parallel multicore architecture needs to support, and how efficient such support needs to be. Such a background knowledge will be useful when readers move on to future chapters that discuss the architecture of parallel multicores.

This chapter discusses the author's perspectives on parallel programming models. The chapter starts by discussing limits of parallel program performance. The discussion points out to the significant challenges for producing scalable performance on a large number of processor cores, which includes the fraction of execution that cannot be parallelized, load imbalance, and various overheads from managing parallel execution, such as communication and synchronization. It then discusses several popular parallel programming models that are widely used, important differences between them, and the relationship between the programming models and the architecture of the system. The choice of programming model has important implications on communication and synchronization overheads, hence it is a critical factor in parallel program performance.

The book's coverage on parallel programming is not meant to give readers a comprehensive coverage of parallel programming. There are numerous other textbooks that cover parallel programming models and techniques. In this book, the chapters place an emphasis on only one programming model (the shared memory programming model), which is chosen because most multicore systems currently support it. Other programming models are useful and popularly used in other situations, for example message passing is commonly used for large systems containing many multicore nodes, MapReduce is commonly used for data center computation on distributed systems, etc. However, in the author's view, the shared memory programming model is a necessary prerequisite knowledge for readers interested in learning parallel multicore architectures. Thus, it is selected for a deeper coverage.

2.1   Limits on Parallel Program Performance

Fundamentally, what programmers expect from parallel execution of their algorithm or code is to obtain smaller execution time compared to the sequential execution of the algorithm or code. One useful tool for reasoning about parallel program execution time is *Amdahl's Law*. Suppose that the sequential execution of the algorithm or code takes T_1 time units, while parallel execution of the algorithm or code on p processors (assuming p threads) takes T_p time units. Suppose that out of the entire execution of the program, s fraction of it is not parallelizable while $1 - s$ fraction is parallelizable. Recall from Equation 1.4 that the idealized (or Amdahl's) *speedup* of the parallel execution compared to the sequential execution is:

$$speedup_p \quad = \quad \frac{1}{s + \frac{1-s}{p}} \tag{2.1}$$

and when we have a very large number of processors:

$$speedup_\infty \quad = \quad \lim_{p \to \infty} \frac{1}{s + \frac{1-s}{p}} = \frac{1}{s}$$

The equation above shows that obtaining a high degree of scalability is hard; it requires almost all parts of a program to be almost completely parallelizable perfectly. All other parts that are not parallelized must be very small in order to produce a scalable parallel execution performance. Another implication is that increasing speedups by increasing the number of processors yield diminishing returns. This can be seen in Figure 2.1, which plots Amdahl's speedups for three cases of sequential fraction: 1%, 5%, and 10%. We can observe the declining steepness of all the speedup curves as the number of threads/processors increase. In other words, there is a declining marginal speedup from increasing the number of processors.

In practice, the sequential fraction s is not the only factor affecting speedups. There are other factors that reduce speedups such as load imbalance, synchronization overheads, communication overheads, and thread management overheads. Many of these overheads increase as the number of processors increase. For example, thread management overheads increase at least linearly with the number of threads because threads need to be spawned, assigned tasks from a protected task queue, etc. Synchronization overheads tend to increase at least quadratically with the number of processors. As the number of processors increases, the time to perform barrier synchronization, acquire locks,

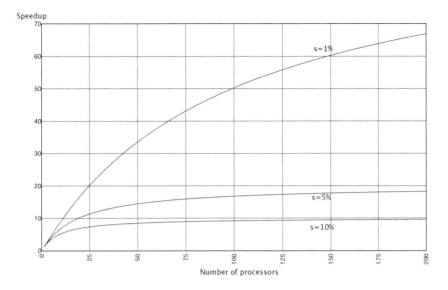

Figure 2.1: Amdahl's speedups illustrated with different values for the sequential fraction s.

etc. is longer and takes a larger fraction of the original execution time. Communication overheads also tend to increase because a higher number of processors cannot be interconnected with very short physical distances. The communication latency between any random pair of nodes increases with the number of processors. Thread management overheads also increase with a higher number of processors because thread management requires synchronization and communication. Hence, if we include these overheads into s, s tends to increase as the number of processors increases, independent of the serial fraction inherent in the algorithm.

■ *Did you know?*

Under the perfect situation in which there is no fraction of the program that cannot be parallelized completely (i.e., $s = 0$), the speedup will be $speedup_p = p$, which is referred to as a linear speedup. *Linear speedup is the* theoretical *maximum speedup attainable. However, in practice some programs have been known to show* super-linear *speedups on some number of processors, where their speedups exceed the linear speedups. The reason for this is that as the number of processors grows, the combined aggregate resources (e.g., the total cache space or memory space) also grow. At some tipping point, adding extra processors changes the situation from the working set of the program exceeding the total cache space to the situation in which the working set fits into the total cache space. When this occurs, cache capacity misses are reduced significantly, and the execution of all threads become much faster, leading to the super-linear speedups.*

Figure 2.2 shows what happens to the speedup curves if we take into account linearly-increasing overheads ($s = 0.01 + \frac{x}{10^4}$) or quadratically-increasing overheads ($s = 0.01 + \frac{x^2}{10^5}$). Note the coefficients in the cost function are arbitrary, hence we should focus on the trends of the curves rather than the magnitude. The figure shows that the effect of linearly-increasing cost is reduced maximum speedup and fewer processors that achieve the maximum speedup. The same observation can be made with quadratically-increasing cost. Note also that with these overheads, there is an speedup-optimum number of threads that when exceeded, speedups decline.

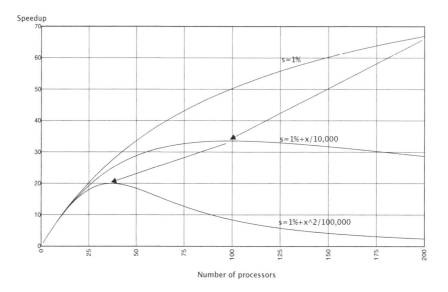

Figure 2.2: Amdahl's speedups if we include parallel overheads in s.

The nature of diminishing return from increasing the number of threads implies that there are only a limited number of low hanging fruits that come from exploiting thread level parallelism. Beyond an inflection point, it is not economical to keep increasing the number of cores in a multicore chip, as the marginal performance benefit is either too small or negative.

From an energy efficiency perspective, thread level parallelism has a declining energy efficiency as the number of threads increases. The reason is that since power consumption is likely increasing at least linearly with the number of processors, speedups increase by a smaller factor compared to the increase in power consumption. Thus, the power-performance ratio increases as the number of threads increases, which is equivalent to a declining energy efficiency. Only when speedups scale perfectly with the number of threads we can maintain energy efficiency. Although moving from an instruction-level parallelism focus to a thread-level parallelism focus brings an improvement in energy efficiency, the gain in energy efficiency cannot be continued by just increasing the number of processors. Therefore, if the power wall problem discussed in Chapter 1 worsens, chip designers need to rely on other approaches to improve energy efficiency.

It is often the case that achieving a highly scalable parallel program requires using a very large input set. Increasing the size of computation often allows the overheads of synchronization, communication, and thread management to contribute to a smaller fraction of execution compared to that of computation. Fortunately, many important scientific simulations do have very large input. The use of input size that is scaled proportionally with the number of threads is often referred to as *weak scaling*, as opposed to *strong scaling* where the input size that is fixed regardless of the number of threads. There is some validity in the arguments for using weak scaling, since large systems will likely be used for computation with larger input sets.

■ *Did you know?*

In the Amdahl's law, there is an ambiguity as to what should constitute as the execution time of a sequential execution of a program (T_1). The choices include:

1. The same parallel program used in parallel execution, but it runs with a single thread on a single processor.

2. The sequential version of the program.

3. The best sequential version of the program.

The first choice is incorrect to use; the sequential execution should not include parallel overheads, such as thread creation, calls to parallel libraries, etc. For example, when a program containing OpenMP directives is compiled with an OpenMP compiler, it includes calls to OpenMP libraries even when it runs on a single thread. However, using thread-safe libraries, which include the overheads of entering and exiting critical sections, for sequential execution may be acceptable if they are the only libraries that are available.

The second choice of using the sequential version of the program is more correct since parallel overheads are not included, but care must also be taken. A potential pitfall of the choice is whether the sequential version of the program is a realistic implementation for sequential execution.

The correct choice is the last option, which uses the best sequential version of the program to measure T_1, both algorithm-wise and code-wise. For example, some algorithms are developed for the purpose of extracting parallelism, but it may not be the best version chosen for a sequential implementation. The second aspect is whether the code is the best sequential code given the algorithm. For example, some aggressive compiler optimizations that can benefit sequential execution are often not performed when the program is compiled for parallel execution, but they can produce a better performing sequential code when they are applied.

2.2 Parallel Programming Models

A programming model is an abstraction of the hardware that programmers can assume. It determines how easily programmers can specify their algorithms into computation tasks that the hardware and compiler understand, and how efficiently those tasks can be executed by the hardware. For non-parallel systems, the sequential programming model has worked really well in hiding the hardware details from programmers, allowing programmers to effectively express their algorithms in an intuitive manner as sequence of steps which are executed sequentially. In contrast, for multiprocessor systems, the programming model that can hide hardware details from the programmer but simultaneously achieve high efficiency remains elusive.

There are at least two major parallel programming models that are widely used: *shared memory* and *message passing* programming models. Both programming models are widely used, with the message passing model more popular for large machines consisting of hundreds to thousands of processor cores, and the shared memory model more popular for smaller machines. There are also other programming models; we will defer their discussion to the later part of the chapter.

Let us define a *parallel task* as a unit of computation that can be executed independently from others. Parallel tasks can run on different processors or cores. Figure 2.3 illustrates the features of the programming models. In the shared memory model, the abstraction is that parallel tasks executed by separate threads or processes can access any location of the memory. Hence, they communicate implicitly, by writing (through a store instruction) and reading (through a load instruction) from common memory locations. This is analogous to threads from a single process which share a single address space. In message passing, threads have their own local memory and one thread cannot access another thread's memory. Hence, to communicate data, they have to rely on explicit messages containing data values sent to each other. This is similar to the abstraction of processes which do not share an address space.

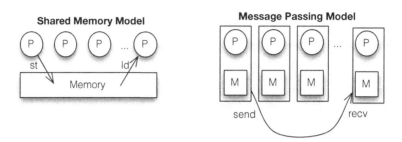

Figure 2.3: Illustrating different parallel programming models.

There have been ongoing debates as to which one of the programming models is superior. In the author's view, the reason why they are widely used programming models is that they fulfill different needs and work better under different circumstances. Therefore, it is not clear if one will render the other unnecessary. Instead of debating which model is superior, it is more helpful to discuss each model's relative merits and drawbacks. As an analogy to the difference between the first two models, consider threads that want to communicate versus processes that want to communicate on a single processor system. Suppose that we are to create two threads (or processes) in which the main thread (process) asks the worker thread (process) to add two numbers and print the resulting sum.

In the thread model shown in Code 2.1, threads from a single process share a single address space, so the child thread automatically knows the value of variables a and b that are initialized by the main thread. However, the child thread must be prevented from accessing a and b until after the main thread initializes them. Hence, the `signal` is initially set to 0 and the child thread waits until it is set to 1. Finally, the main thread must not continue until the child thread finishes its execution, hence it waits until the signal is set back to 0 by the child thread.

In the process model, since processes have their private address spaces, a child process does not automatically know the values of a and b. The main and the child process must communicate through explicit message sending and receiving, as shown in Code 2.2. The code example assumes a simplified messaging interface in which `sendMsg(destID, d1, d2, ...)` represents sending a message containing data d1, d2, etc. to destination process `destID`. Similarly, `recvMsg(srcID, &d1, &d2, ...)` means receiving a message from source process `srcID` containing values that will be assigned to variables d1, d2, etc.

Because the processes do not share an address space, the main process must send a message containing the value of a and b, which must be received by the child process.

Overall, the simple code examples illustrate a few things. The thread model is lighter in the sense that it does not incur much communication overhead since data is not explicitly communicated. However, it needs synchronization in order to control the order in which the operations are performed by various threads. The process model is heavier in the sense that it suffers from the overheads of sending and receiving explicit messages that contain the data that is communicated.

Code 2.1 Thread model of communication.

```
1   int a, b, signal;  // all shared variables
2   ...
3   void dosum() {
4     while (signal == 0) {}; // wait until instructed to work
5     printf(``child thread> sum is %d\n'', a + b);
6     signal = 0; // my work is done
7   }
8
9   void main() {
10    signal = 0;
11    thread_create(&dosum)        // spawn child thread
12    a = 5, b = 3;
13    signal = 1;                  // tell child to work
14    while (signal == 1) {}       // wait until child done
15    printf(``all done, exiting\n'');
16  }
```

Code 2.2 Process model of communication.

```
1   int a, b;
2   ...
3   void dosum() {
4     recvMsg(mainID, &a, &b);
5     printf(``child process> sum is %d'', a + b);
6   }
7
8   void main() {
9     if (fork() == 0) { // i am the child process
10      dosum();
11    }
12    else {             // i am the parent process
13      a = 5, b = 3;
14      sendMsg(childID, a, b);
15      wait(childID);
16      printf(``all done, exiting\n'');
17    }
18  }
```

On the other hand, the explicit sending and receiving of messages also serve to synchronize the sequence of operations in both processes. These differences also exist when we compare shared memory versus message passing programming models.

2.2.1 Comparing Shared Memory and Message Passing Models

Table 2.1 summarizes the differences between shared memory and message passing programming models. The first two aspects (communication and synchronization) are similar to the differences that exist in comparing the thread versus process programming models. The shared memory programming model does not communicate data between threads but explicit synchronization is needed to order data accesses among threads. The message passing programming model communicates data between threads through sending and receiving messages, which also implicitly act as synchronization that control the relative ordering of data access by different threads.

Table 2.1: Comparing shared memory and message passing programming models.

Aspects	Shared Memory	Message Passing
Communication	implicit (via loads/stores)	explicit messages
Synchronization	explicit	implicit (via messages)
Hardware support	typically required	none
Development effort	lower	higher
Tuning effort	higher	lower
Communication granularity	finer	coarser

Providing an abstraction of shared memory is typically achieved through special hardware support. For small systems, such as multicore systems, processor cores may already share the last level cache; supporting the shared memory abstraction is simple and in some cases automatic. However, when multiple nodes, each of which has its own processor and memory, are interconnected to form a shared memory system, hardware support is necessary to give an illusion that all nodes' memories form a single memory that is addressable by all processors. For that reason, the cost of providing shared memory abstraction increases with the number of processors. A message passing programming model, on the other hand, does not require such hardware support. Providing a shared memory abstraction is difficult to achieve with a low cost when the number of processors is large. A current shared memory system is often limited to a few hundred to a few thousand processors (e.g., 128 processors in SGI Origin 2000 in 1998-1999, 2048 processors in SGI Altix 3700 in 2000). For very large systems with thousands or more processors, shared memory abstraction is typically not provided, due to the cost of providing it.

Shared memory parallel programs are often easier to develop initially. The reason is that programmers need not worry about how data is laid out and how it is mapped to processors because data can be communicated between processors regardless of where it is located or how it is laid out. In addition, since a shared memory abstraction provides implicit communication, a typical shared memory program code structure is often not much different than its sequential version. In fact, in many cases, all programmers need to do is to insert into the program source code directives that identify parallel tasks, scope of variables, and synchronization points. The compiler translates those directives into code that spawn and control parallel threads. On the other hand, writing a message passing program requires the programmers to immediately think about how to partition data among processors and how to communicate data among them through explicit message sending and receiving. Hence, the initial development effort tends to be lower (sometimes significantly) in shared memory programs.

However, once the parallel program is up and running, and when programmers want the program to scale to a large number of processors, where data is located and how it is laid out start to impact performance significantly. For example, accessing a remote memory may take multiple times longer than accessing the local memory. Hence, it is important to lay out data closest to the processors which access it the most. While message passing programmers already think about this issue when they develop their programs, shared memory programmers eventually face the same issue during post-development time. Hence, the effort to tune the programs to be highly scalable is often higher in shared memory programs than in message passing programs.

In terms of communication granularity, typically the message passing model is used when communications between tasks are less frequent and involve larger amounts of data. The shared memory model is used when communications between tasks may be more frequent and involve small amounts of data in each instance. The reason for this is that typically sending a message involves a higher latency, as data needs to be bundled as a message and unbundled at the destination. This is reinforced by the message passing model being used more when dealing with a larger system (larger processor counts). A larger system incurs larger communication latencies hence the programming model that encourages fewer communications and larger messages fit better with such a system.

Most multicore chips have hardware support for supporting the shared memory abstraction. Thus, this book will place more emphasis on the shared memory programming model.

■ *Did you know?*

Naturally, the shared memory programming model fits better with shared memory multiprocessor systems. However, shared memory programs can also be run on distributed computers with the abstraction of shared memory provided by a software layer at the page granularity. Such systems are referred to as software virtual shared memory *(SVM) systems. In general, SVMs suffer from a high inter-processor communication latency, which limits their practicality.*

Interestingly, the message passing programming model benefits from running on a shared memory multiprocessor. Without shared memory, to send a message, the message must be bundled into packets and sent off the network. With shared memory, sending and receiving a message is simple: sending a message involves writing the message into a message buffer in memory and passing the pointer to the buffer to the receiver, while receiving a message involves reading the message from the message buffer using the pointer that was passed by the sender. Since passing a pointer is faster than sending packets of a message, even message passing programs benefit from shared memory abstraction.

2.2.2 A Simple Example

This section shows a simple example contrasting the shared memory and message passing models. The codes used for comparison are for illustration purposes only, and they are not optimal in terms of performance. The codes are written in pseudo-code style, so they do not correspond directly to any particular syntax required for popular shared memory programming standards (e.g., OpenMP) or message passing programming standards (e.g., MPI).

Suppose we want to perform matrix multiplication in Code 2.3 on two processors. Suppose that there are two 2-dimensional rectangular matrices A and B that we want to multiply together, and the result is stored in the third matrix Y.

Without regard to performance overheads and scalability, suppose that we want to parallelize the innermost "for k" loop of the matrix multiplication (there are much less overheads to parallelize the outer "for i" loop). Suppose that we want to run half of the iterations of the loop on one thread, and run the remaining half of the loop on the other thread. The threads have IDs of 0 and 1, respectively.

Code 2.3 Matrix multiplication code.

```
1  #define MATRIX_DIM 500
2
3  double A[MATRIX_DIM][MATRIX_DIM],
4    B[MATRIX_DIM][MATRIX_DIM],
5    Y[MATRIX_DIM][MATRIX_DIM];
6  int i, j, k;
7
8      for (i=0; i<MATRIX_DIM; i++) {
9        for (j=0; j<MATRIX_DIM; j++) {
10         Y[i][j] = 0.0;
11         for (k=0; k<MATRIX_DIM; k++)
12           Y[i][j] = Y[i][j] + A[i][k] * B[k][j];
13         } // for k
14       } // for j
15     } // for i
```

We will assemble a shared memory parallel program version of the code above, without assuming any popular parallel programming standards. We use self-explanatory pseudo commands when necessary. The purpose for this is to illustrate what language and compiler supports should be provided in a shared memory programming model. The shared memory program corresponding to it is shown in Code 2.4.

In the code above, notice that first we have to define which section of the code must be executed by multiple threads, and which section must be executed by just one thread. That parallel code section is delimited by `begin_parallel()` and `end_parallel()`. We assume that the operating system (OS) or the thread library is involved in creating or dispatching the second thread, and return a different `tid` to different threads, i.e., the original (or parent) thread receives a return value of 0, while the child thread receives a return value of 1. Next, the two threads need to compute different iterations of the loop so they have to calculate the loop index range that they should compute on. This is accomplished by having thread-specific copies of `startiter` and `enditer` computed using the `tid`, and having the loop index variable that is specific to each thread (`kpriv`), so that each thread can track its own current loop index. Note that if the original loop index variable `k` was used, both threads would interfere with one another by overwriting each other's `k`. Thus all occurrences of `k` must be replaced by a private version of it: `kpriv`. With private variables, the threads no longer interfere with one another because each thread uses a different version of the variable, i.e., thread 0 uses `kpriv[0]` while thread 0 uses `kpriv[1]`. The term for this transformation is *privatization*. The new variable is not really private in the sense that threads cannot access or modify each other's privatized variable. The new privatized variables are still allocated in the shared memory, but their usage is private, in that in a bug-free code, each thread accesses only its variable.

The body of the loop is enclosed in `begin_critical` and `end_critical`. The update to variable `Y[i][j]` may be performed simultaneously by the two threads, so there is a possibility of them both reading the same old value, individually produce new values, and simultaneously write the new values, thereby one overwriting the new value of the other. Such an outcome is referred to as a *race*, and may produce both incorrect and unpredictable results. To avoid the races, we can only let one thread to read-modify-write `Y[i][j]` at a time. Thus, the thread library must provide primitives to achieve that, in the example code above, we assume the primitives are

Code 2.4 The shared memory code corresponding to Code 3.28.

```
1 #define MATRIX_DIM 500
2
3 double A[MATRIX_DIM][MATRIX_DIM],
4   B[MATRIX_DIM][MATRIX_DIM],
5   Y[MATRIX_DIM][MATRIX_DIM];
6 int i, j, k, tid;
7 int kpriv[2], startiter[2], enditer[2];
8 . . .
9   for (i=0; i<MATRIX_DIM; i++) {
10     for (j=0; j<MATRIX_DIM; j++) {
11       Y[i][j] = 0.0;
12
13       tid = begin_parallel(); // spawn one extra thread
14       startiter[tid] = tid * MATRIX_DIM/2;
15       enditer[tid] = startiter[tid] + MATRIX_DIM/2;
16
17       for (kpriv[tid]=startiter[tid]; kpriv[tid]<enditer[tid];
18       kpriv[tid]++) {
19         begin_critical();
20           Y[i][j] = Y[i][j] + A[i][kpriv[tid]] * B[kpriv[tid]][j];
21         end_critical();
22       } // for k
23       barrier();
24       end_parallel(); // terminate the extra thread
25
26     } // for j
27   } // for i
28 . . .
```

begin_critical and end_critical, marking the beginning and the end of a *critical section*. A critical section allows only one thread to enter it at a time. Thus, in this case the critical section serializes the execution and negates the parallelism between the two threads. While this is not desirable for performance, it illustrates that synchronization in a shared memory parallel program needs to be explicitly inserted into the code, to ensure that a certain computation is carried out in some order relative to other computations. Finally, the statement barrier is another synchronization primitive that ensures that all threads must reach that point before any of them is allowed to move past it. The barrier may be omitted if there is no further computation that depends on the completion of results from the previous parallel execution.

The message passing program corresponding to it is shown in Code 2.5. In the message passing model, processes do not share a single memory, hence all declared variables and data structures are not the same ones in both processes. In the code, we assume that initially only the main process has the correct content of matrices A and B. Hence, before the main process is able to ask the other process to execute a part of the loop, it must send parts of the matrices that the other process will need. The other process will execute the second half of the loop iterations, which will read the right half of matrix A and the bottom half of matrix B. Thus, before the child process can perform its computation, the parent process must send halves of matrices A and B (line 16-17) while the child process must receive the halves of matrices A and B sent by the parent process (line 20-21). After the content of the matrices are communicated, both threads start the computation using their own values of `startiter` and `enditer`. The result of the multiplication of elements from matrices A and B is accumulated to a temporary variable `temp`. At the end of the computation, the partial result from the child process is sent to the main process. The main process receives the partial result, and then combines it with its own partial result into `Y[i][j]`.

Code 2.5 The message passing code corresponding to Code 3.28.

```
1 #define MATRIX_DIM 500
2
3 double A[MATRIX_DIM][MATRIX_DIM],
4   B[MATRIX_DIM][MATRIX_DIM],
5   Y[MATRIX_DIM][MATRIX_DIM];
6 int i, j, k, tid;
7 int startiter, enditer;
8 double temp, temp2;
9 . . .
10    tid = begin_parallel(); // spawn one extra process
11    startiter = tid * MATRIX_DIM/2;
12    enditer = startiter + MATRIX_DIM/2;
13
14    if (tid == 0) {
15      send(1, A[0][MATRIX_DIM/2-1]..A[MATRIX_DIM-1][MATRIX_DIM-1]);
16      send(1, B[MATRIX_DIM/2-1][0]..B[MATRIX_DIM-1][MATRIX_DIM-1]);
17      }
18    else
19      recv(0, A[0][MATRIX_DIM/2-1]..A[MATRIX_DIM-1][MATRIX_DIM-1]);
20      recv(0, B[MATRIX_DIM/2-1][0]..B[MATRIX_DIM-1][MATRIX_DIM-1]);
21    }
22
23    for (i=0; i<MATRIX_DIM; i++) {
24      for (j=0; j<MATRIX_DIM; j++) {
25        Y[i][j] = 0.0;
26
27
28        temp = Y[i][j];
29        for (k=startiter; k<enditer; k++) {
30          temp = temp + A[i][k] * B[k][j];
31        } // for k
32
33        if (tid == 0) {
34          recv(1, &temp2);
35          Y[i][j] = temp + temp2;
36        }
37        else
38          send(0, temp);
39
40      } // for j
41    } // for i
42  end_parallel();
43
```

There are several interesting things we can observe from the code above. First, data needs to be communicated explicitly, the main process sending whatever data the other process needs for its part of the computation. The processes keep a copy of the data in their local memory, even for read-only data. In shared memory programs, there is only one copy of most data (especially the read-only one) kept in the main memory. Hence, shared memory programs have smaller code and data footprints in the main memory. In addition, the total physical memory is the addition of all local memories in a shared memory system, while in a non-shared memory system each processor's main memory is limited by its own physical memory size. In some cases, the latter benefit alone is sufficient for some programmers to choose to run their applications on shared memory multiprocessor systems over distributed systems.

The code above also assumes that both send and recv are blocking, in that send blocks if the message buffer is full, while recv blocks when the message it is waiting for has not arrived. Therefore, send and recv actually act as synchronization, serving to order computation in one process relative to another. Overall, the examples in Code 2.4 and Code 2.5 reiterate the differences in explicit synchronization in shared memory programs versus explicit communication and implicit synchronization in message passing programs.

2.2.3   Other Programming Models

Partitioned Global Address Space (PGAS)

As discussed earlier, the shared memory programming model allows all threads to share a single address space transparently. While it simplifies writing a parallel program, it also hides data layout from the programmer. Since data layout and data locality are very important aspects for tuning parallel program performance, such transparency tends to defer some complexity of parallel programming to the latter (tuning) stage, and may even increase the difficulty of tuning. Giving the programmer some control over how data should be laid out and assigned to different threads early in the programming stage may allow the programmer to achieve better tuning productivity. To facilitate that, a hybrid programming model has been proposed. The programming model, PGAS (partitioned global address space) is an attempt to achieve the benefits of both shared memory and message passing programming models: data locality (partitioning) features of the message passing model and the simple data referencing of the shared memory model.

The memory model of PGAS is illustrated in Figure 2.4(a). The address space is comprised of a private portion and a shared portion. Each thread is allocated a private portion that can only be accessed by the thread itself, and in a non-uniform memory architecture (NUMA) system, it automatically has affinity with the thread. The shared portion can be accessed (read and written) by all threads, and can be partitioned into regions with different affinities. Data affinity only specifies lay out, i.e., which memory data should be allocated in the shared space, hence it is useful to improve locality but cannot be used to restrict accesses by other threads.

Programmers can control whether a data structure should be allocated in a thread's private space or in the shared space. Programmers can assign which portions of the data structure are given different affinities if it is allocated in the shared space. Figure 2.4(b) shows an illustration of variables or data structures that can be declared with universal parallel C (UPC), a PGAS programming language. A declaration `int a` allocates variable a in a private space, i.e., one instance of a in the private space of each thread. A declaration `shared int b` allocates a single variable in the shared space, with a default affinity of thread 0. For a matrix, block-wise affinity assignment can be specified: `shared [2] x[8][8]` interleaves the affinity of the matrix, where each two consecutive elements of the matrix are assigned one affinity, and the next two consecutive elements

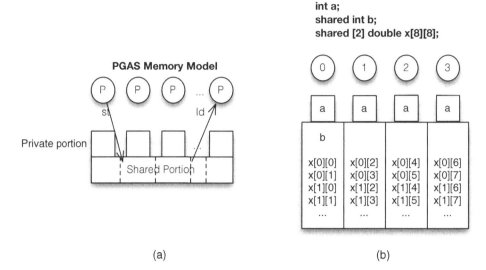

Figure 2.4: Illustrating PGAS memory model (a) and example data structure allocation and affinity with UPC (b).

are assigned the next affinity, and so on until it wraps around. There are rules regarding pointer allocation as well. For example, a pointer may be declared as a private or shared variable, and may point to an object in the private or shared space. A private pointer can only point to an object in the private space or a local object in the shared space.

> ■ *Did you know?*
>
> *Since its inception in early 2000s, there have been multiple programming languages that support PGAS programming model, including Unified Parallel C (UPC), Co-Array Fortran, Titanium, X-10, and Chapel. These languages not just define a memory model, but they also define various forms of synchronizations and memory consistency models. Interested readers are referred to* http://www.pgas.org.

Figure 2.4(b) illustrates how a programming model allows the programmer to have more control over how data should be laid out. To illustrate how data layout can be useful in improving locality, Code 2.6 shows a matrix multiplication example. In the example, matrix multiplication $C = A \cdot B$ is performed. All the matrices are allocated in the shared space. Matrices A and C have their rows distributed evenly across all threads: every $\frac{N \times P}{THREADS}$ rows are assigned the affinity of a unique thread since only the thread accesses matrix elements from those rows. However, each thread will access all elements of matrix B, hence matrix B does not benefit from being associated with any particular affinity. Hence, simply declaring shared B[P][M] does not hurt locality. In the code example, B is distributed column-wise to avoid a hot spot where all threads accessing the portion of the shared memory with the default affinity.

For NUMA systems, PGAS allows the programmer to place different parts of data close to the threads that will access them. Fundamentally, there is a trade off between flexibility (how much the programmer can specify or control in a parallel program) with complexity (how many issues the programmer has to deal with for parallel programming). PGAS increases programming flexibility

---

Code 2.6 Example code showing matrix multiplication with UPC.

Code that computes $C = A \cdot B$, where A is a matrix of size $N \times P$, B is a matrix of size $P \times M$, and C is a matrix of size $N \times M$. It is assumed that $N \times P$ is divisible by the number of threads.

`upc_forall` specifies that all loop iterations can be executed independently from one another. The first three arguments specify the same arguments as C's `for` statement. The last argument `&A[i][0]` specifies that the ith iteration should be executed by the thread that has affinity to element a[i][0].

The code is as follows.

```
1 shared [N*P /THREADS] double A[N][P]; // distribute rows of matrix A
2 shared [N*P /THREADS] double C[N][M]; // distribute rows of matrix C
3 shared [M /THREADS] double B[P][M] ; // distribute columns of matrix B
4
5 void main(void) {
6    ... // matrices are initialized
7
8    upc_forall(i=0;i<N;i++;&A[i][0])
9      for (j=0; j<M; j++) {
10        C[i][j] = 0;
11        for(l=0; l< P; l++)
12          C[i][j] +=A[i][l]*B[l][j];
13      }
14    upc_barrier;
15
16    ...
17 }
```

---

but also complexity compared to the standard shared memory programming model. However, since data locality is a critical determinant of performance in NUMA systems, PGAS programming model may be necessary to get high-performing parallel programs in NUMA systems.

Data Parallel Programming Model

Data parallel programming model is a programming model associated with the single instruction stream multiple data stream (SIMD) machine. Essentially there is just one instruction stream that can operate on a large number of data. A non-data parallel instruction typically takes two source operands, performs an operation on them, and produces a single result. A data parallel instruction can take multiple sets of two source operands and produces a set of results. It requires that data that forms source operands to be organized in a vector format. The number of sets of operands and results are the width (or number of lanes) of the vector.

Data that feed vector lanes may be organized as vector data by grouping a set of registers into a single vector register. Alternatively, small data may be packed into a single wide register. Figure 2.5(a) shows a single 128-bit wide register may pack multiple data items depending on the size of the data item: two 64-bit data items, four 32-bit data items, eight 16-bit data items, or 16 8-bit data items. For example, two double precision floating points (double) can fit into one vector register creating a 2-wide vector, four single precision floating points (float) can fit into one vector register creating a 4-wide vector, 16 byte-sized data items can fit into one vector register creating a 16-wide vector, etc. Moving multiple data items into the vector register requires packing and storing the resulting vector requires unpacking.

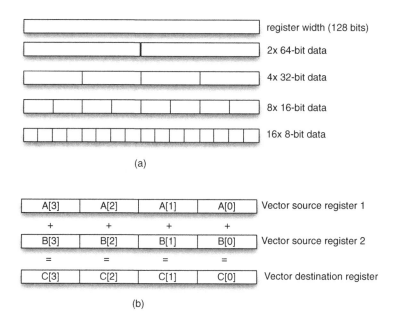

Figure 2.5: A vector register can pack various counts of data items of different sizes (a) and an example vector addition involving two source vector registers, each containing four data items (b).

Code 2.7 Example 4-wide vector addition operation using Intel SSE instructions.

```
1 // A 128-bit vector struct with four 32-bit floats
2 struct Vector4
3 {
4   float x, y, z, w;
5 };
6
7 // Add two constant vectors and return the resulting vector
8 Vector4 SSE_Add ( const Vector4 &Operand1, const Vector4 &Operand2 )
9 {
10   Vector4 Result;
11
12   __asm
13   {
14     MOV EAX Operand1      // Load pointers into CPU regs
15     MOV EBX, Operand2
16
17     MOVUPS XMM0, [EAX]    // Move unaligned vectors to SSE regs
18     MOVUPS XMM1, [EBX]
19
20     ADDPS XMM0, XMM1      // Vector addition
21     MOVUPS [Result], XMM0 // Save the return vector
22   }
23   return Result;
24 }
```

An example code performing a 4-wide vector addition is shown in Code 2.7. In the code, packing is performed by first placing pointers of four data items into the EAX (and EBX) register, and loading these items into the vector register XMM0 (and XMM1) using the MOVUPS instruction. Once four data items are packed in both the XMM0 and XMM1 vector registers, they can be added together with just one instruction ADDPS. The illustration of the addition is shown in Figure 2.5(b).

Data parallel execution is very efficient. For example, to add the four pairs of data items shown in Code 2.7, without vector one needs to write a loop with four iterations where each iteration adds a pair of data items. The loop introduces not just four addition instructions, but also instructions to update the loop index, a conditional branch, etc. However, data parallel programming model is not very flexible: it requires the same type of computation to be applied to many data items. Some flexibility is possible, for example a mask can be specified to a vector operation so that it only performs the operation on data items that are not masked. Thus, the mask achieves the effect of a simple conditional branch on vector operation.

The data parallel programming model typically requires the system to have shared memory, due to several reasons. First, there is a need for reading/writing data from/to the memory into/from vector registers. Vector data typically comes from elements of a matrix data structure. Data read-/written by one vector lane may at some point be read/written by scalar instructions or a different vector lane. It is convenient to support vector execution when memory is shared across processor cores. Furthermore, packing/unpacking is quite tied to the addressing mode supported by the processor. The data parallel programming model is thus tied to the instruction set architecture of a processor. Thus, the data parallel programming model is often supported within the shared memory model.

Another example of the data parallel programming model is SIMT (single instruction multiple thread) that is implemented in some graphics processing units (GPUs), where cores run threads that execute the same instruction in lockstep, and the instruction operates on different data. The SIMT programming model is discussed in greater detail in Chapter 12.

MapReduce

MapReduce is a programming model proposed by Google for cluster computing. It has enjoyed widespread commercial adoption by various companies, including Amazon, Facebook, and Yahoo. Perhaps the most popular MapReduce implementation is an open source Hadoop library. In MapReduce programming, programmers provide (at least) two functions: map() and reduce(), which are executed as separate phases. During the map phase, the map function accepts input data to produce intermediate output in the form of a list of $< key, value >$ pairs. In the reduce phase, the list of key-value pairs are read by the reduce function, and all values having the same key are aggregated.

To give an illustration, suppose we are given a document, and we want to tabulate the frequency of each distinct word in a histogram. In word count, each map worker takes a chunk from the text document input, and for each word w that it encounters, it produces a $< w, 1 >$ pair as intermediate output. After the map phase, the reduce phase starts. Each reduce worker works on a specific key (a distinct word) to sum up the list of values (counts) associated with the key.

Let us examine key features of the MapReduce programming model. One notable feature is that data is not accessed directly using its location. Instead, the location of data is abstracted, and data is stored into the intermediate output using its key during the map phase and retrieved from the intermediate output during the reduce phase also using its key. This carries an important implication: the intermediate output can change its location as well as organization without affecting the MapReduce programs. Whereas in the shared memory and message passing models, programmers need to be aware of where data is stored (location in the shared memory or which process has data), in MapReduce they do not need to be aware of where data is stored. As a result, MapReduce can be implemented in systems where processors do not share the memory or in systems where processors share the memory. Figure 2.6 illustrates this. In the former case, the intermediate output can be implemented in a file system, such as in Hadoop File System (HDFS). Map processes emit intermediate output into the HDFS through file writes and reduce processes read from the intermediate output from HDFS through file reads. Between map and reduce, data is shuffled in the file system so that ones that share the same key are moved to the same node where the reduce process will run on. An alternative implementation for the intermediate output is to keep it in a data structure in memory. An example data structure is a hash matrix (Figure 2.6), which is used in shared memory implementation of MapReduce, such as Phoenix.

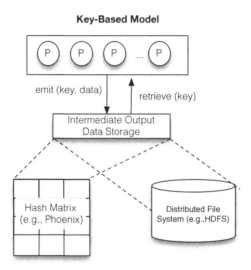

Figure 2.6: Illustrating MapReduce programming model.

Another key feature of MapReduce is the type of parallelism it allows. In the map phase, input records are distributed across map workers, and map workers perform the same computation on different input records they are assigned to. The reduce phase reads from the intermediate output to aggregate values from the same key, in effect performing a key-based reduction. The association of data with keys enable parallel reduction because threads/processes can work on different keys, without interfering with one another. Thus, from a parallelism point of view, the map workers achieve data parallelism, while reduce workers perform parallel reduction.

MapReduce parallelism model, at least in its basic form, carries some restrictions. For example, MapReduce cannot handle pipelined parallelism among map or reduce workers. However, the restrictions also bring benefits. For example, since MapReduce deals only with data parallelism and parallel reduction, threads or processes are guaranteed not to conflict in the map or reduce phases, hence there is no need for the threads or processes to synchronize. The only synchronization required is a barrier between the end of the map phase and the start of the reduce phase. No deadlock is possible since no locks are used in the user programs. In addition, concurrency management, such as when and how many threads are spawned, and task queue management, can be hidden from programmers.

> ■ *Did you know?*
>
> *Another implication of abstracting data location using keys is that the performance of MapReduce program is no longer just determined by where data is located, but by what keys data is associated. This is because when a $< key, value >$ pair is inserted into the intermediate output, the performance of the insertion depends on the value of the key and the value of keys that were already inserted into the intermediate output prior to this one. For example, in the word count application, it was reported that when the document contains only unique words, the performance is $67\times$ slower than when the document contains only one single word replicated many times [64]. Such data content-dependent performance is not usually present in the more traditional shared memory or message passing models.*

For a more vivid illustration of the MapReduce programming model, let us consider an example for *inverted index* computation. The goal of the computation is: given a list of HTML documents, each containing links to other HTML documents, it should produce an output that lists all HTML documents that contain each link. This is illustrated in Figure 2.7. The input to the computation consists of four documents each containing different links. In the map phase, different files may be assigned to different map workers. Each worker parses the files assigned to it, and whenever it encounters a link L in document D, it emits an $< L, D >$ pair. Thus, L is the key, and D is the value in the pair. At the end of the map phase, the intermediate output contains many $< L, D >$ pairs, and they are sorted by L's. In the reduce phase, different key values (i.e., different L's) may be assigned to different reduce workers. Each worker merges all values for a single key value. For example, a reduce worker may process $< LinkA, Doc1 >$, $< LinkA, Doc3 >$, $< LinkA, Doc4 >$ and produce the final output for "LinkA: Doc1, Doc3, Doc4". Other reduce workers may work on different keys (links) and produce the final output for them. In this example, map workers work in parallel with respect to one another, and reduce workers work in parallel with respect to one another. However, reduce is started only after map is completed. The intermediate output allows map and reduce to be decoupled because data is identified using its key, rather than address.

Overall, MapReduce is a parallel programming model that shows that restricting the type of parallelism that can be expressed in the model can bring desirable properties which simplify parallel programming. For specific domains that do not require all-flexible parallel programming, such a model may be highly attractive.

Transactional Memory

Transactional memory (TM) is a programming model where programmers specify sections of code that should be executed as a transaction. The concept of transactions is derived from database programming for the purpose of isolating concurrent activities. In database systems, a transaction must have the following ACID properties: *atomicity*, *consistency*, *isolation*, and *durability*. Atomicity requires that each transaction either fully succeeds (it completes and all its effects reflected) or fully fails (none of its effects are reflected). Consistency refers to in any events, the transaction must re-

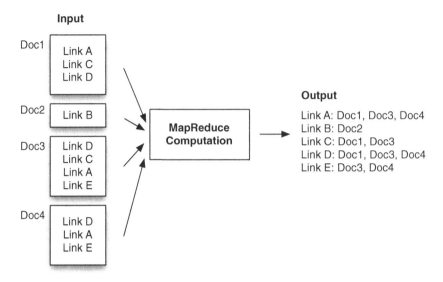

Figure 2.7: Illustrating an inverted index computation using MapReduce programming model.

sult in a correct state, even when there are programming errors. Isolation refers to a property where the state of the system matching what would be obtained if transactions were executed sequentially. Durability refers to a property where when a transaction commits, it remains so, even in the event of failures such as power loss, crashes, or other errors.

In the context of parallel programming, transactions were proposed primarily as a programming abstraction that frees up programmers from dealing with lower level thread synchronization constructs such as locks. Therefore, a transaction has a narrower role compared to that in database programming, it is designed to satisfy only atomicity and isolation. In TM, transactions must be fully executed or not at all, and they must result in states that might have resulted if they were to execute sequentially. However, the notion of atomicity is weaker, in that a transaction must succeed or fail completely only in the events of other transactions interfering with a transaction's execution, but not in the event of failures, or interacting with the outside world (e.g., system calls). Durability is not of a concern because we are dealing with memory states that are volatile, hence they are not designed to survive failures. Therefore, for parallel programming, the word "memory" is specifically added to form "transactional memory".

To illustrate how programmers can use TM, consider an image histogram kernel, where we collect the number of occurrences of every red, green, and blue intensity values in an image by visiting every pixel in the image. Code 2.8 shows the implementation of the kernel using coarse-grain locks versus fine-grain locks. In the coarse-grain lock version, to avoid races involving multiple threads trying to update the same red, green, or blue histogram element, we enclose the histogram update with a pair of lock and unlock. The semantics of a lock is that it only allows one thread to acquire it, and all other threads must be waiting until the lock is released. Therefore, only one thread updates the red, green, and blue histogram at a time. There is not much concurrency between the execution of multiple threads. To improve the concurrency, we have to resort to a fine-grain lock version. In this version, we can associate a lock with each histogram element. Thus, each of the red elements, green elements, and blue elements is associated with a lock of its own (line 2). Further-more, each thread only acquires a lock that is associated with the histogram element that it wants to update. Thus, it acquires one red lock before updating a red histogram element, acquires one green lock before updating a green histogram element, and acquires one blue lock before updating a blue histogram element. In this case, now multiple threads can update different histogram elements concurrently. Threads have conflict and wait only when they want to update the same histogram element simultaneously. This histogram implementation allows concurrent execution of threads, at the expense of complexities and overheads associated with fine-grain lock programming.

Code 2.8 Image histogram computation code.

Coarse-grain lock version:

```
1   image = Image_Read(fn_input);
2
3   for (i=0; i<image->row; i++) {
4     for (j=0; j<image->col; j++) {
5       lock();
6       histoRed[image->red[i][j]]++;
7       histoGreen[image->green[i][j]]++;
8       histoBlue[image->blue[i][j]]++;
9       unlock();
10    }
11  }
```

Fine-grain lock version:

```
1   image = Image_Read(fn_input);
2   lock_t redLock[256], greenLock[256], blueLock[256];
3
4   for (i=0; i<image->row; i++) {
5     for (j=0; j<image->col; j++) {
6       lock(&redLock(image->red[i][j]));
7       histoRed[image->red[i][j]]++;
8       unlock(&redLock(image->red[i][j]));
9
10      lock(&greenLock(image->red[i][j]));
11      histoGreen[image->red[i][j]]++;
12      unlock(&greenLock(image->red[i][j]));
13
14      lock(&blueLock(image->red[i][j]));
15      histoBlue[image->blue[i][j]]++;
16      unlock(&blueLock(image->red[i][j]));
17    }
18  }
```

In TM, programmers define the code section that should have atomicity and isolation proper-ties. For example, rather than relying on locks, programmers can declare the block of code that updates histogram elements as an atomic block (transaction), as shown in Code 2.9. TM provides *optimistic concurrency* where rather than blocking, each thread proceeds executing the code block. If a conflict is encountered, i.e., two threads updating the same histogram element while executing the code block, the conflict must be detected and the corrective action is to roll back the execu-tion of both threads or to prevent their execution from updating memory state to preserve atomicity (so that it does not appear the threads have executed the code block at all), and to let the threads reexecute the code block. Therefore, a TM system needs the following components: a conflict detection mechanism, a rollback mechanism or a mechanism to gate memory writes, and a reexecution mechanism.

Code 2.9 Image histogram computation with transactional memory.

Transactional memory version:

```
1   image = Image_Read(fn_input);
2
3   for (i=0; i<image->row; i++) {
4     for (j=0; j<image->col; j++) {
5       atomic {
6         histoRed[image->red[i][j]]++;
7         histoGreen[image->green[i][j]]++;
8         histoBlue[image->blue[i][j]]++;
9       }
10    }
11  }
```

To some degree, TM may simplify parallel programming by reducing or eliminating the use of locks in parallel programs. This reduces the potential occurrences of deadlocks (where a cyclic lock dependency between two threads prevent any of them from continuing execution). Due to its simpler abstraction, TM has been touted as composable, allowing a more complex code with transactions to be built using code components that themselves rely on transactions. However, it has been repeatedly shown that in both software and hardware implementations of TM, the TM performance is closely tied to the choice of the granularity of the atomic code blocks. If the code block is too large, the probability of conflicts is large and conflicts and rollbacks may become too frequent. Furthermore, the cost of providing atomicity abstraction increases as the transaction size increases. In hardware implementations of TM, the size of transactions is limited by the size of the buffer (or cache) that can hold updates that are not yet committed to the memory or otherwise performance degrades steeply. If the code block is too small, the amount of concurrency is also reduced. Therefore, programmers still need to be intimately familiar with their code in order to choose the appropriate transaction size.

There are two implementations of TM: software (STM) or hardware (HTM). STM is typically data structure specific. It allows modifications to a node to be performed on a duplicate copy of the node, and to commit a transaction, the pointer to the node is modified to point to the now-modified duplicate node. HTM uses the cache or special buffer to keep values updated by an uncommitted transaction, and the values are either discarded if the transaction rolls back, or allowed to merge to the rest of the memory hierarchy if the transaction is committed.

TM does not replace all synchronization primitives. Transactions only provide an illusion of mutual execution, but do not express thread dependency. For example, if a thread needs to block waiting for another thread to complete certain computation, programmers still need to rely on flags or semaphores. Quite a few processors today support HTM, but typically have a limit on the transaction size (transactions that are too large cannot be guaranteed to commit). It remains to be seen in what way programmers will use transactions in legacy and future code.

2.3 Exercises

Homework Problems

1. Consider a linear transformation computation $Y = A \times B + C$, where Y, A, B, C have a dimension $n \times p, n \times m, m \times p, n \times p$, respectively. Assume that all n, m, and p are divisible by 2. The algorithm for the computation is shown below:

```
int i, j, k;
float A[n][m], B[m][p], Y[n][p], C[n][p], x;
...
for (i=0; i<n; i++) {
  for (j=0; j<p; j++) {
    x = 0;
    for (k=0; k<m; k++)
      x = x + A[i][k] * B[k][j];
    Y[i][j] = x + C[i][j];
  }
}
```

   (a) Parallelize the algorithm for the "for i" loop, using the message passing programming model on two processors. Use *send(destination-thread, list-of-data)* and *recv(source-thread, list-of-data)*. Assume originally only thread 0 has all the data. Determine which data thread 0 must send to thread 1 and vice versa.

   (b) Parallelize the algorithm for the "for i" loop, using the shared memory programming model on two processors. Use "begin parallel" and "end parallel" to mark your parallel region, and insert proper synchronization (e.g., locks and barriers). Identify what data should be private-per-thread or common (shared) for all threads.

Chapter 3

Shared Memory Parallel Programming

Contents

In the previous chapter, we mentioned that in this book, we will focus mostly on the shared memory programming model, because its concepts are important for understanding the architecture of multicore architectures, and also because currently it is a dominant programming model for multicore architectures. The objective of this chapter is to discuss steps needed to create shared memory parallel programs. The focus is on identifying parallel tasks by analyzing the code or algorithm, how to determine the scope of variables, coordinate the parallel tasks, and express parallelism to the compiler. By the end of this chapter, readers will have learned basic shared memory parallel programming techniques.

It is a good idea to study shared memory parallel programming prior to studying the architecture of shared memory multiprocessors, in order to get a handle on how software uses the systems, what constructs are important, and what software issues are relevant when considering the design space of a shared memory multiprocessor.

3.1 Steps in Parallel Programming

In general, shared memory parallel progi.e., ramming involves several steps shown in Figure 3.1. The first step in creating a parallel program is identifying sources of parallelism in the code. Various analyses techniques at different levels (e.g., code level and algorithm level) can be performed to identify parallelism. These will be discussed in Sections 3.3, 3.4, and 3.5. Once parallel tasks are identified, they may be grouped into larger ones if they are too small. At this step, a task becomes the smallest unit of execution that may be executed by a thread. Then, we need to determine the scope of each variable used by the tasks (Section 3.6). Because two tasks may be executed by different threads, the choice is whether the variable should be shared by all threads or should be private to each thread. The next step involves coordinating the execution of tasks through thread synchronization. We will discuss what types of synchronization should be inserted and where they should be inserted (Section 3.7). Then, we will discuss how tasks can be assigned to threads (Section 3.8) and how threads can be mapped to processors (Section 3.9). Collectively, the parallelism identification step, variable scope determination, and synchronization, can be referred to as *task creation* since during these steps we create tasks that can cooperate to perform a single computation. Task creation is relatively machine independent. Programmers do not have to worry much about the number of processors, how processors are interconnected, and how data is laid out.

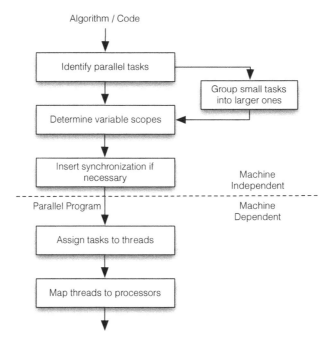

Figure 3.1: Steps in shared memory parallel programming.

The next step deals with assigning tasks to threads. Typically, there are many more tasks than available processors, and it is counter-productive to spawn more threads than processors (which would lead to threads time-sharing a single processor), so multiple tasks may be assigned to a single thread. A goal of task-to-thread mapping may be to balance the work load of the threads. The final step deals with mapping the threads to processors, and laying out data in memory. The goal of this step is to achieve communication locality, in which processors that communicate with each other are located in close proximity to one another, and data locality, in which data accessed by each processor is located as close as possible to the processor. These last two steps can be collectively referred to as *task mapping*. Sometimes task mapping can be hidden from programmers, for example, by using the default mapping that the system employs. However, relying on such default mapping sometimes produces suboptimal performance and scalability.

The first step in task creation is identifying parallel tasks. There are three levels at which this can be done: *program-level*, *algorithm-level*, and *code-level*. An example of parallel tasks at the program level is parallel compilation of files. For example, parallel make tools (e.g., `pmake`) spawn processes that compile different source files independently from one another. Program-level parallelism is effective, but is restricted to the case in which multiple instances of a program are run simultaneously. In addition, exploiting program-level parallelism is sometimes trivial. Consequently, we will focus our discussion on identifying parallelism at the code level and algorithm level. Identifying code-level parallelism is a versatile technique since we only need to analyze code structures, without needing to know the algorithms that the code represents. However, sometimes knowing the algorithms can give extra parallelism opportunities that are missed in code-level parallelism.

3.2 Dependence Analysis

The goal of dependence analysis is to discover if there are sections of code that can be executed in parallel. In general, two sections that have no dependence relationship can be executed in parallel, whereas two sections that have dependence relationship may not be executed in parallel (although some code transformation may remove some dependences). Dependence analysis identifies parallelism at the code-level using only information embedded in the source code. Other information, such as the knowledge of the algorithms, is not considered. Dependence analysis is useful not just for shared memory parallel programming which is the focus in this chapter, but also message passing parallel programming.

The first issue that we need to deal with is what granularity of code sections we should perform dependence analysis on. That choice is largely up to the programmer, however there are some limits. For example, the smallest granularity may be single machine instructions. Dependences between them are largely due to register dependences, for example one instruction produces a register value that another instruction reads. Exploiting dependences or the lack of dependences on register values require a common register file, which is more appropriate for instruction-level parallelism on a single processor. Thus, the smallest granularity we should consider for parallel programming is at the source-code statement level. A larger granularity that can be considered is at the loop body (across different iterations of a loop or a loop nest), or at a small function body. An even larger granularity may be at the level of large function bodies or abstract algorithm steps.

To allow a systematic way of performing dependence analysis, it is necessary to define a framework. We will start by defining several notations. Let S denote a statement or a group of statements in the source code. If there are two statements $S1$ and $S2$, let $S1 \rightarrow S2$ denote that statement $S1$ comes before $S2$ in the order of program execution. Furthermore, let us define the following dependence relationships (or simply "dependences"):

- $S1 \rightarrow^T S2$ denotes *true dependence*, i.e., $S1 \rightarrow S2$, and $S1$ writes to a location that is read by $S2$. In other words, $S1$ is the *producer* of data that is read by the *consumer* ($S2$).

- $S1 \rightarrow^A S2$ denotes *anti dependence*, i.e., $S1 \rightarrow S2$, and $S1$ reads a location written by $S2$.

- $S1 \rightarrow^O S2$ denotes *output dependence*, i.e., $S1 \rightarrow S2$, and $S1$ writes to the same location written by $S2$.

To illustrate the dependences, Code 3.1 shows a code section with four statements.

Code 3.1 A simple code with four statements.

```
1 S1: x = 2;
2 S2: y = x;
3 S3: y = x + z;
4 S4: z = 6;
```

The dependences corresponding to the code are:

- $S1 \rightarrow^T S2$ because x is written in statement $S1$ and read in statement $S2$.

- $S1 \rightarrow^T S3$ because x is written in statement $S1$ and read in statement $S3$.

- $S3 \rightarrow^A S4$ because z is read in statement $S3$ and written in statement $S4$.

- $S2 \rightarrow^O S3$ because y is written in statement $S2$ and also written in statement $S4$.

Anti and output dependences are also referred to as *false* dependences, for the reason that the later instruction is not dependent on any value produced by the earlier instruction. The dependences are there only because they involve the same variable or memory location. Thus, false dependences can actually be removed through renaming the variables. For example, if $S3$ writes to "y2" instead of "y", then the output dependence between $S2$ and $S3$ disappears. Similarly, if $S4$ writes to "z2" instead of "z", then the anti dependence between $S3$ and $S4$ disappears. True dependences are in general difficult to remove, hence they are a real hinderance to parallelization. In a parallel program, renaming is only necessary if two statements will execute in parallel on different threads. Thus, the renaming typically creates a "private" copy of a variable for each thread. For this reason, the typical method to remove false dependences in parallel programs is referred to as *privatization*. Privatization will be discussed in more details in Section 3.6.

■ *Did you know?*

Dependence analysis can also be performed for a larger granularity by arbitrarily grouping adjacent statements. One reason to do this may be because we would like to identify parallelism between groups of statements, rather than between statements. For example, suppose that we group statements $S1$ and $S2$ from the above example into group S_{12}, and statements $S3$ and $S4$ into group S_{34}. With the grouping, we wish to consider only dependences across groups of statements, which leads us to identify the following:

- *$S_{12} \rightarrow^T S_{34}$ because statement group S_{12} produces a value x that is read by statement group S_{34}.*

- *$S_{12} \rightarrow^O S_{34}$ because statement group S_{12} writes onto y that is later written in statement group S_{34}.*

Notice from the example above that we can arbitrarily define our statement groups and perform dependence analysis on the groups. We have an intuition that the larger the statement group, the smaller parallel overheads will be relatively. We also have an intuition that if the statement group is very large, the statement groups will be increasingly diverse and likely to have more cross-group dependences. Thus, a question arises: what statement group granularity is likely to be more profitable than others for identifying a lot of parallelism between sufficiently large statement groups?

One such statement group granularity is loop or loop nest bodies. Loop structures show promising features. First, they are often regularly structured and easily analyzable. Second, they tend to contribute significantly to the execution time for many scientific applications. Scientific applications, which have been a key driver for parallel computers, typically rely on simulations of physical phenomena. Many models of physical phenomena heavily use matrices as their main data structures to model objects in the physical space. Accessing these multi-dimensional data structures (the matrices) requires the use of nested loops to iterate over different dimensions and often across time steps. Therefore, analyzing loop structures is a very fruitful way to identify parallelism for these applications. Non-numerical applications seldom use matrices. Instead, they use linked data structures such as linked lists, hash tables, trees, and graphs. While traversing these structures also often involve loops, the code structures of these loops are much more complex since many addresses of pointers cannot be inferred until run-time, and sometimes the loops involve recursion. As a result, loop-level code-analysis is less fruitful in identifying parallelism in non-numerical applications.

3.2.1 Loop-Level Dependence Analysis

Let us augment our dependence analysis so that it is suitable to use for loops. Let us denote loop iteration space inside a bracket []. For example, for a doubly nested loop with i iterating on the outer loop and j iterating on the inner loop, we will denote the iteration space as $[i, j]$. We can express a statement S executed in a particular iteration $[i, j]$ as $S[i, j]$. If we treat the entire loop body as a statement group, we can let $S[i, j]$ denote the entire loop body at iteration $[i, j]$.

Next, let us define *loop-carried dependence* as a dependence that exists between a statement in one iteration with another statement in a different iteration, while *loop-independent dependence* as a dependence that exists between statements within a loop iteration. The difference between them is illustrated via Code 3.2.

Code 3.2 A code segment illustrating dependences in loop structures.

```
1 for (i=1; i<n; i++) {
2   S1: a[i] = a[i-1] + 1;
3   S2: b[i] = a[i];
4 }
5 for (i=1; i<n; i++)
6   for (j=1; j< n; j++)
7     S3: a[i][j] = a[i][j-1] + 1;
8 for (i=1; i<n; i++)
9   for (j=1; j< n; j++)
10     S4: a[i][j] = a[i-1][j] + 1;
```

In the first statement in the first loop ($S1$), we have a write to $a[i]$ and a read from $a[i - 1]$, which means that a value written to $a[i]$ will be read in the next iteration (the $(i + 1)^{th}$ iteration). Hence, we have $S1[i] \rightarrow^T S1[i + 1]$ dependence, which is loop-carried. For example, in iteration $i = 4$, statement $S1$ writes to $a[4]$ and reads from $a[3]$, which was earlier written in iteration $i = 3$. In addition, the value written to $a[i]$ is read by statement $S2$ in the same iteration, so we have a loop-independent dependence of $S1[i] \rightarrow^T S2[i]$.

In the second loop, a value written to $a[i][j]$ will be read in the next j iteration, hence we have a dependence $S3[i, j] \rightarrow^T S3[i, j + 1]$, which is loop-carried for the $for\ j$ loop but is loop-independent for the $for\ i$ loop.

Finally, in the third loop, a value is written to $a[i][j]$ will be read in the next i iteration, hence we have a dependence $S4[i, j] \rightarrow^T S4[i + 1, j]$, which is loop-carried for the $for\ i$ loop but is loop-independent for the $for\ j$ loop. Overall, the dependences are:

- $S1[i] \rightarrow^T S1[i + 1]$

- $S1[i] \rightarrow^T S2[i]$

- $S3[i, j] \rightarrow^T S3[i, j + 1]$

- $S4[i, j] \rightarrow^T S4[i + 1, j]$

3.2.2   Iteration-Space Traversal Graph and Loop-Carried Dependence Graph

An *iteration-space traversal graph* (ITG) shows graphically the order of traversal in the iteration space. ITG does not show dependences; it only shows the order in which loop iterations are visited.

Loop-carried dependence graph (LDG) shows true/anti/output dependences graphically, in which a node is a point in the iteration space and the directed edge shows the direction of the dependence. In other words, LDG treats statements in the innermost loop body as a single statement group. Since a node represents all statements in a single iteration, so the LDG does not show loop-independent dependences.

An LDG can essentially be obtained by drawing the dependences for each of the iterations. For example, Example 1 in Code 3.3 has the ITG and LDG shown in Figure 3.2. The LDG is essentially an *unrolled* version of the dependence $S3[i, j] \rightarrow^T S3[i, j + 1]$. In the figure, we can visually observe that the dependence is loop-carried on the $for\ j$ loop but not on the $for\ i$ loop.

Examples 2 and 3 of Code 3.3 show more complex cases. In Example 2, the $for j$ iteration goes from a larger index value to a smaller value with an increment of -1, hence the ITG will be different

---

Code 3.3 A simple code with loop-carried dependence.

Example 1:

```
1 for (i=1; i<4; i++)
2   for (j=1; j<4; j++)
3     S3: a[i][j] = a[i][j-1] + 1;
```

Example 2:

```
1 for (i=0; i<n; i++) {
2   for (j=n-2; j>=0; j--) {
3     S2: a[i][j] = b[i][j] + c[i][j];
4     S3: b[i][j] = a[i][j+1] * d[i][j];
5   }
6 }
```

Example 3:

```
1 for (i=n; i<=n; i++)
2   for (j=1; j<=n; j++)
3     S1: a[i][j] = a[i][j-1] + a[i][j+1] + a[i-1][j] + a[i+1][j];
```

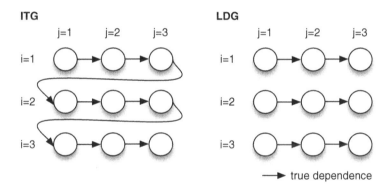

Figure 3.2: ITG and LDG corresponding to Code 3.3 (Example 1).

from the previous example. For dependences, a value read from $b[i][j]$ in statement $S2$ is written in statement $S3$ in the same iteration. So we have an anti-dependence $S2[i, j] \rightarrow^A S3[i, j]$, which is loop independent.

Across loop iterations, a value written to $a[i][j]$ in statement $S2$ is read in the next j iteration in statement $S3$. To visualize this case better, we can choose two adjacent points in the iteration space and compare which value is read in one iteration and written in another. For example, if we choose iteration $[i = 3, j = 6]$, statement $S2$ is equivalent to $a[3][6] = b[3][6] + c[3][6]$. If we choose the next j^{th} iteration, i.e., $[i = 3, j = 5]$, statement $S3$ is equivalent to $b[3][5] = a[3][6] * d[3][5]$. Note that $a[3][6]$ appears twice: it is written at iteration $[3, 6]$ and read at iteration $[3, 5]$. Hence, we have a true dependence $S2[3, 6] \rightarrow^T S3[3, 5]$. Generalizing, we have a true dependence relation $S2[i, j] \rightarrow^T S3[i, j - 1]$ which is loop dependent on the $for\ j$ loop but not $for\ i$ loop. The ITG and LDG are as shown in Figure 3.3. Notice that the precise iteration number is no longer tracked, replaced by "increasing i" and "increasing j", because what is important is tracking dependences for the entire iteration space rather than for specific iterations. Readers may also notice that the direction of dependence from a source node to a destination node in the iteration space is only possible if there is an edge or path in the ITG from the source node to the destination node. Since the ITG contains edges from a node to another node on its left, the dependences in the LDG show the same direction.

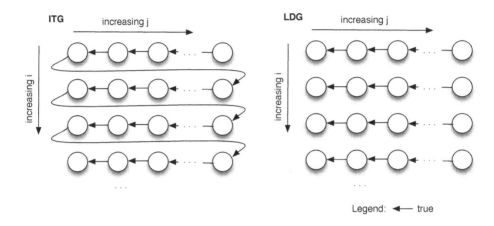

Figure 3.3: ITG and LDG corresponding to Code 3.3 (Example 2).

In Example 3, a value written to $a[i][j]$ is read in the next j iteration (by a part of the statement "$a[i][j-1]$") and in the next i iteration (by a part of the statement "$a[i-1][j]$"). Hence, there are two true dependences: $S1[i,j] \to^T S1[i,j+1]$ and $S1[i,j] \to^T S1[i+1,j]$.

In addition, the part of the statement $a[i][j+1]$ reads in iteration $[i,j]$ the value that is not yet written as it will be written at iteration $[i][j+1]$. Hence, we have an anti-dependence $S1[i,j] \to^A S1[i,j+1]$. Similarly, the part of the statement $a[i+1][j]$ reads in iteration $[i,j]$ the value that will be written at iteration $[i+1][j]$, hence we have an anti-dependence $S1[i,j] \to^A S1[i+1,j]$. The ITG and LDG are as shown in Figure 3.4.

3.3 Identifying Parallel Tasks in Loop Structures

In this section, we will discuss how we can analyze loop structures to identify various types of parallelism, including DOALL, DOACROSS, and DOPIPE. A loop nest structure may have to be modified by splitting it, rewriting it, etc. before parallel tasks can be easily expressed in the parallel programming language or compiler.

3.3.1 Parallelism between Loop Iterations and DOALL Parallelism

One of the most fruitful ways to identify parallelism is by analyzing which loop iterations can be executed in parallel. In order to do that, we start by analyzing the loop-carried dependences. The first principle is that dependences must be obeyed, especially true dependences. Note that anti and output dependences can be removed through *privatization* (discussed later in Section 3.6.1); for now we assume that all the dependences must be obeyed. The dependence between two iterations can

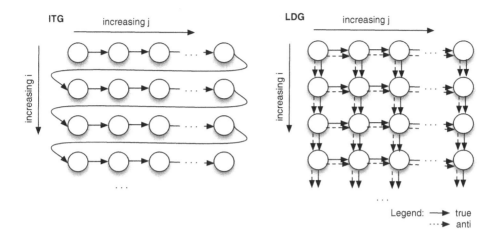

Figure 3.4: ITG and LDG corresponding to Code 3.3 (Example 3).

be observed visually in the LDG in the form of an edge connecting the two nodes that represent the iterations. It may also be observed as a path (a series of edges) connecting the two nodes. Only when there is no edge or path that connects two nodes can we say that the two nodes have no dependences between them. Iterations that do not have dependences with each other can be executed in parallel. For example, a very simple loop is shown in Code 3.4. Its LDG is shown in Figure 3.5.

Code 3.4 A simple example.

```
1 for (i=2; i<=n; i++)
2   S: a[i] = a[i-2];
```

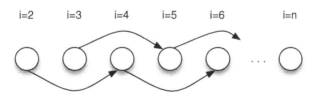

Figure 3.5: The LDG corresponding to Code 3.4.

From the LDG, we can see that odd iterations do not have edges pointing to even iterations, and even iterations do not have edges pointing to odd iterations. Hence, we can extract two parallel tasks: one task executing odd iterations and another executing even iterations. To achieve that, we can split the loop into two smaller loops. The two loops can now be executed in parallel with respect to each other, although each loop still needs to be executed sequentially.

For another example of identifying loop-level parallelism, consider the code in Example 2 in Code 3.3 with its LDG shown in Figure 3.3. The LDG shows loop-carried dependences (edges in the graph) across the j iterations, but not across i iterations. This means that all for i iterations are independent of one another and each of them can be a parallel task. When all iterations of a loop are parallel tasks, we refer to the loop as exhibiting a *DOALL* parallelism. Considering that a typical loop that works on large matrices has a large number of iterations, the degree of DOALL parallelism can be immense. In many parallel languages, expressing a DOALL parallelism is simple. For example, in OpenMP, we only need to add a directive right above the *for i* statement (we will discuss it more later).

A more complex example is in Example 3 of Code 3.3 and its corresponding LDG in Figure 3.4, showing loop-carried dependences across the i as well as the j iterations. It may at first seem that no parallel tasks can be extracted from the code. However, note that there are no loop-carried dependences between *anti-diagonal* loop iterations. In each anti-diagonal, no two nodes in the graph have edges or paths of edges that point to each other (Figure 3.6). However, the same cannot be said for nodes in diagonals. While no direct edges exist between nodes in a diagonal, but paths between them exist.

Code 3.5 Split loops from the original loop in Code 3.4.

```
1 for (i=2; i<=n; i+=2)
2    S: a[i] = a[i-2];
3 for (i=3; i<=n; i+=2)
4    S: a[i] = a[i-2];
```

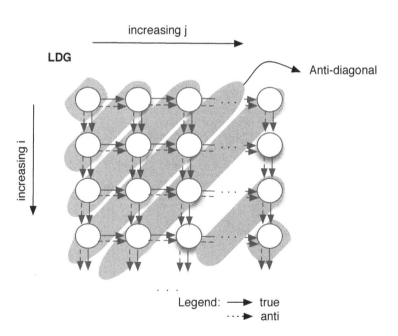

Figure 3.6: The LDG from Example 3 of Code 3.3 shows no dependences between nodes in anti-diagonals. Anti-diagonals are shaded in grey.

Unfortunately, it is not easy to specify such parallel tasks to the compiler. For example, OpenMP parallel directives only allow us to specify DOALL parallelism for a particular loop but do not allow us to specify anti-diagonal parallelism across two loops in a loop nest. One way to remedy this limitation is to restructure the code so that one loop iterates over anti-diagonals, and an inner loop iterates over nodes in an anti-diagonal. We can then specify DOALL parallelism for the inner loop. The pseudo-code for this is shown in Code 3.6.

Code 3.6 Restructured pseudo-code that iterates over anti-diagonals, performing an equivalent computation to the original loop in Example 3 of Code 3.3.

```
1 Calculate number of anti-diagonals
2 foreach anti-diagonal do {
3   Calculate number of points in current anti-diagonal
4   foreach point in the current anti-diagonal do {
5     compute the current point in the matrix
6   }
7 }
```

3.3.2 DOACROSS: Synchronized Parallelism between Loop Iterations

The DOALL parallelism described in the previous section is simple as it specifies that all iterations of a loop are parallel tasks. Typically, the number of parallel tasks in a DOALL parallel loop is very high, so identifying DOALL parallelism should be attempted before identifying other types of parallelism. However, in some loops such parallelism is not available due to loop-carried dependences across loop iterations. How can we extract parallelism in such cases? In this section, we will look at other avenues for extracting parallelism, leading up to DOACROSS, a type of parallelism that allows us to extract parallel tasks even for loops that exhibit loop-carried dependences.

For example, take a look at the code shown below (Code 3.7).

Code 3.7 A loop with loop-carried dependence.

```
1 for (i=1; i<=N; i++)
2   S: a[i] = a[i-1] + b[i] * c[i];
```

The loop has loop-carried dependence $S[i] \to^T S[i+1]$ so clearly it does not have a DOALL parallelism. However, upon a closer inspection we can notice that part of the statement that multiplies $b[i]$ with $c[i]$ do not have loop-carried dependence. This presents an opportunity for parallelism. There are two ways to exploit this opportunity. The first choice is to split the loop into two loops: the first loop only executing the part of the statement that is free from loop-carried dependence, and the second loop only executing the part of the statement with loop-carried dependence. The resulting code is shown below (Code 3.8). The code shows that in order to separate the two statements, the first loop must store its multiplication of $b[i]$ and $c[i]$ results temporarily in an array $temp[i]$. With this solution, the first loop has DOALL parallelism and the second one does not. Unfortunately, the solution has a high storage overhead since we have to introduce a new array $temp[i]$, whose size increases with the array size used in the code.

Code 3.8 A split version of the loop in Code 3.7.

```
1 for (i=1; i<=N; i++)        // this loop has DOALL parallelism
2   S1: temp[i] = b[i] * c[i];
3 for (i=1; i<=N; i++)        // this loop does not
4   S2: a[i] = a[i-1] + temp[i];
```

Another solution for extracting parallel tasks in a loop with a partial loop-carried dependence is to express a DOACROSS parallelism, in which each iteration is still a parallel task (similar to DOALL), but synchronization is inserted in order to ensure that the consumer iteration only reads data that has been produced by the producer iteration. This is achieved by inserting *point-to-point synchronization* between parts of the statements that show loop-carried dependence. The synchronization primitives needed are: *post*, which is called by the producer of data to signal that the data is ready, and *wait*, which is called by the consumer to block until data is ready. To simplify the discussion, we assume that the primitives are named, i.e., `wait(x)` unblocks only when there is a corresponding `post(x)`, where x is the variable name that uniquely identifies the synchronization. A simple way to think of post(x) is incrementing a counter associated with x, while wait(x) is waiting until the counter value is non-zero, and then decrementing the counter value associated with x.

The loop now becomes:

Code 3.9 Exploiting DOACROSS parallelism in the loop from Code 3.7.

```
1 post(0);
2 for (i=1; i<=N; i++)   {
3   S1: temp = b[i] * c[i];
4   wait(i-1);
5   S2: a[i] = a[i-1] + temp;
6   post(i);
7 }
```

In Code 3.9, the original statement is broken into two: $S1$, that has no loop-carried dependence, and $S2$, that has loop-carried dependence. The temporary multiplication result is stored in a private (per-thread) variable `temp` in statement $S1$ and is read in statement $S2$. With DOACROSS, `temp` is now a private scalar rather than a shared array. Thus, the storage overheads only scales with the number of threads rather than the number of iterations. Note the statement `post(i)`. It is a signal by the producer that the value of $a[i]$ has been produced and is ready for consumption by whoever is waiting on it. Also note the statement `wait(i-1)`. It is a signal by the consumer that it must wait until the value $a[i-1]$ has been produced by the producer, which in this case the previous i iteration. Also note that in the first iteration, statement $S2$ reads from $a[0]$ which is not produced by any iteration. Hence, we can add `post(0)` to ensure that the first iteration does not block forever. With the transformation and insertion of synchronization, the iterations of the loop are now parallel tasks, and the execution is shown in Figure 3.7.

One may wonder what execution time saving we obtain. Let us for now assume that the synchronization latency is zero. Let T_{S1} and T_{S2} denote the execution time of statement $S1$ and $S2$ respectively. If the loop is executed sequentially, the execution time is $N \times (T_{S1} + T_{S2})$. If executed with DOACROSS, $S1$ can be executed in parallel with respect to all statements in other iterations.

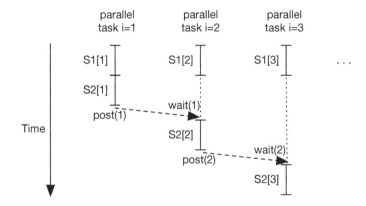

Figure 3.7: Execution of the first three iterations of the DOACROSS code in Code 3.9.

The statement that gets serialized is $S2$, in which each $S2$ waits until the same statement from the previous iteration has produced the data it waits for. Hence, the execution time is $T_{S1} + N \times T_{S2}$, which is an improvement over the original execution time. If we assume a simple case in which $T_{S1} = T_{S2} = T$ and $N \gg T$, the speedup ratio is $\frac{2NT}{(N+1)T} \approx 2\times$. In practice, how much improvement we actually get depends on how large is the execution time of parts of the loop that do not have loop-carried dependence (e.g., T_{S1}) versus the parts of the loop that have to be serialized due to loop-carried dependence (e.g., T_{S2}), and the magnitude of synchronization overheads. Since synchronization overheads are often substantial, programmers must be careful when using DOACROSS parallelism. One way to reduce the synchronization overheads is to group many parallel tasks (iterations) into a thread, so since the synchronization can be performed between threads rather than between tasks, the frequency of synchronization can be greatly reduced.

3.3.3 Parallelism Across Statements in a Loop

When a loop has loop-carried dependence, another way to parallelize it is to *distribute* the loop into several loops that execute different statements from the original loop body. For example, consider the loop in Code 3.10.

Code 3.10 An example of loop distribution.

```
1 for (i=0; i<n; i++) {
2   S1: a[i] = b[i+1] * a[i-1];
3   S2: b[i] = b[i] * coef;
4   S3: c[i] = 0.5 * (c[i] + a[i]);
5   S4: d[i] = d[i-1] * d[i];
6 }
```

The loop has loop carried dependence $S1[i] \rightarrow^T S1[i+1]$ and $S4[i] \rightarrow^T S4[i+1]$, and anti-dependence $S1[i] \rightarrow^A S2[i+1]$. It also has a loop-independent dependence $S1[i] \rightarrow^T S3[i]$. The lack of loop-carried dependences in all statements presents an opportunity for parallelism. For example, note that S4 has no dependences with other statements in the loop body. Hence the loop can be distributed into two loops where one of them executes the first three statements and the second loop executes the last statement. The resulting code is shown in the first part of Code 3.11. The two loops can now be executed in parallel with respect to each other, although each loop must still be executed sequentially.

Instead of each parallel task performing similar computations on different data as in DOALL and DOACROSS parallelism, here each parallel task performs different computations on different sets of data. We can refer to it as *function parallelism* as opposed to *data parallelism* exhibited by DOALL and DOACROSS parallelism. The characteristics of function parallelism are that the degree of parallelism is typically modest and does not increase with a larger input size. This is because the source of parallelism is the code structure rather than the data that the code works on. Since different parallel tasks execute different computations, it is often difficult to balance the load across tasks. Hence, most scalable programs have abundant data parallelism. However, function parallelism can enhance parallelism when data parallelism is limited.

To get an idea of how much speedup can be obtained through the transformation shown in the first part of Code 3.11, let $T_{S1}, T_{S2}, T_{S3}, T_{S4}$, denote the execution time of statement $S1, S2, S3, S4$ respectively. If the loop is executed sequentially, the execution time is $N \times (T_{S1} + T_{S2} + T_{S3} + T_{S4})$. With the transformation, the new execution time is $max(N \times (T_{S1} + T_{S2} + T_{S3}), N \times T_{S4})$. If we assume a simple case in which $T_{S1} = T_{S2} = T_{S3} = T_{S4} = T$ and $N \gg T$, the speedup ratio is $\frac{4NT}{3NT} \approx 1.33\times$, which is nice but quite limited.

Code 3.11 An example of loop distribution.

After distributing statement $S4$, the resulting two loops can be executed in parallel with respect to one another:

```
1 for (i=0; i<n; i++) {
2   S1: a[i] = b[i+1] * a[i-1];
3   S2: b[i] = b[i] * coef;
4   S3: c[i] = 0.5 * (c[i] + a[i]);
5 }
6 for (i=0; i<n; i++)
7   S4: d[i] = d[i-1] * d[i];
```

After distributing statement $S2$ and $S3$:

```
1 for (i=0; i<n; i++)               // Loop 1
2   S1: a[i] = b[i+1] * a[i-1];
3 for (i=0; i<n; i++)               // Loop 2
4   S4: d[i] = d[i-1] * d[i];
5 for (i=0; i<n; i++)               // Loop 3
6   S2: b[i] = b[i] * coef;
7 for (i=0; i<n; i++)               // Loop 4
8   S3: c[i] = 0.5 * (c[i] + a[i]);
```

Note the dependence of $S1[i] \rightarrow^A S2[i+1]$ implies that statement $S2$ in iteration $i+1$ must be executed after statement $S1$ in iteration i. Hence, the dependence is not violated if all $S2$'s are executed after all $S1$'s. Similarly, the dependence of $S1[i] \rightarrow^T S3[i]$ implies that statement $S3$ in iteration i must be executed after statement $S1$ in iteration i. Hence, no dependence is violated if all $S3$'s are executed after all $S1$'s. Therefore, we can further distribute the loop into four loops, as shown in the second part of Code 3.11. The execution of the loops is illustrated in Figure 3.8.

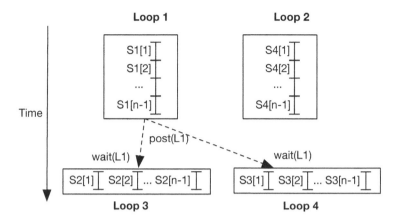

Figure 3.8: Execution of distributed loops from Code 3.11.

The first two loops executing statements $S1$ and $S4$ can be executed in parallel with respect to one another. Once the first loop completes, the third loop executing statement $S2$ and the fourth loop executing statement $S3$, can both run with DOALL parallelism. The mechanism for ensuring that the third and fourth loops execute only after the first loop completes execution can be enforced with a point-to-point synchronization, or with a barrier.

With the new strategy, the execution time for the loop is $max(N \times T_{S1} + max(T_{S2}, T_{S3}), N \times T_{S4})$. Again, if we assume a simple case in which $T_{S1} = T_{S2} = T_{S3} = T_{S4} = T$ and $N \gg T$, the speedup ratio is $\frac{4NT}{(N+1)T} \approx 4\times$, which is a significant improvement over the $1.33\times$ speedup ratio achieved by the previous strategy.

3.3.4 DOPIPE: Parallelism Across Statements of a Loop

We can also exploit pipelined parallelism for loops that exhibit loop-carried dependence. For example, consider the loop shown in Code 3.12. One dependence the loop has is $S1[i] \to^T S1[i+1]$, hence the loop does not have DOALL parallelism. Let T_{S1} and T_{S2} denote the execution time of statements $S1$ and $S2$, respectively. Note that one option is using the technique from the previous section to distribute the loop. The first statement can be executed in the first loop sequentially, and the second loop executed with DOALL parallelism after the first loop completes execution. In such a case, the execution time becomes $N \times T_{S1} + \frac{N}{P} \times T_{S2}$, where N is the number of iterations of the loop, and P is the number of processors. Unfortunately, if we only have a few processors, then the speedup is not much.

Code 3.12 A loop amenable to pipelined parallelism.

```
1 for (i=1; i<=N; i++) {
2   S1: a[i] = a[i-1] + b[i];
3   S2: c[i] = c[i] + a[i];
4 }
```

An alternative solution that can achieve better parallelism in this case is by distributing the loop and introducing pipelined parallelism. With pipelined parallelism, right after $a[i]$ is produced by the statement $S1$ in the first loop, the second loop executes statement $S2$ that reads the just-produced value of $a[i]$. This type of parallelism is referred to as DOPIPE, and the resulting code is show in Code 3.13. The illustration of how DOPIPE parallelism is executed is shown in Figure 3.9.

Code 3.13 DOPIPE parallel version of the loop from Code 3.12.

```
1 for (i=1; i<=N; i++) {
2   S1: a[i] = a[i-1] + b[i];
3   post(i);
4 }
5 for (i=1; i<=N; i++) {
6   wait(i);
7   S2: c[i] = c[i] + a[i];
8 }
```

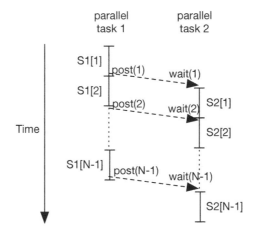

Figure 3.9: Execution of the iterations of the DOPIPE code in Code 3.12.

Assuming zero-latency synchronization and that statement $S1$ takes the same amount of time to compute as statement $S2$, the execution time becomes $N \times T$.

This compares favorably to the alternative of executing the first loop to completion before starting the second loop. Of course, just like any function parallelism, DOPIPE parallelism suffers from a limited degree of parallelism and difficulty in ensuring load balance across parallel tasks.

■ *Did you know?*

The amount of synchronization overheads can be reduced in the DOPIPE parallelism by introducing a synchronization interval. Rather than calling a post(a[i]) *each time one $a[i]$ is produced, we can use one* post(a[i]) *for every n iterations instead, where n is the synchronization interval. This is simple to do as programmers only need to wrap the* post *and* wait *statements by* if (i % n == 0) { ... }.

In a multicore architecture, multiple processor cores often share the last level cache. In such architectures, one unique benefit of DOPIPE parallelism is that it is cache efficient in that data values produced by the producer task are almost immediately consumed by the consumer task.

Hence, its temporal locality is good. This is in contrast to DOALL parallelism in which each task works on a different iteration using largely different sets of data. If there are many tasks assigned to a thread, many threads will compete for the cache space, and there is a possibility of the cache being thrashed between different working sets that belong to different threads.

DOPIPE parallelism is a form of pipelined parallelism applied at the loop level. For some applications, pipelined parallelism may exist at other levels, such as across loops, across functions, or across logical stages in the algorithm. Such task-level pipelined opportunities require dependence analysis that is rarely provided by a compiler. It is usually up to the programmer to identify and exploit pipelined parallelism.

3.4 Identifying Parallelism at Other Levels

While parallelism at the loop level is usually the most fruitful, sometimes there are applications that do not have regular loop structures due to their key data structures. When there are little parallelism opportunities in loops, programmers may have to analyze non-loop granularities. The dependence analysis framework that we discussed earlier is applicable for analyzing other statement groups as well.

For example, suppose that we would like to analyze dependences between some functions and its caller. We would like to analyze whether it is possible to run the functions in parallel with respect to one another or with respect to the caller. To do that, we can divide the code into three groups of statements: the code prior to the function call (pre-code), each function being called, and the code that follows the function call (post-code). True dependences between the pre-code, the functions, and the post-code, determine the parallel tasks that we can identify. The lack of true dependence between any of the pre-code, the functions, and the post-code present parallelism opportunities.

Code 3.14 An example code with function calls.

```
1 // search_tree returns number of nodes that match data value
2 int search_tree(struct tree *p, int data)
3 {
4   int count = 0;
5   if(p == NULL)
6     return 0;
7   if (p->data == data)
8     count = 1;
9   count = count + search_tree(p->left);
10  count = count + search_tree(p->right);
11  return count;
12 }
```

Code 3.14 shows a binary traversal code that traverses the entire tree in a depth-first search manner and counts the number of nodes having data that matches with data being searched. There are two recursive function calls in the body of the function which we will treat as two statement groups ($S2$ and $S3$), in addition to the pre-code statement group ($S1$) and post-code statement group ($S4$). Dependence analysis reveals the following dependences:

- $S1 \rightarrow^T S2$ due to true dependence on `count`

- $S1 \rightarrow^T S3$ due to true dependence on `count`

- $S1 \rightarrow^T S4$ due to true dependence on `count`

- $S2 \rightarrow^T S3$ due to true dependence on `count`

- $S2 \rightarrow^T S4$ due to true dependence on `count`

- $S3 \rightarrow^T S4$ due to true dependence on `count`

Fortunately, the dependence on `count` is easy to remove by renaming, yielding to the code in Code 3.15.

Code 3.15 An example code with function calls.

```
1 // search_tree returns number of nodes that match data value data
2 int search_tree(struct tree *p, int data)
3 {
4    int count1 = 0, count2, count 3;
5    if(p == NULL)
6      return 0;
7    if (p->data == data)
8      count1 = 1;
9    count2 = search_tree(p->left);
10   count3 = search_tree(p->right);
11   return (count1 + count2 + count3);
12 }
```

The new code has fewer true dependences:

- $S1 \rightarrow^T S4$ due to true dependence on `count1`

- $S2 \rightarrow^T S4$ due to true dependence on `count2`

- $S3 \rightarrow^T S4$ due to true dependence on `count3`

We can draw dependence graph similar to the LDG we used for loop structures, as shown in Figure 3.10. The original dependence graph (left portion) does not show opportunities for parallelism, but the new dependence graph (right portion) shows that statement groups $S1$, $S2$, and $S3$ can be executed in parallel with respect to one another. However, they all have to complete prior to executing $S4$. Much of the benefit of parallelism comes from parallel execution of $S2$ and $S3$ with respect to one another because they involve a more substantial computation compared to $S1$, although as we have discussed in Amdahl's law, non-parallel fraction of execution tends to be the one that limits speedups.

One can go further to larger code section granularities to find further parallelism, for example to see if the first function call to `search_tree` has any dependences with the surrounding pre-code and post-code, and with other nearby function calls. The decision of which granularity to perform dependence analysis and thus identifying parallel tasks is a complex one that depends on the size of code being parallelized, amount of parallelism, the degree of load imbalance, and the parallel overheads on a particular target machine.

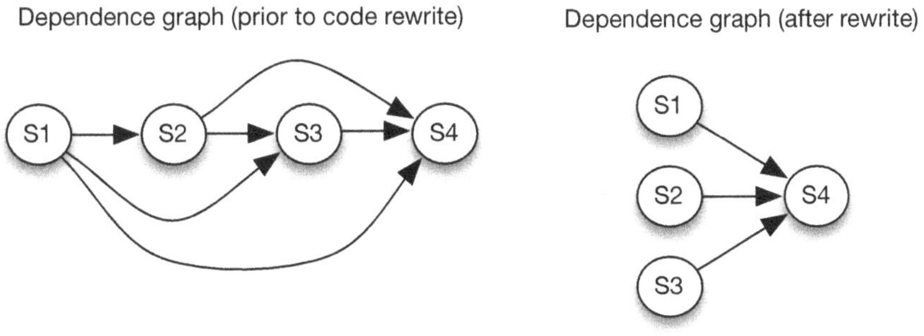

Dependence graph (prior to code rewrite)   Dependence graph (after rewrite)

Figure 3.10: Dependence graph corresponding to Code 3.14 (left) and Code 3.15 (right).

3.5 Identifying Parallelism through Algorithm Knowledge

Sometimes, only analyzing code structure does not give us the maximum amount of parallelism. Analyzing the algorithm may reveal more opportunities for extracting parallel tasks. This is because the code structure embeds unnecessary serialization that is the artifact of a sequential programming language.

For example, consider an algorithm that updates the force of a water particle by its four neighbors, shown in Code 3.16.

Code 3.16 A code that simulates ocean current.

The algorithm for the computation of the main loop is:

```
1 While not converging to a solution do:
2   foreach timestep do:
3     foreach cross section do a sweep:
4       foreach point in a cross section do:        // main loop
5         compute force interaction with neighbors
```

and the actual main loop code introduces an artificial traversal order:

```
1 for (i=1; i<=N; i++) {
2   for (j=1; j<=N; j++) {
3     S1: temp = A[i][j];
4     S2: A[i][j] = 0.2 * (A[i][j]+A[i][j-1]+A[i-1][j]
5                         +A[i][j+1]+A[i+1][j]);
6     S3: diff += abs(A[i][j] - temp);
7   }
8 }
```

Analyzing the code reveals that the only parallelism opportunity is within anti-diagonals, and the code must be restructured to exploit it. However, the basic algorithm for the computation does not actually specify any particular order in which the elements of the cross section must be updated first. The algorithm only specifies that in one sweep, each point in a cross section must be updated once by considering the interaction with its neighbors. Once the algorithm is translated into code, a specific traversal order is artificially introduced: following column order first, then following row order, as can be observed from the ITG. One can legitimately question whether any update order will produce acceptable results. If the answer is yes, then we can change the iteration traversal order as follows.

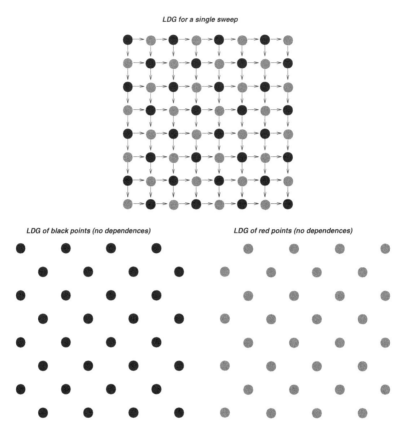

Figure 3.11: LDGs of the original sweep versus after black and red iterations (shown in grey) are separated.

First, we can assign a color of either black or red to each iteration in the iteration space. If the row number plus the column number of the iteration is even, then we color it black, otherwise, we color it red. For example, iteration $[i = 1, j = 4]$ will be red because $1 + 4 = 5$ is odd, while iteration $[i = 2, j = 2]$ will be black because $2 + 2 = 4$ is even. We can see that there are no direct dependences (direct edges in the LDG) between red and black iterations, although they do have indirect dependences (paths in the LDG) between them. Since in a single sweep (one instance of the main loop) only direct dependences are relevant, the new value of any black iteration is independent of the old values of all other black iterations. This can be observed from Figure 3.11. Similarly, the new value of any red iteration is independent of the old values of all other red iterations. Therefore, we do not violate loop-carried dependences if we traverse through black iterations in parallel or red iterations in parallel. If we use a loop that makes a sweep over black iterations first, then the loop exhibits a DOALL parallelism. Similarly, if we use a loop that makes a sweep over red iterations, then the loop exhibits a DOALL parallelism. However, updating all black iterations first before updating any red iterations necessitates changing the traversal order of points in the cross section. If the algorithm can tolerate this, as is the case here, then the transformation can be applied, as shown in Code 3.17.

Code 3.17 Red-black partitioning on the ocean simulation.

```
1 // Black sweep with DOALL parallelism for both outer and inner loops
2 for (i=1; i<=N; i++) {
3   offset = (i+1) % 2;
4   for (j=1+offset; j<=N; j+=2) {
5     S1: temp = A[i][j];
6     S2: A[i][j] = 0.2 * (A[i][j]+A[i][j-1]+A[i-1][j]
7                         +A[i][j+1]+A[i+1][j]);
8     S3: diff += abs(A[i][j] - temp);
9   }
10 }
11
12 // Red sweep with DOALL parallelism for both outer and inner loops
13 for (i=1; i<=N; i++) {
14   offset = i % 2;
15   for (j=1+offset; j<=N; j+=2) {
16     S1: temp = A[i][j];
17     S2: A[i][j] = 0.2 * (A[i][j]+A[i][j-1]+A[i-1][j]
18                         +A[i][j+1]+A[i+1][j]);
19     S3: diff += abs(A[i][j] - temp);
20   }
21 }
```

Another algorithm analysis technique that may yield even more parallelism is by analyzing whether the algorithm can tolerate non-deterministic execution. That is, whether it can tolerate dynamic changes in the order of update. If it can, we can simply ignore dependences and execute all iterations of the sweep in parallel, without needing to partition the sweep into black and red sweeps. The iteration traversal order will now be timing dependent, in that whichever thread executes an iteration, it will update the value of that matrix element using its nearby neighbors regardless of whether the neighbors have been updated or not. One may think that the result will be chaotic. However, the results may not be as chaotic as one may expect because the non-determinism is limited within a single sweep and not across sweeps.

Another example is an algorithm that performs smoothing of an image shown in Code 3.18. The image is greyscale two-dimensional, and each pixel has greyscale intensity that is stored in each element of the `gval` matrix.

Code 3.18 A smoothing filter of a 2-D greyscale image.

```
1 for (i=1; i<N-1; i++) {
2   for (j=1; j<N-1; j++) {
3     gval[i][j] = (gval[i-1][j-1]+gval[i-1][j]+gval[i-1][j+1]+
4                   gval[i][j-1]+gval[i][j]+gval[i][j+1]+
5                   gval[i+1][j-1]+gval[i+1][j]+gval[i+1][j+1])/9;
6   }
7 }
```

Analyzing the code reveals no parallelism opportunity since there are loop-carried dependences across rows, columns, and even anti-diagonals, so here even red-black partitioning cannot be applied. However, the main goal of the smoothing algorithm is to replace each pixel's intensity value by the average of pixel intensities of itself and all neighboring pixels. The ITG introduces artificial serialization in the order in which pixels are updated (i.e., following column order first, then following row order). One can, again, legitimately ask if any update order will produce acceptable results. In this case, the answer is likely to be yes since a slight change in image resulting from smoothing is likely not noticeable. Consequently, we can ignore all dependences and extract DOALL parallelism on both the *for i* loop and the *for j* loop.

3.6 Determining the Scope of Variables

After we identify parallel tasks either through code analysis or algorithm analysis, we have parallel tasks that can execute in parallel with respect to one another. Typically, there are more parallel tasks than the number of available processors, so multiple tasks are often grouped into larger tasks before they are assigned to a thread for execution. The number of threads that execute tasks are typically chosen to be the same or less than the number of available processors. In this section, we assume that we have an unlimited number of processors, and each task is assigned to a unique thread.

The next step to perform is what we will refer to as *variable partitioning*, which in essence is a step that determines whether variables should have a *private*-per-thread scope or a *shared*-by-all-threads scope. This step is specific to shared memory programming; in the message passing model, all variables are private since each process has its own address space.

In this step, we need to analyze the use of different variables by parallel tasks that we have identified, and categorize them into the following behavior categories:

- *Read-Only*: a variable is only read by all tasks.

- *R/W Non-conflicting*: a variable is read, written, or both by only one task; or if the variable is a matrix, different elements are read/written by different tasks.

- *R/W Conflicting*: if tasks execute in parallel, a variable written by one task may be read by a different task.

Consider the example in Code 3.19. If we define each iteration in the *for i* loop as a parallel task, then read-only variables include n, matrix c, and matrix d, since none of them is modified by any tasks. Read/write non-conflicting variables include matrices a and b since the matrix elements modified by each task are disjoint from elements modified by other tasks. For example, iteration $i = 1$ only reads and modifies $b[1][j]$ whereas iteration $i = 2$ only reads and modifies $b[2][j]$, so there is no overlap or conflict since different tasks read/write to different elements of the matrix. Similarly, iteration $i = 1$ only reads $a[1][j - 1]$ which is produced by the same task at the previous j iteration, without overlaps with data read or written by other iterations. Finally, the loop index variables themselves i and j are read/write conflicting. At each i iteration, the loop index variable i is read and used for accessing the matrices, and then incremented at the end of the iteration. Since i is written at the end of the iteration, its value may be read by another task of a different iteration, hence it is a read/write conflicting variable. Regarding j, each i iteration sets it to zero, then increments it until reaching $n - 1$. In the mean time, other tasks may overwrite the value of j as they also use j in the same way. Thus, j is also a read/write conflicting variable.

Code 3.19 A code example.

```
1 for (i=1; i<=n; i++)
2   for (j=1; j<=n; j++) {
3     S2: a[i][j] = b[i][j] + c[i][j];
4     S3: b[i][j] = a[i][j-1] * d[i][j];
5   }
```

Similarly, consider the following code (Code 3.20). If we define each iteration in the $for\ j$ loop as a parallel task, then read-only variables include n, matrix c, i, and matrix d. Note that i is a read-only variable because given a $for\ i$ iteration, none of $for\ j$ iterations modify its value. Read/write non-conflicting variables include matrices a, b, and e since the matrix elements modified by each task are disjoint from elements modified by other tasks. For example, iteration $j = 1$ only reads and modifies $b[i][1]$ whereas iteration $j = 2$ only reads and modifies $b[i][2]$, so there is no overlap or conflict since different tasks read/write to different elements of the matrix. Similarly iteration $j = 1$ only reads $a[i-1][j]$ which is produced by the same task at the previous i iteration, without overlaps with data read or written by other iterations. Finally, the loop index variable itself, i.e., j, is read/write conflicting since it is read and incremented by different tasks. However, i is not written inside a $for\ j$ iteration, hence it is read-only variable.

Code 3.20 A code example.

```
1 for (i=1; i<=n; i++)
2   for (j=1; j<=n; j++) {
3     S1: a[i][j] = b[i][j] + c[i][j];
4     S2: b[i][j] = a[i-1][j] * d[i][j];
5     S3: e[i][j] = a[i][j];
6   }
```

Read/write conflicting variables prevent parallelization because they introduce dependences between threads. Therefore, we need techniques to remove such dependences. One of such techniques is *privatization*, through which per-thread copies of a read/write conflicting variable are created so that each thread can work solely on its own copy. Another technique is *reduction*, through which per-thread copies of a read/write conflicting variable are created so that each thread can produce a partial result in its own copy, and at the end of the parallel section all partial results are combined into a global result. We will now describe these techniques in more detail.

3.6.1 Privatization

Read/write conflicting variables prevent parallelization. So one important concept is called *privatization*. Privatization involves making private copies of a shared variable, so that each thread works on its local copy rather than the shared copy. This removes read/write conflicts and allows parallelization. By default, in the shared memory model, any memory location is addressable by all threads. Hence, local copies are created by compiling a single variable into several different variables stored at different memory locations.

Under what situation is a variable privatizable? One situation is when in the original sequential program execution order, a variable is defined (or written) by a task before being used (or read) by the same task. In this case, a task can write to a private copy of the variable (rather than to the shared copy) and read from that private copy. It does not matter what values other tasks write to the variable since in program order, the value read from the variable is always the same value that was earlier written by the same task.

Another situation in which a variable is privatizable is when a variable is not defined before it is read by the same task, but the values that the task is supposed to read from the variable are known ahead of time. In this case, the local copy of the variable can be defined (or initialized) with the correct value regardless of other tasks.

Privatization can be applied to both *scalar* variables and *arrays* or *matrices*. Of course, when applied to scalar variables, the additional space overhead is small. When applied to arrays or matrices, the additional space overhead and the overhead to initialize them can be substantial since they typically scale with the input size.

As an example, consider the previously-discussed code (Code 3.19), which has read/write conflicting variables i and j. Note that here i is incremented in each $for\ i$ iteration, so its value is always known ahead of time. For example, the task that executes the fifth iteration can assume that i should have a value of 5 at the beginning of its execution, without waiting for the task corresponding to the fourth iteration to produce its value. The variable j, on the other hand, is always defined (written to) by each $for\ i$ iteration task when it enters the inner loop. Hence, variable j can also be privatized. The result of privatization is that each thread has private copies of both variables i and j. All tasks that are assigned to the thread will be executed sequentially by the thread, thus they can reuse privatized variables.

One way to think of private copies is to think that the scalar variables are replaced with references into arrays of variables with the task IDs as the index. For example, Figure 3.12 shows a variable v that is privatized: the original shared copy remains there (v) and private copies are created ($v[0], v[1], v[2], \ldots$). Each thread will then read from or write to its own private copy by replacing references to v with references to $v[ID]$ where ID is a unique thread identification number, ensuring different threads accessing different elements of the privatized variable. Consequently, with privatization, the read/write conflicting variable v has been changed into read/write non-conflicting variable $v[.]$.

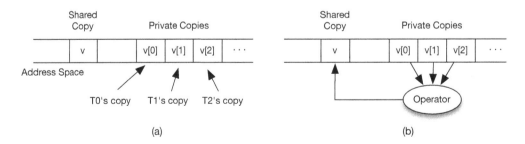

Figure 3.12: Illustration of a privatized variable (a) and a reduction variable (b).

Another example is in Code 3.20, in which each $for\ j$ iteration is a parallel task. Here, the read/write conflicting variable is j. j is incremented in each $for\ j$ iteration, so its value is known ahead of time for any tasks. For example, the task that executes the fifth iteration can assume that $j = 5$, without waiting for the fourth iteration to produce its value. Hence, j is privatizable.

Privatization eliminates inter-thread dependence because each thread works on its own copy of a variable. Since no thread needs to read a value that is produced by another, the threads become independent and can execute in parallel. However, in cases when a read/write conflicting variable cannot be privatized or reduced (discussed in the next section), its access must be guarded by synchronization in order to ensure that a thread that consumes the value of the variable waits until the value has been produced by another thread.

Note that there are variables that are automatically privatized by the compiler. For example, variables declared inside a parallel region are automatically privatized. Stack and local variables of a function declared inside a parallel region are also automatically privatized.

3.6.2   Reduction Variables and Operation

A technique related to privatization is *reduction*. Reduction is a type of computation in which the result of the computation can be composed of partial results computed by parallel tasks. The parallelism strategy for reduction operation involves having each thread compute a partial result and store it in the private copy of the variable, and at the end the partial results of all tasks are combined to form the final result. This is illustrated in Figure 3.12(b). The figure shows variable v privatized into $v[.]$. However, unlike regular privatization, the values in the private copies are merged using a *reduction operator* into the shared copy. Because the shared copy is also involved in storing the computation result at the end, a reduction variable v is sometimes referred to as semi-private.

What operations are amenable to reduction? One basic requirement is that a reduction should reduce elements of some array or matrix down to one scalar value. The second requirement is that the final result must be composable from partial results computed by all tasks. Operations performed on all array elements that are *commutative* and *associative* satisfy these requirements. For example, let us say that we want to add up all array elements into its sum. This satisfies the first requirement. We can divide the work by having each thread summing up a part of the array and storing the partial sum into its private variable. In the end, we can have the master thread add all partial sums into the final sum. The final sum will be correct because addition is commutative and associative, which implies that regardless of the order of summation performed across threads, when we sum up the partial sums, we get the right global sum value.

More specifically, suppose that the computation is the following: $y = y_{init} \circ a[0] \circ a[1] \circ \ldots \circ a[n]$. An operator $\circ$ is commutative if $u \circ v = v \circ u$, and is associative if $(u \circ v) \circ w = u \circ (v \circ w)$. We refer to $\circ$ as the *reduction operator* and y as the reduction variable. From here, we can derive that reduction operators include sum (addition of elements), product (multiplication of elements), maximum, minimum, and logical operations (and, or, xor, etc.). In OpenMP, programmers can specify the reduction operator and variable to the compiler, which will break down the computation among threads into partial results and combine them into the final result. However, there are operators other than addition, multiplication, and logical operations that may not be expressible in OpenMP but exhibit commutativity and associativity. Such operators require programmers to modify their own code to implement reduction. An example of that is shown in Example 3.1.

Reduction allows parallel execution of threads as it removes data dependences between them due to read/write conflicting variables. It allows each thread to store a partial result in its own copy of a variable. In the end, the main thread can gather all partial results and generate the full (global) result.

■ **Example 3.1** Example of exploiting reduction.

Consider the following code:

```
1 sum = 0;
2 for (i=0; i<8; i++) {
3   a[i] = b[i] + c[i];
4   if (a[i] > 0)
5     sum = sum + a[i];
6 }
7 Print sum;
```

For the code above, manually exploiting reduction involves rewriting the code as:

```
1 begin parallel // spawn a child thread
2 private int start_iter, end_iter, i;
3 shared int local_iter = 4, sum = 0;
4 shared double sum = 0.0, a[], b[], c[], localSum[];
5
6 sum = 0;
7 start_iter = getid() * local_iter;
8 end_iter = start_iter + local_iter;
9 for (i=start_iter; i<end_iter; i++)
10   a[i] = b[i] + c[i];
11   if (a[i] > 0)
12     localSum[id] = localSum[id] + a[i];
13 barrier;
14 end parallel // kill the child thread
15
16 for (k=0; k<getNumProc(); k++)
17   sum += localSum[k];
18 Print sum;
```

3.6.3 Summary of Criteria

A variable that is read-only should be declared as shared to avoid storage overheads that may reduce performance. The program is still correct if a read-only variable is declared as private and is initialized to a correct value. However, this comes at the expense of unnecessary storage overheads.

A variable that is read/write non-conflicting should also be declared as shared for performance reasons. Similar to the prior case, privatizing a read/write non-conflicting variable introduces unnecessary storage overheads.

For a variable that is read/write conflicting, care must be taken. Normally, such variable needs to be declared as shared but accesses to it must be protected by a critical section. Furthermore, point-to-point synchronization may be needed if the correctness of program execution depends on the proper sequencing of instructions. Note that a critical section is expensive since it serializes accesses to a shared variable and implementations of locks are often not scalable to a high number of processors. Hence, as much as possible, critical sections should be avoided. The most straightforward strategy is to check whether the variable satisfies the criteria for a reduction variable. If it does, it should be made a reduction variable and the operation that is performed on it should be treated as a reduction operation. If it is not a reduction variable, the next step is to check whether it is privatizable. If it is privatizable, then it should be privatized if it is profitable to do so, i.e., the performance impact of extra storage overheads is tolerable and is smaller than the performance impact from having a critical section.

Another alternative is to reanalyze the code and choose a different parallel region. It is often the case that a read/write conflicting variable may change into a read/write non-conflicting variable when the scope of parallelism changes. For example, consider the following code (Code 3.21) which shows multiplication of matrices A and B, and the result is stored in matrix Y. If the parallel region is the $for\ k$ loop (i.e., the parallel tasks are $for\ k$ iterations), $Y[i][j]$ is a read/write conflicting variable since different tasks may read and write to it simultaneously. So it needs to be protected using a critical section. However, if the parallel region is changed to, say, the $for\ i$ loop, then for any i and j, $Y[i][j]$ is only written to or read from by a single task. The variable becomes read/write non-conflicting, and there is no longer a need to protect its access with a critical section.

Code 3.21 A matrix multiplication code example.

```
1    for (i=0; i<N; i++) {
2      for (j=0; j<N; j++) {
3        Y[i][j] = 0.0;
4        for (k=0; k<N; k++) {
5          Y[i][j] = Y[i][j] + A[i][k] * B[k][j];
6        }
7      }
8    }
```

3.7 Synchronization

In the shared memory programming model, synchronization acts as a mechanism through which programmers control the sequence of operations that are performed by parallel threads. Note that synchronization is performed among threads, rather than among tasks. So, at this step we have assumed that tasks have been assigned to threads. For simplicity, however, we assume that there are as many threads as tasks, such that the mapping of a task to a thread is one-to-one.

Three types of synchronization primitives are in wide use. The first one is *point-to-point* synchronization involving two parallel tasks. The example is *post* and *wait* that we used while describing DOACROSS and DOPIPE parallelism. A post operation acts like depositing a token signifying that data is produced, and a wait operation blocks until there is a token deposited, preventing the consumer from continuing, until data is ready.

The second type of popular synchronization is a *lock*. A lock can be obtained by only one parallel thread, and once the lock is held by that thread, other threads cannot obtain it until the current thread releases the lock. The two operations that can be performed on a lock are acquiring the lock (`lock(name)`) and releasing the lock (`unlock(name)`). Therefore, essentially a lock is useful for enforcing exclusivity. If a code region is protected by a lock, then one can create a *critical section*, which is a region of code that only allows at most one thread to execute it at any time. A critical section is useful for ensuring that only one thread at a time access a read/write conflicting variable that is not privatizable and for which reduction cannot be applied. If a data structure is protected by a lock, then only one thread can access the data structure at a time.

The third type of popular synchronization is *barrier*. A barrier defines a point that a thread is allowed to go past only when all threads have reached it (illustrated in Figure 3.13). In the figure, there are four threads reaching the barrier points at different times. Threads 1, 3, and 4 have to wait inside the barrier until the last thread (Thread 2) reaches it. Only then, can they execute code after the barrier. This example illustrates that a barrier is simple and easy to use, it makes the total execution time of the parallel execution dependent on the execution time of the slowest thread. Hence, when using barriers, load balance is very important. The efficiency of the barrier implementation is also a critical goal in designing parallel computers.

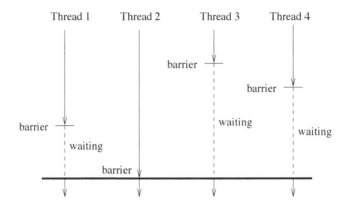

Figure 3.13: Illustration of a barrier.

A barrier should be inserted if the code section following it uses values that are written by the parallel code section preceding it. For example, numerical simulations often work in time-steps where in one time-step the main data structure (matrices) are updated. Barriers are a logical synchronization to use between these time-steps. They ensure that before going to the next time-step, all threads have completed computation for the current time-step.

3.8   Assigning Tasks to Threads

Task mapping deals with two aspects. The first aspect is how to map tasks to threads. Often, there are more tasks than threads, so two questions are what tasks should be assigned to a thread and how they should be assigned? The important issues are the task management overheads (larger tasks incur lower overheads), load balance (larger tasks may reduce load balance), and data locality. The second aspect is how to map threads to processors, so as to make sure that the communicating processors are as close to each other as possible.

One consideration in task mapping is whether to assign tasks to threads *statically* or *dynamically*. Static task mapping means that tasks are preassigned to threads before execution. For example, this is achieved by specifying which iterations of a DOALL loop are to be executed by a thread. Dynamic task mapping means that tasks are not assigned to threads prior to execution. Instead, a task queue will be created and maintained during execution to keep tasks that are not yet assigned to threads. During execution, whichever thread becomes idle, it grabs a task from the task queue and executes it. This is repeated until the task queue is empty. Dynamic task mapping introduces extra overheads for the task queue management, but sometimes makes it is easier to ensure that all threads' loads are balanced. It also tends to increase the amount of communication and reduces locality, since it is difficult to lay out data to the thread that will use it when we do not know at compile time which thread will use it. Finally, it is possible to have a hybrid mapping in which the mapping is largely static, but periodically the load balance is assessed, and the mapping is adjusted accordingly.

Let us consider how tasks may be assigned to threads. In a static assignment, tasks are assigned to threads. For a DOALL loop where loop iterations or groups of consecutive iterations form tasks, tasks may be assigned in a round robin fashion to threads, which is a reasonable policy. Let us refer to the number of consecutive iterations that are grouped as a single task as *chunk size*. How important is the choice of chunk size in determining load balance? Let us consider an example shown in Code 3.22. In the code, the number of iterations of the inner loop changes for different iterations of the outer loop. For illustration purposes, let us assume n and p have the values of 8 and 2, respectively. Therefore, the outer loop will execute 8 iterations, while the inner loop will execute $1, 2, 3, \ldots, 8$ iterations. The choice of chunk size determines how much imbalance there is between threads.

Code 3.22 Code illustrating load balance and OpenMP schedule clause.

```
1 sum = 0;
2 #pragma omp parallel for reduction(+:sum) \
3     schedule(static, chunksz)
4 for (i=0; i<n; i++) {
5   for (j=0; j<=i; j++) {
6     sum = sum + a[i][j];
7   }
8 }
9 Print sum;
```

Figure 3.14 shows the impact of various chunk sizes in a static task assignment on load balance. For example, if the chunk size is 4, then the first thread (thread 0) executes the first four iterations of the outer loop, while the second thread (thread 1) executes the last four iterations of the outer loop. The total number of inner loop iterations (or the number of times the "sum" statement is executed) is 36. Using a chunk size of four, thread 0 executes $1 + 2 + 3 + 4 = 10$ inner loop iterations while thread 1 executes $5 + 6 + 7 + 8 = 26$ inner loop iterations. Hence, the imbalance, expressed as the difference in the number of iterations executed by the two threads divided by all iterations, is $\frac{16}{36} = 44\%$.

Using a chunk size of 2, thread 0 executes the first and third two outer loop iterations, resulting in a total number of inner loop iterations of $(1+2)+(5+6) = 14$. Thread 1 executes $(3+4)+(7+8) = 22$ inner loop iterations. The imbalance has reduced to $\frac{8}{36} = 22\%$. Finally, using a chunk size of 1, thread 0 executes all odd outer loop iterations, with the total number of inner loop iterations of $1 + 3 + 5 + 7 = 16$. Thread 1 executes all even outer loop iterations, with a total number of inner loop iterations of $2 + 4 + 6 + 8 = 20$. The imbalance is reduced even more to $\frac{20-16}{36} = 11\%$. This example illustrates that smaller chunk sizes tend to achieve better load balance. The strategy is helpful when there is a large number of loop iterations.

An alternative way to achieve a better load balance is to use dynamic task assignment. However, even with dynamic assignment, the chunk size is still an important parameter. If it is too small, there may be too few tasks, and load imbalance can still occur.

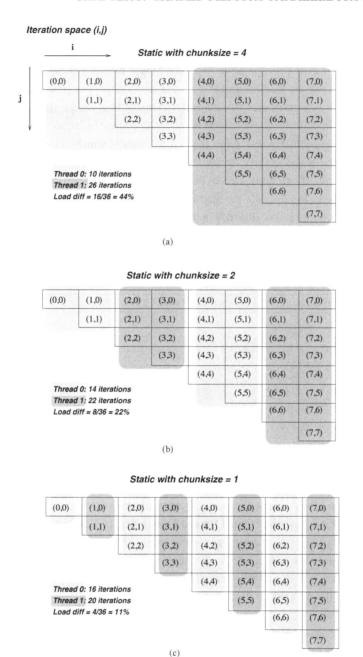

Figure 3.14: Number of iterations executed using `static` schedule with various chunk sizes: four (a), two (b), and one (c).

Load balance and task overheads are not the only important factors in task mapping. Communication cost is also an important factor. Let us distinguish two communication overheads: *inherent* communication from the impact of task mapping on the algorithm, and *artifactual* communication from the impact of task mapping considering the way data is laid out and the architecture. Artifactual communication overheads cannot be inferred without first understanding how parallel architectures are designed, so we will first discuss inherent communication.

One metric that is useful in evaluating inherent communication is the *communication to computation ratio* (CCR). To compute CCR, we can estimate the amount of communication of a thread divided by the amount of computation of the thread. The parameters are the number of processors and the input size.

To illustrate how inherent communication is computed, consider the ocean application from Code 3.16. In one sweep the loop iterates over i and over j to visit all elements of the matrix. Suppose that we have p processors and the matrix dimension of $N \times N$ greatly exceeds p. There are at least three possible ways to assign tasks to threads, as shown in Figure 3.15.

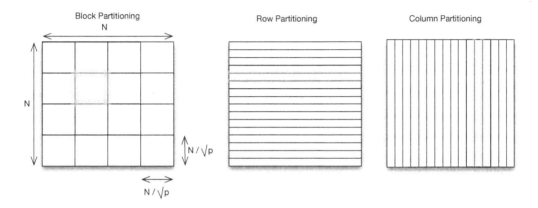

Figure 3.15: Assigning tasks to threads block-wise (a), row-wise (b), and column-wise(c).

The figure assumes that all iterations are parallel (i.e., we relax the loop-carried dependences). In this case, we can partition the tasks block-wise, row-wise, or column-wise, as shown in the figure. For all cases, the amount of computation for each thread, expressed in the number of matrix elements that need to be updated, are identical, which is $\frac{N \times N}{p}$. However, the amount of communication among threads differs with different mapping strategies. Recall that in ocean, each iteration updates one matrix element, using neighboring matrix elements, which are updated by neighboring iterations. Hence, for the block-wise partitioning strategy, in each block, all border elements are accessed by more than one thread (shown in grey for one block in the figure), but interior elements are only accessed by the thread that the block is assigned to. There are approximately $4 \times \frac{N}{\sqrt{p}}$ elements at the borders (top, bottom, left, and right borders). Therefore, amount of communication, expressed in the number of elements that are communicated between the thread and other threads is $4 \times \frac{N}{\sqrt{p}}$. Consequently, the CCR is as follows:

$$
\begin{aligned}
CCR &= \frac{4 \times \frac{N}{\sqrt{p}}}{\left(\frac{N^2}{p}\right)} \\
&= \frac{4 \times \sqrt{p}}{N} \\
&= \Theta\left(\frac{\sqrt{p}}{N}\right)
\end{aligned}
\tag{3.1}
$$

For row-wise partitioning, for each partition ($\frac{N}{p}$ rows), there are $2 \times N$ border elements that are communicated with other threads. Hence, the CCR can be computed as:

$$
\begin{aligned}
CCR &= \frac{2 \times N}{(\frac{N^2}{p})} \\
&= \frac{2 \times p}{N} \\
&= \Theta(\frac{p}{N})
\end{aligned}
\tag{3.2}
$$

For column-wise partitioning, each partition consists of $\frac{N}{p}$ columns, and there are $2 \times N$ border elements that are communicated with other threads. Hence, the CCR is identical to that of row-wise partitioning.

If the problem size stays constant, and we increase the number of processors, CCR increases too, but at different rates in different mapping schemes. In block-wise partitioning, it increases at the rate of $\sqrt{p}$, while at row-wise and column-wise partitioning, it increases at the rate of p. Hence, clearly in terms of inherent communication, block-wise mapping is superior.

However, when artifactual communication is considered, the answer differs. Artifactual communication must consider the ping-pong effect of sharing data between two processors, i.e., as data is shuffled back and forth between communicating processors. The overhead of such communication not only depends on the frequency of data shuffling, but also on the latency of each data shuffle. The frequency of data shuffling depends on the layout of data in memory. For example, matrix elements in consecutive columns of a row are laid out contiguously in C/C++, but in Fortran, matrix elements in consecutive rows of a column are laid out contiguously. Data shuffling occurs at the granularity of a cache block (typically 64 or 128 bytes), which can hold 16 to 32 float-type matrix elements, or 8 to 16 double-type matrix elements. The amount of total (inherent plus artifactual) communication does not depend on how many matrix elements are communicated. Rather, it depends on how many cache blocks are shared between processors.

To illustrate the problem, suppose that each processor must compute 64 matrix elements and that we have a cache block that can hold 2 consecutive matrix elements. In block-wise partitioning (see Figure 3.16(a)), in the top and bottom rows, the matrix elements are contained in ten cache blocks. However, each matrix element in the left and right border requires one cache block. In all, there are up to 22 cache blocks that are shared with other processors. In a row-wise partitioning (see Figure 3.16(b)), the elements in the top and bottom rows only occupy up to16 cache blocks, so only 16 cache blocks are shared among processors. Finally, in a column-wise partitioning (see Figure 3.16(c)), each of the element occupies one cache block, so overall there are up to $2 \times 16 = 32$ cache blocks that are shared. Hence, row-wise partitioning achieves the least artifactual communication, followed by block-wise partitioning, and finally by column-wise partitioning.

This example illustrates a few points. First, despite having an identical amount of inherent communication, row-wise and column-wise partitioning differ significantly in terms of total communication. Hence, it is very important to select a partitioning strategy that minimizes such communication. Secondly, block-wise partitioning may be less cache efficient than row-wise partitioning if it incurs much artifactual communication due to communicated matrix elements at the extreme columns within the block. Overall, while inherent communication reflects the communication requirement of an algorithm, the actual real-world performance is more determined by the amount of

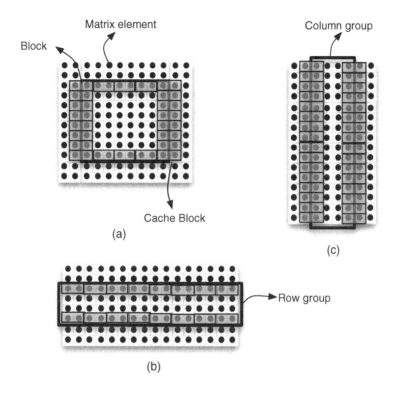

Figure 3.16: Number of cache blocks shared by more than one processor in the block-wise partitioning (a), row-wise partitioning (b), and column-wise partitioning (c), assuming the memory layout is as shown.

total communication, which is not necessarily identical to the behavior of inherent communication.

In conclusion, there are multiple factors we need to consider when we map tasks to threads: load balance, task management overheads, and communication costs between threads. The latter two factors are machine-specific in terms of their magnitudes and how the magnitudes scale with a larger number of processors being utilized to execute threads.

3.9 Mapping Threads to Processors

We have discussed how tasks are mapped to threads. The next question naturally is how threads should be mapped to processors. One simple approach to this question is to do nothing, i.e., leaving the OS thread scheduler to decide. The OS thread scheduler decides when ready threads should run and which processors they should run on. It takes into account response time, fairness, thread priority, utilization of processors, and overheads of context switching. For a system where a collection of threads from different processes run, the OS thread scheduler does a reasonably good job at mapping threads to processors.

However, in the case of parallel programming, there are several unique challenges in mapping threads to processors. One challenge is with regard to when threads are scheduled, with respect to one another. Unrelated threads can be scheduled at any time as they do not have synchronization with one another. However, parallel threads often synchronize, either using locks, barriers, or others. Scheduling of threads in a parallel program has to be coordinated to avoid scheduling inefficiencies. An example situation that leads to such inefficiency is when a thread that holds a global lock is switched out. Other threads that want to acquire the lock cannot obtain the lock, hence they cannot make forward progress even when they are running on processors. Processor resources will be wasted unnecessarily, until the thread holding the lock is switched in again. Another situation is when multiple threads have reached a barrier, and a thread that has not reached a barrier is switched out. Similar to the lock situation, the thread that is switched out prevents the other threads from making forward progress. Processor resources are again wasted until the switched out thread is switched in. Finally, in a point-to-point synchronization, if a thread that wants to send a message is switched out, another thread that expects to receive the message may be blocked waiting, unable to make forward progress. Thus, for a parallel program, there is a need to ensure that either all of its threads simultaneously run or neither of them runs.

Some OS thread schedulers have been augmented with a *gang scheduling* capability, where all threads are scheduled to run, or none of them runs. This eliminates wasteful processor resources. Such a gang scheduling support is needed even more for large systems, as the cost of scheduling errors is higher for a larger system. In some cases, gang scheduling alone may not be sufficient in insuring high performance of parallel program execution. For example, in a study on ASCI Q super-computer [47], it was found that OS kernel activities (called noises) may produce brief but frequent interrupts, which significantly reduce parallel program performance. Even with gang scheduling, the OS in each compute node still has to preempt a thread to run its routine activities. Each compute node may incur its own noise asynchronously compared to other compute nodes. Each time a node suffers from a noise, all threads in all nodes participating in a barrier are slowed down. When noises in different nodes are synchronized, i.e., OS activities are deferred and scheduled together across nodes, the threads are slowed down much less frequently, and their performance improves.

Another important aspect of mapping threads to processors is data locality. This is applicable in a NUMA system where an access to remote memories may take far longer time than an access to the local memory. In this case, it is important for threads to run on the same nodes where data needed by the threads reside. This can be achieved using two methods: data mapping or explicit mapping of threads to processors. Let us discuss data mapping first.

Data mapping allows data to be allocated or mapped to nodes where threads that will access it will run on. In some cases, the programming model (such as PGAS) may allow data mapping to be specified. In other cases, some programming language extension is provided for programmers to specify data mapping in traditional programming languages such as C or Fortran.

Another approach is to allocate or migrate data to the thread that accesses it. One way to achieve this is through page allocation and migration policy. A parallel program begins its execution suffering from a lot of page faults because its pages have not been allocated. The OS can choose which frame to allocate a page through a *page allocation policy*. One popular page allocation policy that the OS can use is to allocate the page at a frame in which the least recently used page resides. The old page at that frame is evicted to make room for the new page. Such a policy or its approximation is widely implemented in many OSes. However, in a NUMA system, such a policy is not aware of how close the page is to the processor that needs it, so it may not produce an optimal performance. Thus, in a NUMA system, other policies can be used. One policy is to allocate the frame on the node that incurs the page fault, e.g., on the same node where the processor that accesses it resides. Such a policy is referred to as the *first touch* policy. The rationale behind this policy is that the processor that first accesses the data in a page is likely to be the same processor that accesses data in the page the most. Clearly, this is an approximation, a heuristic.

■ *Did you know?*

Some hypervisors implement a mechanism similar to gang scheduling when it schedules a virtual machine (VM) on processors. A hypervisor is a layer between hardware and the OS (called a guest virtual machine) which gives an abstraction to the guest VM that it is running directly on hardware. A hypervisor allows multiple guest VMs to share the same processor hardware, thereby improving processor utilization. To allow guests sharing the same processor hardware, processors are virtualized into virtual processors or vCPUs. The hypervisor maps vCPUs to actual processors, and time share the processors among multiple guest virtual machines. A guest requests n vCPUs, and it is up to the hypervisor whether it allocates n physical processors, or fewer - by letting some vCPUs to time share the same physical processor.

Similar to a parallel program, a guest VM consists of an OS with threads that synchronize. If a guest VM requires n vCPUs, and the hypervisor only allocates less than n processors, the guest may suffer from significant performance degradation, where some vCPUs may make execution progress but others stall. Thus, the hypervisor may implement some forms of gang scheduling. For example, VMware hypervisor version 2.x employs a strict co-scheduling where when a vCPU makes execution progress more than a threshold compared to other vCPUs in a guest VM, the entire guest VM is stopped, and is started only when the hypervisor can allocate n processors to the guest VM, thus ensuring gang scheduling of vCPUs. Strict co-scheduling or gang scheduling may cause processor resource fragmentation if the requested number of vCPUs is larger than the typical number of available processors, since the guest VM has to wait until the number of available processors reaches n (in version 3.x, the co-scheduling policy is relaxed to reduce processor resource fragmentation).

The pitfall of the first touch policy occurs when the main data structure (e.g., the matrices) are initialized by different threads than the threads that use the data structure in the main computation. Allocating pages according to the initialization pattern which is inconsistent with the access pattern in the main computation leads to many remote memory accesses during the main computation. Worse, if the initialization is performed only by the main thread, all pages of the data structures will be allocated on a single node. During main computation, all but one node will access a single remote memory. Not only does this incur a high remote memory access latency, but this also causes contention on that node, which increases the memory access latency significantly. Such a scenario may be quite common when programmers use an automatic parallelizing compiler. The compiler typically employs (reasonable) heuristics that skip parallelization of loops or loop nests that have a very small body. Since an initialization loop or loop nest often has a small body, it is often not parallelized, resulting in one thread to be the first in touching much of the data structure. A common solution for this problem is to manually force the parallelization of the inner loop, and ensure that the traversal order used in the initialization loop is the same with that used by the loops in the main computation.

An alternative page allocation policy is *round robin*, in which pages are allocated in different memory nodes in a round robin manner. Round robin page allocation sounds like a bad idea since it virtually guarantees that there will be many remote memory accesses. However, it spreads pages across nodes in a balanced manner so contention on any particular node rarely occurs with this policy. Thus, round robin may perform better than the worst case performance of the first touch policy.

An alternative solution to the non-optimal page allocation policy is an adaptive policy in which usage of pages are monitored and pages can be migrated from one node in which they have been allocated on, to the node that accesses them the most. *Page migration* is implemented in the SGI Origin 2000 system [38]. Unfortunately, however, page migration is an expensive operation because the physical address of a page changes. There is a possibility that many processors cache the address mapping (called the *page translation entry* or PTE) in a hardware structure referred to as the *translation lookaside buffer* or TLB. Unfortunately, it is difficult to know which processors cache the PTE of a page. Hence, to migrate a page, the OS must conservatively invalidate every processor's TLB. This is a very expensive operation that may reverse the benefit that comes with page migration.

Instead of allocating or moving data to the threads that access them, we can also map threads to where data is allocated. An OS used in NUMA systems typically provide commands to specify which processors threads are restricted to run on. An example is `cset` in Linux OS. In NUMA systems, the goal of thread mapping is to map threads to the nodes that has data that they will access, and to map threads that communicate with each other on nodes that are physically adjacent. Thread mapping can be specified using a command line tool, or can also be specified through a programming language extension.

Code 3.23 shows an example of a programming language support for data and thread mapping. It shows the `affinity` clause for SGI Origin 2000 NUMA system that allows programmers to specify where a loop iteration should be executed. The `distribute` clause specifies that matrix a should be allocated in an interleaved manner across processors at the granularity of *block*, across rows and across columns. The `affinity` clause specifies that iteration (i, j) should be assigned to a thread that runs on the same node where data $a(i, j)$ is allocated. Similar support is provided in programming models oriented for NUMA, such as PGAS.

Code 3.23 Example of computation affinity that can be specified in a programming language extension in Origin 2000 system [38].

```
1 !$sgi distribute a(block,block)
2 !$omp parallel do private(i,j), shared(a)
3 !$sgi+ nest(i,j), affinity(i,j) = data(a(i,j))
4       do j = 1, n
5         do i = 1, n
6           a(i,j) = 0.0
7         enddo
8       enddo
9       end
```

3.10 A Brief Introduction to OpenMP

This section briefly introduces the OpenMP standard version 3.0. More comprehensive information can be found at http://www.openmp.org. In this book we only cover the basics of OpenMP related to expressing various parallelism concepts that were covered earlier.

OpenMP (open multi-processing) is an application programming interface (API) that supports shared memory programming. OpenMP is jointly standardized by a group of major computer hardware and software vendors. OpenMP is an evolving standard. OpenMP supports C/C++ and Fortran languages. The OpenMP standard consists of a set of compiler directives with which programmers can express parallelism to a compiler that supports OpenMP. The compiler replaces the directives into code that calls library routines or reads environment variables that influence the run-time behavior of the program.

OpenMP was initially designed to express DOALL parallelism in loop structures. It uses a fork-join model of execution, where in serial sections, one thread (the master thread) executes computation. When a parallel section is encountered, the master spawns slave threads to run together, until the end of the parallel section where the slave threads join the master thread.

The primary way programmers use OpenMP is to use directives inserted into the source code of their program. The directive in OpenMP follows the following format:

```
#pragma omp directive-name [clause[ [,] clause]...]  new-line
```

For example, to express a DOALL parallelism for a loop, we can insert the following directive right above the loop.

```
#pragma omp for [clause[[,] clause] ...  ]  new-line
```

where a clause is one the following:

- private(variable-list)
- firstprivate(variable-list)
- lastprivate(variable-list)
- reduction(operator: variable-list)
- ordered
- schedule(kind[, chunk_size])
- nowait

To start a parallel section, we can insert #pragma omp parallel followed by curly braces that indicate the start and end of the parallel section, as shown in Code 3.24. Any code inside the parallel section is executed by all threads. When a DOALL loop is encountered, instead of each thread executing all iterations, we can split the iterations among the threads using a work-sharing construct #pragma omp for.

To express a *for* loop that has DOALL parallelism, we can insert the following directives to a code (Code 3.24). The source file must include the header file omp.h which contains OpenMP function declarations. A parallel region is started by #pragma omp parallel and is enclosed by curly brackets. The start of a parallel region will spawn threads, and the number of threads spawned can be specified by an environment variable (e.g., setenv OMP_NUM_THREADS n) or directly in the code by calling a function (e.g., omp_set_num_threads(n)). The code inside the brackets is executed by all threads. Within a parallel region, we can have multiple parallel loops and each of the loops does not spawn new threads as they have been created when entering the parallel region. If we only have one loop that we want to execute in parallel, we can combine the start of the parallel loop and the start of the parallel region with one directive `#pragma omp parallel for`.

Code 3.24 A DOALL parallelism example in OpenMP.

```
1 #pragma omp parallel
2 {  // start of parallel region
3   #pragma omp parallel for default(shared) private(i)
4   for(i=0; i<n; i++)
5     A[i]= A[i]*A[i]- 3.0;
6 } // end of parallel region
```

OpenMP allows parallel section and work-sharing directives to be combined into one as follows:

```
1 I#pragma omp parallel for default(shared) private(i)
2 for(i=0; i<n; i++)
3   A[i]= A[i]*A[i]- 3.0;
```

In the code, the `default(shared)` clause states that unless otherwise specified, all variables within the scope of the loop are shared. Note that the loop index variable `i` needs to be private per thread, hence `private(i)` is added.

To express function parallelism in which we want to execute some code section in parallel with another code section, we can use the following construct (Code 3.25). The code shows that the two loops should be executed in parallel with respect to one another, although each loop is sequentially executed.

Code 3.25 A function parallelism example in OpenMP.

```
1 #pragma omp parallel shared(A,B)private(i)
2 {
3   #pragma omp sections nowait
4   {
5     #pragma omp section
6     for(i=0; i<n; i++)
7       A[i]= A[i]*A[i]- 4.0;
8     #pragma omp section
9     for(i=0; i<n; i++)
10      B[i]= B[i]*B[i] + 9.0;
11  } // end omp sections
12 } // end omp parallel
```

In OpenMP, a variable can have a type of `shared`, `private`, `reduction`, `firstprivate`, or `lastprivate`. `shared` and `private` are variable scopes that we have discussed in Section 3.6. Note that if a variable exists outside the parallel region and has the same name as the variable inside the parallel region and the variable is declared private, then they do not share any storage, meaning that a write to them will write to different locations in memory.

`reduction` variable is a privatized variable that are combined at the end of the parallel section to produce a single result value and has been discussed in Section 3.6.1. Only certain operators are built-in in the programming language and provably associative and commutative to the compiler, hence, only certain operators are allowed in the reduction clause, for example arithmetic (+ and *) and logical (&, |, &&, ||, etc.).

`firstprivate` and `lastprivate` are special types of private variables. `firstprivate` initializes the private copies of a variable from the value of the original variable prior to entering the parallel region. `lastprivate` means that upon loop exit, the value of the original copy of the variable is assigned the value seen by the thread that is assigned the last loop iteration (for parallel loops only).

For synchronization primitives, OpenMP implicitly inserts a barrier after each parallel loop or parallel sections. If programmers find that no barrier is necessary, they can insert a `nowait` clause. For example, in the following code, any thread that finishes execution of its tasks is allowed to move on to the next section of code (Code 3.26):

Code 3.26 Removing implicit barriers in OpenMP.

```
1 #pragma omp parallel for nowait default(shared) private(i)
2 for(i=0; i<n; i++)
3   A[i]= A[i]*A[i]- 3.0;
4 ...
```

In OpenMP, we can also indicate a critical section with the following directive: `#pragma omp critical` and enclose in curly brackets the code that is inside the critical sections. If the enclosed code contains simple operations such as an increment, an add, or a subtraction, sometimes there is a corresponding single machine instruction that can accomplish it quickly and atomically. In such a case, we can use `#pragma omp atomic` instead. The critical clause makes it unnecessary for programmers to declare lock variables and to use a pair of lock and unlock. However, OpenMP also allows named lock variables. Named locks are useful when we need several locks associated with different parts of a data structure. Named locks are not available as directives, but instead can be invoked through library calls: `omp_init_lock()` for initializing a named lock, `omp_set_lock()` and `omp_unset_lock()` for locking and unlocking, `omp_test_lock()` for testing whether the lock is currently held by a thread or not, and `omp_destroy_lock()` for deallocating the lock.

It is also possible to specify that only a single thread should execute a portion of the code, using the directive `#pragma omp single` and enclosing in curly brackets the code that is to be executed by just one thread. If that single thread needs to be the master thread, then the directive to use is `#pragma omp master`.

When assigning iterations, we can also specify that the iterations should be executed in program order using the clause `ordered`. However, this should not be used unless there are reasons to do this as it is an expensive construct that introduces serialization.

The `schedule` clause allows how iterations can be grouped into tasks and how tasks can be assigned to threads. It has two parameters: type of scheduling and *chunk* size. A chunk is a group of consecutive iterations. The type of scheduling is one of the following:

- `static`: each chunk is assigned to a processor statically.

- `dynamic`: each chunk is placed in a task queue. Each processor, when it is idle or when it finishes computing a task, grabs the next one in the task queue and executes it.

- `guided`: the same as dynamic, except that the task sizes are not uniform, early tasks are exponentially larger than later tasks.

- `runtime`: the choice of scheduling is not determined statically. Rather, the OpenMP run-time library checks the environment variable `OMP_SCHEDULE` at run time to determine what scheduling to use.

Specifying the number of threads to run an OpenMP programs can be achieved by embedding it in the code, such as using a library call `omp_set_num_threads()`, or through setting up an environment variable `OMP_NUM_THREADS` prior to launching the program. The program will read this environment variable and set the number of threads for the entire execution.

A new feature in OpenMP 3.0 is tasking. `#pragma omp task` allows us to define an irregular task to be executed by threads. Tasking is more flexible to use compared to sections, for example sections do not permit additional code outside the sections. An example of tasking can be seen in Code 3.27, which parallelizes the binary tree traversal that was shown in Code 3.14.

Code 3.27 An example use of tasking for binary tree traversal from Code 3.14.

```
1 int search_tree(struct tree *p, int data)
2 {
3   int count1 = 0, count2, count 3;
4   if(p == NULL)
5     return 0;
6   if (p->data == data)
7     count1 = 1;
8   #pragma omp task untied firstprivate(p)
9   {
10    count2 = search_tree(p->left);
11   }
12   #pragma omp task untied firstprivate(p)
13   {
14    count3 = search_tree(p->right);
15   }
16   return (count1 + count2 + count3);
17 }
18 ...
19 #pragma omp parallel
20 {
21   #pragma omp single
22   {
23     search_tree(root,sleep_time);
24   }
25 }
26 ...
```

In the code, we invoke `#pragma omp single` to ensure only one thread executes the first call to the search tree function. In the function itself, `#pragma omp task` defines a task that will be queued in the task queued and can later be executed by a thread. Immediately after setting aside a task (to traverse the left subtree), the program execution can continue execution to set aside a task for the right subtree. The `untied` clause allows flexibility in reassigning a task from a thread to another, helping to achieve load balance.

Let us look at a simple example of using OpenMP for parallelizing matrix multiplication. Suppose that there are two 2-dimensional rectangular matrices A and B that we want to multiply together, and the result is stored in the third matrix Y. The code for the multiplication is shown below

(Code 3.28). In this example, we will discuss simple parallelization strategies with OpenMP, and ignore more advanced optimizations such as blocking, tiling, etc.

Code 3.28 Matrix multiplication code.

```
1 #define MATRIX_DIM 500
2
3 double A[MATRIX_DIM][MATRIX_DIM],
4   B[MATRIX_DIM][MATRIX_DIM],
5   Y[MATRIX_DIM][MATRIX_DIM];
6 int i, j, k;
7 . . .
8
9   for (i=0; i<MATRIX_DIM; i++) {
10     for (j=0; j<MATRIX_DIM; j++) {
11       Y[i][j] = 0.0;  // S1
12       for (k=0; k<MATRIX_DIM; k++) {
13         Y[i][j] = Y[i][j] + A[i][k] * B[k][j]; // S2
14       } // for k
15     } // for j
16   } // for i
17 . . .
```

From the code, we can see a loopnest consisting of three loops. The two outer loops iterate over each dimension of the matrix. Each iteration in the second loop assigns a value to one element of the result matrix Y. The innermost loop visits a row in matrix A and a column in matrix B, and their sum of products is accumulated to the current element in matrix Y.

Applying dependence analysis of the loopnest, we find that the innermost statement first reads the last value of $Y[i][j]$ set by the previous k iteration, then adds it with $A[i][k] \times B[k][j]$, and writes the new value to $Y[i][j]$. The new value will be read by the same statement in the next k iteration. Therefore, the we have a true dependence $S2[i][j][k] \rightarrow^T S2[i][j][k+1]$, where $S2$ represents the innermost statement. There are no other dependences, except between $S1$ and $S2$ for the first k iteration. The true dependence is loop-carried for the $for\ k$ loop but is loop independent for both $for\ i$ and $for\ j$ loops. Therefore, both the $for\ i$ and $for\ j$ loops exhibit DOALL parallelism.

Moving on to determining the scope of variables, we can see from the code that matrices A and B are never written, so they are read-only variables. Loop index variables i, j, k are read-write conflicting but are privatizable since we know their values for all iterations beforehand. Finally, consider elements of array Y. If the parallel tasks are iterations of the $for\ i$ loop, elements of array Y are read/write non-conflicting variables since each parallel task reads from and writes to different rows of the matrix. Likewise, if the parallel tasks are iterations of the $for\ j$ loop, elements of array Y are read/write non-conflicting variables since each parallel task reads from and writes to different columns of the matrix, for a single row. Hence, for both loops, all variables should be declared shared except the loop index variables. Finally, if the parallel tasks are iterations of the $for\ k$ loop, elements of array Y are read/write conflicting, because each k iteration reads from the value written by the previous k iteration. Examining the operation performed on Y, it is a summation of the products of elements from a row of matrix A and a column of matrix B. Since an addition operation is commutative and associative, it is a reduction operator, and each element of array Y can be made a reduction variable. All other variables (except the loop index variables) can be declared as shared.

Using OpenMP, if we want to parallelize the $for\ i$ loop only, we can place the OpenMP directive `#pragma omp parallel for default (shared)` right before the $for\ i$ loop to parallelize the $for\ i$ loop, or right before the $for\ j$ loop to parallelize the $for\ j$ loop, or at both places to parallelize both loops. If instead we want to parallelize the $for\ k$ loop, we can put the OpenMP directive `#pragma omp parallel for default(shared)` right before the $for\ k$ loop, but in addition, we either have to guard the access to $Y[i][j]$ with `#pragma omp critical` (Code 3.29), or transform $Y[i][j]$ into a reduction variable. Unfortunately, the latter choice cannot be implemented using the OpenMP reduction clause because the reduction variable must be scalar, and $Y[i][j]$ is a part of a matrix.

Code 3.29 Matrix multiplication code.

```
1 .  .  .
2     for (i=0; i<MATRIX_DIM; i++) {
3       for (j=0; j<MATRIX_DIM; j++) {
4         Y[i][j] = 0.0;
5 #pragma omp parallel for default(shared)
6         for (k=0; k<MATRIX_DIM; k++) {
7 #pragma omp critical {
8             Y[i][j] = Y[i][j] + A[i][k] * B[k][j];
9           } // critical
10        } // for k
11      } // for j
12    } // for i
13 .  .  .
```

The resulting parallel program was compiled using Intel icc compiler with −O3 optimization level on a workstation having two Intel Xeon CPU running at 2.0 GHz, with each core capable of running two threads simultaneously (two-way hyperthreaded). Each CPU has a 512KB L2 cache. The matrix multiplication is executed 10 times.

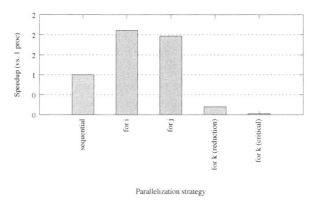

Figure 3.17: Speedup ratio from parallelizing different loops in a loop nest.

Figure 3.17 shows the speedup ratios by using different parallelization strategies: parallelizing only the $for\ i$ loop, only the $for\ j$ loop, only the $for\ k$ loop with reduction, and only the $for\ k$ loop with critical section guarding the innermost statement. The sequential execution time is 20 seconds. Parallelizing the $for\ i$ loop gives an execution time of 9.47 seconds, yielding a speedup ratio of 2.11. This is not surprising because while all four threads can run simultaneously, the threads that share processor resources are slowed down due to contention. Hence, a perfect speedup ratio of four cannot be approximated. Parallelizing the $for\ j$ loop gives an execution time of 10.13 seconds, yielding a speedup ratio of 1.97. The reason for the slight increase in execution time is because while in the $for\ i$ loop only one parallel region is encountered, in the $for\ j$ loop parallelization, each $for\ i$ iteration corresponds to one parallel region. Since there are a total of 500 parallel regions, the overhead for setting up a new parallel region, entering and exiting it is approximately $\frac{10.13-9.47}{500} \times 1000 = 1.3$ milliseconds or less. Parallelizing the $for\ k$ loop with reduction loop slows it down further to 101.32 seconds, due to the overheads of a lot more parallel regions. Finally, parallelizing the $for\ k$ loop with a critical section guarding the innermost statement requires more than 720 seconds to execute.

Overall, the evaluation results show that the granularity of parallel regions is very important because parallel overheads can be quite significant. A higher priority should be given to parallelizing the outermost loop in a loopnest compared to parallelizing inner loops. In addition, critical sections that are frequently encountered can greatly degrade performance.

3.11   Exercises

Worked Problems

1. **Code Analysis**. For the code shown below:

```
...
for (i=1; i<=N; i++) {
  for (j=1; j<=i; j++) {   // note the index range!
    S1: a[i][j] = b[i][j] + c[i][j];
    S2: b[i][j] = a[i][j-1];
    S3: c[i][j] = a[i][j];
  }
}
```

   (a) Draw its iteration-space traversal graph (ITG).

   (b) List all the dependences, and clearly indicate which dependence is loop-independent vs. loop-carried.

   (c) Draw its loop-carried dependence graph (LDG).

   Answer:

   Loop-carried dependences:

$$S1[i, j-1] \to^T S2[i, j] \tag{3.3}$$

   Loop-independent dependences:

$$S1[i, j] \to^T S3[i, j] \tag{3.4}$$
$$S1[i, j] \to^A S2[i, j] \tag{3.5}$$
$$S1[i, j] \to^A S3[i, j] \tag{3.6}$$

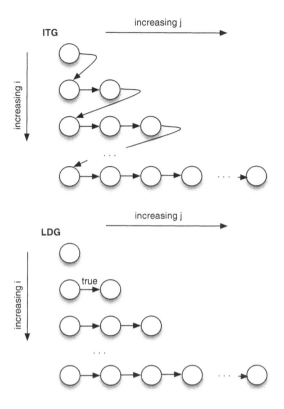

2. **Code Analysis**. For the code shown below:

```
...
for (i=1; i<=N; i++) {
   for (j=2; j<=N; j++) {
     S1: a[i][j] = a[i][j-1] + a[i][j-2];
     S2: a[i+1][j] = a[i][j] * b[i-1][j];
     S3: b[i][j] = a[i][j];
   }
}
```

(a) Draw its iteration-space traversal graph (ITG).

(b) List all the dependences, and clearly indicate which dependence is loop-independent vs. loop-carried.

(c) Draw its loop-carried dependence graph (LDG).

Answer:

Loop-carried dependences:

$$S1[i, j-1] \to^T S1[i, j] \tag{3.7}$$

$$S1[i, j-2] \to^T S1[i, j] \tag{3.8}$$

$$S2[i, j] \to^O S1[i+1, j] \tag{3.9}$$

$$S3[i-1, j] \to^T S2[i, j] \tag{3.10}$$

Loop-independent dependences:

$$S1[i,j] \rightarrow^T S3[i,j] \tag{3.11}$$

$$S1[i,j] \rightarrow^T S2[i,j] \tag{3.12}$$

$$\tag{3.13}$$

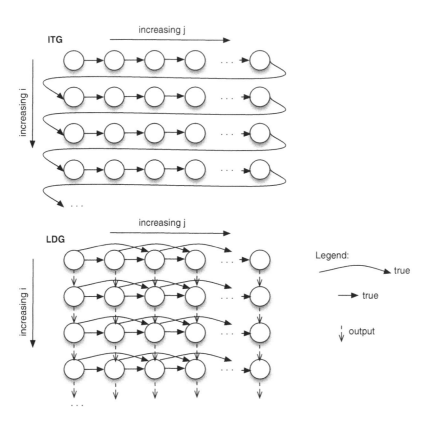

3. **Other Parallelism**. For the code shown below:

```
...
for (i=1; i<=N; i++) {
  for (j=1; j<=i; j++) {  // note the index range!
    S1: a[i][j] = b[i][j] + c[i][j];
    S2: b[i][j] = a[i-1][j-1];
    S3: c[i][j] = a[i][j];
    S4: d[i][j] = d[i][j-1] + 1;
  }
}
```

   (a) Show the code that exploits function parallelism.

   (b) If S4 is removed from the loop, exploit DOACROSS parallelism to the fullest and show the code.

   (c) If S4 is removed from the loop, exploit DOPIPE parallelism using as many threads as possible and show the code.

Answer:

(a) Since there is no dependence relation between S4 and all of S1, S2, and S3, the loop can be distributed into two loops, one with statements S1, S2, and S3, while another with statement S4. After loop distribution, the two "for i" loops can be executed in parallel with respect to each other:

```
...
for (i=1; i<=N; i++)
  for (j=1; j<=i; j++)
    S1: a[i][j] = b[i][j] + c[i][j];
    S2: b[i][j] = a[i-1][j-1];
    S3: c[i][j] = a[i][j];
  }
}

for (i=1; i<=N; i++)
  for (j=1; j<=i; j++)
    S4: d[i][j] = d[i][j-1] + 1;
  }
}
```

(b) In order to exploit the DOACROSS parallelism to the fullest, we need to consider both "for i" and "for j" loops. They are parallelizable with proper synchronization.

```
...
for (i=1; i<=N; i++)
  for (j=1; j<=i; j++)   // note the loop index range!
    S1: a[i][j] = b[i][j] + c[i][j];
    signal(i,j);

    if (i>1 && j>1)
      wait(i-1,j-1);
    S2: b[i][j] = a[i-1][j-1];
    S3: c[i][j] = a[i][j];
  }
}
```

(c) In order to exploit the DOPIPE parallelism to the fullest, we need to break the three statements inside the loop to three threads/processors, each executing only statements S1, S2, or S3, respectively. We assume here that wait(x) needs to have one corresponding signal(x).

```
...
// code for Thread 1:
for (i=1; i<=N; i++)
  for (j=1; j<=i; j++)
    S1: a[i][j] = b[i][j] + c[i][j];
    signal(i,j);
    signal(i,j);
  }
}
// code for Thread 2:
for (i=1; i<=N; i++)
  for (j=1; j<=i; j++)
    wait(i,j);
    S2: b[i][j] = a[i-1][j-1];
  }
```

```
      }
      // code for Thread 3:
      for (i=1; i<=N; i++)
        for (j=1; j<=i; j++)
          wait(i,j);
          S3: c[i][j] = a[i][j];
        }
      }
```

Note that for P2's code, the synchronization needs to satisfy two dependence constraints: a true dependence on a[i-1][j-1] produced at iteration i-1,j-1 by statement S1, but also an anti-dependence on b[i][j] that is read by statement S1 at the same iteration. So, the synchronization that is inserted should be the more restrictive of the two constraints, which is `wait(i,j)` rather than `wait(i-1,j-1)`.

4. Consider an algorithm to compute matrix $Y = A \times B + C$, where Y, A, B, C are matrices with dimension $n \times p, n \times m, m \times p, n \times p$, respectively. Assume that all n, m, and p are divisible by 2. The algorithm is shown:

```
int i, j, k;
float A[n][m], B[m][p], Y[n][p], C[n][p], x;

...
// begin linear transformation
for (i=0; i<n; i++) {
  for (j=0; j<p; j++) {
    x = 0;
    for (k=0; k<m; k++)
      x = x + A[i][k] * B[k][j];
    Y[i][j] = x + C[i][j];
  }
}
```

With appropriate directives, all the loops (for i, for j, for k) can be parallelized. Indicate for each variable, whether it should be declared private or shared variable when we parallelize the "for i" loop only, "for j" loop only, or the "for k" loop only.

Answer:

for i only:

Variable	Private	Shared
i	X	
j	X	
k	X	
A		X
B		X
C		X
Y		X
x	X	

for j only:

Variable	Private	Shared
i		X
j	X	
k	X	
A		X
B		X
C		X
Y		X
x	X	

for k only:

Variable	Private	Shared
i		X
j		X
k	X	
A		X
B		X
C		X
Y		X
x		X

Note: variable x needs to be protected with synchronization, or declared as reduction variable with '+' as the reduction operator.

Homework Problems

1. **Code analysis**. For the code shown below:

```
for (i=4; i<=n; i++)
    A[i] = A[i] + A[i-4];
```

   (a) Draw the loop carried dependence graph.

   (b) By analyzing the loop carried dependence graph, identify the parallelism in the code, rewrite it, and express the parallel loop(s) by using appropriate OpenMP directives.

2. **Code analysis**. For the code shown below:

```
...
for (i=1; i<=N; i++) {
    for (j=1; j<=i; j++) {  // note the index range!
        S1: a[i][j] = b[i][j] + c[i][j];
        S2: b[i][j] = a[i-1][j-1];
        S3: c[i][j] = a[i][j];
    }
}
```

   (a) Draw its iteration-space traversal graph (ITG).

    (b) List all the dependences and clearly indicate which dependence is loop-independent vs. loop-carried.

    (c) Draw its loop-carried dependence graph (LDG).

3. **Code analysis**. For the code shown below:

```
...
for (i=1; i<=N; i++) {
   for (j=1; j<=i; j++) {   // note the index range!
     S1: a[i][j] = b[i][j] + c[i][j];
     S2: b[i][j] = a[i-1][j-1] * b[i+1][j-1]
           * c[i-1][j];
     S3: c[i+1][j] = a[i][j];
   }
}
```

    (a) Draw its iteration-space traversal graph (ITG).

    (b) List all the dependences and clearly indicate which dependence is loop-independent vs. loop-carried.

    (c) Draw its loop-carried dependence graph (LDG).

4. **Code analysis**. Draw the ITG, find all dependence relations, and draw the LDG for the following code:

```
for (i=2; i<N; i++)
    for (j=2; j<N; j++)
        S: a[i][j] = a[i-2][j] + a[i][j+2]
```

5. **DOACROSS and DOPIPE**. For the code shown below assume that we want to parallelize it for two threads. ... for (i=2; i<N; i++) S1: a[i] = a[i-1] + b[i-2]; S2: b[i] = b[i] + 1; ...

    (a) Exploit DOACROSS parallelism and show a single code that works for both threads.

    (b) Exploit DOPIPE parallelism and show the code for each thread.

6. **Variable scope analysis**. Consider the following code section. All matrices have a dimension of N N , and all arrays have a dimension of N. Assume that N is divisible by 2. ... for (i=0; i<N; i++) k = C[N-1-i]; for (j=0; j<N; j++) A[i][j] = k * A[i][j] * B[i/2][j]; ...

As can be seen from the code, all the loops (for i and for j) are parallelizable. Indicate each variable whether it should be declared as shared or private when we parallelize: for i loop only and for j loop only.

7. **Data vs. function parallelism**. The following loop is taken from tomcatv, a Spec benchmark, translated into an equivalent C code:

```
for (j=2; j<n; j++) {
   for (i=2; i<n; i++) {
     x[i][j] = x[i][j] + rx[i][j];
     y[i][j] = y[i][j] + ry[i][j];
   }
}
```

Assume that n is a multiple of 2. Using OpenMP directives, show the parallel version of the loop that exploit:

(a) Function parallelism only.

(b) Data parallelism only.

(c) Both function and data parallelisms.

8. **Data vs. function parallelism**. This following loop is taken from tomcatv of Spec benchmark, translated into an equivalent C version:

```
for (j=2; j<n; j++) {
  for (i=2; i<n; i++) {
    x[i][j] = x[i][j] + rx[i][j];
    y[i][j] = y[i][j] + ry[i][j];
  }
}
```

Assume that n is a multiple of 2. Using OpenMP directives, show parallel version of the loop that exploit:

(a) Function parallelism only.

(b) Data parallelism only.

(c) Both function and data parallelisms.

9. **Reduction Operation**. For the following code, parallelize the code by identifying the reduction variable and reduction operation. When necessary, rewrite the code so that you can use the reduction clause in an OpenMP directive.

```
// pre: x and y contain a value > 1
for (i=0; i<n; i++)
  y = y * exp(x,A[i]);
print y;
```

where $exp(a, b) = a^b$.

10. Identify all correctness problems in the following code:

```
#pragma omp parallel for shared(i,j,N,B) private(A,C,temp,sum)
for (i=1; i<N; i++) {
    S1: temp = A[i][i];
    S2: sum = 0;
    #pragma omp parallel for shared(i,j,N,B) private(A,C,temp) reduction(+:su
    for (j=1; j<N; j++) {
        S3: A[i][j] = A[i/2][j] + B[i-1][j-1];
        S4: C[N-i][N-j] = temp * B[i][j];
        S5: sum = sum + A[i][j] * C[N-i][N-j];
    }
}
```

Chapter 4

Parallel Programming for Linked Data Structures

Contents

In Chapter 3, we have discussed parallel programming techniques that are applicable for applications that rely on matrices as their data structures. Accesses to a matrix are characterized by a nest of loops in which each loop iterates over elements in one dimension of the matrix. Since matrices are commonly used for scientific simulations and multimedia processing, the techniques described are useful for these applications.

The objective of this chapter is to look at parallelization techniques for non-scientific applications that mainly rely on *linked data structures* (LDS) as their main data structures. LDS include all data structures that use a collection of nodes that are linked together with pointers, such as linked lists, trees, graphs, hash tables, etc. Many classes of applications heavily use LDS, including compilers, word processors, and database systems. Some of them, such as database systems, have a need for a very high degree of parallelism in order to be able to serve a large number of transactions simultaneously.

LDS accesses exhibit a high degree of loop-carried dependence, preventing the loop parallelization techniques from Chapter 3 to be applied successfully. Hence, they require a different set of techniques for an effective parallelization. In this chapter, we will focus on these techniques, and we will illustrate the practical application of the techniques on a linked list. Unfortunately, some

LDS parallelization techniques are data structure-specific. For each type of LDS, there may be a large number of parallel algorithms for it. Since it is impossible to cover all of them in this chapter, we will focus our discussion on features that are common in these techniques and apply them to a simple LDS – a linked list. This will provide a basic framework on which readers can build further investigation into parallelization techniques for LDS.

Note that the goal of this chapter is not to exhaustively cover techniques for LDS parallelization. Instead, it is to give readers appreciation of how locks may be used in non-scientific applications that utilize LDS, and how lock granularity is related to the amount of concurrency that can be exploited and the programming complexity. Understanding how locks are used helps in figuring out what requirements are important when designing hardware support for lock synchronization.

4.1 Parallelization Challenges in LDS

LDS consists of different types of data structures such as linked lists, trees, hash tables, and graphs. The common feature of an LDS is that it has a collection of nodes which are linked to one another with pointers. A pointer is a data type that stores an address. To construct a singly linked list, for example, each node contains a pointer that stores the address of the next node in the list. For a doubly linked list, each node contains two pointers, one to store the address of the next node, and another to store the address of the previous node. A tree is organized hierarchically, with a root node at the top of the hierarchy, and leaf nodes at the bottom of the hierarchy. A node in a tree structure contains pointers that point to its children nodes, and sometimes also contains a pointer that points to its parent node. A graph is a collection of nodes in which each node can point to any nodes and may have an arbitrary number of pointers to other nodes.

While diverse, LDS traversal shares a common characteristic. It relies on reading a node to discover the addresses of other nodes it points to, read those nodes, follow next nodes that are pointed by the read nodes, and so on. Therefore, unlike the traversal of a matrix that uses an arithmetically-computed matrix index, in LDS the next node to be visited in a traversal is not known until the current node's content is read. This pattern creates a loop-carried dependence in a LDS traversal.

4.1.1 Loop-Level Parallelization is Insufficient

Code 4.1 illustrates the data structure declaration of a singly-linked list, with a function `AddValue` that finds a node with a key value specified in the function parameter `int key`, and adds a value `x` to the `data` field. Note that the key statement in the traversal is "`p = p->next`". When `p` points to a node, in order to get the next pointer value, the content of the node must be read before the value `p->next` is known. Therefore, there is a loop-carried dependence in the traversal loop. Such a dependence makes it hard to parallelize an LDS traversal loop.

There is another challenge. The loop-carried dependence may exist beyond just the traversal statement. For example, it is possible for the LDS to contain a cycle, that is there is a path from the current node to its successors until it reaches the current node again. This is common in a graph, but can also occur in linked lists such as in a circular list. When a node is revisited in a traversal, the code may read from the node's data that was changed in an earlier iteration, such as in the statement "`p->data = p->data + x;`", creating an additional loop-carried dependence. In general, this situation is created by design by the programmer as he/she precisely knows how

---

Code 4.1 An example of a function that finds a node in a linked list and modifies it.

```
1  typedef struct tagIntListNode{
2    int key;  // unique for each node
3    int data;
4    struct tagIntListNode *next;
5  } IntListNode;
6  typedef IntListNode *pIntListNode;
7
8  typedef struct {
9    pIntListNode  head;
10 } IntList;
11 typedef IntList* pIntList;
12
13 void AddValue(pIntList pList, int key, int x)
14 {
15   pIntListNode p = pList->head;
16   while (p != NULL) {
17     if (p->key == key)
18       p->data = p->data + x;
19     p = p->next;
20   }
21 }
```

---

the LDS is organized. However, it may not be immediately apparent to performance tuners or the compiler.

Another challenge is that some LDS use recursive functions for its traversal. Recursive traversal is common in a tree. A recursive traversal is not necessarily a hindrance in exploiting parallelism. For example, in a tree traversal, we can spawn a thread to traverse the left subtree and another to traverse the right subtree. So a recursive tree traversal presents an opportunity for extracting parallelism. However, such parallelization opportunities are specific to the data structure being used.

Considering the existence of loop-carried dependence in the traversal loop, applying loop-level parallelization in LDS is difficult. However, there are other parallelism opportunities, that will be discussed in the next few sections.

4.2 Approaches to Parallelization of LDS

4.2.1 Parallelizing Computation vs. Traversal

A simple approach to parallelize LDS is to parallelize the computation vs. traversal. Suppose that we want to traverse a linked list and perform computation on each node. Loop-carried dependence only affects the traversal but not node computation. Thus we can bundle each node computation into a task to be executed in parallel with respect to other nodes' computation, while keeping the traversal sequential. This approach is illustrated in Figure 4.1.

Figure 4.1(top) illustrates traditional code for traversing a singly-linked list starting with p until its is NULL. Since it is sequential, it performs traversal and computation alternatingly. The bottom part of the figure shows a parallel version where one thread performs the traversal sequentially, but

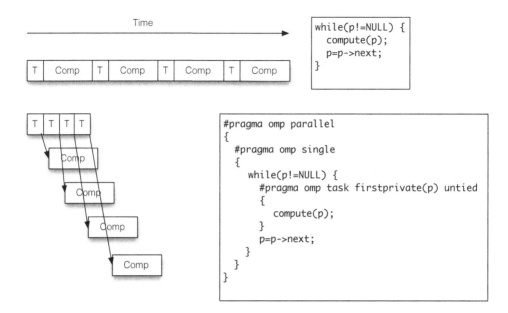

Figure 4.1: Sequential linked list traversal and computation (top) versus parallel node computation (bottom).

it specifies each node computation as a parallel task. These tasks can then be assigned dynamically to available threads. Therefore, the node computations can be performed in parallel with respect to one another, as illustrated in the figure.

Overall, this approach is straightforward and is relatively easy to implement. However, the performance aspect of the approach is interesting. There is a potential performance benefit due to a prefetching effect. If threads run on processors that share a cache, as the master thread performs the LDS traversal, it brings in nodes of the LDS into the shared cache before the slave threads need to access them. thereby eliminating some of the future cache misses that the slave threads may otherwise suffer from.

Perhaps the most important factor determining the performance of this approach is the time to perform node computation compared to the time to perform traversal of each node and the task management overhead. The task management overhead is substantial due to the large number of tasks. If, say the computation time is equal or smaller than the traversal time plus the task management overhead, this approach will yield a maximum speedup of 2. We can think of the traversal time and task management overhead as the Amdahl law's serial fraction, which eventually determines the maximum speedup. Achieving a large speedup in proportion to the number of threads requires the computation time to be much larger than the traversal and task management overhead time.

Figure 4.2 shows the speedup curves for the linked list traversal program shown earlier on a 32-core AMD Opteron system. The compute() function is implemented as a dummy loop that is calibrated to compute for a specified amount of time in nanoseconds, which is shown in the x-axes. The y-axes shows speedups with respect to the sequential traversal version. We plot the speedups for 2, 4, 8, 16, and 32 threads. The figure shows that all number of threads start off suffering from significant slowdowns when the compute time is small. They start to enjoy speedups when as the computation time increases until they reach near-perfect speedups. The smaller the number of

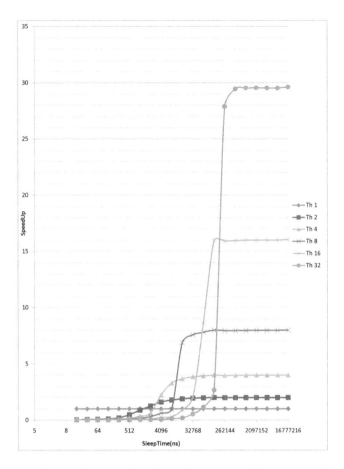

Figure 4.2: The speedup ratio as a function of amount of time spent in computation per node, for different number of threads.

threads, the earlier it enjoys speedup. For example, for 2 threads, $4\mu s$ is required before we get a speedup of almost $2\times$. For 32 threads, the computation time must be at least 0.26ms before we get a speedup of almost $32\times$.

In other data structures that have more than one pointer per node such as trees and graphs, traversal and computation of nodes may even be overlapped, as shown in the binary tree traversal in Code 3.27.

4.2.2 Parallelizing Operations on the Data Structure

Another approach in LDS parallelization is parallelizing operations that are performed on the LDS. At the algorithm level, we can view an LDS as a data structure that comes with a set of basic primitives/operations that can be performed on it, such as *node insertion*, *node deletion*, *node search*, and *node modification*. In some LDS, there may be additional primitives such as *tree balancing* in a tree LDS. In this section, we will discuss how to exploit parallelism at such a level.

If we consider allowing various operations to be executed in parallel, we must know in what way the parallel execution is correct or incorrect. It fits our intuition that parallel execution should not produce different results compared to a sequential execution. More formally, such a constraint is defined in a concept called *serializability* which states that "*a parallel execution of a group of operations or primitives is serializable if there is some sequential execution of the operations or primitives that produce an identical result*". For example, if there is a node insertion operation and a node deletion operation that are executed in parallel, to achieve serializability, the result of the execution must be either equal to the result achieved when we sequentially perform the insertion followed by the deletion, or when we sequentially perform the deletion followed by the insertion.

The key to correct parallelization for LDS is to ensure that parallel execution of LDS operations always produces serializable outcomes. Before discussing how such techniques can be constructed, in the next section we will first discuss how unregulated parallel execution of linked list primitives can produce non-serializable outcomes.

> ### ■ *Did you know?*
>
> The concept of serializability is borrowed from, and is central to, database man-agement systems (DBMS). A DBMS consists of many tables containing records that are accessed and modified by many transactions that are processed concurrently. Serializability ensures the isolation property of transactions, where the effect of exe-cuting one transaction is independent of the execution of other transactions. Ensuring serializability makes it easy to reason about the correctness of concurrent execution of transactions.

Challenges in Parallelizing LDS Operations

Consider the key code portion of the node insertion, deletion, and search for a singly-linked list which are shown in Code 4.2, Code 4.3, and Code 4.4. In the node insertion function, the steps involved are the memory allocation of the new node through calling the `IntListNode_Create()` function, finding where to insert the node (which is required to keep the list sorted), and finally the insertion of the new node either at the head of the list, or between `prev` and `p`. Note that up until the last step, the list is only read and not modified. Only in the last step the list is modified by changing `prev`'s next pointer to point to the new node.

In the node deletion function, the steps involved are finding the node that contains the key value to be deleted as specified by the function argument variable `key`, deleting the node from the list, and finally freeing up the deleted node by calling the `free()` function. Note that the modification to the list occurs when the node is deleted, by changing the `prev`'s next pointer to point to `p`'s next pointer, effectively removing the node to be deleted from the list.

Suppose that there are two insertion operations that are executed in parallel. If handled incorrectly, they may conflict and cause a non-serializable outcome. An example is shown in Figure 4.3, in which two insertion operations conflict, with one that wants to insert a node with a key value of "4", and another that wants to insert a node with a key value of "5". Initially, the list has a node with a key value of "6" as the successor of a node with a key value of "3" (Figure 4.3(a)). Note that the pointer variables `p`, `prev`, and `newNode` are local function variables. Hence, they are all allocated in the respective stack of each thread, and therefore are private to each thread. However, the nodes pointed by these variables are a part of the linked list and hence they are shared by all threads.

Suppose that the two insertion operations are executed in parallel at almost the same stage. Both thread 0 and thread 1 have allocated the new nodes to insert, and have executed the statement "`newNode->next = p`", which link the new node's next pointers to point to node 6 (Fig-

Code 4.2 A node insertion function.

```
1  void Insert(pIntList pList, int key)
2  {
3    pIntListNode prev, p,
4      newNode = IntListNode_Create(key);
5
6    if (pList->head == NULL) { // first element, insert at head
7      pList->head = newNode;
8      return;
9    }
10
11   // traverse to find where to insert
12   p = pList->head;  prev = NULL;
13   while (p != NULL && p->key < newNode->key) {
14     prev = p;
15     p = p->next;
16   }
17
18   // insert the node at head or between prev and p
19   newNode->next = p;
20   if (prev != NULL)
21     prev->next = newNode;
22   else
23     pList->head = newNode;
24 }
```

Code 4.3 A node deletion function.

```
1  void Delete(pIntList pList, int key)
2  {
3    pIntListNode prev, p;
4
5    if (pList->head == NULL) // list is empty
6      return;
7
8    // traverse to find the node
9    p = pList->head;  prev = NULL;
10   while (p != NULL && p->key != key) {
11     prev = p;
12     p = p->next;
13   }
14
15   if (p == NULL)  // node not found
16     return;
17   if (prev == NULL) // delete the head node
18     pList->head = p->next;
19   else  // or delete a non-head node
20     prev->next = p->next;
21   free(p);
22 }
```

ure 4.3(b)). At this point, suppose that thread 0 is slightly faster and executes "prev->next = newNode". This will link node 3's next pointer to point to the new node (node 4) (Figure 4.3(c)).

Code 4.4 A node search function.

```
1 int Search(pIntList pList, int key)
2 {
3   pIntListNode p;
4
5   if (pList->head == NULL) // list is empty
6     return 0;
7
8   // traverse to find the node
9   p = pList->head;
10  while (p != NULL && p->key != key)
11    p = p->next;
12
13  if (p == NULL)  // node not found
14    return 0;
15  else
16    return 1;
17 }
```

Next, thread 1 also executes the same statement slightly later, and because its `prev` variable still points to node 3, it overwrites node 3's next pointer to point to the new node (node 5). The result is incorrect because node 4 has been accidentally removed from the linked list. In contrast, in a serializable execution, regardless of whether the insertion of node 4 or insertion of node 5 happens first, the final list contains both node 4 and node 5.

A similar non-serializable outcome may arise between an insertion and a deletion operation. Suppose that the insertion and the deletion are executed in parallel, as shown in Figure 4.4. The figure shows that thread 0 wants to insert a node with a key value of "4", while thread 1 wants to delete the node with key value of "5" from the linked list. Initially, the list has node 3, which is linked to node 5, which is linked to node 6 (Figure 4.3(a)). Suppose that both threads have finished the traversal. Thread 0 has discovered that it wants to insert node 4 after node 3, hence its `prev` pointer points to node 3. Thread 1 has found node 5, and hence its `prev` pointer points to node 3 while its `p` pointer points to node 5.

Assume that thread 0 runs slightly ahead and executes statements that insert node 4. It changes node 4's next pointer to point to node 5, and then changes node 3's next pointer to point to node 4 (Figure 4.3(b)). Thread 1 is oblivious to the fact that the linked list has changed, and its `prev` and `p` pointers still point to node 3 and node 5, respectively. When thread 1 executes the statement that deletes node 5, it overwrites node 3's (pointed by its `prev` variable) next pointer to point to node 6 (pointed by its `p`'s next pointer). The result is incorrect because node 4 has now been accidentally removed from the linked list. In contrast, in a serializable execution, regardless of whether the insertion of node 4 or deletion of node 5 happens first, the final list has node 4.

Note that this is not the only possible incorrect outcome involving insertion and deletion operations. If the deletion of node 5 is executed first by thread 1, prior to the insertion of node 4, then the insertion fails and node 4 is missing from the list. If thread 1 attempts to delete node 3 instead of node 5, incorrect outcomes can also result. Overall, any insertion as a successor or predecessor of a node that is to be deleted can yield to a non-serializable outcome.

We have discussed how two insertion operations, and an insertion and a deletion can conflict and produce an incorrect outcome. In a similar manner, two deletion operations can also conflict

Conflict between 2 insertion operations

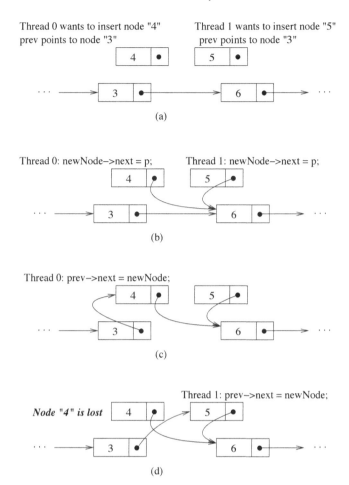

Figure 4.3: Non-serializable outcome from parallel execution of two insertions.

and produce an incorrect outcome (readers are invited to work out this outcome as an exercise). In general, when two operations modify the linked list simultaneously, involving nodes that are adjacent, then an incorrect outcome may arise.

So far we have discussed non-serializable outcomes resulting from parallel execution of two operations that modify some nodes in the list. We have not discussed what outcome may arise when one of the operations modifies the list, while another operation only reads from the list without modifying it. Can an incorrect outcome occur as a result of their parallel execution?

To answer the question, Figure 4.5 illustrates the parallel execution of deletion and node search operation. The node search code is similar to what is shown in Code 4.1 except that the statement that modifies the node's `data` field is omitted. Suppose that initially, thread 0, which attempts to search the node with the key value of "5", has reached node 3. Thread 1 has found node 5 and is ready to delete it. Its `prev` pointer points to node 3 and its `p` pointer points to node 5. This initial situation is illustrated in Figure 4.5(a).

Suppose that next, thread 1 performs the deletion by changing node 3's next pointer to point to node 6 (Figure 4.5(b)). In this case, when thread 0 continues its traversal by following node 3's next

Conflict between an insertion and a deletion operation

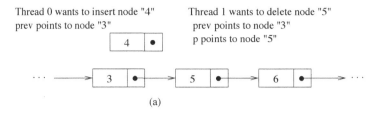

Thread 0 wants to insert node "4"   Thread 1 wants to delete node "5"
prev points to node "3"   prev points to node "3"
                                                        p points to node "5"

(a)

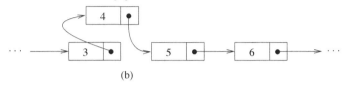

Thread 0: newNode–>next = p; prev–>next = newNode;

(b)

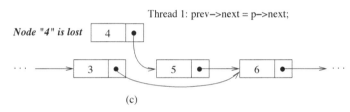

Thread 1: prev–>next = p–>next;

Node "4" is lost

(c)

Figure 4.4: Non-serializable outcome from parallel execution of an insertion and a deletion operation.

pointer, it will reach node 6, and continues traversal from there. The outcome of the traversal is that node 5 is not found.

Alternatively, suppose that thread 0 is slightly faster than thread 1 and follows node 3's next pointer and visits node 5. Then, thread 1 deletes node 5 by changing the node 3's next pointer to point to node 6 (Figure 4.5(c)). In this case, thread 0 reports that node 5 is found.

The two possible outcomes of thread 0 finding node 5 or not are actually not a problem as they reflect serializable outcomes. If the insertion is performed sequentially after the node search, the node search will find node 5. Alternatively, if the node search is performed sequentially after the insertion, then node search will not find node 5. Therefore, the outcomes are serializable in this case. However, note that in the former case in which node 5 is found, there is still a possible error. When node 5 is deleted, and the traversal is pointing to the node, it is possible that thread 1 follows it up directly with freeing the heap memory allocated to node 5 by calling `free()`. The memory deallocation routine in the heap library may then overwrite the content of node 5. Although thread 0 has found node 5, its content may have been so corrupted by the heap library, that it cannot rely on whatever it reads from node 5. Therefore, a conflict can occur not only between the basic primitives of the list, but also between them and memory management functions.

Finally, we will look at whether an incorrect outcome can occur when parallel execution of a node search and a node insertion can occur. Figure 4.6 illustrates the parallel execution of an insertion and a node search operation. Suppose that initially, thread 0, which attempts to search the node with the key value of "6", has reached node 3. Thread 1 has found a place to insert a new node

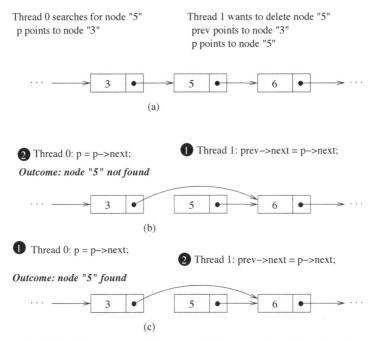

Figure 4.5: Serializable outcome from parallel execution of a deletion and a node search operation.

with a key value of "5" between node 3 and node 6. Its prev pointer points to node 3 and its p pointer points to node 6. This initial situation is illustrated in Figure 4.6(a).

The code for insertion consists of a statement to set the new node's next pointer to node 6 (i.e., newNode->next = p;), and a statement to link node 3's next pointer to the new node (i.e., prev->next = newNode;). In a sequential execution, the order of these two statements does not affect the outcome. In parallel execution, however, it affects the outcome. Suppose that thread 1 links the new node to node 6 first. After that, thread 0 continues its traversal by following the next pointer of node 3 and moves on to node 6 (the current state of the linked list is shown Figure 4.6(b)). The outcome is that thread 0 finds node 6. Finally, thread 1 updates node 3's next pointer to point to the new node (not shown in the figure). The outcome is correct in this case.

However, suppose that thread 1 first links node 3 to the new node first, before attempting to link the new node's next pointer to node 6 (the current state of the linked list is shown Figure 4.6(c)). Then, thread 0 continues its traversal by following node 3's next pointer. Thread 0's traversal reaches node 5 (the new node), then continues traversal by following node 5's next pointer. Unfortunately, node 5's next pointer does not point to node 6 yet. The pointer may have a NULL or an undefined value. In this case, the outcome of the node search is that node 6 is not found. This is a non-serializable outcome as in sequential execution, node 6 will always be found. Overall, this case illustrates different reordering of statements in the program that does not make any difference in sequential execution and can cause a very different outcome in parallel execution.

To conclude the discussion, based on the examples that we have discussed, we can make the following observations:

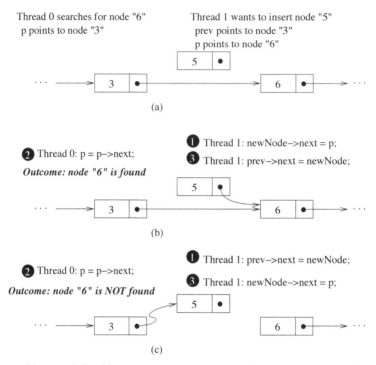

Figure 4.6: Non-serializable outcome from parallel execution of an insertion and a node search operation.

1. *Parallel execution of two operations that access a common node, in which at least one operation involves writing to the node, can produce conflicts that lead to non-serializable outcome.* We have illustrated this using two parallel insertions, an insertion and a deletion, and an insertion/deletion and a node search. Note that if two operations affect completely different sets of nodes, then they will not lead to a conflict.

2. *Under some circumstances, serializable outcome may still be achieved under a conflict mentioned in point (1).* We have illustrated this point by showing that node deletion and a node search operation can go on in parallel without resulting in a non-serializable outcome. Unfortunately, this is highly circumstantial and is not generally true for all types of LDS, e.g., it cannot be said that a node deletion and search in a tree or graph structure to be always serializable. Thus, exploiting such a parallelism opportunity requires deep analysis of a particular LDS and the algorithm that is used in the LDS operations.

3. *Conflicts can also occur between LDS operations and memory management functions such as memory deallocation and allocation.* We have illustrated that even when a node search can execute in parallel with a node deletion, we still have to ensure a node that is found is not corrupted by deallocation of the node.

Knowing the basic observations of how a non-serializable outcome can arise, in the next section we will discuss parallelization techniques for the singly linked list.

4.3 Parallelization Techniques for Linked Lists

There are several parallelization techniques possible for the linked list LDS. They differ in terms of the amount of parallelism extracted and the programming complexity of the solution. In general, in LDS parallelization, a higher degree of parallelism requires a higher programming complexity. Programmers need to assess their situations carefully before deciding on which parallelization strategy best suits their needs and constraints.

4.3.1 Parallelization among Readers

From the discussion in the previous section, we have learned that when there are two operations that affect a common node, in which one of them modifies the node, an incorrect outcome may result. If the operations do not modify the list, then they cannot produce an incorrect outcome. Therefore, the most straightforward way to exploit parallelism is to allow parallel execution between read-only operations, but not between read-only and read-write operations.

Out of the primitives of the linked list, node insertion, deletion, and node modification, they modify some nodes in the list. On the other hand, node search does not modify the list. We can allow parallel execution of multiple node searches, but serialize primitives that modify the list, as illustrated in Figure 4.7. If the LDS is infrequently modified, this approach can yield a substantial degree of parallelism. Otherwise, the degree of parallelism will be modest.

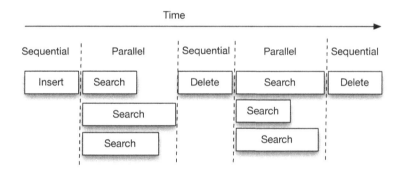

Figure 4.7: Illustration of the parallelism among readers approach.

To implement this approach, we need to ensure mutual exclusion between a read-write operation and a read-only operation, but not between two read-only operations. To achieve that, we can define two types of locks: a *read lock* and a *write lock*. A read only operation must obtain a read lock prior to execution and release it after execution. A read-write operation must obtain a write lock prior to execution and release it after execution. If a read lock is already granted to an operation, a request for another read lock can be granted, but a request for a write lock cannot be granted until all read locks are released. In addition, when a write lock is already granted to an operation, a request for a read lock or another write lock cannot be granted until the current write lock is released. It is helpful to visualize this behavior using a *lock compatibility table* as shown in Table 4.1.

Lock implementations in some thread libraries do not distinguish between read and write locks, hence programmers may have to write their own lock implementations. One way to implement read

Table 4.1: Lock compatibility table.

		Requested Lock	
		Read Lock	Write Lock
Already Granted Lock	Read Lock	Yes	No
	Write Lock	No	No

and write locks is by using a regular data structure protected by a traditional lock. The data structure keeps track of the type of lock currently acquired, and if it is a read lock, it keeps a counter that tracks how many readers currently hold the lock. Each request to acquire a read lock increments the counter while a release decrements the counter. Accesses to the data structure can be protected using a regular (untyped) lock.

Another way to implement the read or write lock is by using a single counter. This counter approach does not require using a traditional lock, but requires the processor to support an instruction to perform addition and subtraction atomically, for example fetch-and-add. Assuming the number of threads n is known ahead of time, a read lock acquisition increments the counter, while a read lock release decrements the counter. A write lock acquisition subtracts the counter by n, and a write lock release increases the counter by n. A read lock acquisition fails if the old counter value is negative, indicating there is an existing write lock. A write lock acquisition fails if the old counter value is not zero, indicating there is an existing write lock or one or more read locks.

Code 4.5 A node search function.

```
1 void Insert(pIntList pList, int key)
2 {
3   setLock(global, WRITE);
4   OrigInsert(pList, key);
5   unsetLock(global);
6 }
7
8 void Delete(pIntList pList, int key)
9 {
10   setLock(global, WRITE);
11   OrigDelete(pList, key);
12   unsetLock(global);
13 }
14
15 int Search(pIntList pList, int key)
16 {
17   setLock(global, READ);
18   int result = OrigSearch(pList, key);
19   unsetLock(global);
20   return result;
21 }
```

To implement this solution, each operation can be wrapped in a wrapper function, which makes a call to obtain a read or write lock, depending on the operation type, and a release of the lock at the end of the operation. Suppose that the lock compatibility table is implemented through an interface setLock(lock_p lock, lock_type_t type) for acquiring a lock of a certain type (read or write) or to change the lock type, and unsetLock(lock_p lock, lock_type_t type) for releasing the lock. Suppose that setLock is a blocking function, e.g., the caller blocks in the function until it successfully obtains the lock of the requested type. The original functions Insert(), Delete(), and Search() are replaced with OrigInsert(), OrigDelete(), and OrigSearch(). In their place, we create wrapper functions Insert(), Delete(), and Search(). The code for the wrapper functions are shown in Code 4.5. The wrapper functions attempt to acquire a write lock for node insertion and deletion, and read lock for node search. Let us name our lock variable global to indicate that all operations of an LDS rely on the same lock variable.

> ■ *Did you know?*
>
> For transaction processing in a database management system (DBMS), read and write locks are only a subset of lock types that are used. Another lock type is the upgrade lock, *used for avoiding a deadlock when multiple transactions hold read locks for a single object and both want to upgrade the lock to a write lock. There are also* intention read *and* intention write *locks which are used for nested locking mechanisms, for example, rather than read locking all records in a table one at a time, a transaction can request an intention-read lock on the table itself. Similarly, we can adopt additional types for a lock in order to improve parallelism.*

4.3.2 Parallelism among LDS Traversals

While the previous approach enables parallelism among read-only operations, a higher degree of parallelism can be obtained if parallelism is also allowed between a read-write operation and other operations. There are at least two approaches for providing parallelism in this case. The finer grain approach is to associate a lock with each node in the list. Individual nodes affected by an operation can be locked separately. A simpler approach uses a global lock, that is, one lock for the entire LDS. The fine-grain lock approach introduces complexities in managing the locks, such as avoiding or handling deadlocks and livelocks. Using a single lock for the LDS avoids deadlocks and livelocks since no cyclic dependence in lock acquisition can occur when there is only one lock.

The key observation in allowing parallelism between read-write operations is to decompose the operations into components that only read from the linked list, and components that modify the linked list. Logically, a linked list insertion or deletion involve a traversal to determine where to insert a node or where the node to be deleted is located. Once they are located in a traversal, modifications are made. Since the traversal only reads from the linked list, we can allow multiple operations doing the traversals at the same time. Only when the operation needs to modify the linked list, it acquires a lock and makes the modification. This is illustrated in Figure 4.8.

Note, however, as discussed in Section 4.2.2, an incorrect outcome can arise when the linked list is changed (by another thread) between the time a thread finishes traversal and the time when it makes modification to the list. Therefore, when a thread obtains a write lock to modify the list, it must ensure that the nodes that will be modified or relied upon to be correct have not changed since the last time they were read. If they have not changed, then the modification can be performed. This is shown in Code 4.6.

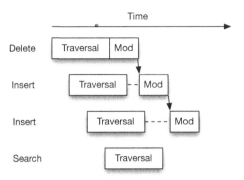

Figure 4.8: Parallel traversal but sequentialized modifications.

In the code, the data structure of each node is modified slightly. A new field `deleted` is added to indicate whether a node has been deleted or not. A node that is deleted is not immediately freed. Instead it is marked as deleted using the new field, and the deallocation is postponed until a more convenient time.

In Code 4.6, we can see that the insertion function is split into two: `TryInsert()` which attempts to perform the node insertion and returns 0 if it fails, and the wrapper function `Insert()` which attempts the insertion until it is successful. In the `TryInsert()`, the traversal portion finds where the new node needs to be inserted, i.e., between the node pointed by the `prev` variable and the node pointed by the `p` variable. Note here that for brevity, the code only shows the case where `prev` and `p` are not NULL.

After traversal is completed, the function acquires a write lock, ensuring that no other threads also attempt to modify the list simultaneously. What could have changed between the end of traversal and the successful acquisition of the write lock? Several things. For example, the node pointed by `prev` may have been deleted. Or the node pointed by `p` may have been deleted. It is incorrect to insert the new node to point to a deleted node, or to link a deleted node to point to the new node. Another possibility is another node insertion may have completed and inserted a new node between the node pointed by `prev` and a node pointed by `p`. To check for that scenario, the code tests whether `prev->next` is still equal to `p` or not. If any of the scenarios above have occurred, the new node should not be inserted, and the traversal should be repeated. These tests are one of the reasons why when a node is deleted, it should not be deallocated immediately, since otherwise the tests will access a deallocated node and may result in a segmentation fault.

The code shown has a risk of not making forward progress, for example when the insertion repeatedly fails. A possible variation of the code is placing the repeat traversal inside the locked region, which ensures that the execution will have forward progress because the repeat traversal is sequentialized and thus guaranteed to succeed.

An important additional note is the importance of the statement i.e., `newNode->next = p` appearing above the `prev->next = newNode` statements (line 35 and 36). In a sequential version, there is no difference if they appear in a different order. However, in the parallel version, there is a difference. Suppose that we reverse the order of the two statements. Suppose also that there is another traversal on another thread that goes on in parallel and that thread has reached the same node pointed by `prev`. Its next step is to go to the next node pointed by `prev->next`. If

Code 4.6 Node insertion function with parallel traversal.

```
1 typedef struct tagIntListNode{
2   int key;
3   int data;
4   struct tagIntListNode *next;
5   int deleted;          // =1 if deleted, =0 otherwise
6 } IntListNode;
7 typedef IntListNode *pIntListNode;
8
9 void Insert(pIntList pList, int key)
10 {
11   int success;
12
13   do {
14     success = TryInsert(pList, key);
15   }
16   while (!success);
17 }
18
19 int TryInsert(pIntList pList, int key)
20 {
21   int success = 1;
22   ...
23   p = pList->head; prev = NULL;
24   while (p != NULL && p->key < newNode->key) {
25     prev = p;
26     p = p->next;
27   }
28
29   // for brevity, only show the case where prev and p are not NULL
30   setLock(global, WRITE));
31   if (prev->deleted || p->deleted || prev->next != p) { // test assumptions
32     success = 0;
33   }
34   else {
35     newNode->next = p;
36     prev->next = newNode;
37   }
38   unsetLock(global);
39
40   return success;
41 }
```

the next pointer has been overwritten to point to newNode by the current thread, while newNode's next pointer still points to NULL (it has not been written to point to the node pointed by p yet), then the traversal has incorrectly concluded that it has reached the last node in the list. Thus, programmers using this approach must be more vigilant in coding compared to when they write a sequential program.

A node deletion can be parallelized using a similar strategy, as shown in Code 4.7. Note here that for brevity, the code only shows the case where prev and p are not NULL. After a traversal to locate the node to be deleted, a write lock is acquired. To ensure that the list has not changed between the time of traversal until this point, we can check to make sure that no node has been inserted between `prev` and `p` by checking whether `prev`'s next pointer still points to `p`. It also checks whether any nodes pointed by `prev` or `p` have been deleted. In either case, the function returns 0 so that the node deletion can be repeated. When finally node pointed by `p` is deleted, it is not directly deallocated to avoid corrupting the node, in case there are other threads that rely on the values stored in the node. Rather, the node is marked as deleted.

Code 4.7 A parallelizable node deletion function.

```
1 void Delete(pIntList pList, int key)
2 {
3   int success;
4
5   do {
6     success = TryDelete(pList, key);
7   }
8   while (!success);
9 }
10
11 void TryDelete(pIntList pList, int x)
12 {
13   int success = 1;
14
15   p = pList->head; prev = p;
16   while (p != NULL && p->key != key) {
17     prev = p;
18     p = p->next;
19   }
20
21   // for brevity, only show the case where prev and p are not NULL
22   setLock(global, WRITE);
23   if (prev->deleted || p->deleted || prev->next != p)
24     success = 0;
25   else {
26     prev->next = p->next;
27     p->deleted = 1;  // mark node as deleted
28     unsetLock(global);
29   }
30 }
```

When is it safe to deallocate and reclaim the storage of a node? The minimum requirement is that the node is not currently involved in any operation, that is, no threads have any active pointers pointing to the node. However, keeping such information requires keeping a reference count on each node, which is costly. A simpler alternative is to wait until all current pending operations complete, and then schedule a garbage collection phase that deallocates and reclaims all deleted nodes. This can be achieved through several modifications. First, the pointer to a deleted node can be inserted into a list, in addition to the deleted field to be set to 1. This allows the garbage collector to quickly deallocate deleted nodes without having to search for them. Second, in order to achieve mutual exclusion between the garbage collector and other operations, we may add a lock that must be held exclusively by the collector, but can be held by multiple other operations such as node insertion, deletion, and search.

In general, despite some cases programmers must be cautious, the global lock approach is relatively easy to implement, regardless of the type of LDS. This is because we have only one lock and do not need to handle deadlocks and livelocks. What is needed for applying the global lock approach is to write each operation on the LDS in a way that traversal can be separated with the code that modifies the LDS.

■ *Did you know?*

How much parallelism can we expect from the global lock approach? Suppose that the time taken to locate a node through traversal is T_{trav}, the time taken to actually modify the node is T_{mod}, and the list has n nodes. As the linked list adds more nodes and increases in size, T_{trav} increases along with the linked list size as well (for random searches). T_{mod}, on the other hand, remains constant as the modifications to the list still involve only one or two nodes. Thus, $T_{trav} = \mathrm{O}(n)$ while $T_{mod} = \mathrm{O}(1)$.

By keeping the traversal parallel, the global lock approach parallelizes a larger fraction of the execution time as the data structure size increases. We can think of the T_{mod} as the Amdahl's law sequential fraction of execution. Therefore, when the data structure increases in size, the parallelism benefit (and potential speedup) from the global lock approach increases because T_{mod} becomes relatively smaller. When the number of threads increases, however, T_{mod} becomes a more important limiting factor in speedups.

4.3.3 Fine-Grain Lock Approach

While the global lock approach allows multiple operations to execute in parallel, it is still limited in the sense that only one thread is allowed to modify the linked list at a time. Even when different threads modify different parts of the linked list, they have to perform the modification sequentially in the critical section. In this section, we will look at how modifications to different parts of the list can be allowed to proceed in parallel.

To achieve that, we need a finer lock granularity. Rather than using a single global lock, we can associate a lock with each node. The basic principle is that when an operation needs to modify a node, it locks the node so that operations that want to write or read from the node cannot do so, but other operations that write or read other nodes can proceed in parallel without a conflict.

The question is now how to figure out what nodes to lock for each operation. To answer the question, we first need to distinguish between nodes that will be modified in an operation, versus nodes that will only be read in an operation but must remain valid in order for the operation to complete correctly. The principle for handling them is that: *nodes that will be modified must be write locked*, while the *nodes that are read and must remain valid must be read locked*. Note that locking both types of nodes too strongly (e.g., using write locks) is largely inconsequential as it only results in reduced concurrency. However, locking them too weakly (e.g., using read locks) affects the correctness of the operation. Hence, this analysis must be performed carefully.

For the node insertion operation, the node pointed by `prev` will be modified to point to the new node, so it needs to be write locked. The node pointed by `p` will not be modified, but it must remain valid for the operation to be performed correctly, e.g., it cannot be deleted before the operation is completed. Therefore, it needs to be read locked.

For the node deletion operation, the node pointed by `prev` will have its next pointer changed, so it must be write locked. The node pointed by `p` will later be deleted, so it needs to be write locked. Note that the successor node (the node pointed by p's next pointer) must also remain valid for the delete operation to complete correctly, so it needs to be read locked. The reason is that if it is deleted, then at the end of the operation, prev's next pointer will point to a deleted node, which is incorrect.

Based on the principles, we can see that the two insertions shown in Figure 4.3 cannot occur simultaneously. The first insertion must write lock node 3, write lock node 4, and read lock node 6. The second insertion must also write lock node 3, write lock node 5, and read lock node 6. Thus, they conflict, and hence the insertions (of node 4 and 5) are now serialized. Similarly, between an insertion (of node 4) and a deletion (of node 5) on Figure 4.4, the insertion must write lock node 3. write lock node 4, and read lock node 5, while the deletion must write lock node 3 and node 5, and read lock node 6. Thus, their lock requests conflict at node 3 and node 5, ensuring that they are serialized.

After all involved nodes are locked appropriately, the next step before modifying them is to retest the validity of the nodes, in the same way as with the global lock approach. This is because in between the time of the traversal and the first lock acquisition, as well as between lock acquisition of various nodes, the linked list may have been changed by another thread.

Code 4.8 and code 4.9 show the node insertion and deletion using the fine-grain locking approach, respectively. Code 4.8 shows that the node data structure is augmented with a field lock that implements a typed (read and write) lock. The primitives for locking a particular node are setLock() and unsetLock().

The code shows that after traversal, the code acquires a write lock for the node pointed by prev because it intends to modify it, and a read lock for the node pointed by p because it needs the node to be unchanged during the deletion. Then it tests for validity of assumptions, by checking whether the node pointed by prev has not been deleted, the node pointed by p has not been deleted, and whether prev->next still equals p. If any of those conditions is violated, the function returns 0 so that the insertion can be retried.

Code 4.9 shows that after traversal, the code acquires a write lock for the node pointed by prev because it intends to modify it, a write lock for the node pointed by p because it intends to delete it, and a read lock for the node pointed by p->next because it needs the node to be unchanged during the deletion (for example, the node pointed by p->next should not be deleted). Then it tests for validity of assumptions, by checking whether the node pointed by prev has not been deleted, the node pointed by p has not been deleted, and whether prev->next still equals p. If any of those conditions is violated, the function returns 0 so that the deletion can be retried.

One caution in implementing the fine grain locking approach is that deadlocks are a possibility if we are not careful with the order of lock acquisition. In the shown implementation, the lock acquisition is always performed from the left-most node first. If, on the other hand, the node insertion acquires locks starting from the left-most node but the node deletion acquires locks starting from the right-most node, then cyclic dependence of lock acquisition between node insertion and deletion can occur and cause a deadlock. An alternative approach to ensure a uniform order of lock acquisitions for all threads is to acquire locks in the order of increasing or decreasing node addresses. This approach is useful when the data structure itself does not have natural ordering information, such as graphs.

Another subtle issue is that while Code 4.8 and 4.9 have prevented simultaneous modifications to neighboring nodes that may violate serializability, they have not prevented an issue of serializability

---

Code 4.8 Parallelization of node insertion using the fine-grain locking approach.

```
1 typedef struct tagIntListNode{
2   int key;
3   int data;
4   struct tagIntListNode *next;
5   int deleted;   // =1 if deleted, =0 otherwise
6   lock_t lock;
7 } IntListNode;
8 typedef IntListNode *pIntListNode;
9
10 void Insert(pIntList pList, int key)
11 {
12   int success;
13
14   do {
15     success = TryInsert(pList, key);
16   }
17   while (!success);
18 }
19
20 int TryInsert(pIntList head, int x)
21 {
22   int succeed = 1;
23
24   p = pList->head; prev = NULL;
25   while (p != NULL && p->key < newNode->key) {
26     prev = p;
27     p = p->next;
28   }
29
30   // for brevity, only show the case where prev and p are not NULL
31   setLock(prev, WRITE);
32   setLock(p, READ);
33   if (prev->next ! = p || prev->deleted || p->deleted)
34     success = 0;
35   else {
36     newNode->next = p;
37     prev->next = newNode;
38   }
39   unsetLock(p);
40   unsetLock(prev);
41
42   return success;
43 }
```

---

between an insertion or deletion with traversal that was illustrated in Figure 4.5(c) and Figure 4.6(c). The issue has to do with a traversal that visits a node that either has newly been inserted or newly deleted, but before the insertion or deletion are completed. In insertion, there is a possibility that the list has been linked to a newly inserted node but the newly inserted node has not been linked to the remainder of the list. In deletion, there is a possibility that the newly deleted node no longer points to the remainder of the list (it points to NULL), and the traversal incorrectly detects the end of the list without ever visiting the remainder of the list. There are two possible solutions to this

---

Code 4.9 Parallelization of node deletion using the fine-grain locking approach.

```
1 void Delete(pIntList pList, int key)
2 {
3   int success;
4
5   do {
6     success = TryDelete(pList, key);
7   }
8   while (!success);
9 }
10
11 int TryDelete(pIntList head, int x)
12 {
13   int succeed = 1;
14
15   p = pList->head; prev = NULL;
16   while (p != NULL && p->key != key) {
17     prev = p;
18     p = p->next;
19   }
20
21   //  only show the case where prev, p, and p->next are not NULL
22   setLock(prev, WRITE);
23   setLock(p, WRITE);
24   setLock(p->next, READ);
25   if (prev->next ! = p || prev->deleted || p->deleted)
26     success = 0;
27   else {
28     prev->next = p->next;
29     p->deleted = 1;   /* don't deallocate, mark it deleted */
30   }
31   unsetLock(p->next);
32   unsetLock(p);
33   unsetLock(prev);
34 }
```

---

problem. The first solution is *careful programming*. When a new node is inserted, programmers have to ensure a correct sequence: (1) the new node's next pointer is made to point to the part of the list that it is supposed to point, and (2) the predecessor node in the list's next pointer is made to point to the new node. The solution shown in Code 4.8 already implements this sequence. If the sequence is violated, however, a non-serializable outcome can result. On the other hand, when a node is deleted, programmers have to ensure the following: (1) the previous node's next pointer is made to be equal to the current pointer's next pointer value, (2) the deleted node's next pointer cannot be overwritten, and (3) the deleted node cannot be deallocated. The solution shown in Code 4.9 already implements this, as it leaves the deleted node unchanged other than setting its `deleted` field to 1. This solution works, however, it is prone to programmers accidentally making a mistake of violating the sequence or requirements. Is there an alternative?

An alternative solution is to use locking even during traversal, to ensure that nodes that are traversed are also locked. This prevents current nodes that are traversed to be modified by any operations. The drawback of this approach is the overheads involved in locking and unlocking nodes during traversal will significantly slow down the traversal. This scheme is referred to as *spider locking*, because of the analogy of spider (the locks) crawling along the data structure during traversal. Code 4.10 shows a traversal using the spider locking scheme used in the `Search()` function. The same technique can also be used for the traversal portion of the node insertion and node deletion functions.

Code 4.10 Parallelization of node search using a spider locking approach.

```
1  int Search(pIntList pList, int key)
2  {
3    pIntListNode p, prev;
4
5    if (pList->head == NULL) // list is empty
6      return 0;
7
8    // traverse to find the node
9    p = pList->head;  prev = NULL;
10   setLock(p, READ);
11   while (p != NULL && p->key != key) {
12     prev = p;
13     if (p->next != NULL)
14       setLock(p->next);
15     p = p->next;
16     unsetLock(prev);
17   }
18   unsetLock(p);
19
20   if (p == NULL)   // node not found
21     return 0;
22   else
23     return 1;
24 }
```

Comparing the fine-grain lock approach with the global lock approach, for the singly linked list they are not much different in programming complexity. This is because of the regularity of the linked list structure makes it is easy to separate the following three steps: (1) traversal, (2) locking of nodes that will be modified or relied upon as valid, and (3) the modification of the nodes. We can cleanly separate the steps because we can easily identify what nodes will be written or read prior to modifying the nodes. For more complex types of LDS, the fine-grain locking approach will be more complex as well because the three steps may not be as easy to separate. For example, in a tree LDS, the algorithm that performs the tree balancing operation hardly knows how many nodes will be written or read until the balancing itself is being carried out. In addition, node modifications and locking may be intermingled unless the algorithm is designed to separate them. A similar issue arises with node insertion and deletion in a balanced tree. Furthermore, determining the ordering of node acquisition that avoids deadlocks is also more challenging because in the natural algorithms of some operations, lower level nodes may be visited first (thus need to be locked first), while in others, higher level nodes may be visited first (thus need to be locked first). For these cases, the algorithm may have to be split into two phases: a phase in which we figure out which nodes will need to be locked and/or modified, and a phase in which we actually lock the nodes and perform the modification.

Overall, we have shown that parallelization techniques for LDS are very different than parallelization techniques for loop-based scientific applications. Whereas loop-level parallelization is very fruitful in scientific applications, it is not so fruitful in LDS. In addition, loop-level parallelism is easy to express using simple directives. Thus, it lends itself to the ease of exploiting parallelism without many changes to the source code or the algorithms. Unfortunately, exploiting parallelization at the LDS primitives level requires many changes to the algorithms and source code that implement the LDS primitives.

4.4　The Role of Transactional Memory

Transactional memory (TM) can simplify LDS parallel programming to some extent. The simplest way to use TM is to wrap each LDS operation in a transaction. For example, we can write `atomic{Insert(...)}` or `atomic{Delete(...)}`. This automatically ensures that each operation is performed in isolation with respect to other concurrent operations. If during node insertion a conflict is detected, the transaction encapsulating the insertion will be aborted and the insertion is retried. We can also wrap the searching operation in a transaction, allowing the search to be aborted when any of the nodes traversed or searched are modified before the search transaction is able to commit. This greatly simplifies the LDS programming.

There are potential pitfalls, however. As the size of LDS increases, each operation takes a longer time to complete, mainly due to a longer time to traverse and search the LDS. This lengthened time reduces performance by increasing the probability of two transactions conflicting with one another, resulting in a rollback and retry of at least one of the transactions. This rollback can happen even when two operations modify different nodes in the LDS that do not intersect. In TM, a rollback is triggered when a conflict is detected, and a conflict is detected when the write set of one transaction intersects with the read/write set of another transaction. Such a situation is referred to as a *false conflict* because if the conflict is ignored and the two non-overlapping operations are allowed to execute simultaneously, they actually produce serializable outcome.

As with any optimistic concurrency techniques, the performance of TM relies on a low transaction conflict probability. A high conflict probability can result in an excessive number of transaction conflicts, aborts, and retries. In a pathological worst case, it is possible for a transaction to conflict repeatedly and not make forward progress, reducing the TM performance to below lock-based programs or even below sequential execution. Finally, some hardware TM supports impose a restriction on the maximum size of the speculative data touched by the transaction. Any transactions that touch more data than the maximum speculative buffer size may abort, even when there are no conflicts with other transactions.

Therefore, with TM, programmers have to carefully choose the granularity of transactions. They may have to perform LDS traversal in parallel and only wrap the code that modifies the LDS in a transaction, similar to the fine-grain lock-based programming. An example for node deletion can be seen in Code 4.11.

Notice in Code 4.11 that due to the use of small granularity transactions, we still need to worry about races between two threads modifying the same nodes concurrently. Therefore, after the traversal stage, inside the transaction, we still need to check the condition that determines whether pointers and nodes involved in the deletion are still valid.

Code 4.11 Parallelization of node deletion using fine-grain transactional memory.

```
1 void Delete(pIntList pList, int key)
2 {
3   int success;
4
5   do {
6     success = TryDelete(pList, key);
7   }
8   while (!success);
9 }
10
11 int TryDelete(pIntList head, int x)
12 {
13   int succeed = 1;
14
15   p = pList->head; prev = NULL;
16   while (p != NULL && p->key != key) {
17     prev = p;
18     p = p->next;
19   }
20
21   // for brevity, only show the case where prev and p are not NULL
22   atomic {
23     if (prev->next ! = p || prev->deleted || p->deleted)
24       success = 0;
25     else {
26       prev->next = p->next;
27       p->deleted = 1;  /* don't deallocate, mark it deleted */
28     }
29   }
30 }
```

Overall, it appears that regardless of using fine-grain locks or TM, one has to approach LDS programming with the consideration of concurrency and granularity in mind. Similar to programming with locks, the finer the transaction, the more races can occur and the more complexity is involved in programming. However, once the decision on granularity has been made, TM simplifies fine grain lock programming by removing the need to maintain locks, their data structures, and risks associated with locks (e.g., deadlocks). It is likely that locks will still be needed at coarser granularities due to the high probability of transaction aborts, and hence programmers should judiciously examine which situations warrant the use of locks, and which situations warrant the use of transactions, and how transactions may interact with the portion of codes that rely on locks.

4.5   Exercises

Worked Problems

1. Consider the following doubly-linked list, showing four nodes with keys 4, 5, 6, and 7. At the moment, Thread 1 and Thread 2 intend to delete node 5 and node 6, respectively, and have completed traversal. The code for deleting a node is shown in the figure.

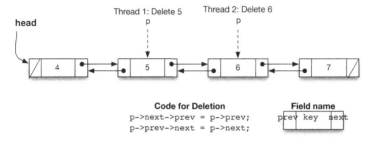

Code for Deletion
```
p->next->prev = p->prev;
p->prev->next = p->next;
```

Field name
prev key next

   (a) What will be the outcome of the list if Thread 1 and Thread 2 perform the deletion code in parallel (without any synchronization)? Show graphically the outcome.

   (b) Is the outcome in part (a) serializable or not? Answer and explain briefly.

   (c) If we want to ensure correct execution with fine-grain locking, what nodes need to be locked by Thread 1 and Thread 2?

   (d) Is there a need to associate a lock with the **head** pointer? If so, list situations that require such a lock to be acquired.

Answer:

   (a) There is a minor difference as to what node 5 and node 6 point to, depending on whether T1 executes first or T2 executes first. However, from the point of view of the resulting linked list, the serializable outcome produces the same effect: both node 5 and node 6 are deleted from the node.

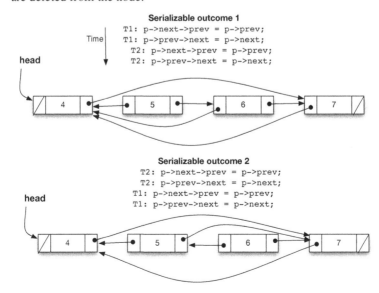

(b) The interleaved execution leads to one of the following four outcomes depending on the way the statements are interleaved. They are shown below. Interleaved outcome 1 leads to a serializable outcomes. However, interleaved outcomes 2, 3, and 4 lead to non-serializable outcome. Some outcomes make the linked list inconsistent. Consider outcome 2. Traversing from left to right, node 5 appears to have successfully deleted but node 6 does not. Traversing from the right to left, node 5 and node 6 appear to have been deleted successfully.

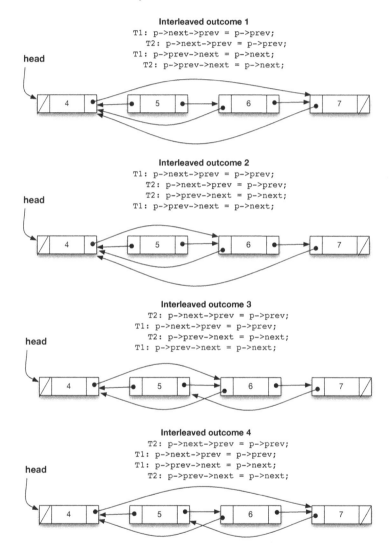

(c) Nodes that need to be write locked by Thread 1: node 4, node 5, and node 6. Nodes that need to be write locked by Thread 2: node 5, node 6, and node 7.

(d) Yes, the head pointer needs to be associated with a lock, and the lock needs to be acquired prior to any of the following situations: (1) any insertion of nodes at the head of the list including when the list is initially empty, (2) any deletion of nodes pointed by the head, and (3) list creation or deletion/deallocation.

Homework Problems

1. **Serializable outcome**. Consider the following doubly-linked list, showing four nodes with keys 3, 5, 7, and 9. At the moment, Thread 1 intends to add node 4, while Thread 2 intends to delete node 5. Both threads have completed traversal. The code for insertion and deletion are shown in the figure.

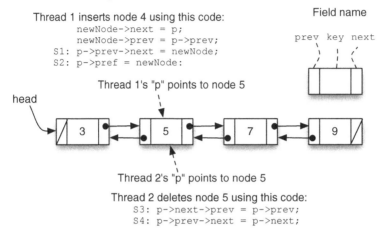

Thread 1 inserts node 4 using this code:
```
        newNode->next = p;
        newNode->prev = p->prev;
    S1: p->prev->next = newNode;
    S2: p->pref = newNode:
```

Field name

prev key next

Thread 1's "p" points to node 5

head

3   5   7   9

Thread 2's "p" points to node 5

Thread 2 deletes node 5 using this code:
```
    S3: p->next->prev = p->prev;
    S4: p->prev->next = p->next;
```

(a) What is the outcome of the list if Thread 1 and Thread 2 run in parallel, resulting in an execution with the following sequence in time: S1, S3, S2, S4. Show the outcome by drawing the resulting linked list, including where all pointers point to.

(b) If we want to ensure correct execution with fine grain locking, what nodes need to be locked by Thread 1 and Thread 2? Determine whether the lock for each node should be a read or a write lock.

2. **Non-serializable outcome**. In a singly-linked list, show how two deletion operations can produce non-serializable outcome. Be specific in showing all possible outcomes.

3. **Non-serializable outcome**. In a singly-linked list, suppose that a deletion operation attempts to delete a node from the list (i.e., node x), while an insertion operation attempts to insert a node between node x and its successor node. If they execute in parallel without any locks, what are all the possible outcomes?

4. **Doubly-linked list**. In a doubly-linked list, each node has two pointer fields: `pred` which points its predecessor node, and `succ` that points to its successor node.

(a) Show the pseudo code for node insertion and node deletion.

(b) Specify what nodes need to be write locked and read locked for an insertion operation.

(c) Specify what nodes need to be write locked and read locked for a deletion operation.

5. **Deadlock avoidance**. In order to avoid the possibility of a deadlock in a fine-grain lock approach, typically the nodes are globally ordered so that the order of lock acquisition on nodes performed by multiple threads cannot form a cycle. For a graph or tree algorithms, one way to achieve this is to acquire locks in the order of ascending (or descending) node addresses.

What constraints does this lock acquisition ordering place on algorithms and programming complexity?

6. **Read vs. write locks**. Replacing all read locks with write locks simplifies programming of a fine-grain lock approach, but at the same times reduces concurrency. Estimate the degree of the loss of concurrency on a linked list data structure, assuming that each node has a random but equal probability of being deleted or linked to a new node inserted as its successor. Assume that insertions and deletions balance out each other, keeping the number of nodes in the linked list relatively constant at n nodes.

7. **Unsafe deletion**. In the fine-grain lock approach, explain why the following code snippet for deleting a node is not safe to use:

```
1   // ... lock acquisition here
2   // ... assumptions  found to be valid here
3   prev->next = p-> next;
4   p->next = NULL;
5   p->deleted = 1;
```

Propose two solutions of how this problem can be avoided.

8. **ABA problem**. One challenge that the fine grain lock approach faces is referred to as the ABA problem. Suppose we would like to delete a node from a linked list at an address pointed by p, having a key value 5. The deletion thread T_1 has found the node, but before it can perform the deletion, another thread T_2 successfully performs two operations. The two operations are: (1) delete the node pointed by p and free up its memory chunk, and (2) reuse the chunk as a new node having a key value of 10 and insert the new node into the list. Suppose that the new node is inserted by T_2 into the list at exactly the same position as the old node was. When T_1 continues with acquiring locks and testing its assumptions, it finds that the assumptions are valid, i.e., the node pointed by `prev` and `p` are not in a deleted state, and `prev->next == p`. Thus, T_1 deletes the node with a key value of 10, rather than the one it intended to delete. Give three possible solutions to avoid this ABA problem, and list their advantages and disadvantages.

Chapter 5

Introduction to Memory Hierarchy Organization

Contents

The objective of this chapter is to give a brief overview of the memory hierarchy used in current multicore architecture. In these architectures, the memory hierarchy consists of hardware-managed temporary memory referred to as *caches*, and occassionally software-managed temporary storage referred to as *scratchpad memory*. This chapter primarily covers basic cache architectures. The coverage is divided into general concepts and organizations of a cache (Sections 5.1 – 5.4), and multicore-focused organizations of caches (starting from Section 5.5 until the end of the chapter). The chapter ends with a section containing two case studies of cache organizations in recent multi-core systems (Section 5.8).

In previous chapters, we have discussed how parallel programs are constructed. To get the most performance from a parallel program, it is necessary to tune it to conform to the machine architecture on which it runs. One of the biggest obstacles in parallel program performance tuning is probably the complex memory hierarchy present in current computer systems. It makes a difference in performance where a thread can get most of its data from: from an inner level cache with an access time of only a few processor clock cycles, from an outer level cache with an access time of tens of clock cycles, from the local main memory with an access time of hundreds of clock cycles, or from a remote memory with an access time of up to thousands of clock cycles. Therefore, a good understanding of how memory hierarchy is organized is crucial for (1) knowing how to tune the performance of parallel programs, and (2) knowing what other hardware support is needed to build a shared memory multiprocessor.

5.1   Motivation for Memory Hierarchy

For decades, the increase in CPU speed has been much faster than the decrease in the access latency of the main memory. Up until roughly 2001-2005, CPU speed as measured in its clock frequency grew at the rate of 55% annually, while the memory speed grew at the rate of only 7% annually [24]. This speed gap produced an interesting implication. While in the past, a load instruction could get the needed datum from main memory in one CPU clock cycle, in recent systems it requires hundreds of processor clock cycles to get a datum from the main memory. Dependences between a load instruction (producer) and instructions that use the loaded value (consumers) dictate that the consumer instructions must wait until the load obtains its datum before they can execute. With the latency of loading datum from the main memory in the order of hundreds of cycles, the CPU may stall for much of that time because it runs out of instructions that are not dependent on the load. Hence, it is critical to performance that most data accesses are supplied to the CPU with low latencies. Caches provide such support.

A cache is a relatively small memory for keeping data that is likely needed by the requestor. The concept of a cache is universal since it can be used as a software construct or a hardware component. In this chapter, we focus on hardware caches that exist between the processor and the main memory.

An example of a memory hierarchy is shown in Figure 5.1. It shows a configuration in which there are twelve processor cores on a chip. Each core has a private Level 1 (L1) data cache and a Level 1 instruction cache. Each core has a Level 2 (L2) cache that holds both instructions and data (referred to as "e.g., unified"). There is a Level 3 (L3) cache that is shared by all cores. Due to its size, the L3 cache may be banked, and each bank may be local to each core, but remote to other cores, meaning that it is accessible by all cores but at differing latencies. The typical range of access latencies in 2013 (in terms of CPU clock cycles) and capacity of each cache is shown in the figure. After the L3 cache, there may be an off-die L4 cache and the main memory.

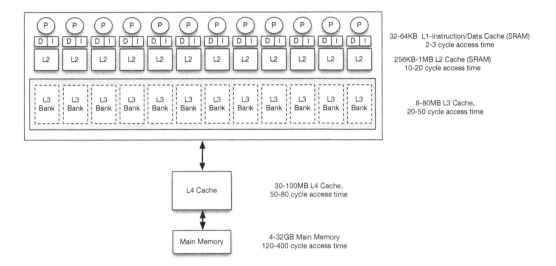

Figure 5.1: A memory hierarchy configuration in a multicore system in 2013.

The example in the figure is similar to the memory hierarchy of the IBM Power8 processor. In the Power8, each core has 4-way *simultaneous multithreading* (SMT), which means that it can execute four threads simultaneously by fetching from two different program counters. Most of the processor core resources such as register files and functional units are shared by the four threads. A Power8 die also has twelve cores, so there are a total of 48 threads that can run simultaneously. Each of the cores has a 32KB L1 instruction cache and a 64KB L1 data cache. Each core also has a private 512KB L2 cache, so in total the L2 caches have 6MB of capacity. Both the L1 and L2 caches use SRAM cells. The L3 cache is 12-way banked, and each bank has an 8MB capacity, for a total of 96MB over all banks. The L4 cache is located off the die on the memory buffer controller, which is connected to the main memory. The L3 and L4 caches are implemented on DRAM on logic process, a technology referred to as embedded DRAM (eDRAM).

Due to temporal locality behavior naturally found in programs, caches are an effective structure to keep most useful data closer to the processor. By simply keeping more recently used data in the cache while discarding less recently used data, caches achieve that goal. For example, if data access is completely random, the *hit rate* of each cache (the fraction of accesses that find their data in the cache) will be proportional to the ratio of the cache size to the size of the program working set (which will be minuscule for small caches). However, cache hit rates are often much higher than that, 70-95% hit rates are not uncommon both for the L1 and L2 caches.

5.2 Basic Architectures of a Cache

Figure 5.2 shows a simple analogy in which at a very high level, a cache structure can be thought of as a table, with multiple rows referred to as *sets* or *congruence classes*, and multiple columns referred to as *ways*.   To exploit spatial locality and reduce management overheads, multiple bytes are fetched as a *cache block* which is then stored in a placeholder called a *cache line*, which is analogous to a cell in the table. The basic parameters of a table are the number of rows, the number of columns, and the cell size. Similarly, the basic parameters of a cache structure are therefore the number of sets, *associativity* (or the number of ways), and the cache block size. *Cache size* can be computed simply by multiplying the number of sets, associativity, and the block size. Since cache size often has a more direct impact on performance than the number of sets, typically cache parameters are specified in terms of cache size, associativity, and block size.

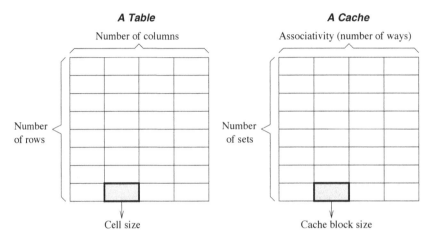

Figure 5.2: Analogy of a table and a cache.

To manage a cache, several aspects must be considered. The first is *placement policy* that decides where a memory block can be placed in the cache. The second is *replacement policy* that decides which block needs to be evicted to make room for a new block. The third is *write policy* that decides that when parts of a cache block are written, when the new value should be propagated to the outer level memory hierarchy component.

5.2.1   Placement Policy

The placement policy decides where a block in memory can be placed in the cache. This decision affects performance significantly, since a block stored in the cache must be locatable in future accesses to the block. To simplify the process of searching a block, the placement of a block is restricted to a *single* set, although it can be placed in any way in that set. Therefore, the organization of the cache in terms of number of sets and ways determine the placement of a block. This is illustrated in Figure 5.3. In one extreme, a block in memory can only be stored at a particular line in the cache. Such a policy requires a *direct-mapped* cache organization in which the cache only has one-way associativity. At the other extreme, a block in memory can be stored at any of the lines in the cache. Such a policy requires a *fully-associative* cache organization in which we only have one set. A direct-mapped cache easily suffers from conflicts in which multiple blocks in memory map to the same cache line and end up evicting each other. A fully-associative cache does not suffer from conflicts but is expensive to implement due to the need to search all ways when a block needs to be found. A compromise is to limit the associativity using a *set-associative* cache organization

(Figure 5.3 shows 2-way and 4-way associative caches). In a set-associative cache, a block can be kept at any way in a single set. A set-associative cache organization is much more resistant to conflicts than a direct-mapped cache, and yet is much cheaper to implement than a fully-associative cache.

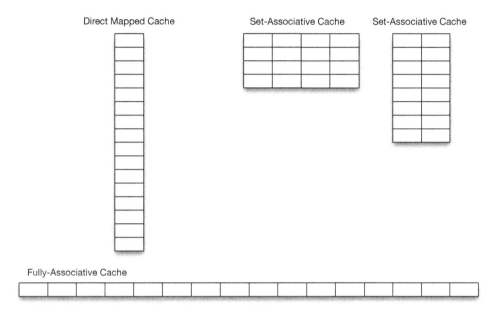

Figure 5.3: Various cache associativities.

To locate a block in the cache, a cache employs three steps:

1. Determine the set to which the block may map to.

2. Access the set to determine if any of the blocks in the set matches the one that is being requested, and access the requested block if found.

3. If the block is found, access the appropriate block, select the byte or word that is requested, and return it to the processor.

The first task, determining the set to which a block can map, is accomplished through a *cache indexing function*. Typically, the cache indexing function used is simple: the index to the set is obtained by taking the modulo of the block address by the number of sets:

$$setIdx = blkAddr \ \mathbf{mod} \ numSets \qquad (5.1)$$

Figure 5.4 illustrates cache indexing. The top figure shows that an address produced by a memory reference instruction issued by the processor can be split into the part that addresses the particular byte in a block (block offset) and the part that addresses the block (block address). If the block size is N bytes, to locate any byte in a cache block, we need $log_2(N)$ bits as the block offset. For example if the block size is 64 bytes, we need $log_2(64) = 6$ lowest order bits as the block offset.

In the traditional cache indexing, the number of sets is a power of two, and hence the simple modulo function of Equation 5.1 does not require any computation in order to obtain the set index:

the result is simply a few lower bits of the address (called the index bits). Note that since the main memory is much bigger than the cache, there are many blocks that may map to a particular set. When a block is stored in the cache, the cache must remember which blocks are stored so that it has the ability to check whether the requested block is one of the blocks stored in a cache set. Multiple blocks that map to the same set will have the same values in the index bits, so for that purpose, when a cache block is stored, the address bits that are not part of the block offset or index bits must be stored along with the block. These bits are referred to as the *tag* bits. For the simple modulo indexing function, the block address bits that are not parts of the index bits are treated as the tag bits.

The simple modulo indexing ensures that contiguous blocks in memory are mapped to different (and contiguous) sets – which helps in distributing memory blocks evenly across sets in the cache. The number of index bits needed depend on the number of sets in the cache. For example, if there are 2048 sets, then the number of bits that are used for locating the correct set is $log_2(2048) = 11$ bits.

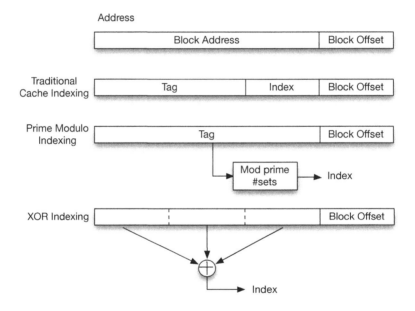

Figure 5.4: How different parts of an address are used for locating a block in a cache.

The simple modulo indexing strategy is not the only way to index a cache. It has been shown that in some cases, some access patterns visit addresses that follow multiples of a power-of-two striding, which leads to the addresses mapping more to certain cache sets but less to others, leading to non-uniform set utilization. An alternative strategy would be to use a non-power-of-two number of sets, in particular a prime number of sets. A prime number of sets guarantees that any stride amounts will result in uniform mapping of addresses to sets. For example, instead of having 2048 sets, we can use 2039 sets (2039 is the nearest lower prime number). Such an indexing function is referred to as *prime modulo indexing* and is illustrated in Figure 5.4. A prime modulo index needs to be derived from the entire block address, and the entire block address must be stored as the tag of a block. While it seems that computing a modulus with a prime number requires a long chain of divisions, there are ways to greatly simplify the computation [34]. Another possibility for a cache indexing function is to pseudo-randomize the value of the index by using XOR function of various parts of the block address (an example is shown in the bottom portion of Figure 5.4). As with the prime module indexing, with the XOR-based indexing, the entire block address needs to be stored as the tag. Overall, both the prime modulo and XOR-based indexing are likely to reduce the non-uniform set utilization of caches. However, due to the additional computation required to derive an index, designers must compare the benefit versus the cost before choosing a particular indexing function.

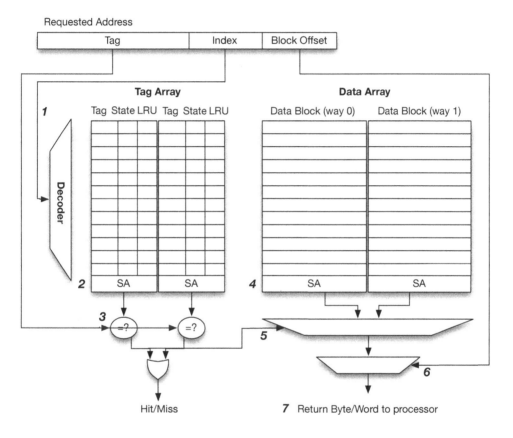

Figure 5.5: Locating a block in the cache. A two-way associative cache bank is shown.

The process of locating a block is illustrated in Figure 5.5, assuming a traditional cache indexing. The figure shows a single cache bank that is organized as a two-way set associative bank. A cache bank contains an address decoder for selecting a set corresponding to a particular address, tag and data arrays, sense amplifiers that temporarily retrieve tags and data blocks, multiplexers, tag comparison logic, and other logic circuits. A large cache may contain more than one cache bank.

Several steps are involved in locating data: accessing the set that the block may map to in the tag array (Step 1). The tag array stores tag bits for blocks that are currently cached. The two tags in the set are pulled down into the sense amplifiers or SA (Step 2) and then compared against the tag of the requested addressed (Step 3). In parallel to Steps 2 and 3, the data blocks from both ways are also read out into the sense amplifiers (Step 4). If any of the tags match, then we have a cache hit, else we have a cache miss. When we have a tag match in a particular way, the correct block from the same way is selected (Step 5). Finally, the requested byte/word/words are selected using the block offset bits of the address (Step 6), and returned to the processor (Step 7). In a high-performance cache, these steps may be pipelined to improve the cache access throughput, so that multiple accesses can be served (at different stages) by the cache simultaneously. For example, Steps 1 and 2 may be grouped into one stage, Step 3 may be another stage, Step 4 may be another stage, and Steps 5 and 6 may be grouped into another stage. The decisions of which stages to group depend on the length of the critical logic delay of each step.

Note that the steps of accessing the tag array (Steps 1 and 2) and the data array (Step 4) can be performed *sequentially*, or both in *parallel*. The advantage of accessing them sequentially is that after a cache hit to a way is determined, the cache only accesses the way of the data array in which the hit occurs. In the case of a cache miss, the data array is not accessed at all. So this approach is more power efficient. The alternative to it is to access both the tag array and data array in parallel. Such an approach is faster since by the time hit or miss is determined, data blocks from all ways have been read and the remaining thing to do is to select the correct block and the correct byte or word from the block. However, it is less power efficient because all cache ways of the corresponding set in the data array are always activated and read, even when the access results in cache misses. Such a power-performance trade-off is common in cache design. In some cases, the L1 caches use parallel tag and data array access in order to keep the access latency short, while outer level caches (L2 and L3) may use sequential tag array and data array access to conserve power consumption, especially considering outer caches may have higher associativities than the L1 caches.

> ■ *Did you know?*
>
> Another interesting power-performance trade-off occurs when determining the timing of tag lookups at various cache hierarchy levels. For the Intel Itanium 2 processor, a design decision was made to prioritize reducing the L2 cache access latency. Right after the physical address is available, the L2 tag lookup is performed immediately, even before the L1 data cache hit or miss is determined. An advantage of the decision is quick determination of L2 cache hit or miss. In the case that the L1 data cache misses but the L2 cache hits, the L2 cache can supply the block early. In the case that the L2 cache misses, the miss request can be forwarded to the L3 cache early. A cost of the decision is that in the case of L1 data cache hit, power has been unnecessarily consumed for checking the L2 cache tag. The early L2 tag access becomes more attractive when the L1 data cache hit rate is relatively low, the L2 cache hit rate is relatively low, and the L2 or L3 cache access latencies are relatively low. In the case of Itanium 2, the L1 data cache and L2 cache are relatively small (16KB and 256KB) and the L2 cache access latency is relatively fast (as fast as 5 clock cycles).
>
> Pushing it to the extreme, one may envision a scheme that performs L1, L2, and L3 cache tag lookups simultaneously, which is a high-power and high-performance solution. When power budget is abundant, such a scheme may pay off. However, if power budget is constrained, figuring out which lookups should be performed in parallel or sequentially to achieve optimum power-performance trade offs requires a lot of simulation experiments with actual workloads.

Another possibility is to employ *way prediction*. Way prediction is a technique that relies on a small table that given a block address, it produces the cache way where the block is likely residing at. With way prediction, one can get the best of parallel and sequential tag and data array lookups, assuming the way prediction is accurate. With way prediction, Steps 1 and 2, and Step 4, are performed in parallel. However, data array lookup in Step 4 is only performed for the predicted way; all non-predicted ways are not read. Thus, tag array and data array lookups are performed in parallel. In Step 3, the cache tags are compared against the block address' tag, which not only determines cache hit or miss, but also confirms if the way prediction was correct. If the predicted way is correct, we already have the desired data block, and the requested bytes can be returned to the processor. If the predicted way is incorrect, the block that was read is an incorrect block, and data array lookup has to be repeated in the correct way. With way prediction, if the prediction is correct, the cache is as fast as parallel lookup, and as power efficient as sequential lookup. If the prediction is incorrect, the cache consumes more power and takes a longer access latency than the sequential lookup. An accurate way prediction scheme is critical to produce a net benefit.

5.2.2 Replacement Policy

Suppose that we have a set-associative cache. When a new block is read from the outer level hierarchy and needs to be placed in the cache, it needs to evict a block from among blocks currently cached in the set. The criteria for an optimum replacement [7] is that *the block that will be accessed the farthest in the future should be the one that is evicted.* However, the optimum replacement is theoretically guaranteed to produce the least number of cache misses, it is not implementable because it requires information from the future. Hence, most cache implementations use a *least recently used* (LRU) replacement or its approximations. In the LRU policy, the cache block that was accessed the farthest back in the past is selected to be evicted to make room for a new block. The LRU replacement exploits temporal locality in code because recently accessed data tend to be accessed again in the near future. It has been shown that LRU performs well overall, although it trails the performance of optimum replacement, sometimes by a large margin. There is a case in which LRU performance is pathological: when a program accesses more blocks in a circular pattern than what the cache can hold, LRU replacement performs terribly. For example, suppose that the program accesses block A, B, C, A, B, C, A, and so on. If all the blocks map to a single cache set, and the cache has a 2-way associativity, then every block access incurs a cache miss.

LRU can be implemented in several ways. One way to implement LRU replacement is to use a matrix of bits stored in the LRU information portion of the tag array. In the matrix implementation, the number of rows and columns are the same as the number of ways, and each row and column are associated with a particular way. Figure 5.6 illustrates this. Suppose that initially a 4-way associative cache set contains block A, B, C, and D, a stream of accesses B, C, A, and D occur, and the LRU matrix is initialized to all 0's. The LRU matrix is organized as a 4×4 matrix. Every cache hit to a particular way will update the matrix by setting all bits in the way's row to 1's, and then setting all bits in the way's column to 0's.

Figure 5.6 illustrates step by step the content of the LRU matrix after each access. An access to B (which resides in way 1), sets the second row bits to 1, and then the second column bits to 0. An access to C (which resides in way 2), sets the third row bits to 1, and then the third column bits to 0. An access to A (which resides in way 0), sets the first row bits to 1, and then the first column bits to 0. Finally, an access to D (which resides in way 3), sets the fourth row bits to 1, and then the fourth column bits to 0. Suppose that at this time a replacement needs to be made. By scanning the rows, we discover that way 1 (containing block B) has the least number of 1's (it has none), hence B is the least recently used block that should be selected for eviction. More generally, the access recency order is represented by the number of 1's in each row: the least recently used way has the

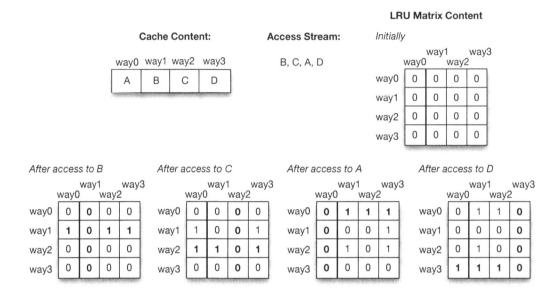

Figure 5.6: Illustrating matrix implementation of the least recently used (LRU) replacement policy.

least number of 1's (way 2 has no 1's), whereas the most recently used way has the most number of 1's (way 3 has three 1's).

The LRU matrix incurs a space overhead of N^2 bits for an N-way associative cache. Thus, it is cheap to implement for small associativities, but becomes expensive to implement for a highly associative cache. As a result, some designs for highly-associative caches use approximations to LRU instead of true LRU. One such approximation is the *first in first out* (FIFO) policy, which evicts a cache block that was brought into the cache the earliest, regardless of whether the block was recently used or not.

> ■ *Did you know?*
>
> For more discussion on various alternative cache indexing functions and their impact on performance, readers are referred to the study by Kharbutli and Solihin [34]. The performance of LRU is not graceful, i.e., when the working set of a program becomes larger than the cache, the performance may degrade abruptly rather than gradually. Replacement policies that rely more on randomness often exhibit more gracefulness, although they perform slightly worse than LRU in many cases. Readers are referred to a study by Guo and Solihin [20] for more discussion.

Another possible approximation to LRU is by keeping track of only a few most recently used blocks, and on replacement, a block from among blocks that are not the few most recently used ones is selected, either randomly or based on a certain algorithm. The simplest example of this approach is a scheme that tracks the most recently used (MRU) block, and on a replacement, pseudo-randomly selects a block from among non-MRU blocks. Another example that belongs to this approach is the tree-based pseudo LRU replacement policy [2], illustrated in Figure 5.7.

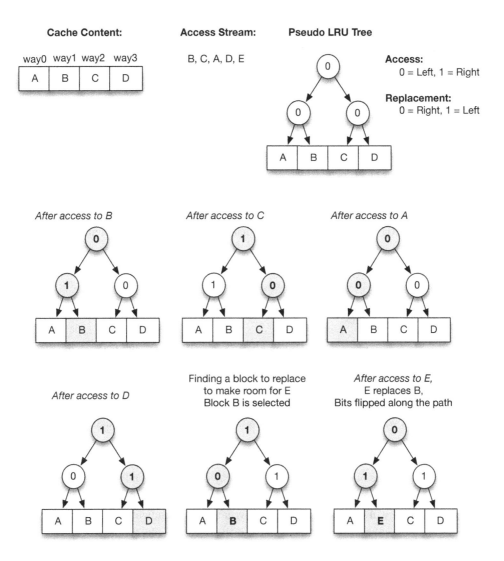

Figure 5.7: Illustration of pseudo-LRU replacement on a 4-way set associative cache.

In the pseudo-LRU replacement policy, for an A-way associative cache, $A-1$ bits are maintained and logically organized as a binary tree. The purpose of the tree is to record the path of recent accesses. During accesses, the path from the root of the tree to the accessed block is recorded in the nodes of the tree, with '0' indicating the left turn and '1' indicating the right turn. Figure 5.7 illustrates an example. Suppose that we have a 4-way associative cache set containing block A, B, C, and D; we have a stream of accesses B, C, A, D, and E; and the initial content of the pseudo LRU bits are zero. What happens to the bits after each access is shown in the figure. First, the access to block B is recorded in the tree as a left turn from the root, and a right turn from the left child node. The root node is reset (to 0) and the left child node is set (to 1). The next access is to block C, which causes the root node to be set and the right child node to be reset, to indicate the path from the root to block C. The next access is to block A, which causes the root node to be reset and the left child node to be reset, to indicate the path from the root to block A. The next access is to block D, which causes the root node to be set and the right child node to be set, to indicate the path from the root to block D. The next access is to block E, which is a cache miss. Thus, a victim block needs to be determined to make room for block E. Starting from the root node, we observe a value of '1' which for replacement purpose indicates turning left. At the left child node, the value '0' indicates turning right, leading to block B. In this example, B is the pseudo-LRU victim, which coincidentally is the same as victim had LRU replacement been used. Finally, block E is placed in the cache line that used to hold block B, and then the pseudo LRU tree is updated to reflect that. Note that finding a victim block and updating the tree can be combined, e.g., by flipping the bits as we traverse from the root to the victim block.

Comparing the LRU and pseudo-LRU replacement, for an N-way associative cache, the space overheads for the LRU matrix is N^2 bits while for the pseudo-LRU tree is $N - 1$ bits, which means that the pseudo-LRU replacement is cheaper than the LRU matrix to implement, especially for a highly associative cache.

5.2.3   Write Policy

Write Through vs. Write Back

A cache is a temporary memory. The main place to store programs and data are the main memory. So intuitively, an important question in cache design is that when a processor changes the value of bytes at a cache block, when should that change be propagated to the outer level memory hierarchy? There are two choices for implementation: *write through* and *write back* policies. In a write through policy, any bytes written by a single write event in the cache are immediately propagated to the outer level memory hierarchy component.

In contrast, in a write back policy, the change is allowed to occur at the cache block without being propagated to the outer level memory hierarchy component. Only when the block is evicted, is the block "written back" or propagated, and it overwrites the stale version at the outer level. In the write back policy, if every evicted block is written back, bandwidth consumption may be high. Hence, an obvious optimization is to write back cache blocks that have been modified while they are in the cache. To achieve this, each cache block's tag is augmented with a state field, which includes a *dirty* bit or state. When a new cache block is installed in the cache, its dirty bit is cleared. When there is a write to any byte or word in the block, the dirty bit is set. When the cache block is evicted, it is written back if its dirty bit has a value of one, or *silently* discarded if its dirty bit has a value of zero.

Comparing the write through versus write back policies, the write back policy tends to conserve bandwidth usage between the cache and its outer level memory hierarchy component because there are often multiple writes to a cache block during the time the cache block resides in the cache. In the write through policy, each write propagates its value down so it consumes bandwidth on each write. As a result, the outermost level cache in a processor chip typically uses a write back policy since off-chip pin bandwidth is a limited resource. However, the choice incurs less penalty for on-chip bandwidth which tends to be much higher. For example, the L1 cache is usually backed up by an outer level L2 cache, and both of them are on-chip. The bandwidth between the L1 cache and L2 cache is quite high compared to the off-chip bandwidth.

Another factor that determines the choice of write through vs. write back policy is fault tolerance against hardware faults. A bit stored in the cache can flip its value when it is struck by alpha particles or cosmic rays (a phenomenon called *soft errors*). The cache cell is not damaged but it loses its value. In a write through cache, if this fault is detected, then it is safe to discard the block and refetch it from the outer level hierarchy. However, in a write back cache, detecting the fault is not enough because, assuming a block is dirty, the only valid copy of the data has been changed (the outer level memory hierarchy component does not have a valid copy yet). Hence, a write back cache needs to be protected not just by error detection, but also by *error correction*. Redundant bits called *error correcting code* (ECC) are added to enable error correction. However, since ECC computation is more expensive than simple *parity bits* which can detect but not correct errors, ECC can negatively impact cache access latencies. Therefore, in many implementations, the L1 cache uses a write through policy (so that it can use simpler parity bit protection), while the L2 cache uses a write back policy (so it can conserve off-chip bandwidth) and is protected with ECC.

■ *Did you know?*

Another factor that is critical to consider when deciding write through vs. write back policy is the power consumption of the outer cache (e.g., the L2 cache), which has to be written whenever there is a write occurring to the inner cache (e.g., the L1 cache). The writes may be to different or to the same bytes in a single cache block, resulting in frequent writes to the L2 cache, which would have been filtered at the L1 cache had a write back policy been used. These writes cause frequent L2 cache accesses, incurring high power consumption and increase the occupancy of the L2 cache ports and controller. One way to mitigate this is to insert a write buffer to temporarily keep updates to several recently written L1 cache blocks. Instead of going to the L2 cache, the writes now happen at the write buffer rather than the L2 cache. When the buffer is full, the oldest (or least recent) block is written through to the L2 cache. On an L1 cache miss, the write buffer must be checked, and if the block is found, it is returned to the L1 cache.

Write Allocate vs. Write No Allocate

Another aspect of the write policy is whether the block that contains the byte or word to be written needs to be brought into the cache if it is not already in the cache. In the *write allocate* (WA) policy, upon a write miss, the block is brought into the cache before it is written. In the *write no-allocate* (WNA) policy, upon a write miss, the write is propagated down to the outer level memory hierarchy component without bringing the block into the cache.

The write no-allocate policy is more beneficial when there is only a small probability that adjacent bytes in the block will be read or written in the near future, i.e. there is little spatial locality after a write. It is also more beneficial when there is only a small probability that the written bytes in the block will be read or written again in the near future, i.e., there is little temporal locality after a write. If the written bytes or adjacent bytes in the block will be read or written in the near future, then a write allocate policy works better. Since increasing the cache block size increases the probability that a block will be accessed multiple times, the write allocate policy tends to perform better relative to the write no-allocate policy on larger cache block sizes.

A write through policy may use a write allocate or write no-allocate policy. However, a write back cache typically has to use write allocate policy since without a write allocate policy, a write miss will have to be propagated down similar to a write through cache.

■ *Did you know?*

> *Although a fixed policy for cache allocation and replacement can be tuned to work well in general, it is a "one size fits all" approach that cannot cater to differences in application behavior. Recent processors have added new instructions to enable programmers and compilers to fine tune the policies used by the cache to fit specific application behavior. These instructions target specific cases that a general cache policy does not handle very well. For example, some applications exhibit streaming behavior, where it writes (or reads) consecutive bytes once and rarely accesses them again in the near future. A write allocate policy unnecessarily keeps them in the cache. Instead, non-temporal store instructions (e.g., MOVNTI, MOVNTQ, etc. on x86 instruction set) were added to allow programmers/compilers to specify write no allocate policy for data being written (if a block containing data is already cached, it will be evicted). Another special case is zeroing a region in memory for the purpose of initializing a large data structure. Rather than fetching the block only to overwrite it with zero, instructions were provided to allocate a zero block in the cache (e.g., DBCZ in PowerPC instruction set). Other cache-control instructions that are commonly supported include ones that allow a specific block to be written back, invalidated, and prefetched.*
>
> *Perhaps one of the richest sets of instructions for controlling cache behavior can be found in the Intel Itanium processor (IA-64 instruction set), which relies on sophisticated compiler analysis to control data management in the cache by providing to different cache levels. The following table shows hints that can be attached to load/store instructions and their meaning.*

Hint	Allocate at L1?	Allocate at L2?	Allocate at L3?
NTA	*No*	*Yes (but replace next)*	*No*
NT2	*No*	*Yes (but replace next)*	*Yes*
NT1	*No*	*Yes*	*Yes*
T1 (default)	*Yes*	*Yes*	*Yes*

5.2.4   Inclusion Policy on Multi-Level Caches

In a multi-level cache configuration, another issue that is relevant is whether the content of the inner level cache (which is smaller) should be contained in the outer level cache (which is larger). If an outer level cache includes the content of the inner level cache, then the outer cache is said to be *inclusive*, and the property is referred to as an *inclusion property*. If, on the other hand the outer cache can only hold blocks that are not in the inner cache, then the outer cache is said to be *exclusive* of the inner cache. Inclusion and exclusion require certain protocols to enforce. If neither protocols are enforced, neither inclusion nor exclusion may be achieved. Such a policy is sometimes referred to as *non-inclusive non-exclusive* (NINE).

Figure 5.8 illustrates the differences between the policies shown in different columns. There are two levels of caches, with the L2 cache being inclusive, exclusive, or NINE. Suppose that initially the L2 cache has a block Z. If there are L1 and L2 cache misses to block X, block X is fetched into the L1 and L2 caches in the inclusive and NINE cases, but only into the L1 cache in the exclusive case. All the affected cache lines are shown in grey so that they are highlighted. Now suppose that block X is evicted from the L1 cache. In both the inclusive and NINE cases, block X will simply be evicted out of the L1 cache, and the L2 cache is not involved (unless block X is dirty, in which case its value is written back to the L2 cache). In the exclusive case, block X is then allocated in the L2 cache. In effect, an exclusive L2 cache acts to hold victim blocks from the L1 cache, making it a *victim cache*. Next, suppose block Y is evicted out of the L2 cache. In the inclusive case, evicting block Y from the L2 cache necessitates the block to be evicted from the L1 cache as well, otherwise inclusion is violated. Thus, the L2 cache sends a *back invalidation* to the L1 cache (illustrated by the arrow). In the NINE case, block Y is simply evicted from the L2 cache, and the L1 cache is not notified. This step is not applicable to the exclusive cache as block Y is not present in the L2 cache. Finally, suppose that there is an L1 cache miss to block Z. In both the inclusive and NINE case, block Z is found in the L2 cache and is fetched into the L1 cache. In the exclusive case, block Z is removed from the L2 cache before it is allocated in the L1 cache (to preserve exclusivity), as illustrated with the arrow.

Let us now discuss the merits and drawbacks of different policies. An interesting property of an inclusive cache is that since all blocks held in the inner cache are also held in the outer cache, contra-positively, all blocks not held in the outer cache are not held in the inner cache. The latter property is very important. In some parallel systems with per-processor private cache, a cache miss to a block is handled by checking other peer caches to see if any of them holds a copy of the block. In some cases, a peer cache (at the same level) may hold the only valid copy of the block in the system and must supply the block to the cache that suffers the miss. Thus, every cache miss at that level anywhere in the system must result in checking for presence of the block at all other caches. If the cache being checked is inclusive, when it is determined that it does not hold the block, the inclusion property ensures that its inner caches also do not hold the block. Thus, the checking stops at the inclusive cache, and the cache can simply provide a response for the check. In contrast, if the cache being checked is not inclusive (either exclusive or NINE), the checking must continue to all its inner caches. For example, if both the L2 and L3 caches are private to a processor and are exclusive or NINE, checking for the presence of a block at the L3 cache is not sufficient, the checking must continue to the L2 caches and L1 caches other than the one where the miss originates from. If the L2 cache is inclusive instead, the checking must continue from the L3 cache to the L2 cache, but it stops at the L2 cache. If the L3 cache is also inclusive, then the checking stops at the L3 cache.

There are two implications of this. First, cache miss latency is shorter in an inclusive cache, and is longer in an exclusive or NINE cache. An inclusive cache can post a response quickly to an external request for a block, whereas an exclusive or NINE cache must wait until all inner caches are checked before it can post a response. Second, checking the presence of blocks in inner caches mean that there is an increase in occupancy in the cache controller and the tag array of the inner cache. Requests from the processor now must contend with checks requested by the outer cache, and the contention may slow down accesses by the processors. It is possible to mitigate the contention by duplicating the inner cache tag array, with one tag array used by the processor and the other used by external requests. This solution does not completely remove the contention problem because while simultaneous tag checks can be supported, a change in one tag copy must be propagated to the other tag copy, making both tags unavailable in the mean time.

Despite the benefits, there is a cost for enforcing inclusion. In an inclusive cache, the total number of unique cache blocks that can be held is dictated by the size of the outer cache, rather than by the total size of the outer and inner level caches. If the outer level cache size is relatively

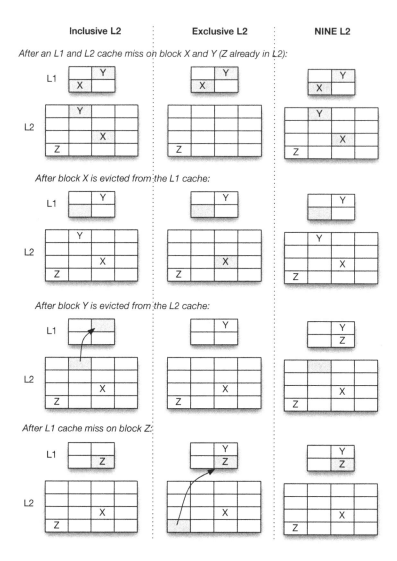

Figure 5.8: Illustration of various inclusion policies: inclusive, exclusive, and not-inclusive and not-exclusive (NINE) L2 cache.

small, then the wasted cache capacity can be significant. For example, if we have 32-KB L1 data cache, 32-KB L1 instruction cache, and a 512-KB L2 cache, then the wasted space is 64-KB, which is equivalent to 12.5% of the L2 cache size. So 12.5% of the L2 cache capacity is dedicated to hold blocks that are redundant in the L1 caches. However, if we have a 2-MB L2 cache, then the wasted space of 64-KB only corresponds to 3.1% of the L2 cache size. Therefore, the cost of an inclusive cache is proportional to the ratio of the inner cache to the capacity of the inclusive cache itself.

Comparing the exclusive and NINE policies, an exclusive cache does not keep redundant blocks in the inner caches hence overall it is able to keep a larger number of unique blocks. For example, if an L2 cache of 512KB is exclusive of an L1 cache that is 64KB, then overall the L1 and L2 caches are able to keep 576KB unique data, or 9,216 64B blocks. A NINE cache does not guarantee the lack of redundancy. However, while enjoying the benefit of keeping the maximum number of unique blocks, an exclusive cache suffers from a drawback of frequent filling of new blocks. Since an exclusive cache must be filled with every evicted block from an inner cache, the rate of fill is equal to the rate of the inner cache's misses. In contrast, a NINE cache is filled with a new block only when it suffers from a cache miss. Therefore, an exclusive cache uses up more bandwidth between the inner cache and itself, and incurs a higher occupancy on its tag and data array.

As an example, suppose that a processor suffers from 40 million L1 cache misses per second. In an L2 exclusive cache, it must accept blocks evicted from the L1 cache at the rate of $40 \cdot 10^6 \times 64 = 2.56$ GB/sec. If the L2 cache is NINE, suppose it suffers from 4 million L2 cache misses per second and must accept write backs of dirty L1 blocks. Assuming 25% of evicted L1 cache blocks are dirty, the NINE L2 cache must support $0.1 \times 2.56 \cdot 10^9 + 0.25 \times 2.56 \cdot 10^9 = 0.896$ GB/sec, significantly lower than an exclusive cache.

> ■ *Did you know?*
>
> *Another cost of inclusion is that in some cases, a block may be evicted from a larger outer cache while the block is still needed in the inner cache. This can occur when a block has a tight temporal locality, it is repeatedly accessed by the processor in the inner cache, the inner cache filtering the accesses such that the block is rarely accessed in the outer cache. Thus, the block drifts into the least recently used position and is evicted out of the outer cache, causing a back invalidation to the inner cache, which is forced to invalidate the block that the processor is still actively using. The risk for such a scenario increases as the ratio of the inner cache size to the inclusive outer cache size increases. One promising solution to this problem [30] is to split the back invalidation into two steps: the first step sends an intention to back invalidate (for example when the block becomes an LRU block or a near-LRU block in the L2 cache), and the second step sends an actual back invalidation. During the time between the first and second step, the block in the inner cache is marked with a flag. If the inner cache turns out still needing the block by accessing it, it can clear the flag and send a refresh signal to the outer cache. The outer cache can respond by refreshing the block's LRU information, making it a most-recently-used block again.*

In a multicore architecture that relies on a shared last level cache, the storage overhead of an inclusion property is more pronounced. For example, in the AMD Barcelona quad-core processor, each core has a private 512-KB L2 cache (for a total of 2-MB over four cores), while the shared-by-all-cores L3 cache size is 2-MB. If the inclusion property is enforced, 2-MB of cache space, equivalent to 100% of the L3 cache size, will be wasted! Therefore, designers tend to choose between inclusive, exclusive, or NINE based on the cost relative to the benefit of inclusion.

A related concept to inclusion is what I refer to as *value inclusion*. When inclusion is maintained, and a block is cached in both the inner level and outer level caches, can the block's data values differ in both caches? If value inclusion is maintained, the data values must be the same. Otherwise, a difference in data values is allowed. A difference in data value can happen if the inner level cache uses a write back policy, and the block is modified by the processor. The modification is not seen yet by the outer level cache. In a multiprocessor system, this creates a problem because the outer level cache does not know whether the block in the inner level cache is dirty or not. One way to avoid this situation is to use a write through policy at the inner level cache, so that value inclusion is maintained, i.e., the outer level cache always has the latest values of all blocks currently cached in the inner level cache. Another way to avoid this situation is not to maintain value inclusion, but on a write to a block in the inner level cache, the outer level cache is informed. The outer level cache can keep a bit or a special state that indicates the block is dirty in the inner level cache. When necessary, the outer level cache can request the inner cache to write back the dirty block. One benefit of value inclusion is the fast response an outer cache can supply data block when there is a cache miss on a peer outer cache to the same block.

5.2.5   Unified/Split/Banked Cache Organization and Cache Pipelining

Another important design goal of a cache is high access bandwidth. A cache that may be accessed simultaneously each clock cycle needs to provide high access bandwidth. An example is the L1 cache of a high-performance superscalar processor: it should provide at least one instruction block per cycle, and at least two data reads or writes per cycle. For a *unified cache* to provide such a high bandwidth, it has to contain at least two read ports and one write port. Each additional port in a cache adds an extra decoder, wires for word lines, wires for bit lines, sense amplifiers, and multiplexers. A two-ported cache can have a much larger structure than a single-ported cache, a three-ported cache can have a much larger structure than a two-ported cache, etc. A large cache structure increases the cache access time, resulting in possible reduction in performance.

One way to mitigate the high bandwidth requirement without substantially increasing the cache size, distinct contents can be split into different caches. An example of a split cache configuration is the typical L1 cache used in most processors today. The L1 cache is typically split into the instruction cache and the data cache. This split is effective because instruction fetches are easily distinguished from data fetches. Instruction fetches are issued by the fetch unit of the processor, while data fetches are issued by the load/store unit of the processor. For the most part, load/store instructions do not fetch data from the code region, unless in special cases such as self-modifying code or just-in-time compilation. Figure 5.9 illustrates a dual ported cache versus split instruction and data caches. The split caches shown are single ported hence can be smaller and faster (in some implementations, even with split organization, the L1 caches are typically multi ported, but the number of ports would have been higher without the split organization). An alternative organization is, rather than distinguishing types of data held in the split caches, splitting the cache over different addresses in an interleaved manner. This organization is referred to as *multi-banked cache*. In a multi-banked cache, multiple accesses to different banks can be performed in parallel, while accesses to the same bank result in conflict and are sequentialized. This results in a higher bandwidth from a smaller and faster cache. If addresses of accesses are completely random, for a dual-banked cache, the probability of any pair of accesses going to the same bank is 50%. The conflict probability will decrease further as the number of banks increases. Clearly, the split instruction-data cache is more effective because and instruction and data accesses rarely go to the same cache. However, the multi-banked cache does not require distinguishing types of data.

In many processor implementations, the L1 cache is split into instruction and data caches, but all outer caches such as the L2 cache and L3 cache are unified. The L1 caches are often multi-ported, but outer caches are accessed infrequently (the L2 cache is only accessed on L1 cache misses, and the L3 cache is only accessed on L2 cache misses), hence it is sometimes sufficient to have them single ported.

Another technique to improve cache access bandwidth is pipelining. Steps in accessing the cache shown in Figure 5.5 may be turned into different pipeline stages. Suppose that if not pipelined, all the steps take T seconds of time to complete, hence the cache can achieve a throughput of $\frac{1}{T}$ access/sec (or equivalently, if each access is to a B block size, then the cache access bandwidth is $\frac{B}{T}$

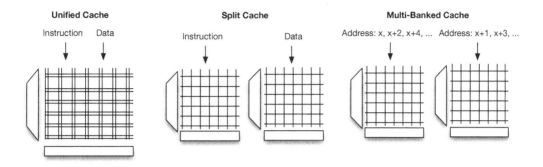

Figure 5.9: Illustration of unified vs. split vs. banked cache organizations.

bytes/sec). If the cache access can be divided into N balanced pipeline stages, then the cache can run at an $N\times$ the original clock frequency and can process $\frac{N}{T}$ accesses per second. One drawback for providing high bandwidth is the high power consumption that comes with a higher clock frequency. Thus, it is common for an outer cache such as the L2 cache to run at a lower clock frequency than an inner cache such as the L1 cache.

■ *Did you know?*

A multi-banked organization is sometimes implemented not only to provide high bandwidth, but because the cache would be too large to be accessible within a reasonable wire delay. The last point is especially acute for the last level cache. The IBM Power8 chip has a 12-banked L3 cache (similar to Figure 5.1).

C0 Priority Resource checking	C1 Directory lookup Cache model update	C2 Hit/miss result EDRAM access	C3 Reject/needs	C4 Cache ECC Intervention to L2 Broadcast to L4 Store to EDRAM	C5 Response to L2	C6 Data return to L2

Figure 5.10: The L3 cache pipeline of IBM zEC12 processor.

An example of a cache pipeline is shown in Figure 5.10. The figure shows the L3 cache pipeline of IBM zEC12 processor system. The pipeline has seven stages. The first stage (C0) is used for selecting a request among competing requests and for resource checking and arbitration. The requests may come from one of six L2 caches or from an L4 cache, hence arbitration is necessary. The second stage (C1) is used for looking up the tag and state at the tag array. The third stage (C2) is when the hit/miss result from the tag lookup becomes available and is used to initiate data array lookup. The data array is implemented with DRAM cells utilizing a process referred to as embedded DRAM or EDRAM. At C2, the state of the cache block is also input to the cache controller which determines what appropriate action to take. The description of C2 and C3 make it clear that sequential tag-data lookup is used. What is performed at stage C3 is somewhat unclear; it is likely to be related to the cache controller's response based on the block state. In the fifth stage (C4) error detection and correction are performed. Also performed in C4 are cache coherence actions (intervention to L2 or broadcast to L4), and data store to the EDRAM. The last two stages (C5 and C6) are used to send the response to the request to the L2 cache and sending the data to the L2 cache, respectively.

5.2.6   Cache Addressing and Translation Lookaside Buffer

Most microprocessor systems today support *virtual memory*. In a virtual memory system, a program (and its compiler) can assume that the entire address space is available for its use, even though in reality, the physical memory may be smaller than the address space viewed by the program, and it may be partitioned for simultaneous use by multiple programs. This address space illusion is provided by the system through providing two types of addresses: virtual address (the address program sees) and physical address (the actual address in the physical memory). Figure 5.11 illustrates a virtual memory system at a very high level.

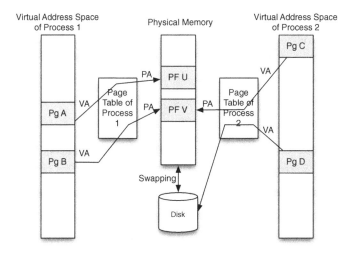

Figure 5.11: Illustration of the role of virtual memory.

The figure shows two processes, each having its own *page table* managed by the OS. Each process' page table maintains a mapping between the virtual address space that the process sees and the actual physical memory available in the system. The page table is a data structure that translates virtual address (VA) of the application to the physical address (PA) in the physical memory. As will be discussed later, an address presented to the cache that is used for indexing and tag comparison can be either of the addresses. The operating system (OS) manages the translation of virtual address to physical address at the granularity of pages (typically 4 KBytes, but larger page sizes are often supported as well). Thus, a page in the virtual address space of a process is mapped to a placeholder called a *page frame* in the physical memory. In the figure, pages A and B of process 1 map to page frames U and V in the physical memory. Page C of process 2 maps to page frame V in the physical memory, indicating that processes 1 and 2 are sharing data in the physical memory through different virtual addresses. Page D is currently not resident in the physical memory, as indicated by the page table. Non-resident pages are kept in the swap area in the disk, allowing multiple processes to run simultaneously and only data pages needed by a process are brought into the physical memory.

, While initially the virtual memory system was created for hiding the physical memory size from programs and allowing programs to run simultaneously, over time it added more functionalities such as protection, sharing, and security. By keeping separate page tables, one process's memory can be isolated from another. At the same time, by letting page table entries of different processes mapping to the same page frame, virtual memory allows sharing between multiple processes. In addition, since one can attach attributes to a page in the page table, the page table can increase protection and security by assigning a read only attribute to a page or even a non-executable attribute to a page. This allows protecting code region from being overwritten either accidentally or maliciously (e.g., security attacks) and avoiding executing injected code in the data region.

The page table is a structure maintained by the OS and is stored in the main memory, so accessing it requires a high latency. In some systems, due to the very large virtual address space supported, the page table is hierarchically organized, hence multiple memory accesses are required to translate a virtual page address to a physical page frame address. Requiring page table access for each memory access (a load or store instruction) in order to get the physical address to supply to the cache will cause the cache access time to be very high. Hence, most processors employ a *translation lookaside buffer* (TLB), which is a cache that stores most recently used page table entries. The TLB is structured like a cache, with a tag array and data array. Each entry in the TLB contains a page table entry, including the physical page frame address for a given virtual page address and all meta information (protection, whether the page has been read or written, etc.). However, there are subtle differences. First, since a page size is much larger than a cache block size, the TLB only needs to have fewer entries to cover as much memory as the L1 cache or the L2 cache. For example, 16 entries in the TLB cover $16 \times 4 = 64KB$ of memory, which is as much memory as covered by a large L1 data cache. Thus, a TLB can get by with fewer entries compared to the L1 cache or L2 cache. Another difference is that a TLB miss may be more expensive compared to a regular cache miss, since on a TLB miss, we must invoke either a hardware or software handler to traverse the page table at multiple hierarchy levels (called a *page table walk*). Thus, page table entries are made cacheable in the L1 and L2 cache, while in newer systems special "translation caches" are deployed. Still, in the rare events where no page table entries are found in the cache, multiple memory accesses are required to service a TLB miss. Considering these differences, the TLB is usually structured as small but highly (or fully) associative cache. In more recent systems, the TLB itself is organized as multi level caches, with L1 TLB being small but backed up by a larger L2 TLB.

Let us go back and discuss cache addressing. Figure 5.12 illustrates three options in cache addressing. One option is to use *virtual addressing* (top left), that is, to index the cache using the index bits from the virtual address, and store tag bits of the virtual address in the cache's tag array. This option is also referred to as *virtually indexed and virtually tagged cache*. Using virtual addressing, the physical address is not needed for accessing the cache, hence the TLB and the L1 cache can be accessed in parallel, and the latency of accessing the TLB is completely hidden. However, a drawback of this approach is that since each process has its own page table, the mapping between the same virtual page address (of different processes) to physical page address is different in different processes. Thus, a virtually-addressed cache cannot be shared by multiple processes, either simultaneously in a multicore or multithreading manner, or in a time-shared manner. For example, upon a context switch, a different process is loaded into the processor, and the cache content is invalid for that process. Hence, the cache must be flushed on a context switch. The TLB also needs to be flushed if its entries are not tagged with the *address space identifiers* which identify different processes. The cost of L1 cache flushing, which includes the latency to invalidate the entire cache and the loss of data, may not be acceptable if context switches are frequent.

An alternative option is to use *physical addressing* (right), that is, to index the cache using the index bits of the physical address, and store tag bits of the physical address in the cache's tag array. A drawback of this approach is that since the TLB or page table is accessed for address translation to generate the physical address that is needed for indexing the cache, TLB access time is directly added to the cache access time. A TLB is typically designed to be small so that it can be accessed in a few processor cycles. The access time may be comparable to the L1 cache access time, hence, adding the TLB access time to the L1 cache access time effectively doubles the latency to access the L1 cache. This can significantly degrade performance.

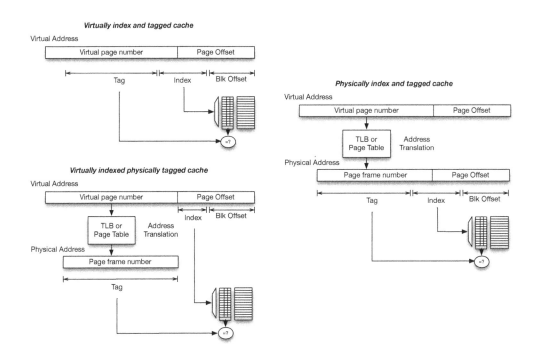

Figure 5.12: Various cache addressing options.

The third option is to use a mixed addressing referred to as *virtual indexing and physical tagging* (bottom left). The key observation utilized in this approach is that the page offset bits (bits used to index a particular byte or word location in a page) are valid for both virtual and physical address, hence, these bits can be used prior to accessing the TLB. If we ensure that the cache index bits are a subset of these bits, then the cache index is the same regardless of whether we use the virtual or physical address. For example, for a 4KB page, we need the lowest $log_2(4096) = 12$ bits as the page offset. For a 32-byte cache block size, we use the lowest $log_2(32) = 5$ bits as the block offset. Hence, we can use up to $12 - 5 = 7$ bits for cache indexing, which means that we can have $2^7 = 128$ sets in the cache. For a direct mapped cache, we can support an L1 cache size of $128 \times 1 \times 32 = 4096$ bytes. For a four-way associative cache, we can support an L1 cache size of

$128 \times 4 \times 32 = 16\text{KB}$. More generally, the relationship between the maximum cache size that can be used is:

$$MaxCacheSize = \frac{PageSize}{CacheBlockSize} \times Associativity \times CacheBlockSize$$
$$= PageSize \times Associativity \qquad (5.2)$$

With virtual indexing and physical tagging, the cache can be accessed immediately and in parallel with TLB access (Figure 5.12). When the TLB access is complete, the physical address tag can be compared with the tag stored in the cache to determine whether we have a cache hit or a cache miss. The drawback of this addressing is that the L1 cache size is limited. However, this is not a serious drawback because the L1 cache size is already limited for performance purpose. In addition, the L1 cache size can be increased beyond the maximum size if we are willing to increase the cache associativity. Therefore, many cache implementations choose this mixed addressing approach.

5.2.7 Non-Blocking Cache

A high performance processor may generate memory accesses even as an earlier memory access already suffers from a cache miss. In early cache designs, these memory accesses will stall until the access that misses in the cache is satisfied. This can obviously hurt performance. Modern cache architectures overcome this limitation by introducing a structure referred to as *miss status handling registers* (MSHRs). When a cache access suffers a cache miss, an MSHR is allocated for it to keep track of the status of the miss. This frees up the cache to service new accesses. Such a cache is referred to as a *non-blocking* or *lockup-free cache*. After an outstanding miss is satisfied, the MSHR that it corresponds to is deallocated.

The role of the MSHR depends on what type of access is kept track of there. For a store instruction that misses in a write back cache, the new value of the byte or word to be stored must be held in the MSHR until the data block is fetched from the outer level memory hierarchy. When the block arrives, the new value from the store must be merged into the block. For a load instruction that misses in the cache, the MSHR must link up with the processor register that is the destination of the load instruction. When the block arrives, the MSHR extracts the corresponding byte or word and passes that to the register for which the load instruction stalls.

The number of cache misses that can be outstanding at any given time is limited by the number of MSHRs. Hence, the number of MSHRs influences the degree of memory-level parallelism. The number of MSHRs must be designed by taking into account the number of instructions that the processor can execute in a cycle, the latency and bandwidth to access the outer level memory hierarchy, and the configuration of the inner level memory hierarchy that provides access filtering.

Note that non-blocking caches are required for implementing certain architecture features, among them are software prefetching (to be discussed in Section 5.4) and relaxed memory consistency models (to be discussed in Chapter 9). This is because without memory-level parallelism provided by a non-blocking cache, they cannot bring the performance benefit that they are designed for.

5.3 Cache Performance

The performance of the processor due the cache hierarchy depends on the number of accesses to the cache that find the blocks in the cache (*cache hits*) versus those which do not find the blocks in the cache (*cache misses*). There are various basic types of cache misses, known as the 3 Cs of cache misses:

1. *Compulsory misses* are misses that are required to bring blocks into the cache for the first time. They are also referred to as *cold misses* because they occur when the cache is cold (empty).

2. *Conflict misses* are misses that occur in the cache due to limited cache associativities.

3. *Capacity misses* are misses that occur in the cache due to limited cache size.

Distinguishing compulsory misses from other types of misses is easy: the first miss to a memory block is a compulsory miss and subsequent misses are not. However, it is not always easy to distinguish between conflict and capacity misses. Typically, conflict misses are measured by subtracting the number of misses of a limited associativity cache by the number of misses of a fully-associative cache of the same size and cache block size.[1] The remaining misses after subtracting the compulsory misses and conflict misses can be categorized as capacity misses.

There are other types of cache misses that are mentioned less frequently in literature:

1. *Coherence misses* are misses that occur due to the need to keep the cache coherent in shared memory multiprocessor systems. This will be discussed in more detail in later chapters.

2. *System-related misses* are misses that occur due to system activities such as system calls, interrupts, and context switches. When a process is suspended due to an interrupt, system call, or context switch, its cache state is perturbed by an interfering entity (another thread/process or the OS). When the process resumes execution, it will suffer from new cache misses to restore cache state that has been perturbed. These misses are system-related misses.

Coherence misses matter a lot in a multiprocessor system. They are one of the sources of bottlenecks in scalability of parallel programs. System-related misses also matter overall, and we need to take them into account as they tend to increase when the cache size increases, precisely when the number of conflict and capacity misses decreases.

Figure 5.13 shows the breakdown of the L2 cache misses for twelve SPEC2006 benchmarks when each benchmark is co-scheduled with one other interfering benchmark for various cache sizes. Since there are eleven other benchmarks, there are eleven possible co-schedules. The number of L2 cache misses for each benchmark is the average over eleven co-schedules the benchmark can have, normalized to the case in which 512-KB cache is used. The context switch misses are divided into two types: *replaced* misses that occur due to misses to blocks that were replaced during the cache perturbation caused by a context switch, and *reordered* misses that occur due to misses to blocks that were not replaced but were reordered in the recency positions in the cache during the cache perturbation. A time slice of 5ms is used for both benchmarks in a co-schedule. The Linux kernel version 2.6 assigns time quanta between 5 ms to 100 ms based on the process/thread priority level, so 5ms corresponds to the lowest priority level.

The figure shows that as the cache size increases, the number of "natural misses" (the sum of cold, capacity, and conflict misses) decreases, the total number of context switch misses may decline

---

[1]However, this approach sometimes fails. It is well known that in certain uncommon pathological cases, the number of cache misses on a fully-associative cache may be higher than in a set associative or a direct mapped cache. Using this approach will yield a negative number of conflict cache misses!

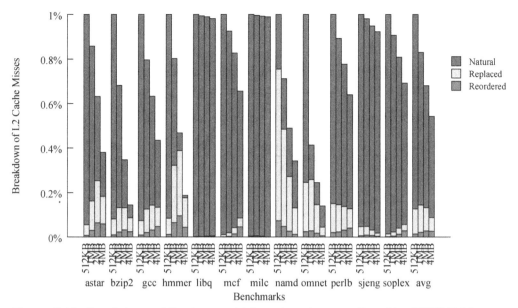

Figure 5.13: Breakdown of the types of L2 cache misses suffered by SPEC2006 applications with various cache sizes. Source: [39].

(in namd, perlbench), increase (in mcf, soplex), or increase then decline (in astar, bzip2, gcc, hmmer, omnetpp, and sjeng). The reason for this behavior is because when the cache is small, there are not many cache blocks that can be displaced by a cache perturbation that occurs in a context switch, so the number of context switch misses is low. As the cache becomes larger, a cache perturbation may displace more cache blocks, causing more context switch misses when the process resumes execution. However, when the cache becomes large enough to hold the total working sets of both benchmarks, cache perturbation only displaces very few blocks, so the number of context switch misses declines. Rather than being displaced, most blocks are now reordered, but reordered blocks do not incur context switch misses if there are no other misses to cause them to be displaced when the thread resumes execution. Hence, the absolute number of reordered misses also declines as the cache becomes large enough. Overall, system-related misses should not be ignored when context switches occur frequently and when the cache is large but is still smaller than the combined working set size of processes that time-share a processor.

Cache parameters affect the different types of misses. Intuitively, increasing the cache size reduces the number of capacity misses, while increasing cache associativity reduces the number of conflict misses. However, capacity misses and conflict misses are sometimes intermingled. For example, increasing the cache size while keeping cache associativity constant (hence increasing the number of sets) changes the way blocks in memory map to sets in the cache. Such a change in mapping often influences the number of conflict misses, either increasing or decreasing it. Increasing the cache size while keeping the number of sets constant (hence increasing the associativity) does not change how blocks in memory map to cache sets, but since associativity is increased, both conflict and capacity misses may also be reduced.

Although compulsory misses are "compulsory", they are measured by the number of times new blocks are fetched into the cache, hence they are affected by the cache block size. Larger cache block sizes reduce the number of compulsory misses when the program has good spatial locality.

The number of capacity and conflict misses may also decrease because more bytes are fetched upon each miss, thus fewer misses are required to load the same number of bytes. However, when there is little or no spatial locality, the number of capacity misses may increase. This is because increasing block sizes while keeping the cache size constant reduces the number of blocks that can be cached.

To summarize, Table 5.1 shows the impact of various cache parameters on various types of cache misses.

Table 5.1: Impact of various cache parameters on cache misses.

Parameters	Compulsory	Conflict	Capacity
Larger cache size	unchanged	unchanged	reduced
Larger block size	reduced	reduced/ increased	reduced/ increased
Larger associativity	unchanged	reduced	unchanged

5.3.1 The Power Law of Cache Misses

Researchers have long made an interesting empirical observation with regard to how a sequential application's number of cache capacity misses is affected by the cache size. In a single core/processor system, the capacity miss rate of an application tends to follow a certain trend known as the *power law* [22]. Mathematically, the power law states that if m_0 is the miss rate of a workload for a baseline cache size C_0, the miss rate (m) for a new cache size C can be expressed as:

$$m = m_0 \cdot \left(\frac{C}{C_0} \right)^{-\alpha} \tag{5.3}$$

where α is a measure of how sensitive the workload is to changes in cache size. Hartstein et al. in [22] validated the power law on a range of real-world benchmarks, and found that α ranges from 0.3 to 0.7, with an average of 0.5. When $\alpha = 0.5$, Equation 5.3 can be rewritten as:

$$\frac{m}{m_0} = \sqrt{\frac{C_0}{C}} \tag{5.4}$$

Let us suppose that $C = 4 \times C_0$, then $m = \frac{m_0}{2}$, which means that for an average workload, Equation 5.3 states that in order to decrease the capacity miss rate by a factor of two, the cache size must be increased by a factor of four. Hence, there is a diminishing number of cache misses that can be eliminated for each constant increase in the cache capacity.

How good are applications tracking the power law? Figure 5.14 plots the cache miss rate of each application we evaluate normalized to the smallest cache size as a function of cache size for a single level of cache. Note that both axes are shown in logarithmic scale; the miss rate curve will follow a straight line if it obeys the power law, because $log\ m = log\ m_0 + \alpha\ log\ C_0 - \alpha\ log\ C$. In the figure, the base cache size is 8KB, and each subsequent data point doubles the size until it reaches 2MB.

The figure shows that these applications tend to follow the power law of cache miss rate quite closely. Also, note the four bold lines in the figure correspond to the power law fit for all commercial applications, for all SPEC 2006 benchmarks, for the commercial application with the smallest α

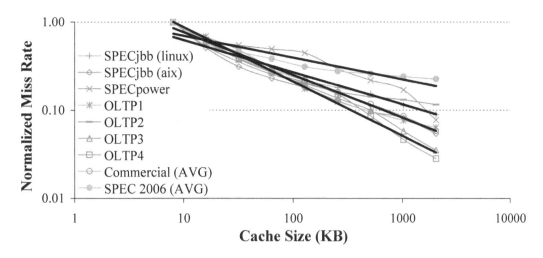

Figure 5.14: Normalized cache miss rate as a function of cache size. Source: [49].

(OLTP-2), and for the commercial application with the largest α (OLTP-4). The larger the α value, the steeper the negative slope of the line. The curve-fitted average α for the commercial workloads is 0.48, close to 0.5 in Hartstein et al.'s study [22], while the minimum and maximum α for the individual commercial applications are 0.36 and 0.62, respectively. The smallest α (SPEC 2006) has a value of 0.25.

While the power law is a useful tool for coming up with a back-of-envelope projection of cache performance, there are several aspects that need to be taken into account before using it. First, note that the power law has a finite range of cache sizes for which it applies. This is because at some large enough cache size, the number of capacity misses will drop to zero and the total number of cache misses stagnates, whereas the power law continues to predict a decrease in the number of cache misses. It is important to apply the power law only in the range before the number of capacity misses flattens. In addition, there are applications which have their miss rate figures exhibiting shapes that are stepwise linear. Typically, this is because the application has a discrete number of loops, where at a certain cache size, the entire working set of a loop fits, resulting in a large drop in miss rate. Then, there is no improvement in miss rate until the cache size is large enough for another loop's working set fits. For this reason, simpler applications (including SPEC 2006 benchmarks) exhibit more stepwise linear miss rate figure compared to commercial applications which exhibit a much more linear trend.

5.3.2 Stack Distance Profile

The power law captures a rough approximation of an application's miss rate as affected by the cache size. The power law enables us to represent the average behavior of a group of applications, and in some cases, individual applications. However, there are situations in which the power law does not fit the behavior of individual applications. To come up with a better representation of the behavior of an application's miss rate as affected by the cache size, researchers have demonstrated a useful profiling information referred to as the *stack distance profile*.

A stack distance profile captures the temporal reuse behavior of an application in a fully- or set-associative cache [42]. To collect the stack distance profile of an application on an A-way associative cache with LRU replacement algorithm, $A + 1$ counters are maintained: $C_1, C_2, \ldots, C_A, C_{>A}$. On each cache access, one of the counters is incremented. If it is a cache access to a block in the ith position in the LRU stack of block the set, C_i is incremented. Note that our first block in the stack is the most recently used block in the set, and the last block in the stack is the least recently used block in the set. If it is a cache miss, the block is not found in the LRU stack, resulting in incrementing the miss counter $C_{>A}$. A stack distance profile can be estimated by the compiler [10], by simulation, or directly on hardware with an appropriate hardware support [61].

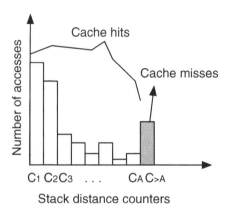

Figure 5.15: Illustration of a stack distance profile.

Figure 5.15 shows an example of a stack distance profile. Applications with regular temporal reuse behavior usually access more-recently-used data more frequently than less-recently-used data. Therefore, typically, the stack distance profile shows decreasing values as we go to the right, as shown in Figure 5.15. Using the stack distance profile, the number of cache misses for a smaller cache can be easily computed assuming LRU replacement policy. For example, for a smaller cache that has A' associativity, where $A' < A$, the new number of misses can be computed as:

$$miss = C_{>A} + \sum_{i=A'+1}^{A} C_i \tag{5.5}$$

Hence, for a cache that employs the LRU replacement policy, the miss rate as a function of the cache capacity can be directly derived from the stack distance profile of an application.

5.3.3 Cache Performance Metrics

In many sequential program execution cases, the number of cache misses correlates almost linearly with program throughput (instruction per cycle or IPC). However, how much each cache miss contributes to the reduction in IPC depends on the characteristics of the program, such as how much computation can be overlapped with cache misses (due to *instruction-level parallelism* or ILP) and how much of a cache miss can be overlapped with other cache misses (due to *memory-level parallelism* or MLP). If one ignores the impact of ILP and MLP on performance, then one of meaningful metrics to evaluate cache performance is the *average access time* (AAT), which is defined as the average time a memory access takes, and is computed by taking into account hit rates at various cache levels. For example, for a system with two levels of caches, let T_{L1}, T_{L2}, T_{Mem} denote the access time of the L1 cache, L2 cache, and memory, respectively, and M_{L1} and M_{L2} are the cache miss rates of the L1 and L2 caches. AAT can be computed as follows:

$$AAT = T_{L1} + M_{L1} \cdot T_{L2} + M_{L1} \cdot M_{L2} \cdot T_{Mem}$$

While the AAT provides a way to approximate cache performance, there are several problems. First, it does not take into account the impact of ILP and MLP. With ILP, some of the cache hit or miss latencies are hidden because the processor keeps busy executing instructions that have no dependence on the load instructions that miss on the cache. With MLP, multiple cache misses may be serviced simultaneously, effectively spreading the access latency across multiple misses. To account for ILP and MLP, the numbers used for T_{L1}, T_{L2}, and T_{Mem} can be chosen to be non-hidden latencies that are amortized by the average MLP. To give an example, Figure 5.16 illustrates this with the L1 cache access latency. Suppose that the execution is interleaved between computation and two L1 cache accesses. There are three choices of L1 cache access latencies to use. The first one is the theoretical time to access the L1 cache, which assumes there is one L1 cache access that occurs in isolation, shown as T_{L1_a} in the figure. Another version one counts only the latency that is not overlapped with computation, shown as T_{L1_b}. It represents the actual performance cost suffered by the program as it is not overlapped with execution, and it takes into account the ILP techniques used by the processor. Finally, T_{L1_c} shows the non-hidden part of L1 cache access latency, divided by the number of L1 cache accesses. In this case, $T_{L1\_c} = \frac{T_{L1\_b}}{2}$ because there are two L1 cache accesses. Thus, it represents the amortized (per-access average) non-hidden latency of the L1 cache access, and it takes into account the MLP. T_{L1_c} represents the best estimate of the effective L1 cache access latency that should be used when computing the AAT. However, both T_{L1_b} and T_{L1_c} are not always easily available and often require detailed simulation to measure.

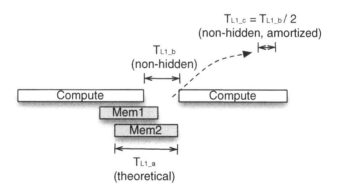

Figure 5.16: Illustration of various types of memory access latencies.

Another problem with the AAT is that it does not correspond directly to execution time, which is the ultimate measure of performance. To account for the impact of cache performance on the overall program performance, we can consider the cycles per instructions (CPI). Imagine a system with an ideal memory hierarchy, i.e., an L1 cache that never suffers from cache misses and has a zero cycle access latency. The CPI for the ideal memory hierarchy is referred to as CPI_{ideal}. Any additional clock cycles per instruction added on top of that is due to the imperfection of the memory hierarchy, caused by both cache access and miss latencies, and their rates of accesses or misses. In other words, AAT is a main contributor that adds to CPI_{ideal}. Thus, if the fraction of instructions that are memory references (loads or stores) is f_{mem}, the CPI is related to AAT as follows.

$$CPI = CPI_{ideal} + f_{mem} \times AAT \qquad (5.6)$$

The equation above does not distinguish between load instructions, which tend to contribute more to CPI because it is harder to overlap them with computation, and store instructions, which tend to contribute less to CPI because it is easier to overlap them with computation. If desired, it can be further separated into the contribution of loads vs. stores, at the expense of additional difficulties in estimating load- and store-specific AATs.

Finally, for parallel programs, however, the relationship cache performance metrics such as miss rates and execution time is not as straightforward due to the relative timing of execution progress of different threads. For example, a thread that arrives at a barrier early will either spin in a loop or block waiting for all other threads to arrive at the barrier. While spinning, it executes a series of reads and compares on a memory location in the cache. Such spinning code executes a lot of instructions and may produce a lot of cache accesses and cache hits with very few cache misses. This leads to a high IPC and low miss rates. Unfortunately, none of the high IPCs and low miss rates of spinning contributes to shorter execution time since it is due to useless work. Another example is the number of coherence misses which highly depends on the relative timing of execution of different threads. Overall, regular cache performance metrics cannot be blindly used for diagnosing parallel program performance.

5.4   Prefetching

Modern cache designs often employ *prefetching*, a technique which attempts to bring data into the cache before the program accesses it. Prefetching reduces the time a program waits for data to be fetched, so it can speed up program execution. However, it comes at the expense of extra bandwidth usage since it employs prediction of what data may be needed in the future by the processor. Such prediction can never be perfect, hence some blocks that are prefetched may never be used by the processor.

Many processors provide a special instruction for specifying an address to prefetch. While such prefetching instruction is supported in hardware, it is up to the software (i.e., the compiler) to use it, and where to insert it. Therefore, using prefetch instructions for performing prefetching is referred to as *software prefetching*. The alternative to software prefetching is to make hardware structures that dynamically observe the program's behavior and generate prefetch requests, transparently to software. Such an approach is referred to as *hardware prefetching*.

There are three metrics that are traditionally used to characterize the effectiveness of a prefetching technique: coverage, accuracy, and timeliness. *Coverage* is defined as the fraction of original cache misses that are prefetched, and therefore, the cache misses become cache hits or partial cache misses. *Accuracy* is defined as the fraction of prefetches that are useful, i.e., they result in cache hits. Figure 5.17 illustrates the difference between coverage and accuracy. And finally, *timeliness* measures how early the prefetches arrive, which determines whether the full cache miss latency is hidden, or only a part of the miss latency is hidden. An ideal prefetching technique should exhibit

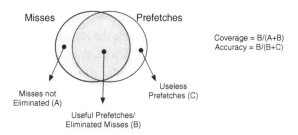

Figure 5.17: Illustration of prefetching coverage vs. accuracy.

high coverage so that it eliminates most of the cache misses, high accuracy so that it does not increase memory bandwidth consumption, and timeliness so that most of the prefetches hide the full cache miss latency. Achieving this ideal is a challenge. By aggressively issuing many prefetches, a prefetching technique may achieve a high coverage but low accuracy. By conservatively issuing only prefetches that are highly predictable, a prefetching technique may achieve a high accuracy but a low coverage. Finally, timeliness is also important. If a prefetch is initiated too early, it may pollute the cache, and may be replaced from the cache or prefetch buffer before it is used by the processor. If it is initiated too late, it may not hide the full cache miss latency.

The three metrics (coverage, accuracy, and timeliness) are complete metrics if prefetched blocks are stored in a special storage (called *prefetch buffers*). If on the other hand they are placed directly in the cache, they can cause an extra problem, which requires different metrics to be collected. For example, if a prefetch causes a cache block to be evicted and there is a miss that occurs to that block due to the eviction, then the prefetch is potentially harmful. If the prefetch itself results in a future cache hit, then its harmfulness is offset. Therefore, collecting the statistics on the number of useful vs. useless but harmless vs. useless and harmful prefetching can give good insights into the effectiveness of a prefetching scheme.

In addition to evaluating prefetching schemes based on their performance metrics, they must also be evaluated based on other important measures, such as the cost and complexity of a hardware implementation and whether they require the code to be recompiled.

We will now focus our discussion on basic hardware prefetching techniques since they are the ones that are directly related to the cache design. Based on the type of data access patterns that can be handled, *sequential prefetching* detects and prefetches for accesses to contiguous locations. *Stride prefetching* detects and prefetches accesses that are s-cache block apart between consecutive accesses, where s is the amount of the stride. Therefore, an s-strided access pattern would produce an address trace of $A, A + s, A + 2s, \ldots$. Note that sequential prefetching is a stride prefetching where $s \leq 1$. With large cache block sizes in current processor architectures, sequential prefetching is often sufficient in detecting most strided access patterns.

There are different places where prefetching can be initiated and the destination where the prefetched data can be placed. Prefetching can be initiated in the L1 cache level, L2 cache level, L3 cache level, the memory controller, or even in the memory chips to preload DRAM row buffers. Prefetched data is usually stored at the level at which the prefetch is initiated, such as in the prefetch-initiating cache or in a separate prefetch buffer to avoid polluting the cache with prefetched data.

5.4.1 Stride and Sequential Prefetching

Early stride and sequential prefetching studies include the Reference Prediction Table by Chen and Baer [13], and also stream buffers by Jouppi [33]. This section will describe stream buffers scheme, which is attractive due to its simplicity. A stream buffer allows prefetching sequential accesses. A stream buffer is a first in first out (FIFO) buffer, where each entry contains a cache-block worth of data, an address (or tag) of the block, and an "available" bit. To prefetch for multiple streams in parallel, more than one stream buffer can be used, in which each buffer prefetches from one stream.

On a cache access, the cache is checked for a match. The head entries of stream buffers are also checked in parallel to that (or alternatively, after the cache access is found to suffer a cache miss). If the requested block is found in the cache, no action on the stream buffers is performed. If the block is not found in the cache, but found at the head of a stream buffer, the block is moved into the cache. The next entry in the stream buffer now becomes the head entry, and the freed up slot triggers a prefetching request to an address sequential to address in the last entry of the buffer. If the block is not found in both the cache and all the stream buffers, a new stream buffer is allocated. The block's successors are prefetched to fill the stream buffers.

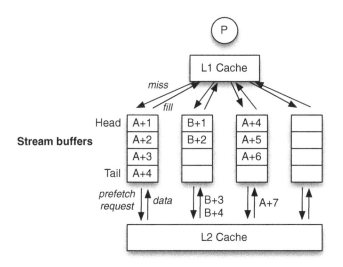

Figure 5.18: Illustration for stream buffer operation.

Figure 5.18 illustrates the stream buffer operation with four stream buffers. Suppose that the block addresses from access streams are $A, B, A+3, B+1, \ldots$ and that the cache and stream buffers do not contain any of the blocks initially. The access to A results in a cache miss, which results in allocating a stream buffer for A's successors, which are $A+1, A+2, A+3, A+4$. The figure shows all A's successors have been prefetched into the stream buffer. Similarly, the access to B results in a cache miss, and a stream buffer is allocated for $B's$ successors $B+1, B+2, B+3, B+4$. The figure shows that currently, only blocks $B+1$ and $B+2$ have been stored in the stream buffer, while $B+3$ and $B+4$ are still being prefetched. Next, for an access to $A+3$, the cache and the head entries of the stream buffers are checked for a match. Since there is no match, a new stream buffer is allocated for $A+3$'s successors $A+4, A+5, A+6, A+7$. However, an access to $B+1$

will find a match in the stream buffer, and $B + 1$ will be moved into the L1 cache, and the freed entry is used to prefetch the successor of the tail entry.

Note that now we have two stream buffers allocated for A's successors and $A + 3$'s successors, and some entries overlap in two stream buffers ($A + 4$). This is caused by the inability to identify a stride of 2 for A's stream. In fact, stream buffers cannot handle any non-sequential accesses efficiently, including non-unit strides ($s > 1$) or even a negative sequential accesses ($s = -1$). For non-unit stride accesses, each access could result in a stream buffer miss because the address is only compared to the head entries of the buffers. Not only does this produce overlapping entries, a single stream may also occupy several stream buffers. To overcome that, Palacharla and Kessler [45] suggested two techniques to enhance the stream buffers: allocation filters and a non-unit stride detection mechanism. The filter waits until there are two consecutive misses for the same stream before allocating a stream buffer, making sure that a stream buffer is only allocated for strided accesses.

Overall, prefetching for sequential and strided accesses can be achieved with relatively simple hardware. Several recent machines, such as Intel Pentium 4 and IBM Power4 architectures implement a hardware prefetcher that is similar to stream buffers at the L2 cache level [25, 27]. For example, the L2 cache in the Power4 can detect up to eight sequential streams. The L2 cache block is 128 bytes, and therefore, a sequential stream detector can catch most strided accesses. On a cache miss to a block in the L2 cache, the fifth successor block is prefetched. This is similar to 4-entry stream buffers. The L3 cache block is four times larger than the L2 (512 bytes), and therefore it only prefetches the next successive block on an L3 miss. Since the prefetching is based on physical addresses, prefetching of a stream is terminated when a page boundary is encountered. However, for applications with long sequential accesses, continuity in the prefetching can be supported if large pages are used.

■ *Did you know?*

In embedded systems which are used for processing tasks with hard real-time constraints, predictability in the worst-case execution time is paramount as missing the deadline of a task processing will result in catastrophic consequences. Such systems often strip out components that contribute to execution time variation that is hard to predict, such as virtual memory, branch prediction, and also caches. Since the number of cache misses and the additional execution time due to cache misses are hard to bound, these systems replace them with software-managed storage called scratchpad memory. *Various policies that are managed by hardware in caches are managed by software, including placement policy, replacement policy, allocation policy, and write back policy. Transfer to and from the scratchpad memory may involve an on-chip DMA engine. Since the software knows exactly which data access will be to the scratchpad memory as opposed to the main memory, it can bound the worst case execution time much more tightly. However, the complexity in managing the scratchpad memory is quite high, and increases when the applications grow in complexity. Therefore, some embedded systems include both caches and scratchpad memory.*

5.4.2 Prefetching in Multiprocessor Systems

In a multiprocessor system, ensuring that prefetching does not cause unintended negative performance impact is harder. A block that is prefetched by a processor too early may be useless since it may be stolen by another processor before the processor has a chance to access the block. In the mean time, the prefetched block has already evicted another block that may be more useful. Therefore, in multiprocessor systems, prefetching must ensure that a block is prefetched not only sufficiently early to hide the latency of future misses, but also not too early that it ends up stolen by other processors. In a single processor environment, prefetching that is too early is risky if the cache capacity is limited because the prefetched block may evict a more useful block (this does not happen if the cache is large enough to keep both blocks). In multiprocessor systems, even when the cache is really large, prefetching too early can still hurt performance by unnecessarily stealing a cache block from another processor, which may have to steal it back.

5.5   Cache Design in Multicore Architecture

Cache architecture has grown a lot more complex in current multicore processors, adapting to the demand for low access time and large capacity, and enabled by growing transistor budgets. To have a framework for discussion, it is useful to distinguish between physical versus logical organization of caches.

Physical organization refers to how caches are organized on the die, i.e., whether a core and a cache are directly connected physically. If the cache can be directly accessed by all cores, the cache is said to be *physically united*.   In some cases, the cache may consist of one or multiple banks. As long as all the banks are connected directly to all cores, we refer to such a cache as a united cache. If, however, the cache is physically divided into parts where each part is assigned to a core, and a core is only directly connected to the part of the cache that is assigned to it, we will refer to the cache as *physically distributed*.   Each part may consist of one or more banks. The terms united and distributed are used in order to distinguish a cache's physical organization from its logical organization. Logical organization refers to which caches a core is allowed to access, i.e., whether a core is allowed to access the entire cache, or only the part of the cache that is coupled to the core. If the entire cache can be accessed by any core, then the cache is said to be *logically shared*.   A physically distributed cache can be aggregated to form a logically shared, for example by allowing a core to access any part of the cache even parts that are not directly connected to the core. If only a part of the cache is allowed to be accessed by a core, then the cache is said to be *logically private*.   A logically private cache configuration can be built on top of a physically distributed cache by allowing a core to access only the part of the cache that is directly connected to it. A logically private cache configuration can also be built on top of a physically united cache by dividing the cache into partitions where a core is allowed to access only a certain partition. The distinction between physical and logical organization is quite important to avoid ambiguity when discussing various cache organization choices for a multicore architecture.

We will first discuss the physical organization of caches in Section 5.6. We will discuss how a physically united cache is a suitable design for a small-scale multicore, but is increasingly difficult to scale to a larger scale multicore, due to the cost of directly interconnecting a large number of cores and a large number of cache banks. In Section 5.7, we will discuss various logical organization choices for united caches. In one option, we can let the logical organization exactly follow the physical organization, which is a simple approach. In another option, we can aggregate the entire caches to form a single large shared cache. We introduce a concept called tile associativity that defines which tiles a block address can map to. We will show how the arrangement of tiles in forming tile associativity determines the physical proximity of data from cores. We will also discuss an alternative configuration that falls in between physical and shared logical configuration. This hybrid configuration has several attractive features. We will also discuss some techniques to alleviate the main drawback of a logically shared cache, i.e., the large distance between data and cores, by allowing blocks to be replicated. On the other hand, some techniques have also attempted to alleviate the main drawback of logically private caches, i.e., the lack of capacity sharing, by allowing neighboring caches to share their cache capacity.

5.6 Physical Cache Organization

5.6.1 United Cache Organization

Early multicore designs relied on a united cache organization. For example, IBM's first dual-core architecture, IBM Power4, connects two processor cores with a united L2 cache. Newer multicore systems such as AMD quad core and Intel Nehalem, use distributed L2 caches backed up by a large united L3 cache.

In the IBM Power4 chip, the L2 cache is fairly large, so it is split into three banks, with each bank having the capacity of 0.5 MB. The L2 cache is united, hence each core is connected directly to all cache banks. To achieve fast access for all cores to all cache banks, a crossbar is used to interconnect cores with cache banks. A crossbar has a set of buses that directly connect each core with all cache banks. It allows cores to access different banks simultaneously. Only when two cores access the same bank, their accesses collide and have to be serialized.

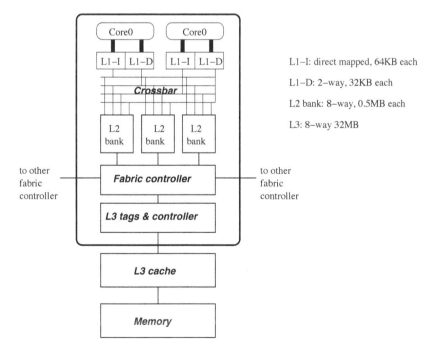

Figure 5.19: High-level diagram of a dual-core chip architecture similar to IBM Power4.

To implement a crossbar needed in the united cache configuration shown in Figure 5.19, multiple buses may be used. We can use one address bus per core that connects to all banks, one data bus per core that connects to all banks to send a block value from a core's L1 cache to the L2 cache, and one data bus for each L2 cache bank that connects to all cores' L1 caches to send a block value from the L2 cache to an L1 cache. Hence, the total number of buses scales with the sum of the number of cores and the number of L2 cache banks. In addition, the length of each bus also scales with the number of cores or number of L2 cache banks. Hence, the complexity of a crossbar scales quadratically with the number of cores and L2 cache banks.

Most of the wires in a crossbar's buses can be implemented in the metal layers of the chip, possibly on top of memory arrays. Thus, some components of the crossbar do not necessarily take much die area overhead. However, some components must still be implemented on the silicon. For example, each bus has an arbiter, a queue, and possibly repeaters. These components are implemented in silicon, and they take up a larger die area when the buses become longer. Thus, a unique characteristic of a multicore architecture is that the cores, caches, and interconnection compete for the same die area (for quantification of this aspect, readers are referred to [36]). Scaling the crossbar to a large number of cores will essentially reduce the die area available to implement the cores themselves and the cache.

In addition to the complexity of providing a crossbar, a large united cache suffers from a high access latency, due to the physical length of wires that form the cache structure (e.g., word lines, bit lines). Even for a single processor system, it has been demonstrated that the performance of applications improves when the cache is broken into smaller banks, allowing the applications to access cache banks that are close by with a low access latency; only accesses to far-away cache banks incur a high access latency [35].

Overall, the high-access latency of a large united cache and the complexity of interconnecting a large number of cores and cache banks put a limitation on the scalability of a united cache. This leads to an alternative physical organization of distributed caches.

5.6.2 Distributed Cache Organization

In light of the inherent non-scalability of a physically united cache, more multicore architectures rely less on a physically united L2 cache architecture. As discussed in Chapter 1, a convenient and logical way to scale a multiprocessor system is to move the interconnection down the memory hierarchy. In this case, multicore architectures will likely implement physically distributed L2 caches that are connected together using an interconnection network or backed up by a united L3 cache.

The interconnection of choice depends on the number of cores that are implemented on a single chip. Similar to the scalability issues facing traditional multichip multiprocessors, some medium-scale interconnection network such as rings can be used when the number of cores is still relatively small but is larger than what can be supported using a bus. A larger scale multicore system is likely to use some low-dimensional networks or high-dimensional networks if the number of cores continues to grow. The configuration in which a multicore system uses distributed caches and use point-to-point interconnection is often referred to as tiled multicore architecture because of its regular tile-like layout on the die. Figure 5.20 shows examples of a tile-based multicore architecture with ring and 2-D mesh interconnection. The "R" box in the picture denotes a router. From this point on, we will refer to a section of the L2 cache that is associated with a core as a *cache tile*.

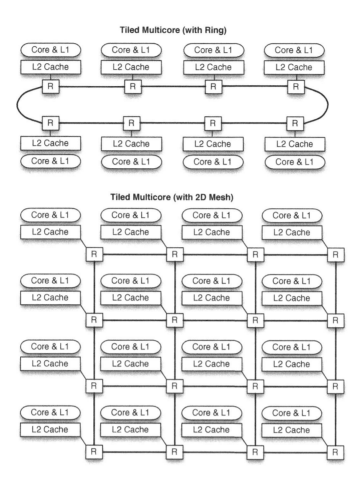

Figure 5.20: Examples of a tiled multicore with a ring (top) and a 2D mesh (bottom) interconnection.

5.6.3 Hybrid United+Distributed Cache Organization

There are possible physical cache organizations that fall in between distributed and united cache configurations. For example, we may have a group of cores sharing a cache or having distributed caches at the L2 level but the L3 cache is united (Figure 5.21). Backing up distributed L2 caches with a united L3 cache moves the complexity of the interconnection down to the L3 cache that is less frequently accessed than the L2 cache. However, a single large cache will be uniformly slow for all cores to access. In addition, the united L3 cache must now handle cache coherence across L2 caches, so it is relatively complex to design. The L3 cache will act as a transaction serializing point for all requests from the L2 caches. It also broadcasts intervention or invalidation requests to other L2 caches. Overall, a united large L3 cache is a reasonable compromise design, but ultimately it suffers from the scalability and complexity drawbacks of a united cache design.

An alternative design will be the hybrid distributed+united physical cache shown in Figure 5.21. Such a hybrid organization is attractive for several reasons. First, physical sharing is limited to only a few cores, hence the design of each united cache is relatively simple. In addition, since there

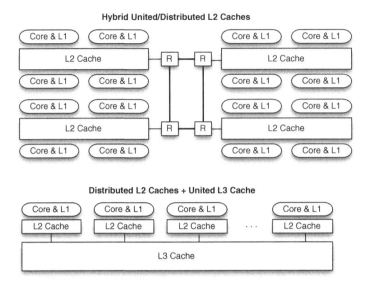

Figure 5.21: Hybrid physical configuration of L2 caches (top) and distributed L2 caches backed up by a united L3 cache (bottom).

are fewer caches, fewer routers and links are needed to interconnect them, allowing data to be sent over the interconnection with a smaller latency. However, there is a limit to this approach. As we include more cores to share an L2 cache, the L2 cache becomes too large to offer small access latencies to the cores that share it. Eventually, if the L2 cache is too large, the overall performance is degraded. The reason for this is shown in Figure 5.22. The figure plots the overall cache access latency as a function of cache size. The x-axis starts with a very small united cache on the left, thus many of such caches are needed for a given number of cores on a chip. As we go to the right along the x-axis, the united cache size increases, thus each cache is shared by more cores, and fewer of them are needed to achieve the same aggregate cache capacity. There are three curves in the figure. One curve, labeled *access latency*, shows the time to access one united cache. As the cache becomes bigger, the access time increases due to the large structure of the cache. Another curve shows *routing latency*, representing the time to route request and response on the interconnection network. As each united cache becomes larger, fewer of them are needed for the same aggregate capacity, which reduces the number of routers in the interconnection network. As the number of routers is reduced, the average distance from a core to a cache, in terms of the number of network hops, declines as well, which reduces the total routing latency. The total cache access latency is the addition of each cache's access latency and the routing latency. The figure shows that the total cache access latency declines then increases as the size of each cache increases. Thus, there is an optimum cache size beyond which the total cache access latency degrades.

To summarize, a single large united cache shared by all cores does not provide scalability as the number of cores on a chip increases in the future, due to the increasing complexity, die area overhead, and a high access time. Distributed caches are more amenable to scaling. However, if each cache is too small, the resulting routing latency may become too high. It is important to size the cache in such a way to optimize for the total cache latency, which includes access latency of

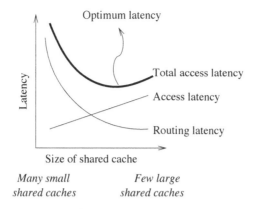

Figure 5.22: Total cache access time as a function of the size of a cache tile in a tiled multicore.

each cache tile as well as the routing latency. This may lead to a hybrid distributed+united cache in which each cache is shared by several cores and the caches are kept coherent.

5.7   Logical Cache Organization

On multicore configurations in which the L2 cache is distributed into tiles associated with different cores, several logical organization choices are possible: shared, private, or hybrid. In a logically shared configuration, the cache tiles are treated as components of a single large cache. In this case, each tile is made accessible by any core and can be used to store data for any core. Such a shared cache organization was not feasible to implement in traditional multiprocessor systems because caches are located in different chips and hence accessing a remote cache is very expensive. In a multicore architecture, on the other hand, accessing a remote (non-local) cache tile can be performed relatively quickly as all the cache tiles are located on a single die.

There are many ways to aggregate cache tiles into a logically shared cache, as illustrated in Figure 5.23. The figure shows a 4×4-tiled multicore, physically with private L2 cache tiles assigned to different cores. One possible logical cache organization is to keep them private, in line with the physical organization. With a private cache configuration, each core can only place blocks that it fetches on its own cache tile. A block may be replicated at other cache tiles if other cores access the block too, and their values are kept consistent by the cache coherence protocol.

Alternatively, although the L2 cache tiles are distributed, they can be aggregated to form a large shared L2 cache in various ways. For example, we can organize the tiles to form a 1-way tile-associative shared cache. With this configuration, given an address, a hash function determines which tile the address maps to. This hash function is static, so to find a particular block, a core knows exactly which tile to look up. The lookup request is routed through the interconnection network. Note that an important concept to consider is how close the data can be found relative to the core that accesses the data, which is referred to in literature as *distance locality*. The drawback of a logically shared configuration is that the distance locality is quite poor for a large multicore system. For example, in the figure, if the core that accesses a data block is core 0, and the data block maps to tile 15, the network distance (assuming a two-dimensional mesh) is 6 hops. To get a message across, each router likely introduces at least a 3-cycle delay, corresponding to the number of pipeline stages implemented in the router. The transmission time depends on the link width, which is likely 1 to 2 cycles for a cache block worth of data. Hence 6 network hops will take at least $6 \times 3 + 1 = 19$ additional cycles (assuming cut-through routing), and can be as high as $6 \times 5 + 2 = 32$ additional cycles if the routing delay is 5 cycles. Even with three-cycle routing, a worst-case round trip latency when the network runs at half the core frequency will be $2 \times 2 \times 19 = 76$ clock cycles. Thus, accessing a remote cache is expensive in a large multicore with a logically shared cache configuration.

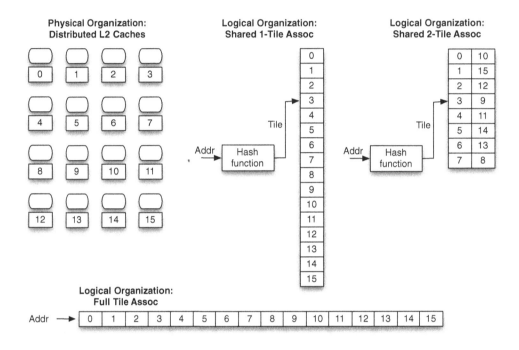

Figure 5.23: Several logical organization choices for distributed caches.

Another possible configuration is to organize the tiles with a higher tile associativity, as illustrated in the figure with a 2-tile associative configuration. In this case, a block can map to any of two cache tiles. For example, a block with address 0 can map to tile 0 or tile 10 with a 2 tile-associative configuration. Note that the tiles that form a tile set appear randomly grouped, e.g., tiles 0 and 10 are in a set, tiles 1 and 15 are in a set, etc. There is a purpose behind the arrangement. While the main purpose of set associativity in a cache is to reduce the number of conflict misses, tile associativity can be used for another purpose: to improve distance locality (i.e., reduce distances to data). Since a data block can be placed in any tile in a tile set, the placement policy can be tailored in such a way to allocate the block in the tile closest to the core that accesses the block. For example, if core 1 accesses a block that maps to a tile set consisting of tile 2 and tile 12, the block can be placed in tile 2, allowing core 1 to access the block with only one network hop. However, if core 14 accesses a block that maps to the same tile set, the block can be placed in tile 12 instead, so that the distance is two network hops, instead of three network hops if the block was stored in tile 2. The decision of which tile a block should be placed in a tile set can be made at placement time, after a cache hit, or even after several cache hits by the same core. For example, if after a block is placed in a cache tile, it is repeatedly accessed by a core that is far away, the block can be migrated to another tile in the same tile set that is closer to the core. Other policies are possible.

In the arrangement shown in the figure, any core can access at least one tile in any tile set with at most three network hops, a huge reduction compared to the six network hops worst case in a 1-tile associative organization. If the grouping of tiles into tile sets is more spatial and less random, the reduction will be a lot smaller. Consider a grouping of consecutive cache tile IDs into sets, i.e., tiles 0 and 1 form a set, 2 and 3 form a set, etc. With such a grouping, the worst case distance from a core to a tile set is as high as 5 network hops.

However, there are drawbacks to tile associativity. The higher the associativity, the more tiles must be checked simultaneously to locate a data block. This consumes additional power, as well as incurs a higher network traffic compared to a single tile-associativity. Such drawbacks can be mitigated to some extent by requiring a core to look up the closest tile in a tile set first, and look up farther tiles only when the block is not found on the closest tile. However, an L2 cache miss will still have caused multiple lookups. In addition, even with a higher tile associativity or with spread-out tile arrangement, good distance locality is still difficult to achieve in a parallel program in which many threads access a single data item. Wherever the data item is placed will be quite far away from some of the threads. In such a case, good distance locality can only be achieved by replicating a block.

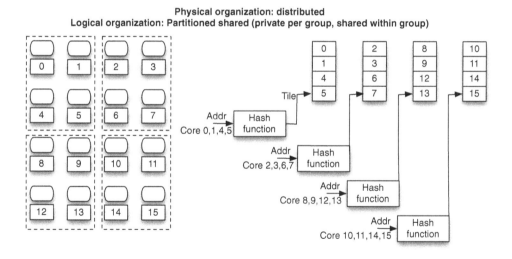

Figure 5.24: Partitioned shared cache organization.

Note that it is possible to have a hybrid private and shared cache configuration, as illustrated in Figure 5.24. In the figure, tiles are partitioned into groups, where each group of four cache tiles are logically shared. However, each group is private, and coherence is maintained between groups. With coherence, a block can be replicated in different tile groups. However, within a group, there can only be one copy of the block.

Figure 5.25 visualizes the differences between various logical cache organizations in a multicore architecture: private, shared, shared with tile associativity, and hybrid. On the x-axes is distance locality, a measure of how close data is physically to the processor using it. On the y-axes is capacity and fragmentation, a measure of how much aggregate capacity is available (capacity) and how much of the aggregate capacity is accessible to a processor core (fragmentation). On one extreme is the private organization, where each processor can only access one cache tile (worst fragmentation). If an application running on a core has a working set that exceeds the local cache tile size, the application will suffer from a high number of capacity misses. At the same time, there may be excess cache capacity elsewhere for various reasons, for example there may not be any threads running there, or there are threads running there but they have a small working set. Such excess cache capacity cannot be donated to other cores, hence the worst fragmentation. Furthermore, data may be replicated at different tiles, meaning that the aggregate capacity to hold unique data declines as replicas occupy some capacity. However, data can always be found in the local cache tile directly connected to the processor, hence it has the best distance locality.

On the other extreme is shared cache configuration. It has the best (or least) cache fragmentation because each processor has access to the aggregate cache capacity. It also has the best aggregate capacity because no data is replicated. However, data may be spread out over many tiles, meaning that data is on average far away from each processor, hence it has the worst distance locality.

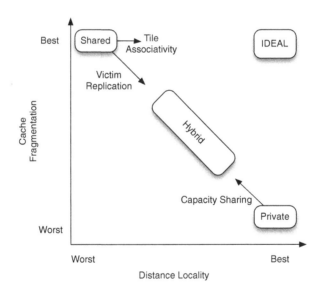

Figure 5.25: Comparing the merits and drawbacks of logical organization choices for distributed caches.

Adding tile associativity to a shared cache configuration improves its distance locality as data can be placed in a tile nearer to the processor requesting it, while cache fragmentation and capacity remain unchanged. The cost of tile associativity is latency and power consumption for locating data, as multiple cache tiles may have to be looked up. For a multicore system with a low core count (e.g., 4-16 cores), the poor distance locality of a shared cache may be tolerable. However, for a higher core count, say 64 cores or more, a shared cache configuration's poor distance locality imposes a severe cost. First, most data will be located in remote tiles, very little of it will be found in the local tile. Secondly, having a large fraction of cache accesses going to remote cache tiles is wasteful in terms of the average cache hit latency, high network traffic, and high energy use due to the high traffic. Hence, it is likely that a large core count multicore system will not use a shared cache organization.

In between the two extremes is a hybrid configuration, where the cache tiles are partitioned and processors within a partition share either one or multiple cache tiles. The processors cannot access remote cache tiles. It has better cache fragmentation than private because the cache tiles in a partition aggregate their capacity for use by any processor in the partition. It has better aggregate capacity than private because data is only replicated across partitions. It also has better distance locality than shared because data is contained in the local partition. Therefore, a partitioned shared configuration is likely to emerge as a relatively attractive alternative compared to fully private or fully shared configurations. Some capacity sharing is allowed within a group, removing the much of the capacity fragmentation problem. At the same time, if a group is relatively small, e.g., 4 tiles, the distance locality will still be good, as data is never far away from any core in a group, and can be found at up to two network hops away.

Finally, there are some techniques that improve upon the shared configuration as well as the private configuration. One of them is *victim replication*, an attempt to improve the distance locality of shared cache configuration by allowing blocks mapped to a remote cache tile to be replicated in the local cache tile. Specifically, blocks evicted from an inner cache (victims) may be temporarily cached in the local cache tile. Such replication reduces aggregate cache capacity but improves distance locality. It also introduces a new coherence problem that needs to be addressed. For the private configuration case, *capacity sharing* is a technique that allows blocks evicted from the local cache tile to be allocated in a remote cache tile. Later when the processor requests for the block again, it can find it in a remote cache tile rather than having to fetch it from an outer memory hierarchy level. Capacity sharing reduces cache fragmentation at the expense of distance locality. We will look into these techniques in greater detail.

5.7.1 Hashing Function

For a shared cache organization, a hashing function maps a block to a cache to a cache tile or to a tile set. The hashing function needs to be simple and easy to generate, and at the same time should be absence of uneven distribution of blocks into tiles. Simple hashing functions that interleave block or page addresses across cache tiles should not be used, as they suffer from pathological behavior, where some sets are utilized but others are not. Figure 5.26 illustrates an example.

Figure 5.26(a) shows that with block interleaving, four bits in the address are used to index a tile in the 16-tile system. Unfortunately, the same bits are also used for indexing a set in a tile. Suppose four bits for indexing a cache tile have a value of "0100". In the tile itself, the same bits are used to index a set, hence only a certain group of sets are indexable with an index value containing "0100". Other sets are not indexable at all. Similarly, page interleaving may produce a pathological hashing as well (Figure 5.26(b)), depending on the number of sets on a cache tile versus the size of a page. For example, if a cache tile has a 512KB size, 8-way associativity, and 64B block size, and a page has 4KB size, then the set index contains $\frac{512KB}{8 \times 64} = 10$ bits beyond the block offset bits (i.e., bit 6 to bit 15), whereas the tile index contains 4 bits beyond the page offset bits (i.e., bit 12 to bit 15). Hence, they overlap by three bits.

Figure 5.26(c) illustrates the selection of higher order bits from the address that avoids the overlap problem. However, it is well known that higher order bits do not vary as much as lower

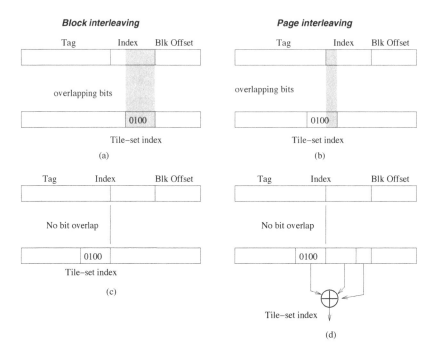

Figure 5.26: Bad tile hashing function due to block interleaving (a) and page interleaving (b), an improved hashing function (c), and an improved hashing function with bit randomization (d).

order bits because a single value in higher order bits corresponds to a large address region. Hence, it is possible that there are only a few distinct values used by a program if we use higher order bits as the tile index, which implies non-uniform use of tiles. Thus, it may be beneficial to spread them out further by XOR-ing the higher order bits with lower order bits in order to produce more combinations of tile index values (Figure 5.26(d)).

■ *Did you know?*

Note that if the address-to-tile hashing function is exposed to the operating system (OS), the OS may be able to improve distance locality by allocating pages that are used by a core to page frames that map to the tiles that are near to the core. Such an approach relies on page coloring in which page frames are assigned colors where each color corresponds all page frames that map to a particular tile. The OS page allocator can be modified to allocate a new page on a page frame that has the same color as the tile from which the page fault occurs [14]. This approach can significantly improve the distance locality of a logically shared cache. It can also be used to manage the cache capacity assigned to a core, by spreading data across several neighboring cache tiles. One drawback to this approach is that if for some reason a thread migrates to a different tile, the distance locality degrades, unless all pages of the thread are moved to frames that have a different color. However, moving a page in the main memory is a very expensive operation as it involves a large amount of memory copying, page table modification, and TLB shootdown.

5.7.2   Improving Distance Locality of Shared Cache

We have discussed how shared cache configuration in a large multicore suffers from the distance locality problem. We have also discussed how a hybrid private+shared cache can improve the distance locality quite significantly. However, there are more advanced solutions targeted to improve the distance locality of a shared cache configuration in a tiled multicore.

One observation for a shared cache is that distance locality is the outcome of not being able to replicate a block. Hence, if a block maps to a cache tile that is far away from a core, the core must retrieve the block from that faraway tile every time it misses on the block. If a core is allowed to replicate the block in its local cache tile, then distance locality is greatly improved. While replication is automatic in a private cache configuration as it is allowed by the cache coherence protocol, allowing replication in a shared cache requires us to support a new mechanism. This mechanism can come in different forms.

One example mechanism to replicate data in a shared cache in order to improve distance locality is *victim replication* (VR) [67]. In VR, the local L2 cache tile is allowed to act as the victim tile of a core's L1 cache. A block that is fetched from a remote L2 cache tile is stored in the core's L1 cache. If the block is evicted from the L1 cache, it is stored in the local L2 cache as a victim. This is performed without the knowledge of the *home* tile, i.e., the tile to which a block address maps. When later the core accesses the block again, it will suffer from an L1 cache miss. At that time, it should first check if the local L2 cache keeps a replica of the block. If so, there is no need to fetch the block from the home tile. It can just retrieve the block from its local L2 cache, invalidate it from the L2 cache, and place the block in the L1 cache.

Replication can introduce a data coherence problem that has to be handled correctly. To ensure coherent view of replicated data, a cache coherence protocol is needed to at least propagate a change of value in one cache to other caches that keep a copy of the block. For example, when a dirty L1 cache block is evicted, the block can still be replicated at the local L2 cache, but the copy at the home tile must be updated with the new value. Write propagation due to a remote writer must also be ensured. For example, when a remote core wants to write to a block, it sends the request to the home tile, which then sends an invalidation message to all L1 caches that may have a copy of the block. When an L1 cache receives this invalidation message, it must not just check its own tag. Since it is possible that the block is replicated at the local cache, it must also check the local L2 cache tag to invalidate the block.

There is also an issue of how to manage the use of L2 cache space between local blocks versus replica. VR uses a policy in which to make room for a new block (either real or replica), the victim block is selected from the local L2 cache based on the following priority order: (1) an invalid block, (2) a global block that is not being shared by cores, and (3) another replica.

One drawback of allowing a victim block to be replicated in the local L2 cache is that there is competition for L2 cache capacity between victim blocks and regular data blocks. Such capacity contention likely results in an increased local L2 cache capacity miss rate. Thus, VR attempts to reduce cache hit latency (by converting remote hits to local hits) at the expense of increased cache miss rate. Since a cache miss latency is usually much more expensive than a remote hit latency, VR must be able to convert many remote hits into local hits for each additional cache miss that it incurs. Due to this property, one may think of strategies to distinguish between different types of data in order to assess which data gives the most benefit from distance locality with the least drawback from increased capacity misses.

An example study that proposed selective replication *adaptive selective replication* (ASR) [6] found that for commercial workloads, there is a type of data that is shared by many threads but is mostly read only. Such read-only data was found to have a small capacity footprint but causes a disproportionally large number of misses. Thus, shared read-only blocks should be the most important candidate for replication, in comparison to shared read-write blocks.

Note that replication techniques for a shared cache configuration allow a shared cache to evolve to absorb some of the advantages of the private cache configuration, namely good distance locality. However, at the same time, some of the disadvantages of the private cache configuration are also absorbed. For example, replication invariably reduces the aggregate cache capacity as in the private cache configuration.

5.7.3   Capacity Sharing in the Private Cache Organization

In the previous subsection, we discussed how an important limitation of a logically shared cache configuration, namely poor distance locality, could be addressed by selective replication. In this subsection, we will discuss ideas to address main limitations of the private cache configuration, namely cache capacity fragmentation due to the lack of capacity sharing.

The lack of capacity sharing can cause a significant system performance loss in a multicore system, especially when a diverse mix of sequential programs run on different cores. Some programs may over-utilize the local L2 cache (due to their large working set), while others may under-utilize the local L2 cache (due to their small working set). Recent trends in enterprise IT toward service-oriented computing, server consolidation, and virtualization, help create an environment in which increasingly a diverse set of applications run on a single CMP.

Such uneven cache utilization can result in a significant loss in the overall performance, due to the inability of the programs that require a large cache capacity from utilizing the excess cache capacity that may exist at the neighboring tiles. For example, with 512KB private L2 caches, several SPEC CPU2006 benchmarks (e.g., namd, milc, povray, libquantum) suffer almost no decrease in performance when half of their private L2 cache capacity is taken away, indicating a significant amount of excess cache capacity. Without capacity sharing, such excess cache capacity cannot be donated to other cores which need more cache capacity.

Recognizing the need to provide capacity sharing in private caches, prior work, such as, cooperative caching (CC) [11] and dynamic spill receive (DSR) [48], have proposed capacity sharing mechanisms. CC allows each core to spill an evicted block to any other private cache on-chip, if the block is not already replicated. While this allows capacity sharing, allowing any core to spill into other caches regardless of the temporal locality of the application running in the core may produce an unwanted effect of polluting other caches without providing much performance improvement to the application, when the application has little temporal locality. DSR attempts to remove this drawback by distinguishing between applications that can benefit from extra cache capacity beyond that provided by their local L2, versus applications that can tolerate a reduction in L2 cache capacity without much performance loss. The former applications are referred to as spillers and the latter, as receivers. In DSR, only cache blocks evicted by a spiller are allowed to spill into caches belonging to receivers, while receivers, which cannot benefit from additional cache capacity, are not allowed to spill their blocks. In a sense, receiver caches have a new role of being the victim caches of spiller caches.

Both CC and DSR allow remote caches to be treated as the victim cache of the local cache. This reduces the number of off-chip misses. However, in terms of the number of remote cache hits, is it the best policy for managing capacity sharing? Not necessarily. The optimality of treating remote caches as a large victim cache relies on the premise that victim blocks are less likely to be reused by the core than blocks that are currently in the local cache. Interestingly, this premise is not always true, and is often false for spiller applications. This is due to a behavior common in spiller applications in which blocks that were less recently used are more likely to be accessed in the near future. In other words, spillers often exhibit anti-LRU behavior.

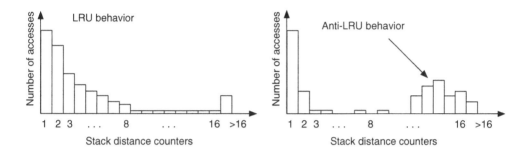

Figure 5.27: Different shapes of stack distance profiles, showing perfect LRU vs. anti-LRU behavior.

To illustrate this anti-LRU temporal reuse pattern behavior, Figure 5.27 shows two different shapes of stack distance profiles. The x-axis shows the cache ways sorted based on their recency of accesses, with an up to 16-way associative cache, and the y-axis shows the percentage of cache accesses that hit in a given stack or recency position. Thus, the leftmost point represents the percentage of accesses to the most recently used blocks. As we go to the right along the x-axis, the figure shows the percentage of accesses to less and less recently used blocks. Finally, the right-most point on the x-axis accounts for all the misses which cannot be avoided by a 16-way associative cache

Suppose the local cache is 8-way associative. If the cache associativity is increased to 16, while keeping the number of sets constant, the cache size also doubles. Applications showing significant cache accesses between the 8th and 16th stack positions can benefit from doubling the cache capacity, since these accesses change from misses to hits. These applications can be categorized as *spillers*. Applications with few or no cache accesses between the 8th and 16th stack positions can be categorized as *receivers*, since they do not gain performance with more cache space, and can potentially donate some portions of their cache space without performance degradation.

Let us now consider the different types of LRU behavior. If an application has a perfect LRU temporal reuse behavior, blocks more recently accessed have a higher likelihood of being accessed again. The stack distance profile will show monotonically decreasing values. This can be sen in the left diagram of Figure 5.27. If an application has an anti-LRU temporal reuse behavior, the stack distance profile does not show monotonically decreasing values. This can be sen in the right diagram of Figure 5.27. Due to the perfect LRU's monotonically decreasing values, it is common for such applications to be receivers, since it is difficult for them to have many accesses beyond the 8th stack position. Similarly, anti-LRU applications tend to be spillers as they often exhibit elevated number of accesses at higher stack positions.

An interesting consequence of the anti-LRU behavior is that because DSR uses remote caches to store victim blocks evicted from the local L2 cache, remote L2 caches strictly hold blocks that are farther away in the recency order than the local L2 cache. The anti-LRU behavior hence ensures that many occurrences of remote cache hits, where blocks in the last eight ways are found in the remote L2 caches.

A large number of remote L2 cache hits is costly from both performance and an energy point of view. A remote hit has a significantly longer latency compared to a local hit due to the coherence action needed for the remote cache to source the block into the local cache. In addition, it also incurs more energy consumption due to the coherence request posted on the interconnection, snooping and tag checking activities in all remote caches, and data transfer across the interconnection. Thus, performance and energy consumption can be improved if one converts the remote cache hits to local cache hits. In order to improve the number of local hits, we can *selectively* place blocks locally vs. remotely when they are brought into the L2 cache from the outer level memory hierarchy. This highlights the importance of placement policy in addition to replacement policy in managing capacity sharing. A recent study [51] investigates how such a selective placement policy can be implemented in hardware to improve local hit rates.

5.8   Case Studies

5.8.1   IBM Power7 Memory Hierarchy

IBM Power7 is a recent multicore processor, rolled out by IBM in 2010. It was manufactured using IBM's 45nm silicon-on-insulator technology using copper interconnects. It contains 1.2 billion transistors and occupies a 567 mm^2 die area. Figure 5.28 shows the photo of the Power7 die, showing eight cores on the die, each core having its own L2 cache. Each core provides four thread contexts through simultaneous multithreading, hence the entire chip can execute 32 threads simultaneously. Due to the need to support a high number of threads running simultaneously, the chip is designed with high cache capacity and high memory bandwidth in mind. The processor is capable of running at 4GHz.

The L3 cache architecture has noteworthy aspects. The L3 cache is split up into tiles/regions accessible to all cores, but at different latencies, with the local L3 region being faster than other regions. Thus, the L3 cache is an example of a physically distributed cache that is logically shared by all the cores. The characteristic that different regions of cache have differing cache access latencies makes the Power7 L3 cache an example of an NUCA (non-uniform cache access latency) cache. The L3 cache also occupies a relatively small die area, even though it has a large capacity of 32MB. This is due to the implementation of the L3 cache using DRAM cells (using embedded DRAM/eDRAM technology), rather than SRAM cells.

The chip also has two memory controllers supporting four DDR3 memory channels. The top and the bottom area of the die contains logic and interconnect that allows it to be connected to other Power7 chips to enable scaling up to 32 sockets.

Let us visit the memory hierarchy in greater details. The L1 instruction and L1 data caches are highly banked (64 banks total) in order to allow simultaneous reads and writes to different banks without resorting to the lower-density many-ported cache design. Each bank has three ports, supporting either two reads or one write per cycle. The L1 data cache has a 32KB capacity, 8-way

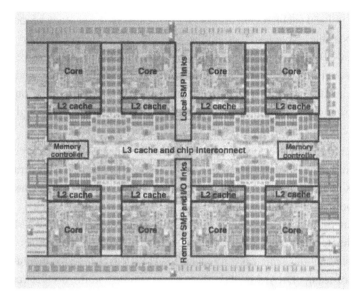

Figure 5.28: IBM Power7 die photo.

associativity, and 128-byte block size. Due to the large block size, a cache fill requires a burst of four transfers from the L2 cache (each 32 bytes is referred to as a sector). The L1 cache uses a write through policy, thus as we have discussed, can use error detection (i.e., parity bits) instead of error correction. It also implies that the L2 cache must use a policy of inclusion to guarantee that a write through from the L1 cache can be satisfied at the L2 cache. The write through is capable of writing between 1 to 16 bytes in a sector of 32 bytes. This conserves L1-to-L2 bandwidth as even a byte write will write through only 1 byte of data. Another bandwidth-conserving feature is the 16-deep 32-byte entry write buffer to absorb and combine writes from the L1 cache.

The L2 cache is physically distributed and is private per core. It has 256KB size, 8-way associativity. It uses a write back policy, thus it conserves bandwidth to the L3 cache but also requires error correction. Parts of the L2 cache is running at half the core clock frequency. The L2 cache also uses a 128-byte cache block size. The consideration for the L2 cache size is driven by several factors. One factor is the wasted cache capacity due to the inclusion policy, which favors a larger L2 cache size. Since the ratio of the L1 data cache of 32KB to the L2 cache of 256KB is 1:8, the wasted cache capacity is 12.5%, which can be lowered further if the L2 cache size is larger but is still acceptable at the current size. Another factor is access latency, at 256KB it is reported that the L2 cache can be accessed in 2 ns, or 8 clock cycles if the clock frequency is 4GHz. Reducing the L2 cache size can reduce the access latency, but in the case of the Power7, it is already quite small. Increasing the L2 cache size may reduce the cache miss rate, but it is less crucial to do so since the L3 cache (access latency of 6ns or 24 clock cycles) backs it up with 32MB capacity. Another factor to consider is the power consumption due to the frequent write through from the L1 cache. A larger L2 cache will consume more power, and this factor favors a smaller L2 cache size. Overall, designing the cache hierarchy requires balancing such competing goals.

The L3 cache consists of eight regions of 4-MB size. The total L3 cache capacity is thus 32MB. This is the first NUCA cache in the IBM Power processor family, where a local L3 cache region requires only 6ns access time while the remote L3 cache regions require 30ns access time. Thus, the ratio of remote to local cache region access is 5:1, indicating the urgency of making as many local region hits as possible. Note also that a typical off-chip DRAM main memory access time is in a similar range (30-60ns) thus remote region cache access is almost as expensive as off-chip DRAM access. However, it offers a much larger access bandwidth (512 GB/sec) and less overall power consumption compared to off-chip DRAM bandwidth (typically providing only a few to tens of GB/sec) and power consumption, thus it plays a crucial role supporting the high number of threads that run on the chip.

Each L3 cache region is 8-way associative. While the data array of a 4MB region is implemented in DRAM, the tag array is implemented in SRAM. Using SRAM for the tag array gives the benefits of faster access and non-destructive read, allowing fast determination of cache hit or miss. Using eDRAM for the data array allows higher density and thus higher capacity. Each eDRAM cell consists of 1 transistor and 1 capacitor, as opposed to 6 transistors in an SRAM cell. According to IBM's own estimate, the overall area of the L3 cache in eDRAM is three times denser than the area required to implement the same capacity using SRAM. In exchange for the much higher capacity, the drawbacks of using eDRAM include slower access time and the need to refresh eDRAM cells periodically, and IBM attempted to mitigate the drawbacks. For example, the refresh latency is hidden using a parallel engine that refreshes unused subarrays in the part of the cache that is being accessed. IBM estimated that the eDRAM dissipates only one fifth of the standby energy of an equivalent SRAM macro [53].

How are the L2 and L3 caches arranged? The L3 cache is not inclusive of the L2 cache, but it is not exclusive either. Thus, it is an example of a NINE (non-inclusive non-exclusive) policy. When a block missed by the L2 cache is found in the L3 cache, the block is allocated in the L2 cache but the copy in the L3 cache is retained. The block may subsequently be evicted out of the L3 cache without invalidating the copy in the L2 cache. A feature common in an exclusive cache is used, where a block evicted from the L2 cache is allocated in the L3 cache, if it is not already there. Recall that a drawback of an exclusive cache is that it is frequently accessed because it has to allocate a line for a block evicted from the inner cache. Frequent accesses to the L3 cache in this case is expensive due to the DRAM operations needed in the L3 cache. Thus, it makes sense to retain a copy of a block in the L3 cache even as the block is allocated in the L2 cache. When the block is evicted from the L2 cache, the L3 cache tag can be checked and if the copy of the block is still there, the block can be evicted from the L2 cache outright, skipping an allocation at the L3 cache.

Figure 5.29 shows the path for cache block fill (shown with dashed arrow lines) and eviction (shown in solid arrow lines). An L1 cache miss fills the block from the L2 cache. If the L2 cache misses as well, it will fetch the block from the L3 cache. If the L3 cache misses, it will fill from the off-chip main memory. Eviction from the L1 cache is silent, since (due to value inclusion) the L2 cache already has the latest copy of the block. A block evicted from the L2 cache will be processed in one of the following ways: it is allocated in the L3 cache (if it is not found in the L3 cache), it updates the block in the L3 cache (if the evicted block is dirty and the block is found in the L3 cache), or it updates the state/directory of the block in the L3 cache tag array and discards the block (if the evicted block is clean and the block is found in the L3 cache).

Recall that the L3 cache is NUCA, with a ratio of 5:1 access time between remote region and local region. This makes it important and profitable to keep local L3 region hit rate higher than remote L3 region hit rate. Thus, it makes sense that the Power7 allocates an evicted L2 block in the local L3 region, rather than a remote L3 cache region. However, if the L2 cache can only use the

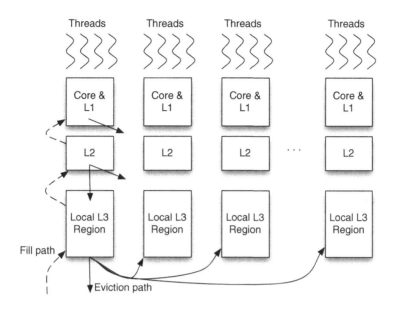

Figure 5.29: IBM Power7 fill and eviction path.

local L3 cache region, then the usage of the L3 cache may become imbalanced where some regions are heavily utilized while others are not. Therefore, Power7 allows movement of blocks between regions of L3 cache (lateral cast-out). When a block is evicted from a local L3 cache region, the block may be allocated in one of the remote L3 regions (based on heuristics). Which L3 region is chosen to host the cast-out and whether it accepts the cast-out are decided by some heuristics as well. In order to prevent the block from moving from a region to another forever, a lateral cast-out block is distinguished from one that is allocated as a result of L2 eviction (local cast-out). Upon a local cast out, a block that is distinguished as lateral cast-out (along with invalid block and block that is already allocated in the local L2 cache) is considered as a second type and is preferred for eviction to make room for the local cast-out block (first type). If no second type blocks are found, then a first type block is selected for eviction. Since second type blocks are always selected for eviction ahead of the first type blocks, over time there may not be second type blocks left. Thus, a mechanism is needed to add to the supply of second type blocks. This is achieved in Power7 by converting LRU blocks among first type blocks to the second type.

Overall, the Power7's memory hierarchy is designed to support the high number of threads that may be running simultaneously. The use of eDRAM in the L3 cache (instead of SRAM) is aimed to provide a large cache capacity to support the threads, at the expense of cache access time. However, designers seem to be genuinely concerned about the performance impact of using eDRAM L3 cache that they took steps in reducing the number of L3 cache accesses. As noted earlier, the L2 cache is inserted between the L1 and L3 cache to filter not only L1 cache misses, but also L1 cache write throughs. Also, when a clean block is evicted from the L2 cache, the L3 cache tag array is checked first in order to avoid updating data in the L3 cache unless the tag check result indicates the necessity. The capacity sharing through lateral cast-out employed at the L3 cache allows threads to share the L3 cache capacity in a fluid manner in order to reduce off-chip memory accesses as much as possible. A main concern is on avoiding the off-chip memory bandwidth becoming the bottleneck for data supply, because the off-chip memory access time is comparable to remote L3 cache region access time.

5.8.2   Comparing AMD Shanghai and Intel Barcelona's Memory Hierarchy

In this case study, we will discuss the design of AMD and Intel quad core processors' memory hierarchy, mainly focusing on the implications of the inclusion policy choice. Note that the treatment of this subject is incomplete without discussing cache coherence policy differences between them. However, since cache coherence is not discussed yet at this point, we will focus the discussion on the inclusion policy and its implication. The discussion in this section is based on results from a thorough experimental study by Hackenberg et al. [21].

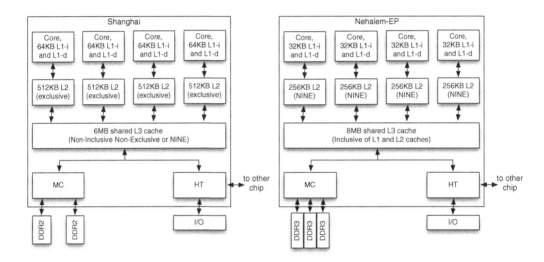

Figure 5.30: AMD Shanghai and Intel Nehalem-EP quad core memory hierarchy.

Figure 5.30 shows the memory hierarchy of the system being compared. The figure shows that both the AMD and Intel quad core chips at the very high level have similar cache configurations, where each core has its own L1 caches and L2 cache. The L1 instruction and data caches are smaller in the Intel at 32KB each, compared to 64KB each in the AMD. All cores share the L3 cache. Memory controller is integrated on chip, as well as a communication hub (Hypertransport in AMD, and QuickPath Interconnect in Intel) that can connect to other chips to increase the size of the system.   Note, however, the L3 caches employ different inclusion policies: non-inclusive non-exclusive (NINE) policy in the AMD, and inclusive in the Intel. The Intel L3 cache inclusiveness extends to cover all blocks in the L1 and the L2 caches.

Let us first focus on the L3 cache and consider the wasted capacity aspect of the policy. The L2 cache size is 512KB in the AMD, therefore the sum of L2 cache capacity for all four cores is 2MB. The L3 cache size is 6MB. If AMD had chosen an inclusive policy, one third of the L3 cache will be used to keep blocks that are cached in the L2 cache, which represents a significant loss of cache capacity. On the other hand, the L2 cache size is 256KB in the Intel, therefore the sum of L2 cache capacity for all four cores is 1MB. The L3 cache size is 8MB. If Intel chooses an inclusive L3 cache (it does), the wasted cache capacity is only one eighth, which is much more acceptable compared to the AMD. Note that the AMD uses a NINE policy, rather than an exclusive policy, therefore the L3 cache will keep some blocks that are also cached in the L2. Thus, the AMD will suffer some wasted capacity as well, but less than one third that would have been the case with an inclusive policy. Recall that an exclusive policy requires much higher bandwidth connecting the L2 and L3 caches (and there are four L2 caches), and a NINE policy may achieve a good compromise between the wasted capacity problem and constraining the bandwidth demand between the L2 caches and the L3 cache.

Let us look at the implications of the inclusion policy on other aspects of performance. Suppose that the core suffers from an L1 cache and L2 cache miss. The miss then goes to the L3 cache, and suppose it also misses in the L3 cache. In the case of an inclusive L3 cache, an L3 miss also implies that the data block does not reside in any of the L1 or L2 caches. Thus, for an inclusive L3 cache, the request can be forwarded directly to the memory controller. On the other hand, for a NINE L3 cache, even when the L3 cache misses, the block may reside in a different L2 cache. While in some cases the request can still be forwarded to the memory controller, in other cases the block may have been written in an L2 cache which becomes the only cache that holds valid value of the block. Therefore, absence of more advanced filtering mechanisms, the L3 cache has to probe all the L2 cache tags, before it can forward the miss to the memory controller. In [21], it was reported that the latency for the case described above is 65ns for the Intel, but it is higher at 77ns for the AMD. Furthermore, with a NINE L3 cache, every L3 cache miss requires a probe to all L2 cache tags and L1 cache tags (if the L2 cache is not inclusive of L1 caches as well). This means there is an increased occupancy for L1 and L2 cache controllers, which must be taken into account in design. In an inclusive cache, all L3 cache misses go directly to the memory controller without probing other L1 and L2 caches.

Let us now discuss the L2 cache design. The AMD uses an exclusive policy, while the Intel uses a NINE policy. While the Intel achieves an L2 cache read bandwidth of 31 GB/sec, the AMD achieves a read bandwidth of only 21.5 GB/sec. This is likely affected by the fact that an exclusive L2 cache has to be accessed twice on each L1 cache miss: once to fetch a block from the L2 cache, and another time to allocate the block evicted from the L1 cache as a result of the L1 cache miss. In contrast, a NINE L2 cache is only accessed once when an L1 cache miss occurs. The AMD compensates for this by providing larger L1 caches (to reduce L1 miss rates) as well as using more read ports for the L1 cache (two 128-bit read ports versus the Intel's one 128-bit port). This results in a higher L1 data cache read bandwidth (79.9 GB/sec in the AMD compared 41.3 GB/sec in the Intel).

5.9   Exercises

Worked Problems

1. **Average access time**. Suppose a processor has an L1 cache and an L2 cache. The L1 cache access time is 1ns, the L2 cache access time is 9ns, and the L2 miss penalty is 90ns. The average workload suffers miss rates of 10% at the L1 caches and 20% at the L2 cache. The L2 miss rate is computed as the number of L2 cache misses divided by the number of L2 cache accesses.

   (a) Compute the average access time (AAT).

   (b) Suppose that as the L2 cache size is doubled (everything else kept the same), and the L2 cache miss rate decreases to 10%. What is the maximum L2 cache access time such that AAT decreases, compared to before doubling the L2 cache size?

   (c) What is the CPI, if 30% of all instructions are memory reference instructions (loads and stores), and the CPI on an ideal cache is 0.5. An ideal cache is one that has zero-cycle access latency and has a miss rate of 0%. The processor clock frequency is 2 GHz.

   Answer:

   (a) $AAT = 1 + 0.1 \times 9 + 0.1 \times 0.2 \times 90 = 3.7$ ns.

   (b) $AAT' = 1 + 0.1 \times x + 0.1 \times 0.1 \times 90 = 1.9 + 0.1x$. If we require that $AAT' < AAT$ then $1.9 + 0.1x < 3.7$, which means the access latency of the new L2 cache has to be lower than 18 ns.

   (c) The clock cycle time of a 2 GHz processor is 0.5ns. Thus, 3.7ns = 7.4 clock cycles. $CPI = CPI_{ideal} + frac_{mem} \times AAT = 0.5 + 0.3 \times 7.4 = 2.72$.

2. **Cache replacement policy**. Suppose that you have a 4-way associative cache. In one of the sets of the cache, you see a stream of accesses to the following block addresses: A B C D E A G H F G G C D F G E B A. Determine whether each of the access would result in a cache hit, a cache miss, or a cache miss and replacement. Show what block is replaced for each of the following replacement policies: LRU, OPT, FIFO, and Pseudo-LRU. For Belady's, assume that after the stream, future accesses are going to be G F A C D B E. For the pseudo LRU, suppose initially that all bits are zero. Use the following notation: "H" for hit, "M" for miss, "MR-x" for miss and replace block x.

Answer:

Accessed Blk	LRU	Pseudo-LRU	FIFO	OPT
A	M	M	M	M
B	M	M	M	M
C	M	M	M	M
D	M	M	M	M
E	MR-A	MR-A	MR-A	MR-B
A	MR-B	MR-C	MR-B	H
G	MR-C	MR-B	MR-C	MR-A
H	MR-D	MR-D	MR-D	MR-D
F	MR-E	MR-E	MR-E	MR-H
G	H	H	H	H
G	H	H	H	H
C	MR-A	MR-A	MR-A	H
D	MR-H	MR-F	MR-G	MR-C
F	H	MR-H	H	H
G	H	H	MR-H	H
E	MR-C	MR-C	MR-F	H
B	MR-D	MR-D	MR-C	MR-E
A	MR-F	MR-F	MR-D	MR-D

3. **Cache replacement and indexing**.

   (a) Is it possible for a direct-mapped cache to achieve a lower miss rate than a fully-associative cache with LRU replacement policy? Provide a proof for your answer.

   (b) Suppose that you have a cache with n sets, and the block size is b. Now suppose you run a program that shows striding accesses with a stride of s starting from address 0. That is, the addresses generated would be $0, s, 2s, 3s, 4s, \ldots$. If $n = 32$, $b = 8$ bytes, and $s = 32$ bytes, identify which sets of the cache would be more heavily utilized than others?

   (c) Suppose that instead of using a number of sets that is a power of two, we switch to a number of sets that is prime, i.e., $n = 31$. Can you identify which sets of the cache would be more heavily utilized than others? Explain your observation.

Answer:

   (a) Yes. For example, when a cache with 2 blocks and the access pattern is A, B, C, A, B, C, and so on. Suppose that A and C map to set 0 (for a direct-mapped) cache) and B maps to set 1 (for a direct mapped cache). For a direct-mapped cache, all accesses to B will be cache hits, while all accesses to A and C will be cache misses. Hence we have a 33% hit rate. For a fully-associative LRU cache, we have 0% hit rate because all blocks map to the same set.

   (b) The sets that are heavily used are set 0, 4, 8, 12, 16, 20, 24, 28, and back to 0, 4, 8, 12, 16, 20, 24, 28, and so on. Other sets are not used at all.

(c) The sequence of sets that are used is 0, 4, 8, 12, 16, 20, 24, 28, then 1, 5, 9, 13, 17, 21, 25, 29, then 2, 6, 10, 14, 18, 22, 26, 30, then 3, 7, 11, 15, 19, 23, 27, and back to 0, and so on. Hence, all sets are equally utilized. In fact, as long as the stride amount is not a multiple of the number of sets (this includes all strides with power of twos), all sets will be equally utilized.

4. **Inclusion policy**. Suppose that we have a fully associative L2 cache that has four lines, and a direct mapped L1 cache with two sets. The cache uses write back write allocate policy. For a given stream of accesses shown below, determine the outcome of each access for an *inclusive* L2 cache. Blocks A, B, C, D map to the second L1 cache set, while blocks U and V map to the first L1 cache set. Indicate the outcome as: H (hit), M (miss), M-X (miss with X as victim block), for all caches. The L2 cache uses LRU replacement policy. Also show the final content of the cache. The access stream is: Read(V), Read(B), Read(D). The initial content of the caches are:

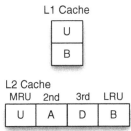

Answer:

Access	L1 cache's outcome	L2 cache's outcome
Read(V)	M-U	M-B (back invalidate B at L1)
Read(B)	M	M-D
Read(D)	M-B	M-A

The final content of the cache:

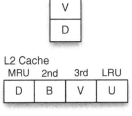

Homework Problems

1. **Average access time**. Suppose that we have a system with two levels of caches. L1 cache has a hit latency of 1 clock cycle, while L2 cache has a hit latency of 9 clock cycles. An L2 cache miss costs 100 clock cycles to service.

   (a) Calculate the average access time (AAT) if an application suffers from the following miss rates: 20% on the L1 cache and 10% on the L2 cache.

(b) Suppose that you aim to double the L2 cache to reduce its miss rate, but the larger L2 cache now needs 12 clock cycles to access. What is the minimum reduction in miss rate in order for the new L2 cache to reduce AAT?

(c) In the situation in part (b), suppose that the miss rate follows the power law with =0.5. Does the new L2 design improve or decrease AAT? Is the new L2 cache design worth adopting?

2. **Replacement policy**. Suppose that we have a fully associative cache that has four lines. The cache uses write back write allocate policy. Each block in the cache has one of the following states: D (dirty), V (valid clean), and I (invalid). For a given stream of accesses shown below, determine the outcome of each access for the following two cache replacement policies: least recently used (LRU), first in first out (FIFO), pseudo-LRU, and Belady's optimal. Indicate the outcome as one of these: H (hit), M (miss), M-X (miss that causes block X to be victimized). In the end, show the final content of the cache. The access stream is: R(A), R(B), W(C), R(D), W(A), R(C), R(E), R(A), R(B). For Belady's, assume that after this, future accesses are going to be A C D E, etc. For the pseudo LRU, suppose initially that all bits are zero.

3. **Inclusion policy**. Suppose that we have a fully associative L2 cache that has four lines, and a direct mapped L1 cache with two sets. The cache uses write back write allocate policy. For a given stream of accesses shown below, determine the outcome of each access for the L2 cache. Blocks A, B, C, D map to the second L1 cache set, while blocks U and V map to the first L1 cache set. Indicate the outcome as: H (hit), M (miss), M-X (miss with X as victim block), for all caches. The L2 cache uses LRU replacement policy. Also show the final content of the cache. The access stream is: Read(V), Read(B), Read(D).

(a) Assume that the L2 cache is non-inclusive and the initial content of the caches are:

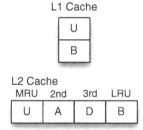

(b) Assume that the L2 cache is exclusive and the initial content of the caches are:

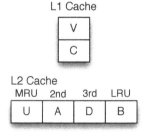

4. **Power law**. How much bigger a cache size needs to be in order to reduce the miss rate of a workload by 50%, if the workload has a cache size sensitivity (α) value of 0.3, 0.5, 0.7, or 0.9?

5. **Power law and stack distance profile**. Suppose a workload with $\alpha = 0.5$ suffers a miss rate of 10% on an 8-way associative cache with size C_0. Calculate the stack distance counters $C_1, C_2, \ldots, C_8$ in terms of the fraction of accesses to various stack positions. Repeat the exercise for $\alpha = 0.3$ and $\alpha = 0.8$.

6. **Stack distance profile**. Suppose a program running on a processor that has an 8-way associative cache has the following fractions of cache accesses to different stack positions:

7. **Non-uniform cache architecture (NUCA)**. Suppose a program running on a single processor has the following fractions of cache accesses to different stack positions:

Stack position	App1's fraction of accesses	App2's fraction of accesses
1	60%	50%
2	10%	10%
3	5%	8%
4	3%	7%
5	2%	5%
6	0%	1%
7	8%	1%
8	7%	1%
9 and higher	5%	17%

Suppose that the system implements multiple cache banks with various latencies. The closest cache bank has an access latency of 3 cycles and holds blocks that are the first two stack positions (most recently and next most recently used blocks). The next farther cache bank has an access latency of 6 cycles and holds blocks in the next two stack positions. The next farther cache bank has an access latency of 9 cycles and holds blocks in the next two stack positions. The farthest cache bank has an access latency of 12 cycles and holds blocks in the last two stack positions.

(a) What is the average cache access time for App1?

(b) What is the average cache access time for App2?

Chapter 6

Introduction to Shared Memory Multiprocessors

Contents

In Chapter 5, we discussed the memory hierarchy organization of single-processor as well as parallel/multicore systems. The objective of this chapter is to answer the question of what hardware support is needed in order to guarantee the correctness of executing shared memory parallel programs on a multiprocessor system. This chapter highlights that there are three main types of support needed: a (1) *cache coherence protocol*, which ensures a coherent view of cached values as seen by multiple processors, a (2) *memory consistency model*, which ensures consistent view of the ordering of memory operations, and (3) hardware *synchronization* support, which enables a simple, correct, and efficient primitive that enable programmers to orchestrate their parallel programs. It discusses at a high level that any shared memory multiprocessors need the three types of support and present how they are related to one another. This chapter also serves as an introduction, or an entry point, to chapters in the rest of the book.

As we have mentioned in earlier chapters, we focus the discussion on multiprocessor systems that support the abstraction of shared memory. The abstraction of shared memory does not always come automatically; it requires special hardware support. This is in contrast with systems that do not provide the shared memory abstraction and rely on explicit message communication for processors to communicate with one another. Such systems only require a message passing library to ease sending and receiving messages.

There are several advantages of organizing a multiprocessor system as a shared memory system. First, programs that were created assuming a shared memory system, such as shared memory parallel programs, and multi-threaded programs created for a single processor system, will work automatically on a shared memory multiprocessor. They need to be significantly modified to run on systems that do not provide shared memory. Secondly, there is only one OS image running on the system, which simplifies maintenance and co-ordinated scheduling of threads. Thirdly, the total memory size of a shared memory multiprocessor that consists of multiple nodes is the multiplication of the number of nodes with the size of memory of each node. This makes shared memory multiprocessor systems attractive for applications with large memory footprint sizes. For example, an anecdotal evidence on the profile of applications that ran on the 128-processor shared memory Origin 2000 system (in the late 90s) indicated that an important fraction of applications were non-parallel applications that required a huge memory to perform well without thrashing. These programs would cause an excessive number of page faults on systems that do not provide shared memory. Fourthly, fine grain sharing is naturally supported in shared memory multiprocessors. Communicating a few bytes or a cache block takes a few hundred to a few thousand cycles, whereas in a system without shared memory, the overheads of message bundling, sending, receiving, and unbundling can be orders of magnitude higher. Therefore, in a non-shared memory system, algorithms in a program must be structured in such a way that a large collection of data items are sent together using few large messages rather than many small messages, in order to make message sending and receiving infrequent events. Finally, common data structures that are read by all threads do not need to be replicated in a shared memory system but they need to be replicated in systems without shared memory, incurring storage overheads.

Providing shared memory abstraction requires hardware support that may be expensive depending on the platforms. On small-scale systems such as a multicore, or a small number of multicore chips interconnected using a bus, the hardware complexity is relatively low. In fact, on a multicore processor with cores sharing a cache, shared memory can be automatically provided. However, the cost of providing shared memory grows super-linearly as the number of processors increases. In contrast, the cost of non-shared memory systems grows relatively linearly with the number of processors, as long as the demand for high bandwidth and low latency is not too high (allowing less scalable interconnection to be used). Shared memory multiprocessors may be prohibitively expensive to support for very large systems consisting of thousands of nodes. To provide larger systems, a group of shared memory nodes can be interconnected together, with the shared memory abstraction provided within nodes but not across nodes.

6.1   The Cache Coherence Problem

write back Let us assume a system with multiple processors, each processor with a private cache, and we want to aggregate them to form a shared memory multiprocessor system. Suppose that we glue these processors with a shared bus, as shown in Figure 6.1. The question that arises naturally is then: can the abstraction of a *single* shared memory be automatically achieved? The answer is no for several reasons that will be discussed further. It is important to understand what problems occur, so that we can develop an intuition into what hardware support is required to provide the shared memory abstraction.

For example, consider the following code (Code 6.1), which has two threads executing on two processors accumulating the values of $a[0]$ and $a[1]$ to the variable sum.

Let us assume that $a[0] = 3$ and $a[1] = 7$. The correct outcome of the computation is that the sum reflects the addition of $a[0]$ and $a[1]$ at the end of the computation, which corresponds to a value of 10. Suppose that synchronization has been properly inserted such that the access to sum occurs one at a time. In a system without caches, thread 0 reads the initial value of sum from memory, accumulates a value of 3 to it, and stores it back to memory. Thread 1 reads a value of

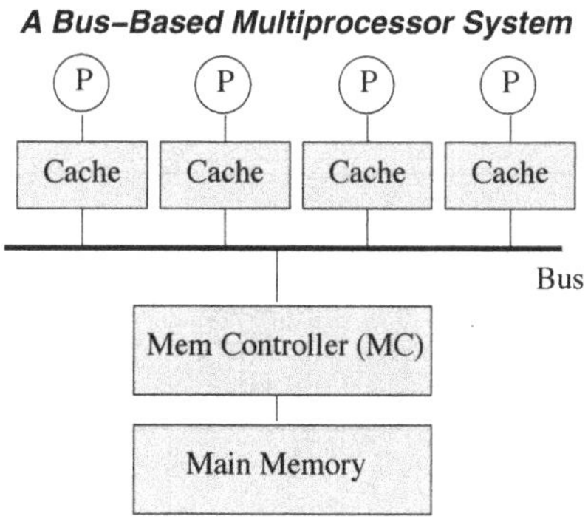

A Bus–Based Multiprocessor System

Figure 6.1: A simple bus-based multiprocessor system with four cores.

Code 6.1 A simple code to accumulate two values to a sum.

```
1 sum = 0;
2 #pragma omp parallel for
3 for (i=0; i<2; i++) {
4   #pragma omp critical {
5     sum = sum + a[i];
6   }
7 }
8 ... = sum;
```

---

sum (which is now 3) from memory, accumulates 7 to it, and stores back a value of 10 to memory. When thread 0 reads sum from memory, it will read 10, which is correct.

Now imagine that each processor has a cache (Figure 6.1), more specifically, a write back cache. Suppose that initially, the value of sum in memory is 0. The sequence of operations that occurs is shown in Table 6.1. Thread 0 starts out by reading (with a load instruction) from the memory location where the variable sum is located, into a register. This results in the memory block that contains sum to be cached by processor 0. Then, thread 0 performs an addition instruction for adding sum and $a[0]$. The result of the addition, currently still in a register, is then written to the memory location of sum using a store instruction. Since the block containing sum is cached, the cache block is modified and the dirty bit is set. In the mean time, the main memory still contains the stale copy of the block, in which the value of the sum is 0. When thread 1 performs a read to sum from the main memory, it will see the value of sum as 0. It adds $a[1]$ and sum, and stores the result to the cache. The value of sum in its cached copy is 7. Finally, when thread 0 reads the value of sum, it reads from the memory location of sum, and it will read it from the cache because it has a valid copy in its cache (a cache hit). It will read "3" as the final value, which is incorrect.

At this point, readers may wonder whether the problem is resolved when write through caches are employed instead of write back caches. The answer is no. In the sequence shown in Table 6.1, the problem is partially mitigated, because when thread 0 updates the value of sum, it is propagated to the main memory. So when thread 1 reads the value of sum, it reads a correct value of 3. It then adds 7 to the sum, so the sum becomes 10, and when it writes to sum, it is propagated to the main memory. Therefore, the main memory has a value of 10. However, when thread 0 prints the value of sum, it finds a valid copy in the processor 0's cache (a cache hit) and it prints a value of "3", which

Table 6.1: Illustration of the cache coherence problem.

Action	P0's Cache	P1's Cache	Memory
Initially	–	–	$sum = 0$
P0 reads sum	$sum = 0$	–	$sum = 0$
P0 adds sum with a[0]	$sum = 3$, Dirty	–	$sum = 0$
P1 reads sum	$sum = 3$, Dirty	$sum = 0$	$sum = 0$
P1 adds sum with a[1]	$sum = 3$, Dirty	$sum = 7$, Dirty	$sum = 0$

is also incorrect (despite the fact that the main memory has an up-to-date value of sum, which is 10).

Overall, the write policy of caches (either write through or write back) only dictates how a change of value in a cached copy should be *propagated to the outer level* (e.g., main memory), but does not dictate how a change of value in a cached copy should be *propagated to other copies in peer caches*. The problem, of course, does not exist in systems that do not have caches. Since the root of the problem is a non-coherent view of values of a single data item in different caches, it is referred to as the *cache coherence* problem.

To enable a coherent view of data values in multiple caches, we need to support cache coherence. At the very least, there has to be a mechanism to propagate changes in one cache to other caches. We refer to this requirement as the *write propagation* requirement. There is another (subtler) requirement for supporting cache coherence which is referred to as *transaction serialization*. Transaction serialization is essentially a requirement that multiple operations (reads or writes) to a single memory location are seen in the same order by all processors.

Let us discuss the need for transaction serialization. We will first discuss the need for serialization between two writes, and later discuss the need for serialization between a write and a read. The former case is illustrated in Figure 6.2(a). In the figure, let us assume we have four processors: P1, P2, P3, and P4. P1 writes a value of 1 to a location/address x in its cache while simultaneously P2 writes a value of 2 to the same address x in its cache. If we only guarantee write propagation but not serialization, P3 and P4 may see a different order of changes. P3 may see that P2's write occurs before P1's write, therefore it sees a final value of 1. In contrast, P4 may see that P1's write occurs before P2's write, therefore it sees a final value of 2. As a result, P3 and P4 see different values for the same memory location, resulting in incoherent cached data value. Therefore, serialization between writes is required in order for all processors to have a coherent view of cached values.

Figure 6.2(b) illustrates the need to serialize write and read operations. In the figure, let us assume we have three processors: P1, P2, and P3. P1 writes a value of 1 to a location/address x in its cache, which gets propagated at different times to P2 and P3. If we only guarantee serialization of writes but not serialization writes/reads, P2 and P3 may see different final values in x. Suppose that P2 performs a read operation which is forwarded to P3. P3 has not received the write propagation from P1, thus it supplies an old value of x, which is 0. Finally, P3 receives write propagation from P1 and now has a new value of $x = 1$. Note that at the end, P2 thinks the latest value of x is 0, while P3 thinks that the latest value of x is 1. Since P2 and P3 see different final values for the same memory location, incoherent cached data value has occurred. Therefore, serialization between reads and writes is also required in order for all processors to have a coherent view of cached values.

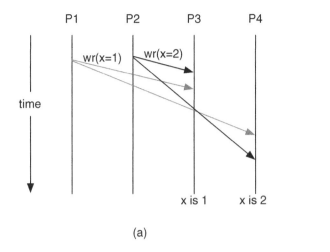
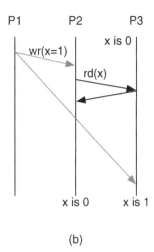

Figure 6.2: Illustrating the need for transaction serialization between writes (a) and between a write and a read (b).

Because of the need to serialize writes and read operations, we often refer to a write operation as a *write transaction* and a read operation as a *read transaction*, implying that each operation has to be atomic with respect to one another. Note, however, that serialization between two read operations is not required because in the absence of writes, as long as the value is coherent initially, the reads will return the same value.

Cache coherence is supported using a mechanism called the *cache coherence protocol*. The requirement for the correctness of a cache coherence protocol is that it must ensure write propagation and transaction serialization.

Cache coherence protocols will be discussed in more detail in Chapter 7.

6.2 Memory Consistency Problem

There is another problem that multiprocessor systems must address, which is more subtle than that of the cache coherence problem: the *memory consistency* problem. Whereas the cache coherence determines the requirement for propagating a change of value in a single address in one cache to other caches and the serialization of those changes, the memory consistency deals with the *ordering* of *all* memory operations (loads and stores) to *different* memory locations. The problem is referred to as *memory* consistency because unlike *cache* coherence problem that only occurs for systems with caches, memory consistency problem exists even on systems without caches, although caches may exacerbate it.

To illustrate the problem, consider a pair of signal-wait synchronization. Readers may recall that such synchronization is needed for DOACROSS and DOPIPE parallelism (see Chapter 3), among others. Suppose that thread 0 produces a datum that is to be consumed (read) by thread 1. Thread 0 executes the *post* in order to let thread 1 know that the datum is ready. Thread 1 executes a *wait* which makes it block until the corresponding post is executed. One simple way to implement a pair of signal-wait is to use a shared variable initialized to 0. The post operation sets it to 1, while the wait operation waits until the value of the variable is set to 1. This is illustrated in Code 6.2. In the illustration, the shared variable that implements the signal-wait pair is `datumIsReady`. Processor 1 (executing thread 1) waits in a loop until `datumIsReady` is set to 1, which indicates that `datum` has been produced.

Code 6.2 A code containing signal-wait synchronization.

P0:	P1:
₁S1: datum = 5;	₁S3: while (!datumIsReady) {};
₂S2: datumIsReady = 1;	₂S4: print datum;

Let us consider whether Code 6.2 works as intended on a single processor system, and then whether it works on a multiprocessor system. In a single processor system, the correctness of execution of the code depends on the requirement that statement S1 is executed before statement S2. If for some reason S2 is executed before S1, then `datumIsReady` is set to 1 before the value of `datum` is produced. Similarly, if S4 is executed before S3, then it may print the value of `datum` that is not yet produced. Hence, the correctness of execution of the code depends on the proper execution ordering of S1 and S2, and S3 and S4. It is crucial that the binary code corresponding to program source code preserves the ordering of the statements. We refer to the order of instructions as they occur in the program source code as the *program order*.

Let us first consider how the program ordering of S3 and S4 is preserved in a single processor. A typical processor today implements out-of-order execution which may reorder instruction execution to exploit instruction-level parallelism, but preserve dependences (data and control flow) and commit instructions in program order. The execution of S4 is dependent on whether the loop condition in S3 is satisfied or not, hence S3 has a control flow dependence with S4. Since the processor obeys control flow dependence, we know that S3 and S4 will be executed in program order.

Let us now consider S1 and S2. The store instructions corresponding to S1 and S2 have neither data dependence (true, anti, or output) nor control flow dependence. During execution, S2 may be performed before S1, but since a processor implements in-order instruction commit, it is guaranteed that instructions corresponding to S1 are committed before S2. Hence, the code will execute correctly unless the program binary itself does not preserve the program order. There needs to be a way to tell the compiler to preserve program order when generating the binary code. To tell the compiler to preserve the program order, the typical solution is to provide a language construct that the compiler understands. One example is that in C/C++, if `datumIsReady` is declared as `volatile`, the compiler knows that any load or store to the variable must not be eliminated or reordered with other instructions that precede or follow it. While such a solution may be overly restrictive (not all loads and stores to a volatile variable need strict ordering), it is very simple to use. Programmers only need to remember which variables are used for synchronization purposes and declare them volatile.

Overall, in a single processor system, for the code to execute correctly, one only needs to ensure that the compiler preserves the program order when there are accesses to synchronization variables. How about in a multiprocessor system? In a multiprocessor system, thread 0 and thread 1 are executed on different processors, so an extra problem arises. First, even though with respect to processor 0, the instructions of S1 and S2 are committed in program order, they may not appear so to processor 1. For example, the write to `datumIsReady` may be propagated sooner to processor

1 (e.g., due to a cache hit), while the write to datum may be propagated later to processor 1 (e.g., due to a cache miss). Hence, preserving program order on a single processor is insufficient for ensuring the correctness of the execution of the code. In a multiprocessor system, therefore, there need to be mechanisms to ensure that acesses of one processor appear to execute in program order to all other processors, at least partially. However, as one may expect, ensuring full program order across processors is expensive in terms of performance, hence some processors only enforce partial program ordering. What types of program ordering are enforced, and what are not, are specified in a *memory consistency model* of the processor.

Basically, system programmers must be aware of the memory consistency model that the multiprocessor system guarantees, and write their code accordingly. Various memory consistency models trade off performance with the ease of programming. Since the optimum point between performance and ease of programming is unclear, various processors today support different memory consistency models. It is critical for programmers to know what model the system they use provides, know how to produce correct code for it, and also realize its performance characteristics.

Memory consistency models will be discussed in more detail in Chapter 9.

6.3 Synchronization Problem

Even if cache coherence is supported, the example in Code 6.1 assumes that synchronization primitive required by the #pragma omp critical clause is implemented in the system. It leaves the question of how mutual exclusion required by the critical section is enforced. *Mutual exclusion* requires that when there are multiple threads, only one thread is allowed in the critical section at any time.

Mutual exclusion is not a problem that is unique to multiprocessor systems. In a single processor system, for example, multiple threads may time-share a processor, and accesses to variables that are potentially modified by more than one thread must be protected in a critical section. A brute-force way to achieve critical section is by disabling interrupts when mutual exclusion is needed for a specific code segment. Disabling all interrupts ensure that the thread that is executing will not be context switched or interrupted by the OS. Such an approach is costly to use in a single processor system. In a multiprocessor system, besides being costly, disabling interrupts does not achieve mutual exclusion because other threads in different processors still execute simultaneously.

In order to provide mutual exclusion, suppose that a primitive lock (lockvar) that acquires a lock variable lockvar, and unlock (lockvar) that releases the lock variable lockvar, are provided. Also suppose that lockvar has a value of 1 if it is acquired by a thread, otherwise its value will be 0. To enter a critical section, a naive implementation of these functions is shown in the following code (Code 6.3).

The code shows that to acquire a lock, a thread will go in a loop waiting for the value of lockvar to become 0, indicating a released lock. Then, the thread acquires the lock by setting lockvar to 1. This prevents other threads from entering the critical section once the lock is successfully acquired. Finally, when a thread exits the critical section, it resets the lockvar to 0.

The problem with the naive implementation is that the sequence of instructions that reads the value of lockvar and writes to it is not atomic, as evident in the corresponding assembly language version. The load that reads the value of lockvar and the store to it are distinct instructions, and there are other instructions between them such as the compare and the branch instructions. The

Code 6.3 An incorrect implementation of lock/unlock functions.

The high-level language implementation:

```
1 void lock(int *lockvar) {
2   while (*lockvar == 1) {} ;   // wait until released
3   *lockvar = 1;  // acquire lock
4 }
5
6 void unlock(int *lockvar) {
7   *lockvar = 0;  // release lock
8 }
```

The corresponding assembly language version:

```
1 lock:  ld  R1, &lockvar     // R1 = lockvar
2        bnz R1, lock         // jump to lock if R1 != 0
3        st  &lockvar, #1     // lockvar = 1
4        ret                  // return to caller
5
6 unlock: st  &lockvar, #0    // lockvar = 0
7         ret                 // return to caller
```

sequence of instructions is not atomic since it can be interrupted in the middle and can overlap with the same sequence at other processors. This non-atomicity causes a correctness problem as it allows multiple threads to read the same value of lockvar, say 0, and acquire it simultaneously. For example, consider the sequence of events shown in Figure 6.3. Say two threads running in processor 0 and processor 1 execute the lock() code at about the same time (the example shows thread 1 slightly lagging). Both read lockvar and discover its value to be 0. Both compare the value with zero, and the branch is not taken because the value is found to be zero by both processors. Then, thread 0 acquires the lock and writes a value of 1 to lockvar. It then enters the critical section. Thread 1 does not know that the lock has been acquired, and it also writes a value of 1 to lockvar and enters the critical section. Now there are more than one thread in the critical section at the same time, which is incorrect.

	Thread 0	**Thread 1**
	lock: ld R1, &lockvar	
	bnz R1, lock	lock: ld R1, &lockvar
Time	sti &lockvar, #1	bnz R1, lock
		sti &lockvar, #1

Figure 6.3: Incorrect execution resulting from the naive lock implementation.

Note that the incorrect outcome is unaffected even when the system correctly implements a cache coherence protocol. Cache coherence protocol ensures that a new value written to a location will be propagated to other cached copies. In this example thread 1's lockvar copy may get invalidated as a result of thread 0's write to lockvar. However, since thread 1 does not attempt to reread the value of lockvar that it has read earlier, it will not see the new value. Instead, thread 1 attempts to write (or overwrite) lockvar with a value of 1.

One way to fix the problem is to introduce a support for an *atomic instruction* that performs a sequence of load, modify, and store as a single, unbreakable unit of execution. The word atomic here implies two meanings. First, it implies that either *the whole sequence is executed entirely*, or none of it appears to have executed. Second, it also implies that *only one such instruction from any processor can be executed at any given time*. Multiple such instructions from several processors will have to be serialized. How can an atomic instruction be supported? Certainly, software support cannot provide any atomicity of the execution of several instructions. Thus, hardware support is required and will be discussed in more detail in Chapter 8.

In this chapter, we will look at the need for hardware support from a different angle, that is, is there an alternative that does not require hardware support? If there is, is it efficient? To answer the questions, consider a software solution for guaranteeing mutual exclusion, such as the Peterson's algorithm [62]. Peterson's algorithm guarantees mutual exclusion for two threads through the following code (Code 6.4), To enter a critical section, a thread calls the `void lock(..)` function, while to exit a critical section, the thread calls the `void unlock(..)` function.

Code 6.4 Acquiring and releasing a lock in Peterson's algorithm.

```
1 int turn;
2 int interested[n];  // initialized to 0
3
4 void lock (int process) {      // process is 0 or 1
5   int other = 1 - process;
6   interested[process] = TRUE;
7   turn = process;
8   while (turn == process && interested[other] == TRUE) {} ;
9 }
10 // Post: turn != process or interested[other] == FALSE
11
12 void unlock (int process) {
13   interested[process] = FALSE;
14 }
```

Let us see how Peterson's algorithm works. First of all, notice in `lock(..)` that the condition in which the code exits the while loop and successfully acquires the lock is either because `turn` is not equal to `process`, or `interested[other]` has a FALSE value. When there is only one thread attempting to acquire the lock, it will successfully acquire the lock because `interested[other]` is FALSE. When a thread exits the critical section, all it needs to do is to set the `interested[process]` to FALSE, allowing the other thread to enter the critical section.

Figure 6.4 shows how the algorithm ensures mutual exclusion when there is no race in acquiring the lock. The figure illustrates thread 0 which successfully acquires the lock, and while it is in the critical section, thread 1 attempts to acquire the lock. Because thread 0 is in the critical section, `interested[0]` is TRUE and therefore, thread 1 waits in the while loop. When thread 0 exits the critical section, it sets `interested[0]` to FALSE. That allows thread 1 to exit its while loop and enter the critical section. Mutual exclusion is ensured because thread 1 cannot enter the critical section while thread 0 is still in it.

Figure 6.5 shows how the algorithm ensures mutual exclusion when two threads try to simultaneously acquire the lock. Suppose that both threads assign a value TRUE to `interested [process]` simultaneously. Then, they try to write their own thread ID to `turn`. Since `turn`

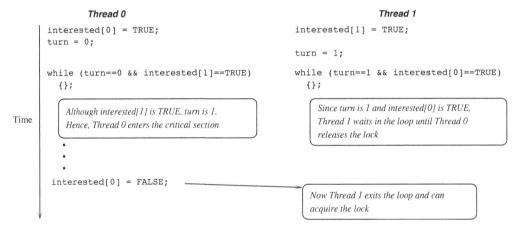

Figure 6.4: Execution of the Peterson's algorithm without races.

is a shared variable, one thread will overwrite the value written by the other. The figure assumes that thread 0 is slightly faster and writes 0 to `turn`, while thread 1 which is slightly late overwrites `turn` with a value of 1. Then, both threads execute the while loop. Because the value of `turn` is 1, thread 0 exits the loop, successfully acquires the lock, and enters the critical section. Thread 1 must wait in the loop because `turn` is 1, and `interested[0]` is TRUE. Only after thread 0 exits the critical section and sets `interested[0]` to FALSE, thread 1 can enter the critical section.

```
                Thread 0                                            Thread 1
        interested[0] = TRUE;                           interested[1] = TRUE;
        turn = 0;
                                                        turn = 1;

        while (turn==0 && interested[1]==TRUE)          while (turn==1 && interested[0]==TRUE)
          {};                                             {};
```

      Although interested[1] is TRUE, turn is 1.   *Since turn is 1 and interested[0] is TRUE,*
      Hence, Thread 0 enters the critical section   *Thread 1 waits in the loop until Thread 0*
Time   *releases the lock*

        `interested[0] = FALSE;`

                                                           Now Thread 1 exits the loop and can
                                                           acquire the lock

Figure 6.5: Execution of the Peterson's algorithm with a race in acquiring the lock.

While the software solution (the Peterson's algorithm) can also achieve mutual exclusion, it suffers from a lack of scalability. Consider the condition for exiting the while loop in Peterson's algorithm when the algorithm is modified to work for $n > 2$ threads rather than two threads. If there are n threads, the complexity increases substantially. We may need to arrange threads in pairs of two and let each pair of threads compete in obtaining the lock. The winning threads from the previous round can be paired again and compete in a new round. This can go on until there is only one thread winning all the rounds, and the thread gets the lock. Such a tournament incurs significant latency.

Compare this against Code 6.3, which only tests one variable `lockvar` in order to acquire a lock. Of course, Code 6.3 is incorrect unless it is used in conjunction with an atomic instruction supported by the hardware. This points out that it is important to have hardware support for synchronization in order to reduce synchronization overheads and enable scalable synchronization.

Finally, it is important to note that the correctness of a synchronization primitive is related to the memory consistency model provided by the processor. By nature, synchronization operation is used to impose ordering between memory accesses performed by different threads. However, the ordering of the memory accesses performed by a synchronization operation and those performed outside the synchronization cannot be guaranteed unless the hardware provides either a strict memory consistency model, or an explicit mechanism that can order memory accesses. This will be discussed further in Chapter 8.

6.4 Exercises

Worked Problems

1. **Register allocation**. Suppose that you are writing a compiler algorithm that decides what variable can be allocated in a register. A register allocation allows the variable to be accessed in the register without involving a load or store to read from or write to it. In order not to create cache coherence problem, which of the following types of variables can be register allocated vs. cannot be register allocated: read-only, read/write non-conflicting, and r/w conflicting? Explain. (see Section 3.6 for what each variable type refers to).

   Answer:

Variable type	Can be register allocated?
Read-only	Yes
R/W Non-Conflicting	Yes
R/W Conflicting	No

   R/W conflicting variables are written and read by different threads. Hence, they cannot be register allocated because a write by a processor to its registers is not visible to other threads, hence write propagation no longer occurs.

2. **Cache coherence**. Assume that we have a two-processor system (P1 and P2). These processors run different threads (T1 and T2, respectively) that access a data block containing variable *sum*, in the following sequence in time:

   T1: prefetch the block containing sum from &sum (i.e., the location of sum)

   T2: read the value of sum from &sum

   T2: add 7 to sum and write into &sum

   T1: read the value of sum from &sum

   T1: add 3 to sum and write into &sum

   T1: read sum to print its value

   Each access may hit or miss in the cache, depending on the cache configuration that will be specified. For each situation below, determine if there is a correctness issue. Also give the final values in all caches and in the main memory.

   (a) The two processors P1 and P2 share an only single level cache (the L1 cache) that uses a write back policy.

   (b) Each processor has its own single-level write through cache. Does your answer depend on whether the cache has a write allocate or write no-allocate policy?

   (c) Each processor has its own L1 cache that uses evict-on-write policy, i.e., a block is replaced immediately after it is written to. There are no other levels of caches in the system.

   (d) Each processor has a cache, but the block containing *sum* is not allowed to be cached.

Answer:

(a) No correctness problem because data block containing "sum" is only cached at a single location (the shared L1 cache).

L1 cache	10, dirty
Memory	0

(b) Correctness problem exists because a block may be kept in several L1 caches. A write through write allocate L1 cache only guarantees that a write will be propagated to the outer level memory hierarchy but does not guarantee write propagation to other L1 caches.

P1's cache	3
P2's cache	7
Memory	3

Furthermore, the problem persists even with a write no-allocate policy. This is because the block was brought into the cache through a prefetch instruction, not a write instruction.

(c) Correctness problem exists: although evict-on-write ensures that after a write, the written value is propagated to the outer memory hierarchy, it does not ensure that future reads in other caches will see that new value.

P1's cache	3
P2's cache	-
Memory	3

(d) No correctness problem since sum is uncached. There is only one copy of sum in the system.

P1's cache	-
P2's cache	-
Memory	10

Homework Problems

1. **Register allocation**. Suppose that you are writing a compiler algorithm that decides what variable can be allocated in a register. A register allocation allows the variable to be accessed in the register without involving a load or store to read from or write to it. In order not to create cache coherence problem, which type of variable can be register allocated vs. cannot be register allocated?

Variable type	Can be register allocated?
Read-only	
R/W Non-Conflicting	
R/W Conflicting	

If there are variable types that you think cannot be safely allocated in registers, give explanation of why it is so (see Section 3.6 for what each variable type refers to).

2. **Cache coherence**. Assume that we have a two-processor system (P1 and P2). These processors run different threads (T1 and T2, respectively) that access a data block containing variable sum, in the following sequence in time:

T1: prefetch the block containing sum from &sum (i.e., the location of sum)

T2: read the value of sum from &sum

T2: add 7 to sum and write into &sum

T1: read the value of sum from &sum

T1: add 3 to sum and write into &sum

T1: read sum to print its value

Each access may hit or miss in the cache, depending on the cache configuration that will be specified. For each situation below, determine if there is a correctness issue. Also give the final values in all caches and in the main memory.

(a) Each processor has its own write through L1 cache, and both processors share a single write back L2 cache.

(b) Each processor has its own write back L1 cache, however, each block can be cached in at most one cache. More specifically, if a block is cached at Px, and Py requests the block on a read or a write, the block is removed from Px's cache and placed in Py's cache. Assume a block is not evicted from the cache unless when it is moved to another processor's cache.

(c) Each processor has its own write back L1 cache. Suppose we run the two threads T1 and T2 in only one processor (either P1 or P2, but not both) in a time-sharing manner.

(d) Each processor has its own write back L1 cache. Suppose that instead of executing with two threads, only one thread executes. Thus, in the sequence of events shown above, all the events occur due to T1's execution while T2 does not exist. Furthermore, to achieve balanced processor utilization, the operating system migrates T1 from P1 to P2 after the first three events, i.e. right after adding '7' to sum but before reading from sum for the second time.

3. **Peterson's algorithm.** Modify Peterson's algorithm for lock acquisition and release so that it can be used for four threads that compete for a lock.

Chapter 7

Basic Cache Coherence Issues

Contents

As we have discussed in Chapter 6, hardware support for building a shared memory multiprocessor system that guarantees correct and efficient execution of parallel programs must address cache coherence, memory consistency, and support for synchronization primitives.

The objective of this chapter is to discuss basic issues when designing cache coherence protocols. Despite having the seemingly simple objectives of ensuring a consistent view of cached values through write propagation and transaction serialization, there is a wide range of design choices for implementing a cache coherence protocol. At the most basic levels, we must choose how write propagation is performed: either through directly updating all cached values upon a write by a processor, or through invalidating all other cached values upon a write by a processor – forcing other caches to reload the new values when the processors access them. The former strategy is referred to as *write update*, while the latter is referred to as *write invalidate*. They differ in characteristics and suit different program behavior. The write invalidate strategy is advantageous when a write to a cache block tends to be followed by subsequent writes to the same block. In such a case, the invalidation occurs only once and subsequent writes do not generate any more traffic. The write update strategy is advantageous when a write to a cache block tends to be followed by reads by other processors. Updating other cached values allow other processors to immediately obtain the new value by reading them from the caches. In such a case, the write invalidate strategy is disadvantageous because when copies of a heavily shared data block are invalidated, each processor will suffer a cache miss to reload the block. Such "coherence misses" do not occur in the write update strategy. However, the write update strategy sometimes keeps unnecessary data fresh for too long in other caches, hence, there are fewer cache blocks available for more useful data, leading to an increase in other types of misses (capacity and conflict).

Another important way to categorize cache coherence protocols is based on whether coherence requests are broadcast to all caches or only to select caches. Coherence protocols that fit the former description are referred to as *broadcast/snoopy* protocols. In the latter case, sending coherence requests to only select caches require a directory to keep track of which caches should be involved to serve a coherence request. Such protocols are then referred to as *directory* protocols. Broadcast protocols are fundamentally less scalable because as the number of caches increases, the number of requests that each cache must listen to increases as well. Directory protocols are fundamentally more scalable because only caches that should be involved in coherence transactions receive the requests. In exchange for better scalability, however, directory protocols require storage overheads for keeping directory information, and require indirection, i.e., all coherence requests must be sent to the directory first before sent to participating caches. In this chapter, we will cover broadcast coherence protocol design and leave directory protocol design to Chapter 10.

In some cases, the type of interconnect that connects coherent caches determine which coherence protocol is easier to implement. For example, certain interconnects such as a bus and ring naturally supports broadcast. Other interconnects where caches are interconnected point-to-point, broadcast is not naturally supported. However, broadcast protocols can still be implemented on point-to-point interconnected caches, as we will cover later in this chapter.

We will start describing the write invalidate strategy, and discuss different protocols that rely on this strategy. The protocols are described in increasing sophistication, and one builds upon another. More sophisticated protocols use less bandwidth but are more complex to implement. Readers are advised to read the protocols sequentially. We will then discuss one write update coherence protocol. Finally, we will discuss broadcast vs. directory protocols.

7.1 Overview

Figure 7.1 shows several ways how multiple processors can be interconnected. They differ in the level of the memory hierarchy they are interconnected at, and what interconnection is used. In a shared cache organization, the cache is shared by all processors. Each processor can access any part of the cache directly. The advantage of this organization is that cache coherence support is not needed because there is only a single cache, and any block can be cached at only one location. The disadvantages of this organization are that it requires the processors and caches to be in a very close proximity to one another, otherwise the time to access the cache will be very high. In addition, the interconnect must provide high bandwidth because all memory requests must go through it. A cache is a good traffic filter for memory accesses, thus the closer the interconnect to the processor, the less memory accesses are filtered, and the higher the bandwidth that must be provided by the interconnect. Finally, when there are multiple cache banks, the interconnection between processors and cache banks is all-to-all, which is expensive to support. Therefore, such an organization is only appropriate for a small number of cores and is not scalable.

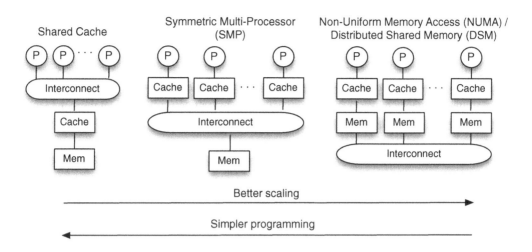

Figure 7.1: Various ways to organize a shared memory multiprocessor system.

The interconnection can be moved to an outer level between the caches and the main memory. This organization is referred to as *symmetric multi-processor* (SMP) configuration, since all processors have approximately equal memory access latency. Note, however, that SMP is an over-used term that sometimes refers to multiprocessor systems in which the memory latencies of different processors do not differ by *much*, with "much" being ambiguous. A SMP configuration may use various interconnect but the most common interconnect is a bus. This organization allows better scaling compared to the shared cache organization, since the interconnect only needs to handle traffic that has been filtered by the caches and is less latency sensitive. As a back-of-envelope calculation, if the caches together filter 90% of memory requests, the interconnect only handles 10% of memory access traffic and thus can accommodate $10\times$ the number of processors compared to the shared cache organization. Furthermore, an SMP organization also allows a fast cache access time to the local cache. However, programming will be more complex than in the shared cache organization, due to the need for data locality in caches. For example, if a data block is read and written alternatingly between two processors, the block will ping pong between two caches and the processors suffer from cache misses alternatingly. In contrast, in a shared cache organization, there is no such concern the data block remains shared in the cache. However, in an SMP, programmers do not need to worry about where their threads run in the processors as they can equally access the memory fast. Another disadvantage of an SMP organization is that while it can scale to a higher number of processors compared to the shared cache organization, its scalability is still limited. As the number of processors increases, the interconnect becomes saturated and access to memory will become slower.

Another organization is *distributed shared memory* (DSM), in which memories are interconnected. This organization is the most scalable. With a large number of processors, the interconnection does increase the average access time to memory, although access to the local memory is still fast. However, a DSM is more scalable than the SMP organization because the access time to main memory is already high to begin with (in the order of tens to hundreds of nanoseconds), so adding extra few tens or hundreds of nanoseconds in latency to access remote memories only increase the overall latency by less than an order of magnitude. In contrast, adding tens to hundreds of nanoseconds to the access time of some segments of the cache that are remote will significantly reduce the overall cache performance. In addition, caches filter out most memory accesses, so the main memory is accessed a lot less frequently compared to caches. Hence, an increase in the access time to main memory makes a smaller impact on the overall performance than the same amount of increase in the access time to caches.

■ *Did you know?*

 The SMP organization has been around for a long time. Some of the early machines that rely on SMP configurations include a mainframe computer system with IBM dual-processor system based on System/360 model, produced in the late 60s. In contrast, the DSM organization is much younger. It was developed during the 90s by various companies. One of the key challenges in a NUMA system is supporting cache coherence protocol that is highly scalable but provides low overheads.

 A different machine that attempts to improve data locality in the memory is cache only memory architecture (COMA). In COMA, the local memories at each node are used as cache. Data is not assigned to any particular memory. It can be migrated across memories and even replicated in multiple memories. With COMA, programmers do not need to be worried about data locality in memories. Data is automatically replicated and attracted to the nodes that use the data. However, COMA adds complexity to the hardware that manages data in memory. Hardware needs to know how to locate data in memories (it can rely on a directory), and ensures that the last copy of data does not get evicted from a memory. A hybrid NUMA/COMA mechanism was implemented in the Sun Microsystem's Wildfire system.

Since a processor can access its local memory directly, without going through the interconnect, it can access its local memory faster than accessing a remote memory. Even remote memories may have different latencies depending where they are connected to the interconnect topology. Thus, a DSM is also an example of a non-uniform memory architecture (NUMA) system. In a NUMA system, programming is more complex as programmers have to be concerned about data locality in memory. In particular, programmers want to ensure that data is allocated in the local memory. Since data is allocated in memory by the operating system (OS) in unit of pages, programmers have to take into account OS page allocation policy and algorithm. Not only that, programmers have to carefully orchestrate the placement of threads in processors so that they run near where data is laid out in memory.

Note that the organizations are not exclusive. In reality, various levels may be interconnected with different organizations. For example, a multiprocessor system may consist of multicore chips. In each multicore chip, it is feasible to have the shared cache or SMP organization at the L2 or L3 cache level, while across chips we may have a DSM configuration.

The choice of multiprocessor organization and interconnect has a significant impact on how the cache coherence protocol should be designed. Cache coherence protocol choice must support the scale of the system, which is affected by the organization. Supporting scalability is expensive, thus a cache coherence protocol should not be over-designed. In this chapter, we will consider the simplest class of cache coherence: broadcast/snoopy protocols. Initially, we will start with an interconnect that naturally supports broadcast, which is a bus. A bus-based cache coherence protocol is a broadcast/snoopy coherence protocol that is relatively simple to develop and validate, due to the bus providing serializing point for all coherence transactions. Later in the chapter, we will discuss how a broadcast cache coherence protocol can be designed over point-to-point interconnect.

The attractiveness of the bus-based multiprocessors, which is the focus of this chapter, is that it only requires a few modifications to a single processor system, which already relies on a bus for the connection to the main memory. In addition, as will be discussed later, the support needed for cache coherence also includes a finite-state machine (FSM) of cache state that is an extension to what are already used in a single processor system. For example, a write back cache already associates each cache block with a state, in which the state values include *invalid*, *valid clean*, and *dirty*. Finally, the cache coherence protocol for a bus-based multiprocessor is simpler than for other organizations, so we first use a bus-based multiprocessor as a starting point to introduce basic concepts and techniques used in cache coherence protocols.

7.1.1 Basic Support for Bus-Based Multiprocessors

Bus is perhaps the simplest interconnection fabric that can be used to connect multiple processors into a single multiprocessor system. At the high level, a multiprocessor bus is a set of wires shared by multiple processors. In order for a processor to communicate with another, it must post its command, address, and data on the bus, and other processors must listen to the bus to check if the bus contains any command, address, or data that are relevant to them.

A bus logically has three different types of lines: command lines, address lines, and data lines. The command lines are used to place a bus command such as a read or a write command. In a write back cache, a read miss will generate a bus read command, and a write miss will also generate a bus read command because of the write allocate policy. A bus write command is generated when a block needs to be written back to the memory, such as when a dirty block is evicted. The address lines are used to place the address that the command is to be applied to. The data lines are used to place the data that is returned by the memory on a bus read, or data that is sent to the memory on a bus write. In some buses, the lines are *physically* separated, while in others, they are shared and multiplexed (e.g., Hypertransport [26]). When lines are multiplexed, messages sent on the lines must be distinguished from one another. This can be done by encapsulating each message into a series of packets, with the head packet containing information to identify the following packets.

A bus can be *synchronous* or *asynchronous*. In a synchronous bus, all devices connecting to the bus share the same clock signal, transmitted through the control lines. In an asynchronous bus, the devices do not share a common clock signal. Transmitting data through a synchronous bus is simple because the devices agree on the timing of when a particular message (command, address, or data) is sent. Each device can follow a finite state machine to know what message will be posted next and at which bus cycle. In contrast, in an asynchronous bus, the device must establish communication through a series of requests and replies in a handshake protocol. Such a protocol makes the device more complex and communication slower. Since a processor-memory bus or a multiprocessor bus are co-designed with the devices that will connect to it, the number of such devices are fixed, and the bus is relatively short, a synchronous design is usually used. I/O buses, on the other hand, must be designed with a wide range of numbers and types of devices in mind. I/O buses also tend to be relatively long, hence a common clock signal in a synchronous design cannot provide a high frequency due to the high clock skew. Hence, I/O buses tend to use an asynchronous design.

Depending on the design, a bus can transmit data only once per cycle, or can also transmit data at both the rising and falling edges of the clock. The latter is known as a *double rate* bus.

A bus transaction goes on three phases. The first phase is *arbitration* which selects the requester that is allowed to use the bus. Arbitration is important in a multiprocessor system to prevent requests from different processors to collide. A bus grant signal is given by the arbiter to the requestor that wins. In a bus-based multiprocessor system, the requestors are the processors or their caches, and the memory controller at the memory side. When the requestor receives a bus grant signal, it places the block address on the address lines, and for a bus read, it waits for data to be returned by the memory. In an *atomic* bus, the bus is reserved for the entire duration of the transaction (until data is returned by the memory). In a *split transaction* bus, the bus lines are released as soon as the transfer of address or data is completed. Obviously, with the access time to the DRAM main memory taking 30-70 ns, reserving the bus for the entire duration of a transaction significantly reduces the available bus bandwidth. Hence, many recent systems rely on a split transaction bus. These phases (arbitration, command, and data transfer), can be pipelined with respect to one another to improved throughput.

Each type of bus in a multiprocessor system may need a separate arbiter. Arbitration logic tries to give a higher priority to a more important device but still ensure fairness. For example, requests from caches may be given a higher priority compared to requests from I/O devices.

Bus-based multiprocessors extend the existing mechanisms of the bus (bus transactions), and the cache (cache states). Figure 7.2 illustrates the components added or modified. The cache tag array is augmented with extra bits for encoding new cache states (shown in shaded regions). Each cache block is associated with a state value, which means that coherence is maintained at the granularity of cache blocks.

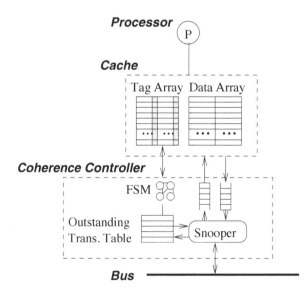

Figure 7.2: Support for a bus-based multiprocessor system at each node.

A new component called a *coherence controller* is added to the processor side, and also to the memory side. The *outstanding transaction table* keeps track of bus transactions that have not completed. This is a structure required in the split transaction bus organization. In the split transaction bus, multiple requests to different addresses can be placed on the bus even when the oldest request has not obtained its data. Therefore, the controller must be able to keep track of multiple outstanding bus transactions. Using the table, when the data block is returned, the transaction id is checked against entries in the table to determine which transaction it corresponds to. The table needs to be sized appropriately based on speed of the processor, cache miss rates, and the latency to the off-chip memory, in order to prevent the processor from stalling when its request finds the table already full.

Each coherence controller has a component called a *bus snooper*. The role of the snooper is to snoop each bus transaction. For each snooped bus transaction, the coherence controller checks the cache tag array to see if it has the block that is involved in the transaction, checks the current state of the block (if the block is found), and reacts accordingly by responding with data or by changing the state of the block. To determine what new state a block should transition into upon an event, a finite state machine (FSM) implementing the cache coherence protocol is employed. Data that is sent out is placed in a queue called the *write back buffer*. The write back buffer keeps a cache block that needs to be written back (or *flushed*) either due to natural cache eviction of a dirty block, or due to the need to respond to snooped bus transaction.

If the next level of the memory hierarchy is the main memory, at the memory side, the memory controller must also have a snooper to monitor all bus transactions. Depending on the type of bus transaction it sees, it must choose whether to respond by supplying or accepting data, or ignore it. However, the memory controller does not keep states for blocks in memory, so it operates differently than the coherence controllers at the processor side.

Note that we have been implicitly assuming that the coherence unit is a cache block, which is common in implementations. The reason why this assumption is reasonable is because other cache management functions (placement, eviction, and state bookkeeping) are all performed at the granularity of cache blocks. Thus, it is natural and simple to use the same granularity for the purpose of keeping caches coherent. Later, we will see how this assumption may introduce a problem in *false sharing*, a special type of cache misses that occur due to keeping coherence at the granularity of the cache block size.

Recall that the requirements for supporting cache coherence are write propagation and transaction serialization. There are two major strategies for ensuring write propagation. In *write update* protocols, when a write is snooped on the bus by a snooper, the snooper reacts by updating the local cached copy, in effect propagating the new value to the local cache. In *write invalidate* protocols, when a write is snooped on the bus by a snooper, the snooper reacts by making the local cached copy invalid. So the new value is not propagated right away. Only later when a processor accesses the block that was invalidated, it suffers a cache miss that requires the new block to be brought into the cache. At that time, the processor sees the new value.

For transaction serialization, the bus is a shared medium that already introduces serialization of all reads and writes. Hence, the bus introduces a natural mechanism to serialize transactions, so as long as all coherence controllers obey the bus ordering, then a correct coherence protocol can be supported in a straightforward manner. For example, say a processor wants to write to a block address. It tries to get access to the bus in order for the read/write transaction to be serialized. In the mean time, the coherence controller snoops a bus write request to the same block address. To preserve transaction serialization, the controller must obey the bus order. Since its write request has not been granted access to the bus, it has lost the competition. It has to respond to the bus write transaction it snoops from the bus, by updating or invalidating the corresponding cache block first. It also has to cancel its bus write request, and retry the write request on the cache block (which may now generate a new bus request that is different than the cancelled one). Overall, as long as the write order on the bus is obeyed by all cache controllers by responding to transactions in bus order, then transaction serialization can be guaranteed.

7.2   Cache Coherence in Bus-Based Multiprocessors

7.2.1   Coherence Protocol for Write Through Caches

The simplest cache coherence protocol is the one that is built over write through caches. Let us assume a single level cache, which may get requests from the processor side, as well as from the bus side as snooped by the snooper. Processor requests to the cache include:

1. **PrRd**: processor-side request to read to a cache block.

2. **PrWr**: processor-side request to write to a cache block.

 Snooped requests to the cache include:

1. **BusRd**: snooped request that indicates there is a read request to a block made by another processor.

2. **BusWr**: snooped request that indicates there is a write request to a block made by another processor. In the case of a write through cache, the BusWr is a write through to the main memory performed by another processor.

 Each cache block has an associated state which can have one of the following values:

1. **Valid** (V): the cache block is valid and *clean*, meaning that the cached value is the same with that in the lower level memory component (in this case the main memory).

2. **Invalid** (I): the cache block is invalid. Accesses to this cache block will generate cache misses.

There is no dirty state in the write through cache since all writes are written through to the lower level, all cached values are clean. The write through mechanism is designed to propagate writes to the lower level of the memory hierarchy. We will see how cache coherence controllers in other processors can snoop these bus transactions and use them for propagating values to caches, not just to the lower level memory hierarchy. We assume that the caches use *write no-allocate* and *write invalidate* cache coherence policies.

The finite state machine corresponding to the coherence protocol for write through caches is shown in Figure 7.3. In the figure, the response to processor-side requests is shown on the left part, while the response to the snooper-side requests is shown on the right part. They are separated for ease of illustration purpose only; the actual implementation uses a single finite state machine that can respond to both processor-side and snooper-side requests. The figure shows the transition from one state to another, and the label of the edge shows the triggering event and the action or response taken as a result of the event.

The key to a write invalidation protocol is that a processor can modify a cache block after invalidating other copies (in other caches). Hence, the cache block that is being modified resides in only one cache, the one that belongs to the processor that writes to it. By obtaining an *exclusive*

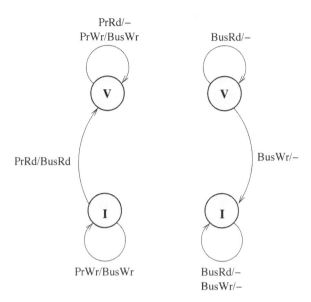

Figure 7.3: State transition diagram for the cache coherence protocol for write through caches.

ownership of the block, the processor has ensured that no other processors are also writing to the block.

In Figure 7.3, the *I* state represents two cases: a case in which the block is not cached, or when the block is cached but its state is invalid. Note that no state is actually maintained for blocks that are not cached. However, they are treated in the same way as blocks that are cached and in an invalid state. Let us consider the left part of the figure that shows a reaction to a processor read or write request. First, consider the case when the cache block is in "I" (invalid) state. When there is a processor read request, the processor suffers a cache miss. To load the datum into the cache, a BusRd is posted on the bus, and the memory controller responds to the BusRd by fetching the block from the main memory. When the block is fetched, it is placed in the cache, and the state is set to "V" or valid. When there is a processor write request, since the cache uses a write no-allocate policy, the write is propagated down to the lower level using the BusWr transaction without fetching the block into the cache. Therefore, the state remains invalid.

Let us consider the case in which the cache already has the block in the valid state. On a processor read, the block is found in the cache and data is returned to the processor. This does not incur a bus transaction since it is a cache hit, and the state remains unchanged. On the other hand, on a processor write, the block is updated, and the change is propagated down to the main memory through the BusWr transaction. The state remains valid (unchanged).

Now let us look at how the finite state machine reacts to snooped bus transactions. If the cache does not have the block or the block is in invalid state, all snooped BusRd or BusWr should not affect it, so they are ignored. If the cache block is in a valid state, when a BusRd transaction is snooped, that means another processor suffers a read miss and tries to fetch the block from the main memory. Therefore, the state remains valid, and no action is taken. However, if a BusWr is snooped, it indicates that another processor wants to write to the block and attempts to obtain an exclusive ownership of the block. Hence, in this case, the state must be invalidated by transitioning from the valid to invalid state.

Write propagation is ensured through two mechanisms. First, by invalidating other copies on a write to a cache block, other caches are forced to suffer a cache miss to reload the block. Secondly, by relying on the write through mechanism, the reload can be supplied by the main memory which has the latest value of the block.

The drawback of using a write through cache is that it requires a high amount of bandwidth. This is because there tends to be temporal and spatial locality of writes to a cache block. Each write in the write through cache incurs a BusWr transaction that takes up bus bandwidth. In contrast, in a write back cache, if a byte/word in a cache block is written multiple times, or if there are multiple writes to different bytes/words in the same cache block, it only uses the bus bandwidth once to invalidate other caches. Therefore, using write through caches in a bandwidth-restricted architecture prevents scalability of the system since bandwidth gets saturated more quickly.

7.2.2   MSI Protocol with Write Back Caches

Using write back caches can save bandwidth consumption significantly over using write through caches. In this section, we will discuss how a cache coherence protocol can be built over write back caches. The simplest of such protocols is the MSI protocol. Note that a write back cache has a dirty state that indicates whether any part of the block has changed since it was loaded into the cache. The same concept of cache states is extended to build a coherence protocol.

In the MSI protocol, processor requests to the cache include:

1. **PrRd**: processor-side request to read to a cache block.

2. **PrWr**: processor-side request to write to a cache block.

Bus-side requests include:

1. **BusRd**: snooped request that indicates there is a read request to a cache block made by another processor.

2. **BusRdX**: snooped request that indicates there is a *read exclusive* (write) request to a cache block made by another processor.

3. **Flush**: snooped request that indicates that an entire cache block is written back to the main memory by another processor.

Each cache block has an associated state which can have one of the following values:

1. **Modified** (M): the cache block is valid in only one cache, and the value is (likely) different than the one in the main memory. This state extends the meaning of the dirty state in a write back cache for a single processor system, except that now it also implies exclusive ownership. Whereas dirty means the cached value is different than the value in the main memory, modified means both the cached value is different than the value in the main memory, and it is cached only in one location.

2. **Shared** (S): the cache block is valid, potentially *shared* by multiple processors, and is clean (the value is the same as the one in the main memory). The shared state is similar to the valid state in the coherence protocol for write through caches.

3. **Invalid** (I): the cache block is invalid.

We will also define several terms that will be used throughout. The first is that the cache block state is analogous with a permission to perform read/write on the block without having to go to the bus. The invalid state is analogous to a no-read/no-write permission because accessing it is Invalid and generates a cache miss that goes to the bus. The shared state is analogous to a read/no-write permission because reading the block does not generate a bus transaction but writing will generate a bus transaction to invalidate other caches. Finally, the modified state is analogous to a read/write permission because reading from or writing to the block is permitted without generating a bus transaction; we know that there are no other cached copies. Using this analogy, changing the state from less restrictive permission to more restrictive permission (e.g., from M to S) can be referred to as a *downgrade*, while changing the state from more restrictive permission to less restrictive permission (e.g., from S to M) can be referred to as an *upgrade*.

A downgrade request in which the final state is "invalid" is referred to as *invalidation*. A downgrade request in which the final state is "shared" is referred to as *intervention*.

We assume that the caches use *write allocate* and *write invalidate* cache coherence policy. The finite state machine corresponding to the MSI coherence protocol for write back caches is shown in Figure 7.4. In the figure, the response to processor-side requests is shown on the left part, while the response to the snooper-side requests is shown on the right part. They are separated for ease of illustration purpose only; the actual implementation uses a single finite state machine that can respond to both processor-side and snooper-side requests.

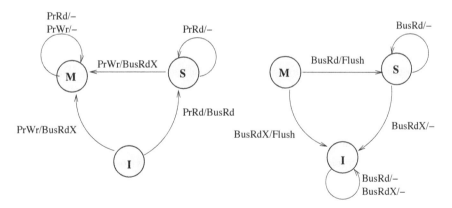

Figure 7.4: State transition diagram for the MSI cache coherence protocol for write back caches.

As before, the invalid (I) state represents two cases: a case in which the block is not cached, or when the block is cached but its state is invalid. Let us consider the left part of the figure that shows a reaction to a processor read or write request. First, consider when the cache block is in "I" (invalid) state. When there is a processor read request, a cache miss occurs. To load the data into the cache, a BusRd is posted on the bus, and the memory controller responds to the BusRd by fetching the block from the main memory. When the block is fetched, it is placed in the cache, and the state is set to "S" or shared. The shared state does not distinguish between the case in which there is only one cached copy, and the case in which there are multiple copies in different caches. When there is a processor write request, the cache must allocate a valid copy of the cache block, and to do that, it posts a BusRdX request on the bus. Other caches will respond by invalidating their cached copies (to be discussed later), and the memory responds by supplying the requested block. When the requestor gets the block, it is placed in the cache in the "M" or modified state. Then, the processor can write to the cache block.

Suppose now the cache already has the block in the shared state. On a processor read, the block is found in the cache and data is returned to the processor. This does not incur a bus transaction since it is a cache hit, and the state remains unchanged. On the other hand, on a processor write, there may be other cached copies that need to be invalidated, so a BusRdX is posted on the bus, and the state transitions to modified.

If the cache block is present in the cache in the modified state, reads or writes by the processor do not change the state, and no bus transaction is generated since we are sure that no other cached copies exist; an earlier invalidation has invalidated all other cached copies.

Now let us look at how the finite state machine reacts to snooped bus transactions. If the cache does not have the block or the block is in an invalid state, any snooped BusRd or BusRdX should not affect it, so they are ignored.

If the cache block is in a shared state, when a BusRd transaction is snooped, that means another processor suffered a read miss and is trying to fetch the block. Since the memory supplies the data, no action is taken by the cache and the cache block state remains shared. However, if a BusRdX is snooped, it indicates that another processor wants to write to the block, and therefore the local cached copy is invalidated (by transitioning into the invalid state).

If the cache block is in the modified state, the copy in the cache is the only valid copy in the entire system (no other cached copies exist and the value in the main memory is stale). Therefore, when a BusRd transaction is snooped, indicating that a processor suffered a read miss and trying to fetch the block, the processor that has the modified copy of the block must respond by flushing the block on the bus. After flushing, the resulting state is the shared state. The cache that issues the BusRd request must pick up the flushed block as a reply to its request and place it in its cache in a shared state. In addition, the main memory must also snoop the flushed block and update the corresponding block in the main memory. This is due to a requirement called *clean sharing* in which if a block is shared in multiple caches, its value has to be clean, i.e., the same with the one in the main memory. Other protocols that allow *dirty sharing* will be discussed in later sections.

If a BusRdX transaction is snooped, the processor that has the modified copy of the block must respond by flushing the block on the bus, and then transitioning into the invalid state. This flush may sound redundant since the processor that issues a BusRdX is going to overwrite the cache block. So why flush the block that is going to be overwritten? The answer to this is that a typical cache block is large, containing multiple bytes or words. The bytes that have been modified are not necessarily the same bytes that another processor wants to overwrite or modify. Another processor may want to write to other bytes, but read from the bytes that have been modified. Therefore, flushing the entire block is a correctness requirement, and the processor that issues the BusRdX must pick the block up and place it in the cache prior to writing to it.

Table 7.1: Illustration of MSI protocol operations.

	Request	P1	P2	P3	Bus Request	Data Supplier
0	Initially	–	–	–	–	–
1	R1	S	–	–	BusRd	Mem
2	W1	M	–	–	BusRdX	Mem
3	R3	S	–	S	BusRd	P1's cache
4	W3	I	–	M	BusRdX	Mem
5	R1	S	–	S	BusRd	P3's cache
6	R3	S	–	S	–	–
7	R2	S	S	S	BusRd	Mem

Write propagation is ensured through two mechanisms. First, by invalidating other copies on a write to a cache block, other caches are forced to suffer a cache miss to reload the block. Secondly, by flushing a modified block upon snooping a BusRd or BusRdX request, the flushed block can be picked up by the requesting processor/cache, ensuring that it gets the latest value of the block.

Compared to the write through cache, the MSI protocol requires a much smaller amount of write bandwidth. If a block is written multiple times (due to temporal or spatial locality), only one invalidation is generated, and the rest of the writes occur locally in the cache since the cache block is in the modified state.

However, there is a serious drawback with the MSI protocol. Consider a processor that wants to read blocks and then write to them, without other processors sharing the blocks. In this case, for each read-then-write sequence, two bus transactions are involved: a BusRd to fetch the block into the shared state, and a BusRdX to invalidate other cached copies. The BusRdX is useless since there are no other cached copies, but the coherence controller has no way to know that there are no other cached copies. This problem penalizes the system performance in two cases. The first case is when a sequential application is running. No other threads run and share the data with the application, yet the application uses more bandwidth compared to when it runs on a single processor system. In addition, the snoopers and cache coherence controllers' occupancy are increased due to having to react to more bus requests. The second case is for parallel programs that have been heavily tuned to reduce data sharing across threads. Such programs incur very little sharing, so most cache blocks are only stored in one cache. Hence, most BusRdX requests are unnecessary since they do not result in invalidations. Unfortunately, they are penalized in the same way as programs that have heavy sharing.

To remove the drawback of the MSI protocol, a state can be added in order to distinguish between a block that is clean and exclusively cached versus one that is stored at multiple caches. Such a protocol will be detailed in the next section when we discuss the MESI protocol.

To illustrate how MSI works, consider the example in Table 7.1. The table shows requests made by various processors in the following format: Rx or Wx, where R stands for a read request, W stands for a write request, and x stands for the ID of the processor making the request. The bus request generated as a result of the processor request is also shown. The new states at the different caches *resulting* from the request, are shown in the table. The last column shows where data for the request is supplied to the local cache from: the main memory or another cache. In the example, assume that initially the cache is empty.

On a read from Processor 1 (the first request), a BusRd is posted, the main memory responds with the block; Processor 1 gets the block and stores it in its cache with a shared state.

On a write from Processor 1, it does not know if other caches have the same block or not, so a BusRdX is posted on the bus to invalidate the same block in other caches. The main memory snoops the BusRdX and responds with the block. Note that here the memory controller does not know whether supplying the data is necessary or not, since it cannot distinguish between the case in which Processor 1 already has the block but needs to upgrade its state to modified, or it does not have a block and needs to fetch it from memory. After posting the BusRdX on the bus, effectively, the write has been serialized, so the cache state can safely transition to modified, and the block can be written to. Note that at some time later, the reply from memory comes. The processor can either ignore the reply, or put it in its cache in the modified state while delaying its write until it has finished doing so.

When Processor 3 makes a read request, a BusRd is posted on the bus. Processor 1's snooper picks it up, checks its cache tag, and finds that it has the block in modified state. This means that Processor 1 has the latest (and the only valid) copy, and flushes it in response to the snooped request. The block state transitions to shared after that. In the mean time, the memory controller also attempts to fetch the block from the main memory because it does not know if eventually a cache will supply the data or not. Processor 3 snoops the flush, and by matching the address of the block being flushed with its outstanding read transaction, it knows that the flushed block should be treated as the reply to its read request. So the block is picked up and stored in its cache in the shared state. The main memory which has been trying to fetch the block from memory will also snoop the flushed block, pick it up, cancel its memory fetch, and overwrite the stale copy of the block in memory. Supporting this mechanism means that the memory controller must also have a table keeping its outstanding fetches to the main memory. If a flush is detected, it must cancel its outstanding fetch to the same address, perhaps by marking the outstanding entry so that when the fetched block arrives, it can be discarded. It must also create a new entry that writes to the block with the flushed block.

■ *Did you know?*

At this point, readers may intuit that there is a potential correctness problem if the main memory has supplied a stale version of the cache block before the owner (the processor that has the block in modified state) has a chance to flush/supply its block. To avoid this situation, several solutions are possible. One possible solution is to give enough "fixed amount" of time for all processors to finish snooping and responding to a bus request, before the memory controller replies with a block. For example, even if the memory controller has fetched a block from main memory, the block must be kept in a table until it is verified that no cache will supply the block through a flush. Another possible solution is to collect all snoop responses, for example by having have a special "SNOOP-DONE" bus line that is asserted by all coherence controllers after they finish snooping the transaction and checking their cache tags. The line logically implements an AND operation, which means that it is asserted only when all processors have responded. Only when the SNOOP-DONE is set and no flush has been posted, can the memory controller safely supply the block.

Next, Processor 3 has a write request. It posts a BusRdX on the bus to invalidate copies in other caches. Processor 1's coherence controller responds by invalidating its copy. Processor 3's cache block state transitions to modified.

When Processor 1 attempts to read the block, it suffers a cache miss as a result of the earlier invalidation that it received. This type of miss is referred to as a *coherence miss* because it arises due to coherence actions (invalidations). So Processor 1 posts a BusRd, and Processor 3 responds by flushing its cache block and transitions its state to shared. The flushed block also updates the main memory copy; as a result, the cache blocks are now clean.

When Processor 3 reads the block, it finds it in the shared state in its cache. Since it has a valid copy, it has a cache hit and does not generate a bus request.

Finally, Processor 2 attempts to read the block and posts a BusRd on the bus. The memory controller fetches the block from the memory and the value in the main memory is valid because it has been updated by the earlier flush. Note that in this case, actually both Processor 1 and Processor 3 have the same valid copy of the block. Should Processor 1 or Processor 3 flush the block to supply the block? Although not required for correctness, they can definitely do that, and performance-wise it makes sense if they can supply the block faster than the memory can read from DRAM and supply the same block. In fact, in the MESI protocol, *cache-to-cache transfer* is employed that allows this to occur.

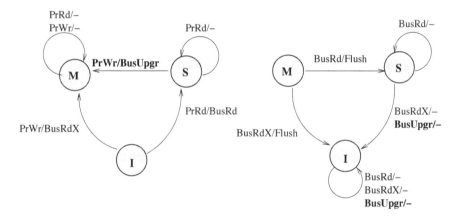

Figure 7.5: State transition diagram for the MSI cache coherence protocol with BusUpgr.

Earlier we have pointed out that on a BusRdX, the memory controller has no way to distinguish between the case in which the requesting cache already has a copy of the block but needs to upgrade its state, or it does not have a copy in the cache block and needs to fetch the block from the main memory. In the former case, the memory controller performs a useless task fetching the block from the main memory and supplies it on the bus, only to be discarded by the requesting cache. To avoid this waste, we can distinguish between the two cases by introducing a new bus request called a bus upgrade (*BusUpgr*). If a cache already has a valid copy of the block and only needs to upgrade its permission, it posts a BusUpgr instead of BusRdX. On the other hand, if it does not have the block in the cache and needs the memory or another cache to supply it, it posts a BusRdX. The memory controller responds differently in these two cases. It ignores the BusUpgr, but fetches the block when it snoops a BusRdX. With this small modification, the state transition diagram becomes one

Table 7.2: Illustration of MSI protocol operations with BusUpgr.

	Request	P1	P2	P3	Bus Request	Data Supplier
0	Initially	–	–	–	–	–
1	R1	S	–	–	BusRd	Mem
2	**W1**	**M**	–	–	**BusUpgr**	**–**
3	R3	S	–	S	BusRd	P1's cache
4	**W3**	**I**	–	**M**	**BusUpgr**	**–**
5	R1	S	–	S	BusRd	P3's cache
6	R3	S	–	S	–	–
7	R2	S	S	S	BusRd	Mem

shown in Figure 7.5 with the BusUpgr shown in bold fonts. The affected operation in the example in Table 7.2 are also shown in bold fonts.

Another choice in the coherence protocol is the state a cache block should transition into when it receives an intervention request, i.e., when the snooper snoops a BusRd to a locally cached block that is in modified state. In the MSI protocol shown earlier, it transitions into a shared state. An alternative is to transition into an invalid state. The rationale for this is that if a read from another processor is often followed immediately by a write, then if a cache block immediately transitions to invalid, then the requesting processor only needs to incur one bus transition. Does this optimization always improve performance? The answer depends on how often we have a situation in which all processors have a read-write sequence versus read-read sequence. If there are many read-write sequences, then we have saved one bus transaction for each of this sequence. However, if there are mostly read-read sequence, then we have unnecessarily invalidate cached copies which may result in more cache misses when a processor attempts to read from the cached copy that was just invalidated. Many synchronization operations have a read-write sequence, especially atomic instructions, however this is not always the case, especially when more optimized synchronization operations are used. This will be discussed in more details in Chapter 8.

7.2.3 MESI Protocol with Write Back Caches

As mentioned earlier, there is a serious drawback with the MSI protocol in that each read-write sequence incurs two bus transactions regardless of whether the block is stored in only one cache or not. This penalizes programs that have little data sharing, such as sequential program (no data sharing), and highly-optimized parallel programs (little data sharing). Clearly, this is not acceptable. Hence, to remove such problem, the MESI protocol adds a state to distinguish between a block that is clean and is exclusively cached versus a block that is clean and stored at multiple caches.

In the MESI protocol, the same as the MSI protocol, processor requests to the cache include:

1. **PrRd**: processor-side request to read to a cache block.

2. **PrWr**: processor-side request to write to a cache block.

Bus-side requests, the same as the MSI protocol, include:

1. **BusRd**: snooped request that indicates there is a read request to a cache block made by another processor.

2. **BusRdX**: snooped request that indicates there is a *read exclusive* (write) request to a cache block made by another processor which does not already have the block.

3. **BusUpgr**: snooped request that indicates that there is a write request to a cache block that another processor already has in its cache.

4. **Flush**: snooped request that indicates that an entire cache block is written back to the main memory by another processor.

5. **FlushOpt**: snooped request that indicates that an entire cache block is posted on the bus in order to supply it to another processor. We distinguish FlushOpt from Flush because while Flush is needed for write propagation, FlushOpt is not required for correctness. It is implemented as a performance enhancing feature that can be removed without impacting correctness. We refer to such an optional block flush as *cache-to-cache transfer*.

Each cache block has an associated state which can have one of the following values:

1. **Modified** (M): the cache block is valid in only one cache, and the value is (likely) different than the one in the main memory. This state has the same meaning as the dirty state in a write back cache for a single processor system, except that now it also implies exclusive ownership.

2. **Exclusive** (E): the cache block is valid, clean, and *only resides in one cache*.

3. **Shared** (S): the cache block is valid, clean, but may reside in multiple caches.

4. **Invalid** (I): the cache block is invalid.

One challenge in implementing the MESI protocol is that on a read miss, how does the coherence controller know whether to load the block into the cache in the exclusive or shared state? It depends on whether there are other cached copies. If there are no other copies, the block should start out in the exclusive state. Otherwise, it should start out in the shared state. How can we check whether there are existing copies in other caches? To achieve that, a new bus line can be added, which we will refer to as COPIES-EXIST or "C" bus line. The bus line has a high value when there is at least one cache that asserts it, and thus has a low value only when there are no cached copies.

We assume that the caches use *write allocate* and *write invalidate* cache coherence policies. The finite state machine corresponding to the MESI coherence protocol for write back caches is shown in Figure 7.6. In the figure, the response to processor-side requests is shown on the top part, while the response to the snooper-side requests is shown on the bottom part.

As before, the *I* state represents two cases: a case in which the block is not cached, or when the block is cached but its state is invalid. Let us consider the top part of the figure that shows a reaction to a processor read or write request. First, consider when the cache block is in "I" (invalid) state. When there is a processor read request, it suffers a cache miss. To load the data into the cache, a BusRd is posted on the bus, and the memory controller responds to the BusRd by fetching the block from the main memory. Other snoopers will snoop the request and check their caches to

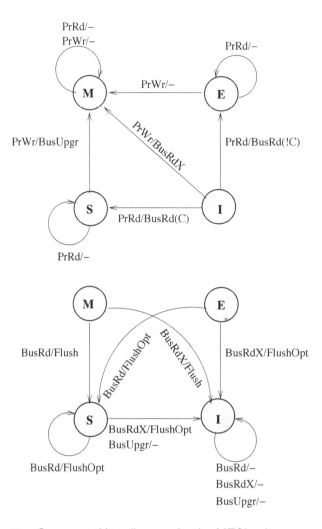

Figure 7.6: State transition diagram for the MESI coherence protocol.

determine if any of them has a copy. If a copy is found, the cache asserts the COPIES-EXIST bus line (indicated as "C" in the figure). In that case, the fetched block is placed in the requestor's cache in the shared state. If, on the other hand, the COPIES-EXIST bus line is not asserted (indicated as the "!C" in the figure), the fetched block is placed in the requestor's cache in the exclusive state. When there is a processor write request, the cache must allocate a valid copy of the cache block, and to do that, it posts a BusRdX request on the bus. Other caches will respond by invalidating their cached copies, while the memory responds by supplying the requested block. When the requestor gets the block, it is placed in the cache in the "M" or modified state.

Suppose now the cache already has the block in the exclusive state. Any read to the block is a cache hit and proceeds without generating a bus transaction. A write to the block, in contrast to the MSI protocol which has no exclusive state, does not generate a bus transaction because a block in the exclusive state implies that it is the only cached copy in the system. So the write can proceed after the state transitions to modified.

Suppose now the cache already has the block in the shared state. On a processor read, the block is found in the cache and data is returned to the processor. This does not incur a bus transaction since it is a cache hit, and the state remains unchanged. On the other hand, on a processor write, there may be other cached copies that need to be invalidated, so a BusUpgr is posted on the bus, and the state transitions to modified. The memory controller ignores a BusUpgr because it does not need to fetch the block from the main memory and supplies it to the requesting processor.

If the cache block is present in the cache in the modified state, reads or writes by the processor do not change the state, and no bus transaction is generated since it can be sure that no other cached copies exist.

Now let us look at how the finite state machine reacts to snooped bus transactions. If the cache does not have the block or the block is in invalid state, any snooped BusRd or BusRdX/BusUpgr should not affect it, so they are ignored.

If the cache block is in an exclusive state, when a BusRd transaction is snooped, that means another processor suffered a read miss and is trying to fetch the block. Since the result is that the block is stored in more than one cache, the state must transition into the shared state. Furthermore, the Illinois MESI protocol proposed a performance optimization referred to as *cache-to-cache transfer* [46], in which a valid and clean block can be supplied by a cache that has a copy rather than by just the main memory. Such a cache-to-cache transfer can shorten the read miss latency since the time to transfer the block from another cache is typically faster than the time for the memory controller to fetch the block from the main memory.

■ *Did you know?*

The benefit of cache-to-cache transfer is predicated upon the lower latency of obtaining data from a peer cache compared to obtaining from the main memory. While this is in general true in a bus-based system in which the coherence is maintained at the outermost level on chip cache, it may become less valid or invalid in other scenarios. For example, in a multicore architecture in which coherence is maintained at the level of L2 caches, and there is an on-chip shared L3 cache, it may be faster to fetch the missed block from the L3 cache rather than from another L2 cache. Another example is on a 3D chip where memories are stacked on top of processors. It may be faster to obtain data from a memory vertically than from a peer cache on a remote area of the same die.

If a BusRdX is snooped, it indicates that another processor wants to write to the block. In this case, the local cached copy is flushed and then invalidated. The cache-to-cache transfers labeled as FlushOpt are optional and are performed as a performance enhancement rather than for satisfying correctness requirements.

If the cache block is in a shared state, when a BusRd transaction is snooped, that means another processor suffers a read miss and tries to fetch the block. Therefore, the state remains shared, and one of the caches supplies the block through FlushOpt. If a BusRdX is snooped, one of the copy is flushed to the bus through the FlushOpt, and the local cached copy is invalidated. Note that the main memory does not need to be updated when a FlushOpt is seen on the bus. This is because the cache block involved in the FlushOpt is clean, i.e., the copy in the main memory is also fresh and valid.

Table 7.3: Illustration of MESI protocol operations.

	Request	P1	P2	P3	Bus Request	Data Supplier
0	Initially	–	–	–	–	–
1	R1	E	–	–	BusRd	Mem
2	W1	M	–	–	–	–
3	R3	S	–	S	BusRd	P1's cache
4	W3	I	–	M	BusUpgr	–
5	R1	S	–	S	BusRd	P3's cache
6	R3	S	–	S	–	–
7	R2	S	S	S	BusRd	**P1/P3's cache**

If the cache block is in the modified state, the copy in the cache is the only valid copy in the entire system (no other cached copies exist and the value in the main memory is stale). Therefore, when a BusRd transaction is snooped, the block must be flushed for ensuring write propagation, and the state transitions to shared. The cache that puts the BusRd request must pick up the flushed block as the reply to its request and place it in its cache in a shared state. In addition, the main memory must also snoop the flush and update the main memory.

Write propagation is ensured through two mechanisms. First, by invalidating other copies on a write to a cache block, other caches are forced to suffer a cache miss to reload the block. Secondly, by flushing a modified block upon snooping a BusRd or BusRdX request, the flushed block can be picked up by the requesting processor/cache, ensuring that it gets the latest value of the block.

Compared to the MSI protocol, the MESI protocol eliminates the need to incur two bus transactions on a read-then-write sequence coming from a processor. This avoids penalizing sequential programs and highly-tuned parallel programs. However, the MESI protocol incurs additional complexity compared to the MSI protocol. First, there is the addition of the COPIES-EXIST bus line and its associated logic. Secondly, the cache-to-cache transfer in the form of FlushOpt incurs additional complexity in the coherence controller. This is especially the case when the FlushOpt is performed when a cache block has a shared state. There are potentially multiple caches that have the block in the shared state and all of them read the cache block from their caches and attempt to perform the FlushOpt. One of them will get to the bus faster than others and flushes its block on the bus. Other coherence controllers must snoop this, realize that somebody else has flushed the same block, and cancel their plans to flush the block. The cost of this mechanism is that potentially many cache controllers have performed useless work (and waste power) by reading the cache, try to obtain the bus access, and cancel it when someone supplies the block earlier than they can.

To illustrate how MESI works, consider the example in Table 7.3 which shows the same sequence of requests made by various processors as in Table 7.1. The example in the table assumes that initially the cache is empty. The difference between MESI and MSI are highlighted in bold fonts. In the example, we assume that BusUpgr is used when a processor write request is made to a block that is already cached, whereas BusRdX is used when the block is not yet cached.

On a read from Processor 1, a BusRd is posted, the main memory responds with the block, and Processor 1 gets the block, stores it in its cache with an exclusive state. On a write from Processor 1, in contrast to MSI, the cache state transitions to modified without incurring a bus transaction, since we know that in the exclusive state, no other cached copies exist.

When Processor 3 makes a read request, a BusRd is posted on the bus. Processor 1's snooper picks it up, checks its cache tag, and finds that it has the block in a modified state. This means that Processor 1 has the latest (and the only valid) copy, and flushes it in response to the snooped request. The block state transitions to shared after that. In the mean time, the memory controller also attempts to fetch the block from the main memory because it does not know if eventually a cache will supply the data or not. Processor 3 snoops the flush, and by matching the address of the block being flushed with its outstanding read transaction, it knows that the flushed block should be treated as the reply to its read request. So the block is picked up, stored in its cache in the shared state. The main memory which has been trying to fetch the block from memory will also snoop the flushed block, pick it up, cancel its memory fetch, and overwrite the stale copy of the block in memory.

Next, Processor 3 has a write request. It posts a BusUpgr on the bus to invalidate copies in other caches. Processor 1's coherence controller responds by invalidating its copy. Processor 3's cache block state transitions to modified.

When Processor 1 attempts to read the block, it suffers a cache miss as a result of the earlier invalidation that it received. Processor 1 posts a BusRd and Processor 3 responds by flushing its cache block and transitions its state to shared. The flushed block also updates the main memory copy, so as a result the cache blocks are now clean.

When Processor 3 reads the block, it finds it in state shared in its cache. Since it has a valid copy, it has a cache hit and does not generate a bus request.

Finally, Processor 2 attempts to read the block and posts a BusRd on the bus. Unlike MSI that does not employ cache-to-cache transfer, in MESI both Processor 1 and Processor 3's cache controllers attempt to supply the block by flushing it on the cache through FlushOpt. One of them wins and supplies the block, and Processor 2 will pick up the block. The memory controller cancels its fetch upon snooping the FlushOpt block.

While the MESI protocol has improved various performance aspects of the MSI protocol, it still suffers from a remaining problem that is potentially quite serious. When a cache block is read and written successively by multiple processors, each of the read incurs an intervention that requires the owner to flush the cache block. While the flushed block must be picked up by the requestor as a means to ensure write propagation, the flushed block updating the copy in the main memory is not a correctness requirement for write propagation. Unfortunately, the definition of the shared state is that the cache block is clean, in that the value of the block is the same with that in the main memory. Therefore, in order to preserve the meaning of the shared block, the main memory has no choice but to update its copy. This is referred to as *clean sharing* in that when a block is shared by multiple caches, it has to be clean. Note also that clean sharing implies that evicting a shared cache block can be performed silently, i.e., the block is simply discarded. Unfortunately, by keeping clean sharing, the main memory is updated too many times. In some systems, the bandwidth to the main memory is already restricted, so updating the main memory on each cache flush uses an excessive amount of bandwidth. For example, if multiple cores in a multicore architecture maintain coherence at the L2 cache level, the L2 caches can communicate with each other using an on-chip interconnection, but updating the main memory must be performed by going off-chip. Off-chip bandwidth is severely restricted in a multicore architecture because of the limited availability of pins and slow off-chip interconnection. Thus, it will be nice if a cache flush does not need to update the main memory, by allowing dirty block to be shared by multiple caches. Supporting *dirty sharing* can be provided with an additional state in the MOESI protocol which is described in the next section.

7.2.4 MOESI Protocol with Write Back Caches

As mentioned earlier, the bandwidth to the main memory can be reduced by allowing dirty sharing. The MOESI protocol allows dirty sharing. The MESI protocol is used by Intel processors such as the Xeon processor while the MOESI protocol is used by processors such as the AMD Opteron [4]. In the MOESI protocol, the same as the MSI protocol, processor requests to the cache include:

1. **PrRd**: processor-side request to read to a cache block

2. **PrWr**: processor-side request to write to a cache block

   Bus-side requests include:

1. **BusRd**: snooped request that indicates there is a read request to a cache block made by another processor.

2. **BusRdX**: snooped request that indicates there is a *read exclusive* (write) request to a cache block made by another processor which does not already have the block.

3. **BusUpgr**: snooped request that indicates that there is a write request to a cache block that another processor already has in its cache.

4. **Flush**: snooped request that indicates that an entire cache block is placed on the bus by a processor to facilitate a transfer to another processor's cache.

5. **FlushOpt**: snooped request that indicates that an entire cache block is posted on the bus in order to supply it to another processor. We refer to it as FlushOpt because unlike Flush which is needed for write propagation correctness, FlushOpt is implemented as a performance enhancing feature that can be removed without impacting correctness.

6. **FlushWB**: snooped request that indicates that an entire cache block is written back to the main memory by another processor, and it is not meant as a transfer from one cache to another.

   Each cache block has an associated state which can have one of the following values:

1. **Modified** (M): the cache block is valid in only one cache, and the value is (likely) different than the one in the main memory. This state has the same meaning as the dirty state in a write back cache for a single system, except that now it also implies exclusive ownership.

2. **Exclusive** (E): the cache block is valid, clean, and *only resides in one cache*.

3. **Owned** (O): the cache block is valid, possibly dirty, and may reside in multiple caches. However, when there are multiple cached copies, there can only be one cache that has the block in owned state, other caches should have the block in state shared.

4. **Shared** (S): the cache block is valid, possibly dirty, but may reside in multiple caches.

5. **Invalid** (I): the cache block is invalid.

The idea behind the owned state is that when a cache block is shared across caches, its value is allowed to differ from that in the main memory. One cache is assigned as the owner and caches the block in state "O" or owned, while others cache it in the shared state. The existence of the owner simplifies how data is supplied in a cache-to-cache transfer. For example, when a BusRd is snooped, we can let the owner to provide data through FlushOpt, while other controllers take no action. The main memory does not need to pick up a Flush or FlushOpt to update the block in main memory. In addition, we can also assign the owner to be responsible for writing back the block to the main memory when the block is evicted. Hence, when a cache block in the shared state is evicted, regardless of whether it is clean or dirty, it can be discarded. Only when the cache block that is evicted is in the owned state, it is written back to the memory to update it. To indicate that a block in the owned state is evicted and needs to update the main memory, a different bus request type is needed, which we refer to as FlushWB.

Who should be the owner of a cache block? To answer this question, consider that when there is dirty sharing, a block in the shared state can be replaced silently, but a block in the owned state must be written back to the main memory. Bus bandwidth can be conserved if the frequency of write backs is minimized. To reduce the frequency of write backs, the cache that will hold the block the longest should be selected as the owner. Although predicting which cache will hold a particular shared block the longest is difficult, good heuristics can often help. Since applications tend to exhibit temporal locality, a good heuristic for predicting such a cache is selecting the cache that last wrote to or read from the block as the owner. However, reads to valid blocks do not incur any bus transactions, so it is inconvenient (and expensive) to change the ownership when a processor reads from a shared block in the cache. Thus, one heuristic that can be used (implemented in AMD Opteron systems) is to select the last cache that wrote to the block as the owner. More specifically, the cache that has the block in the modified state, when it receives an intervention request, downgrades the block state to owned – in effect becoming the owner of the block.

We assume that the caches use *write allocate* and *write invalidate* cache coherence policies. The finite state machine corresponding to the MOESI coherence protocol for write back caches is shown in Figure 7.7. In the figure, the response to processor-side requests is shown on the top part, while the response to the snooper-side requests is shown on the bottom part.

As before, the *I* state represents two cases: a case in which the block is not cached, or when the block is cached but its state is invalid. Let us consider the top part of the figure that shows a reaction to a processor read or write request. First, consider when the cache block is in "I" (invalid) state. When there is a processor read request, it suffers a cache miss. To load the data into the cache, a BusRd is posted on the bus, and the memory controller responds to the BusRd by fetching the block from the main memory. Other snoopers will snoop the request and check their caches to determine if any of them has a copy. If a copy is found, the cache asserts the COPIES-EXIST bus line (indicated as "C" in the figure). In that case, the fetched block is placed in the requestor's cache in the shared state. If, on the other hand, the COPIES-EXIST bus line is not asserted (indicated as the "!C" in the figure), the fetched block is placed in the requestor's cache in the exclusive state. When there is a processor write request, the cache must allocate a valid copy of the cache block, and to do that, it posts a BusRdX request on the bus. Other caches will respond by invalidating their

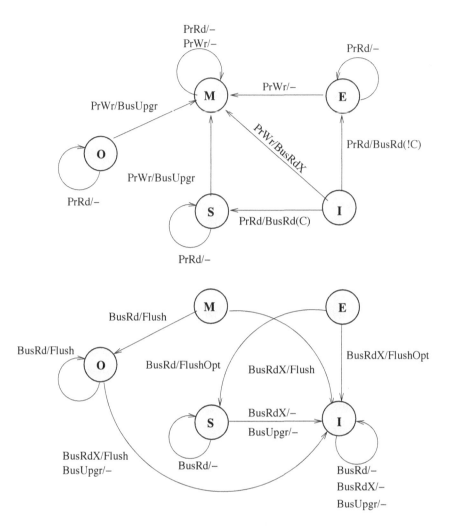

Figure 7.7: State transition diagram for the MOESI coherence protocol.

cached copies, while the memory responds by supplying the requested block. When the requestor gets the block, it is placed in the cache in the "M" or modified state.

Suppose now the cache already has the block in the exclusive state. Any read to the block is a cache hit and proceeds without generating a bus transaction. A write to the block, as in the MESI protocol, does not generate a bus transaction because a block in the exclusive state implies that it is the only cached copy in the system. So the write can proceed after the state transitions to modified.

Suppose now the cache already has the block in the shared state. On a processor read, the block is found in the cache and data is returned to the processor. This does not incur a bus transaction since it is a cache hit, and the state remains unchanged. On the other hand, on a processor write, there may be other cached copies that need to be invalidated, so a BusUpgr is posted on the bus, and the state transitions to modified.

If the cache block is present in the cache in the modified state, reads or writes by the processor do not change the state, and no bus transaction is generated since it can be sure that no other cached copies exist, since through an earlier invalidation, we have made sure that only one modified copy can exist in the system.

If the cache block is present in the cache in an owned state, this means that it is dirty and the block is shared in other caches. A processor read can just fetch the value from the cache. A processor write must invalidate other cached copies by posting a BusUpgr transaction.

Now let us look at how the finite state machine reacts to snooped bus transactions. If the cache does not have the block or the block is in invalid state, any snooped BusRd or BusRdX/BusUpgr should not affect it, so they are ignored.

If the cache block is in an exclusive state, when a BusRd request is snooped, the block is flushed to the cache using FlushOpt, and the state transitions to shared. When a BusRdX request is snooped, the block is flushed using FlushOpt and the state transitions to invalid.

If the cache block is in a shared state, when a BusRd transaction is snooped, that means another processor suffered a read miss and is trying to fetch the block. Therefore, the state remains shared, and since only the owner is responsible for flushing the block, the local cache does not flush the block. Note that there may be an owner (in case of dirty sharing) or there may not be an owner (clean sharing). In the case that there is no owner (clean sharing), the main memory can supply the block, although using a MESI-like FlushOpt is also possible here. If a BusRdX or BusUpgr is snooped, the block's state transitions to invalid. Again, the owner (if there is one) is responsible for flushing the block, so, in contrast to MESI, the non-owner caches do not need to flush their block copies.

If the cache block is in the modified state, the copy in the cache is the only valid copy in the entire system (no other cached copies exist and the value in the main memory is stale). Therefore, when a BusRd transaction is snooped, the block must be flushed for ensuring write propagation, and the state transitions to owned. The reason for transitioning to the owned state is based on a heuristic that has been discussed earlier. Note that by transitioning to the owned state, the local cache has become the supplier of the block and is responsible for flushing it when required.

If the cache block is in the owned state, it indicates that there is dirty sharing, with the local cache being responsible as the supplier of the block. Hence, when a BusRd is snooped, it flushes the block and remains in the owned state (i.e., remains the owner). If a BusRdX is snooped, it supplies the block by flushing it, and transitions into the invalid state. If a BusUpgr is snooped, it transitions into the invalid state without flushing the block. Note that because or dirty sharing, the flushes from this state is a correctness requirement, rather than a performance enhancement because potentially, nobody else in the system has a valid copy of the block (some sharers which obtain the block from the owner may have a valid copy, but there is no guarantee that there are sharers).

When the block in the owned state is evicted from the cache, the ownership disappears since other caches have the copy in the shared state. Hence, at this point dirty sharing must be *converted* into clean sharing. The owner is responsible for flushing the block to the memory so that the memory can update its copy. This is achieved by posting a FlushWB request on the bus. In contrast to Flush or FlushOpt requests that are ignored by the memory controller, a FlushWB request is picked up by the memory controller to update the value in the main memory.

Two mechanisms ensure write propagation. First, by invalidating other copies on a write to a cache block, other caches are forced to reload the block through cache misses. Secondly, with dirty sharing, a cache acts as an owner and flushes the block when it snoops a BusRd or BusRdX, ensuring the correct block value is passed on. With clean sharing, the memory supplies the block.

Table 7.4: Illustration of MOESI protocol operations. * indicates dirty sharing, in which the main memory is not updated when a block is flushed on the bus.

	Request	**P1**	**P2**	**P3**	**Bus Request**	**Data Supplier**
0	Initially	–	–	–	–	–
1	R1	E	–	–	BusRd	Mem
2	W1	M	–	–	–	–
3	R3	O	–	S	BusRd	P1's cache*
4	W3	I	–	M	BusUpgr	–
5	R1	S	–	O	BusRd	P3's cache*
6	R3	S	–	O	–	–
7	R2	S	S	O	BusRd	**P3's cache**

Compared to the MESI protocol, the MOESI protocol does not reduce the bandwidth usage on the bus, but it does reduce the bandwidth use to the main memory. There are cases in which this introduces benefits. For example, in the AMD K7, two processor chips are connected to a common memory controller, and the memory controller connects to DRAMs. The interconnection between one processor and the memory controller is approximately equal to the bandwidth available between the memory controller and the main memory. However, when two processors are interconnected to the main memory controller, the combined bandwidth between processors is higher than the bandwidth to the main memory. Hence, MOESI was selected for the obvious benefit that it reduces the bandwidth requirement to the main memory. Another example in which reduced memory bandwidth may be useful is in a multicore architecture in which each core has a private last level cache, and the private caches are kept coherent. The caches can communicate using on-chip bandwidth, but the bandwidth to the main memory is limited by off-chip pin bandwidth. Since on-chip bandwidth is more abundant than off-chip bandwidth to the main memory, MOESI can reduce the off-chip bandwidth requirement.

To illustrate how MOESI works, consider the example in Table 7.4 which shows the same sequence of requests made by various processors as in Table 7.1. The example in the table assumes that initially the cache is empty. The difference between MOESI and MESI are highlighted in bold fonts.

On a read from Processor 1, a BusRd is posted, the main memory responds with the block, Processor 1 gets the block and stores it in its cache with an exclusive state. On a write from Processor 1, the cache state transitions to modified without incurring a bus transaction, since no other cached copies exist.

When Processor 3 makes a read request, a BusRd is posted on the bus. Processor 1's snooper picks it up, checks its cache tag, and finds that it has the block in a modified state. Processor 1 downgrades its cache state to owned, supplies the block through Flush on the bus. Processor 3 picks up the flushed block and places it its cache in the shared state. In the mean time, the memory controller ignores the flush that it snoops on the bus. Only if an owned block is written back, the memory controller needs to pick it up to update the main memory. Note that to distinguish an owner's flush due to natural block replacement versus that due to supplying the block to a remote requestor, another bus transaction needs to be used.

Next, Processor 3 has a write request. It posts a BusUpgr on the bus to invalidate copies in other caches. Processor 1's coherence controller responds by invalidating its copy. Processor 3's cache block state transitions to modified.

When Processor 1 attempts to read the block, it suffers a cache miss as a result of the earlier invalidation that it received. Processor 1 posts a BusRd and Processor 3 responds by flushing its cache block and transitions its state to owned. The flushed block does not update the main memory, allowing dirty sharing.

When Processor 3 reads the block, it finds it in state shared in its cache. Since it has a valid copy, it has a cache hit and does not generate a bus request.

Finally, Processor 2 attempts to read the block and posts a BusRd on the bus. Unlike MESI in which both Processor 1 and 3 try to flush the block, in MOESI the owner (Processor 3) flushes the block, while others (Processor 1) knows that it does not need to react.

> ■ *Did you know?*
>
> *While MOESI protocol allows dirty sharing and quick supply of dirty block from a peer cache to the cache that misses the block, it suffers from several limitations. One limitation is that when a clean block is kept by multiple caches, just like MESI, it has no simple way to designate a particular cache to supply a block to a cache that misses on the block. One protocol that addresses this problem is Intel's MESIF, where a new state (F = Forward) is created to designate (at most one) cache as a clean data block supplier, in the event another cache misses the block. When such an event occurs, the supplier cache transitions to a shared state after supplying the block, passing its forward state to the cache that suffered the miss. MESIF still does not allow dirty sharing as MOESI does.*
>
> *Another limitation of MOESI is that it is possible to lose the owner state, which happens when the cache that holds the dirty block in the O state evicts the block. The block will then be written back to main memory and the dirty sharing is converted into clean sharing. This is the case even when there may be other caches that hold the block as well. One possible solution [58] to this is to incorporate an ownership transfer mechanism, where when a dirty block owner wants to evict a block, it posts a query on the bus. If there is a positive snoop response by another cache, indicating that there is another cache who keeps the block, the owner state is transferred to the cache, which avoids the write back and retains dirty sharing. A complementary solution is to proactively transfer ownership to a cache that most recently missed on the block, since such a cache has a higher probability to retain the block the longest.*

7.2.5   Update-Based Protocol with Write Back Caches

One of the drawbacks of an invalidate-based protocol is that it incurs a high number of coherence misses. Each read to a block that has been invalidated incurs a cache miss, and the latency to serve the miss can be quite high. In this section, we will look at an update-based protocol that relies on directly updating cached values to achieve write propagation compared to using invalidation and subsequent misses to ensure write propagation. The update protocol that will be discussed is called the Dragon protocol [43]. The protocol assumes the following requests from the processor and bus transactions.

1. **PrRd**: processor-side request to read to a cache block that already resides in the cache.

2. **PrRdMiss**: processor-side request to read to a cache block that *does not* already reside in the cache.

3. **PrWr**: processor-side request to write to a cache block that already resides in the cache.

4. **PrWrMiss**: processor-side request to write to a cache block that *does not* already reside in the cache.

Bus-side requests include:

1. **BusRd**: snooped request that indicates there is a read request to a cache block made by another processor.

2. **Flush**: snooped request that indicates that an entire cache block is placed on the bus by another processor.

3. **BusUpd**: snooped request that indicates a write to a word results in propagating the written value on the bus. Only a word of data is posted on the bus, rather than an entire cache block.

Each cache block has an associated state which can have one of the following values:

1. **Modified** (M): the cache block is valid in only one cache, and the value is (likely) different than the one in the main memory. This state implies exclusive ownership.

2. **Exclusive** (E): the cache block is valid, clean, and *only resides in one cache*.

3. **Shared Modified** (Sm): the cache block is valid, possibly dirty, and may reside in multiple caches. However, when there are multiple cached copies, there can only be one cache that has the block in shared modified state, other caches should have the block in state shared clean. This state is similar to the owned state in MOESI that allows dirty sharing.

4. **Shared Clean** (Sc): the cache block is valid, possibly not clean, but may reside in multiple caches. This state is similar to the shared state in MOESI.

Similar to MOESI, the Dragon protocol allows dirty sharing in which the owner is assigned a state shared-modified, while other caches are assigned the shared-clean state. Note that since a cache block may be updated but never invalidated, there is no invalid state. If a block is cached, it has a valid value, although the value may be dirty.

We assume that the caches use *write allocate* and *write update* cache coherence policy. The finite state machine corresponding to the Dragon coherence protocol for write back caches is shown in Figure 7.8. In the figure, the response to processor-side requests is shown on the top part, while the response to the snooper-side requests is shown on the bottom part. Arrows that do not originate from a state represent the case in which prior to the transition, the block is not present in the cache.

Note that there is no invalid state. Hence, an arrow that goes from nowhere to a state represents a newly loaded block. Let us consider the top part of the figure that shows a reaction to a processor read or write request. First, consider when a read miss to a block occurs. BusRd is posted on the bus, and if there is no copy of the block in any cache (!C), then the block is placed in the cache in

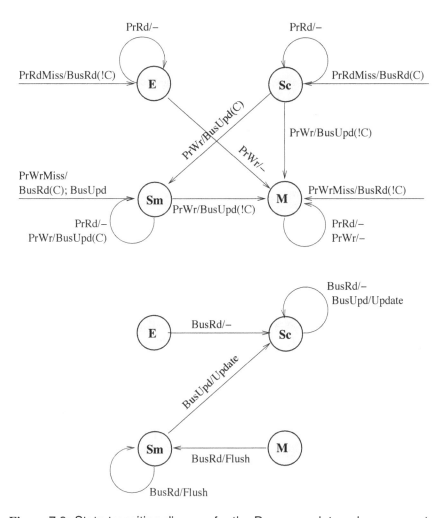

Figure 7.8: State transition diagram for the Dragon update coherence protocol.

the exclusive state. If there is already a copy in some caches (C), then the block is placed in the cache in the shared-clean state. Now consider when a write miss to a block occurs. If there is no copy of the block in any cache (!C), the block is placed in the cache in the modified state. If there is already a copy of the block in some caches (C), then the block is placed in the cache in the state shared-modified. After that, the write is performed and BusUpd is posted on the bus in order to update other copies.

If a block is already cached in the exclusive state, a processor read does not change its state and does not incur a bus transaction. A processor write changes it to the modified state without incurring a bus transaction.

If a block is already cached in the shared-clean, a processor read does not change its state and does not incur a bus transaction. A processor write changes it to the shared-modified because now it is the new owner of the block. In addition, since this is a processor write, it must propagate the written value by posting a BusUpd on the bus. Since it goes to the bus, the COPIES-EXIST line can also be checked, so that if there is no longer another cached copy, the state can transition to modified instead of shared-modified. Note that this is necessary for good performance because in the modified state, processor writes no longer incur bus update transactions, preserving bus bandwidth.

If a block is already cached in the shared-modified, a processor read does not change its state and does not incur a bus transaction. A processor write either keeps the state unchanged at shared-modified because it remains the owner of the block, or transitions to modified if it becomes the only cache that has a copy. In either case, BusUpd is posted in order to update other cached copies.

If a block is already cached in the modified state, a processor write or read does not change the state, and no bus transaction is incurred because we know no other cached copies exist.

Now let us look at how the finite state machine reacts to snooped bus transactions. If the cache does not have the block (not shown in any state), any snooped transaction is ignored.

If the cache block is in an exclusive state, when a BusRd request is snooped, the block is supplied from the main memory, so the state transitions to shared-clean without incurring further bus transactions. A BusUpd cannot occur in this state because there are no other caches that have the block; nobody else can update the block.

If the cache block is in a shared-clean state, when a BusRd transaction is snooped, that means another processor suffers a read miss and tries to fetch the block. Since the block is supplied by the main memory or the owner of the block, no action is taken. If there is dirty sharing, the owner is responsible for flushing the block. If a BusUpd is snooped, the update for the word is picked up and used to update the currently cached block.

If the cache block is in the shared-modified state, it means that the local cache is the owner of the block. Hence, if there is a BusRd, the block is flushed on the bus so that it can be picked up by the requestor. If there is a BusUpd, a requestor is trying to write to the block, hence the requestor will be the new owner of the block, so the ownership is relinquished by transitioning into the shared-clean state, and the update is merged into the cache block.

If the cache block is in the modified state, the copy in the cache is the only valid copy in the entire system. Therefore, when a BusRd transaction is snooped, the block must be flushed for ensuring write propagation, and the state transitions to shared-modified. A BusUpd is impossible to be snooped at this state because no other cached copies exist.

Unlike MSI, MESI, or MOESI, in the Dragon update protocol, write propagation is ensured by directly updating all other copies on a write. The BusUpd can propagate the needed bytes or words, so it may occupy the bus for a shorter time compared to a regular Flush.

To illustrate how the Dragon protocol works, consider the example in Table 7.5 which shows the same sequence of requests made by various processors as in Table 7.1. The example in the table assumes that initially the cache is empty.

On a read from Processor 1, a BusRd is posted, the main memory responds with the block, and Processor 1 gets the block, stores it in its cache with an exclusive state. On a write from Processor 1, the cache state transitions to modified without incurring a bus transaction, since no other cached copies exist.

When Processor 3 makes a read request, a BusRd is posted on the bus. Processor 1's snooper picks it up, checks its cache tag, and finds that it has the block in a modified state. Processor 1 downgrades its cache state to shared-modified, supplies the block through Flush on the bus. Processor 3 picks up the flushed block and places it its cache in the shared-clean state. In the mean time, the memory controller ignores the flush that it snoops on the bus, allowing dirty sharing. Only if a shared-modified block is written back, the memory controller needs to pick it up to update the main

Table 7.5: Illustration of the Dragon protocol operations. * indicates dirty sharing, in which the main memory is not updated when a block is flushed on the bus.

	Request	P1	P2	P3	Bus Request	Data Supplier
0	Initially	–	–	–	–	–
1	R1	E	–	–	BusRd	Mem
2	W1	M	–	–	–	–
3	R3	Sm	–	Sc	BusRd	P1's cache*
4	W3	Sc	–	Sm	BusUpd	–*
5	R1	Sc	–	Sm	–	–*
6	R3	Sc	–	Sm	–	–*
7	R2	Sc	Sc	Sm	BusRd	P3's cache*

memory. Note that to distinguish this with a regular flush, a different bus transaction needs to be used.

Next, Processor 3 has a write request. It posts a BusUpd on the bus to update other cached copies. Processor 1's coherence controller responds by transitioning to the shared-clean state, relinquishing the ownership of the block, and updates its own cached copy. Processor 3 becomes the new owner and the state of the block becomes shared-modified.

When Processor 1 attempts to read the block, it has a cache hit since the block is valid because it has been updated earlier. The state is unchanged and the no bus transaction is involved.

When Processor 3 reads the block, it also finds a valid copy in its cache. So it reads the copy and no bus transaction is generated.

Finally, Processor 2 attempts to read the block and posts a BusRd on the bus. Similar to MOESI, the owner (Processor 3) supplies the block through a flush which is picked up by Processor 2, which can then cache the block in the shared-clean state.

There are several low-level protocol choices. One of them is that one can remove dirty sharing by requiring that any BusUpd should be snooped by the memory controller to update the block in the main memory. If this is implemented, then the state shared-modified can be eliminated since we now only have clean sharing. However, clean sharing increases the frequency of updating the lower level memory hierarchy component.

7.3 Impact of Cache Design on Cache Coherence Performance

Let us now revisit different types of cache misses: compulsory, conflict, capacity, coherence, and system-related (refer to Chapter 5 for more discussion). One of the types of cache misses is coherence misses. Let us define coherence misses more explicitly: *coherence misses are misses that occur due to accessing cache blocks that have been invalidated due to coherence events.*

Clearly, coherence misses only affect write invalidate protocols since an update protocol does not invalidate a cache block, which does not lead to subsequent misses on the block. This is not to say that an update protocol does not incur a performance problem in caches. For example, an update protocol may keep updating a block in another cache that is no longer used. In this case the block stays in the cache longer than needed, and this reduces the number of useful cache blocks that can be stored. Hence, while using an update based protocol does not incur coherence misses, it incurs a hidden cost of increased number of conflict and capacity misses.

There are two types of coherence misses: *true sharing* and *false sharing* misses. A true sharing miss occurs due to multiple threads sharing the same variable (same byte/word), and they invalidate one another. A false sharing miss occurs due to multiple threads sharing different variables in different bytes or words that reside in a single cache block. Because the coherence granularity is a cache block, the block is invalidated by one another while they have no actual sharing.

How do cache parameters affect the number of coherence misses? Table 7.6 shows the relationship. First, larger cache block sizes typically reduce the number of any type of cache misses if there is spatial locality on the block due to their *prefetching effect*, i.e., it takes fewer misses to fetch the same number of bytes. The exception is the number of false sharing misses. The number of true sharing misses tends to decrease as the prefetching effect of large cache block sizes allows multiple bytes that may have true sharing to be fetched together. However, the number of false sharing misses increases with a larger cache block size because false sharing is more likely to occur as more bytes are grouped in a cache block.

Table 7.6: Impact of various cache parameters on coherence misses.

Parameters	True Sharing	False Sharing
Larger cache size	increased	increased
Larger block size	decreased	increased
Larger associativity	unclear	unclear

The impact of cache size on coherence misses is less subtle. A larger cache size allows more blocks to be cached, and more of them will likely suffer from true sharing and false sharing misses. With a small cache size, these blocks would not be cached, so they incur capacity misses rather than coherence misses. Finally, the impact of associativity on coherence misses is unclear.

7.4 Performance and Other Practical Issues

7.4.1 Prefetching and Coherence Misses

Employing prefetching carries some risks in multiprocessor systems. Prefetching of a block generates an intervention through a BusRd transaction on the bus. If currently there is a cache that holds the block in an exclusive or modified state, then it must supply the block and downgrade its state to shared. Unfortunately, doing this incurs three risks. First, there is the usual risk that the prefetched block evicts a more immediately useful block in the cache. This risk is inherent in prefetching as long as the prefetched blocks are placed in the cache and not in a separate buffer, and also exists in single processor prefetching. The second risk is that the prefetched block may be stolen before it is used by the processor. Such risk increases when the prefetching acts aggressively in bringing in blocks into the cache early. For example, if an invalidation is received, the prefetched block must be invalidated and refetched later. When the processor needs to access it, it suffers from a cache miss despite the fact that prefetching was accurate in identifying the block that the processor will be accessing. The third risk occurs when the block is supplied from a cache that held the block in the exclusive or modified state. If the supplier processor still needs to write to the block, its write will be delayed now that it needs to send an invalidation on the bus. Consequently, prefetching, if done too early, may hurt the performance of the processor that supplies the data as well as the one that performs prefetching. Overall, prefetching in a multiprocessor system is a lot trickier than in a single processor system.

7.4.2 Multi-Level Caches

So far, we have assumed a system in which each processor has a cache. If a processor has multi-level caches, the cache coherence protocol needs to be modified in order to work on them. Consider a system where each processor has L1 caches and an L2 cache, and the coherence is maintained at the L2 cache level.

Ensuring cache coherence protocol correctness requires ensuring write propagation, even in the case of multi-level caches. Write propagation must be performed *downstream*: when a processor writes to its local L1 cache, it must be propagated not just to the L2 cache, and from there to other processors' caches. It must also be performed *upstream*: when another processor's attempt to write is snooped on the bus, the write must not only be propagated to the L2 cache, but also to the L1 cache.

Let us first consider the downstream write propagation. At the very least, a write attempt in the L1 cache must notify the L2 cache so that the L2 cache can generate an appropriate bus transaction to invalidate other processors' caches. This can be accomplished by simple changes to the L1 cache controller. Secondly, when another processor suffers a subsequent miss on the block, the latest value of the block must be supplied to the requestor through a bus flush. One relevant question here is whether the latest value of the block resides in the L1 cache or the L2 cache. If it is in the L2 cache, the L2 cache can supply the block on the bus. If it is in the L1 cache, the L2 cache must not supply the block directly. Instead, it must obtain the block from the L1 cache, before supplying it on the bus.

The write policy of the L1 cache determines how that mechanism should be implemented. If the L1 cache uses a write through policy, then all writes at the L1 cache are always propagated down to the L2 cache. Thus, the L2 cache always has the latest version of the block and can supply a modified block on the bus directly. If, on the other hand, the L1 cache uses a write back policy, the L2 cache does not always have the latest version of a block. Dirty blocks may be kept at the L1 cache without the knowledge of the L2 cache. To support write propagation correctly, the L2 cache must (1) know that the L1 cache has a dirty copy, and (2) ask the L1 cache to write back its cache block so that the L2 cache can pick up the latest version of the block. Therefore, the L1 cache controller must be modified to notify the L2 cache upon a write. The L2 cache also needs to keep a special cache state to keep track that a block is dirty in the L1 cache. Finally, when the snooper notifies the L2 cache controller that there is an intervention request to a block that is dirty in the L1 cache, the L2 cache controller must request the block to be written back from the L1 cache, and request the block state to be updated in the L1 cache. The write back updates the copy in the L2 cache as well and modifies the state appropriately. Then, the L2 cache supplies the block on the bus.

Table 7.7: Illustration of protocol operation for a multicore with three cores, private L1 caches, and a shared L2 cache.

	Request	P1.L1	P2.L1	P3.L1	L2	Data Supplier
0	Initially	–	–	–	–	–
1	R1	V	–	–	E	Mem
2	W1	V	–	–	M	–
3	R3	V	–	V	M	L2 Cache
4	W3	I	–	V	M	–
5	R1	V	–	V	M	L2 Cache
6	R3	V	–	V	M	–
7	R2	V	V	V	M	L2 Cache
8	EvictL2	I	I	I	I	–

Let us consider the upstream write propagation. When an invalidation is received by the L2 cache, it must invalidate its block, but such invalidation must also be propagated to the L1 cache, in case the L1 cache also has a copy of the block. This is required to force a cache miss when the processor wants to access the block later on. Readers may recall that such policy is already enforced if the inclusion property between the L2 and L1 cache is enforced (refer to Section 5.2.4). Therefore, when an inclusive L2 cache is used, the upstream write propagation is automatic. However, if an inclusive L2 cache is not used, each invalidation must still be sent to the L1 cache. Note that sending an invalidation to the L1 cache on each snooped write request is expensive as the L1 cache tag must be accessed to determine if the block is stored at the L1 cache or not. The benefit of the inclusion property is that since it is guaranteed that the blocks that are stored in the L1 caches are also stored in the L2 cache, if a snooped bus transaction has verified that the block involved is not found in the L2 cache, no invalidation or intervention need to be sent to the L1 cache since the block cannot be stored in the L1 cache either.

Cache Coherence in a Shared Cache

To illustrate how coherence in a multi-level caches works, consider a 3-core system with private caches and a shared L2 cache. Table 7.7 shows states of a data block in all caches after various transactions. The example assumes that the L1 caches, private to each core, use a write through policy, and keep two states for each block: Valid and Invalid. The L2 cache, which is shared by all cores, on the other hand, uses a write back policy, an inclusive policy, and keeps MESI states. The L2 cache keeps MESI states because it may be designed to keep data coherent with other L2 caches in a larger system.

On a read from Processor 1 (the first request), the block is fetched from off-chip memory and placed in the L1 cache of Processor 1 in a Valid state, as well as in the L2 cache in an exclusive state. When Processor 1 later writes to the block, since the L1 cache is a write through cache, the write request is sent to the L2 cache. The L2 cache may send invalidation to the L1 caches of Processor 2 and Processor 3. However, if the L2 cache keeps a directory of L1 caches, or if it keeps duplicates of the L1 cache tags of all the processors, it only needs to check the tags to see if any other L1 caches have a copy of the block, and only sends invalidation to the L1 caches that may have a copy of the block (none in this case). The write request also writes the new value to the block that resides in the L2 cache, and the state at the L2 cache changes to modified.

On a read request from Processor 3, the L2 cache has the latest value of the data block so it directly supplies the block to the L1 cache of Processor 3. When later Processor 3 wants to write to the block, the request is sent to the L2 cache, which in turn sends invalidation to Processor 1's L1 cache. Processor 3 can then proceed with its write, while the block is invalidated at the L1 cache of Processor 1. The newly written block value is also propagated down to the L2 cache. Later, when Processor 1 wants to read the block, it suffers an L1 cache miss, and the block is supplied by the L2 cache. A read by Processor 3, on the other hand, is a cache hit. When Processor 2 wants to read the block, the block is again supplied by the L2 cache as the L2 cache has the latest value of the block.

Finally, if the block is ever evicted from the L2 cache, either due to the replacement policy making room for a new block, or due to invalidation received from an external source (such as from another chip), to keep the inclusion property between the L2 cache and L1 caches, invalidation is sent to all L1 caches.

7.4.3 Snoop Filtering

In well-optimized programs, threads do not share much data. So most of the time, most snooped bus transactions do not find the block in the local cache. However, even in that case, the snooper has incurred unnecessary work: snooped the bus transaction, and checked the cache tag to determine whether the cache has the block. Snooping each bus transaction is unavoidable in a bus-based multiprocessor. However, checking the cache tag on each snooped transaction is expensive and often unnecessary. First, if the coherence level is at the L2 cache level, then the L2 cache tags are accessed by both the processor as well as by the snooper. Accesses from the processor and the snooper compete and such competition may increase contention-related delay. The degree of such contention depends on the number of L2 cache ports. Hence, one way to reduce the contention delay in accessing L2 cache port is to add an additional port. However, this comes at the expense of a significant area overhead and power, which reduces the overall cache size. Alternatively, the L2 cache tag can be duplicated to eliminate contention between the processor and the coherence controller. But again, this solution comes at the cost of a significant area overhead.

One possible solution to reduce contention between the processor and the snooper is to introduce a *snoop filter*, which determines whether a snooper needs to check the L2 cache tag or not. By reducing the number snooped transactions that need to check the cache tags, contention and power consumption can be reduced, allowing a single ported L2 cache to perform well.

An example of snoop filter implementations can be found in the IBM BlueGene/P processor [50], which is a 4-core multicore processor. Each core has private L1 and L2 caches, and an L3 cache shared by all cores. Coherence is maintained between the L2 caches. The snoop filter implements several types of filter. The first filter is a *history filter* which records blocks that have been verified not to be in the cache, i.e., recently checked against the cache tags and found to mismatch, or recently invalidated blocks. When there are bus read or read exclusive requests snooped on the bus to these blocks, the requests are ignored and the L2 cache tags are not checked. Another filter is *stream filter* which records recent stream-like cache misses made by the processor. If a snooped request on the bus matches the stream, they are further checked against the L2 cache tags. A third filter is referred to *range filter*. A range filter records address ranges that are not cached, e.g., because they are specified as non-cacheable. Snooped bus transactions to these addresses are ignored.

7.5 Broadcast Protocol with Point-to-Point Interconnect

The choice of cache coherence protocol highly depends on the size of the multiprocessor or multi-core system, i.e., the number of caches that need to be kept coherent. A small number of processors can benefit from a bus-based interconnection with broadcast coherence. However, since a bus is not scalable due to its physical constraints (clock skew, central arbitration limit, etc.), for a medium or large multiprocessor, a different alternative is needed. For a medium-scale multiprocessor system, a more suitable alternative is to use *point-to-point interconnection*, while still relying on a broadcast or snoopy protocol. A point-to-point interconnect is a network that utilizes a set of routers and links, where a link connects only a pair of routers. Together, the routers and links form a network *topology*, i.e., the overall shape of the network, such as a ring, a mesh, a torus, etc. The key characteristic of a point-to-point interconnect is that there is no link that is shared by all processors or caches. Therefore, it is absent of a shared medium that can easily be used for broadcasting messages, and for ordering of requests made by various processors.

In this section, we will discuss how a broadcast/snoopy protocol can still be designed on top of a point-to-point interconnected system. Such a protocol makes sense as we scale up the system to a larger number of processors, if the shared medium becomes a scalability bottleneck at a lower processor count compared to the processor count where the broadcast protocol becomes a scalability bottleneck. Eventually, however, broadcast/snoopy protocol cannot scale to a large-scale multiprocessor. For them, the only choice to keep cache tiles coherent is to use a directory protocol; it is the only scalable protocol for a large number of caches. In this section, we will discuss snoopy cache coherence protocol implemented on multiprocessor system with a point-to-point interconnect.

Recall from an earlier discussion of coherence protocol that to implement a coherence protocol correctly, we need to ensure the following properties: write propagation and transaction serialization. Write propagation can be enforced through invalidation and maintaining cache coherence states. Ensuring write propagation is performed by broadcasting invalidation to all caches in a broadcast protocol. In this regard, broadcast coherence over a point-to-point network relies on the same strategy as a broadcast protocol over a shared bus.

Transaction serialization requires two things: (1) a way to determine the sequence of transactions that is consistently viewed by all processors, and (2) a way to provide the illusion that each transaction appears to proceed atomically, absence of overlap with other transactions. Transaction serialization in a bus-based broadcast protocol is achieved by ensuring that all processors obey the order in which requests are posted on the shared bus. For example, if a processor wants to write but snoops an invalidation request before it has a chance to place its upgrade request on the bus, the processor has to cancel its write, invalidate its cache block, and reissue the write request as a read exclusive request. Avoiding overlap in processing of multiple requests that are already sequenced is trivial in a shared bus as long as snooped requests are serviced based on the order in which they appear on the bus.

Let us now assess the situation with regard to achieving a broadcast protocol over point-to-point interconnection network, such as a ring or a mesh. Write propagation can be ensured by guaranteeing that invalidation will reach all tiles, and all tiles will react to it.

Globally sequencing requests is more challenging due to the absence of a natural sequencer since there is no shared medium such as the bus. In general, there are two alternatives to achieve global sequencing of requests. The first approach is to assign a *sequencer* whose role is to provide an ordering point for colliding requests and ensuring that requests are processed and seen by all cores in that order. The second approach is to design the protocol to work in a distributed fashion, without having to assign a single sequencer.

In the first approach, there are several possible choices for the component we assign as the global sequencer, depending on which cache level the cache coherence protocol is provided. For example, if we are keeping the L2 caches coherent and there is a shared L3 cache, we can designate the L3 cache as the global sequencer. If on the other hand the L3 caches need to be kept coherent and they are the outermost level caches, we can designate a directory or memory controller as the sequencer.

All requests are sent to the sequencer, and the order in which they are received by the sequencer determines the order in which the requests are serviced. The same order must also be the same one observed by all processors. The latter requirement is not straightforward to ensure. It requires that all transactions that may be processed concurrently appear as if they occurred atomically in the same order determined by the sequencer.

How does the sequencer handle a request? A write request that arrives at the sequencer is handled by broadcasting an invalidation to all processors, which respond by sending an invalidation acknowledgment message to the sequencer or the requestor (this is a design choice). A read request that arrives at the sequencer will also be broadcast to all processors, so that it can be determined where the block may be cached. If a cache holds the block in a dirty state, it will supply the block. When the requestor obtains the block, it sends acknowledgment to the sequencer, which then considers the request processing complete. During the time request processing has started but has not completed, new requests that arrive at the sequencer will be rejected or serviced at a later time when the current request is complete. Note that this approach locks up the sequencer for the block address until the current request is fully processed. Such an approach reduces concurrency for request processing, but may be acceptable if the number of caches is relatively small.

In a more general design, the global sequencer does not have to be centralized. It can be distributed across tiles or chips, where each sequencer handles a set of block addresses distinct from other sequencers. Block addresses may be assigned to home tiles in an interleaved manner, and the interleaving granularity may vary.

Illustration of Global Sequencing

Figure 7.9 illustrates how a cache coherence protocol that relies on a global sequencer works. No assumption is used as to what type of device is assigned the role of the sequencer. One possibility is to assign the memory controller the role of the sequencer, such as in the AMD Opteron-based "Magny Cours" system. Figure 7.9(a) shows an example 6-node system interconnected using a point-to-point interconnect with a 2-dimensional mesh topology. The topology does not actually matter to the protocol discussion, it is chosen merely for ease of illustration. For simplicity, we will assume each node to have a processor/core and a cache. In the figure we label three nodes that we will use for illustration: node A, B, and S. Now suppose that node A and B simultaneously want to write to a block that they already cached in a clean state. Without sequencing the writes, we cannot guarantee that we achieve transaction serialization. Hence, suppose that node S is assigned the role of sequencing requests for the block. Hence, both node A and B send the write request to node S (part (b) of the figure). Suppose that the request from node A arrives at node S before the request from node B, and hence S needs to ensure that the write by A is seen by all cores as happening before the write by B. To achieve that, S serves the request from A, but replies to B with a negative acknowledgment so B can retry its request at a later time.

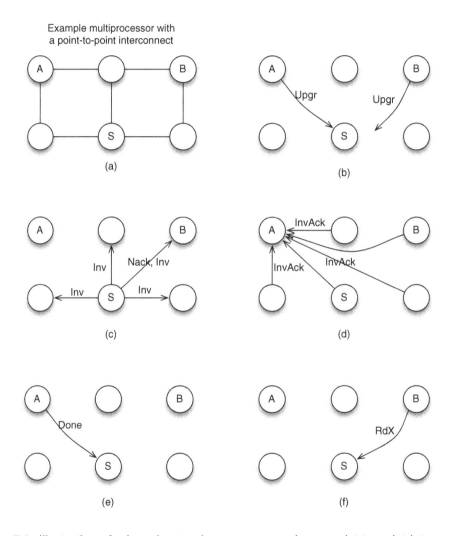

Figure 7.9: Illustration of a broadcast coherence protocol over point-to-point interconnection with a global sequencer.

To process the write request from A, S can broadcast an invalidation message to all nodes (c). S also sends a negative acknowledgement to B indicating that S cannot serve B's request due to being busy processing another transaction. S also needs to record that at the moment there is an outstanding transaction affecting the block so that it will not serve further requests until the outstanding transaction is completed. This may be achieved by transitioning the block's state to a transient state at S. Next, all nodes receive the invalidation message, invalidate the copy of the block if the block is found in the local cache, and send invalidation acknowledgment to node A (d). After receiving all invalidation acknowledgement messages, A knows it is safe to transition the block state to modified, and to write to the block. It then sends a notice of completion to the sequencer S (e). Upon receiving the notice, the sequencer knows that the write by A is completed, so now it can serve the next request. B, which received a negative acknowledgement, has to retry its write request, this time as a read exclusive (RdX) request, because after getting an invalidation, it no longer has a copy of the block (e).

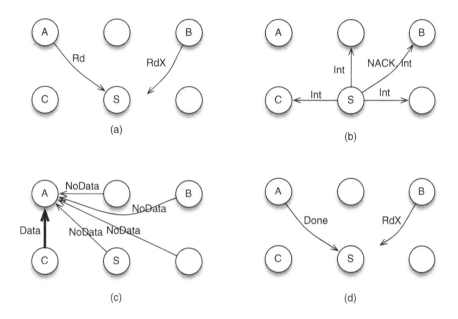

Figure 7.10: Illustration of a broadcast coherence protocol over point-to-point interconnection with a global sequencer.

Figure 7.10 illustrates another case of how the global sequencer works, in the case where a read request and a read exclusive request are sent simultaneously by node A and B, respectively. Suppose that the read request by A arrives earlier at the sequencer S. Since the sequencer determines the overall order at which transactions are (or appear to be) serialized, it responds to the read request while negatively acknowledge the read exclusive request from B. In part (b) of the figure, S sends intervention messages to all nodes except A. Each node receiving the intervention message check their cache to see if it has a copy of the block. If it does not have a copy of the block, it responds with a message indicating it has no copy of the message (NoData). If it has a copy of the block, such as node C, it responds with a message containing the data block (Data). This is shown in part (c). After collecting all the responses, node A can send a message to S to indicate that its request has been fully processed (d). Afterward, if B sends its read exclusive request to S, it will be processed.

Figure 7.11 illustrates another case with simultaneous read requests. This situation is unique since it does not involve a write request, therefore we are not dealing with two different versions (or values) for the data block. Thus, it is possible to overlap the processing of the two requests. Suppose that node A and B simultaneously want to read to a block that they do not find in their local caches.

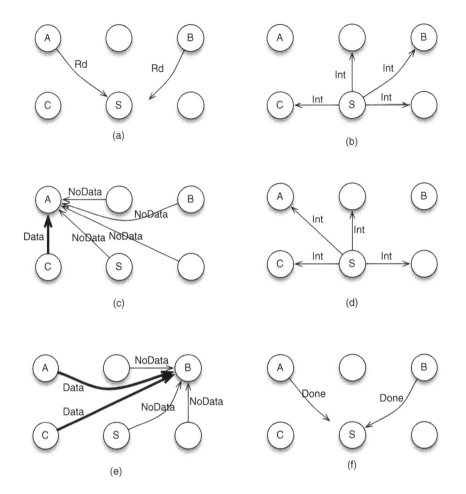

Figure 7.11: Illustration of a broadcast coherence protocol over point-to-point interconnection with a global sequencer.

Both node A and B send the read request to node S (part (a) of the figure). Suppose that request from node A arrives earlier in node S (a), and hence it is served first by S. The sequencer S can mark the block to indicate that the read has not completed. S does not know if the block is currently cached or not, or which cache may have the block. So it has to send an *intervention* message to all nodes (except the requestor A), inquiring if any of them has the data block (b). Suppose that node C has the block and supplies the block to A, while other nodes reply with NoData message to A (c). In the mean time, let us suppose that the sequencer receives a new read request by node B. Since this is a read request, the sequencer can overlap the processing safely, without waiting for the completion of the outstanding transaction. In the figure part (d), it sends intervention message to all nodes except the requestor B.

Nodes A and C have a copy of the block, and hence both may send the data block to node B (e). Notice here that in this basic example protocol, traffic is wasted when multiple nodes send the data block to the requestor. This problem arises because there is no single designated supplier of data block. This problem can be mitigated with the addition of an "owner" state as in AMD's MOESI (for dirty sharing) or "forward" state as in Intel's MESIF (for clean sharing), or both.

Finally, nodes A and B can send a notice of completion, the Done message, to the sequencer S. Part (f) of the figure shows a case where node B sends the Done message earlier than node A. This is fine because both read transactions deal with the same data value, hence they can be overlapped and their completion reordered. However, the sequencer S must know how many Done messages it has to receive in order to determine that all the outstanding read transactions have been completed, for example to determine when it can process a future read exclusive request.

The illustrations of the protocol so far have assumed the case in which data is found on some of the nodes. The case where data is not found in any of the nodes and must be fetched from the main memory is more complicated to handle, because we have to deal with the issue of when to issue a memory fetch. In general, there are two approaches to decide when to issue a memory fetch. The first approach is a *late memory fetch* approach, where the system does not issue a memory fetch until it determines that there is no copy of the block currently cached in any of the nodes. Another approach is a *early memory fetch* approach, where the system issues a memory fetch before it can be determined that there is no copy of the block in any of the nodes. Thus, the memory fetch is speculative. The memory fetch is useful in reducing the cache miss latency if it turns out that the block is not cached in any of the nodes. The memory fetch is useless if it turns out that data can be supplied by some node. Moreover, the fetch has to be cancelled and the fetched block discarded if it turns out the data is in a dirty state in a node, as the fetched block is stale.

Figure 7.12 illustrates the two approaches. The request arrives at the sequencer (a). In the late fetch approach, the sequencer sends out intervention messages to the rest of the nodes (b). As a response to receiving the intervention messages, each node sends a NoData response message the requestor A, indicating it does not have the block (c). The rest of the processing is shown in part (d), in three consecutive steps. The requestor, knowing the block is not found on any of the nodes, issues a request to fetch from the main memory (Step 1). The sequencer fetches the block from the main memory (Step 2), and supplies it to A (Step 3). Contrast this with the early fetch approach, where the memory fetch is issued speculatively, immediately upon receiving the read request (part (e)). The block is fetched from the main memory without knowing whether the block may be found in a node, and whether the block in the node is in a clean or dirty state. Suppose that the node S finds the data block in its cache and supplies it to the requestor, while other nodes do not find the data block and send NoData response messages to the requestor (f). If the requestor (node A) receives multiple data replies, it is responsible in determining which version of data to keep and which one to discard. For example, if it obtains a data reply for a block that is currently cached in a dirty state in a node, the block being fetched from memory is stale and should be the one discarded.

Comparing the early and late fetch approaches, the late fetch approach suffers from high memory access latency. The early fetch approach has a lower memory access latency. However, it comes with significant costs. It performs fetches speculatively even when they may not be needed. These fetches increase power consumption and off-chip bandwidth demand.

Due to the need for the sequencer to issue memory fetches, it makes sense to place the sequencer close to the memory controller, or assigns the memory controller a sequencer role, to reduce the fetch latency. As an example, in the AMD Opteron-based Magny Cours system, the memory controllers act as the sequencers, based on addresses assigned to them.

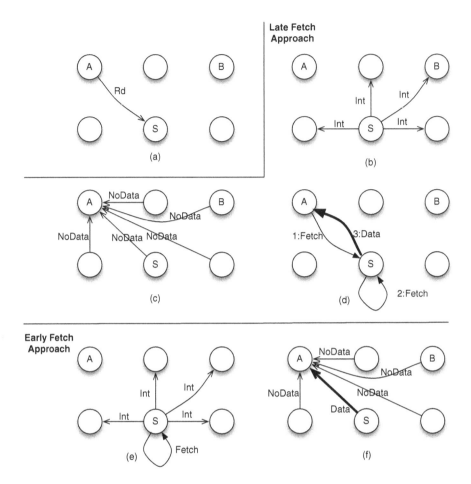

Figure 7.12: Illustration of a broadcast coherence protocol over point-to-point interconnection with a global sequencer.

■ *Did you know?*

Let us look at how the AMD Magny Cours system deals with the early vs. late fetch dilemma. The memory controller is augmented with a structure referred to as a probe filter, which tracks the state of blocks that are cached. When a request arrives at the sequencer (the memory controller), following an early fetch approach, it immediately issues a fetch to the main memory, in parallel with looking up the directory. If a block is cached in a shared state or is uncached, the sequencer supplies the block, after the fetch from the main memory has returned. This policy avoids the possibility of multiple caches supplying the block, which may happen under an alternative approach of broadcasting an intervention message. If a block is in a modified or exclusive state, however, at most only one node has the block and can supply it. In this case, the directory maintains precise information of which cache has the block, forwards the request to the cache, which then supplies the block to the requestor.

The early fetch approach is more attractive when the directory lookup latency is high, the memory access latency is low compared to the directory lookup, and memory bandwidth and power are relatively abundant. In the Magny Cours, the directory is kept in the L3 cache and has a relatively high access latency.

Global Sequencing with Overlapped Request Processing

The protocol discussed in the previous section suffers from not being able to overlap request processing completely, except between multiple read transactions. This may cause a high coherence transaction latency due to the high waiting time as requests from different nodes for a single address collide at the sequencer.

One way to allow overlapped request processing while still giving the appearance that requests are not overlapped is to use an ordered network. Using an ordered network to overlap request processing has been used in some distributed shared memory system [19], and can be applied to a multicore system as well. The basic idea is to impose or use the property of the network to ensure that all nodes see the order of transactions in the same way as the sequencer. For example, we can define a deterministic path for messages sent from the sequencer to every node. Different destination nodes may share a path or have their own paths, but all messages sent by the sequencer to a node must follow this predetermined path. Hence, messages sent by the sequencer are guaranteed to arrive at the destination node in the same order as the sequencer sending them.

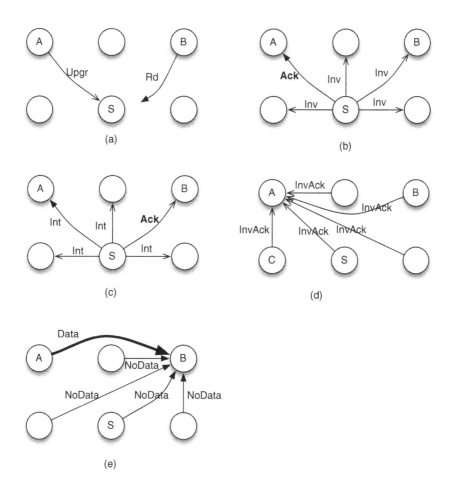

Figure 7.13: Overlapping request processing using an ordered network.

Figure 7.13 illustrates how the ordered network property can be used to overlap request processing. Suppose node A sends an upgrade request to S and in the mean time B sends a read request to S. Suppose the write request from A arrives at the sequencer before the request from B arrives (a). Upon receiving the read exclusive request, the sequencer sends out invalidation messages to all other nodes, while sending an acknowledgment message to the requestor node A, indicating that the request has been accepted by the sequencer (b). The messages may use different paths as shown in the figure, but for each destination node, only one path is allowed. While this is still going on, the sequencer assumes that the transaction is already completed and serves a new request. When it receives the read request from node B, it forwards intervention messages to all other nodes, and sends an acknowledgment to node B indicating that the request has been accepted by the sequencer (c). Because the network message delivery is ordered, it is guaranteed that each node will first receive the invalidation message before it receives the intervention message. Each node also needs to respond to messages in the order of their arrival. Thus, each node will have invalidated its own copy of the block by the time it receives or responds to the intervention message (d). In this case, they would respond indicating that they do not find the block in their cache. This guarantees that it will be node A who will supply the data to B.

Note that A will receive the acknowledgment message from the sequencer before the intervention message. Hence, A knows that its request is accepted by the sequencer earlier than the read request by node B. However, node A may receive the intervention message before it has collected all invalidation acknowledgments. It will be incorrect to supply data to B until after all the invalidation acknowledgments are collected and its write completed. Therefore, node A must wait until its own acknowledged transaction is complete before it reacts to other requests. In the mean time, node A can buffer the intervention message or negatively acknowledge it until it has collected all invalidation acknowledgments and has performed the write to the data. After that occurs, it can supply the newly written data directly to node B (e). Similarly, node B must wait until it receives data before it can service other requests that it receives after the arrival of the acknowledgment message from the sequencer.

Compared to the non-overlapped processing approach, with the overlapped request processing may require additional mechanism and buffering at each node. However, since transactions can be processed at a lower latency and higher bandwidth, the overlapped processing approach is likely more attractive. Requiring ordered message delivery in the network often requires restricting paths that can be used to deliver the message. On a larger network, this results in reduced *path diversity*, which in turn leads to more pathological cases exhibiting network performance problems. However, for a small network, there is not much path diversity to start with, and hence the effect of the reduced path diversity is less significant.

Distributed Sequencing

It is possible also to rely on distributed protocol determining the order of transactions affecting a single block address, instead of relying on just one fixed sequencer. The idea here is that requests can be broadcast, and any node that can supply the requested data block is a good candidate to act as the sequencer. However, the remaining nodes must observe the same order of transactions as determined by the sequencer. The order observed by other nodes is inferred through the order in which messages are sent out by the sequencer. Thus, distributed sequencing requires the interconnect to route messages in a certain way to guarantee global ordering of message arrivals. This requires beyond what an ordered network can provide. It requires nodes to be fully ordered with respect to one another, with an ordering that is statically fixed, any time messages involved in transaction are sent. An example of a network that satisfies such a requirement is a ring. Each link in a ring connects two routers in a single direction (if the link is unidirectional), and together the routers and links form a closed loop. In a ring, messages sent from nodes will travel through the same path that is statically fixed, thereby satisfying the requirement.

A ring provides several benefits compared to a more general interconnect topology. Each router in a ring can have a simple design, because it only has to choose whether to forward a message to the next link or not, hence it can be implemented with low routing latency and modest amount of buffering. However, a ring's network distance increases linearly with the number of nodes, hence a ring becomes less attractive as the size of the system grows. In this section, we will look at an example of a cache coherence protocol that uses distributed sequencing exploiting the property of a ring interconnect.

In a ring protocol, the data supplier is typically assigned the role of a sequencer for transactions affecting the block. All requests are placed on the ring and travel through the ring until they go the entire circle back to the requestors. Let us define *transaction window* as the time between when a node places a request on the ring until its response has returned to the node. In some cases, a request can be responded by just one node, such as when a read request is satisfied by a node that caches the block supplying the block. In some cases, a request must be responded by all nodes, such as when an upgrade request needs to involve all nodes invalidating their copy of the block.

One important property that needs to be guaranteed in a ring is that the *data supplier supplies responds with a message (containing data) in the same order of requests arriving at the data supplier.* Such a property is important in ensuring that there is one order of transactions being processed that is seen consistently by all nodes. For example, if there are two requests arriving at the supplier, the request that reaches the supplier earlier will also be responded earlier than the other request. This ensures that a requesting node, if its request reaches the supplier earlier than anybody else, will see a response earlier than anybody else. It also ensures that a requesting node, if its request reaches the supplier later than another requesting node, will see the other requesting node's response before its own response. The latter is a condition where a ring collision between two requests is detected.

More precisely, if during the transaction window a node receives a response to a request other than its own, it has detected a collision with that other request. On the other hand, if no other responses are received in the transaction window, no collision has been detected. Absence of collision, the request has been satisfied as if it were the only request in the system. A collision may be benign if it involves two overlapping read transactions. A *benign collision* can be allowed to occur without causing a coherence problem, since they only involve a block with a single value. A collision between two write transactions or between a write and a read transaction is not benign, as it has a potential to cause coherence problems, because they involve multiple data values. Due to this distinction, a benign collision may be ignored, but a non-benign collision cannot be ignored. A non-benign collision may be dealt with by canceling both transactions involved in the collision, or canceling one of the transactions by prioritizing one over the others.

Let us look at an illustration of how a basic ring coherence protocol works. Figure 7.14 shows four nodes being connected in a ring. Part (a) of the figure shows simultaneously, node A and B send a read request for the same data block. The message is shown in the following format: command type (Rd, RdX, or Upgr) dot the requestor, comma, then the response in parentheses. The response

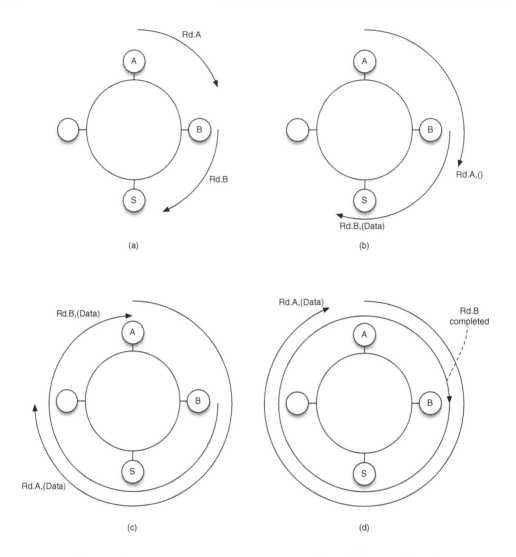

Figure 7.14: Ring cache coherence protocol illustration showing a situation with two simultaneous reads.

may contain an acknowledgement by the data supplier (Ack), data block (Data), and or invalidation acknowledgement (InvAck).

The requests from node A (Rd.A) and from node B (Rd.B) travel through the ring in the same clockwise direction. Suppose that node S has the data block being requested and therefore will act as the sequencer. As each request message arrives at a node, the node checks its cache to see if it has the block requested, augments the request message with data as a snoop response if it finds the requested block, or forwards the message on the ring if it does not find the requested block in its cache. In part (b), the read request from B has reached the supplier node S, which responds by augmenting the message with the data block. Meanwhile, the read request from A has reached node B, and node B forwards the request on the ring. In part (c), the messages have traveled even further on the ring. The read request from A has reached node S, and S has responded with data in the forwarded message. The read request from B has reached node A. At this point, node A detects a collision with a different request for the same data block, because it receives a response to B's request rather than its own request. Furthermore, A can also conclude that its request has lost out in the collision to the request from B because the supplier has responded to the request from B before the request from A. In this case, A has a choice to make. It can mark its own read request as having lost in a collision, so that it can cancel the request, and retry it later. Alternatively, since the winning request is a read request as well, the collision is a benign case. Multiple read transactions can be validly overlapped, hence A can just forward the request from B and not cancel its own request. Part (d) shows a situation where the Rd.B message has finally arrived at node B. Since no intervening responses has been received by B, it concludes that its request is now complete.

When a collision occurs between a read request and a write request, the collision is not benign and can potentially result in incorrect transaction serialization. In this case, one of the read or write transaction must be cancelled (to be retried at a later time). One way to address the collision is by canceling both transactions. However, such an approach is costly because we only need to cancel one transaction to remove the collision. To avoid unnecessary cancellations, we can prioritize one transaction over another so that the prioritized transaction succeeds while the non-prioritized transaction is cancelled. Which transaction should be cancelled? One possibility is to prioritize read over write, with a rationale that a read is often more time critical, as it results from a load instruction of which its result is needed by another instruction. Another possibility is to prioritize write over read, with a rationale that a write causes cached copies to be invalidated, which lead to future cache misses. By prioritizing the write over read, the write will succeed and will not cause more invalidations due to a retry in the future. Which prioritization policy is more attractive depends on complex trade-offs including the likelihood of collisions, the cost of a cache miss, whether a write may cause processor stall, etc. Several ring protocols proposed in literature have chosen to prioritize write over read.

An example collision between a write transaction and a read transaction is shown in Figure 7.15, assuming a policy that prioritizes read over write. Part (a) of the figure shows a read exclusive request from node A (RdX.A) and the read request from node B (Rd.B) travel through the ring in the same clockwise direction. Suppose that node S has the data block being requested and therefore will act as the sequencer. In part (b), the read request from B has reached the supplier node S, which responds by augmenting the request message with the data block. Meanwhile, the read exclusive request from A has reached node B. Node B detects a collision, however since it knows that a read exclusive request has a lower priority, it continues on by adding an invalidation acknowledgement to the message and forwarding it on the ring. B does not mark its ongoing read transaction for cancellation. In part (c), the messages have traveled even further on the ring. The read exclusive request from A has reached node S, and S adds invalidation acknowledgement, supplies a data block, and forwards the message. The read request from B has reached node A. At this point, node A detects a collision with its own read exclusive request. Since the protocol prioritizes read over write, A marks its read exclusive request for cancellation. It also forwards the read request of B along the ring. Part (d) shows a situation where the Rd.B message has finally arrived at node B and is now considered complete. The read exclusive request is retried by node A. Note that the basic ring protocol illustrated thus far does not guarantee an upper bound for transaction cancellations and retries. It is possible in a rare case to have transactions cancelled and retried repeatedly.

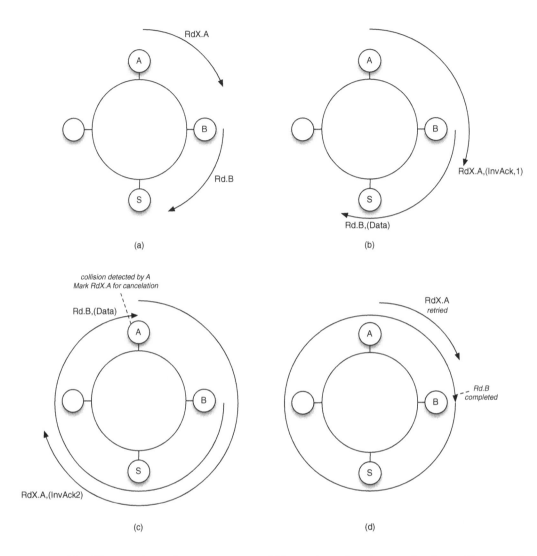

Figure 7.15: Ring cache coherence protocol illustration showing a situation with a read colliding with a write.

Finally, when there are two simultaneous write requests (e.g., two RdX, two Upgr, or one RdX and one Upgr), it is less clear the best way to handle it. It is possible to cancel both write requests and retry them. It is also possible to prioritize one write over the other, however, this requires a single node arbitrating between them, acknowledging the winning request and not acknowledging (or negatively acknowledging) the losing request.

Let us now consider how the basic ring protocol can request a fetch from the memory controller. In a ring, in order to discover whether there is a node that can supply a block or not requires, a request must travel for one rotation along the ring, collecting responses from nodes visited by the request. The memory controller(s) may be integrated into the ring as node(s). Similar to the case with global sequencing, we face two choices: early or late fetch policy.

Figure 7.16 illustrates the difference in the two policies. The ring shows three regular nodes A, B, and S, and one memory controller node MC integrated into the ring. Parts (a) and (b) illustrate the late fetch policy, while parts (c) and (d) illustrate the early fetch policy. Part (a) shows that initially node A issues a read request that reaches back itself with a negative (no data) response (Step 1). It then issues a non-snoop request to the memory controller (Step 2). The memory controller fetches data (Step 3), and replies the fetch with data (Step 4). If collision is detected during the fetch, the request needs to be cancelled and retried. The drawback of the late fetch policy is it takes a full ring rotation to determine a cache miss, and the fetch request adds more latency in order for the memory controller to start fetching the data block from the main memory. However, the memory controller fetches data only when no copy of the block exists in a cache and therefore needs to be supplied by the main memory.

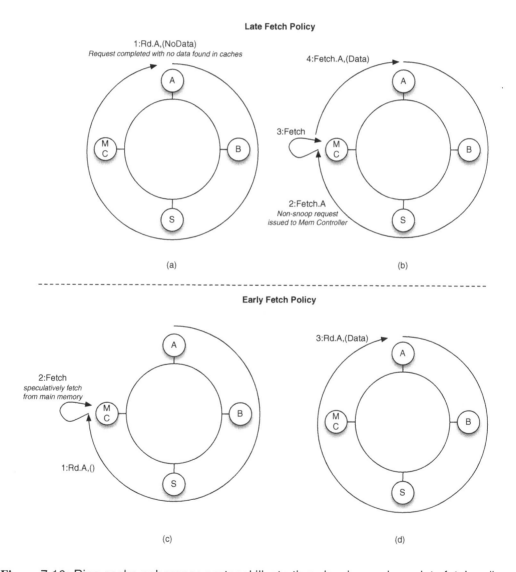

Figure 7.16: Ring cache coherence protocol illustration showing early vs. late fetch policy.

The early fetch policy is illustrated in parts (c) and (d) of Figure 7.16. In part (c), the read request sent by node A reaches the memory controller (Step 1). The memory controller speculatively fetches data from the main memory (Step 2), not knowing whether it will need to supply data. Part (d) shows the request/response message including the requested data is being sent to node A (Step 3). Node A is responsible in deciding whether to use the data supplied by the memory controller or not. For example, if it turns out that there is a data supplied by a node that has the block in a dirty state, the data sent by the memory controller is stale and needs to be discarded by node A.

Note that so far we have assumed that there is only one message corresponding to each request. The message serves multiple roles. It contains the request. It provides a consistent ordering of requests in the ring. It serves to detect collision between requests. It also transports data from data supplier. While simple, the use of a single message to serve multiple roles incurs costs. One cost is the high latency for the message to traverse the ring. When a message transits at a node, the node needs to look up its tag to determine if it has the block, and integrates a snoop response into the message before placing it back on the ring. An exception is when valid data is already found and supplied in the response message. In such a case, the snoop can be skipped at the next nodes. The larger the ring, the costlier the scheme becomes.

An alternative to the single message scheme is to split the message into several messages with distinct roles. We can have one message to carry the request. As soon as a node receives a request message, it can forward it immediately on the next link of the ring without waiting for a snoop response. We can have another message carrying the snoop response, which contains responses of nodes visited by the request message. The response message travels slower, as it must wait at each node until the node finishes checking its cache. As it travels along the ring, it collects and aggregates the snoop responses. Finally, we may have another message to carry data supply, provided by a regular node or the memory controller node. Using a separate message for data may allow the snoop response message to be forwarded more quickly without slowed down by data.

Splitting a transaction into request and response messages reduces the ring latency, and may reduce the probability of request collisions. The request message can race ahead, suffering from only the link delay and routing delay at each router. In contrast, if the request and response travel on one message, the combined message must wait for link, routing, and snoop delay at each node. The snoop delay may be quite high because it needs to check a large SRAM tag structure to produce a snoop response. With the split message, only the response message needs to wait for snoop response at each node. Everything else the same, the transaction window's size is not affected much in the split message approach. The transaction window remains the time between the time the request message is placed on the ring by the requestor until the response message reaches the requestor. However, the split message approach allows interesting optimizations which can reduce the transaction window's size. Take for example a ring with bidirectional links.

Figure 7.17 illustrates the situation with a bidirectional ring. Suppose that node A has a way of accurately predicting which node is the likely supplier of data block that it wants to read, and that node is S. In part (a) of the figure, A places a read request message on the ring in a counter clockwise direction (Step 1a), and places a response message on the ring in a clockwise direction (Step 1b), simultaneously. As the request and response messages traverse the ring, the request message reaches the supplier earlier. Part (b) of the figure shows what happens next. The supplier S responds to the request message by sending data to the requestor A (Step 2a). The data supply is speculative, in the sense that it is not known yet whether the data is valid to use (not stale) and that the request will be collision-free. In the mean time, the response message traverse the ring further (Step 2b), so far indicating that no nodes visited have a copy of the block. Next, in part (c) the data supply message reaches A, which promptly uses the data, speculatively (Step 3). Next, the response message arrives at node S, which augments the response by a positive snoop result indicating that it has the data and that it has sent the data to the requestor separately (Step 4). Finally, part (d) of the figure shows that the response message finally reaches node A. Since during this time no collision is detected, node A has used the correct data for its execution. Hence the read transaction can be closed, and node A continues execution. If, on the other hand, collision is detected, node A has to roll back its execution to the point before sending the read request, cancel the read request, and retry it.

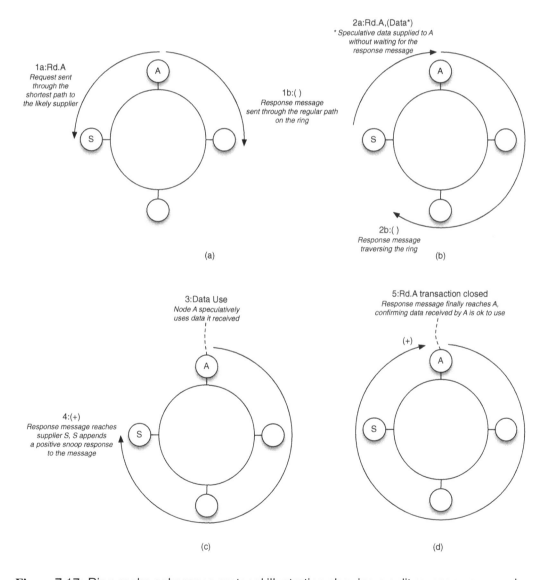

Figure 7.17: Ring cache coherence protocol illustration showing a split message approach.

In the example above, the message is split into three parts. The request and data messages travel without using the ring path. Only the response message travels using the ring path. Due to this, the split message approach reduces the ring protocol latency, especially in getting data supplied earlier. However, this comes with a cost of higher number of messages in the ring. Finally, the supplier is still required to forward the response message in the same order as it receives (and processes) the request message in order to ensure consistent ordering of transactions in the system.

■ *Did you know?*

Another way of utilizing a bidirectional ring is to use different directions for requests involving different addresses, for example by using clockwise direction for even block addresses, and counter-clockwise direction for odd block addresses.

The ring protocol can also be implemented for multiprocessor or multicore systems that are not interconnected with a ring topology. The ring may be "embedded" in a path in the network that is designated to be used as a ring. In such an implementation, the split message approach may be even more flexible. For example, the request message can be sent through non-ring shortest path to reach the supplier, and likewise, the data supply can also travel through non-ring shortest path. However, the response message is crucial in ordering transactions and detecting collisions, hence it must still travel through the embedded ring [60].

To summarize, we have discussed a broadcast/snoopy cache coherence protocol over point-to-point interconnection that relies on a global sequencer. We have discussed a variant of that protocol that does not overlap request processing at all, and another variant that overlaps request processing by exploiting the property of an ordered network. We have also discussed a ring protocol, where no global sequencer is used, but a certain message (snoop response message) has to visit all nodes in a static ordering.

7.6 Exercises

Worked Problems

1. For each of the memory reference streams given in the following, compare the cost of executing it on a bus-based machine that supports (a) MSI, (b) MESI, and (c) MOESI protocols. All the references (read/write) in the streams are to the same location, and the digit refers to the processor issuing the reference. Assume that all caches are initially empty, and use the following cost model: a read/write cache hit takes 1 cycle to complete; a read/write cache miss that does not involve a whole block to be transferred on the bus takes 60 cycles to complete; and a read/write cache miss that involves data block to be transferred on the bus takes 90 cycles to complete. Assume all caches are write back and write allocate. For MSI, assume that BusUpgr is not used.

The first stream is: R1 (read by processor 1), W1 (write by processor 1), R1, W1, R2, W2, R2, W2, R3, W3, R3, W3.
The second stream is: R1, R2, R3, W1, W2, W3, R1, R2, R3, W3, W1.
The third stream is: R1, R2, R3, R3, W1, W1, W1, W1, W2, W3.

Answer:

Stream 1 (MSI):

Processor	P1	P2	P3	Bus Action	Data From	Cycles
Read1	S	-	-	BusRd	Mem	90
Write1	M	-	-	BusRdX	Mem	90
Read1	M	-	-	-	-	1
Write1	M	-	-	-	-	1
Read2	S	S	-	BusRd/Flush	P1.C	90
Write2	I	M	-	BusRdX	Mem	90
Read2	I	M	-	-	-	1
Write2	I	M	-	-	-	1
Read3	I	S	S	BusRd/Flush	P2.C	90
Write3	I	I	M	BusRdX	Mem	90
Read3	I	I	M	-	-	1
Write3	I	I	M	-	-	1
TOTAL						546

Stream 1 (MESI):

Processor	P1	P2	P3	Bus Action	Data From	Cycles
Read1	E	-	-	BusRd(!C)	Mem	90
Write1	M	-	-	-	-	1
Read1	M	-	-	-	-	1
Write1	M	-	-	-	-	1
Read2	S	S	-	BusRd(C)/Flush	P1.C	90

Write2	I	M	-	BusUpgr	-	60
Read2	I	M	-	-	-	1
Write2	I	M	-	-	-	1
Read3	I	S	S	BusRd(C)/Flush	P2.C	90
Write3	I	I	M	BusUpgr	-	60
Read3	I	I	M	-	-	1
Write3	I	I	M	-	-	1
TOTAL						397

Stream 1 (MOESI):

Processor	P1	P2	P3	Bus Action	Data From	Cycles
Read1	E	-	-	BusRd(!C)	Mem	90
Write1	M	-	-	-	-	1
Read1	M	-	-	-	-	1
Write1	M	-	-	-	-	1
Read2	O	S	-	BusRd(C)/Flush	P1.C	90
Write2	I	M	-	BusUpgr	-	60
Read2	I	M	-	-	-	1
Write2	I	M	-	-	-	1
Read3	I	O	S	BusRd(C)/Flush	P2.C	90
Write3	I	I	M	BusUpgr	-	60
Read3	I	I	M	-	-	1
Write3	I	I	M	-	-	1
TOTAL						397

Stream 2 (MSI):

Processor	P1	P2	P3	Bus Action	Data From	Cycles
Read1	S	-	-	BusRd	Mem	90
Read2	S	S	-	BusRd	Mem	90
Read3	S	S	S	BusRd	Mem	90
Write1	M	I	I	BusRdX	Mem	90
Write2	I	M	I	BusRdX/Flush	P1.C	90
Write3	I	I	M	BusRdX/Flush	P2.C	90
Read1	S	I	S	BusRd/Flush	P3.C	90
Read2	S	S	S	BusRd	Mem	90
Read3	S	S	S	-	-	1
Write3	I	I	M	BusRdX	Mem	90
Write1	M	I	I	BusRdX/Flush	P3.C	90
TOTAL						901

Stream 2 (MESI):

Processor	P1	P2	P3	Bus Action	Data From	Cycles
Read1	E	-	-	BusRd(!C)	Mem	90
Read2	S	S	-	BusRd(C)/FlushOpt	P1.C	90
Read3	S	S	S	BusRd(C)/FlushOpt	P1/2.C	90
Write1	M	I	I	BusUpgr	-	60
Write2	I	M	I	BusRdX/Flush	P1.C	90
Write3	I	I	M	BusRdX/Flush	P2.C	90
Read1	S	I	S	BusRd(C)/Flush	P3.C	90
Read2	S	S	S	BusRd(C)/FlushOpt	P1/3.C	90
Read3	S	S	S	-	-	1
Write3	I	I	M	BusUpgr	-	60
Write1	M	I	I	BusRdX/Flush	P3.C	90
TOTAL						841

Stream 2 (MOESI):

Processor	P1	P2	P3	Bus Action	Data From	Cycles
Read1	E	-	-	BusRd(!C)	Mem	90
Read2	S	S	-	BusRd(C)/FlushOpt	P1.C	90
Read3	S	S	S	BusRd(C)	Mem	90
Write1	M	I	I	BusUpgr	-	60
Write2	I	M	I	BusRdX/Flush	P1.C	90
Write3	I	I	M	BusRdX/Flush	P2.C	90
Read1	S	I	O	BusRd(C)Flush	P3.C	90
Read2	S	S	O	BusRd(C)/Flush	P3.C	90
Read3	S	S	O	-	-	1
Write3	I	I	M	BusUpgr	-	60
Write1	M	I	I	BusRdX/Flush	P3.C	90
TOTAL						841

Stream 3 (MSI):

Processor	P1	P2	P3	Bus Action	Data From	Cycles
Read1	S	-	-	BusRd	Mem	90
Read2	S	S	-	BusRd	Mem	90
Read3	S	S	S	BusRd	Mem	90
Read3	S	S	S	-	-	1
Write1	M	I	I	BusRdX	Mem	90
Write1	M	I	I	-	-	1
Write1	M	I	I	-	-	1
Write1	M	I	I	-	-	1

Write2	I	M	I	BusRdX/Flush	P1.C	90
Write3	I	I	M	BusRdX/Flush	P2.C	90
TOTAL						544

Stream 3 (MESI):

Processor	P1	P2	P3	Bus Action	Data From	Cycles
Read1	E	-	-	BusRd(!C)	Mem	90
Read2	S	S	-	BusRd(C)/FlushOpt	P1.C	90
Read3	S	S	S	BusRd(C)/FlushOpt	P1/2.C	90
Read3	S	S	S	-	-	1
Write1	M	I	I	BusUpgr	-	60
Write1	M	I	I	-	-	1
Write1	M	I	I	-	-	1
Write1	M	I	I	-	-	1
Write2	I	M	I	BusRdX/Flush	P1.C	90
Write3	I	I	M	BusRdX/Flush	P2.C	90
TOTAL						514

Stream 3 (MOESI):

Processor	P1	P2	P3	Bus Action	Data From	Cycles
Read1	E	-	-	BusRd(!C)	Mem	90
Read2	S	S	-	BusRd(C)/FlushOpt	P1.C	90
Read3	S	S	S	BusRd(C)	Mem	90
Read3	S	S	S	-	-	1
Write1	M	I	I	BusUpgr	-	60
Write1	M	I	I	-	-	1
Write1	M	I	I	-	-	1
Write1	M	I	I	-	-	1
Write2	I	M	I	BusRdX/Flush	P1.C	90
Write3	I	I	M	BusRdX/Flush	P2.C	90
TOTAL						514

2. **Dragon Protocol**

For each of the memory reference streams given in the following, compare the cost of executing it on a bus-based machine that supports Dragon protocol. All the references (read-/write) in the streams are to the same location, and the digit refers to the processor issuing the reference. Assume that all caches are initially empty, and use the following cost model: a read/write cache hit takes 1 cycle; a read/write cache miss which does not involve transferring a whole block on the bus takes 60 cycles to complete; and a read/write miss which involves BusUpd. Assume all caches are write back and write allocated.

The first stream is: R1 (read by processor 1), W1 (write by processor 1), R1, W1, R2, W2, R2, W2, R3, W3, R3, W3.

The second stream is: R1, R2, R3, W1, W2, W3, R1, R2, R3, W3, W1.

The third stream is: R1, R2, R3, R3, W1, W1, W1, W1, W2, W3.

Answer:

Stream 1 (Dragon):

Processor	P1	P2	P3	Bus Action	Data From	Cycles
Read1	E	-	-	BusRd(!C)	Mem	90
Write1	M	-	-	-	-	1
Read1	M	-	-	-	-	1
Write1	M	-	-	-	-	1
Read2	Sm	Sc	-	BusRd(C)/Flush	P1.C	90
Write2	Sc	Sm	-	BusUpd(C)	-	60
Read2	Sc	Sm	-	-	-	1
Write2	Sc	Sm	-	BusUpd(C)	-	60
Read3	Sc	Sm	Sc	BusRd(C)/Flush	P2.C	90
Write3	Sc	Sc	Sm	BusUpd(C)	-	60
Read3	Sc	Sc	Sm	-	-	1
Write3	Sc	Sc	Sm	BusUpd(C)	-	60
TOTAL						515

Stream 2 (Dragon):

Processor	P1	P2	P3	Bus Action	Data From	Cycles
Read1	E	-	-	BusRd(!C)	Mem	90
Read2	Sc	Sc	-	BusRd(C)	Mem	90
Read3	Sc	Sc	Sc	BusRd(C)	Mem	90
Write1	Sm	Sc	Sc	BusUpd(C)	-	60
Write2	Sc	Sm	Sc	BusUpd(C)	-	60
Write3	Sc	Sc	Sm	BusUpd(C)	-	60
Read1	Sc	Sc	Sm	-	-	1
Read2	Sc	Sc	Sm	-	-	1
Read3	Sc	Sc	Sm	-	-	1
Write3	Sc	Sc	Sm	BusUpd(C)	-	60
Write1	Sm	Sc	Sc	BusUpd(C)	-	60
TOTAL						573

Stream 3 (Dragon):

Processor	P1	P2	P3	Bus Action	Data From	Cycles
Read1	E	-	-	BusRd(!C)	Mem	90
Read2	Sc	Sc	-	BusRd(C)	Mem	90

Read3	Sc	Sc	Sc	BusRd(C)	Mem	90
Read3	Sc	Sc	Sc	-	-	1
Write1	Sm	Sc	Sc	BusUpd(C)	-	60
Write1	Sm	Sc	Sc	BusUpd(C)	-	60
Write1	Sm	Sc	Sc	BusUpd(C)	-	60
Write1	Sm	Sc	Sc	BusUpd(C)	-	60
Write2	Sc	Sm	Sc	BusUpd(C)	-	60
Write3	Sc	Sc	Sm	BusUpd(C)	-	60
TOTAL						631

Homework Problems

1. Suppose a 4-processor system uses a bus-based broadcast/snoopy coherence protocol. Assume that the cost of processing a protocol transaction depends on where data is supplied and whether it involves a bus transaction. A cache hit not involving a bus transaction costs 1 cycle, a cache hit involving a bus transaction costs 10 cycles. A cache miss with data supplied by another cache costs 50 cycles. A cache miss with data supplied by the main memory costs 80 cycles. The caches uses MSI coherence protocol. Show what happens to cache states after each memory reference. The memory reference stream is: R1 (read by processor 1), R2, R3, R2, W3 (write by processor 3), E3 (eviction by processor 3), W4, R2, R3, W1.

2. Repeat homework problem (1) for MESI protocol.

3. Repeat homework problem (1) for MOESI protocol.

4. Repeat homework problem (1) for Dragon protocol. Additionally, assume that any memory reference that involves a BusUpd transaction requires 50 clock cycles to complete.

5. Some systems have implemented MOSI protocol to allow dirty sharing, which consists of four states: modified, owned, shared, and invalid. The meaning of the states are:

   - Modified: data is dirty and can only be kept in one cache
   - Owned: data is dirty and may be kept in multiple caches, but only one of them has it in the owned state
   - Shared: data may be clean/dirty, and may be kept in multiple caches
   - Invalid: data is uncached or invalid

   Assume a bus-based multiprocessor with write back caches. The following bus transactions are available: BusRd, BusRdX, BusUpgr, and Flush. FlushOpt is not implemented. Show the state transition diagram for processor-initiated requests, and state transition diagram for snooped bus requests.

6. Compare the latencies of MSI and MESI for the following cases: (a) read latency for data that was earlier read by one other processor, (b) write latency for data that is read then written by only one processor, and (3) read latency for data that is written by one processor and then read by another processor.

7. Compare the latencies of MESI and MOESI for the following cases: (a) read latency for data that was earlier read by one other processor, (b) write latency for data that is read then written by only one processor, (c) read latency for data that is written by one processor then read by another processor, (d) read latency for clean data kept in other caches, and (e) bandwidth to the main memory for a read to data recently written by another processor.

8. **Non-Silent Replacement** Suppose that the MESI protocol is modified so that the replacement of a clean block is no longer silent, i.e., it is broadcasted on the bus. This way a cache can detect if it becomes the only cache that holds a copy of the block, and can transition the state of the block from shared (S) to exclusive (E). Explain the advantages and drawbacks of this modification. Draw the cache coherence protocol diagram for the modified MESI protocol.

9. **MOESI Problem** In the MOESI protocol, if a block in the owned (O) is evicted from the cache, the block is written back to the main memory, even though there may be other caches which hold the block in a shared (S) state. This write back incurs an unnecessary off-chip bandwidth consumption. Propose a solution to avoid having to write back the block, or at least reduce the frequency of such write backs. Draw the cache coherence protocol diagram for your solution.

Chapter 8

Hardware Support for Synchronization

Contents

As we have discussed in Chapter 6, hardware support for building a shared memory multiprocessor system that guarantees correct and efficient execution of parallel programs must address cache coherence, memory consistency, and support for synchronization primitives. The objective of this chapter is to discuss hardware support for implementing synchronization primitives. From the point of view of software, synchronization primitives that are widely used are locks, barriers, and point-to-point synchronizations such as signal-wait pairs. Recall for example that locks and barriers are heavily used in DOALL parallelism and in applications with linked data structures, whereas signal-wait synchronization is essential in pipelined (e.g., DOACROSS) parallelism.

There are many ways of supporting synchronization primitives in hardware. A common practice today is to implement the lowest level synchronization primitive in the form of atomic instructions in hardware, and implement all other synchronization primitives on top of that in software. We will discuss the trade-offs of various implementations of locks and barriers. We will show that achieving fast but scalable synchronization is not trivial. Often there are trade-offs in *scalability* (how synchronization latency and bandwidth scale with a larger number of threads) versus *uncontended latency* (the latency when threads do not simultaneously try to perform the synchronization). We will also discuss several software barrier implementations. For very large systems, software barriers implemented on top of an atomic instruction and lock may not give sufficient scalability. For these systems, hardware barrier implementation is common, and we will discuss one example.

Finally, we will discuss transactional memory which is supported in recent multicore architecture. Transactional memory provides a higher abstraction level for coordinating parallel execution, in some cases removing the need to use lower level primitives such as locks. We will discuss one implementation of transactional memory in hardware.

8.1 Lock Implementations

In this section, we will discuss hardware support for lock implementations, and in the next section, we will discuss hardware support for barrier implementations.

8.1.1 Evaluating the Performance of Lock Implementations

Before discussing various lock implementations, first we will discuss what performance criteria need to be taken into account in a lock implementation. They are:

1. **Uncontended lock-acquisition latency**: the time it takes to acquire a lock when there is no contention between threads.

2. **Traffic**: the amount of traffic generated as a function of number of threads or processors that contend for the lock. Traffic can be subdivided into three: the traffic on *lock acquisition when a lock is free*, traffic on *lock acquisition when a lock is not free*, and traffic on *lock release*.

3. **Fairness**: the degree in which threads are allowed to acquire locks with respect to one another. One criteria related to fairness is whether in the lock implementation, it is possible for a thread to be *starved*, i.e., it is unable to acquire a lock for a long period of time even when the lock became free during that time.

4. **Storage**: the amount of storage needed as a function of number of threads. Some lock implementations require a constant storage space independent of the number of threads that share the lock, while others require a storage space that grows linearly along with the number of threads that share the lock.

8.1.2 The Need for Atomic Instructions

Recall the discussion in Chapter 6 in which we compare software versus hardware mechanisms for guaranteeing mutual exclusion. We have shown that a software mechanism (i.e., Peterson's algorithm) does not scale because the number of static instructions executed and the number of variables that need to be tested in order for a thread to check the condition for a lock acquisition increases along the number of threads. In contrast, if an *atomic instruction* that can perform a sequence of load, compare or other instructions, and a store, is available, a simple lock implementation that relies on testing only one variable is sufficient.

In current systems, most processors support an atomic instruction as (almost) the lowest level primitive on which other synchronization primitives can be built. An atomic instruction performs a sequence of read, modify, and write in an indivisible manner as one indivisible operation. Consider the lock implementation in the following code (Code 8.1).

Code 8.1 An incorrect implementation of lock/unlock functions.

```
1 lock:  ld  R1, &lockvar   // R1 = lockvar
2        bnz R1, lock        // jump to lock if R1 != 0
3        st  &lockvar, #1    // lockvar = 1
4        ret                 // return to caller
5
6 unlock: st  &lockvar, #0 // lockvar = 0
7         ret                 // return to caller
```

In order for the code to work correctly, the sequence of load, branch, and store instructions must be performed *atomically*. The term atomic implies two things. First, it implies that either *the whole sequence is executed entirely*, or none of it appears to have executed. Second, it also implies that *only one atomic instruction from any processor can be executed at any given time*. Multiple instruction sequences from several processors will have to be serialized. Certainly, software support cannot provide any atomicity of the execution of several instructions. Thus, most processors support atomic instructions, instructions that are executed atomically with respect to other processors. Different processors may support different types of atomic instructions. Below are some of the commonly used ones:

- `test-and-set Rx, M`: read the value stored in memory location M, test the value against a constant (e.g., 0), and if they match, write the value in register Rx to the memory location M.

- `fetch-and-op M`: read the value stored in memory location M, perform `op` to it (e.g., increment, decrement, addition, subtraction), and then store the new value to the memory location M. In some cases, an additional operand may be specified.

- `exchange Rx, M`: atomically exchange (or swap) the value in memory location M with the value in register Rx.

- `compare-and-swap Rx, Ry, M`: compare the value in memory location M with the value in register Rx. If they match, write the value in register Ry to M, and copy the value in Rx to Ry.

Out of the instructions listed above, the most versatile one is the compare and swap (CAS). Compared to the test-and-set, it is able to perform a comparison, but with an arbitrary value in a register operand instead of with a constant. Compared to an exchange, It can swap values in a register and a memory location, but with an attached condition. However, it cannot perform what fetch-and-op does except in some situations.

Two natural questions that readers may ask include: (1) how can atomicity be ensured for an atomic instruction? and (2) how can an atomic instruction be used to construct synchronization? We will discuss the answer to the first question first.

An atomic instruction essentially provides a guarantee to programmers that a sequence of operations represented by the instruction will be executed in its entirety. Using this guarantee, programmers can implement a variety of synchronization primitives they need (to be discussed later).

■ *Did you know?*

In the x86 instruction set, in addition to atomic instructions, regular integer instructions can also be made atomic by prefixing it with LOCK. When a memory location is accessed by an instruction that is LOCK-prefixed, assuming a bus-based multiprocessor, the LOCK# bus line is asserted to prevent other processors to read or modify the location while the prefixed instruction executes. For example, the following instructions can be LOCK-prefixed:

- *Bit manipulation instructions such as BT, BTS, BTR, and BTC.*
- *Arithmetic instructions such as ADD, ADC, SUB, and SBB.*
- *Logical instructions such as NOT, AND, OR, and XOR.*
- *Some unary instructions such as NEG, INC, and DEC.*

Atomic instructions are also provided. They start with "X", such as XADD, and XCHG. These atomic instructions do not require the "LOCK" prefix to make them atomic.

To illustrate the use of the prefix, let us say there is a variable counter *that we want to increment atomically. To do that, we can prefix the INC instruction with the LOCK prefix, as shown in the following example:*

```
1 void __fastcall atomic_increment (volatile int* ctr)
2 {
3     __asm {
4         lock inc dword ptr [ECX]
5         ret
6     }
7 }
```

The actual mechanism that guarantees atomicity of a sequence of operations itself must be provided correctly by the hardware.

Fortunately, the cache coherence protocol provides a foundation on which atomicity can be guaranteed. For example, when an atomic instruction is encountered, the coherence protocol knows that it must guarantee atomicity. It can do so by first obtaining an exclusive ownership of the memory location M (by invalidating all other cached copies of blocks that contain M). After the exclusive ownership is obtained, the protocol has ensured that only one processor has an access to the block (all other processors will suffer from a cache miss if they try to access the block). The atomic instruction can then be executed. For the duration of the atomic instruction, the block must not be allowed to be stolen by other processors. For example, if another processor requests to read or write to the block, the block is "stolen" (i.e., it is flushed and its state is downgraded). Exposing the block before the atomic instruction is completed breaks the atomicity of the instruction, similar to the non-atomic execution of a sequence of instructions in the naive lock implementation case (Code 8.1). Therefore, before the atomic instruction is completed, the block cannot be stolen. One way to prevent stealing of the block (on a bus-based multiprocessor) is to lock or reserve the bus until the instruction is complete. Since the bus is the serializing medium in the system, if it is locked, no other bus transactions can access the bus until it is released. A more general solution (which also applies to non-bus based multiprocessors) is not to prevent other requests from going to the bus, but for the coherence controller of the processor that executes the atomic instruction to defer responding to all requests to the block until the atomic instruction is completed, or negatively acknowledge the requests so that the requestors can retry the requests in the future. Overall, through exclusive ownership of a block and preventing it from being stolen until the atomic instruction is complete, atomicity is ensured. A simpler solution to provide atomicity will be discussed later in Section 8.1.5.

8.1.3 Test and Set Lock

How is the atomic instruction used to implement a lock? It depends on the type of the atomic instruction. The following code illustrates a lock implementation using a test-and-set instruction (Code 8.2). The first instruction in the lock acquisition attempt is the atomic test-and-set instruction, which performs the following steps atomically: it reads from the memory location where `lockvar` is located (using an exclusive read such as BusRdX or BusUpgr), into register R1, compares R1 with zero. If it finds that R1 is 0, writes "1" to `lockvar` (indicating a successful lock acquisition). If R1 is not 0, it does not write "1" to `lockvar` (indicating a failed lock acquisition). The second instruction branches back to the label `lock` if R1 is not zero, so that the lock acquisition can be retried. If the value of R1 is zero, then we know that when the branch instruction is reached, the test-and-set instruction is successful due to its atomicity. Note that releasing the lock is simply performed by storing a zero to `lockvar` without using an atomic instruction. This works because there is only one thread in the critical section, so there is only one thread that can release the lock. Hence, no races can occur.

Code 8.2 An implementation of test-and-set lock.

```
1 lock: t&s R1, &lockvar // R1 = lockvar
2                        // if (R1==0) lockvar=1
3        bnz R1, lock    // jump to lock if R1 != 0
4        ret             // return to caller
5
6 unlock: st  &lockvar, #0 // lockvar = 0
7          ret             // return to caller
```

Let us see how the execution of two threads now allows only one thread to enter the critical section. Figure 8.1 illustrates the case. Let us assume that thread 0 executes the test-and-set instruction slightly earlier than P1. If the memory block where `lockvar` is stored initially has a value of 0, then after the execution of the test-and-set instruction, it holds a value of 1. Note that the atomicity of test-and-set serializes the execution of other test-and-set instructions. Hence, while test-and-set from thread 0 is ongoing, test-and-set from thread 1 is not allowed to proceed. When the test-and-set instruction of thread 1 executes, it sees the value of 1 in the memory location where `lockvar` is located. Hence, its lock acquisition fails, and thread 1 goes back to retry the test-and-set, on and on until it finally succeeds when the lock is released by thread 0.

Let us now evaluate the test-and-set lock implementation. The uncontended lock-acquisition latency is low since only one atomic instruction, plus a branch instruction, are needed to successfully obtain a lock. The traffic requirement, however, is very high. Each lock acquisition attempt causes invalidation of all cached copies, regardless of whether the acquisition is successful or not. For example, look at the example in Table 8.1, in which three threads running on three processors all trying to obtain a lock once. Initially, no one holds the lock. Then, P1 executes a test-and-set and successfully obtains the lock. The test-and-set instruction incurs a BusRdX bus transaction since the block is not already cached in P1's cache. Suppose that after P1 obtains the lock (while P1 is in

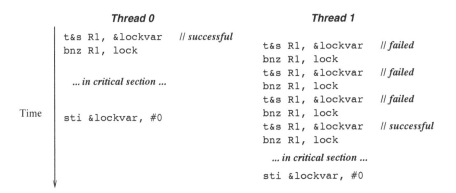

Figure 8.1: The execution of test-and-set atomic instructions from multiple processors.

the critical section), P2 and P3 attempt to acquire the lock. P2 executes a test-and-set, followed by an attempt by P3, and then by P2 for the second time. Each of these attempts involves a test-and-set instruction, so it incurs a BusRdX transaction to invalidate other cached copies and transitions the state of the block that contains `lockvar` to modified. Note that despite the fact that the lock is held by P1, P2 and P3 will keep incurring bus transactions to invalidate each other's copy in attempts to acquire the lock. This is one significant drawback of the test-and-set lock implementation. In fact, there may be many more failed attempts than shown in the table.

When later P1 releases the lock, it writes "0" to the lock variable, causing invalidation through the BusRdX transaction. Then, both P2 and P3 try to acquire the lock, but P2 succeeds and P3 fails. P3 keeps trying and failing to acquire the lock that is held by P2 for as long as P2 is in the critical section (the table shows only two failed attempts, but in reality they can occur many more times). After P2 releases the lock, P3 can acquire the lock successfully. Since no processor is contending for the lock now, when P3 releases the lock, it still has the cache block in modified state and does not incur a BusRdX bus transaction to store "0" to the lock address.

The table shows that a bus transaction is incurred at every attempt to acquire the lock, regardless of whether the lock is currently held or not. The amount of traffic for a single critical section that appears in the source code is quite high: $\mathcal{O}(p^2)$. This is because there are $\mathcal{O}(p)$ processors which will enter the critical section, which means that there are $\mathcal{O}(p)$ lock acquisitions and releases. After each lock release, there will be $\mathcal{O}(p)$ attempts to acquire the lock, with one processor succeeding in acquiring the lock, and the rest failing in acquiring the lock.

Obviously, the traffic incurred by the test-and-set lock can be excessively high. The traffic due to the lock acquisition attempts can slow down regular and coherence cache misses. Indeed, the critical section itself may be slowed down if traffic is saturated by failed lock acquisition attempts, delaying the lock to release, which further exacerbates the traffic situation.

One way to reduce the traffic requirement is to use a *back-off* strategy, in which after a failed lock acquisition attempt, a thread "waits" (or backs off) before performing another attempt. A delay can be inserted between subsequent retries. The delay in the back-off strategy needs to be carefully tuned: if it is too small, high amount of traffic remains; and if it is too large, the thread may miss an opportunity to acquire the lock when the lock becomes available. In practice, an *exponential back-off* strategy, in which the delay starts small but gradually increases exponentially, works quite well.

Table 8.1: Illustration of test-and-set lock implementation performance.

	Request	P1	P2	P3	Bus Request	Comments
0	Initially	–	–	–	–	lock is free
1	t&s1	M	–	–	BusRdX	P1 obtains lock
2	t&s2	I	M	–	BusRdX	P2 lock acq fails
3	t&s3	I	I	M	BusRdX	P3 lock acq fails
4	t&s2	I	M	I	BusRdX	P2 lock acq fails
5	unlock1	M	I	I	BusRdX	P1 releases lock
6	t&s2	I	M	I	BusRdX	P2 obtains lock
7	t&s3	I	I	M	BusRdX	P3 lock acq fails
8	t&s3	I	I	M	–	P3 lock acq fails
9	unlock2	I	M	I	BusRdX	P2 releases lock
10	t&s3	I	I	M	BusRdX	P3 obtains lock
11	unlock3	I	I	M	–	P3 releases lock

8.1.4   Test and Test and Set Lock

Another way to reduce the traffic requirement is to have a criteria that tests whether a lock acquisition attempt will likely lead to failure, and if that is the case, we defer the execution of the atomic instruction. Only when a lock acquisition attempt has a good chance of succeeding do we attempt the execution of the atomic instruction. Using this approach, the test-and-set lock can be improved and the improved version is referred to as the *test-and-test-and-set lock* (TTSL) implementation. The code for TTSL is shown in Code 8.3.

Code 8.3 An implementation of test-and-test-and-set lock (TTSL).

```
1 lock: ld  R1, &lockvar // R1 = lockvar
2       bnz R1, lock      // jump to lock if R1 != 0
3       t&s R1, &lockvar // R1 = lockvar
4                         // if (R1 == 0) lockvar=1
5       bnz R1, lock      // jump to lock if R1 != 0
6       ret               // return to caller
7
8 unlock: st  &lockvar, #0 // lockvar = 0
9         ret               // return to caller
```

The load instruction and the following branch instruction form a tight loop that keeps reading (but not writing) the address where `lockvar` is located until the value in the location turns 0. Therefore, while a lock is being held by a processor, other processors do not execute the test-and-set atomic instructions. This prevents repeated invalidations that are useless as they lead to failed lock acquisitions. Only when the lock is released, will the processors attempt to acquire the lock using the atomic instructions. The uncontended lock-acquisition latency is higher than the test-and-set lock implementation due to the extra load and branch instructions. However, the traffic during the time a lock is held is significantly reduced. Only a small fraction of lock acquisition attempts generate traffic.

Table 8.2 illustrates the performance of the TTSL implementation. Suppose that each processor needs to get the lock exactly once. Initially, no one holds the lock. Then, P1 executes a load and finds out that the lock is available. So it attempts a test-and-set and successfully obtains the lock. The test-and-set instruction does not incur a BusRdX bus transaction since the block is exclusively cached. Suppose that after P1 obtains the lock (while P1 is in the critical section), P2 and P3 attempt to acquire the lock. Compared to the test-and-set lock implementation, in TTSL, P2 executes a load, followed by a load by P3. Both find that the value in `lockvar` location is one, indicating the lock is currently held by another processor. So they keep reading from the cache block, waiting until the value changes. While they are waiting, no bus transaction is generated since they are spinning using a load instruction rather than a test-and-set instruction. One of such loads is shown in line 5. In reality, it is likely that many loads are executed, rather than just one, so the advantage of TTSL over the test-and-set lock implementation increases. Note that an additional benefit of spinning using loads is that since bus bandwidth is conserved, the thread that is in the critical section does not experience the bandwidth contention that could slow it down.

Next, when P1 releases the lock, suppose that P2 is the first to suffer from a miss and discover that the lock has been freed; P2 then acquires the lock using the test-and-set instruction. This sequence produces two bus transactions: a bus read for loading the value, and a bus upgrade caused by the test-and-set instruction to write to the block. In contrast, in the test-and-set lock implementation, only one bus transaction is involved. Hence, the lock acquisition in TTSL incurs slightly more bandwidth usage than the test-and-set lock implementation, although overall, less bandwidth is used due to the use of loads for spinning.

Next, suppose that P3 spins on the lock variable (lines 9 and 10). When the lock is released by P2 (line 11), P3 attempts to read, and successfully acquires the lock, and succeeds. And finally, P3 releases the lock.

8.1.5   Load Linked and Store Conditional Lock

Although TTSL is an improvement over the test-and-set lock implementation, it still has a major drawback in its implementation. As mentioned before, one way to implement an atomic instruction requires a separate bus line that is asserted when a processor is executing an atomic instruction. Such an implementation is not general enough as it only works for bus-based multiprocessors. In addition, it works well only if lock frequency is low. If programmers use fine-grain locks, they use many lock variables simultaneously. There are many instances of lock acquisitions and releases, and many of them are unrelated as they are used, not for ensuring a critical section, but rather, for ensuring exclusive access to different parts of a data structure. If each of these lock acquisition asserts a single bus line, then unnecessary serialization occurs.

Another implementation, which reserves a cache block for the entire duration of the atomic instruction, is more general. It does not assume the existence of a special bus line so it can work with other interconnects as well. However, to prevent a cache block from being stolen by other processors, requests to the block must be deferred or negatively acknowledged. Such a mechanism can be costly to implement. Deferring requests requires an extra buffer to queue the requests, while negative acknowledgments waste bandwidth and incur delay when requests are retried in the future.

Table 8.2: Illustration of TTSL implementation performance.

	Request	P1	P2	P3	Bus Request	Comments
0	Initially	–	–	–	–	lock is free
1	ld1	E	–	–	BusRd	P1 reads from &lockvar
2	t&s1	M	–	–	–	P1 obtains lock
3	ld2	S	S	–	BusRd	P2 reads from &lockvar
4	ld3	S	S	S	BusRd	P3 reads from &lockvar
5	ld2	S	S	S	–	P2 reads from &lockvar
6	unlock1	M	I	I	BusUpgr	P1 releases lock
7	ld2	S	S	I	BusRd	P2 reads from &lockvar
8	t&s2	I	M	I	BusUpgr	P2 obtains lock
9	ld3	I	S	S	BusRd	P3 reads from &lockvar
10	ld3	I	S	S	–	P3 reads from &lockvar
11	unlock2	I	M	I	BusUpgr	P2 releases lock
12	ld3	I	S	S	BusRd	P3 reads from &lockvar
13	t&s3	I	I	M	BusUpgr	P3 obtains lock
14	unlock3	I	I	M	–	P3 releases lock

In order to avoid complexity associated with supporting an atomic instruction, an alternative is to provide an *illusion of atomicity* on a sequence of instructions, rather than true instruction atomicity. Note that the lock acquisition essentially consists of a load (ld R1, &lockvar), some instructions such as the conditional branch (bnz R1, lock), and a store (st &lockvar, R1). Atomicity implies that either none or all of the instructions appear to have executed. From the point of view of other processors, only the store instruction is visible, as it changes a value that may be seen by them. Other instructions (the load and the branch) have their effect on the registers of the local processor but their effect is not visible to other processors. Hence, from the point of view of other processors, it does not matter if the load and the branch have executed or not. From the point of view of the local processor, these instructions can be canceled easily by ignoring their register results and reexecuting them later. Therefore, the instruction that is critical to the illusion of atomicity is the store instruction. If it is executed, its effect is visible to other processors. If it is not executed, its effect is not visible to other processors. Therefore, in order to give the illusion of atomicity to the sequence of instructions, we need to ensure that the store fails (or gets canceled) if between the load and the store, something has happened that potentially violates the illusion of atomicity. For example, if there is a context switch or interrupt that occurs between the load and the store, then the store must be canceled (servicing the interrupt may result in the value of the block to change without the knowledge of the processor, which breaks atomicity). In addition, with respect to other processors, if the cache block that is loaded has been invalidated before the store executes, then the value in the cache block may have changed, resulting in a violation to atomicity. In this case, the store must be canceled. If, however, the block remains valid in the cache by the time the store executes, then the entire load-branch-store sequence can appear to have executed atomically.

The illusion of atomicity requires that the store instruction is executed conditionally upon detected events that may break the illusion of atomicity. Such a store is well known as a *store conditional* (SC). The load that requires a block address to be monitored from being *stolen* (i.e., invalidated) is known as a *load linked* or *load locked* (LL). The LL/SC pair turns out to be a very powerful mechanism on which many different atomic operations can be built. The pair ensures the illusion of atomicity without requiring an exclusive ownership of a cache block.

An LL is a special load instruction that not only reads a block into a register, but also records the address of the block in a special processor register which we will refer to as a *linked register*. An SC is a special store instruction that succeeds only when the address involved matches the address stored in the linked register. To achieve the illusion of atomicity, the SC should fail when another processor has raced past it, successfully performed an SC, and stolen the cache block. To ensure the failure of SC, the linked register is cleared when an invalidation to the address stored in the linked register occurs. In addition, when a context switch occurs, the linked register is also cleared. When an SC fails (due to mismatch of the SC address and the address in the linked register), the store is canceled without going to the caches. Hence, to the memory system, it is as if the SC is never executed. All other instructions in the atomic sequence (LL included) can simply be repeated as if they have also failed.

Code 8.4 shows the code that implements a lock acquisition and release using an LL/SC pair, which is identical to Code 6.3 except that the load is replaced with the LL, and the store is replaced with an SC.

Code 8.4 An implementation of LL/SC lock. The code assumes that a failed SC returns a 0.

```
1 lock: LL    R1, &lockvar    // R1 = lockvar;
2                             // LINKREG = &lockvar
3        bnz  R1, lock        // jump to lock if R1 != 0
4        add  R1, R1, #1      // R1 = 1
5        SC   &lockvar, R1    // lockvar = R1;
6        beqz R1, lock        // jump to lock if SC fails
7        ret                  // return to caller
8
9 unlock: st  &lockvar, #0    // MEM[&lockvar] = 0
10        ret                 // return to caller
```

The LL instruction and the following branch instruction forms a tight loop that keeps reading (but not writing) the location where `lockvar` is until the value in the location turns 0. Thus it behaves similarly to a TTSL implementation which spins using loads. Therefore, while a lock is being held by a processor, the SC is not executed. This prevents repeated, useless, invalidations that correspond to failed lock acquisitions. Only when the lock is released, will the processors attempt to acquire the lock using the SC instruction. It is possible that multiple processors attempt to perform the SC simultaneously. On a bus-based multiprocessor, one of the SCs will be granted a bus access and performs the store successfully. Other processors snoop the store on the bus and clear out their linked registers, causing their own SC to fail. In contrast to a test-and-set atomic instruction, when an SC fails, it does not generate a bus transaction (a test-and-set instruction always generates a BusRdX or BusUpgr).

> ■ *Did you know?*
>
> *LL/SC instruction pairs are supported in various instruction sets such as Alpha* (`ldl_l`/`stl_c` *and* `ldq_l`/`stq_c`), *PowerPC* (`lwarx`/`stwcx`), *MIPS* (`LL`/`SC`), *and ARM* (`ldrex`/`strex`). *The conditions that make SC fails can vary across implementations although sometimes the failure is not strictly necessary given the conditions. For example, in some implementations, SC fails when another LL is encountered, or even when ordinary loads or stores are encountered.*

Table 8.3 illustrates the performance of the LL/SC lock implementation. Suppose that each processor needs to get the lock exactly once. Initially, no one holds the lock. The sequence of bus transactions generated is identical to ones in the TTSL implementation, except that the LL replaces the regular load, and SC replaces the test-and-set instruction.

Table 8.3: Illustration of LL/SC lock implementation performance.

	Request	**P1**	**P2**	**P3**	**Bus Request**	**Comments**
0	Initially	–	–	–	–	lock is free
1	ll1	E	–	–	BusRd	P1 reads from &lockvar
2	sc1	M	–	–	–	P1 obtains lock
3	ll2	S	S	–	BusRd	P2 reads from &lockvar
4	ll3	S	S	S	BusRd	P3 reads from &lockvar
5	ll2	S	S	S	–	P2 reads from &lockvar
6	unlock1	M	I	I	BusUpgr	P1 releases lock
7	ll2	S	S	I	BusRd	P2 reads from &lockvar
8	sc2	I	M	I	BusUpgr	P2 obtains lock
9	ll3	I	S	S	BusRd	P3 reads from &lockvar
10	ll3	I	S	S	–	P3 reads from &lockvar
11	unlock2	I	M	I	BusUpgr	P2 releases lock
12	ll3	I	S	S	BusRd	P3 reads from &lockvar
13	sc3	I	I	M	BusUpgr	P3 obtains lock
14	unlock3	I	I	M	–	P3 releases lock

Therefore, performance-wise, the LL/SC lock implementation performs similarly to a TTSL implementation. A minor difference is when multiple processors simultaneously perform SCs. In this case, only one bus transaction occurs in LL/SC (due to the successful SC), whereas in the TTSL, there will be multiple bus transactions corresponding test-and-set instruction execution. However, this is a quite rare event since there are only a few instructions between a load and a store in an atomic sequence, so the probability of multiple processors executing the same sequence at the same time is small.

However, the advantages of LL/SC over using atomic instructions are numerous. First, LL/SC implementation is relatively simpler (extra linked registers). Secondly, it can be used to implement many atomic instructions, such as test-and-set, compare-and-swap, etc. Hence, it can be thought of as a lower level primitive than atomic instructions.

However, the LL/SC lock implementation still has a significant scalability problem. Each lock acquisition or lock release triggers invalidation of all sharers that spin on the lock variable because the value of the lock variable has changed. They in turn suffer from cache misses to reload the block containing the lock variable. Hence, if there are $\mathcal{O}(p)$ lock acquisitions and releases, and each acquisition or release triggers $\mathcal{O}(p)$ subsequent cache misses, then the total traffic of an LL/SC lock implementation scales quadratically to the number of threads in the system, or $\mathcal{O}(p^2)$. This is in addition to the issue of lock fairness in which there is no guarantee that the thread that attempts to acquire the lock the earliest can actually acquire the lock earlier than others. The following two lock implementations will address each of these problems.

8.1.6 Ticket Lock

The *ticket lock* is a lock implementation that attempts to provide fairness in lock acquisition. The notion of fairness deals with whether the order in which threads first attempt to acquire a lock corresponds to the order in which threads acquire the lock successfully. This notion of fairness automatically guarantees that a thread is not starved out from failing to acquire a lock for a long period of time because other threads always beat to it.

To achieve such fairness, the ticket lock implementation uses a concept of a queue. Each thread that attempts to acquire a lock is given a ticket number in the queue, and the order in which lock acquisition is granted is based on the ticket numbers, with a thread holding the lowest ticket number is given the lock next.

To implement that, two variables are introduced. The first one is `now_serving` and the other is `next_ticket`. The role of `next_ticket` is to reflect the next available ticket number (or the order position) that a new thread should get. The role of `now_serving` is to reflect the position of the current holder of the lock. Necessarily, $next\_ticket - now\_serving - 1$ is the number of threads that are currently waiting for the lock, i.e., they have attempted to acquire the lock but have not obtained it. To obtain a lock, a thread reads the `next_ticket` into a private variable (say, `my_ticket`) and atomically increments it, so that future threads will not share the same ticket number. Then, it waits until `now_serving` is equal to the value of `my_ticket`. A thread that is currently holding the lock releases the lock by incrementing the `now_serving` variable so that the next thread in line will find that the new value of `now_serving` is equal to its `my_ticket`, and the thread can successfully acquire the lock. The complete code for lock acquisition and release are shown in Code 8.5.

Note that the code shows the implementation in a high-level language, assuming that there is only one lock (so a lock's name is not shown) and fetch the atomic primitive `fetch_and_inc()` is supported. As we have seen in the discussion of LL/SC lock implementation, such primitive can be implemented easily using a pair of LL and SC. The only thing that needs to be inserted between the LL and SC is an instruction that increments the value read from memory by LL. We also assume that `fetch_and_inc()` is implemented as a function that returns the old value of the argument prior to incrementing it. Finally, the values of `now_serving` and `next_ticket` are both initially initialized to 0 before use.

Code 8.5 Ticket lock implementation.

```
1 ticketLock_init(int *next_ticket, int *now_serving)
2 {
3   *now_serving = *next_ticket = 0;
4 }
5
6 ticketLock_acquire(int *next_ticket, int *now_serving)
7 {
8   my_ticket = fetch_and_inc(next_ticket);
9   while (*now_serving != my_ticket) {};
10 }
11
12 ticketLock_release(int *now_serving)
13 {
14   now_serving++;
15 }
```

To illustrate how the ticket lock works, consider three processors contending for the lock and each of them will acquire and release the lock exactly once. Table 8.4 shows the values of the important variables at each step: now_serving, next_ticket, P1's my_ticket, P2's my_ticket, and P3's my_ticket. First, P1 tries to acquire lock, it executes fetch_and_inc(next_ticket) atomically, resulting in the value of next_ticket to increase to 1. It then compares my_ticket and now_serving, and since their values are equal, it successfully acquires the lock and enters the critical section. P2, contending for the lock, also attempts to acquire the lock by executing fetch_and_inc(next_ticket), resulting in the next_ticket to increase to 2. It then compares my_ticket, which has a value of 1, and now_serving, which has a value of 0 (since the lock is still held by the thread having the ticket number 0). Since their values are not equal, P2 fails the lock acquisition, stays in the loop to keep on testing the values of now_serving. P3, also contending for the lock, attempts to acquire the lock by executing fetch_and_inc(next_ticket), resulting in the next_ticket to increase to 3. It then compares my_ticket, which has a value of 2, and now_serving, which still has a value of 0 (since the lock is still held by P1). Since their values are not equal, P3 fails the lock acquisition, and like P2, it stays in the loop to keep on testing their values. When P1 releases the lock, it executes the now_serving++ statement, incrementing the now_serving to a value of 1. Now P2's my_ticket and now_serving match, P2 gets out of its loop and enters the critical section. Similarly, when P2 releases the lock, it executes the now_serving++ statement, incrementing the now_serving to a value of 2. Now P3's my_ticket and now_serving match, P3 gets out of its loop and enters the critical section.

The performance of ticket lock depends on how the fetch_and_inc atomic operation is implemented. If it is implemented with an atomic instruction, then its scalability is similar to that of the atomic instruction. If the fetch_and_inc is implemented using an LL/SC pair, then its scalability is similar to that of LL/SC lock implementation. In particular, the fetch_and_inc on next_ticket will cause a processor to invalidate all copies of the block containing next_ticket, and each processor subsequently suffers from a cache miss to reload the block. Similarly, since all processors are monitoring and spinning on the now_serving, when a processor releases the lock, all copies of the block containing now_serving are invalidated, and each processor subsequently suffers from a cache miss to reload the block. Since there are $\mathcal{O}(p)$ number of acquisition and

Table 8.4: Illustration of the ticket lock mechanism.

Steps	next_ ticket	now_ serving	P1	P2	P3	Comments
				my_ticket		
Initially	0	0	0	0	0	all initialized to 0
P1: f&i(next_ticket)	1	0	0	0	0	P1 tries to acq lock
P2: f&i(next_ticket)	2	0	0	1	0	P2 tries to acq lock
P3: f&i(next_ticket)	3	0	0	1	2	P3 tries to acq lock
P1: now_serving++	3	1	0	1	2	P1 rels, P2 acqs lock
P2: now_serving++	3	2	0	1	2	P2 rels, P3 acqs lock
P3: now_serving++	3	3	0	1	2	P3 rels lock

releases, and each acquire and release causes $\mathcal{O}(p)$ invalidations and subsequent cache misses, the total traffic scales on the order of $\mathcal{O}(p^2)$.

The uncontended latency of a ticket lock implementation is slightly higher than that of LL/SC because it has extra instructions that read and test the value of now_serving. However, the ticket lock provides fairness, which is not provided by the LL/SC lock implementation.

8.1.7   Array-Based Queuing Lock

At this point, readers may wonder if there is a lock implementation that has the fairness of the ticket lock and at the same time better scalability compared to all the previous lock implementations discussed so far. One answer to that lies in a lock implementation called the *array-based queuing lock* (ABQL). ABQL is an improvement over the ticket lock. It starts out from the observation that since threads already queue up waiting for the lock acquisition in the ticket lock, they can wait and spin on unique memory locations rather than on a single location represented by now_serving. The analogy for the new mechanism is for the current lock holder to pass the baton to the next thread in the queue, and for that thread to pass the baton to the next next thread, and so on. Each time the baton is passed, only the next thread needs to be notified.

To implement ABQL, we need to ensure that threads spin on unique memory locations. To achieve that, we can change the now_serving to an array, which we will rename to can_serve to reflect its role better. As with the ticket lock implementation, each thread that wants to acquire a lock obtains a ticket number, say x. It then waits in a loop until the xth element in the can_serve array has a value of 1, which will be set by the thread ahead of it in the queue. When a thread with a ticket number y releases a lock, it passes the baton to the next thread by setting the $(y + 1)^{th}$ element in the can_serve array to 1. The complete code for lock acquisition and release are shown in Code 8.6.

Note that the code shows the implementation in a high-level language, assuming that there is only one lock and the atomic primitive fetch_and_inc() is supported. Initially, the values of next_ticket are initialized to 0. Elements of the array can_serve are initialized to 0 as well, except for the first element which is initialized to 1, in order to allow the first lock acquisition to be successful.

Code 8.6 Array-based queuing lock implementation.

```
1 ABQL_init(int *next_ticket, int *can_serve)
2 {
3    *next_ticket = 0;
4    for (i=1; i<MAXSIZE; i++)
5      can_serve[i] = 0;
6    can_serve[0] = 1;
7 }
8
9 ABQL_acquire(int *next_ticket, int *can_serve)
10 {
11    *my_ticket = fetch_and_inc(next_ticket);
12    while (can_serve[*my_ticket] != 1) {};
13 }
14
15 ABQL_release(int *can_serve)
16 {
17    can_serve[*my_ticket + 1] = 1;
18    can_serve[*my_ticket] = 0;   // prepare for next time
19 }
```

To illustrate how ABQL works, consider three processors contending for the lock and each of them will acquire and release the lock exactly once. Table 8.5 shows the values of the important variables at each step: can_serve (assuming it has four elements), next_ticket, P1's my_ticket, P2's my_ticket, and P3's my_ticket.

First, P1 tries to acquire lock, it executes fetch_and_inc(next_ticket) atomically, resulting in the value of next_ticket to increase to 1, and it obtains a value of 0 for its my_ticket. Then it checks whether can_serve[my_ticket] (can_serve[0]) is 1. Since the value is 1, it successfully acquires the lock and enters the critical section. P2, contending for the lock, also attempts to acquire the lock by executing fetch_and_inc(next_ticket), resulting in the next_ticket to increase to 2, and it obtains the value of 1 for its my_ticket. It then checks whether can_serve[1]==1. But at this point can_serve[1] has a value of 0 since P1 has not released its lock. So P2 fails the lock acquisition and stays in the loop. P3, also contending for the lock, also attempts to acquire the lock by executing fetch_and_inc(next_ticket), resulting in the next_ticket to increase to 3, and it obtains the value of 2 for its my_ticket. It then checks whether can_serve[2]==1. But at this point can_serve[2] has a value of 0 since P1 has not released the lock (P1 has not even acquired the lock). So P3 fails the lock acquisition, stays in the loop. When P1 releases the lock, it resets can_serve[0] to 0 and sets can_serve[1] to 1, allowing P2 to get out of its loop and enter the critical section. When P2 releases the lock, it resets can_serve[1] to 0 and sets can_serve[2] to 1, allowing P3 to get out of its loop and enter the critical section. Finally, P3 releases the lock by setting can_serve[3] to 1, and resets can_serve[2] to 0.

Consider the way a thread releases a lock. It writes to one element of the array can_serve[my_ticket+1]. Assume that the array is padded such that different array elements reside in different cache blocks. Since exactly one thread spins in a loop reading from the element, the element is only stored in one cache. The write only invalidates one cache block, and only one subsequent cache miss occurs. Hence, on each release, only $\mathcal{O}(1)$ traffic is generated. That means

Table 8.5: Illustration of ABQL mechanism.

Steps	next_ ticket	can_ serve	P1	P2	P3	Comments
				my_ticket		
Initially	0	[1, 0, 0, 0]	0	0	0	all initialized to 0
P1: f&i(next_ticket)	1	[1, 0, 0, 0]	0	0	0	P1 tries to acq lock
P2: f&i(next_ticket)	2	[1, 0, 0, 0]	0	1	0	P2 tries to acq lock
P3: f&i(next_ticket)	3	[1, 0, 0, 0]	0	1	2	P3 tries to acq lock
P1: can_serve[1]=1; can_serve[0]=0	3	[0, 1, 0, 0]	0	1	2	P1 rels, P2 acqs lock
P2: can_serve[2]=1; can_serve[1]=0	3	[0, 0, 1, 0]	0	1	2	P2 rels, P3 acqs lock
P3: can_serve[3]=1; can_serve[2]=0	3	[0, 0, 0, 1]	0	1	2	P3 rels lock

that since there are $\mathcal{O}(p)$ number of acquisitions and releases, the total lock release traffic scales on the order of $\mathcal{O}(p)$, a significant improvement over the ticket lock implementation. However, note that the fetch_and_inc's scalability depends on its underlying implementation. If it is implemented with an LL/SC, its scalability may partially restrict the overall scalability of the ABQL implementation.

8.1.8 Qualitative Comparison of Lock Implementations

Table 8.6 compares the various lock implementations based on several criteria: uncontended latency, the amount of traffic following a single lock release, the amount of traffic waiting while the lock is held by a processor, storage overheads, and whether fairness guarantee is provided.

Table 8.6: Comparison of various lock implementations.

Criteria	test&set	TTSL	LL/SC	Ticket	ABQL
Uncontended latency	Lowest	Lower	Lower	Higher	Higher
1 Release max traffic	$\mathcal{O}(p)$	$\mathcal{O}(p)$	$\mathcal{O}(p)$	$\mathcal{O}(p)$	$\mathcal{O}(1)$
Wait traffic	High	–	–	–	–
Storage	$\mathcal{O}(1)$	$\mathcal{O}(1)$	$\mathcal{O}(1)$	$\mathcal{O}(1)$	$\mathcal{O}(p)$
Fairness guarantee?	No	No	No	Yes	Yes

The uncontended latency is the lowest on simpler lock implementations such as the test_and_set, TTSL, and LL/SC. Ticket lock and ABQL implementations execute more instructions so their uncontended lock acquisition latency is higher.

In terms of the traffic following a single lock release, assuming all other threads are waiting to acquire the lock next, test_and_set, TTSL, LL/SC, and ticket lock have the highest amount of maximum traffic. This is because all threads spin on the same variable so they may all cache the same block, and each lock release invalidates all other processors and forces them to suffer misses to reload the block. On the other hand, in ABQL, a single release only invalidates one other cache causing only one subsequent cache miss.

In terms of the traffic generated while a lock is held by a thread, test_and_set performs very poorly because all threads keep on attempting to acquire the lock using an atomic instruction and even a failed attempt still generates an invalidation of all sharers and subsequent acquisition attempts by the sharers. On the other hand, TTSL, LL/SC, ticket lock, and ABQL, spin wait using a load instruction. Hence, once a thread discovers that the lock is held, it does not attempt to execute an atomic instruction.

In terms of storage requirements, all of the lock implementations use one or two shared variables so the storage requirement is constant across number of processors. Only ABQL has a storage requirement that scales with the number of processors due to keeping the array can_serve.

In terms of guarantee of fairness, only the ticket lock and ABQL provide it, due to the use of a queue. In other implementations, it is possible (though in reality may not be likely) that a processor has a better chance at acquiring the lock more than others following a release. For example, that may occur when a thread that releases a lock (and invalidating other caches) quickly acquires the lock to reenter the critical section again. In the mean time, other processors have not even had a chance to reattempt a lock acquisition because they are still reloading the invalidated block. In this case, it is possible that a thread keeps on acquiring and releasing a lock at the expense of other threads' ability to acquire the lock. Other causes may also be possible. For example, if the bus arbitration logic favors some requesters than others, some processors may be granted the bus faster than others. In a distributed shared memory system, one processor may reload an invalidated block faster than others, for example due to reloading the block from its local memory whereas others must reload it from a remote memory. Following a release, the processor that reloads the block from its local memory may race past others to attempt a lock acquisition.

Note, however, fairness guarantee creates a risk in performance. If a thread that is already in the queue waiting to get a lock is context switched out, then even when the lock becomes available, the thread will not attempt to acquire the lock. Other threads with larger ticket numbers cannot acquire the lock either because they must wait until the thread that is switched out has acquired and released the lock. Thus, the performance of all threads are degraded by the context switch of one of the threads. Therefore, care must be taken to ensure context switches do not occur when using the ticket lock or ABQL implementations.

From the point of view of software, it is not immediately clear which lock implementation is the best. For software showing a high degree of lock contention, ABQL offers the highest scalability. However, a high degree of lock contention is often a symptom of a deeper scalability problem, such as the use of lock granularity that is too coarse grain. In such a case, using ABQL improves scalability but may not make the program scalable. Better scalability can be obtained using a finer lock granularity. For example, in the linked list parallelization discussed in Chapter 4, using the fine grain lock approach, in which each node is augmented with its own lock, will likely make the contention level of any particular lock very low. In that case, ABQL is not only unnecessary, it is not even preferred due to a high uncontended latency and the fact that the storage overhead of one array for each node will be too high.

8.2 Barrier Implementations

Barriers are very simple and widely used synchronization primitives in parallel programs. We have discussed in Chapter 3 that in loop-level parallelization, barriers are often used at the end of a parallel loop to ensure all threads have computed their parts of the computation before the computation moves on to the next step. In the OpenMP `parallel for` directive, a barrier is automatically inserted at the end of a parallel loop, and programmers must explicitly remove it if they believe that the lack of barrier does not impact the correctness of their computation.

In this section, we will look at how barriers can be implemented, and compare the characteristics of the implementations in various terms. Barriers can be implemented in software or directly in hardware. Software barrier implementation is flexible but is often inefficient, whereas hardware barrier implementation restricts the flexibility and portability of the software but is often a lot more efficient. The simplest software barrier implementation is an implementation called the *sense-reversal global barrier*. The key mechanism used is for threads to enter the barrier and spin on a location that will be set by the last thread that arrives at the barrier, releasing all threads that are waiting there. Obviously, spinning on a single location often involves a lot of invalidations when the location is written, restricting scalability. One of the more complex but more scalable barrier implementations is *combining tree barrier* in which the threads that participate in a barrier are organized like a tree, and a thread at a particular tree level spins on a common location only with its siblings. This restricts the number of invalidations as threads spin on different locations. Finally, we will look at a hardware barrier implementation support that is implemented in some very large machine with thousands of processors.

The criteria for evaluating barrier performance include:

1. **Latency**: the time spent from entering the barrier to exiting the barrier. The latency in the barrier should be as small as possible.

2. **Traffic**: the amount of bytes communicated between processors as a function of the number of processors.

In contrast to lock implementation, fairness and storage overheads are not important issues because barriers are a global construct involving many threads.

8.2.1 Sense-Reversing Centralized Barrier

A software barrier implementation only assumes that lock acquisition and release primitives to be provided by the system (through software, hardware, or a combination of hardware and software). For example, as long as one of test-and-set, TTSL, LL/SC, ticket, or ABQL lock implementation is available, a barrier implementation can be constructed as well.

We note that from the point of view of programmers, a barrier must be simple, that is, a barrier should not require any arguments passed to it, either variable names or number of processors or threads. In OpenMP standard, for example, a barrier can be invoked simply as `#pragma omp barrier`. In the actual implementation, arguments may be used, as long as they are not exposed to the programmers.

The basic barrier implementation is shown in Code 8.7. The implementation makes use of several variables. `barCounter` keeps track of how many threads have so far arrived at the barrier.

`barLock` is a lock variable to protect a modification to shared variables in a critical section. `canGo` is a flag variable that threads spin on to know whether they can go past the barrier or not yet. Hence, `canGo` is set by the last thread to release all threads from the barrier.

Code 8.7 Simple (but incorrect) barrier implementation.

```
1 // declaration of shared variables used in a barrier
2 // and their initial values
3 int numArrived = 0;
4 lock_type barLock = 0;
5 int canGo = 0;
6
7 // barrier implementation
8 void barrier () {
9   lock(&barLock);
10    if (numArrived == 0) { // first thread sets flag
11      canGo = 0;
12    }
13    numArrived++;
14    myCount = numArrived;
15  unlock(&barLock);
16
17  if (myCount < NUM_THREADS) {
18    while (canGo == 0) {};   // wait for last thread
19  }
20  else {   // last thread to arrive
21    numArrived = 0;   // reset for next barrier
22    canGo = 1;        // release all threads
23  }
24 }
```

For example, suppose that three threads P1, P2, and P3 arrive at the barrier in that order. P1 arrives at the barrier first and enters the critical section. Then it initializes the variable `canGo` to 0 so that itself and other threads will wait until the last thread arrives and sets it to 1. It then increments `numArrived` to 1, assigns its value to `myCount`, and exits the critical section. Next, it enters a loop to wait until canGo has a value of 1. The second thread P2 enters the barrier, increments `numArrived` to 2, discovers that it is not the last thread (`myCount` has a value of 2, smaller than NUM_THREADS) and also enters the loop to wait until canGo has a value of 1. Finally, the last thread P3 enters the barrier, and increments `numArrived` to 3. It discovers that `myCount` is equal to NUM_THREADS so it is the last thread to arrive at the barrier. It then resets the value of `numArrived` to 0 so that it can be used in the next barrier. Then, it releases all waiting threads by setting `canGo` to 1. This allows all waiting threads to get out of the loop and resume computation past the barrier.

Unfortunately, the code described above does not work correctly across more than one barrier. For example, when the last thread P3 sets the value of `canGo` to 1, it invalidates all cached copies of the block where `canGo` is located. Following the invalidations, the block resides in P3's cache, while P1 and P2 try to reload the block. Suppose that before that can happen, P3 enters the next barrier, now as the first thread that arrives at that second barrier. As the first thread, it resets the variable `canGo` to 0. It can do so quickly since it has the block in its cache in a modified state. When P1 and P2 reload the block, they discover that the value of `canGo` is 0 as affected by the second barrier rather than 1 as released from the first barrier. Therefore, P1 and P2 stay in the loop of the first barrier and never get released, while P3 waits in the loop of the second barrier, never to be released either.

One possible solution to the "deadlock" situation discussed earlier is to have a two-step release, in which before the first thread that enters a barrier initializes the `canGo` variable, it waits until all threads have been released from the previous barrier. Implementing such a solution requires another flag, another counter, and extra code, which can be quite costly. Fortunately, there is a simpler solution based on an observation that the error arises when the first thread entering the next barrier resets the value of `canGo`. If we avoid this reset, then the thread that enters the next barrier will not prevent other threads from getting out of the first barrier. To avoid resetting the value of `canGo`, in the second barrier, threads can instead wait until the value of `canGo` changes back to 0, which is accomplished by the last thread that enter the second barrier. With this approach, the value of `canGo` that releases threads alternates from 1 in the first barrier, 0 in the second barrier, 1 in the third barrier, 0 in the fourth barrier, and so on. Because the value is toggling between barriers, this solution is referred to as the *sense-reversing centralized barrier*. The code for the barrier is shown in the following (Code 8.8).

Code 8.8 Sense-reversing barrier implementation.

```
1 // declaration of shared variables used in a barrier
2 int numArrived = 0;
3 lock_type barLock = 0;
4 int canGo = 0;
5
6 // thread-private variables
7 int valueToWait = 0;
8
9 // barrier implementation
10 void barrier () {
11   valueToWait = 1 - valueToWait; // toggle it
12   lock(&barLock);
13     numArrived++;
14     myCount = numArrived;
15   unlock(&barLock);
16
17   if (myCount < NUM_THREADS) {  // wait for last thread
18     while (canGo != valueToWait) {};
19   }
20   else {  // last thread to arrive
21     numArrived = 0;  // reset for next barrier
22     canGo = valueToWait;   // release all threads
23   }
24 }
```

The code shows that each thread, when entering a barrier, first toggles the value that it will wait from 0 to 1 or from 1 to 0. Then, it increments the counter and waits until the value of `canGo` is changed by the last thread. The last thread is the one that toggles the value of `canGo`.

The centralized (or global) barrier implementation uses a critical section inside the barrier routine so as the number of threads grow, the time in the barrier increases linearly. Actually, it may increase super-linearly depending on the underlying lock implementation. In addition, the traffic is high since each thread increments the variable `numArrived`, invalidating all sharers of the block, which then have to reload the block through cache misses. Since there are $\mathcal{O}(p)$ such increments, and each increment can cause $\mathcal{O}(p)$ cache misses, the total traffic for the barrier implementation scales quadratically with the number of processors, or $\mathcal{O}(p^2)$. Hence, unfortunately, the centralized barrier is not very scalable.

8.2.2   Combining Tree Barrier

There have been many attempts to improve the scalability of software barriers. In these scalable barriers, the situation in which all threads sharing and spinning on a single location (e.g., `barCount` or `canGo`) is avoided. The way they avoid spinning on a single location is by organizing the barrier in a hierarchical manner, where groups of threads synchronize within each group, one thread from each group is chosen to advance to the next round and forms a new group with other selected threads, and so on until the last group has finished synchronizing in the barrier. There are several scalable barrier algorithms, including combining tree barrier, tournament barrier, dissemination barrier, etc. that have been proposed in the past. We will discuss one such barrier: combining tree barrier.

The combining tree barrier divides the nodes (or threads) into subgroups with k members. Each group of threads synchronize a simple shared counter, for example by requiring each thread to atomically increment the counter and then wait until all threads in the group reach the barrier (counter value reaches k). Afterward, the first threads from each group form a new group of k members (representing a parent node) and synchronize again. This is repeated until there is one group left representing the root node of the tree. Finally, the root releases all threads by setting a flag that all threads monitor.

A combining tree barrier needs the storage space that is equivalent to the size of the tree, that is, $\mathcal{O}(p)$. The amount of traffic scales with the number of nodes, i.e., $\mathcal{O}(p)$, which is favorable compared to a centralized barrier's $\mathcal{O}(p^2)$. However, the latency is now higher, since to know that all threads have reached the barrier, we need to traverse up the tree, participating in $\mathcal{O}(log\ p)$ barriers at various levels of the tree, versus the centralized barrier's $\mathcal{O}(1)$.

8.2.3   Hardware Barrier Implementation

Hardware barrier implementation is attractive for its low latency as well as its scalability. With software barrier, we have to execute many instructions to implement a barrier primitive and rely on cache coherence mechanism to propagate changes made in the primitive. The cache coherence alone is at the moment unable to scale to thousands or tens of thousands of processors. In contrast, hardware implementation relies on signals traveling on dedicated wires. For a large system, the wires form a dedicated barrier network. The requirement of dedicated wires and network make hardware barrier implementations seem unnecessary for a small multiprocessor system, especially ones that are general purpose. However, for a large multiprocessor system, hardware barrier offers the only way to achieve truly scalable barrier implementations.

The simplest hardware barrier implementation in a bus-based multiprocessor is a special bus line that implements an AND logic. Each processor that arrives at the barrier asserts the barrier line. Since the barrier implements an AND logic, the line is only high when all processors have reached the barrier and asserted the line. Each processor also monitors the barrier line to detect its signal value. When processors sense that the barrier line is high, they conclude that all processors have reached the barrier. At this point, they can exit the barrier and continue execution.

Conceptually, a hardware barrier network is simple. It needs to collect each signal from a processor that has reached the barrier, until signals from all processors have been collected. Then it needs to broadcast a barrier completion signal to all processors. All these need to be performed in as short time as possible. Signals cannot be collected by one node because it requires a very large connectivity. A limited connectivity requires the wires used for barrier signaling to form a network. An example of a scalable network with limited node connectivity is a tree. A k-ary tree allows a node to collect signals from k children nodes (unless the node is a leaf node), before passing a barrier signal to to its parent node. A node that is designated as the root eventually receives signals from all its children and detects the completion of the barrier. The root can then send a barrier completion signal down to its k children nodes, which then propagate the signal down to their children, and so on, all the way until the signal reaches the leaf nodes. The number of steps needed to collect signals from N processors will then be $log_k(N)$. The number of steps determine the latency to collect and broadcast barrier signals. With a log function, the latency increases more slowly than the size of the system, making the network a scalable barrier implementation.

> ■ *Did you know?*
>
> IBM BlueGene supercomputer, designed to scale up to as many as 65 thousand processors, is an example system that requires a scalable barrier that a hardware barrier can provide. The BlueGene/L system [1] has several types of interconnection network among processors. One network, a three-dimensional torus, is used for regular data communication between processors. There is also a fast Ethernet network for accessing a file system and for network management. What is interesting is that there are two additional, special-purpose, networks: the collective network and the barrier network.
>
> The collective network was designed to support global operations such as reduction, such as summing up elements of an array or matrix, taking their maximum, minimum, bitwise logical OR/AND/XOR, etc. The network is organized as a tree, in which each tree node is a node of processors. To sum up elements of an array, the summation starts at the leaves of the tree. A node collects the sum from its children nodes, accumulates the value to its own sum, and propagates it to its parent. Since children nodes can perform the summation in parallel, the total latency for such an operation scales as $\mathcal{O}(log\ p)$. The collective network also supports broadcast of data starting from the root to all nodes going down the tree. This can be done in parallel with regular data communication across the torus. Each link in the collective tree network has a target bandwidth of 2.8 Gb/s so it takes only about 16 cycles to transmit an 8-byte value (excluding the latency at the switch).
>
> The barrier network is a separate network that supports global barrier. Instead of relying on a software barrier and cache coherence protocol, the barrier network works literally by sending signals along the wires in the network. The barrier network is organized as a tree. To perform a global barrier, a node collects signals from its children nodes, and propagate the signal up to its parent node, and this is repeated until the root node gets the signal. When the root node gets a signal, it knows that all nodes have arrived at the barrier. Next, it needs to release the nodes from the barrier. To achieve that, it sends a release signal down the tree to all nodes. The signals that are sent around are processed by special hardware logic at the barrier network controller of each node. Hence, they can propagate very fast. The round-trip latency of a barrier over 64K nodes is reported to take only 1.5 μs, corresponding to only a few hundred 700-MHz processor cycles, which is very fast compared to any software implementation (which easily takes that much time or more for just a few nodes).

8.3 Transactional Memory

In the context of parallel programming, transactional memory (TM) is designed to provide a higher level of programming abstraction that frees up programmers from dealing with lower level thread synchronization constructs such as locks. A code region enveloped as a transaction appears to execute fully or not at all (atomicity) without affected by interference from other threads (isolation). Earlier in Section 2.2.3, we have discussed an overview of transactional memory programming model, and in Section 4.4, we have discussed one application of transactional memory on linked data structure parallel programming. In this section, we will discuss architecture support to support transactional memory (TM) programming model.

There are three approaches for supporting TM. The first approach is to let software implement it while the hardware only provides the most primitive form of support in the form of atomic instructions – which are already in place to support other synchronization primitives. Such an approach is referred to as software transactional memory (STM). A particularly useful atomic instruction is the compare and swap (CAS) instruction. In an STM, a data structure (object) is wrapped by another object that contains a pointer that points to the original object. If an object needs to be modified atomically, it will be copied to a separate space and modified there. This modification is not visible to other threads until commit. After the modification is completed, it is committed by executing the CAS instruction to change the pointer so that it points to the new copy of the object. Thus, a single CAS can commit a large amount of changes to the data structure. Conflicts between concurrent modifications to the thread are detected by ensuring that all data that is read by the committing transaction (*read set*) has not been modified by another transaction (*write set*). STM comes as a library specific to particular data structures that the library provides. STM suffers from a significant overheads in the event of no contention due to the maintenance and bookkeeping of the object meta data. A second, related, approach, is providing hardware support to accelerate STM.

In this section, we will discuss the third approach, hardware transactional memory (HTM), where hardware directly provides transactions. We can think of the LL/SC pair as a primitive form of HTM. The lock implementation of LL/SC provides an illusion of atomicity, where any code between LL/SC appears to be executed completely or not at all. A hardware transaction provides the same illusion, but for an (almost) arbitrary region of code. The illusion of atomicity for a transaction requires several elements. First, it requires a mechanism to detect *conflicts*, i.e., conditions that may violate the illusion of atomicity. Second, if a conflict is detected, it requires a mechanism either to undo all effects the transaction has made. Alternatively, it requires a *buffer and commit* mechanism where changes made by the transaction are buffered and gated (not made visible to other threads) until commit time where the changes are made public. In the LL/SC lock, a conflict with other concurrent attempts of acquiring the lock is detected when the address of the lock variable stored in a linked register is cleared following a write attempt by another thread. Similarly, in a transaction, a conflict is detected when data that is read or written by the transaction (read and write set) intersects with data written by another thread (write set). In the LL/SC lock, no store instructions are allowed between the LL and SC, so as to enable the effects of the lock acquisition attempt to be undone easily. In addition, the SC instruction itself is conditional in that it will not be performed if a conflict has been detected. Unlike the LL/SC lock, a transaction must encapsulate (almost) all types of instructions, including store instructions. Since stores change values in memory, a more sophisticated mechanism is needed to buffer the changed/speculative values until commit time.

■ *Did you know?*

In Intel's HTM implementation (RTM = restricted transactional memory), a transaction is bookended by XBEGIN and XEND instructions. In AMD's HTM implementation (ASF = advanced synchronization facilities), a transaction bookended by SPECULATE and COMMIT instructions. On RTM, programmers can explicitly abort a transaction using XABORT.

As of the time of the writing of this book, transactions are only committed with "best effort", i.e., there is no guarantee that a transaction in RTM or ASF will eventually succeed. A transaction may abort even in the absence of conflicts, in multiple situations. Some instructions (e.g., CPUID) will by default abort a transaction. There are events that will also abort transactions, such as interrupts, I/O requests, (likely) page faults, etc. If the number of speculative values is higher than what the speculative buffer can hold, a transaction will also be aborted. For example, if the cache used for holding speculative values has a cache associativity of four, up to four blocks holding speculative values can be kept in any cache set. A fifth speculative value block will cause a speculative buffer overflow which aborts the transaction. There are mechanisms that can be added to allow the speculative buffer to overflow to the outer memory hierarchy safely and without needing a transaction to abort, but they are relatively costly. As a result, in current HTM, programmers are advised to provide non-transactional code that can be executed as a "Plan B" when a transaction repeatedly aborts.

Before going into the detail of the hardware mechanism, let us review the requirement for transactions to be executed atomically and in isolation from other threads. Recall the concept of serializability: *a parallel execution of a group of operations or primitives is serializable if there is some sequential execution of the operations or primitives that produce an identical result.* In this case, each transaction can be thought of as an operation or a primitive. Thus, transactions may be executed in parallel, but must produce the same outcome as if they are executed one at a time. Figure 8.2 illustrates serializability of transactions.

Figure 8.2(a) shows two transactions T1 and T2. Suppose that T1 writes 1 to x, reads from y, and writes 1 to z. This means that the write set for T1 includes x and z, while the read set for T1 includes y. Suppose that T2 reads from x, writes 2 to y, and writes 2 to z. This means that the write set for T2 includes y and z, while the read set for T2 includes x. A sequential execution of the transactions will either be T1 followed by T2 (shown in part (b)), or T2 followed by T1 (shown in part (c)). The values obtained by the reads are shown in bold italic font, and the final values of x, y, and z are shown at the bottom. These values show the only possible values that result from serializable execution of T1 and T2.

Now let us consider two parallel execution scenarios of T1 and T2, shown in parts (d) and (e). In part (d), T2's read of x sees a value of 1, and T1's read of y sees a value of 2. If we inspect the final values, they are (1,2,1), which agrees with part (c) where T2 executes prior to T1. However, the read from x is not the same in the two cases (0 vs. 1), which indicates non-serializable outcome has been produced in the execution scenario shown in part (d). The conflict in the two cases is the result of the intersection of a read from x from T2's read set and write to x from T1's write set. In part (e), T2's read of x sees a value of 1, and T1's read of y sees a value of 2. If we inspect the final values, they are (1,2,2), which agrees with part (b) where T1 executes prior to T2. However, the read from y is not the same in the two cases (0 vs. 2), which indicates non-serializable outcome has been produced in the execution scenario shown in part (d). The conflict in the two cases is the result of the intersection of a read from y from T1's read set and write to y from T1's read set. This example illustrates that when two transactions have overlapping read vs. write sets, their parallel execution may produce non-serializable outcome.

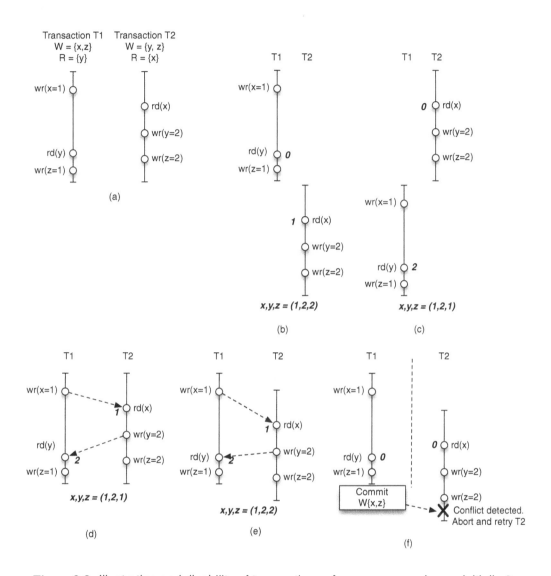

Figure 8.2: Illustrating serializability of transactions. Assume x, y, and z are initially 0.

In parts (d) and (e), we have assumed that the two transactions execute concurrently and propagate their values immediately upon writing new values to memory addresses. While this still allows detection of serializability conflicts, there is no easy way to abort a transaction and undo its effects as the writes have propagated to the memory hierarchy and other threads. In part (f), we assume a buffer and commit approach where the transactions are executed concurrently while we buffer their results to be committed at a later time. In this case, both T1 and T2 execute simultaneously, both assuming old values of x, y, z when they start execution. Conflicts are not detected until T1 commits its transaction where it publishes its write set $\{x,y\}$. At T1's commit, T2 finds out that T1's write set overlaps with its read (both containing x) and its write set (both containing z). Thus, a serializability conflict has been detected, and the right action here is to abort T2, discard its results (easy as they have been buffered and not propagated beyond the buffer), and retry it in the future.

Let us first discuss an approach where speculative values are buffered until commit time. One question is how and where these values should be buffered. Since buffered values should not become visible to other threads, the hardware must provide a space to keep these values without triggering the cache coherence to propagate writes. Several structures that are parts of the memory hierarchy can be used for buffering purposes. Examples of buffer structures include the store queue (used in Sun Rock), the L1 cache (used in Intel Haswell and AMD), and the L2 cache (used in IBM BlueGene/Q). Each of these buffer choices affect the transaction size and performance. The farther away the buffer is from the processor, the larger the capacity for buffering speculative values. For example, the store queue may hold up to a few hundred bytes, the L1 cache may hold a few tens of kilobytes, and the L2 cache may hold hundreds of kilobytes to a few megabytes. At this point, processor makers are not sure yet what maximum capacity they should provide for a transaction, as commercial programs are not yet written or ported massively with transactions.

One possible buffer to hold speculative values is a cache. A consequence of using the cache for this purpose is that tracking of speculative values is that data values will be tracked at a cache line granularity. This introduces a possibility of *false conflict*, where a transaction writing to a non-conflicting data is detected as a conflict with other data that is co-located on the same cache block. Another problem with using the cache for holding speculative values is that the transaction's size limit depends more on the associativity of the cache instead of the aggregate cache capacity. The reason is the transaction overflows the cache as soon as any single cache set holds as many speculative blocks as the cache associativity. For example, in the worst case, a 4-way associative cache may cause an abort after a transaction reads/writes to 5 cache blocks, if the blocks all map to a single cache set. There have been proposals to let speculative cache values to overflow to the main memory to provide an unbounded transaction size, but none of them is simple to implement. Furthermore, there is no proof yet that transactional memory can achieve or sustain high scalability when the transaction size is large.

Let us consider the implementation using a cache to hold speculative values. Each cache line is augmented with a *write bit* (a *read bit* is also added for tracking the read set). When transaction starts execution, any time it writes to a data item, the data is loaded into the cache (if it is not already in the cache) and its write bit is set. This way the block can be tracked as part of the write set of the transaction. In addition, the write bit also pins the block in the cache, making it non-evictable until commit time. If the transaction reads a data item, the data is is loaded into the cache (if it is not already in the cache) and its read bit is set. As with the write bit, the read bit has two roles: marking the read set of the transaction, and pinning the block in the cache until the transaction commits. If the transaction reads and writes a lot of data, there is a chance that the cache fills up and is unable to find a block to victimize. The typical and simple way to handle this is to abort the transaction. Such a policy carries a risk that there may be transactions that can never commit due to their size, and requires programmers to provide a "plan B" code that is invoked in case transactions fail to commit.

Transaction commits must be atomic, i.e., only one transaction commits at a time. For this, there needs to be a mechanism to arbitrate between potentially simultaneous attempts of transaction commits. A transaction commits by making sure that it has the ability to read from its read set and write to its write set. First it has to determine if between the time the transaction starts until it wants to commit, whether there has been other transaction commits that have their write set overlapping with its own read and write set. If so, there has been a conflict and the transaction has to abort and restart. Once it is granted permission to commit, it can publish its write set. One way to publish the write set is by issuing invalidations to all blocks that are in its write set. The write set publication may cause other transactions to be aborted. Invalidating blocks that are in a transaction's write set also instantaneously propagate its writes so that they are visible to other threads. After it has published its write set, it can clear up the write bit and read bit and continue execution past the transaction.

If a transaction snoops another transaction's commit before it has a chance to commit, it has to compare the committing transaction's write set against its own read and write set. If they intersect, it has to abort. It aborts by going to the execution state of the processor prior to the start of the transaction. It has to restore the register state to that point, and invalidate all data in its read and write set.

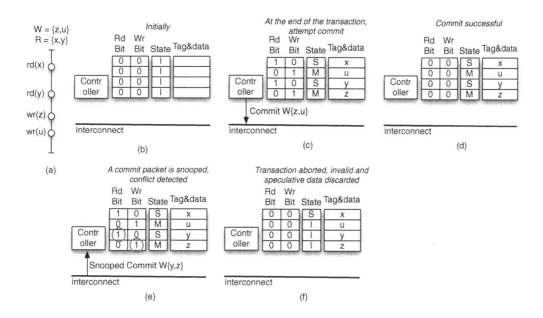

Figure 8.3: Illustration of transaction commit and abort. The transaction (a) and the initial cache state (b). Cache state before commit (c) and after successful commit (d). Cache state before commit upon snooping an external commit (e), and after transaction abort (f).

Figure 8.3 illustrates the scheme. Suppose we have a transaction shown in part (a) of the figure. The transaction reads from x and y, and writes to z and u. Part (b) shows the initial cache state, showing an empty cache with all read and write bits reset. Part (c) shows the cache when the transaction has finished execution, and is attempting to commit, but the commit has not succeeded yet. It shows that block x, y, z, and u are cached. The states of the block do not matter yet at the moment as they are speculative. For illustration, we show x and y in a shared (S) state, and z and u in a modified (M) state. The read bits are set for blocks x and y and the write bit is set for blocks z and u. The commit request attempts to publish the transaction's write set by posting invalidations for z and u, in order to propagate the new value of blocks z and u, and notify other transactions of the write set of the commit. If invalidations to both blocks z and u are successful, then the commit can proceed by clearing/resetting the write and read bits in the cache. After the reset, regular cache coherence operations can be serviced to all data blocks that were involved in the transaction.

Parts (e) and (f) of Figure 8.3 show an alternative situation where before the transaction can commit, it snoops a successful external transaction commit. The external commit affects blocks y and z – which may come as one commit packet or as separate snooped invalidations to blocks y and z. Part (e) shows that a conflict is detected because the external commit's write set intersects with the transaction's read set (block y) and write set (block z). After the conflict is detected, the transaction has to be aborted. It is aborted by invalidating block y and z, and clearing all read and write bits, and retry the transaction. Block u was not involved in the conflict but holds speculative value, hence it has to be discarded and invalidated as well.

We have discussed one particular implementation of an HTM, especially one with the following features: write set published at commit time and speculative values buffered at the cache. It is not the only possible implementations. An alternative approach is to publish the write set early, every time a transaction writes to data. The latter is referred to *eager* conflict detection. With the eager policy, every write results in sending an invalidation message to other caches. Other transactions may abort as a result, and may miss on the block upon retries. However, the intervention requests will not be responded to until the transaction commits. The eager policy can potentially reduce useless work as conflicts can be detected early and transactions can be aborted and retried early. However, it can potentially cause too many aborts and retries. With regard to buffering speculative values, an alternative is to let the memory addresses to be updated with the new values. The old values are recorded in a log so that if the transaction is aborted, the old values can be restored. The approach is referred to as HTM with undo logs. An advantage of using logs is that commit is simple, because values are already propagated. A transaction simply needs to discard the undo log upon commit. A drawback of using logs is slower abort. If a transaction has to abort, it has to restore the old values from the log, one entry at a time. Furthermore, there is a serious drawback of using logs. Using logs requires a write to be changed into one read and two writes (one read of the old data, one write of the new data, and one write of the old data to the log) that must be performed atomically. If any one of them has occurred but a fault occurs before the others can be performed, the data or log can become inconsistent. The OS also has to be involved in allocating memory space for the log, which makes this scheme harder to implement.

■ *Did you know?*

   To illustrate how a transaction is specified, the following code shows an implementation of compare and swap on two memory locations using AMD ASF [5]. The
code reads mem1 and mem2 and compares them with register values held in registers RAX and RBX, respectively. If they are equal, then the swap is performed by
writing register values in registers RDI and RSI to mem1 and mem2. To indicate the
outcome of the swap, register RSX is reset (by XORing register RCX with itself) on
swap, or leave it with a value of '1' otherwise. The code uses immediate retry as the
recovery strategy. Other recovery strategies are possible.

```
 1  DCAS:
 2          MOV R8, RAX
 3          MOV R9, RBX
 4  retry:
 5          SPECULATE ; Speculative region begins
 6          JNZ retry ; Page fault, interrupt, or contention
 7          MOV RCX, 1 ; Default result, overwritten on success
 8          LOCK MOV RAX, [mem1] ; load value in mem1 into RAX
 9          LOCK MOV RBX, [mem2] ; load value in mem2 into RBX
10          CMP R8, RAX
11          JNZ out       ; if R8 != RAX, jump to out
12          CMP R9, RBX
13          JNZ out       ; if R9 != RBX, jump to out
14          LOCK MOV [mem1], RDI ; store value in RDI to mem1
15          LOCK MOV [mem2], RSI ; store value in RSI to mem2
16          XOR RCX, RCX         ; Indicate swap was successful
17  out:
18          COMMIT ; End of speculative region
```

8.4   Exercises

Worked Problems

1. **Lock performance**. Consider a four-processor bus-based multiprocessor using the Illinois MESI protocol. Each processor executes a TTSL or a LL/SC lock to gain access to a null critical section. The initial condition is such that processor 1 has the lock and processors 2, 3, and 4 are spinning on their caches waiting for the lock to be released. Every processor gets the lock once and then exits the program.

   The codes for TTSL lock and unlock implementation:

   ```
   lock: ld   R, L        // R = &L
         bnz R, lock    // if (R != 0) jump to lock
         t&s R, L       // R = &L; if (R == 0) L=1
         bnz R, lock    // if (R != 0) jump to lock
         ret

   unlock: st L, #0      // write ``0'' to &L
           ret
   ```

   Thus, the lock primitive has only two memory transactions: BusRd generated by the `ld` instruction, and a BusRdX generated by the `t&s` instruction.

   The codes for `LL/SC` lock and unlock implementation:

   ```
   lock: ll   R, L        // R = &L
         bnz R, lock    // if (R != 0) jump to lock
         sc   L, #1      // L=1 conditionally
         beqz lock      // if SC fails, jump to lock
         ret

   unlock: st L, #0      // write ``0'' to &L
           ret
   ```

   Thus, the lock primitive has only two memory transactions: BusRd generated by the `ld` instruction, and a BusRdX (or BusUpgr) generated by a successful `sc` instruction (and no bus transaction if `sc` fails).

   Considering only the bus transactions related to lock-unlock operations:

   (a) What is the least number of transactions executed to get from the initial to the final state for test-and-test&set and LL/SC?

   (b) What is the worst-case number of transactions for test-and-test&set and LL/SC?

   Answer:

   Best case for test-and-t&s lock: 7 bus transactions

Bus Trans.	Action	P1	P2	P3	P4	Comment
	Initial State	S	S	S	S	Initially, P1 holds the lock
1	st1	M	I	I	I	P1 releases lock
2	ld2	S	S	I	I	P2 read misses after invalidation
3	t&s2	I	M	I	I	P2 executes t&s and issues BusRdX
	st2	I	M	I	I	P2 releases lock
4	ld3	I	S	S	I	P3 read misses after invalidation
5	t&s3	I	I	M	I	P3 executes t&s and issues BusRdX
	st3	I	I	M	I	P3 releases lock
6	ld4	I	I	S	S	P4 read misses after invalidation
7	t&s4	I	I	I	M	P4 executes t&s and issues BusRdX
	st4	I	I	I	M	P4 releases lock

Best case for LL/SC lock: 7 bus transactions

Bus Trans.	Action	P1	P2	P3	P4	Comment
	Initial State	S	S	S	S	Initially, P1 holds the lock
1	st1	M	I	I	I	P1 releases lock
2	ll2	S	S	I	I	P2 read misses after invalidation
3	sc2	I	M	I	I	P2 executes a successful sc
	st2	I	M	I	I	P2 releases lock
4	ll3	I	S	S	I	P3 read misses after invalidation
5	sc3	I	I	M	I	P3 executes a successful sc
	st3	I	I	M	I	P3 releases lock
6	ll4	I	I	S	S	P4 read misses after invalidation
7	sc4	I	I	I	M	P4 executes a successful sc
	st4	I	I	I	M	P4 releases lock

Worst case for test-and-t&s lock: 15 bus transactions

Bus Trans.	Action	P1	P2	P3	P4	Comment
	Initial State	S	S	S	S	Initially, P1 holds the lock
1	st1	M	I	I	I	P1 releases lock
2	ld2	S	S	I	I	P2 read misses after invalidation
3	ld3	S	S	S	I	P3 read misses after invalidation
4	ld4	S	S	S	S	P4 read misses after invalidation
5	t&s2	I	M	I	I	P2 executes t&s and issues BusRdX
6	t&s3	I	I	M	I	P3 executes t&s and issues BusRdX
7	t&s4	I	I	I	M	P4 executes t&s and issues BusRdX
8	st2	I	M	I	I	P2 releases lock
9	ld3	I	S	S	I	P3 read misses after invalidation
10	ld4	I	S	S	S	P4 read misses after invalidation

11	t&s3	I	I	M	I	P3 executes t&s and issues BusRdX
12	t&s4	I	I	I	M	P4 executes t&s and issues BusRdX
13	st3	I	I	M	I	P3 releases lock
14	ld4	I	I	S	S	P4 read misses after invalidation
15	t&s4	I	I	I	M	P4 executes t&s and issues BusRdX
	st4	I	I	I	M	P4 releases lock

Worst case for LL/SC lock: 10 bus transactions

Bus Trans.	Action	P1	P2	P3	P4	Comment
	Initial State	S	S	S	S	Initially, P1 holds the lock
1	st1	M	I	I	I	P1 releases lock
2	l12	S	S	I	I	P2 read misses after invalidation
3	l13	S	S	S	I	P3 read misses after invalidation
4	l14	S	S	S	S	P4 read misses after invalidation
5	sc2	I	M	I	I	P2 executes a successful sc
	sc3	I	M	I	I	P3's sc fails, no bus transaction generated
	sc4	I	M	I	I	P4's sc fails, no bus transaction generated
	st2	I	M	I	I	P2 releases lock
6	l13	I	S	S	I	P3 read misses after invalidation
7	l14	I	S	S	S	P4 read misses after invalidation
8	sc3	I	I	M	I	P3 executes a successful sc
	sc4	I	I	M	I	P4's sc fails, no bus transaction generated
	st3	I	I	M	I	P3 releases lock
9	l14	I	I	S	S	P4 read misses after invalidation
10	sc4	I	I	I	M	P4 executes a successful sc
	st4	I	I	I	M	P4 releases lock

2. **Using LL/SC**. Use LL/SC instructions to construct other atomic operations listed, and show the resulting assembly code segments.

   (a) fetch&no-op L performs an atomic sequence of reading the value in the location L and storing it back into the same location L.

   (b) fetch&inc L performs an atomic sequence of reading the value in the location L, increment the value by one, and write the new value to L.

   (c) atomic_exch R, L performs an atomic sequence of swapping or exchanging the value held in register R and location L.

Answer:

```
(a) fetch-noop: LL R, L        // R = mem[L]
                SC L, R        // mem[L] = R
```

```
(b) fetch-inc: LL    R, L         // R = mem[L]
                 add  R, R, #1     // R = R + 1
                 SC   L, R         // mem[L] = R
                 bscfail R, fetch-inc // loop back if SC fails
(c) atomic-exch: ll    R2, L       // R2 = mem[L]
                 sc   L, R         // mem[L] = R
                 bscfail R, atomic-exch // loop back if SC fails
                 mov  R, R2        // R = R2
```

Note that the `mov` instruction is purposedly placed after the sc, which is important to make sure that the sc is more likely to succeed. It is safe to do that because the value to be assigned to R is in the register R2, and hence can no longer be affected by an intervention or invalidation of another processor.

3. **Implementing locks**. Implement `lock()` and `unlock()` directly using the atomic exchange instruction. The instruction `atomic_exch R, L` performs an atomic sequence of swapping/exchanging the value held in register R and location L. Use the following convention: a value of "1" indicates that a lock is currently held by a process, and a value of "0" indicates that a lock is free. Your implementation should not repeatedly generate bus traffic when a lock is continuously held by another process.

Answer:

```
lock: mov R, #1         // R = 1
loop: ld R2, L          // R2 = mem[L]
      bnz R2, loop      // Lock not free, loop back
      atomic_exch R, L  // exchange R with mem[L]
      bnz R, loop       // lock attempt fails, loop back
      ret               // lock successfully acquired, return

unlock: st L, #0        // release the lock
        ret
```

4. **Barrier implementation.** A proposed solution for implementing the barrier is the following:

```
BARRIER (Var B: BarVariable, N: integer)
{
  if (fetch&add(B,1) == N-1)
    B = 0;
  else
    while (B != 0) {};   // spin until B is zero
}
```

Describe a correctness problem with the barrier implementation. Then, rewrite the code for `BARRIER()` in a way that avoids the correctness problem.

Answer:

The correctness problem occurs when all but last thread have arrived at the barrier spinning on the while loop. Then the last thread arrives and sets B to 0. The last thread may then continue to the next barrier with the same name, and immediately increments B. Other threads that are about to come out of the barrier have their cached copies of B invalidated, and reload them to find out that the value of B is no longer 0, and stay in the barrier.

The implementation can be corrected by alternating between spinning for 0 and for N-1, i.e.

```
BARRIER (Var B: BarVariable, N: integer)
{
  static turn = 0;

  if (turn == 0) {
    if (fetch&add(B,1) == N-1)
      B = 0;
    else
      while (B != 0) {};    // spin until B is zero
    turn = 1;
  }
  else {
    if (fetch&add(B,-1) == 1)
      B = N;
    else
      while (B != N) {};    // spin until B is zero
    turn = 0;
  }

}
```

Homework Problems

1. **Lock performance**. Consider a three-processor bus-based multiprocessor using MESI protocol. Each processor executes a test-and-test&set or an LL/SC lock to gain access to a null critical section. Consider the following sequence of events:

   - Initially: P1 holds the lock

   - P2 and P3 read the lock

   - P1 releases the lock

   - P2 and P3 read the lock

   - P2 acquires the lock successfully

   - P3 attempts to acquire the lock but is unsuccessful

   - P2 releases the lock

   - P3 reads the lock

   - P3 acquires the lock successfully

   - P1 and P2 read the lock

   - P3 releases the lock

   Considering only the bus transactions related to lock-unlock operations:

(a) Show the states of each cache for the sequence assuming the test-and-test&set lock implementation. Use the following template. Bus transactions corresponding to the first three steps are shown.

Bus Trans.	Action	P1	P2	P3	Comment
-	Initially	M	I	I	Initially, P1 holds the lock
1 (BusRd)	ld2	S	S	I	P2 read misses on the lock
2 (BusRd)	ld3	S	S	S	P3 read misses on the lock
3 (BusUpgr)	st1	M	I	I	P1 releases the lock
4	and so on ...				

(b) Show the states of each cache for the sequence assuming the LL/SC lock implementation. Use the following template. Bus transactions corresponding to the first three steps are shown.

Bus Trans.	Action	P1	P2	P3	Comment
-	Initially	M	I	I	Initially, P1 holds the lock
1 (BusRd)	ll2	S	S	I	P2 read misses on the lock
2 (BusRd)	ll3	S	S	S	P3 read misses on the lock
3 (BusUpgr)	st1	M	I	I	P1 releases the lock
4	and so on ...				

2. **Lock performance**. Consider a four-processor bus-based multiprocessor TTSL lock implementations shown in the book (discussed in lectures). Suppose the cache coherence protocol is MOESI, and we have the following events:

- Initially, P1 holds the lock (and lock variable is cached in modified state)

- P2, P3, and P4 reads the lock variable in that order

- P1 releases the lock

- P2, P3, and P4 reads the lock variable in that order

- P4 acquires the lock successfully

- P2 and P3 attempt but fail to acquire the lock in that order

- P3 reads the lock variable

- P4 releases the lock

- P2 reads the lock variable

- P2 acquires the lock successfully

- P2 releases the lock

Show for each event what bus transaction is generated (ignore Flush and FlushOpt for brevity), what instruction it corresponds to, and the resulting states in the cache.

3. **Lock performance**. Repeat homework problem (2) with LL/SC lock implementation.

4. **Lock performance**. Repeat homework problem (2) with Dragon protocol.

5. **Lock performance**. Repeat homework problem (2) with LL/SC lock implementation on MESI protocol.

6. **Using LL/SC**. Use LL/SC instructions to construct an atomic compare and swap instruction "CAS R1, R2, L" which tests whether data in memory location L is equal to that in R1. If they are equal, write the value in R2 to L, and copy R1 to R2. Otherwise, nothing is done and CAS returns. For example, if initially R1=5, R2=10, L=5, after CAS we have R1=5, R2=5, and L=10. If initially R1=7, R2=10, L=5, nothing changes after CAS. Show your answer in assembly code, and annotate what each instruction does. Keep as few instructions between LL and SC as possible.

7. **Lock implementation**. Use "CAS R1, R2, L" from problem (6) to construct a lock primitive. Lock(Location L) and Unlock(Location L). Keep the implementation short and simple, and avoid generating unnecessary bus transactions when the lock is being held by a thread.

8. **Read and write lock**. Show the machine code for implementing a read and write lock using the LL/SC primitives.

9. **Combining tree barrier**. Write the pseudo code for a combining tree implementation, assuming that the tree is binary (each node receives barrier completion signals from two "children" nodes, except the leaf nodes).

Chapter 9

Memory Consistency Models

Contents

As mentioned in Chapter 6, one important problem that multiprocessor systems must address is the *memory consistency* problem, which deals with how accesses (loads and stores) to any memory address are ordered with respect to one another as seen by all processors. Note that this is not a problem that is covered by the cache coherence protocol, since a cache coherence protocol only deals with how accesses to a single memory block address are ordered. Accesses to different addresses are not the concern of cache coherence protocols. In fact, unlike the cache coherence problem that only occurs for systems with caches, the memory consistency problem exists on systems with and without caches, although caches may exacerbate it.

The objective of this chapter is to discuss the memory consistency problem in more detail, what solutions are offered in current systems, and how they relate to performance. We will begin the discussion with programmers' intuition regarding the ordering of memory accesses. We will show that they in general conform to *full ordering* of memory accesses, and the model that corresponds to such ordering requirements is referred to as the *sequential consistency* (SC) model. [1] We will then discuss how SC can be provided in a multiprocessor system and which parts of the processor or coherence protocol mechanisms must be changed. We will discuss that such changes are too restrictive and likcly produce a high performance overhead. As a result, many processors do not implement

---

[1]Note that this is not related to the *store conditional* instruction discussed in Chapter 8, for which we also abbreviate as SC.

SC. Rather, they implement more relaxed consistency models, such as *processor consistency*, *weak ordering*, and *release consistency*. We will discuss each of them and show how performance is impacted by different consistency models.

9.1   Programmers' Intuition

Our discussion of memory consistency models starts out with inferring what intuition programmers *implicitly* assume with regards to the ordering of memory operations. Consider a pair of post-wait synchronization. Readers may recall that this type of synchronization is needed for DOACROSS and DOPIPE parallelism, among others. Suppose that thread P0 produces a datum to be consumed by thread P1. Thread P0 executes the post in order to let thread P1 know that the datum is ready. Thread P1 executes a wait which makes it block until the corresponding post is executed. To implement the post-wait synchronization, a shared variable is initialized to "0". For the *post* operation, the variable value is set to "1", while for the *wait* operation, a loop waits until the value of the variable is set to "1". This is illustrated in Code 9.1. In the illustration, the shared variable that implements the post-wait pair is `datumIsReady`.

Code 9.1 Example of the use of post-wait synchronization.

P0:	P1:
₁S1: datum = 5;	₁S3: while (!datumIsReady) {};
₂S2: datumIsReady = 1;	₂S4: ... = datum;

In the code above, it is clear that programmers' intention is for the synchronization operation to function properly, that is, for thread P1 to read a value of 5 from `datum`. Programmers do not expect to get a different value from `datum`. However, to get a value of 5 on the read from `datum`, the necessary requirement is that at P0, S1 must be performed before S2. If S2 is performed before S1, then `datumIsReady` is set to 1 before `datum` is set to 5, possibly leading to S4 reading a value of `datum` that is different than 5. Similarly, to get a value of 5 on the read from `datum`, it is also a necessary requirement that S3 is performed before S4, since otherwise, S4 may read a stale value of `datum`. Therefore, *implicitly, programmers expect the order in which memory accesses are executed in a thread to follow the order in which they occur in the source code.* In other words, programmers expect the order of memory accesses expressed in the source code to be obeyed as the source code is compiled into binary code, and as the binary code is executed by the machine. We will refer to such an expectation as the *program order* expectation.

Notice in the previous paragraph we have used the term *performed* casually. From this point on, we will use a strict definition of the term "performed". A load/store instruction is considered performed when all processors can agree that they have completed with respect to all other loads/stores. More specifically, in a system with caches, a load is performed when it has read data from the cache. At that time, the load is no longer affected by other processors' invalidation or intervention requests, hence they can agree that the load is complete. A store is performed when it has propagated its invalidation or update to all other caches. At this point, all processors can agree that the store is complete or will be completed without a problem.

Going back to the programmer's expectation, the program order expectation is not the only implicit expectation made by programmers. Consider the following code (Code 9.2).

Code 9.2 The illustration of the programmers' atomicity expectation. Initially, the values of x, y, z, xReady, and xyReady are zero.

P0:	P1:	P2:
₁S1: x = 5; ₂S2: xReady = 1;	₁S3: while (!xReady); ₂S4: y = x + 4; ₃S5: xyReady = 1;	₁S6: while (!xyReady); ₂S7: z = x * y;

The code makes use of two post-wait pairs of synchronization, one pair between P0 and P1, and another between P1 and P2. The code shows that P0 sets x to a value of 5, then sets xReady to 1 to tell P1 that x now has a new value. P1 waits for the value, uses it to set a new value to y (which should be $5 + 4 = 9$). P1 then sets xyReady to 1 to indicate that both x and y have new values. P2 waits until xyReady has a value of 1, and then proceeds to read the value of x and y.

In the code above, it is clear that the programmers' expectation is for the statement S7 to yield a multiplication result of 45 ($= 5 \times 9$) as a value assigned to z. They expect that first, the value of x is produced by P0, then the value of y is produced by P1, and finally both values of x and y are consumed by P2. However, such an expectation actually *implicitly* assumes the *atomicity* of memory accesses, i.e., an expectation that each memory access occurs in an instant, without being overlapped with other memory accesses. In the example, the expectation assumes that when P0 writes to x, the write is instantly propagated to both P1 and P2. If the write to x is not propagated to P2 instantly, then P2 may read an old value of x. Consider, for example, somehow the write propagation from P0 to P2 is not instantaneous, as illustrated in Figure 9.1. Suppose that all processors execute all memory accesses in program order. P0 executes S1, which writes a value of 5 to x. That write is propagated to P1 and P2, however it reaches P1 faster (Circle 1) than P2 (Circle 3). Then, P0 performs a write to xReady, which is also propagated to P1. Suppose that P1 now sees the new values of xReady and x (in an invalidation-based protocol, P1 has received invalidations and has reloaded blocks containing xReady and x through cache misses). So P1 executes its next statement, assigning a value of 9 to y, and then sets xyReady to 1. Suppose that those writes are propagated to P2 (through invalidations and subsequent cache misses in an invalidation-based protocol). P2 then gets out of its loop and reads the value of x and y. Note that here, P2 reads a fresh value of y since the write to y by P1 has been fully propagated. However, it reads a stale value of x since the write to x by P0 has not been propagated to it yet (i.e., in an invalidation protocol, the invalidation has not reached P2's cache yet). Therefore, P2 reads the old value of x, which is 0, and assigns a wrong value of 0 to z.

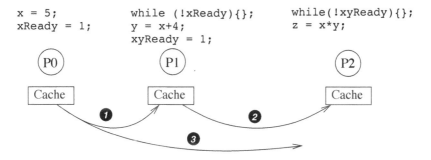

Figure 9.1: Illustration of the violation of store atomicity.

How can an invalidation sent out by P0, corresponding to the write of x, reach P1 but not immediately P2? The answer is that this can happen in some types of interconnection networks. On a bus-based multiprocessor, the write will reach the bus, and all snoopers (P1's and P2's) will see the write and invalidate their corresponding blocks in the caches. So, such a situation would not occur. However, if the multiprocessors are interconnected using a point-to-point interconnection, separate invalidation messages are sent from P0 to P1 and P2. It is entirely possible for the invalidation message sent to P1 to arrive earlier than the invalidation message sent to P2, due to the messages going to different routes, or due to the traffic that delays the delivery of the invalidation going to P2.

Let us get back to the discussion on programmers' expectation. In the code shown above, it is clearly the case that programmers expect the code to function properly, which means that write propagation must happen instantly, or in technical terms, *atomically*. The write by P0 must happen in such a way that it is propagated at once, in a non-divisible step, to both P1 and P2. Thus, by the time P1 gets out of the loop, the write to x would have fully propagated to all processors.

Overall, we can express programmers' implicit expectation of memory access ordering as: *memory accesses coming out of a processor should be performed in program order, and each of them should be performed atomically.* Such an expectation was formally defined as the sequential consistency (SC) model. The following is Lamport [37]'s definition of sequential consistency:

> A multiprocessor is sequentially consistent if the result of any execution is the same as if the operations of all the processors were executed in some sequential order, and the operations of each individual processor occur in this sequence in the order specified by its program.

Let us look at a few more examples to see what results are possible in SC for various cases. Consider the following code (Code 9.3). The code for P0 consists of two writes to a and b. The code for P1 consists of two reads from b and from a. The code contains no synchronization between the two threads, which means that the outcome of the program is *non-deterministic*. Suppose that the system on which the threads run ensure SC. One possible outcome is when S1 and S2 occur before S3 and S4, in which case S3 and S4 will read a value of 1 for both a and b. Another possible outcome is when S3 and S4 both occur before S1 and S2, in which case S3 and S4 will read old values of a and b, which is zero. Another possible outcome arises when S1 is performed first, followed by S3 and S4, then S2. In such a case, S3 will print the old value of b, which is zero, while S4 prints the new value of a, which is 1. However, under SC, it is impossible for S3 to read out a new value of b, which is "1", and for S4 to read out the old value of a, which is "0". Overall, the final values of (a, b) that are possible under SC are (0, 0), (1, 0), and (1, 1), while the final value of (1, 0) is not possible under SC.

Code 9.3 An example illustrating SC and non-SC outcomes. Initially, the values of a and b are both zero.

P0:	P1:
₁S1: a = 1;	₁S3: ... = b;
₂S2: b = 1;	₂S4: ... = a;

To reason about why the final outcome is impossible in SC, note that SC defines program order and atomicity of memory accesses. Let us denote the ordering of memory accesses to be represented by the "→" symbol. In SC, we know that the ordering S1 → S2 and S3 → S4 will be enforced. For statement S3 to read out a new value of b, S3 must have been performed after S2, i.e., S2 → S3. But since S1 → S2 and S3 → S4, it can be concluded that S1 → S2 → S3 → S4. On the other hand, for statement S4 to read out the old value of a, S4 must have been performed before S1, i.e., S4 → S1. But since S1 → S2 and S3 → S4, it can be concluded that S3 → S4 → S1 → S2. However, both conclusions cannot be true simultaneously as they lead to a contradiction. Thus, the result is impossible in a system that guarantees SC.

However, on a system that does *not* enforce SC, this final outcome becomes possible. For example, suppose that the program order between S3 and S4 is no longer ensured. Then it is possible for S4 to be performed earlier than S3. In such a case, we may have S4 performed first (resulting in reading a value of "0" for a), followed by S1 and S2, and followed lastly by S3 (resulting in reading a value of "1" for b).

Now let us consider another example in the following code (Code 9.4). The code for P0 consists of a write to a followed by a read from b. The code for P1 consists of a write to b followed by a read from a. The code contains no synchronization between the two threads, which means that the outcome of the program is *non-deterministic*. Suppose that the system on which the threads run ensure SC. One possible outcome is when S1 and S2 occur before S3 and S4, in which case S2 will read out 0, while S4 will read out 1 (the new value produced by S1). Another possible outcome is when S3 and S4 both occur before S1 and S2, in which case S2 will read out 1 (the new value produced by S3), while S4 will read out 0. Another possible outcome arises when S1 is performed first, followed by S3, then by S2, and finally by S4. In such a case, S2 will read out 1 (the new value of b produced by S3), and S4 will read out 1 (the new value of a produced by S1). However, the final case in which both S2 and S4 read out a "0" is impossible under SC. Thus, the final results of (a, b) may be (1, 0), (0, 1), or (1, 1) under SC, but it cannot be (0, 0).

Code 9.4 A code example illustrating SC and non-SC outcomes. Initially, the values of a and b are both zero.

P0:	**P1:**
₁S1: a = 1;	₁S3: b = 1;
₂S2: ... = b;	₂S4: ... = a;

To reason about why this final outcome is impossible in SC, recall that SC defines program order and atomicity of memory accesses. Hence, we know that the ordering S1 → S2 and S3 → S4 will be enforced. For statement S2 to read out a value of "0", S2 must have been performed before S3, i.e. S2 → S3. But since S1 → S2 and S3 → S4, it can be concluded that S1 → S2 → S3 → S4. For statement S4 to read out a value of "0", S4 must have been performed before S1, i.e. S4 → S1. But since S1 → S2 and S3 → S4, it can be concluded that S3 → S4 → S1 → S2. Both conclusions cannot be true simultaneously since one contradicts another. Therefore, the result is impossible in a system that guarantees SC.

However, on a system that does *not* enforce SC, this final outcome is possible. For example, suppose that the program order between S3 and S4 is no longer ensured. Then it is possible for S4 to be performed earlier than S3. In such a case, we may have S4 performed first (resulting in reading a zero for a), followed by S1 and S2 which reads out zero for b, and followed lastly by S3.

Both Code 9.3 and Code 9.4 are unlikely to be encountered in a majority of programs because of the non-deterministic outcome of the programs. Non-deterministic programs are notoriously difficult to reason for correctness and to debug. However, sometimes they are a legitimate class of programs, such as when the computation can tolerate non-determinism and imprecision (Code 3.16 and Code 3.18 in Section 3.5 are some examples of codes that can tolerate non-deterministic results). Non-deterministic programs can also arise when programmers mistakenly omit synchronization operations, in which case the non-determinism occurs by accident. One relevant and important question is whether programs that have non-deterministic outcomes can tolerate the additional non-determinism that arises from machines that do not ensure SC. The likely answer would be yes for programs that have intentional non-determinism, but it is less clear for programs in which the non-determinism occurs due to accidental omission of synchronization (debugging such programs becomes harder in non-SC machines).

Still, for a large majority of parallel programs, deterministic program output is the case. Therefore, we need to keep in mind when discussing memory consistency models that SC results must be ensured for deterministic programs that have proper synchronization, while also keeping in mind that non-SC results may be tolerable for programmers in non-deterministic programs.

9.2 Architecture Mechanisms for Ensuring Sequential Consistency

From the previous discussion, we have established that in order to ensure SC, memory accesses from a processor must follow program order and each of them must be atomic. In this section, we will see how that can be achieved in a real implementation. First, we will discuss a basic implementation that works. However, while it works, it suffers significantly in terms of performance due to the lack of overlapping of memory accesses. Then, we will discuss techniques that can improve the performance of SC by allowing memory operations to be overlapped with respect to one another. Note that overlapping memory accesses can potentially violate their atomicity. Therefore, a safety mechanism is needed to detect atomicity violation and recover from it. We will discuss such a safety mechanism and how it is implemented in real processors.

9.2.1 Basic SC Implementation on a Bus-Based Multiprocessor

In the basic implementation of SC, memory accesses must be performed atomically with respect to one another. The simplest and correct way to achieve atomicity is to perform one memory access at a time without overlapping them. To perform memory accesses one at a time, we need to know when a memory access starts and ends. Consider a load instruction. A load instruction is logically executed in four steps. First, its effective address is computed in a functional unit. Then, a cache access to the effective address is issued to the memory hierarchy. The memory hierarchy finds the data value associated with that address (which may be in the cache, in memory, or in a remote cache). Finally, it returns the value to the destination register of the load instruction. Note that the first step (computation of effective address) is not affected by other memory accesses and will work the same way regardless of program order, hence, this step can be overlapped with any steps of other memory accesses. The final step (returning the value that has been read from the cache to the destination register of the load) is also unaffected by other memory accesses since the value has already been obtained from the cache, and, hence, it can also be overlapped with any steps from other memory accesses. Therefore, from the perspective of memory access ordering, a load starts when its access is issued to the cache and performs when the value is obtained from the cache (assuming that afterward, the value read can no longer change). These two steps are the ones that must be performed atomically.

Similarly, a store instruction is executed in several steps. First, its effective address is computed in a functional unit. Then, if it is no longer *speculative* (e.g., it is not an instruction in the wrong path of a branch and is free of exception), the store can be committed or retired (readers are referred to textbooks that describe mechanisms for out-of-order execution for more details). It is retired by copying its destination address and value to be written to a structure called the *write buffer*, which is a first-in-first-out (FIFO) queue containing stores that have been retired from the processor pipeline. Later, the store value in the write buffer is released to the cache. The store directly modifies the cached copy if it is the sole copy in the system, or it sends invalidations to other caches if there are other copies. A store is considered performed when it has fully propagated to other processors. In an update protocol, that corresponds to updating all other cached copies. In an invalidation protocol, that corresponds to having invalidated all other copies. Note that the first step (computation of effective address) is not affected by other memory accesses and will work the same way regardless of program order, hence, this step can be overlapped with any steps of other memory accesses. Also, note an important distinction between a store and a load is that the cache access occurs very late in a store instruction (after the store is retired) whereas in a load instruction the cache access occurs early (before the load can be retired). Another important distinction is that whereas a load instruction only involves one processor, a store instruction involves invalidating multiple caches. Hence, from the perspective of memory access ordering, a store starts when its effective address is issued and performed by the time it has been completed globally (i.e., it has finished propagating its value to all processors).

How can the completion of a store be detected? In a basic implementation, one way to detect the completion of the store is to require all sharers to acknowledge the invalidation, and for the store originator to collect all invalidation acknowledgments. In a bus-based multiprocessor, however, simply posting the read exclusive request on the bus ensures that all snoopers will see the store. If we assume that once a snooper sees the request, it *atomically* or *instantaneously* invalidates the cached copy at the node in which the snooper is located, then a store can be considered performed when the read exclusive request reaches the bus. However, in a system that does not rely on broadcast and snooping, it is necessary for the requestor to obtain all invalidation acknowledgment messages from all sharers before it can conclude that the store is performed. Note that in the case that there are no other shared copies (e.g., the block is already exclusively cached when the store is issued to the cache), the store is considered performed right after it accesses the cache to update the value in the cached copy. No write propagation is necessary since there are no sharers.

Now that we have established that a load is performed when it has obtained its value from the cache, and that a store is performed when its read exclusive request has reached the bus, we will illustrate how SC can be enforced in a bus-based multiprocessor. Suppose that we have the following code (Code 9.5), showing five memory accesses coming out of a processor. In the basic implementation, each memory access must performed before the next one (in program order) can start. Hence, before the first load is performed, the second load cannot be issued to the cache. Consider the case in which the first load suffers a cache miss while the second load will have a cache hit if it is allowed to go to the cache. Due to the strict ordering, the second load cannot be allowed to issue to the cache even though the block containing B is in the cache. The second load must wait until the first load finishes its cache miss and obtains the value from the cache.

Code 9.5 Code example illustrating basic SC mechanisms.

```
1 S1: ld R1, A
2 S2: ld R2, B
3 S3: st C, R3
4 S4: st D, R4
5 S5: ld R5, D
```

In the same way, the store in S3 cannot be allowed to access the cache or obtain bus access until the load in S2 has performed (obtained the value from the cache). The store in S4 cannot be allowed to access the cache until the store in S3 has generated a request on the bus. Finally, the load in S5 cannot access the cache until the store in S4 has generated a request on the bus, even when the store and the load are to the same address. Bypassing a store value to a younger and dependent load is not allowed in SC as the atomicity of the store is violated.

In the basic implementation, SC imposes a huge performance restriction as it does not allow memory accesses to be overlapped or reordered. Many techniques in out-of-order execution of instructions which have been shown to be beneficial for exploiting instruction level parallelism (ILP), must be disabled. For example, a write buffer allows a store to be retired, and the following load to performed even before the just-retired store reaches the cache. This must be disabled because the load cannot be issued to the cache until the store has obtained a bus access. Second, two loads cannot be issued to the cache at the same time. A modern cache allows *non-blocking* accesses, in that it can serve a cache access while cache misses from older accesses have not completed. Enforcing SC means that a non-blocking cache loses its effectiveness. Finally, compiler optimizations that reorder memory accesses in the compiled code are not allowable either. Hence, the performance of an SC machine is significantly restricted.

9.2.2   Techniques to Improve SC Performance

We have discussed how a basic SC implementation can be very restrictive in terms of performance. In this section, we will describe what optimizations are possible in order to improve performance while still preserving SC semantics. The key to improving the performance of an SC implementation is to make the execution of memory accesses faster and to allow memory accesses to be overlapped with respect to one another. However, some of these overlaps may violate the atomicity of the accesses. Therefore, a safety mechanism is needed to detect atomicity violation and recover from it.

The first performance enhancement technique that we will discuss avoids overlapping of the execution of loads and stores, but overlaps data fetches that are generated by these loads and stores. The idea is to make the time to perform a load or store as short as possible. For example, a load that hits in the cache will be performed sooner than a load that misses in the cache because it obtains the data from the cache faster than from the main memory. Similarly, a store that finds the block in the cache in an exclusive/modified state does not need to go to the bus since we are sure that there are no other sharers in the system, thus there is no need for an invalidation. In such a case, the store only needs to write to the cached copy, and it performs right away.

How can we maximize the probability that a load hits in the cache and a store finds the block to be written in the cache in an exclusive or modified state? By issuing prefetch requests as soon as the effective addresses of loads and stores are available or can be predicted. For example, when a load's effective address is generated, we can issue a prefetch to the cache even when there are older loads or stores that have not performed. In fact, with a prefetching engine, if the addresses involved in the loads can be predicted, they can be prefetched even before the load instructions are fetched or executed. When the older loads or stores are performed, the load which has already issued a prefetch can access the cache and performs sooner due to the cache hit. Similarly, when a store's effective address is generated, we can issue a prefetch exclusive (essentially an upgrade or a read exclusive request on the bus), even when there are older stores or loads that have not performed. When older loads or stores have performed, and if the prefetch has performed too, the store can access the cache and performs right away without going to the bus.

Note that the prefetches do not obviate the need for loads and stores to access the cache. The loads or stores still must access the cache in a non-overlapped way to guarantee atomicity, however the probability that they find the blocks they need in the cache in the proper state improves with prefetching. Note, however, that prefetching may not always improve performance. One reason is that it is possible for a block that has been prefetched to be stolen before the load or store that generates the prefetching accesses the cache. For example, after a block is prefetched into the cache, it may be invalidated by another processor. Or after a block is prefetched in an exclusive state into the cache, another processor may read from the block, necessitating it to respond with the data and to downgrade its state to shared. In such cases, the prefetches have been useless as the corresponding store still needs to upgrade the block to an exclusive state. In fact, they have not only been useless, but have also been harmful as they incur unnecessary traffic and delay at other caches. Hence, while prefetching helps improve the performance of an SC implementation, it is not a perfect solution.

The second technique for improving the performance of an SC implementation is to rely on speculative accesses. We can overlap the execution of a load with the execution of an older load by speculatively assuming that the older load executes atomically. If we find that the older load has not really executed atomically, then we have wrongly allowed the younger load to proceed without waiting for the older load to perform. In this case, we have to cancel the younger load and reexecute it. Note that the ability to cancel an instruction and reexecute it is already provided by most out-of-order processors to provide a *precise interrupt mechanism*. Hence, all we need to add is the detection on when the atomicity of a load is broken.

To achieve that, we can recall that there is a similar technique for providing an illusion of atomicity between two memory accesses: the load linked (LL) and the store conditional (SC) instructions, used for implementing a lock synchronization. In the LL/SC lock implementation (Section 8.1.5), the load linked instruction appears to have executed atomically if by the time the store conditional instruction is executed, the block that was read by the load linked instruction has not been stolen from the cache. If the block is invalidated before an SC is attempted, then the SC fails and the LL is reexecuted. Or if the program is context switched before the SC is attempted, the SC also fails and the LL is reexecuted.

We can overlap the execution of two loads using a similar mechanism. Suppose we have two loads to different addresses coming from a processor. The first load suffers a cache miss. Under the basic SC implementation (even with the use of prefetching) the second load cannot access the cache until the first load has obtained its data from the cache. With speculation, we can indeed allow the second (the younger) load to access the cache. However, we should mark the second load as speculative. If the block read by the second load has not been stolen (invalidated or naturally evicted from the cache) by the time the first load performs, then the value obtained by the second load would have been the same if it had waited to issue to the cache after the first load performed. Therefore, the second load has executed as if the first load executed atomically. In this case, the speculation is successful, and we have overlapped the execution of two loads. The second load can now be marked non-speculative from the point of view of memory access ordering (it may still be speculative in some other sense such as with regard to an incorrect branch path). However, if the block read by the second load has been invalidated (or evicted from the cache) by the time the first load performs, then the illusion of atomicity has been broken. The second load, if it is issued to the cache now, may obtain a different value compared to when it speculatively accessed the cache. Hence, the speculation has failed and the second load must be reexecuted. The miss-speculation incurs a performance penalty for having to flush the pipeline and reexecute a load and all instructions that are younger than the miss-speculated load.

Similarly, a younger load can be speculative with respect to an older store that is not yet performed. When the older store is performed, the younger load must be reexecuted if its block has been stolen or replaced from the cache. This allows the use of a write buffer in a system that enforces SC.

The discussion on speculative execution primarily deals with speculative loads. Applying speculation to a store instruction is more difficult. The reason is that while a load can be canceled and reexecuted easily, a store cannot be canceled easily. A store, after accessing the cache, has already deposited a new value in the cache and potentially has propagated the value to the main memory and other processors. Hence, canceling a store is a much harder problem. Consequently, speculative execution is typically only implemented for loads. Stores are issued to the cache one at a time.

Overall, we have discussed two very powerful mechanisms for improving the performance of an SC implementation. The first technique (prefetching) does not allow overlapping of memory accesses, but the atomic execution of each memory access is likely to be shorter than without prefetching. The second technique (speculative load accesses) genuinely allows overlapping of memory accesses (loads). Both techniques are implemented in the MIPS R10000 processor, which supports SC, and even in the Intel Pentium architecture, which supports a memory consistency model that is slightly weaker than SC. Both techniques are highly effective in making SC performing better. However, there is still a fundamental performance problem that cannot be dealt with by prefetching or speculative execution: the compiler still cannot reorder memory accesses when compiling the program. Only relaxed memory consistency models allow compilers to reorder memory accesses.

9.3   Relaxed Consistency Models

We have discussed that programmers' intuition largely follows SC, what requirements of execution are needed to guarantee SC and implementations of SC on real systems. We have also discussed that SC is restrictive in terms of what compiler optimizations are allowed. In this section, we will discuss various memory consistency models that relax the memory access ordering restriction of SC. In general, they perform better than SC, but impose an extra burden on the programmer to ensure that their programs conform to the consistency model that the hardware provides.

Relaxing memory access ordering may allow execution that deviates from programmers' intuition. Therefore, typically a safety net is provided in order for programmers to specify strict ordering between a pair of memory accesses. We will first discuss the safety net before discussing relaxed consistency models. Then, we will discuss several relaxed consistency models, focusing on three variants called the *processor consistency* (PC) model, *weak ordering* (WO) model, and *release consistency* (RC) model. There are many more variants implemented in a real system, but PC, WO, and RC provide good representations for them.

9.3.1 Safety Net

The safety net for enforcing strict ordering between two memory accesses typically comes in the form of *fence* instructions (also referred to as *memory barrier* instructions). The semantics of a fence instruction is that *the fence instruction prohibits the execution of the memory accesses following the fence until all memory accesses preceding the fence have performed.* Sometimes the fence only applies to stores, in which case it imposes ordering only between stores that precede it and stores that follow it, and it is referred to as *store fence/barrier*. Sometimes the fence only applies to loads, in which case it imposes ordering only between loads that precede it and loads that follow it, and it is referred to as *load fence/barrier*.

In a real implementation, the fence requires the following mechanism. When a fence is encountered, the memory accesses following the fence are canceled by flushing them from the pipeline (or avoiding fetching them if they are not yet fetched), and all preceding memory accesses are performed. That is, loads must obtain data from the cache, and stores must access the cache and generate bus requests. Once all memory accesses older than the fence complete, the processor state is restored to the state prior to the fence instruction, and execution is resumed from that point.

It is the responsibility of programmers to insert fence instructions in their code for correct execution. Not inserting fence instructions when they are needed may result in incorrect execution and non-deterministic outcome. Inserting fence instructions when they are not needed results in an unnecessary performance degradation.

9.3.2 Processor Consistency

Recall that in SC, each load/store is ordered with regard to the following load/store. In other words, the ordering of the following pairs is enforced: load $\rightarrow$ load, load $\rightarrow$ store, store $\rightarrow$ load, and store $\rightarrow$ store. In the processor consistency (PC) model, the ordering between an older store and a younger load (store $\rightarrow$ load) is relaxed. When a store has not performed, a younger load is allowed to issue to the cache and even complete. The significance of this is that store instructions can be queued in the write buffer, and be performed at a later time without the use of load speculation. In the mean time, loads do not need to wait for the older stores to complete and can access the cache, thereby reducing the load latency.

■ *Did you know?*

There are three variants of memory consistency models that relax store $\rightarrow$ load order. Processor consistency is one of them. These variants differ in whether the processor is allowed to read the value from its own older write that has not globally performed yet. This relaxation allows a load to get a value that it finds in a write buffer belonging to an older write that has not gone to the cache yet, which reduces the load latency. In this regard, both PC and total store ordering (TSO) model allow the relaxation, but IBM 370 model does not. The variants also differ as to whether a read is allowed to obtain a value of a different processor's write before the write has globally complete. In this regard, only PC allows such relaxation. TSO and IBM 370 models do not allow the relaxation.

Using write buffers is no longer a problem in a system that supports PC. Note that the ordering between stores is still enforced, which means that the order in which stores access the cache must follow program order. Hence, the optimization technique used in the SC system that relies on exclusive prefetching is also applicable in PC, although its importance is somewhat diminished because younger loads can issue early despite the completion time of older stores. In addition, the ordering between loads is also enforced. Therefore, prefetching blocks early is also still applicable in PC as it is in SC. One distinction between PC and SC is that when a load is issued to the cache and bypasses an older store, it is not treated as speculative because the reordering is allowed by the PC model, whereas in SC the load is speculative and must be rolled back if the illusion of atomicity is broken. Therefore, recovery techniques for loads that issue to the cache early are no longer needed, resulting in fewer pipeline flush and recovery, and better performance.

How closely does PC correspond with natural programmers' intuition? The answer is quite well. Note that PC only relaxes one ordering constraint out of four, hence it only affects the correctness of code that has a store followed by a load. The behavior of the regular post-wait synchronization pair shown in Code 9.1 in which the producer sets `datum` and `datumIsReady` is not changed because the ordering between two stores is still enforced. In addition, the behavior of the consumer which reads `datumIsReady` and `datum` is also unchanged since the ordering between two loads is still enforced.

There are some cases in which PC yields different results compared to the SC model. For example, consider Code 9.4, in which each processor executes a code that consists of a store followed by a load. Since PC does not guarantee ordering between a store and a younger load, non-SC outcome can result in this case, yielding an outcome in which both a and b have a final value of 0. Note that the example shows code that is not synchronized and can produce non-deterministic outcome even under SC.

In general, for properly synchronized programs, PC yields the same outcome as SC. Consider a post-wait synchronization in which a processor produces a data value and sets a flag to signal the availability of the new value. This involves at least two store instructions, which are ordered with respect to each other in PC. At the consumer, at least two loads are involved, and their ordering is also guaranteed under PC. Thus, a post-wait synchronization produces the same outcome in PC as in SC. In a lock synchronization, the lock release operation involves setting a value to a lock variable using a store instruction. Loads that follow the lock-release store are not in the critical section, so their ordering with respect to the lock-release store is not crucial to correctness. Letting younger loads complete before the lock-release store is executed achieves a similar effect as when the lock is released late, which is a correct behavior. A lock acquire operation involves both loads and a store that changes the value held in the lock variable. The lock-acquire store may be followed by loads that are in the critical section, so their ordering is crucial to correctness. However, a lock-acquire store is often implemented either using an atomic instruction or a store conditional instruction that ensures the atomicity of the store. When such an atomic store fails, the lock acquisition is re-attempted, and the execution of any younger loads will be repeated later. When the atomic store succeeds, the lock acquisition is successful, and in this case, the loads that precede the atomic store must have read a value that indicates the lock was free. This is only possible when no processors were in the critical section. Since all loads are ordered with respect to each other, the loads younger than the atomic store would have obtained the most recent values released by other processors, or when the lock acquire fails, they will be repeated.

9.3.3 Weak Ordering

Another attempt to relax the memory consistency model comes from an observation that a majority of programs are properly synchronized. When programmers want a certain memory access in one thread to occur after another memory access in another thread, programmers will rely on synchronization to achieve it. The synchronization can be in the form of barriers, point-to-point synchronization, etc. For example, a post-wait pair may be used in order to make sure a (consumer) load occurs after a (producer) store has performed. Programs that are not properly synchronized have non-deterministic behavior. For example, without the post-wait synchronization, a consumer load may read a newly produced value or may read an old value, depending on the relative timing of the execution of threads. Since it is rare that programmers tolerate non-deterministic results, we can reasonably assume that most (bug-free) programs are properly synchronized.

If programs are properly synchronized, there is no *data race* that can occur. *Data race* is defined as simultaneous accesses by multiple threads to a single location in which at least one of the access is a write. Data race is a necessary condition for non-deterministic results to occur. Simultaneous loads do not change the outcome of the loads hence they cannot produce data race. Simultaneous stores may overwrite each other depending on the timing, hence they can induce data race. A simultaneous load and store also may cause the load to return different values depending on the timing of the load and store, causing non-deterministic results. Therefore, in a properly synchronized program, programmers' expectation is that no data race can occur.

The implication of the lack of data race in a properly synchronized program is that ordering of memory accesses can be relaxed except at synchronization points. Since data race cannot occur, *it is safe to reorder memory accesses except at synchronization points*. To illustrate this point, assume that synchronization works as it should, and consider the following example. Suppose that different threads enter a critical section protected by a lock, and exit the critical section to do more computation. Note that if the synchronization works correctly, then only one thread will be in the critical section at a time. Therefore, the ordering of memory accesses inside the critical section does not matter and does not need to follow program order, since we know that only one thread executes in the critical section. Furthermore, the ordering of memory accesses outside of the critical section also does not matter and does not need to follow program order, because if programmers had cared about the relative ordering of memory accesses, they would have inserted synchronization to ensure that. Consequently, outside of synchronization points, program order does not need to be maintained. However, ordering of synchronization accesses is still required to ensure the proper behavior of synchronization.

Such an observation is the basis for a relaxed memory consistency model referred to as the weak ordering (WO) model. The WO model uses two assumptions: (1) programs are properly synchronized, and (2) programmers correctly express to the hardware which loads and stores act as synchronization accesses. Based on the assumptions, we can define the correct behavior of a synchronization access: (1) before a synchronization access can issue, all prior loads, stores, and synchronization accesses must have performed, and (2) all loads, stores, and synchronization accesses following it must not have issued. In other words, any pair of accesses in which one occurs prior to the synchronization access and another occurs after the synchronization access, are strictly ordered.

To see why this works, consider the post-wait synchronization pair used for the producer-consumer communication in Code 9.1. If the store to and load from `datumIsReady` are properly identified as synchronization accesses, the code executes correctly. At the producer, the synchronization access cannot issue until all prior memory accesses are complete, including the store to `datum`. Hence, the store to `datum` has fully propagated before the store to `datumIsReady` is allowed to access the cache. At the consumer, all memory accesses following a synchronization access (the load from `datumIsReady`) cannot issue until the synchronization access is complete. That is, before the load from `data` can issue to the cache, the load from `datumIsReady` must have performed first. Hence, WO has guaranteed that the load from `data` gets a newly produced value.

What mechanism is used in the processor to implement WO? When a synchronization access is encountered at the processor pipeline, first, all accesses that follow it are flushed from the pipeline or not fetched into the pipeline, in effect canceling their execution. Then, the synchronization access itself is stalled until all prior memory accesses have performed. That is, all prior loads must have obtained their values, and all prior stores have emptied from the write buffer and have fully propagated their values (through invalidation).

WO is much more relaxed than SC. Compilers can freely reorder loads and stores as long as they do not cross synchronization boundaries. During execution, the execution of loads and stores can be reordered and overlapped, and there is no need to execute them atomically, as long as ordering is enforced around synchronization accesses. Consequently, WO provides better performance than SC. However, it comes at the expense of requiring synchronization accesses to be both properly identified and expressed to the hardware.

Code 9.6 Post-wait synchronization with fences for the weak ordering model.

	P1:
P0:	₁L: ld.SYNC R1, &datumIsReady
₁st &datum, #5 // datum=5;	₂ sub R1, R1, #1 // R1=R1-1
₂st.SYNC &datumIsReady,#1	₃ bnz R1, L
	₄ld R2, &datum // R2 = datum;

Figure 9.2 illustrates execution order allowed under WO. The figure shows a code with two critical sections and memory accesses inside the first critical section (block 1), between the first and second critical section (block 2), and inside the last critical section (block 3). For simplicity, the figure assumes that functions lock and unlock consist of one single memory operation hence we do not show what memory operations are contained within each function. The figure shows the execution of loads/stores from block 1 can be overlapped in any way, but they must be executed after lock(A) and before unlock(A). Similarly, the execution of loads/stores from block 2 can be overlapped in any way, but they must be executed after unlock(A) has completed and before lock(B) executes. Finally, the execution of loads/stores from block 3 can be overlapped in any way, but they must be executed after lock(B) has completed and before unlock(B) executes. Thus, with WO, overlapped execution of memory operations is allowed throughout but punctuated by synchronization operations.

Compared to PC, WO tends to provide better performance due to more relaxed ordering between synchronization points. However, if the size of a critical section is small, or if critical sections are frequently entered and exited, there may be only a few memory accesses between synchronization points. In such a case, only a few memory accesses can be overlapped, and there is little opportunity to improve performance from overlapping their execution. When critical sections are small, PC may outperform WO. In PC, a lock release operation or the *post* part of the post-wait synchronization

Program order   Execution timing

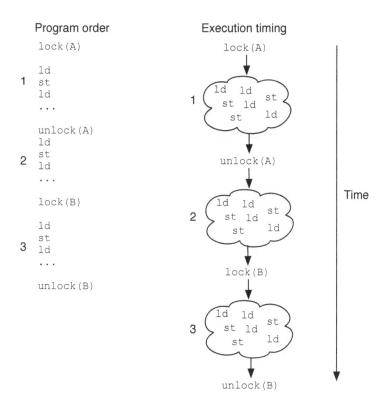

Figure 9.2: Illustration of allowed execution order under WO.

consist of a single store instruction. The store instruction may be followed immediately by loads. With WO, the synchronization store and younger loads will be ordered, whereas in PC they are not ordered. Hence, in this case, PC may achieve a higher degree of overlapping.

9.3.4 Release Consistency

A more aggressive attempt to relax the memory consistency model comes from an observation that there are two types of synchronization accesses: a type that *releases* values for other threads to read, and another type that *acquires* values that are released by another thread. For example, in a post-wait synchronization, the producer thread sets a flag to signal that data is ready. Setting the flag uses a synchronization store that needs to propagate the new flag value and all data values prior to the synchronization store. Hence, the synchronization store acts as a release. The consumer thread reads the flag before it accesses the newly produced data, and, hence, the flag read acts as an acquire.

Similarly, a lock release operation can be considered as a type of release synchronization, and the lock acquire operation as a type of acquire synchronization. To see why this makes sense, consider the sequence of execution shown as follows (Figure 9.3). The figure shows two threads that want to enter a critical section, read the most recent value of sum and accumulate an array element to it, and exit the critical section. The code shows that P0 arrives at the critical section before P1. In order for the code at P1 to execute correctly, it must be the case that when P1 reads from sum, it sees the latest value that was produced by P0 during the time P1 executed in its critical section. With the critical section protecting the access to sum, only one thread can be in the critical section at a time. Hence, the synchronization itself has ensured that the successful lock acquisition at P1 occurs after the lock release by P0, i.e., S3 → S4. In order for the code to perform correctly, P0 must have fully propagated the new value of sum that it wrote in statement S2, by the time it releases the lock, i.e., we must maintain the S2 → S3 ordering. If not, it is possible that when the lock is released and subsequently acquired by another thread, the new value of sum has not propagated completely. In addition, P1 must not have read from sum before the lock is fully acquired, i.e., we must maintain the S4 → S5 ordering. If not, P1 may read a stale value when it executes the statement S5 in its critical section.

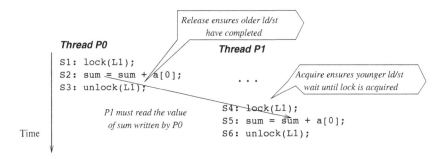

Figure 9.3: Illustration of acquire-release synchronization.

Hence, it is imperative that all memory accesses prior to the lock release have been completed *before* the lock release. In addition, when P1 enters the critical section, it must not have performed any memory accesses in its critical section. Thus, it is imperative that all memory accesses following the lock acquisition to be issued after the lock acquisition is complete.

Note that correctness is not affected if memory accesses following the unlock issue before the unlock completes because its ordering effect is similar to delaying the lock release – lengthening the critical section. Hence, while memory accesses prior to the unlock must be completed prior to the unlock, memory accesses following the unlock can issue early without waiting for the unlock to complete. If there are data dependences between the memory accesses in the critical section and ones after the critical section, they will be handled correctly by uniprocessor dependence detection and enforcement mechanisms. Hence, to ensure correctness, we can conclude that an unlock should prevent *downward migration* of memory accesses but *not upward migration*.

Similarly, correctness is also unaffected if memory accesses prior to a lock issue after the lock acquisition is performed. The effect of allowing that is similar to the case in which the lock is acquired early, before it is really needed in the critical section. However, the code inside the critical section cannot be issued before the lock acquisition is complete because mutual exclusion may not be guaranteed. Hence, to ensure correctness, we can conclude that a lock acquisition should prevent *upward migration* of memory accesses but *not downward migration*.

Now, let us consider the post-wait synchronization pair used for the producer-consumer communication in Code 9.1. The requirement for correctness is that the *post* operation should not issue until all prior memory accesses are complete, especially the store to datum. Otherwise, thread P1 may find that the *post* has been completed only to read the stale value of datum. In addition, the read from datum should not be executed until after the *wait* operation is complete, i.e., a value of "1" in the datumIsReady is observed. Therefore, S2 acts as a release synchronization since it signals the readiness of values produced up to this point, while S3 acts as an acquire synchronization since it reads values released by another thread. Just like in the lock acquire and release example, here S2 (a release synchronization) must also prevent downward migration, while S3 (an acquire synchronization) must also prevent upward migration. S2 does not need to prevent upward migration, since the effect of executing younger loads/stores early is as if S2 is executed late. Likewise, S3 does not need to prevent downward migration, since the effect of executing older loads/stores late is as if S3 is executed early. Finally, note the programming complexity over WO is that while in WO we only need to distinguish the store to and load from datumIsReady as synchronization accesses, in RC, we need to specify that S2 is a release synchronization while S3 is an acquire synchronization.

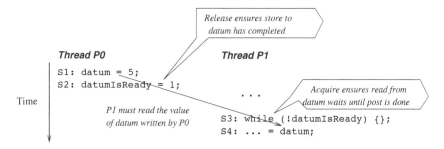

Figure 9.4: Illustration of an acquire and release in post-wait synchronization.

From the intuition of the correct behavior of lock and unlock, and *post* and *wait*, we can now discuss the formal correctness requirements of an acquire and a release synchronization.

> An acquire synchronization must ensure that no younger load/store executes before the acquire is complete. A release synchronization must ensure that all older loads/stores complete before the release is issued. Acquires and releases must execute atomically with respect to one another.

The final requirement states that acquires and releases must be atomic with respect to each other. This implies that they must appear not to have overlapped their execution with respect of one another. This requirement makes sense. For example, a lock acquisition cannot be overlapped with a lock release to fully guarantee mutual exclusion.

Note that the requirements for acquire and release synchronizations imply that the execution of two critical sections on a thread can be overlapped! For example, suppose that a thread acquires and releases lock A and then acquires and releases lock B. The requirement for the acquisition is to prevent upward migration, and hence all younger loads, stores, and even lock acquisitions can be executed as soon as the current lock acquisition is completed. Figure 9.5 illustrates this case, using code that shows two critical sections and memory accesses inside the first critical section (block 1), between the first and second critical section (block 2), and inside the last critical section (block 3). For simplicity, we assume in the figure that the functions lock and unlock are comprised of a single memory operation.

In the figure, the lock release of A prevents downward migration, but not upward migration. Hence, the execution of loads/stores from block 2 can be moved up as far as right after the completion of the acquisition of lock A. So can the execution of the acquisition of lock B. As a result, the execution of loads/stores from blocks 1, 2, and 3, can actually be overlapped. However, lock acquisitions have to be ordered because they both prevent upward migration, while lock releases also have to be ordered because they both prevent downward migration. The ability to overlap the execution of memory accesses in blocks 1, 2, and 3 both dynamically (in hardware) and statically (through memory access reordering by the compiler) stands in contrast to WO. In WO, lock acquisitions and lock releases act to order all loads/stores before and after them. Thus, the execution of blocks 1, 2, and 3 with respect to each other is ordered in WO, and overlap of memory accesses only occurs within each block.

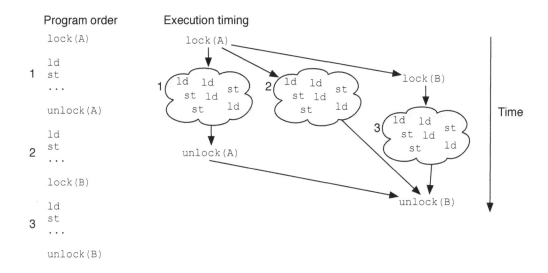

Figure 9.5: Illustration of allowed execution order under RC.

Similar to WO, RC requires all synchronization accesses in a program to be identified correctly and completely, so that the hardware can ensure correct execution of properly synchronized programs. No guarantee is given for programs that are not properly synchronized (e.g., missing synchronization when it is needed), or for programs that are properly synchronized but the synchronization accesses are not properly expressed to the hardware. Furthermore, compared to WO, RC requires more from the programmers. They must label synchronization accesses as acquires or releases, not just as synchronization accesses. Hence, programming complexity is higher in RC than in WO.

What mechanism is used in the processor to implement RC? Recall that a release synchronization must prevent downward migration. When a release synchronization access is encountered in the processor pipeline, the release access is stalled (not committed) until all prior memory accesses have performed. That is, all prior loads must have obtained their values, and all prior stores have emptied the write buffer and have fully propagated their values (through invalidation).

An acquire synchronization must prevent upward migration. When an acquire synchronization access is encountered in the processor pipeline, some of the accesses that are younger than the acquire may have executed in an out-of-order processor pipeline. Such a situation contradicts with the need to prevent them from issuing to the cache and the rest of the memory hierarchy. An out-of-order processor already has a mechanism to cancel the effect of speculative instructions in order to arrive at an instruction-specific state. An acquire synchronization access can rely on such a mechanism. When an acquire synchronization access is encountered in the processor pipeline, all instructions younger than it (including all loads and stores) are canceled, and reexecuted after the acquire synchronization completes. Alternatively, when an acquire synchronization access is decoded in the processor pipeline, all younger instructions are discarded from the fetch and decoded stages and the further fetching is stalled until the acquire synchronization instruction has retired.

Similar to WO, RC allows the compiler to freely reorder loads and stores except that they cannot migrate upward past an acquire synchronization and cannot migrate downward past a release synchronization. However, the flexibility and performance advantage of RC comes at the expense of requiring synchronization accesses to be properly identified and identified as acquires or releases. Unlike in WO, synchronization accesses cannot be easily identified by instruction opcodes alone. For example, the appearance of special instructions such as atomic fetch-and-op, test-and-set, load linked, store conditional, etc. does not give an indication of whether they are acquire or release synchronization. While a release always involves a store, an acquire may involve both loads and stores. Hence, the burden is on programmers' shoulders to properly identify acquire and release synchronization accesses.

9.3.5 Lazy Release Consistency

A further optimization of the release consistency (RC) can be achieved when we consider that the thread that executes an acquire synchronization does not need values written by another thread until the acquire synchronization is completed. For example, as can be observed in Figure 9.3, in a critical section in thread P1, the value of `sum` set by thread P0 in its previous critical section is not needed by P1 until after P1 obtains the lock or until after P0 releases its lock. Also, as can be observed in Figure 9.4, thread P1 does not need the most recent value of `datum` until it has finished its *wait* operation or until P0 has finished its *post* operation. Interestingly, this presents a performance optimization policy through modifications to the behavior of cache coherence. In essence, the timing for performing write propagation can be tweaked when acquire and release synchronization accesses are properly identified.

For example, consider the top portion of Figure 9.6, which shows when propagation is performed on a cache coherent system that relies on the RC model. `datum` is propagated completely before the propagation of `datumIsReady`. However, the value of `datum` is not really needed until after thread P1 completes its acquire synchronization. In a consistency model referred to as *lazy release consistency* (LRC), all values written prior to the release synchronization are propagated together with the propagation of the release synchronization itself. For example, in the bottom part of Figure 9.6, the new values of `datum` and `datumIsReady` are propagated together at the release point.

At this point, readers may wonder why delaying write propagation can be beneficial. Performing write propagation in bulk will slow down the release and subsequent acquire synchronization, and, hence, on a hardware cache coherence system, there may not be any gain. However, in a system that has little bandwidth available between processors, or in a system that suffers from higher overheads due to frequent propagation of small amount of data versus infrequent propagation of a large amount of data, LRC can really help performance. An example in which both of these situations exist is a

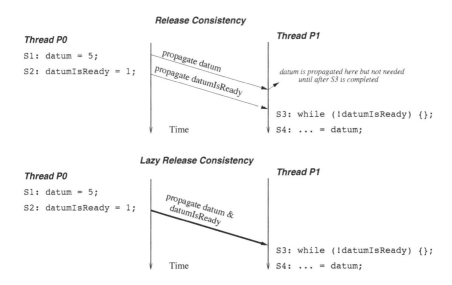

Figure 9.6: Illustration of lazy release consistency.

multiprocessor that does not provide a shared memory abstraction in hardware, but instead employs a software layer that provides a shared memory abstraction. In such a "*software shared memory*" system, write propagation is performed at the page granularity, hence it is extremely expensive to propagate a page each time one block in the page is modified. Hence, write propagation is delayed until the release synchronization point is reached, at which time entire pages that have been modified up to this point are propagated.

LRC is not employed in hardware-supported cache coherent systems because write propagation can be efficiently performed even at a small granularity of a cache block.

9.4   Synchronization in Different Memory Consistency Models

Some programs or thread libraries have been developed for one platform that has a specific memory consistency model. They may not have been programmed for portability to systems with a different memory consistency model. This section discusses how they can be ported from one model to another to achieve equivalent execution. Note that memory consistency models must be considered mostly by programmers dealing with synchronization primitives, such as in thread libraries or in the OS.

The first step programmers must take is to analyze what ordering is guaranteed by the system, and what ordering is required by their software to perform correctly. Then, they need to impose additional ordering requirements for example by inserting fences to their code, or remove unnecessary ordering requirements such as by removing fences. Superfluous fences only reduce performance, but missing fences may produce incorrect execution. Hence, programmers naturally tend to be more conservative than aggressive in relaxing ordering. Anecdotal evidence points to an excessive insertion of fence instructions in complex code such as the operating system (OS). The reason for this is that some OSes needs to run on multiple machines with various memory consistency models. To ease porting, programmers sometimes intentionally sacrifice performance by inserting fence instructions conservatively, assuming the most relaxed memory consistency model. Thus, the code requires very little modification when ported to machines with stricter memory consistency models.

For now, however, let us assume that we start with a program written by programmers with sequential consistency in mind, and that program order is maintained during compilation. We want to implement the program on several different consistency models, and when fences are used, we want to use as few fences and as weak fences as possible in order to still guarantee correct execution. We will use the *post-wait* synchronization example to illustrate the differences in these models. For the machines, we will highlight the differences between a system that provides acquire vs. release types of fences, a system that provides load vs. store vs. full types of fences, and a system that provides labeling of stores and loads as release and acquire synchronization.

Our first example is the IBM PowerPC-style architecture. The architecture style does not support labeling of regular loads/stores as acquire or release synchronization accesses. However, it provides two types of fence instructions: an all-out fence (preventing upward and downward migration), and an acquire fence (preventing upward migration) only. The regular fence is provided through the instruction `lwsync` while the acquire fence is provided through the instruction `isync`. Suppose that we want to implement the post-wait synchronization from Code 9.1. The producer code needs to use the regular fence between the write to `datum` and the write to `datumIsReady`, as shown in Figure 9.7 (top portion).

For the post synchronization, a regular fence strictly orders the two writes. Avoiding only upward migration above the fence does not prevent the write to `datum` from moving below the fence, while avoiding downward migration does not prevent the write to `datumIsReady` from moving up past the fence. Both cases may cause either the write to `datum` to be performed or propagated late, or `datumIsReady` to be performed or propagated too early, which are both incorrect. Therefore, in the absence of labeling acquire or release synchronization, a regular fence instruction is needed to provide strict ordering at the release side.

At the consumer (acquirer) side, two factors together ensure correct execution ordering. First, `isync` prevents read from `datum` from issuing before the `isync` is complete. Second, the `isync` itself is not executed until the program goes out of the loop after the load to `datumIsReady` reads the new value of `datumIsReady`. Notice that the control flow dependence between the loop and the `isync`, together with the ordering between `isync` and read from `datum`, ensure that the load from `datum` will return the new value of `datum`. Without the `isync` instruction, the read from `datum` may access the cache earlier than the read from `datumIsReady`. Control flow dependence alone is not sufficient because the branch may just be predicted, allowing the younger load to access the cache ahead of an older load.

Finally, note also memory operations before the `isync` may be performed later than it because it is an acquire synchronization which only prevents upward migration and not downward migration.

■ *Did you know?*

> `lwsync` *in PowerPC refers to a light-weight memory synchronization fence. While it is a full fence, it works only for accesses to system memory only. It does not create a memory barrier to device memory. A heavy weight version is provided in the form of* `sync` *instruction, which is applicable to both system memory and device memory. The heavy weight version is often needed by adapter device drivers, for ordering system memory accesses made by a driver critical section with accesses made to its I/O adapter.*

IBM PowerPC style

Post synchronization code   Wait synchronization code

```
datum = 5;
lwsync
datumIsReady = 1;
```

```
while (!datumIsReady) {};
isync
... = datum;
```

Lock release code   LL/SC lock acquisition code

```
#end of critical section
lwsync      #full fence
stw r4,r3   #write 0 in r4 to
            #lock address in r3
```

```
loop: lwarx   r6,0,r3 #load linked
      cmpw    r4,r6   #is lock free?
      bne-    wait    #go to wait if not free
      stwcx.  loop    #store conditional
      bne-    loop    #if SC fails, repeat
      isync           #acquire fence
      # begin critical section

wait: ...              # wait until lock is free
```

IA-64 style

Post synchronization code   Wait synchronization code

```
// suppose R1=5, R2=1

st &datum, R1
st.rel &datumIsready,R2
```

```
wait: ld.acq R1, &datumIsReady
      sub R2, R1, #1
      biz R2, wait
      ld R3, &datum
```

Figure 9.7: An example of how a simple post-wait synchronization can be implemented on different platforms.

Let us look at another example, a LL/SC lock implementation in PowerPC-style architecture. The code is shown in Figure 9.7 (middle portion). The lock acquisition code shows isync inserted right at the end of the lock acquisition code and before the code in the critical section. Here the isync is control flow dependent on the lock acquisition code, such that it will not be executed unless the control flow has confirmed a successful store conditional. In addition, the code inside the critical section cannot migrate above the isync. Hence, correctness is ensured. Next, lock release code requires a full fence lwsync instead. This is because the code in the critical section must not be allowed to migrate downward past the store that releases the lock (stw r4, r3), nor can we allow the stw to migrate upward.

The final example is for the IA-64-style instruction set architecture that supports several instructions: mf which is a full memory fence, st.rel which is a release store synchronization instruction, and ld.acq which is an acquire load synchronization instruction. To implement the post-part of the synchronization, we can label the store to datumIsReady as a release synchronization access, as shown in Figure 9.7 (bottom portion).

In the example, the consumer performs a series of loads within the `while` loop that are involved in the *wait* synchronization, and a load that reads from `datum`. Since the loads are involved in an acquire-type of synchronization, we can simply label the load instruction by replacing it with the `ld.acq` instruction, guaranteeing that the load from `datum` does not execute until the load from `datumIsReady` is performed. Similarly, in the post synchronization code, we can replace a regular store to `datumIsReady` with a store release `st.rel`, guaranteeing that the store to `datum` is performed before the store release is executed.

The figure contrasts the PowerPC style of memory consistency programming that relies on the use of fences, with the IA-64 style of memory consistency programming that relies on annotating memory operations. The annotation approach is more efficient for two reasons. First, it uses fewer instructions as no additional instructions are used. Second, the fence approach is more restrictive at the release side because a full fence is used (preventing upward and downward migration) compared to a release synchronization (which prevents only downward migration).

Overall, different architectures support different memory ordering guarantees and safety nets. This prevents low-level code, such as the OS or thread libraries, from being portable. The performance benefits of RC in allowing reordering of memory accesses compared to more restrictive memory consistency models are apparent and appealing. However, the complexity of programming them, especially considering the different ways of expressing synchronizations to different architectures, is potentially daunting. To avoid such complexities in dealing with various architectures, more recently, there has been an effort to incorporate the memory consistency model into the programming language, such as in the *Java Memory Model*. With a memory model at the programming language level, it is the responsibility of a Java compiler to translate code to different architectures in a manner that conforms to those architectures.

9.5 Exercises

Worked Problems

1. Suppose that we want to run a piece of code on a machine that does not impose any ordering of memory operations. However, the machine provides a fence instruction that, if inserted in a code, prevents issuing memory operations that come after the fence before the memory operations that are before the fence are globally performed. For simplicity, assume that lock and unlock functions are comprised of one memory operation that has been annotated as/with acquire synchronization (lock) or as/with release synchronization (unlock). The code to be executed is:

```
lock1
load A
store B
unlock1
load C
store D
lock2
load E
store F
unlock2
```

(a) Insert as few fence instructions as possible to ensure a sequential consistent execution of the code.

(b) Repeat it for processor consistency.

(c) Repeat it for weak ordering.

Answer:

part (a): Sequential consistent execution of the code

```
lock1
FENCE
load A
FENCE
store B
FENCE
unlock1
FENCE
load C
FENCE
store D
FENCE
lock2
FENCE
load E
FENCE
store F
FENCE
unlock2
```

part (b): Processor consistency

```
lock1
FENCE
load A
FENCE
store B
FENCE
unlock1
load C
FENCE
store D
FENCE
lock2
FENCE
load E
FENCE
store F
FENCE
unlock2
```

part (c) Weak ordering:

```
lock1
FENCE
load A
store B
FENCE
unlock1
FENCE
load C
store D
FENCE
lock2
FENCE
load E
store F
FENCE
unlock2
```

2. (*30 Points*) **Performance of memory consistency models**. Given the following code fragment, we want to compute its execution time under various memory consistency models.
Assume a processor architecture with an arbitrarily deep write buffer. All instructions take
1 cycle, ignoring memory system effects. Both read and write instructions that miss in the
cache take 100 cycles to complete (i.e., to perform globally). Assume the cache lines are
not shared (thus, a write hit does not generate invalidations). Lock variables are cacheable
and loads are non-blocking. Assume all the variables and locks are initially uncached and all
locks are unlocked. Further assume that once a line is brought into the cache it does not get
invalidated for the duration of the code's execution. All memory locations referenced here are
distinct and mapped to different cache lines. The processor can only issue one instruction at

any given cycle, and it gives preference to instructions that are earlier in program order. Assume that all lock and unlock primitives have been annotated as/with acquire synchronization while all unlock primitives have been annotated as/with release synchronization, and take the same latency as memory operations.

(a) If the sufficient conditions for sequential consistency (SC) are maintained, how many cycles will it take to execute the code?

(b) Repeat part (a) for weak ordering.

(c) Repeat part (a) for release consistency.

Answer:

Let's use this notation (starting time, ending time)

Instruction	Hit/Miss	SC	WC	RC
Load A	Miss	(0, 100)	(0, 100)	(0, 100)
Store B	Miss	(100, 200)	(1, 101)	(1, 101)
Lock (L1)	Miss	(200, 300)	(101, 201)	(2, 102)
Store C	Miss	(300, 400)	(201, 301)	(102, 202)
Load D	Miss	(400, 500)	(202, 302)	(103, 203)
Unlock (L1)	Hit	(500, 501)	(302, 303)	(203, 204)
Load E	Miss	(501, 601)	(303, 403)	(104, 204)
Store F	Miss	(601, 701)	(304, 404)	(105, 205)

3. **Results under different memory consistency models.** Given the following code segments, specify what read results are possible (or not possible) under sequential consistency (SC), processor consistency (PC), weak ordering (WO), and release consistency (RC). Assume that all variables are initialized to 0 before this code is reached. All the instructions are annotated as regular loads (LD), stores (ST), synchronization operations (SYN), acquire (ACQ), and release (REL).

In addition, if you find results that are impossible under SC, give the ordering of operations that produce those results.

(a)

P1	P2
(ST) A=2	(LD) read A
(ST) B=3	(LD) read B

(b)

P1	P2
(ST) A=2	(LD) read B
(ST) B=3	(LD) read A

Answer:

Part (a):

Possible Result	SC	PC	WO	RC
read A returns 0, read B returns 0	yes	yes	yes	yes
read A returns 2, read B returns 0	yes	yes	yes	yes
read A returns 0, read B returns 3	yes	yes	yes	yes
read A returns 2, read B returns 3	yes	yes	yes	yes

Part (b):

Possible Result	SC	PC	WO	RC
read A returns 0, read B returns 0	yes	yes	yes	yes
read A returns 2, read B returns 0	yes	yes	yes	yes
read A returns 0, read B returns 3	no	no	yes	yes
read A returns 2, read B returns 3	yes	yes	yes	yes

Under SC, we know that A=2 $\rightarrow$ B=3, and read B $\rightarrow$ read A. Additionally, for read A to return 0, an additional ordering of read A $\rightarrow$ A=2 must have occured, which implies that: read B $\rightarrow$ read A $\rightarrow$ A=2 $\rightarrow$ B=3. For read B to return 3, an additional ordering of B=3 $\rightarrow$ read B, which implies that A=2 $\rightarrow$ B=3 $\rightarrow$ read B $\rightarrow$ read A. Since both relations are contradictory, then the result is impossible under SC.

4. **Results under different memory consistency models**. Given the following code segments, specify what read results are possible (or not possible) under sequential consistency (SC), processor consistency (PC), weak ordering (WO), and release consistency (RC). Assume that all variables are initialized to 0 before this code is reached. All the instructions are annotated as regular loads (LD), stores (ST), synchronization operations (SYN), acquire (ACQ), and release (REL).

In addition, if you find results that are impossible under SC, give the ordering of operations that produce those results.

(a)

P1	P2
(ST) A=2	(ACQ) while (flag==0) ;
(REL) flag=1	(LD) print A

(b)

P1	P2	P3
(ST) A = 1	(LD1) read A	(LD2) read B
	(ST) B = 1	(LD3) read A

Answer:

Part (a):

Possible Result	SC	PC	WO	RC
read A returns 0, read flag returns 0	no	no	no	no
read A returns 2, read flag returns 0	no	no	no	no
read A returns 0, read flag returns 1	no	no	no	no
read A returns 2, read flag returns 1	yes	yes	yes	yes

SC imposes an ordering of A=2 $\to$ flag=1, and read flag $\to$ read A. Furthermore, the control structure over multiple "read flag" in the loop would only exit if the following ordering occurs: flag=1 $\to$ read flag. Thus, under SC, only the following ordering is possible: A=2 $\to$ flag=1 $\to$ read flag $\to$ read A, and for this ordering, the only possible result is for read A to return 2 and for read flag to return 1.

Part (b):

Possible Result	SC	PC	WO	RC
LD1 LD2 LD3 = 0 0 0	yes	yes	yes	yes
LD1 LD2 LD3 = 0 0 1	yes	yes	yes	yes
LD1 LD2 LD3 = 0 1 0	yes	yes	yes	yes
LD1 LD2 LD3 = 0 1 1	yes	yes	yes	yes
LD1 LD2 LD3 = 1 0 0	yes	yes	yes	yes
LD1 LD2 LD3 = 1 0 1	yes	yes	yes	yes
LD1 LD2 LD3 = 1 1 0	no	no	yes	yes
LD1 LD2 LD3 = 1 1 1	yes	yes	yes	yes

For LD1 (read A) to return 1, the following ordering must happen: A=1 $\to$ LD1. For LD2 to return 1, the following ordering must happen: B=1 $\to$ LD2 (read B). Together, they imply the following global order: A=1 $\to$ LD1 $\to$ B=1 $\to$ LD2 $\to$ LD3. This global order implies that LD3 (read A) would return 1. If it returns 0, then a contradiction has occurred.

Homework Problems

1. What results are possible under sequential consistency (SC), processor consistency (PC), weak ordering (WO), and release consistency (RC), for the following code. Assume that a and b are memory addresses with initial values of 0. Some of the load or store instructions may be annotated as acquire synchronization (ACQ) or release synchronization (REL). ACQ or REL are interpreted as synchronization annotation in WO. Code for thread 1:

   S1: a = 1;
   S2: b = 1;
   Code for thread 2:
   S3: ... = b;
   S4: ... = a;

2. What results are possible under sequential consistency (SC), processor consistency (PC), weak ordering (WO), and release consistency (RC), for the following code. Assume that a and b are memory addresses with initial values of 0. Some of the load or store instructions may be annotated as acquire synchronization (ACQ) or release synchronization (REL). ACQ or REL are interpreted as synchronization annotation in WO. Code for thread 1:

   S1: a = 1; (REL)
   S2: ... = b;
   Code for thread 2:
   S3: b = 1; (REL)
   S4: ... = a;

3. Given the following code fragment, compute its execution time under various memory consistency models. Each instruction takes 10 cycles if it hits in the cache or 100 cycles if it misses in the cache to complete globally. Assume that cache blocks are not shared (hence no invalidations are involved) and loads are non-blocking. Assume the cache is large and is initially empty. The processor can issue one instruction per cycle, and it prefers issuing instructions that appear earlier in program order. The memory references are: Store A, Load.Acq B, Load C, Store.Rel B, Store D, Load E, Load A. In each cell, show the start time and end time of the instruction. Some loads/stores have been labeled by programmers as synchronizations and their respective types (acquire or release).

4. Suppose you have a machine that does not guarantee any ordering with the exception of fence instruction that allows memory operations after it to execute only after memory operations before it globally complete. Insert fences in such a way to guarantee SC, PC, and WO. The original code is: Lock L1, Rd A, Rd B, Wr B, Wr D, Rd E, Unlock L1, Rd F.

5. Suppose you have a machine that guarantees processor-consistent execution. It also provides fence instruction that allows memory operations after it to execute only after memory operations before it globally complete. Insert fences in such a way to guarantee SC, PC, and WO. The original code is: Lock L1, Rd A, Rd B, Wr B, Wr D, Rd E, Unlock L1, Rd F.

Chapter 10

Advanced Cache Coherence Issues

Contents

In Chapter 7, we have discussed basic issues in cache coherence protocols, focusing on the design of broadcast/snoopy protocols on various interconnects (shared bus and point-to-point). In this chapter, we will look into more advanced issues in cache coherence protocol design. One of the issues is how cache coherence protocols can scale to a larger system size. Broadcast and snoopy protocols hit a scalability issue relatively early because traffic and snoop frequency scale at least linearly with the number of processors. Available interconnect bandwidth gets saturated quickly with broadcast traffic. We will discuss directory cache coherence protocols, which allows for scalable implementation by avoiding broadcasts. We will use them to discuss implementation issues for coherence protocols such as how to deal with protocol races, the use of transient states, etc. Finally, we will discuss contemporary multicore design issues, such as dealing with imprecise directory information, looking into whether coherence should be tracked at a single or multiple granularities, how coherence can be designed to allow a multicore system to be partitioned, and a how thread migration cost may be reduced.

10.1   Directory Coherence Protocols

The most scalable organization uses point-to-point interconnection and, rather than relying on broadcasting and snooping, relies on a *directory* approach. In a directory approach, the information about which caches have a copy of a block is maintained in a structure called the directory. With such an approach, locating cached copies of a block does not rely on broadcasting a request to all processors, but rather by inquiring the directory about which caches may have copies of the block, and sending the request only to those caches. If a block is cached by all processors, then the request must be sent to all processors, which yields comparable traffic to a broadcast/snoopy approach. However, if a block is cached by only a few processors, the traffic savings of the directory approach over a broadcast/snoopy approach is substantial. Which case is more likely in reality? Well-tuned applications exhibit little data sharing for blocks that are frequently read and written because if there is a lot of such data, the applications will suffer from excessive serialization due to the critical sections needed to protect accesses to the data, as well as from coherence misses due to invalidations to the data. Thus, in well-tuned applications, most data sharing occurs only for data that is read only, and there is little sharing for data that is frequently read and written. For such data, a directory approach can yield a substantial traffic savings compared to the broadcast/snoopy approach because most writes will cause only a few caches to be invalidated. One case in which there may be little saving in traffic is when there is highly-contended synchronization in which a variable is frequently read and written by all processors. But again, this case implies a high number of invalidations which restrict the performance and scalability in other ways, which cannot be solved by using a bus.

10.2   Overview of Directory Coherence Protocol

Figure 10.1 shows a basic working of a directory cache coherence protocol. The top diagram shows how a read request is handled, while the bottom diagram shows how a write request is handled. Let us start with the top diagram. Initially, assume that a block B is cached in a modified state in the cache belonging to processor P3. The block is uncached elsewhere. Suppose that P0 wants to read block B and suffers a cache miss. The miss triggers an inquiry to the directory (Step 1). Since the cached copy is the only valid copy in the system, the data block B must be obtained from P3's cache. The directory contains information that enables it. It records that B is cached in the modified state at P3. The directory forwards the request (or intervenes) to P3's cache (Step 2). Finally, P3's cache responds by supplying the block to the requester (Step 3), either directly or through the directory. Note that in this case, the directory has saved traffic compared to a broadcast coherence protocol. A broadcast protocol would have resulted in P0 sending its read miss request to all other processors/caches, since it does not know which cache may have a copy of the block.

The bottom part of Figure 10.1 shows how a write request is handled, assuming initially a block C is cached in shared state in P1's, P2's, and P3's cache. First, the requestor (P1) sends a request to upgrade the state of block C to the directory (Step 1). The requestor may or may not already have the block in its cache (the figure shows the case in which the requestor has the block in its cache). The directory looks up its directory information and discovers that other than the requestor, only P1 and P2 have a copy of block C. Thus, it sends invalidations to the sharers P1 and P2 (Step 2). The sharers (P1 and P2) respond by sending an invalidation acknowledgement either to the requestor or to the directory, indicating they have received the invalidation request and have invalidated the block (Step

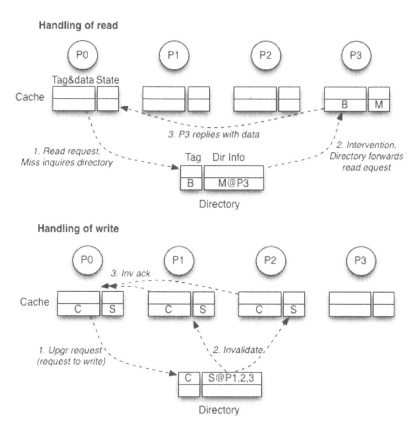

Figure 10.1: Basic operation of a directory cache coherence protocol.

3). As in the prior case, the directory has saved traffic compared to a broadcast coherence protocol, which would have sent invalidations to all other processors/caches.

10.2.1 Directory Format and Location

In the previous section, we have discussed the basic protocol for serving a read or write request. Essentially, when the read/write request reaches the directory, the directory must know: (1) which cache(s) keeps a copy of the block, and (2) in what state the block is cached.

In order to satisfy the first requirement, the directory ideally reflects the state of the block in the caches. For example, if the caches use MESI states for each block, then ideally the directory should also keep a MESI state that perfectly reflects the state of the block in the cache(s). However, the directory state cannot always fully reflect the cache state of a block. For example, in MESI, if a block is in an exclusive state in a local cache, when the processor writes to the block, it can do so silently since no other cached copies exist. Hence, the block state is changed from exclusive to modified silently, and the block value is also changed silently. In this case, the directory never sees the transition from exclusive to modified. Thus, with MESI, the directory cannot distinguish between a block that is cached in exclusive state or modified state. Thus, to cater to MESI cache states, it can keep only three states: exclusive/modified (EM), shared (S), or invalid (I).

To satisfy the requirement of keeping the information of which caches have a copy of a block, there are several possible formats the directory can keep. The important factors in choosing which format to use for a particular case are the *amount of storage overheads* and whether the information can overflow the allocated storage format or not.

One format is to keep a bit that corresponds to each cache that indicates whether the block is cached there or not. This format is referred to as the *full bit vector* directory format. If there are p caches, each block in memory would then require p bits of information. Note that since the cache block size does not change with the number of caches, the ratio of directory storage overhead to the storage for a data block grows linearly with the number of caches. The overhead can be quite high for a larger machine. For example, assuming a cache block size of 64 bytes, when there are 64 caches, the storage overhead ratio is $\frac{64}{64 \times 8} = 12.5\%$, which is substantial. It becomes worse quickly with a larger number of caches. For 1024 caches, the storage overhead ratio becomes $\frac{1024}{64 \times 8} = 200\%$! If the directory information is kept in the main memory, that means that two thirds of the main memory capacity is used up for storing directory information, and only one third is available for storing data. Clearly, the full bit vector is too costly to use in large systems.

A simple way to reduce the storage overhead of the directory is to use one bit to represent a group of caches, rather than just one cache. If any cache in a group has a copy of a block, the bit value corresponding to the group is set to "1". If the block is not cached anywhere in the group, the bit value is set to "0". This format is referred to as the *coarse bit vector* directory format. Since the information is kept per group, when there is an invalidation, the invalidation must be sent to all caches in the group, even when only one cache in the group has the block. Thus, traffic increases compared to the full bit vector approach. However, the storage requirement for the directory decreases as well. If the number of caches per group is g, the storage overhead in the sharing bit vector per group is $\frac{p}{g}$. In the example above, for a 1024-cache system with 64-byte block size, and a group size of 4, the storage overhead ratio is lowered to $\frac{\frac{1024}{4}}{64 \times 8} = 50\%$.

A different approach to reduce the storage overhead is to not keep full directory information of all blocks in the main memory, but instead keep partial directory information, or keep full directory for only a limited number of blocks. One format that uses this approach is the *limited pointer* format, which keeps a limited number of pointers to sharers in the system. For example, for a given block in memory, suppose we keep pointers to only up to n caches. Each pointer requires $log_2(p)$ number of bits to represent the ID of the node. Hence, the storage requirement per block is $n \times log_2(p)$. For a 1024-node system with 64-block size, and 8 pointers per block, the storage overhead ratio is $\frac{8 \times log_2 1024}{64 \times 8} = 15.6\%$, which is significantly lower than a full bit vector format. Of course, the amount of storage overhead reduction depends on how many pointers are kept. However, a particular block is rarely cached in many locations, and hence most of the time four to eight pointers would be sufficient.

One question is in the rare case in which the number of sharers is larger than the number of pointers, how can this situation be handled by the directory? In this case, the directory runs out of IDs that it can keep. There are several strategies to handle this case. One strategy is to not allow the case to occur. That is, when there is a cache which wants to keep a copy of a block, the directory sends an invalidation to a cache that currently keeps a copy of a block to make a room to store the ID of the new cache. This strategy can backfire when the reason that there are many sharers of a block is because the block contains data used for global synchronization, such as a centralized barrier. In this case, naturally many sharers are present, and when the number of sharers is kept artificially low, the barrier can become significantly slower. Other strategies, such as reverting to broadcast when the number of sharers exceeds the number of pointers, suffers from a similar problem. Another possible strategy is to keep a pool of free pointers which can be allocated when such a heavy amount of sharing occurs. Since not many blocks are heavily shared, the number of such free pointers does not need to be large.

The limited pointer format keeps limited directory information (when overflowed) for all blocks in memory. Another way to rely on partial information is to keep full directory information only for a subset of blocks in memory. Note that in a typical configuration, the number of blocks in the main memory greatly exceeds the number of blocks that can be cached, because the main memory size greatly exceeds the cache size. Thus, for most blocks, the directory state will indicate that they are not cached at all. One way to compress the directory storage is to remove the directory information for such blocks, and only keep the directory information for blocks that are cached. This leads to a format referred to as the *sparse directory* format. In the sparse directory format, when there is a request for a block, the request is checked against the entries in a *directory cache*. If the entry for the block is found in the cache, the directory information is retrieved. If it is not found in the cache, the block must not have been cached before. Hence, a new entry is created in the directory cache for that block. With a sufficient directory cache size, the directory information of all cached blocks should fit in it. There is, however, a risk for overflow. The reason for this is that a clean block may be replaced silently from the cache, without notifying the directory cache. Thus, the directory cache may still keep the directory entry for the block, preventing the entry from being used for a block that may actually be cached. When the directory cache runs out of space, there is a possibility of evicting an entry that corresponds to a block that is still cached, while keeping entries corresponding to blocks that are no longer cached. Therefore, an overflow is a possibility, and must be handled with similar strategies used for handling the overflow of the limited pointer scheme.

■ *Did you know?*

Note that the directory formats are not exclusive of one another in their use. We can simultaneously employ several formats. For example, the limited pointer may be combined with the coarse format in that a pointer refers to a group of nodes rather than to a single node. Or, a coarse bit vector format or limited pointer format may be used in conjunction with a sparse directory in order to further reduce their sizes. Finally, we can switch from one format to another as situations change. For example, the SGI Origin 2000 system uses a limited pointer scheme when a block is only cached in one processor, but uses a full bit vector (with a bit corresponding to a node of two processors) when a block is cached by more than one processor, and uses a coarse bit vector for very large machine configurations.

Another issue with the design of the directory is where it is located. There are several aspects to this. One aspect is whether there is only one location where the directory is located (a *centralized* configuration) or the directory is split up into different parts depending on addresses it keeps track (a *distributed* configuration). A centralized directory is simple to design. However, anything centralized at some point becomes a bottleneck to scalability: all cache miss requests will go to the same place and all invalidations have to be sent out from the same place. Thus, a scalable implementation of a directory requires a distributed organization. However, how the directory should be distributed is still an open question.

The consideration of how to distribute the directory structure is affected by several factors. One factor is the minimum number of parts that sufficiently diffuse traffic. There is no convenient rule of thumb here, as the answer depends on the characteristics of the network, e.g., topology, bandwidth, latency, etc. Another factor to consider is in the event that a block is not cached, the proximity of the directory to the supplier of data is important as it determines the cache miss latency. Let us consider a few examples shown in Figure 10.2.

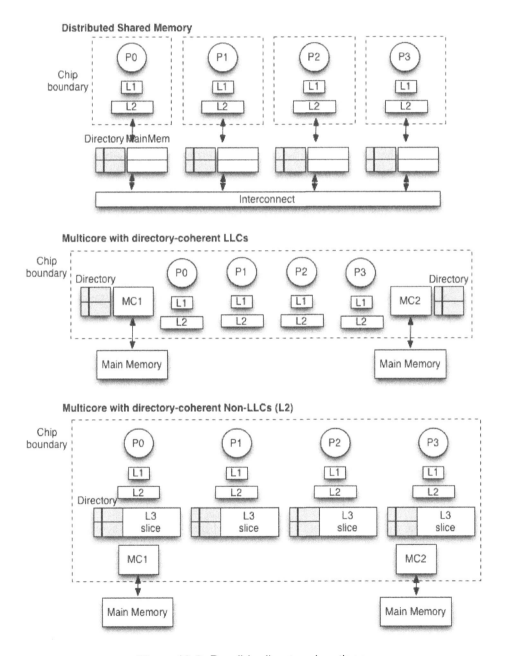

Figure 10.2: Possible directory locations.

The top part of Figure 10.2 shows a classical organization of a *distributed shared memory* (DSM) system. This is a system where nodes, each consisting of a processor, cache hierarchy, and main memory, are interconnected to form a larger shared memory system. Physical addresses are interleaved across the main memories at page granularity, e.g., page frame 0 maps to the first main memory, page frame 1 maps to the second main memory, page frame 2 maps to the third main memory, etc. When the last level cache misses, the miss request is sent to the main memory that corresponds to the page frame address where the data block resides. Such main memory or node is said to be the *home node* of the data block. The home node may be the local node or a remote node, depending on the address of the block that is missed. The directory is divided into parts that are distributed and interleaved in the same way as the main memory. Thus, when a block miss request is forwarded to the home node, the directory is looked up for the status of the block. If the block is uncached, data can be readily obtained from the main memory in the same node, facilitating quick retrieval of data.

The middle part of Figure 10.2 shows a multicore chip with the last level caches kept coherent with a directory coherence protocol. For illustration purposes, the figure shows the L2 caches as the last level caches. However, they can be any other levels, such as the L1 caches, L3 caches, L4 caches, etc. as long as they are the last/outermost level cache on chip. There is a difference between this system and a DSM in that the memory structure associated with the directory protocol is a cache rather than the main memory. A cache can miss, while a main memory cannot. If a data block is missed in the L2 cache, the request is sent to the directory, and if the directory finds that the block is uncached in all other L2 caches, it must fetch the data from the external memory, in this case it is from the main memory through one of the memory controllers that handles the block address. Therefore, to facilitate quick retrieval of data, it makes sense to co-locate the directory with memory controllers in the same interleaved manner. A potential problem here is that there may not be a sufficient number of memory controllers to sufficiently spread traffic evenly across the chip. For example, some multicore chips have only two memory controllers, some may have three or four, but rarely they have much more than that due to the limitation of the number of pins needed by each memory controller.

The bottom part of Figure 10.2 shows a multicore chip with the non-last level caches kept coherent using a directory protocol. For illustration purpose, the figure shows L2 caches being such caches. There is an outer level cache, the L3 cache, that is physically distributed but is logically shared by all cores. In this case, when there is an L2 cache miss, the directory is looked up, and if the block is uncached, it will be retrieved from one of the L3 cache slices. Thus, it makes sense to co-locate the directory with the L3 cache slices and interleave addresses in the same way as the L3 cache slices. However, there is an additional question to consider. Here there is an opportunity to merge the directory with the L3 cache tag array. Essentially, each L3 cache tag array entry is augmented with directory information for the particular block the tag represents. A benefit of the merging is that one lookup can simultaneously determine the directory information of the block and at the same time determine whether the block is present in the L3 cache slice or not, which reduces the L2 cache miss latency as well as the L3 cache hit/miss latency. A drawback of the merging is that the directory can only keep track of as many blocks as the L3 cache (blocks that are not cached in the L3 cache have no directory entries). The drawback leads to a restriction in that the L3 cache must be inclusive of the L2 caches, because a block cached in the L2 must have a corresponding directory entry, and this requires the block to have a cache line reserved for it in the L3 cache.

Another issue is related to where the directory information is physically located. A directory may be implemented in a separate structure or embedded into the existing structure it is paired with. The former requires more engineering effort than the latter, but does not interfere with the capacity of the existing structure. For example, in the DSM example, the directory may be implemented as a separate DRAM structure. Alternatively, the directory can be allocated in a portion of the main memory. At boot time, the hardware sets aside a portion of memory so that it is managed by the coherence controller hardware and is invisible to the OS. The advantage of embedding the directory is that it is simple and can be supported without modifying the main memory. The disadvantage, however, is that accesses to the directory compete for main memory bandwidth with accesses to data. It is possible that this contention introduces a significant delay to data access and to directory access. Another approach is to keep the directory information in the same chip as the processor. The advantage is that accesses from the local processor can quickly determine whether the block can be fetched from local memory or from a remote cache, in contrast to spending a lot of time accessing an off-chip directory. The disadvantage is of course there is less die area available on chip for other uses.

■ *Did you know?*

Here are some examples of directory implementations.

In the IBM Power4 architecture [27], the directory information is kept on the processor chip. To reduce the size of the directory, the information kept in the directory only has one bit that indicates whether the block is only cached by the local processors (there are two processors in one chip), or possibly cached by other, remote, processors. If the block is only locally cached, a read or write request is processed locally. If, however, the block may be remotely cached, the directory information does not have sufficient information to tell which other processors may have a copy of the block. Thus, the request is broadcasted to all other processors. This increases traffic significantly when many blocks are shared by several processor chips. However, this is made rare by the virtue of (1) the multiprocessor system is targeted only for medium scale multiprocessor, and (2) most well-tuned programs have little data sharing between processors.

In the AMD Opteron system [4], the directory keeps the LLCs of multiple chips coherent. Instead of implementing a full blown directory, the system implements a directory with reduced functionality (referred to as a probe filter). A directory entry keeps the state of a cache block as well as one pointer (a limited pointer format) to a cache if the cache has the block in an exclusive or modified state. If a block is cached in a shared state, the system reverts to a broadcast protocol. The directory is embedded into the LLC structure, so that in a system with only one multicore chip, the unused directory does not create any space overheads. The directory takes up 2MB of the 6MB total capacity of the L3 cache. The directory only occupies space when multiple multicore chips are interconnected to form a larger system.

Similar trade offs can be inferred in the multicore organizations. For example, consider the non-LLCs kept coherent with a directory protocol. Consider a case where the directory is embedded into the L3 cache. One benefit is that no separate and dedicated directory structures are needed. Another benefit is flexibility: no overheads are incurred if cache coherence is not activated. Several drawbacks of embedding the directory in the L3 cache include: the directory access and L3 data cache access contend for access to the structure, loss of L3 cache capacity, and directory access may be slower than if it were implemented in a separate structure.

10.3 Basic Directory Cache Coherence Protocol

So far, we have discussed how a basic protocol works and what information needs to be kept in the directory. Now, we will look at implementation details of a directory cache coherence protocol, assuming an implementation for a DSM system (Figure 10.2). Note however that the directory protocol in other configurations will also operate similarly. The discussion will proceed in two steps. First, we will describe a working protocol, while leaving out discussion on some design choices that can be made and what implications the choices cause. After that, we will discuss the correctness and performance issues in more details.

To start off with a base coherence protocol, let us assume that the caches of all nodes use MESI states. Therefore, in the directory, we can keep the following states for each memory block:

1. **Exclusive or modified** (EM): the block is either cached in exclusive or modified state in only one cache.

2. **Shared** (S): the block is cached cleanly, possibly by multiple caches.

3. **Uncached** (U): the block is uncached or cached in invalid state.

Recall the directory's inability to distinguish between a block that is exclusively cached cleanly (in the exclusive state) or dirty (in the modified state). Hence, the directory lumps them together in the EM state.

The following request types are supported:

1. **Read**: read request from a processor.

2. **ReadX**: read exclusive (write) request from a processor that does not already have the block.

3. **Upgr**: request to upgrade the state of a block from shared to modified, made by a processor that already has the block in its cache.

4. **ReplyD**: reply from the home to the requestor containing the data value of a memory block.

5. **Reply**: reply from the home to the requestor *not* containing the data value of a memory block.

6. **Inv**: an invalidation request sent by the home node to caches.

7. **Int**: an intervention (downgrade to state shared) request sent by the home node to caches.

8. **Flush**: the owner of a cache block sends out its cached data block.

9. **InvAck**: acknowledgment of the receipt of an invalidation request.

10. **Ack**: acknowledgment of the receipt of non-invalidation messages.

The first three types of messages (Read, ReadX, and Upgr) are made by the requestor and sent to the home node of the data block, where its directory information resides. Read is a request to read from a block that is not found in the cache (a read miss), while ReadX and Upgr are requests to write to a block that is not found or found in the cache, respectively. The next two types of messages (ReplyD and Reply) are the response of the directory to requests made by the requestor node. The response may contain data (ReplyD) or only contain non-data information (Reply). The next two types of messages (Inv and Int) are messages sent by the home node to sharers (to invalidate them), or to an owner of a block (to downgrade its state to shared). The last three types of messages (Flush, InvAck, and Ack) are the response to Inv and Int messages to write-back/flush a dirty cache block, an acknowledgment of the receipt of an Inv message, or other types of messages. The Ack message here is broadly defined and can include various information that is needed.

Note that some of the messages can be combined into a single message, such as when the current owner of a block flushes the block as well as acknowledges an invalidation request. In this case, we will denote such a combined message as "Flush+InvAck".

The finite state machine corresponding to the coherence protocol employed at the directory is shown in Figure 10.3. The left hand side of the slash symbol ("/") is the request received from a processor by the directory, and the *sender* of the message (the requesting node) is shown in the parenthesis. The right hand side of the slash corresponds to the messages sent by the directory as a response to the request received from the processor. The coherence action in the directory that manipulates the sharing bit vector is not shown in the figure.

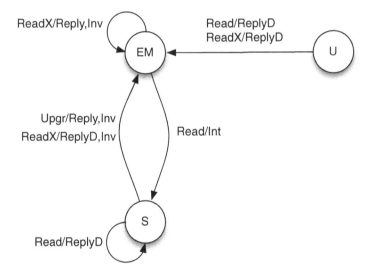

Figure 10.3: Simplified directory state finite state coherence protocol diagram.

Let us first consider when the directory state is uncached (U). If there is a read exclusive request, the directory fetches the block from the local memory and sends a data reply message to the requestor, and transitions to the EM state (it also sets the bit in the sharing bit vector that corresponds to the requesting node – not shown in the diagram). Similarly, if there is a read request, the directory fetches the block from local memory and sends a data reply to the requestor. The requestor will be the first sharer in the system, and the directory transitions to state EM.

When the directory state is shared, when there is a read request, the directory knows it has a valid block in the local memory. Thus, it replies with data to the requestor and updates the sharing vector accordingly. The directory state remains shared. If the request is read exclusive, the directory responds by sending the data value of the block to the requestor, and also invalidation messages to all current sharers. The data reply message sent to the requestor also includes the number of invalidation acknowledgments the requestor can expect to receive. The directory state transitions to EM. If it is an upgrade request, however, the directory sends invalidations to sharers, and a reply without data to the requestor.

Finally, when the directory state is EM, if a read request is received, then the new state will be shared, and an intervention request is sent to the owner of the block. The intervention request also contains the ID of the requestor so that the owner knows where to send the block. If a read exclusive request is received, then a new processor wants to write to the block, so the directory needs to send an invalidation to the current owner. The invalidation request also contains the ID of the requestor so that the owner knows where to send the block. Note that the block may be in either exclusive or modified state at the owner; the directory does not know which is the case. In either case, upon receiving intervention or invalidation, the owner must respond appropriately.

To illustrate the operation of the protocol, consider an example of a stream of memory accesses to a single memory block shown in Table 10.1, assuming a three-node multiprocessor in which each node has a processor, a cache, and a memory with a directory of all local memory blocks. We assume the directory format consists of the directory state and a full-bit sharing vector. The table shows requests made by various processors in the following format: Rx or Wx, where R stands for a read request, W stands for a write request, and x stands for the ID of the processor making the request. Messages generated as a result of the processor request are also shown, in the following format: Msgtype($Src \rightarrow Dest$).

Note that in this illustration, we assume that all messages that correspond to each request occur atomically, i.e., messages from different requests are not overlapped. Overlapping of messages from different requests can introduce potential correctness problems and must be handled correctly. They will be discussed in later sections. For now, we assume that requests are processed one at a time.

The example does not make any assumption on where the home of the block resides. Each time a message is sent from a processor to another processor or the home node, it is counted as one hop and is shown in one line. A message that cannot be sent before a prior message is received indicates message dependence, and they must be sent in two different hops. Messages that do not have dependence can be sent in parallel, denoted with the symbol "//" in the table.

Initially, the block is uncached, and hence the directory content indicates the uncached (U) state, and the full bit sharing vector has 0 in all bits. When processor P1 wants to read the block, it sends a read request to the home node (first hop). The home node checks the directory and finds that the block is uncached, hence it has the latest value of the block. It then sends a ReplyD message containing the data value of the block to P1. It also changes the state of the block to EM, with the sharing vector bit for P1 set to "1" (the sharing full-bit vector becomes "100").

Next, P1 wants to write to the block that it has just brought into its cache. It checks the state of the block, and since the block is in the exclusive state, it changes the state to modified and writes to the block silently, i.e., without sending any messages. The directory is unaware of this action, but it does not need to, because the directory state of the block is already EM.

When P3 wants to read from the block, it suffers a cache miss, and this causes a Read message to be sent to the home node. The home node checks its directory and finds that the state is EM and the block is exclusively cached by P1. Since it does not know whether the block is clean or dirty in P1, it assumes that the block is dirty and sends a intervention message to it. In the message, it includes the ID of P3 so that later P1 can send the data directly to P3. Home then includes P3 as a

Table 10.1: Illustration of directory-based coherence protocol operations.

Request	P1	P2	P3	Directory	Messages	#Hops
Initially	–	–	–	U, 000	–	
R1	E	–	–	EM, 100	Read(P1→H) ReplyD(H→P1)	2
W1	M	–	–	EM, 100	–	0
R3	S	–	S	S, 101	Read(P3→H) Int(H→P1) Flush(P1→H // P1→P3)	3

W3	I	–	M	EM, 001	Upgr(P3→H)
					 Reply(H→P3) // Inv(H→P1)
					 InvAck(P1→P3)
						3

R1	S	–	S	S, 101	Read(P1→H) Int(H→P3) Flush(P3→P1 // P3→H)	3
R3	S	–	S	S, 101	–	0
R2	S	S	S	S, 111	Read(P2→H) ReplyD(H→P2)	2

sharer by updating its sharing vector to "101". When P1 receives the intervention request, it sends its data block to P3 using the flush message. It downgrades its block state to shared. In MESI, the shared state implies a clean block, thus it also needs to send a separate flush message to the home node containing the data value of the block. The home node uses the flushed block to update the block in the local memory. This transaction proceeds in three hops: from P3 to home, home to P1, and P1 to home and P3.

After reading the block, P3 wants to write to it. It finds the block in the shared state in its cache, so it does not have permission to write to the block. Hence, it sends an upgrade request using the Upgr message to the home node. The home node finds that currently P1 also caches the block and must be invalidated. Thus, it sends an Inv message to P1. In parallel, it sends a reply to P3 to notify it to expect an invalidation acknowledgment from P1. Home also changes the directory state to EM, and removes P1 from its sharing vector, so the new sharing bit vector value is "001". When P1 receives the invalidation message from home, it invalidates its block and sends an invalidation acknowledgment message (InvAck) to P3. When P3 receives the InvAck from P1, it knows that it can now change its block state to modified and write to the block.

Later, P1 wants to read from the block that was just invalidated in the previous event. P1 suffers a cache miss as it finds the block in state invalid in its cache, so it sends out a Read message to home. Home finds the block is in state EM and the sharing vector indicates that P3 has the block. So it sends an intervention message to P3, and P3 responds by downgrading its cache state to shared and flushes the block to both P1 and home. Home changes the directory state to shared, updates the sharing vector to "101", and uses the flushed block to update the block value in the local memory.

When P3 wants to read from the block, it finds it in its cache in a shared state. This results in a cache hit, and no messages need to be sent.

Finally, P2 wants to read the block. It sends a read request to home. The directory state at home is shared, indicating that the block is clean. Hence, the home sends a ReplyD message containing the block that it fetches from its local memory.

Let us now compare the basic directory coherence protocol versus a broadcast coherence protocol. First, it is clearly more complicated, with more message types than in a bus-based multiprocessor, the maintenance of a directory at home nodes, and possible protocol races when multiple messages from different requests are overlapped. In addition, in a bus-based multiprocessor, all transactions only incur at most two hops (the request and subsequent reply on the bus), while directory coherence sometimes requires three-hop transactions. In addition, cache-to-cache transfer that can be employed in a bus-based multiprocessor cannot be applied with directory-based coherence. Since all read or write misses need to go to home, the fastest way to supply data is when the home has them in the local memory. In this case, no cache to cache transfer can be exploited.

10.4 Implementation Correctness and Performance

For our simple protocol we discussed in the previous section, we have assumed that (1) the directory state and its sharing vector reflects the most *up to date* state in which the block is cached, and (2) messages due to a request are processed atomically (without being overlapped with one another). In real systems, both assumptions do not necessarily apply. This results in various protocol races that need to be handled properly. Some of them can be handled relatively simply by the directory alone. But in other cases, the directory alone cannot handle them correctly. The behavior of the cache coherence controllers at each node must also be modified to aid the directory. We will now discuss how various races can be handled. Note that it is not the purpose of this chapter to exhaustively discuss all possible races. We will mostly focus on major races to give readers a flavor of the complexity in handling them.

10.4.1 Handling Races Due to Out-of-Sync Directory State

The reason why the directory state and cache states can get out of sync is because they are not updated in lock step, and some events in the caches are *never seen* by the directory state. For example, a block may be replaced from a cache, and the corresponding node is no longer a sharer. However, the directory does not see this event and still thinks that the node is a sharer of the block. Several *odd* situations can occur due to the directory having an inconsistent view of the cache states.

Consider when the directory thinks that a node is a sharer of a block, caching the block in a clean shared state. Let us call the node A. However, the block is replaced by the node A from its cache silently. When the directory receives a read exclusive request to the block from another node, it sends invalidation messages to all nodes that the directory thinks as sharers of the block, including node A. This results in a situation in which a node receives an invalidation message to a block that it no longer has in its cache. In this case, the correct response is to acknowledge the receipt of the invalidation by sending an invalidation acknowledgment message to the requester. No harm is done here since the intended final state for the block is invalid, and the block is already uncached (which is similar to being invalidated).

Another situation is when the directory thinks a node is already a sharer of a block, but the directory receives a read request from the node. This situation occurs because the node that kept the block in its cache has silently evicted the block, while the directory still thinks the node is a sharer.

When the node wants to read from the block, it suffers a read miss, and as a result, a read request is sent to the directory. Handling this case is also simple. The directory can reply with data to the requestor and keep the sharing bit vector unchanged, since the bit vector already reflects the node as a sharer.

When the directory indicates that a block is exclusively cached (the directory state is EM), similar odd situations can occur. For example, a Read or ReadX request may arrive at the directory from a node that the directory thinks as caching the block exclusively (in exclusive or modified state). In this case, apparently the node that owns the block has evicted the block. If the block was clean, no write back (or flush) had occurred, whereas if the block was dirty, the flush message has yet to reach the directory. The directory cannot just reply with data since it may not have the latest data. In contrast to the case in which the directory state is shared, with an EM state, the directory cannot reply with data just yet. However, it cannot just wait for the flushed block to arrive either because it may never come (the block might be clean and was evicted silently by the requestor while it was in the exclusive state). Therefore, this is not a problem that can be solved just by the protocol at the directory alone. The coherence controller at each processor node must also participate. In particular, when the processor evicts a dirty block and flushes the block to the main memory at the home node, it must keep track of whether the write back has been completed or not, with a structure called the *outstanding transaction buffer*. The home node must send an acknowledgment upon the receipt of a flush message. In addition, the coherence controller at the processor side must also delay Read or ReadX requests to a block that is being flushed, until it gets an acknowledgment from the directory that the flushed block has been received. This way, the directory will never see a Read/ReadX request to a block from a node that is still flushing it. Thus, when it receives a Read/ReadX request, the directory knows that it must be the case that the block was clean and evicted silently. Therefore, it can safely reply to the requestor with the data value of the block.

The finite state machine corresponding to the coherence protocol employed at the directory is shown in Figure 10.4. The left hand side of the slash symbol ("/") is the request received from the processor by the directory, and the *sender* of the message (the requesting node) is shown in the brackets. The right hand side of the slash is the messages sent by the directory as a response to the request received from the processor. The *destination* of the message is shown in the brackets. Only state transitions that are new compared to Figure 10.3 are labeled. The coherence action in the directory that manipulates the sharing bit vector is not shown in the figure.

Note that because the directory may be out-of-sync with the cache states, there may be requests arriving to the directory from the owner (i.e., the node that the directory thinks as caching a block in exclusive or modified state). In order to distinguish requests from the current owner versus from other processors, the EM state is split into two: EM_A which indicates that the directory thinks that the current owner is node A, and EM_B which indicates that the directory thinks that the current owner is node B. Nodes A and B can be any nodes as long as they are distinct from one another. When the current state is EM_A, how the protocol reacts depends on whether the request comes from the current owner (A) or from other nodes (B). Likewise, when the current state is EM_B, how the protocol reacts depends on whether the request comes from the current owner (B) or from other nodes (A). Since the EM state is now split into two, there are now two additional edges that represent transitions between the two EM states.

Since the processing of requests from a current sharer or from non-sharer nodes is the same, the shared state is not split into two.

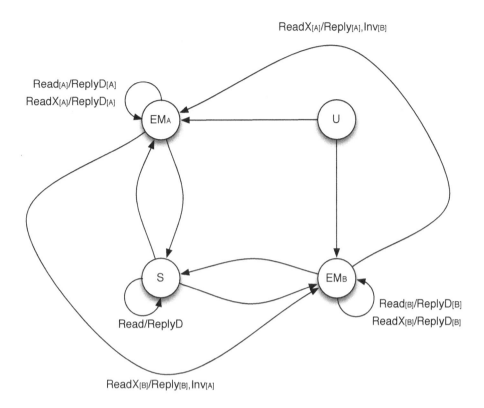

Figure 10.4: Simplified directory state finite state coherence protocol diagram, with modifications to handle out-of-sync view of cache states at the directory.

In the shared (S) state, now it is possible to receive a read request from the node that the directory thinks a sharer. Since the directory already recognizes the node as a sharer, it is correct to respond with the data block through a ReplyD message.

Suppose the directory state is EM_A (identical responses are produced when the state is EM_B). If a read request coming from a different node (B) is received, then the new state will be shared, and an intervention request is sent to the owner of the block (A). The intervention request also contains the ID of the requestor so that the owner knows where to send the block. If a read exclusive request from another node (B) is received, then the directory sends an invalidation message to the current owner (A), sends a reply message to B telling it to expect to receive a reply from A, and ownership transfer is indicated by transitioning from state EM_A to EM_B. The invalidation request also contains the ID of the requestor so that the owner knows where to send the block to. Note that the block may be in state either exclusive or modified at the owner; the directory does not know. In either case, upon receiving intervention or invalidation, the owner must respond appropriately.

Let us now discuss the new case that occurs due to the directory having an out-of-sync view of the cache states. When the state is EM_A, with an out-of-sync view of cache states, the directory may receive a read or read exclusive request from node A. This is because node A suffers a read or write miss after the clean block was silently evicted from its cache (if it had been dirty, the request would have been stalled at the requestor and instead the directory would receive a flush message from node A prior to receiving the read or read exclusive request). Since the directory already notes A as the owner of the block, it can simply react by replying with the requested data block.

Note that it is possible that a block cached in modified state is evicted without the knowledge of the directory. While the block is being written back to the directory, the node may suffer a read miss to the same block, and may send a read request to the directory. It is incorrect for the directory to reply with data in this case. However, this situation arises when the write back is not instantaneously received by the directory. So far, we assume the cache may get out of sync with the directory, but all transactions occur instanteneously. Thus, we defer discussing this case to the next section.

Overall, handling the out-of-sync view of the cache states at the directory can be accomplished by relatively simple modifications to the coherence protocol at the directory and and to each node's cache coherence controller.

10.4.2   Handling Races Due to Non-Instantaneous Processing of a Request

When messages that correspond to a request do not happen instantaneously, then it is possible for messages from two different requests to be overlapped. For example, a processor may try to read from a block and another processor may try to write to the block. Both the read and read exclusive requests to the same block may occur simultaneously in the system. If not handled correctly, overlapped processing of requests may produce incorrect results.

To illustrate the danger of not handling overlapped processing of requests correctly, let us consider one example, which is illustrated in Figure 10.5. Suppose that we have two nodes making requests to a single block: nodes A and B. Home node H keeps the directory information for the block. Let us assume that initially the block has a directory state shared. First, node A makes a read request (Step 1), and since the block is clean, the directory replies with the data (Step 2). Unfortunately, the ReplyD message is delayed in the network, e.g., due to traffic, link failure, etc. In the meantime, the directory sets the bit corresponding to A in its sharing bit vector to indicate that now A is a sharer of the block. Then, node B makes a read exclusive request to the directory (Step 3). Because the directory thinks that the block is cached by A, it sends an invalidation message to A (Step 4). The invalidation message arrives at A sooner than the data reply message that was sent earlier. This is a possibility in a network that allows messages between a pair of nodes to travel using different paths. Hence, the order in which messages are received may be different than the order in which they are sent.

Let us explore the situation in more detail. The problem that arises as a result of the race is with regard to how A should respond to the invalidation message that it receives. From the point of view of the directory, it saw the read request before it saw the read exclusive request. However, because the processing of the prior read request is not complete (A has not received its data reply yet) by the time the directory starts serving the next request, then the processing of both requests is overlapped. The desired outcome is for node A to see the same ordering of the requests as seen by the directory. However, instead, A receives the invalidation message before its data reply, the opposite order that the directory saw. Since A does not know the ordering that the directory saw, it does not know how to respond to the invalidation message.

Without overlapped request processing, when node A receives an invalidation message to a block that it cannot find in its cache, it knows that the invalidation is to a block that it already evicted (as discussed in Section 10.4.1). The correct response in this case is to acknowledge the receipt of the invalidation message because it no longer has the block, as if it has just invalidated

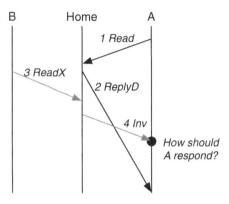

Figure 10.5: An example of a protocol race that arises from overlapped processing of requests. This race is called the *early invalidation race*.

the block. However, with overlapped request processing, receiving an invalidation message to an uncached block may be due to the early invalidation race shown in Figure 10.5. If it applies the same response (replying with an invalidation acknowledgment), the outcome is incorrect. When A acknowledges the invalidation message, it acts as if the write by B has fully propagated. But later, when A receives the data reply message (Circle 2), it places the block in its cache, and allows the processor to read from the block that is supposed to have been invalidated! The final outcome is that to the directory, the read request by A occurs before the write request by another node, while to node A, the write request by another node occurs before its read request.

How can we remedy this situation? The brute force approach will be just to avoid overlapped processing of multiple requests to a block altogether. This can be achieved by serializing the processing of requests at the home node. For example, the directory can require node A to acknowledge the receipt of the data reply it sent out. Before the directory receives this acknowledgment from A, it refuses to service other requests, for example by sending a negative acknowledgment (NACK) to B. Unfortunately, this serialization may significantly delay the processing of the read exclusive request from B and significantly degrade performance. Hence, we need a better solution that minimizes the serialization of request processing at the directory.

Approaches to Overlapping Request Processing

In order to figure out how much processing of requests can be overlapped at the directory, first we need to be able to distinguish when the processing of two requests is overlapped and when it is not. In other words, we need to know the start and end time of request processing. If the end time of the current request processing is greater than the start time of the next request, then their processing is overlapped; otherwise it is not. What is the start time and end time of request processing? It depends on the type of the request, and how the request is handled. Before going into a more specific answer, let us first consider the need to know which is the earlier request and which is the later request out of two requests to a single memory block.

In a bus-based multiprocessor system, the bus provides a medium that determines the order of two requests. Since all read misses and writes to a shared block must go to the bus, one request will be granted the bus sooner than the other, and, therefore, the bus access order provides a consistent view of the order of two requests as seen by all processors. In a directory multiprocessor, no medium is shared and visible by all processors. A request first needs to be sent from the requestor to the home node where the directory is kept. Since requests can be generated from different nodes, it is practically impossible to prevent different requests from being simultaneously issued by different nodes. Therefore, the time at which the requests are issued cannot be used for ordering the request. However, since all of the requests will eventually reach a single node (the home node), the home node can take the role of "deciding" the order of requests to a single memory block.

Relating back to determining when processing of a request starts and when it ends, we can now conclude that the processing of a request starts when the directory receives the request, and not when the request is sent by the requestor. Consider Figure 10.6, showing the processing of a read request. The top part of the figure shows a read request to a block that is clean, i.e., the home has the most up-to-date value of the block, hence, it can reply to the request with the data block. The bottom part of the figure shows a read request to a block that is exclusively cached by another node. In this case, the home responds by sending an intervention message to the current owner, which in turn responds by sending its block to the home (to update the copy at home) and to the requestor (so the requestor can obtain the latest copy as well).

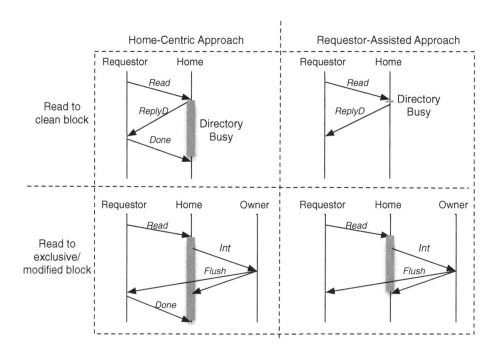

Figure 10.6: The processing period of a read request.

The important question is from the start of the processing of the request, when can the processing be considered complete? An intuitive answer to this is when all nodes involved in the processing have received the message they are supposed to receive, and they have notified home of the receipt of such messages. We refer to this as a *home-centric* scheme, since the home in the end decides when the processing of request is completed. The completion of request processing for the home-centric scheme is shown in the dashed line in Figure 10.6. The drawback of the home-centric scheme is that the processing period is long. The home must wait until the requestor has sent an acknowledgment ("done") of the relevant message before considering the processing is complete. In the mean time, it cannot serve a new request. Such a lengthy processing period and serialization can seriously degrade performance. Hence, a scheme that minimizes the processing period is needed.

An alternative scheme is to use the requestor's help to ensure the ordering of request processing. Note that without modifications at the requestor's cache coherence controller, the protocol race illustrated in Figure 10.5 will occur instead with this scheme. At the requestor, we must now require the coherence controller to maintain an *outstanding transaction buffer* which keeps track of requests that the node has sent but has not received a response yet. For example, if a node has sent a read request to home, it will keep track of the request in the buffer. If it is the first request that the directory decides to process, the node can expect to receive a data reply from home. Otherwise, if the directory is already processing another request, it defers processing this request. The requestor will get a NACK message instead. Therefore, the requestor must wait until the reply (either data or NACK) arrives. If, instead of such reply, it gets another type of message, then it can conclude that there has been a protocol race. It should not handle such a message until either the data reply or NACK is received. Hence, it must keep a buffer that can hold messages that it cannot serve right away. While this *requestor-assisted* scheme introduces extra hardware cost at the cache coherence controller of each node, it enables the home to complete request processing much sooner than in the home-centric scheme. For example, for the read to a clean block request, as soon as the directory sets the sharing bit for the requestor, changes the state if necessary, and sends a data reply message to the requestor, the request processing can be considered complete (Figure 10.6).

For a read request to a block in state EM, the processing period is different because the final state at the directory is shared, but to be in the shared state, the directory must have a clean copy. Therefore, even for the requestor-assisted scheme, the request processing is considered complete only when the home node receives the flush message from the current owner. At that time, the home node can update its copy, and with a clean copy, it can start processing new requests. Note that since the processing in this case is not instantaneous, the directory must keep track of the entire processing period so that it can either buffer new requests and serve them later, or reply with NACKs to new requests so that the requestor can try them at a later time. In order to keep track of the ongoing processing period, the directory state can transition to a special state referred to as the *transient* or *busy* state. A transient state is needed to serve a read request to a block in state EM, but not needed for a read request to a block in the uncached or shared state since the processing ends instantaneously (Figure 10.6).

Figure 10.7 shows the processing period of a read exclusive request for both the home-centric and requestor-assisted scheme. The top part of the figure shows a read exclusive request to a block that is currently uncached. The home responds to this request by sending a data reply message. The second part of the figure shows a read exclusive request to a block that is currently in state shared in the directory. The home responds to this request by sending invalidation messages to all sharers, which in turn send invalidation acknowledgment messages to the requestor. The third part of the figure (without WB race) shows a read exclusive request to a block that is exclusively cached by another node (the directory state is EM). The home responds to this request by sending an invalidation message to the owner, which in turn responds by supplying data to the requestor. The bottom part of the figure (with WB race) will be elaborated on later.

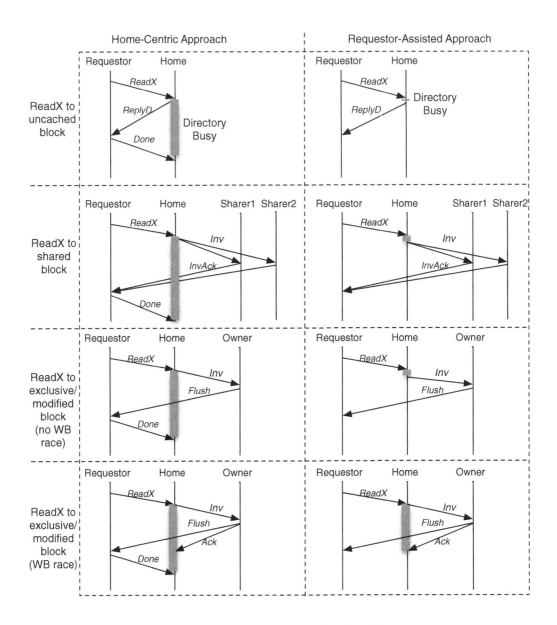

Figure 10.7: The processing period of a ReadX request.

For the home-centric scheme, the processing of a request is considered complete when the requestor has received all messages that it waits for, and after the home receives an acknowledgment ("Done") from the requestor of the receipt of such messages. Note that the home-centric scheme delays the processing of a new request significantly, since the processing involves several steps and potentially a large number of nodes. Thus, a requestor-assisted scheme is again a more attractive solution. In the requestor-assisted scheme, the read exclusive request is complete immediately after the directory has modified its state and sharing vector to reflect the requestor as the new owner of the block, and also after the directory has sent the data reply or invalidation messages to current sharers or to the current owner. As before, to support the requestor-assisted scheme, the cache coherence controller at each node must have an ability to defer the processing of an incoming message until it receives the response message that corresponds to its outstanding request.

For the first case (ReadX to uncached block), it must defer the processing of a message other than the data reply or NACK from the home node. For the second case (ReadX to shared block), it must wait until it gets a NACK from the home node, or an invalidation acknowledgment (InvAck) from all current sharers. How can the requestor know how many invalidation acknowledgment messages to expect? While not shown in the figure, this requires the home node to send a reply message to the requestor containing the number of sharers it finds in the sharing bit vector. For the third case (ReadX to a block in EM state), the requestor should wait until it either gets a NACK or data flush from the current owner of the block. Note that overall, the requestor does not know in advance which case it will encounter at the directory. Hence, after making a read exclusive request, it can wait until it gets a NACK, a data reply, or a reply from the home that indicates it should wait for an InvAck or Flush from another node. All other message types must be deferred.

Note, however, for the last case, there is an additional complexity. We have treated the protocol race due to early eviction write backs (Section 10.4.1) and due to overlapped processing separately, where in reality both can occur simultaneously. While there are several such possible cases, we will discuss one of them (related to the case shown at the bottom of Figure 10.7). The race occurs when the home sends an invalidation message to the current owner based on its knowledge about the node being the owner of the block, while the owner has actually evicted the block. In that case, when the owner receives an invalidation message from home, it no longer has the block as it has written the block back (or evicted it silently if it was clean). Hence, it cannot supply the block to the requestor. In such a case, the home must supply the block to the requestor when it receives the flushed block. Therefore, it cannot consider the processing complete until after it receives either the acknowledgment from the owner or the written back block from the owner, because it may still need to send the block to the requestor. [1]

Finally, to handle the long processing periods in several cases, the directory state needs to be augmented with transient states. One state is needed for handling the read to a block in EM state. Since the final directory state is shared, we will refer to this transient state as $EM2S$ state. Another state is needed for handling a read exclusive request to a block in EM state. Since the initial state is EM and the final state is also EM (but with a different owner), we refer to this state as EM_A2EM_B or EM_B2EM_A state. Adding these transient states to the state diagram of the directory coherence protocol shown in Figure 10.4 results in a more complete protocol shown as follows in Figure 10.8.

In the figure, transient states are shown in rectangles. New transitions into and out of transient states are shown in dashed lines, and the events that trigger such transitions are shown as labels of the dashed lines. To reduce clutter, labels for other state transitions are not shown (they have been shown in Figure 10.4).

Note that in the EM_A state, if there is a read request by a different node (denoted by notA), the directory state transitions to a transient state EM_A2S. In this state, the processing of the request is considered not complete, so any new requests to this memory block are responded to with a NACK message. When the flush message by node A is received by the home, the directory considers the

---

[1] In the Origin 2000 coherence protocol, rather than waiting for the owner's reply, the home node speculatively sends the block to the requestor as soon as it receives the ReadX request. This way, if a clean block was evicted early, the owner can notify the requestor that it no longer has the block. At that time, the requestor already has the valid copy of the block that the home sent earlier. It does not need to suffer from an additional latency for waiting the home node to send the block.

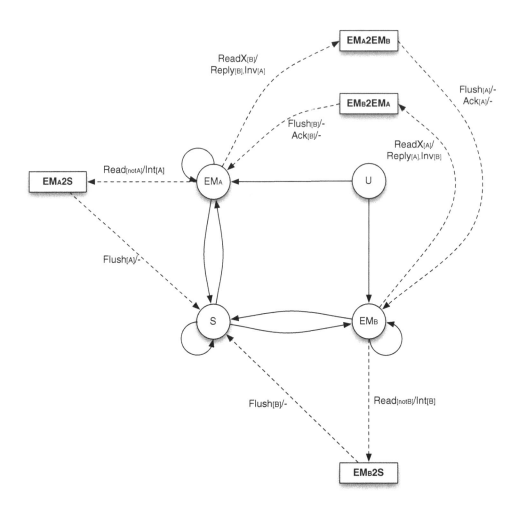

Figure 10.8: A more complete directory state finite state coherence protocol diagram, showing the handling of several protocol races.

request complete, and, hence, the state transitions out of the transient state into the shared state. A similar response occurs when the starting state is EM_B instead.

If while in the EM_A state, a read-exclusive request by a different node arrives at the directory, the directory state transitions to a transient state $EMA2EMB$. In this state, the processing of the request is considered not complete, so any new requests to this memory block are responded to with a NACK message. When the flush message by node A is received by the home (indicating that A wrote back the block early before it received the invalidation message), the directory considers the request as complete and hence the state transitions out of the transient state to the EM_B state. Alternatively, when the acknowledgment message by node B is received by the home (indicating the receipt of the invalidation message, including when B had silently evicted the clean block before it received the invalidation message), the directory considers the request as complete and hence the state transitions out of the transient state into the EM_B state. A similar response occurs when the starting state is EM_B instead.

Overall, we have shown one example of how a directory coherence protocol is implemented, including how an important subset of protocol races are handled. Some protocol races are omitted from the discussion, such as when a write back occurs when the directory is in a transient state. The approach discussed uses a combination of a limited use of requestor-assisted approach relies on using negative acknowledgment. We note that this is not the only possible approach. A different protocol may be constructed when we rely more on the home-centric approach, with the obvious implication of the longer time to process a request. Alternatively, a different protocol may also be constructed when we rely even more on requestor-assisted approach. This may eliminate the transient states, and the negative acknowledgments that correspond to these states. The right choice depends on many parameters, such as the throughput of the node coherence controller, and the availability of bandwidth interconnecting the processors.

■ *Did you know?*

Here are some examples of actual directory coherence protocol implementations. The SGI Origin 2000 [38] system uses a combination of a limited use of requestor-assisted approach and negative acknowledgment, similar to what was covered in the preceding discussion.

One design example that took a more extreme requestor-assisted scheme is the AlphaServer GS320 system [19]. It removes the transient states and negative acknowledgments associated with them by relying on the requestor to correctly order the processing of its request with other requests. A good discussion on the benefits and drawbacks of these approach can be found in [12].

The types of protocol races that can occur also depend on the property of the interconnection network. If the network guarantees that two messages sent by a node to the same destination node arrive in the same order as they were sent, there are fewer cases of protocol races. For example, the race illustrated in Figure 10.5 cannot occur because the invalidation message will not arrive at node A before the data reply message arrives at node A. But races due to an out-of-sync view of cache states at the directory remain and need to be handled correctly.

10.4.3 Write Propagation and Transaction Serialization

In this section, we will discuss the reasoning behind the correctness of the invalidation-based directory coherence that was discussed in the previous section. First, recall that there are two requirements for supporting a correct coherence protocol: *write propagation*, which allows a write to propagate the new value written, and *transaction serialization*, which ensures that two writes are seen in the same order by all processors.

As with a bus-based multiprocessor, ensuring write propagation is simply achieved using the invalidation protocol. When a processor wants to write a block, it sends a ReadX or Upgr request to home, which in response sends invalidations to all other sharers. This forces them to suffer a cache miss when they try to access the block in the future. In addition, on a cache miss to a recently-invalidated block, the directory finds the most recent copy of the block by by looking up its state and the sharing vector, and if the block is dirty, Home requests the processor that has the block to supply the block to the requesting processor.

Transaction serialization is a subset of the issue of avoiding overlapped request processing, which in this case, involves the processing of two requests where at least one of them is a write request. With the home-centric approach, the overlapping is avoided completely at the home node. With the requestor-assisted approach, the overlapping is avoided by the cooperation of the home and the requestor. Figure 10.9 illustrates the case in which three nodes (A, B, and C) want to write to a single block. Each of them issues a ReadX request to home. Recall that the processing period for such a request at home is from the time home receives the request until home obtains an acknowledgment message from the current owner (the bottom part of Figure 10.7). Thus, in this case, while the directory is still processing the ReadX request from A, and has not received the acknowledgment message from node O (current owner), the directory state enters a transient state and either sends NACKs to incoming requests (from B and C) or buffer them for later processing.

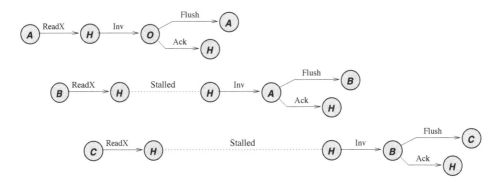

Figure 10.9: Write serialization with a requestor-assisted scheme.

Thus, ReadX from B cannot be processed until the home gets an acknowledgment message from O, at which time the ReadX from A is considered complete. Then, while the ReadX request from B is served, the directory again reenters a transient state and defers the processing of the ReadX request from C, until an acknowledgment is received from A. At that time, the processing of the ReadX request from B is considered complete. Only then, the ReadX request from C can be processed.

> ■ *Did you know?*
>
>   An interesting alternative for handling coherence protocol races and enforcing write serialization is through the use of token coherence [40]. In a token coherence protocol scheme, each block is associated with a limited number of tokens equaling the number of nodes in the system. Each operation is allowed to proceed if it has obtained a sufficient number of tokens. A read operation requires only one token, but a write operation requires all tokens before it can proceed. With token coherence, protocol races manifest in some operations not obtaining all the tokens they need. For example, if there are two write operations that are overlapped, both writes may not get a sufficient number of tokens to proceed, hence they fail and retry. In essence, handling races becomes simpler but there is a possibility of starvation in which nodes keep failing their operations and keep retrying. Hence, there needs to be a mechanism to detect a repeated failure and arbitrate competing operations to guarantee forward progress.

Note, however, that the requestor must still assist home in avoiding ReadX request processing overlap. For example, the flush message sent by node O to node A may arrive later than the invalidation message sent by home to A when home is processing the ReadX from B. Consequently, in a requestor-assisted approach, node A defers the processing the invalidation message until after the flush message from O is received. Similarly, when the ReadX of B is being processed, B defers processing the invalidation message from home until after it receives the flush message from A; when the ReadX of C is being processed, C defers processing the invalidation message from home until after it receives the flush message from B; and so on.

10.4.4 Synchronization Support

Synchronization support in a DSM system is similar to that in a bus-based multiprocessor, which at least includes some kind of atomic memory operations, which are implemented on top of the coherence protocol.

Atomic operations are easy to support with the ability of the directory to avoid overlapped request processing utilizing transient states. For example, consider a system that does not provide an LL/SC instruction pair. To implement an atomic read-write-modify sequence, the node can send a special request to the directory. Upon the receipt of this request, the directory can invalidate all sharers and enter a transient state. During this time, all new requests to the block, including ones due to atomic operations, are negative acknowledged. When the requesting processor has received all invalidation acknowledgments, it performs the operation. After the operation is completed, it can send another message to home signaling that its operation is completed. Having received this message, the directory knows that the operation has completed atomically, hence the directory state can transition out of the transient state to an EM state. It can then serve new requests. Using such a mechanism, we can ensure the processing of operations are not overlapped with one another, hence ensuring atomicity.

If an LL/SC instruction pair is supported, then no special requests or a transient state are needed at the directory. All the directory needs to do is just to perform its normal cache coherence protocol processing.

Interestingly, however, a DSM system can provide an opportunity to minimize the number of invalidations by performing an atomic operation locally (*in-memory*). To achieve this, first the synchronization variables must be placed in an uncacheable page, so that they are never cached by the nodes. Then, an atomic operation executed by a node incurs a special message to the directory that includes the type of operation to be performed and the address for which it is to be performed. The directory can fetch the block, perform the operation, and place the block back in memory. If there are multiple such requests, the directory performs them one at a time sequentially. Such in-memory synchronization greatly limits the amount of traffic generated on a highly-contested synchronization, since each atomic operation no longer generates invalidation messages. The drawback of in-memory synchronization is that in the event of low contention, a cacheable synchronization variable may perform better. Moreover, when the synchronization variable has strong temporal locality, such as when a thread repeatedly acquires and releases a lock without interference from other threads, a cacheable synchronization variable will perform better.

Without an in-memory atomic operation, however, the array-based queuing lock (ABQL) will generate less traffic than other schemes for highly contended locks, at the expense of higher uncontended synchronization latency.

> ■ *Did you know?*
>
> An in-memory synchronization mechanism was supported in the SGI Origin2000
> distributed shared memory multiprocessor [38], which at that time (in 1998) was the
> largest shared memory multiprocessor system ever made, with 128 processors. A
> highly-contended cacheable synchronization can generate, in the worst case, a very
> high amount of coherence traffic in such a large system. Hence, an in-memory syn-
> chronization mechanism was provided.

Finally, centralized barrier implementations can become expensive quite quickly as the size of DSM increases, both due to the increasing number of nodes that must be invalidated, and due to the increasing distance between nodes where invalidation messages must travel. Therefore, a special barrier network becomes more appealing (Section 8.2.3).

10.4.5   Memory Consistency Models

To support sequential consistency (SC), memory accesses coming out of a node must be issued and completed in strict program order, i.e., the start of a read/write (to any address) must be after the completion of the previous read/write (to any address). Detecting the completion of a memory access is the primary challenge in enforcing SC. The completion of a read is simply when the data that needs to be read is returned to the processor from the cache. The completion of a write can be detected when all sharers have sent acknowledgment of the receipt of invalidation messages. Since the requestor eventually has to be notified of the completion of the write (so that it can write to the block and start processing younger requests), it makes sense to collect the invalidation acknowledgments at the requestor directly, rather than at the home which still has to send a message to the requestor after they are fully collected. As described in Chapter 9, the performance of SC can be improved by using load prefetching (so that a read can likely complete faster by finding the data in the cache), and by using read-exclusive prefetching (so that a write is likely to have the block already cached in an exclusive state and can complete faster). In addition, load speculation can be employed. In a DSM system, those optimizations apply as well.

Relaxed consistency models improve the performance of SC by allowing memory accesses to be overlapped and occur out of program order. The larger the DSM system, the larger the advantage of relaxed consistency models over SC, due to higher latencies to process requests. With higher latencies due to the distance between nodes, it is more important to hide them by overlapping their execution.

10.5   Contemporary Design Issues

10.5.1   Dealing with Imprecise Directory Information

One of the key problems with traditional directory coherence protocols is stale information, where many directory entries do not have the most up to date information as to which caches keep a copy of a block. More specifically, the sharing vector field of the directory may indicate a block is stored by a cache even when the cache has evicted the block a long time ago. The problem arises because cache blocks that are clean (unmodified) are usually evicted silently from the cache, without notifying the directory. However, fixing the problem by notifying the directory of each clean bock eviction is expensive because it will result in a large increase in traffic, since most blocks evicted from the cache are clean. Thus, there is a significant trade-off that is fundamentally difficult to reconcile.

What problems arise from stale directory information? There are four significant problems. Figure 10.10 illustrates the inefficiency that arises from stale information. It shows three nodes C1, C2, and C3 and a directory that keeps information of what blocks are being cached in a multicore chip. The example applies to a multicore system where the directory keeps non-LLCs coherent using a directory embedded at the LLC, or a multi chip system where the directory keeps LLCs between chips coherent using a directory. For illustration purposes, let us assume the directory colocated with the on-chip memory controllers. Initially, the directory information is accurate, it depicts that block A is cached in C2 in an exclusive state, B is cached in C2 and C3 in a shared state, C is cached C2 in a shared state, and D is cached in C3 in a shared state. Over time, however, the directory information becomes stale, because evictions in the caches do not notify the directory. For example, C2 evicts block B (Step 1), without notifying the directory, because from the point of view of C2, the block B is clean and thus can be evicted silently. Next, C3 also evicts block B (Step 2) and block D (Step 3), for the same reason. At this point, the directory contain stale information for both block B and D.

The first problem with stale directory information is additional latency and power consumption for locating a data block. Suppose that a core in C1 suffers a cache miss and requests a read access to block C from the directory (Step 4). There are three choices of how the directory can respond. One choice is for the directory to assume its information is stale and fetch the data block from the memory controller (Step 5). The second choice is for the directory to assume its information is valid and forward the request to the tile it believes to be caching the block. The third choice is to hedge by performing both actions (forwarding the read and simultaneously fetching the block from memory). Steps 4 and 5 illustrate the first choice. The drawbacks of this choice is that we waste a lot of power and latency by fetching from off-chip memory if data is actually available on chip (in C2). However, the second choice is also risky because the directory information may be stale. This is illustrated in Steps 6–9. In this alternative strategy, a read miss request by C1 to block D happens (Step 6). Speculating that the directory information is up to date, the read is forwarded to C3 (Step 7). However, C3 no longer has the block as it has evicted it earlier (Step 3), so it responds with NoData (Step 8). At this point, the directory realizes its stale information, updates it, and fetches the block from the memory (Step 9). However, the damage, in terms of wasted latency and power, is already done. The final strategy of fetching from memory and forwarding the request simultaneously does not improve energy efficiency, as the reduced latency comes at the expense of significantly increased energy consumption.

The second problem is the directory unnecessarily occupies a large storage overhead, because some directory entries which are no longer needed (because the corresponding memory blocks are no longer cached) occupy space in the directory. [2] With an up-to-date directory information, the directory can be provisioned with a smaller number of entries to achieve the same performance, since entries containing uncached blocks can simply be dropped off.

The third problem is the replacement policy for directory entries perform sub-optimally due to relying on stale information. For example, suppose that the directory is full. There is a request from

---

[2]For example, even an abbreviated directory format (with some fields omitted) used in the recent AMD Opteron multicore processor occupies 2MB of the 6MB last level cache [4].

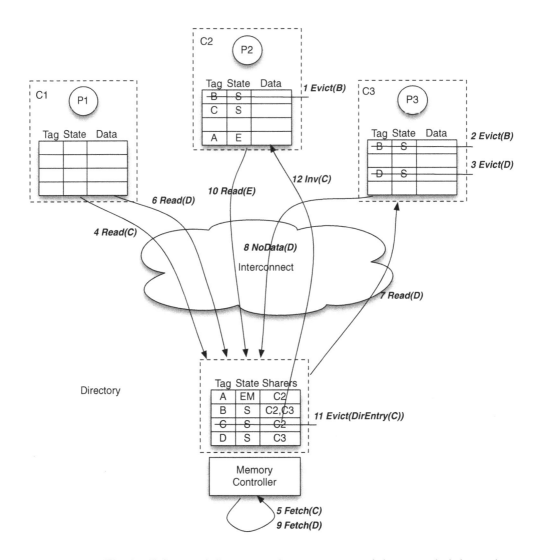

Figure 10.10: The inefficiency of directory coherence protocol due to stale information.

C2 for reading block E (Step 10). Since the directory has no information on block E, it must evict an existing entry and insert a new entry. If the directory does not allow overflow, when an existing entry is evicted, the block must be invalidated from all caches that are indicated in the list of sharers. Since invalidations can result in expensive future cache misses, a good eviction policy may be to choose a victim entry with the fewest number of sharers. Unfortunately, due to stale information, the entry with the fewest sharers may turn out to correspond to a block that is still cached. As an illustration, Figure 10.10 shows that block C has the fewest sharers, which is selected to be evicted (Step 11), and the eviction invalidates block C from C2 (Step 12). If the block is be needed by the core in C2, the core will suffer a cache miss when it accesses the block. In contrast, block B is listed in the directory as being shared by two tiles (C2 and C3), when in fact is no longer cached by either C2 and C3. If it were block B that were selected for eviction, there would not be any performance penalty as the block is no longer cached anywhere.

The fourth problem is excessive invalidation traffic. A write request to the directory must assume that all nodes recorded by the directory as potentially keeping a copy of the block must be invalidated. The invalidation messages that are sent to these nodes could have been avoided if the directory had up-to-date information that all or some of the nodes no longer keep a copy of the block.

■ *Did you know?*

One way the problem of stale directory information is addressed in the AMD Opteron system is by using two methods: not notifying the directory when clean blocks are evicted (incurring the four drawbacks discussed above) or notifying the directory (at the expense of increase in traffic). More specifically:

1. *For a block with E, M, or O state in the cache (correspondingly, EM or O state in the directory), its eviction from the cache must notify the directory.*

2. *For a block with S state in the cache (correspondingly, S state in the directory), its eviction is silent and does not notify the directory.*

3. *A request to a block in state S results in fetching data from the memory, regardless of whether the block is cached on chip or not.*

4. *A directory eviction policy attempts to, as quoted from [4], "avoid victimizing lines that are cached in many CPUs to reduce CPU-side cache perturbation resulting from directory downgrades."*

The system enforces non-stale information for certain states (EM, O, and S1) but not for the S state. Point 1 achieves the non-stale information at the expense of significantly increased traffic to the directory. This increases traffic by 66% according to AMD's own estimate, although the reduction in subsequent traffic needed to locate the block offsets it. Point 2 means that stale information persists for blocks in the S state, and is handled in Point 3 by fetching data block from memory (even though it is possible the block is cached on chip), wasting energy and latency. Finally, Point 4 prioritize evicting blocks that are listed to have few sharers rather than many sharers, regardless of whether the directory information is stale or not.

There are several possible solutions to the problem of stale directory information. One solution is to send a notification message even when a clean block is evicted. However, this would increase traffic substantially. An eviction occurs as a result of processing a cache miss. If a cache miss brings in 64 bytes of data, the resulting eviction requires at least a message the size of the evicted block address, e.g., 8 bytes for a 64-bit address. This results in increasing traffic by roughly $\frac{8}{64} = 12.5\%$. To reduce the amount of traffic overhead, it is possible to aggregate eviction notification messages of several blocks into a single message [56].

For example, Table 10.2 shows how five blocks being evicted can consume different amounts of traffic depending on whether we aggregate and how we aggregate eviction messages. For simplicity, the example in the table only includes the address component of the message (in reality, 1-2 bytes are added to each message to encode other information such as packet header, command type, error detection/correction). The message size assumes 42-bit physical address with 64 byte block size. The table shows that if each block eviction sends a message to the directory, five messages are sent with a total traffic of 22.5 bytes. If these five messages are aggregated into one eviction notification message, the total message size drops significantly, to 6 bytes (with bitmap format) or 6.5 bytes (with pointer format).

Table 10.2: Comparing the size of eviction messages for three schemes: per-block eviction message vs. eviction message aggregation using the bitmap format and pointer format.

Evicted block addresses	Size of eviction message(s)		
	Trad Dir One Blk/Msg	Msg Aggregation (This Invention)	
		Bitmap Format	Pointer Format
4C5FA7A03	4.5B	4C5FA7A0 + 1001001000011000	4C5FA7A0 + 3 + 4 + 9 + C + F
4C5FA7A04	4.5B		
4C5FA7A09	4.5B		
4C5FA7A0C	4.5B		
4C5FA7A0F	4.5B		
TOTAL	22.5B	6B	6.5B

There are two possible formats: bitmap and pointer. In the bitmap format, the root of the address (4C5FA7A0) is encoded, representing a region of 1KB in size, consisting of 16 blocks. To represent which block in the region has been evicted from the cache, we can use a 16-bit bitmap, with the appropriate bit set to 1 to represent the evicted block, and remaining bits are reset to 0. Since five blocks are evicted, there are five '1' bits in the bitmap (i.e., a popcount of five). The message size after aggregation is 4 bytes (root) + 2 bytes (bitmap) = 6 bytes. The next possible format is the pointer format. In the pointer format, the bitmap is replaced by the list of binary values of the block addresses that share the common root. Since five blocks are replaced, each block requires 4 bits, the total message size becomes 4 bytes (root) + 5 blocks * 4 bits/block (pointer) = 6.5 bytes. In this example, message aggregation cuts down the message size (and hence traffic and traffic-related energy use) by 73% and 71%, respectively.

Message aggregation can be achieved using a table that keeps region tag addresses and bitmap of blocks that are recently evicted in the region. When a region has accumulated sufficient number of evictions or when the table runs out of space and has to evict a region information, an eviction notification message for the region can be formed and sent to the directory. At the time of eviction notification message formation, a pointer or bitmap format can be selected based on whichever uses a smaller message size. The region size determines the effectiveness of eviction message aggregation.

Another possible solution to the stale directory information is to employ a predictor at the directory which predicts when an entry is likely to have become stale [54]. The principle behind such a predictor is that when the number of cache misses from a particular LLC has exceeded its size since time t_0, then it is likely that any directory blocks accessed at or before time t_0 will be stale, because the block involved is likely to have been evicted from the cache. Such a time threshold is useful when deciding whether to deploy a late fetch policy (if the directory information is likely to be still fresh) or early fetch policy (if the directory information is likely to be stale). The directory aging threshold can also be useful for selecting a directory entry to evict to make room for a new entry. A stale entry can be prioritized for eviction, although since the prediction is not guaranteed to be correct at all times, invalidation messages still need to be sent to (potentially stale) sharers.

10.5.2 Granularity of Coherence

So far we have assumed that coherence is tracked in the directory at the granularity of cache block size, typically 64 or 128 bytes. This makes management of coherence simpler as coherence management unit and cache management unit coincide. While convenient, it is not necessary for the coherence management to be performed at the cache block size. We can decrease or increase the size of data tracked by the cache coherence protocol. Decreasing the coherence management unit size requires a cache block to be divided into sub-blocks, where each sub-block has its own coherence state. This increases directory space overheads and complicates the protocol, but with a potential benefit of decreasing the occurrence of false sharing. However, increasing the coherence management unit size is simpler to do, and there are good cases supporting it. First, there are cases where a large region of data, especially at the unit of page size, has the same access behavior, for example a page may contain read only data. A page may also contain data that is read/written by only one thread (except when the thread migrates to another processor which produces a situation where data seems shared between two caches). Some pages definitely will not exhibit uniform access behavior, so for them coherence should still be tracked at a block level. However, for pages with uniform behavior, there are advantages of tracking their coherence at the page level. Let us review some of its benefits.

For a broadcast coherence protocol, a benefit of tracking coherence at a region/page level is avoidance of broadcast or snooping [9]. For example, suppose a cache has obtained a region in an exclusive state, but only a few blocks of that page currently reside in its cache. When the cache misses on a block of that page, a non-broadcast or non-snoop read request can be sent to an outer cache or memory directly. For a directory protocol, avoidance of broadcast is not an advantage since the directory already has a role of avoiding broadcast. However, there are other unique advantages.

We will discuss a scheme from [55], illustrated in Figure 10.11. A region state may be one of the following: private read (PR) indicates a region where blocks may be read by a single cache, private read/write (PW) indicates a region where blocks may be read/written by a single cache, shared read (SR) indicates a region where blocks may be shared by multiple caches in a read state, or mixed (MX) state for all other cases. A cache obtains a region in a PR state when it suffers a cache miss to a region which consists of individual blocks that are uncached or in an exclusive state. A cache obtains a region in a PW state when it suffers a cache miss to a region which consists of individual blocks that are uncached, in exclusive or modified states. A cache obtains a region in a SR state when it suffers a cache miss to a region which contain at least one individual block that is in a shared state, with the remaining blocks uncached or in exclusive. Various events may lead to a state transition as appropriate, for example an intervention to a region in a PR state causes a transition to an SR state, a write or read exclusive request to a block belonging in a region in a PR state transitions the region state to PW, etc.

Suppose that initially regions A and B are cached in various nodes with individual blocks cached in various states or are uncached, for example block B.1 of region B is cached in C2 in a shared state while block B.5 of region B is cached in C2 in an exclusive state. This is shown in Figure 10.11. The figure shows that each node keeps a region tag (RT) as well as a regular cache tag, and the directory includes a region directory as well as a block directory.

Suppose C1 reads a block A.3 (Step 1). Without a region tag, the request would be sent to the directory. With a region tag, region A has been acquired by C1 with a private read/write permission, hence, C1 knows that no other nodes has a copy of block A.3. Thus, C1 can directly send the read

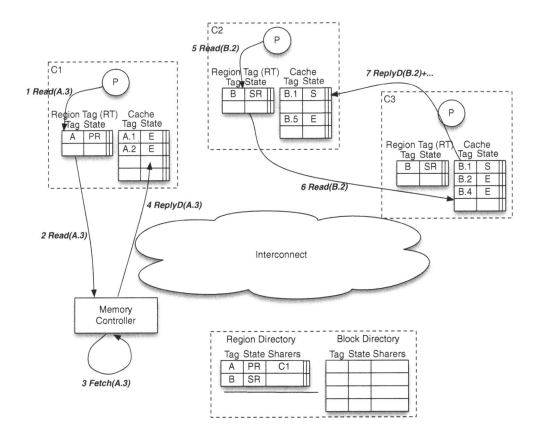

Figure 10.11: Benefits of region directory coherence protocol.

request to the memory controller (Step 2), which fetches the block directly (Step 3) and supplies it to C1's cache (Step 4). Directory lookup is completely avoided in this case, giving a saving in latency and power consumption.

In another example, suppose C2 wants to read block B.2 of region B (Step 5). Without the region protocol, it would have sent the request to the directory. Instead, it looks up its region tag and discovers that it has acquired region B a shared, but read-only permission. There is a unique opportunity for optimization which will be referred to as *direct fetching*, which is a mechanism for a node to directly fetch data from another node without involving the directory. In the Figure 10.11 example, suppose that node C2 makes a prediction that node C3 may have the block B.2. This initial prediction may be made by inquiring the directory or through other prediction mechanisms. Node C2 sends a read request directly to C3 (Step 6). C3 looks up its cache and finds block B.2, changes its state to shared, and replies with the block B.2 (Step 7). Direct fetching avoids directory lookup and saves latency and power consumption.

One challenge with direct fetching is how to predict what blocks are likely present in another cache. As discussed above, the initial direct fetch can be made after getting information from the directory. For subsequent direct fetches to blocks in the same region, we can let the cache that supplies the initial data block to piggyback the information that indicates other blocks in that region that are currently cached. For example, in Step 7, C3 may send a bit vector that indicates what other blocks of region B it has in its cache. C2 can use this bit vector to make a decision of whether to employ direct fetching requests to C3 in the case the bit vector indicates C3 has the block, or issues a read request to the memory controller if the bit vector indicates C3 does not have the block, or issues a read request to the directory, relying on a regular block protocol.

Another possible optimization is bulk transfer. For example, if C2 needs several blocks in a region, it can make a bulk direct fetch request, and C3 can reply with a group of blocks that it can supply from that region. Bulk fetching and transfer may be especially useful when a regular processor dispatches a task to an accelerator integrated into the system bus in a heterogeneous multicore chip (an example of such a system is IBM Power-EN). Typically an accelerator, such as packet processing engine or regular expression engine, works on a few kilobytes of data, a good fit for a region. A region directory protocol allows an entire region of data to be managed as one unit efficiently. A region tag array and directory can be much smaller than regular cache tag array and block directory as they deal with fewer entries.

Overall, the efficiency and performance of cache coherence protocol can be improved by employing a larger granularity for much data that exhibits uniform access and sharing patterns, leaving the remainder handled by block-level protocol.

10.5.3 System Partitioning

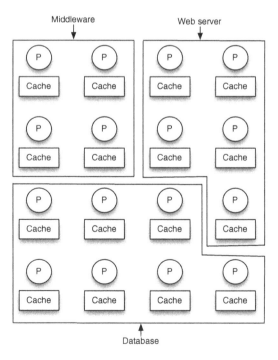

Figure 10.12: Illustration of a partitioned multicore used for server consolidation.

A large number of cores in a multicore chip may be used to run various servers in a virtualized environment, a use case referred to as *server consolidation*. Various servers such as web server, database engine, email server, may be co-hosted on a single multicore. Server consolidation is increasingly enabled by the growth in the number of cores on a chip. Figure 10.12 illustrates a multicore chip used in a server consolidation setting.

Characteristics of such a system is that there is a need for performance isolation (i.e., isolating resources used by one server from other servers), and data sharing mostly occur within a server rather than across servers. Given such characteristics, it makes sense to provide a mechanism for the multicore to be partitioned, if communication within a partition can be made cheaper compared to communication across partitions. To support this, a class of two-level protocols have been proposed. An example of two-level directory protocol can be found in [41], where each partition has its own "first level" directory protocol, and there is another "second level" directory protocol to keep coherence across partitions. A block has two home nodes: one home node is assigned dynamically (when partition changes) in a partition, while another home node is assigned for the second level directory. Mapping of a block address to a home node is achieved by using a table lookup. When partition changes, a home node can be reassigned by writing new entries into the table.

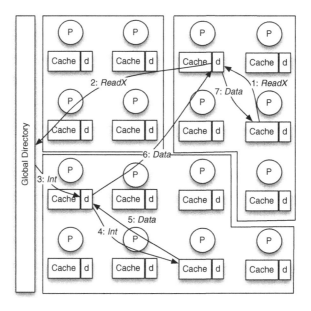

Figure 10.13: Illustration of a two-level directory protocol.

Figure 10.13 shows an illustration of a two-level directory protocol, where 'd' indicates the local directory within a partition. A request is first sent to the first-level home node (Step 1), which is a node within the partition. In some cases, the local home node will be able to satisfy the requests. When it cannot satisfy the request, such as when the requested data block is uncached, or it has no sufficient permission for the request, the home sends the request to the global or second level directory (Step 2). The request is then forwarded to the home node of the partition that has the block (Step 3), which is then forwarded to the owner of the block (Step 4). The owner supplies the data block to the local home (Step 5), which forwards it to the requestor's home node (Step 6). Finally, the requestor home node forwards data to the requesting node (Step 7). Another scheme proposed is for the second level directory protocol to be replaced with a broadcast protocol.

10.5.4 Accelerating Thread Migration

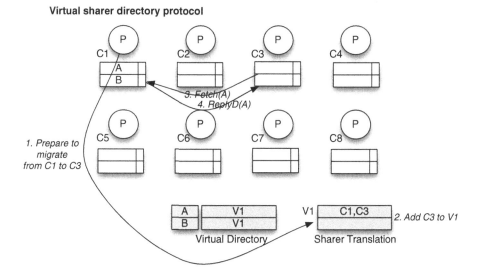

Figure 10.14: Illustration virtual sharer used for accelerating thread migration.

Another interesting possibility in a two level cache coherence protocol is virtualization of sharers, where a directory protocol may keep track of virtual sharers rather than individual caches [59].

Virtual sharers may map to caches, but not necessarily in a one-to-one manner. What is the usefulness of virtualizing sharers? One possible use of virtual sharers is when we want to accelerate thread migration. Imagine a thread wanting to migrate from a core to another. After migration, the thread runs on a core with a cold cache.

Figure 10.14 illustrates the impact of virtualizing sharers. The top part of the figure shows a traditional directory protocol. Suppose that a thread migrates from node C1 to C3 (Step 1), due to a decision made by the operating system or hypervisor. Since the thread runs with a cold cache, it will suffer from many cache misses. In the example, it suffers a cache miss on block A, which inquires the directory (Step 2). The directory looks up the entry for block A, and forwards the request to node C1 (Step 3). C1 then supplies the data block (Step 4). Later, if the thread suffers again from another cache miss, e.g., to block B or other blocks, each cache miss will involve three protocol hops just like the one for block A. Not only does this process incur a high latency for each cache miss, but it is also wasteful in traffic and power consumption.

The bottom part of the figure shows how a virtual sharer directory protocol may help. First, notice that the directory keeps track of virtual sharers V1, V2, etc. rather than physical nodes C1, C2, etc. The directory has a sharer translation that keeps track of which physical nodes each virtual sharer includes. Now, suppose that a thread migrates from C1 to C3. The OS/hypervisor may choose to inform the directory to prepare it for migration (Step 1). Possibly based on cost/benefit calculation, the directory may decide to just add C3 to the virtual sharer V1, which prior to this only included C1. Due to this, then the directory information for all blocks in C1 are valid in the virtual directory. The directory does not need to be modified whenever data blocks move or get replicated between C1 and C3, since they both belong to virtual sharer V1. Node C3 may issue a direct fetch (Step 3) to node C1, which may reply with data block A (Step 4). This two-hop process may be repeated for other blocks until the migration of data is complete. It is also possible for C1 to proactively push its cached data blocks to C3. All these can occur without the involvement of the directory.

As a second use of virtual sharer directory protocol is to define partitions. Each virtual sharer can represent a partition. This allows a flexibility to move and replicate data within a partition, without involving the directory, as long as the state of the data blocks allows such movement or replication. Furthermore, each partition may implement different kinds of first level coherence protocols depending on their needs. For example, a small partition may implement a broadcast protocol. A larger partition may implement a directory protocol within the partition.

10.6 Exercises

Worked Problems

1. **Storage overheads**. Suppose we have a directory coherence protocol keeping caches coherent. The caches use a 64-byte cache block. Each block requires 2 bits to encode coherence states in the directory. How many bits are required and what is the overhead ratio (number of directory bits divided by block size) to keep the directory information for each block, for full-bit vector, coarse vector with 4 processors/bit, limited pointers with 4 pointers per block? Consider 16, 64, 256, and 1024 caches in the system.

   Answer:

Scheme	16-proc	64-proc	256-proc	1024-proc
Full bit vector	$\frac{16+2}{512} = 3.5\%$	$\frac{64+2}{512} = 12.9\%$	$\frac{256+2}{512} = 50.4\%$	$\frac{1024+2}{512} = 200.4\%$
Coarse 4P/bit	$\frac{4+2}{512} = 1.2\%$	$\frac{16+2}{512} = 3.5\%$	$\frac{64+2}{512} = 12.9\%$	$\frac{256+2}{512} = 50.4\%$
Dir_4B	$\frac{4\times4+2}{512} = 3.5\%$	$\frac{4\times6+2}{512} = 5.1\%$	$\frac{4\times8+2}{512} = 6.6\%$	$\frac{4\times10+2}{512} = 8.2\%$

2. **Coherence protocol operations**. Assume a 3-processor multiprocessor system with directory-based coherence protocol. Assume that the cost of a network transaction is solely determined by the number of sequential protocol hops involved in the transaction. Each hop takes 50 cycles to complete, while a cache hit costs 1 cycle. Furthermore, ignore NACK traffic and speculative replies. The caches keep MESI states, while the directory keep EM (exclusive or modified), S (shared), and U (uncached) states.

   Display the state transition of all the 3 caches, the directory content and its state, and the network messages generated for the reference stream shown in the tables.

   Answer:

MemRef	P1	P2	P3	Directory content at home node	List of all network messages	Cost
r1	E	-	-	100, EM	Read(P1 → H), ReplyD(H → P1)	100
w1	M	-	-	100, EM	-	1
r2	S	S	-	110, S	Read(P2 → H), Int(H → P1), Flush (P1 → H&P2)	150
w2	I	M	-	010, EM	Upgr(P2 → H), Reply(H → P2) // Inv(H → P1), InvAck(P1 → P2)	150
r3	I	S	S	011, S	Read(P3 → H), Int(H → P2), Flush (P2 → H&P3)	150
r1	S	S	S	111, S	Read(P1 → H), ReplyD(H → P1)	100

w1	M	I	I	100, EM	Upgr(P1 → H),	150
					Reply(H → P1) // Inv(H → P2&P3),	
					InvAck(P2 → P1) //InvAck(P3 → P1)	
r1	M	I	I	100, EM	-	1
w2	I	M	I	010, EM	ReadX(P2 → H),	150
					Reply(H → P2) // Inv(H → P1),	
					Flush+InvAck(P1 → P2)	
					TOTAL	952

3. **Overlapped processing**. Suppose a 4-processor multiprocessor system uses a directory-based coherence protocol with full bit vector. The directory keeps U, EM, and S states, while the caches maintain MESI states. Assume that cost of a network transaction is solely determined by the number of protocol hops involved in the transaction, and each hop has a latency of 50 cycles.

Suppose that a parallel program incurs the following accesses to a single block address: r1, r2, w3, and r4, where r indicates a read request, w indicates a write request, and the number indicates the processor issuing the request. Suppose that the requests are issued simultaneously to the directory at time 0, but the directory receives them in the following order: r1, r2, w3, r4. Assume that the occupancy of the directory (i.e., the length of time the directory looks up and updates the directory state) is 10 cycles, and fetching data from memory incurs 0 cycles.

(a) What is the latency to complete the processing of all the requests using a home-centric approach?

(b) What is the latency to complete the processing of all the requests using a requestor-assisted approach, which tries to overlap the request processing as much as possible?

Answer:

Suppose that r1, r2, w3, and r4 were issued at time 0.

Part (a): Home-centric approach

Request	Time, Event, and Messages
r1	(0,50) Read (P1 → Home)
	(50, 60) Directory Occupancy
	(60, 110) ReplyD (Home → P1)
	(110, 160) Done (P1 → Home)
r2	(0,50) Read(P2 → Home)
	(50, 160) Waiting for directory to exit busy state
	(160, 170) Directory Occupancy
	(170, 220) Int (Home → P1)
	(220, 270) Flush (P1 → Home and P2)
	(270, 320) Done (P2 → Home)

w3	(0,50) ReadX (P3 → Home)
	(50, 320) Waiting for directory to exit busy state
	(320, 330) Directory Occupancy
	(330, 380) Inv (Home → P1 and P2)
	(380, 430) InvAck (P1 and P2 → P3)
	(430, 480) Done (P3 → Home)
r4	(0,50) Read (P4 → Home)
	(50, 480) Waiting for directory to exit busy state
	(480, 490) Directory Occupancy
	(490, 540) Int (Home → P3)
	(540, 590) Flush (P3 → P4, Home)
	(590, 640) Done (P4 → Home)

Part (b): Requestor-assisted approach

Request	Time, Event, and Messages
r1	(0,50) Read (P1 → Home)
	(50, 60) Directory Occupancy
	(60, 110) ReplyD (Home → P1)
r2	(0,50) Read(P2 → Home)
	(50, 60) Waiting for directory to exit busy state
	(60, 70) Directory Occupancy
	(70, 120) Int (Home → P1)
	(120, 170) Flush (P1 → Home and P2)
w3	(0,50) ReadX (P3 → Home)
	(50, 170) Waiting for directory to exit busy state
	(170, 180) Directory Occupancy
	(180, 230) Inv (Home → P1 and P2)
	(230, 280) InvAck (P1 and P2 → P3)
r4	(0,50) Read (P4 → Home)
	(50, 180) Waiting for directory to exit busy state
	(180, 190) Directory Occupancy
	(190, 240) Int (Home → P3)
	(240, 280) Waiting for receipt of InvAck to complete P3's previous transaction
	(280, 330) Flush (P3 → P4, Home)

Homework Problems

1. **Storage overheads**. Suppose we have a directory coherence protocol keeping caches coherent. The caches use a 128-byte cache block. Each block requires 3 bits to encode coherence states in the directory. How many bits are required to keep the directory information for each block, for full-bit vector, coarse vector with 8 processors/bit, limited pointers with 4 pointers per block, and limited pointers with 8 pointers per block? Consider 16, 64, 256, and 1024 caches in the system.

2. **Coherence protocol operations**. Suppose a 4-node system, each node having a processor and a cache, uses a directory-based coherence protocol with a full-bit directory format. Assume that the cost of processing a protocol transaction depends on the number of protocol hops, and each hop costs 50 cycles. A cache hit costs 1 cycle. The caches maintain MESI states, and the directory maintains EM, S, U states. Show what happens to cache states and directory information after each memory access. The memory accesses are: R1 (read request by node 1), R2, R3, R2, W3 (write request by node 3), E3 (cache eviction by node 3), W4, and W1.

3. **Overlapped processing**. Suppose a 4-processor multiprocessor system uses a directory-based coherence protocol with full bit vector. The directory keeps U, EM, and S states, while the cache maintains MESI states. Assume that cost of a network transaction is solely determined by the number of protocol hops involved in the transaction, and each hop has a latency of 50 cycles.

   Suppose that a parallel program incurs the following accesses to a single block address: w1, r2, w3, w4, where r indicates a read request, w indicates a write request, and the number indicates the processor issuing the request. Suppose that the requests are issued almost simultaneously to the directory, but the directory receives them in the following order: w1, r2, w3, w4. Assume that the occupancy of the directory (i.e., the length of time the directory looks up and updates the directory state) is 10 cycles, and fetching data from memory incurs 0 cycles.

   (a) What is the latency to complete the processing of all the requests using a home-centric approach?

   (b) What is the latency to complete the processing of all the requests using a requestor-assisted approach, which tries to overlap the request processing as much as possible?

Chapter 11

Interconnection Network Architecture

Contents

So far our discussion has been centered on how to build a correct and efficient shared memory multiprocessor, by providing cache coherence, memory consistency, and synchronization primitives. We have assumed that messages are reliably sent from one processor to another with a low latency. However, we have not discussed how messages can be sent reliably and fast from one node to another.

The objective of this chapter is to discuss the fabric that interconnects multiple processors. Two of the most important performance metrics for an interconnection network are *latency* and *bandwidth*. A shared memory multiprocessor has unique requirements for interconnection fabric performance, compared to other systems, such as local area networks (LANs) or the internet, due to the several unique characteristics of communication in a shared memory multiprocessor. First, messages are very short. Many messages are coherence protocol requests and responses not containing data, while some messages contain a small amount (cache-block size) of data, which is 64 or 128 bytes in current systems. Second, messages are generated frequently, since each read or write miss potentially generates coherence messages involving several nodes. Third, since a message is generated due to a processor read or write event, the ability of the processor to hide the message communication delay is relatively low. Therefore, shared memory multiprocessor interconnection fabric must provide very low latency and high bandwidth communication between nodes, optimized for handling small and almost uniformly-sized packets. Fourth, the topology (or shape of the network) is for the most part static.

Such considerations carry several implications. First, while general networks such as TCP/IP rely on many layers of communication protocols to provide a flexible functionality, shared memory multiprocessor interconnection network should be designed with as few layers of communication protocols as possible in order to minimize the communication latency. For example, a shared memory multiprocessor interconnection network may use only two protocol layers: *link-level* protocol to ensure reliable delivery of a single packet over a single link, and *node-level* protocol to ensure reliable delivery of a packet from one node to another node. Secondly, communication protocol should be stripped down to essential features. For example, complex policies, such as end-to-end flow control, and flow control involving packet dropping, can be harmful to performance. Instead, flow control is only performed at the link level, to avoid overflowing the buffers at the receiver. In addition, packet dropping should typically be avoided. Furthermore, routing protocol should not require maintenance and lookups of a large table.

Another unique aspect that needs to be considered in designing the interconnection network for a shared memory multiprocessor is how it interacts with other components of the multiprocessors such as coherence protocol and consistency model.

Overall, choosing the right interconnection fabric design for a given shared memory multiprocessor is a challenging task. It is often the case the optimal interconnection network for a particular shared memory multiprocessor system is not optimal for other shared memory multiprocessor systems, due to the difference in performance, scalability, and cost requirements. To help understand such trade-offs, we will discuss the components of interconnection fabric, and various policies that are applicable for each component, and their implications on performance of the system.

Interconnection network glues multiple processors together to form a shared memory multiprocessor system, as shown in Figure 11.1. A processor, or a group of processors, are encapsulated into a *node*. A node may consist of one or more processor cores, caches or cache hierarchy ($), memories (M), communication controller, which is the logic that interfaces with the network fabric through a *router*, which connects to other routers to form the network. In a small network, sometimes one router is sufficient to connect several processors together. In larger networks, multiple routers are necessary, and they must connect to the communication controller of individual nodes as well as to other routers. In the example in the figure, each router connects to four other routers through four ports (north, east, south, west), and another port to the local controller. The physical wires between two routers are referred to as a *link*. A link can be *unidirectional* in which data can only be sent in one direction, or *bidirectional* in which data can be sent in both directions. One important characteristic of an interconnection network is the shape of the network, referred to as the network *topology*. For example, the network topology shown in the figure is a two-dimensional mesh. In the following sections, we will discuss each of these components in more details.

11.1 Link, Channel, and Latency

A link is a set of wires that connect two nodes. The minimum amount of data that can be transmitted in one cycle is called a *phit*. A phit is typically determined by the width of the link. For example, a 10-bit link may have a phit of 1 byte (8 bits) with the remaining 2 bits used for control signals or parity information. However, data is transferred at the granularity of link-level flow control unit called a *flit*. A flit may consist of one or more phits that are transmitted over several clock cycles, but as a single unit of flow control. A *flit* worth of data can be accepted or rejected at the receiver, depending on the amount of buffering available at the receiver and the *flow control protocol* used.

The flow control mechanism works at the link level to ensure that data is not accepted too fast that it overflows the buffer at the receiving router. In a *lossy network*, overflowing a buffer results

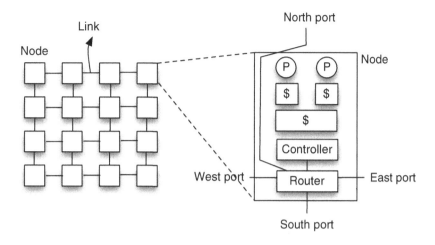

Figure 11.1: Components of an interconnection network.

in flits being dropped and the dropped flits require retransmission in the future. For latency reasons, a *lossless network* is preferred, in which flits should not be dropped and retransmitted. Thus, a typical link-level flow control uses a stop/go protocol. Figure 11.2 illustrates a stop/go protocol. A sender router sends flits of a packet to a receiver router as long as the receiver asserts a "go" signal, which is monitored by the sender. The receiver has an input buffer and monitors how full the buffer is. If the buffer fills up and reaches a threshold, the receiver changes the "go" signal to a "stop" signal. The sender reacts by stopping sending more flits. At some point the input buffer of the receiver is emptied again and the receiver changes the signal to "go" again, at which point the sender resumes sending flits. The stop/go threshold is determined by the round-trip latency between sender and receiver, such that there is no risk of overflowing the buffer. An alternative flow control mechanism, referred to as *credit-based* flow control, requires the receiver to send out the precise number of entries available (or send out the change in the number of entries available) in its buffer, either periodically or whenever the number changes. The sender uses this number to decide whether to send more flits or not.

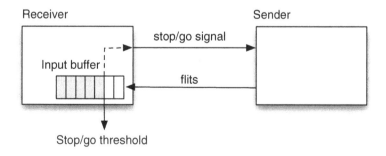

Figure 11.2: Stop/go link-level flow control.

When considering that data will travel over more than just one link, there are two switching policies for a network, as illustrated in Figure 11.3. One policy is *circuit switching*, where a connection between a sender and receiver is reserved prior to data being sent over the connection. This means the sender first sends a command to set up a connection to the receiver. Routers along the path reserve the connection between the appropriate input port and output port where the message will travel. Once the connection set up has been completed, the receiver replies with a message indicating the set up completion. After this, the sender can send a message to the receiver. The message can travel very efficiently from here on. It does not need to be broken into multiple small packets. The single packet does not need to contain routing information. The packet also does not suffer from much routing delay at each router, as the input port's connection with the output port has been reserved.

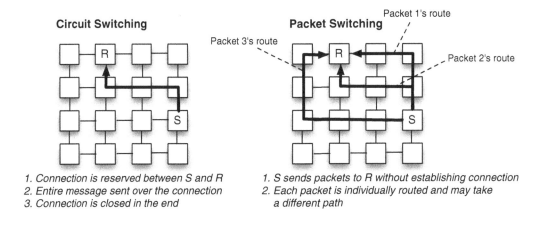

Figure 11.3: Illustration of circuit vs. packet switching.

An alternative switching policy is *packet switching*. With packet switching, when a large message is transmitted on a channel, it is fragmented and encapsulated into *packets*. Figure 11.4 illustrates how a long message is broken into packets. Each part of the message becomes a packet *payload*, which is encapsulated by a *header* and *trailer*. The fragmentation allows a message to be transmitted in parts independently of one another, and the header and trailer ensure reliable delivery of the message and contain sufficient information to reassemble the packets into the original message at the destination. A packet header in packet switching has more information, including the destination and possibly routing information. When a packet is transmitted over a link, it is transmitted over the link in flit granularity, e.g., multiple flits may be required to transmit a packet, depending on the size of a packet relative to the size of a flit. Thus, a message may be broken into one or more packets, a packet into one or more flits, and a flit into one or more phits. When a packet is broken into flits, each flit does not add a "flit header" or "flit trailer" because flits are not designed to be routed individually. Flits of a packet will be transmitted over the link in order, and routing decisions are made only at the packet level. Flits of a packet cannot be routed individually.

The header of a packet typically contains routing and control information that enables the router to determine what to do with the packet. If the packet header is designed to fit the size of a flit, the flit that contains the header is referred to as the *header flit*. Similarly, if the packet trailer is designed

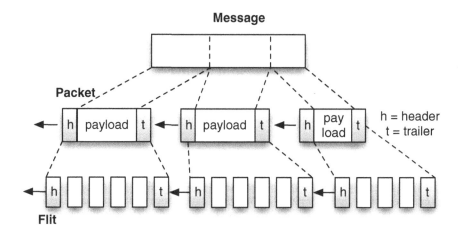

Figure 11.4: Message and packet.

to fit the size of a flit, the flit that contains the trailer is referred to as the *trailer flit*. The packet payload is broken into *body flits*. A router may decide routing for a packet based on inspection of the header flit. By examining the packet header, a router knows which port/link the packet should be sent to next, without having to examine the rest of the packet (payload and trailer). The trailer of a packet follows the packet payload and contains information such as a *checksum*, which is a string of redundant bits that allow the detection or correction of the packet if some bits have changed value due to transmission error. Note that in shared memory multiprocessors, most messages correspond to coherence protocol requests. Hence, they transmit at most one cache block worth of data. In many cases, one packet is sufficient to send a single message. Only when a large number of bytes are transmitted, multiple packets are required.

Comparing circuit switching and packet switching, circuit switching incurs a significant latency for setting up the connection. In addition, once the connection is set up, if it is not used right away, the connection may be under-utilized. Furthermore, if another connection or traffic collides with an existing connection, they have to wait until the existing connection is released. This may produce significant delay to other traffic or connections. However, circuit switching also has advantages. Once the connection is set up, message delivery is very fast as a router only needs to forward the message to the output port, without deciding on routing or allocation of resources. There is only a very small amount of buffering needed as the message can be forwarded to the next router knowing that the resources will be there to accept the message. The lower latency, simpler routing logic, and minimum amount of buffering reduce power consumption at the router. The opposite is true for packet switching. Packet switching incurs significant routing delay and power consumption at each router, but does not incur connection set up or tear down overheads, and can interleave many different traffic easily as resources are managed on a per packet basis.

The maximum rate at which a packet can be streamed through a link is referred to as the link *bandwidth*. The link bandwidth is determined by the clock frequency of the link multiplied by the number of bits of data that can be streamed in one cycle.

How much time does it take to send a single message of size L over a channel in a network with bandwidth B, when there is no contention? We can think of the transfer as being composed of the latency of the first bit being transmitted to the destination, plus the latency for the remaining portion of the message trailing behind the first bit. The former is sometimes referred to as the *header latency* or T_h, and the latter is sometimes referred to as the *serialization latency* or T_s. If the first bit has to travel through H hops and each hop incurs a routing latency of T_r, then the header latency is $H \times T_r$, while the serialization latency is $\frac{L}{B}$. Putting it together, the latency for sending the message is:

$$T = T_h + T_s = H \times T_r + \frac{L}{B} \tag{11.1}$$

The equation hints that to reduce latency, we can reduce the hop count, reduce the routing latency, or increase the channel bandwidth. Reducing the routing latency is difficult. However, the hop count can easily be increased or decreased by changing the overall shape (*topology*) of the network, which will be the focus of the discussion in the next section.

11.2 Network Topology

Network topology is the shape of an interconnection network, i.e., how nodes are interconnected together. It is one of the most important design aspects for an interconnect network because it affects network performance (latency, distance, diameter, bisection bandwidth) and cost significantly. The choice of a network topology is often decided early in the design stage.

For a small multiprocessor, sometimes a single router is sufficient to interconnect all processors. However, when the number of nodes is larger than what a single router can connect to, routers must be interconnected to each other in a certain formation referred to as the topology of the network.

The choice of topologies is an important one as it determines the latency, bandwidth, and cost characteristics of the network. Several metrics are useful for evaluating the characteristics of latency and bandwidth of an interconnection network topology. One useful metric is the network *diameter*, defined as the longest distance between any pair of nodes, measured in the number of *network hops* (i.e., the number of links that the message must travel between two nodes). Another useful metric is *average distance*, computed by dividing the sum of distances between all pairs of nodes by the number of node pairs. Thus, the average distance of a network is the expected distance between two randomly selected nodes. Another useful metric is *bisection bandwidth*, which is the minimum number of links that must be cut in order to partition the network into two equal halves. As a proxy of cost, two metrics are often used. One metric is the number of links required to form the interconnection network. Another metric is the number of in/out links connecting to each router, which is called the *degree*.

The significance of the diameter is that it resembles the worst case latency that can occur in the network (assuming a minimum routing). While the average communication latency in the network can be controlled through placement of threads in such a way to minimize the distances that occur during communication, for global (one-to-all, all-to-one, and all-to-all) communication, diameter is a limiting factor in the communication latency. The significance of the bisection bandwidth is that it is a single metric that characterizes the amount of bandwidth available in the entire system. Especially, it represents the maximum bandwidth that can sustain global communication in the system. Why does bisection bandwidth matter more than the total/aggregate bandwidth? The aggregate bandwidth is a less representative metric here because it does not account for a set of links that become the bandwidth bottleneck in global communication. For example, in a linear array with p nodes, the total link bandwidth is $p - 1$ times the link bandwidth, but bisection bandwidth is equal to one link bandwidth. Since global communication must always travel through one link, bisection bandwidth summarizes the bandwidth characteristic of the network better than the aggregate bandwidth.

Several popular network topologies are shown in Figure 11.5. A bus is different than other topologies in that it allows a direct connection from one node to another, hence, it does not require routing. A two-dimensional mesh is related to the linear array in that the linear array can be thought of as a one-dimensional mesh. A cube is essentially a three-dimensional mesh. The same applies to the hypercube, which is a multi-dimensional mesh with two nodes in each dimension. Due to the similarity, such topologies are grouped into a *k-ary d-dimensional mesh* topology family, where d represents the dimensions, and k represents the number of nodes in each dimension. For example, the linear array in the figure is a 5-ary 1-dimensional mesh, the mesh is a 3-ary 2-dimensional mesh, and the cube in the figure is a 3-dimensional mesh with varying arities. The hypercube is always binary (two nodes in each dimension), so it can be referred to as a 2-ary d-dimensional mesh. Similarly, we can always construct a torus from a mesh by adding links between end nodes at each dimension. For example, ring can be constructed by connecting both end nodes of a linear array. The 2-D torus shown in the figure can be constructed from 2-D mesh shown in the figure. Therefore, a related family of topologies is the *k-ary d-dimensional* torus.

■ *Did you know?*

In an implementation, the number of hops is not the only thing that matters. The length of wire for each network hop also matters, and as much as possible, links should have uniform lengths. An example ring with non-uniform and uniform link lengths are shown below. The arrangement of nodes and links to achieve relatively uniform link length is called folding. *Folding is important in a multicore's interconnect network because a topology must be implemented in a planar layout (unless 3D design with multiple logic layers is used).*

The figure also shows a binary tree, which is an example of a *k-ary tree* where $k = 2$. Note that in the tree, nodes are located at the leaves and are not directly connected to each other. Instead, they are connected through intermediate routers shown by the thin rectangles. A tree suffers from a limited bandwidth problem in that root-level links receive more traffic than leaf-level links. In order to avoid the root-level links from becoming the bottleneck in the system, two related topologies can be used. One topology that can be used is a *fat tree*, which has fatter (i.e., having more wires) upper level links compared to lower level links. Another topology that can be used is a *butterfly* network. A butterfly network can be thought of as a tree with replicated upper level intermediate routers and links. Due to the equal number of links and routers at all levels, a butterfly network does not suffer from limited bandwidth at the root level.

What are the diameter and bisection bandwidth of the topologies? For a k-ary d-dimensional mesh, overall there are k^d nodes in the system. The maximum distance in each dimension is one

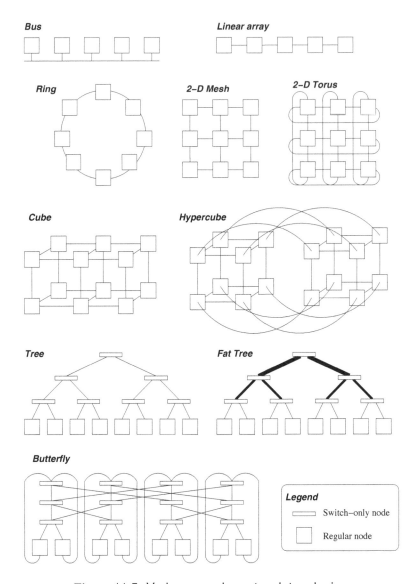

Figure 11.5: Various popular network topologies.

less than the number of nodes in a dimension, i.e., $k - 1$. Since there are d dimensions, the diameter of a k-ary d-dimensional mesh is $d \times (k - 1)$. The bisection bandwidth can be obtained by cutting the network into two equal halves. This cut is performed with a plane one dimension less than the mesh, therefore, the bisection bandwidth is k^{d-1}.

For the tree, the maximum distance is when a node reaches another node through the root of the tree. Since the height of a k-ary tree is $log_k p$, then the diameter of the tree is $2 \times log_k p$. The bisection bandwidth is obtained by cutting the tree into two at the root, hence, it is equal to one link. The fat tree has an equivalent diameter but the bisection bandwidth depends on the number of links at the root level. If the parent link is k-times fatter than child-level links, then the bisection bandwidth is $\frac{p}{2}$.

> ■ *Did you know?*
>
> *A fat tree is difficult to implement because the upper-level links (especially root-level links) must have many wires in order to support a higher bandwidth than lower-level links. In addition, they are often physically longer than lower-level links, reducing the bandwidth they can provide. In some implementations (e.g., Infiniband), the fat tree use different cables for the upper level links. While lower level links use copper cables, upper-level links use fiber optics, which give several benefits over copper cables: (1) they provide much higher bandwidth than the lower-level links that use copper cables, (2) they provide less bulk and weight for upper-level links and routers, and (3) they provide communication latencies that are low and relatively unaffected by the length of the cable (transmission delay of a copper cable deteriorates quickly with the length of the cable).*

Finally, for the butterfly, the path from a node to any other node is by going from the lowest-level link, up the routers to the uppermost-level link, and to the destination node. Thus, for each pair of nodes, there is only a single path connecting them, and all paths have a distance of $log_2 p$ (equaling its diameter). Its bisection bandwidth is the same with the fat tree, that is $\frac{p}{2}$.

Table 11.1 summarizes the characteristics of different topologies assuming bidirectional links, showing latency-related metric (diameter), bandwidth-related metrics (bisection bandwidth), and the cost-related metrics (number of links and node degrees). The degree (radix) assumes an interior node and includes the number of connections of a router to other routers plus one more for the local node. The family of k-ary d-dimensional mesh is shown as well as two of its popular instances: 2-D mesh and hypercube.

Table 11.1: Comparison of various network topologies.

Topology	Diameter	Bisection BW	#Links	Degree
Linear array	p-1	1	p-1	2+1
Ring	$\frac{p}{2}$	2	p	2+1
2-D Mesh	$2(\sqrt{p}-1)$	$\sqrt{p}$	$2\sqrt{p}(\sqrt{p}-1)$	4+1
Hypercube	$log_2 p$	$\frac{p}{2}$	$\frac{p}{2} \times log_2 p$	$log_2 p + 1$
k-ary d Mesh	$d(k-1)$	k^{d-1}	$dk^{d-1}(k-1)$	$2d+1$
k-ary Tree	$2 \times log_k p$	1	$k(p-1)$	$(k+1)+1$
k-ary Fat Tree	$2 \times log_k p$	$\frac{p}{2}$	$k(p-1)$	$(k+1)+1$
Butterfly	$log_2 p$	$\frac{p}{2}$	$2p \times log_2 p$	4+1

While not shown in the table, the average distance of some topologies can also be computed. For example, the average distance of a 2-D mesh is $(\sqrt{p}+1)/3$, while for a hypercube it is $\frac{p}{2}$.

Let us look at a more specific scenario with regard to the bisection bandwidth and diameter for a subset of the network topologies. Given p nodes, we can choose a low dimensional network with a high number of nodes in each dimension, or a high dimensional network with a low number of nodes in each dimension. To give an illustration of which approach (low dimensional vs. high dimensional) is more scalable, we compare a 2-D mesh versus a hypercube and a butterfly for the same number of nodes. Figure 11.6 shows how they scale in terms of diameter and bisection bandwidth as the number of nodes changes from small (4 nodes) to large (256 nodes). The figure shows that a low dimensional network's diameter grows quickly as the number of nodes grows, compared to a high dimensional network's diameter. While they start out with an equal diameter on 4 nodes, 2-D mesh's diameter becomes $3.75\times$ that of the hypercube and butterfly (30 vs. 8) for 256 nodes. The figure also shows that a low dimensional network's bisection bandwidth grows much more slowly compared to a high dimensional network as the number of nodes increases. 2-D mesh, hypercube and butterfly start out with an equal bisection bandwidth on 4 nodes, but on 256 nodes, the bisection bandwidth of hypercube and butterfly is $16\times$ that of 2-D mesh (128 vs. 16 links), if the link has equal width in both cases.

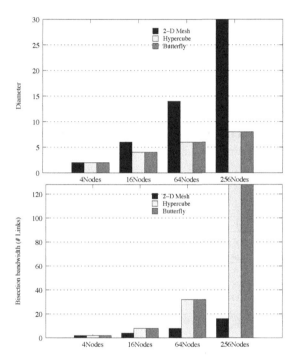

Figure 11.6: Diameter (top) and bisection bandwidth (bottom) comparison for 2-D mesh (left bar), hypercube (middle bar), and butterfly (right bar) for various number of nodes (4, 16, 64, 256).

The figure shows that the hypercube and butterfly have equal diameter and bisection bandwidth. Hence, their scaling characteristics are similar. The difference between them is that a butterfly has only one path connecting a unique pair of nodes, that goes through $log_2 p$ number of routers, while the hypercube has paths that vary in distance depending on the pair of nodes involved in the communication and on the routing algorithm used. Hence, while the hypercube can benefit from mapping threads that frequently communicate to neighboring nodes, a butterfly cannot benefit from thread-to-node mapping.

From performance and scalability perspective, a high dimensional network has significant advantages in terms of diameter, average distance, and bisection bandwidth, compared to a low dimensional network. However, let us discuss cost, which is also an important consideration. For example, in a 2-D mesh, each router is relatively simple and only needs to have a degree of 4. In a hypercube, each router needs to have a degree that is twice the dimension, e.g., for a hypercube with five dimensions, each router has 10 degrees. Note, however, that one can compensate for the hypercube's higher degree by narrowing each port, with a goal of keeping the total number of pins or wire connections constant as a proxy of cost. Thus, for an approximately equal cost, a higher dimension topology still achieves a better diameter and bisection bandwidth compared to a lower dimension topology.

A router architecture often relies on a crossbar switch to connect input to output ports, so the additional ports increase the switch complexity quadratically. With a butterfly, the degree remains 4, but it requires a lot more routers compared to a hypercube. In addition, a higher dimensional network tends to require longer wires (across chips, or within a chip in a multicore system), more metal layers, and more complex wire layout, all of which may contribute to cost.

11.3 Routing Policies and Algorithms

So far we have discussed the topology of the network. Given a network topology, it remains an open question of how a packet can be sent from one node to another. The relevant issues here are whether a packet transmission is pipelined or not, what paths a packet is allowed to travel, and how path restriction is related to various characteristics of the network.

The first issue deals with when a packet needs to travel for several hops (links), does the packet travel in its entirety from one node to the next, or can it be split across multiple links? In a *store and forward* routing policy, a packet must be fully received (and stored) by a node, before it can be forwarded to the next node.

In a *cut-through* or *wormhole* routing policy, parts of a packet can be forwarded to the next router even before the packet has fully arrived at the current router. The difference between them is illustrated in Figure 11.7. In store and forward routing (the top part of the figure), all flits of a packet are buffered completely at each router before the first flit is sent out to the next router. In cut-through or wormhole routing, when each flit is received at a node, it is immediately forwarded to the next node, Thus, a packet may be in transit at multiple links and multiple routers.

The figure illustrates a key benefit of cut-through or wormhole routing: lower packet transmission latency. To see why this is the case, assume that the time to route one packet of size L over a channel with bandwidth B is T_{router}. If a packet travels for H hops, then under store and forward routing the total latency will be the multiplication of the number of hops with the time spent for each hop:

$$T_{stfwd} = H \times (T_r + \frac{L}{B}) \tag{11.2}$$

On the other hand, for a cut-through or wormhole routing, the time to transmit one packet is the same with the time to transmit the first bit over all the hops, plus the time for the rest of the packet to arrive at the final destination node. This is because the trailing bits of a packet follow the first bit without a lag. The first bit only suffers from the time at each router to route it, while the trailing

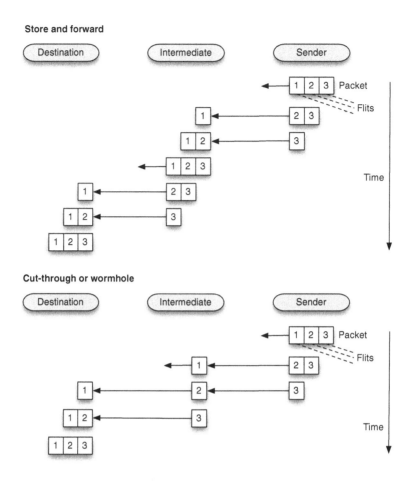

Figure 11.7: Illustration of the difference between store and forward vs. cut-through routing.

bits suffer from the transmission delay. Therefore, the time to send a packet with cut-through or wormhole routing on the network is:

$$T_{cutthrough} = H \times T_r + \frac{L}{B} \tag{11.3}$$

Thus, the difference in the latency to send a packet between the store and forward and the cut through routing is $(H - 1) \times \frac{L}{B}$. This implies that the importance of cut-through routing in reducing the packet latency increases when the number of hops is high (such as on a low dimensional network), and also when the transmission time along a link is high (such as when a link is narrow or has a low clock frequency), or when the packet size is large.

While cut-through and wormhole routing both achieve the same latency advantage over store and forward routing, they differ in the flow control unit. In a cut-through routing, the flow control works on a packet size granularity, while in a wormhole routing, the flow control works on a flit granularity. In a cut-through routing, a packet starts to be sent when the next (or downstream) router has sufficient buffer to hold the entire packet, even though the packet may not be buffered entirely in the router. In a wormhole routing, a packet starts to be sent to the downstream router as soon as the router has one flit available in its buffer. While they behave similarly when there is no contention in the network, they behave differently when a downstream router is contended and blocked. In cut-through routing, flits of the packet continue to be accepted at the blocked router until the entire packet is received at the input buffer. This is because the downstream router guarantees that it has sufficient buffer space for the entire packet before the packet was sent by an upstream router. In wormhole routing, the blocked router's buffer may not have space for the entire packet, hence, it may stop accepting more flits of the packet. As a result, the packet may have flits residing at multiple routers. The flits at other routers may cause blockage there, causing a cascaded blocking, which is less likely to occur with cut-through routing. However, wormhole routing reduces the amount of buffering at each node is reduced because a router only needs to guarantee space for some flits of a packet rather than the entire packet before it can accept a packet. Buffers are one of the most expensive components in a router, so reducing the buffer space significantly reduces the cost of a router.

A routing algorithm decides the paths a packet can travel from one node to another. There are several categories of algorithms, depending on what aspect is being considered. In terms of the hop count, a routing algorithm is *minimal* if a packet always uses a path that has the least number of hops to the destination. If a packet is allowed to use a longer path (e.g., to avoid traffic) then the routing is *non-minimal*. In terms of determinism of the paths, a routing algorithm is said to be *deterministic* if it always uses a single path given a pair of sender and destination nodes, otherwise, it is *non-deterministic*. In terms of whether path selection depends on the state of the network, a non-deterministic routing algorithm is *adaptive* if it uses the state of the network to make its routing decision, otherwise, it is said to be *oblivious*. In terms of whether the path is determined prior to sending a packet, a routing algorithm may use *source routing* if the path is determined at the source, or *per-hop routing* if the path is determined at each hop along the way. Finally, a routing algorithm is *deadlock-free* if its routing cannot introduce a deadlock in packet transmission.

■ *Did you know?*

The choice of routing in the interconnection network affects the design of the cache coherence protocol. For example, if deterministic routing is used, then two messages sent from a node to another node will travel on the same path and arrive at the destination in the same order in which they were sent. Consequently, there are fewer protocol races that can occur compared to when non-deterministic routing algorithms are used.

There are several important aspects when determining a routing algorithm. One important aspect is *path diversity*, which is a property that measures whether the network is able to diversify the paths used to send a packet from a source to a destination. Path diversity increases resilience against pathological traffic situations causing significant decrease in network performance. Ultimately, path diversity results in higher network bandwidth utilization, which leads to higher network performance and lowers cost, because the network can be designed with lower peak bandwidth and yet achieves high sustainable bandwidth.

Another important aspect is whether the routing algorithm ensures there is no deadlock possible. While deadlocks can be expected to be rare, it has to be avoided because resolving deadlocks requires expensive mechanisms while not resolving them is not acceptable as it causes system failure.

A routing algorithm also depends on the topology of the network. In some cases, the topology dictates the routing algorithm. For example, in a butterfly, the routing algorithm is deterministic, oblivious, and employs source routing. Figure 11.8 illustrates the routing. Each router has two output ports: port 0 and port 1. The port selection is based on the destination node ID. In the figure, node 000 and 110 both send a packet to node 011. The destination node ID 011 is used for routing: the first bit '0' is used to select a port in the first router, the second bit '1' is used to select a port in the second router, and the third bit '1' is used to select a port in the third router. Regardless of the senders, the same destination is reached using the port selection just described. There is no path diversity in the butterfly topology routing. This makes butterfly prone to low utilization when an adversarial network traffic pattern occurs.

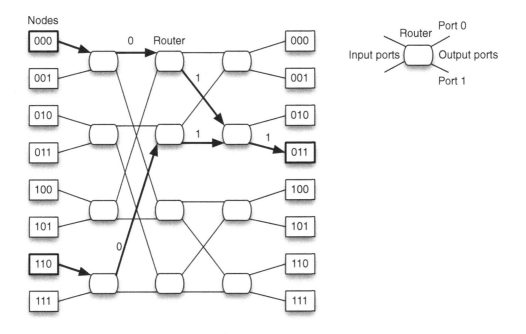

Figure 11.8: Routing in the butterfly network.

In a mesh or hypercube topology, one popular routing algorithm is *dimension-ordered* routing, which requires a packet to travel in one dimension completely before going on another dimension. For example, in a 2-D mesh, a packet must first travel in the west or east direction before it can travel in the north or south direction. Once it travels in the north or south direction, it cannot go back to travel in the west or east direction. On a mesh, a dimension ordered routing algorithm is minimal (because it is guaranteed to use the least number of hops) and deterministic. Such simplicity makes it easy to implement. It is one of the most popular routing algorithms implemented in shared memory multiprocessors that use a mesh topology. However, a dimension-ordered routing policy suffers from several drawbacks. One drawback is that due to its deterministic nature, deterministic routing can lead to contention in certain ports. If a port is congested, a packet will wait until the port becomes free, even if there are other possible paths that go through free ports. Another drawback is some ports are more utilized than others, creating unbalanced utilization of port and link resources.

Deterministic routing also leads to the lack of fault tolerance. If port or link failure occurs, packets that must use that port or link can no longer be delivered, and the entire system may freeze.

There are ways to improve the path diversity of dimension-ordered routing. An example is *O1turn routing*, where out of two dimension-ordered routing algorithms, one is selected randomly: XY or YX-ordered. Another example is *Valiant routing*, which relies on selecting a random intermediate node. To send a packet, the packet is first sent from the sender to the randomly-selected intermediate node (using dimension-ordered routing), and then from the intermediate node to the destination node (again using dimension-ordered routing). This provides path diversity because the intermediate node is selected randomly. It is possible to select multiple intermediate nodes as well for further path diversity. Such routing may become non-minimal. However, if minimal routing is desired, the intermediate node may be restricted to nodes that still guarantee minimal routing, at the expense of path diversity. This is illustrated in Figure 11.9.

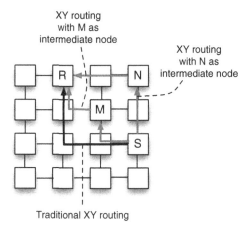

Figure 11.9: Path diversity in XY dimension-ordered routing though the selection of a random intermediate node.

So far we have discussed routing for several topologies such as butterfly and mesh/torus. What routing algorithm is available for other topologies, especially if they are irregular? Is there any routing that applies to any topology? One answer to those questions is a popular routing algorithm called *up*/down** routing. It is unique in that it is applicable to almost all types of topology, even irregular ones. It works by constructing a tree connecting all nodes. To route a packet, a sender sends the packet up the tree until a common ancestor is found, and then down the tree to the destination. In some cases, the destination may be an ancestor node, hence, it only requires a path up the tree. In other cases, the destination may be a descendant node, hence, it only requires a path down the tree. However, paths that go down the tree and then go up the tree are not valid paths.

Figure 11.10(a) shows an example of an original network from which a tree will be constructed, which is a prerequisite of the routing. The construction of the tree works in the following way. First, it starts out choosing a node to be designated as the root of the tree. In the figure, node 2 is chosen as the root of the tree. Second, the root node performs a breadth-first search traversal by sending a special command packet to nodes directly connected to it, which will become the root's children nodes. In the figure, these children include nodes 1, 3, and 6. The children nodes then send out a similar packet to nodes connected to them, and these nodes will become their children. In the figure, nodes 0, 4, 5, and 7 become the second level children nodes in the tree. If there are more nodes, the process is repeated until all nodes become a part of the tree. The resulting tree is shown in the center diagram in Figure 11.10(b). The links connecting a lower level node to an upper level node are assigned "up" direction as shown. In the next step, the breadth first traversal continues until all links are traversed. If a link connects two nodes in the same level in the tree, the direction from lower numbered node to a higher numbered node is also assigned an "up" direction. In Figure 11.10(c), we can see that the "up" links connecting node 1 to 3, 4 to 5, and 5 to 7 are added into the tree.

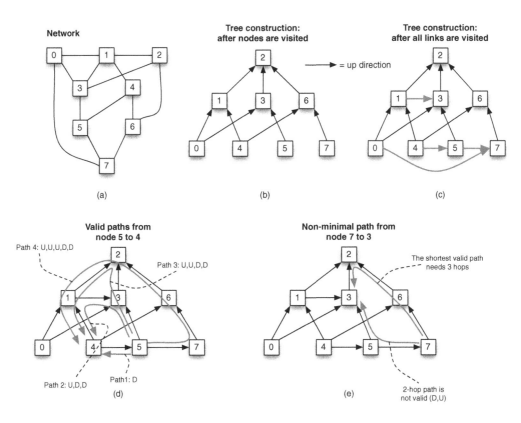

Figure 11.10: Up*/down* routing, showing the original network (a), construction of the spanning tree (b)(c), some valid paths (d), and non-minimal property (e).

Figure 11.10(d) illustrates some example valid paths in the tree from node 5 to node 4. The shortest path is to go down the tree (Path 1) which only takes one hop. Another valid path is Path 2, which requires three hops (up, down, down) through nodes 3, 1, and 4. Path 3 requires 4 hops through nodes 3, 2, 1, and 4. Path 4 requires 5 hops through nodes 7, 6, 2, 1, and 4. There are also other valid paths not shown in the figure. For latency purposes, it is beneficial to choose the shortest path to send a packet. However, the tree shows that alternative paths are available for improving path diversity.

Figure 11.10(e) illustrates one problem that up*/down* routing tends to suffer from: valid paths may not include the shortest path in the network. Thus, up*/down* routing is not minimal. For example, suppose the sender is node 7 and the destination is node 3. In the original network, node 3 is two hops away from node 7, however this requires going through node 5 (down) before reaching node 3 (up). Since the path goes down the tree and then up the tree, the path is not valid. The only valid path requires three hops through node 6 (up), node 2 (up), and finally node 3 (down). Note also that there is no path diversity for sending a packet from node 7 to node 3, whereas sending a packet from node 5 to 4 shows good path diversity. Thus, path diversity is not uniform in up*/down* routing. A final problem with up*/down* routing is that the tree root tends to receive more traffic than other nodes, hence, it may become traffic bottleneck, leading to high latencies even when other routers and links may be under-utilized.

Adaptive routing can also be implemented in a mesh or hypercube topology. The goal of adaptive routing is to achieve less probability of suffering from pathological traffic patterns, where a congestion in one router or link does not put a back pressure to many other traffic. In adaptive routing, a packet can be routed around congestion, or even around a link failure. Adaptive routing typically does not rely on the global state of the network because it is difficult to get a reliable snapshot of the degree of congestion in the entire network. Even if there is a way to capture a global snapshot, by the time information is collected, the situation may have changed. Thus, adaptive routing tends to take into account local information. The proxy for local information is typically buffer occupancy of the next downstream router. High buffer occupancy may indicate severe congestion and changing the path of a packet may not only avoid the congestion, but it may also ease the congestion.

However, adapting to local information does not guarantee that the adaptation is fruitful. In particular, there are several risks from making sub-optimal path decision. First, the new decision may lead to a router or link with worse congestion than the one encountered. Figure 11.11 (left portion) shows a packet sent to the receiver R from the sender S. The thick lines indicate congestion, and the thicker the line the worse the congestion. The packet is deflected upon encountering the first congested link, turns north and then west. Unfortunately, the new west turn suffers from even worse congestion than the one avoided the first time. Figure 11.11 (right portion) shows another problem with an adaptive routing. The packet encounters congestion near the destination and is deflected east. It then encounters another congestion so the packet is deflected south. The packet then turns west and then north, and is deflected again in a loop, such that it may get deflected again in a loop for a long time, producing a livelock situation. A mechanism is needed to avoid livelock, for example by limiting the number of deflections a packet can experience. A limit on deflections may also avoid lengthening the path significantly beyond the minimal path length. Another possible restriction is to avoid a u-turn in a deflection.

Another routing issue is how routing is implemented at the routers along the path. In some cases, the implementation may be as simple as custom logic at the routers. For example, in a butterfly routing, each router can just read the appropriate bit in the header and use the bit value to select an output port. Dimension-ordered routing in a mesh topology is slightly more complex as it needs to perform simple arithmetic to calculate Δx between the sender and destination, and if it is not zero yet, then the selected port should be east or west, otherwise a Δy is calculated and its result determines whether the selected port should be north or south. In this case, a simple logic can be implemented to compute the path.

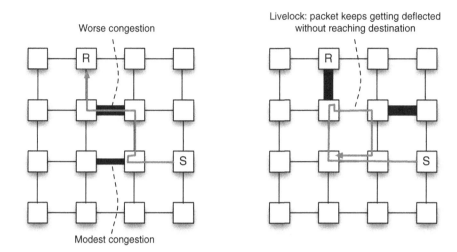

Figure 11.11: Cases where adaptive routing leading to non-desirable outcome.

Implementing adaptive routing requires programmability at the routers, hence simple combinatorial logic is not sufficient. Instead, a routing table may be added to each router and is looked up based on the destination of the packet. One way to implement an adaptive routing is *source routing*, where the entire path is determined at the sender node. At each node, there is a routing table that is indexed by the destination node and contains the full path specification. Figure 11.12 (top diagram) shows an entry for destination node R, and two possible paths for that destination. Path 1 specifies a west turn, north turn, west turn, and north turn, as shown in the diagram. Path 2 specifies north, north, west, and west turn as shown in the diagram. Multiple paths provide path diversity and one of them may be selected at random. The path information is then appended to the header of the packet. At each router along the path, a turn information is stripped off from the header before the packet is placed in the next downstream router. This continues until all turn information has been stripped off from the packet header.

Figure 11.12 (bottom diagram) shows per-hop routing, where the path decision is made on each router along the path. At each router, a routing table contains the next port information for each destination node. In this case, the packet is sent to the first downstream router, which looks up its routing table to determine the next port to forward the packet based on the destination node R. The next router performs similar steps, and so on until the packet reaches the destination node.

In both source and per-hop routing, the routing tables may be reprogrammed periodically either to adapt to changes in the traffic situation, to balance load better, or to route around faults. This fault tolerance ability is in contrast to the lack of it with deterministic routing. An advantage of a per-hop routing is that the routing table is smaller in size and thus is faster to look up. On the other hand, source routing obviates the need for table lookup at routers along the path.

Dealing with Deadlock and Livelock

A deadlock is a situation in which all parties involved are stalled and cannot make any progress. Deadlocks can occur in different components of a multiprocessor, such as in the program due to

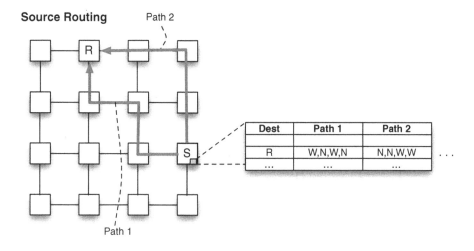

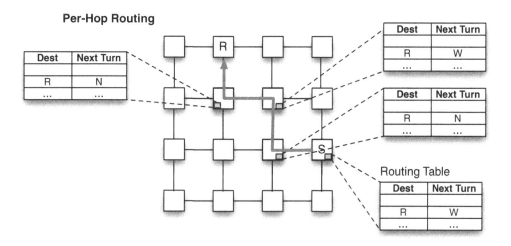

Figure 11.12: Illustration of source vs. per-hop routing.

the order of lock acquisitions, in the coherence protocol due to incorrect handling of protocol races, in the interconnection network, etc. We will focus on the deadlocks that occur specifically in the interconnection network that manifest in the inability to forward packets.

A deadlock in an interconnection network refers to a situation in which packets are stalled and cannot be sent further on a set of links. It occurs due to limited buffers and cyclic dependence in buffer space acquisition. Figure 11.13(a) illustrates such a deadlock. The figure shows four packets being transmitted. Each packet has filled up the input buffer in a channel and needs to be forwarded to the next channel. However, the output buffer in the next channel is already full as it is already occupied by a packet that needs to be transmitted. However, that packet is also stalled because the output buffer in the next node is full, and so on. When such channel acquisition dependence forms a cycle, deadlocks can occur.

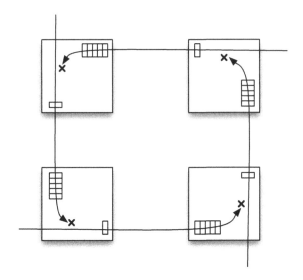

Figure 11.13: An illustration of a deadlock situation.

A deadlock can be detected, broken, or avoided by removing the possibility of a cyclic channel acquisition. While there are deadlock detection algorithms, they are very expensive to deploy on an interconnection network that requires a very low latency communication between nodes. There are also techniques that can recover from deadlocks such as dropping packets. Dropping one of the packets shown in the figure removes the deadlock and allows all other packets to continue. However, again, such a strategy is not desirable to use for a low latency network because when a packet is dropped, it must be detected (likely via a time-out) and retransmitted. A time-out mechanism and its subsequent retransmission introduce an intolerable delay in a shared memory multiprocessor system in which low latencies are paramount for performance. Thus, an acceptable solution must come either from deadlock avoidance, or from deadlock resolution using redundant resources. We will first look at deadlock avoidance techniques.

One popular deadlock avoidance technique for a mesh-family of topologies is a policy referred to as a *turn restriction* routing algorithm. The basis for the algorithm is based on the observation that in order for a deadlock to occur, all four anti clockwise turns shown in Figure 11.13 must occur. Similarly, all four clockwise turns can also cause a deadlock. In order to eliminate the possibility of a cycle forming, we should eliminate at least one of the four anti clockwise turns, and at least one of the four clockwise turns. This is why the algorithms are referred to as "turn restriction" routing algorithms.

A dimension-ordered routing naturally restricts all turns from the y-dimension to the x-dimension, hence, it is naturally deadlock free. However, it imposes deterministic routing. Relaxing the number of turns that are restricted can still give the deadlock freedom benefit while permitting non-deterministic routing. If we restrict one anti clockwise turn and one clockwise turn, we can come up with $4 \times 4 = 16$ pairs of turns that can be restricted to eliminate the possibility of deadlocks. Figure 11.14 shows three of them. The *west first* routing restricts all turns to the west because the west direction must be taken first before any other directions. The *north last* routing restricts turning to any direction when the current direction is north. Hence, going in the north direction must be taken after all turns are completed. Finally, *negative first* restricts turning to the negative direction in each dimension (i.e., turning west on the x-dimension or turning south on the y-dimension). Any hop in the negative direction must be taken first before taking the first turn.

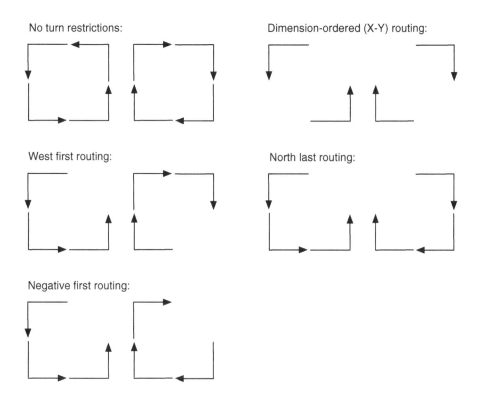

Figure 11.14: Restricting turns to avoid the possibility of deadlocks. Legal turns are shown in the figure.

To illustrate turn restrictions, consider the following example of a 2-D mesh network with bidirectional links, with several paths:

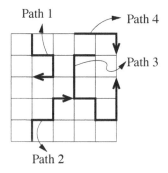

Under *west first* routing, Path 1 is not allowed because it goes to west last, Path 2 and 4 are allowed because they never go west, and Path 3 is allowed because it goes west first before making any turns. Under *north last* routing: Path 1 and 4 are allowed because they never go north, Path 2 is not allowed because it turns north in the middle and makes a turn east after that, while Path 3 is allowed because the last turn goes north and no more turns are made.

Turn restriction algorithms not only improve path diversity, it also allows non-minimum length paths between two nodes. Such a property can be used for routing around a link failure as well as for routing around congested links.

■ *Did you know?*

A reason why up*/down* routing only allows paths that go up the tree, go down the tree, or go up the tree and then go down the tree, but not go down the tree then go up the tree, is to avoid the possibility of deadlocks. By prohibiting going down then up the tree, cyclic dependency in channel acquisition is guaranteed not to occur. Thus, up*/down* routing is deadlock free.

Another way to deal with deadlock is to resolve it when it occurs. One way to achieve that is through using redundant channels. For example, suppose that between each pair of two adjacent nodes, instead of having one channel, we add a redundant channel, consisting of buffers and a link. We only use one channel under a normal situation in which there are no deadlocks. When a deadlock (or congestion) occurs, we can utilize the spare channel to route packets that were potentially deadlocked. In order to avoid the possibility of deadlocks from occurring in the spare channels as well, we can put restrictions, such as only allowing one packet to be using the spare channels at a time, or imposing turn restriction on the spare channels, etc. Hence, deadlocks can be resolved without packet dropping. Note that accurately identifying a deadlock is difficult. However, since a deadlock in the interconnect manifests in long packet delay, we can detect congestion as a proxy for a possible deadlock.

A key drawback, however, is that spare channels are expensive: they require doubling the number of links, and the buffers in a new channel that corresponds to both ends of a channel. Thus, a router becomes more costly. However, there is a way to reduce the cost of spare channels. Note that the deadlock occurs due to the buffers in routers becoming full and cannot receive more flits. When such a situation occurs, the flow control at the link level prevents the sender from sending new flits until the buffer becomes free again. But since there is a deadlock, the buffer does not become free. Hence, while buffers are full, links are free and unused in a deadlock. Therefore, spare channels only need to include buffers at the routers but not extra links. Two or more channels have their own buffers but can share a single link. Such channels are referred to as *virtual channels*. Hence, to the network protocols, it is as if there are multiple separate channels while in fact physically they share common links.

Figure 11.15 illustrates how a virtual channel allows a deadlock to be resolved. The network has two virtual channels, with VC1 used for regular routing, and VC2 used as an *escape channel*, when congestion results in a packet being blocked, or being blocked for more than a threshold amount of time, it is moved to the escape channel. In the figure, the packet that goes north and wants to turn west is moved into the escape channel, allowing it to continue to move in its path. This will eventually unblock other packets, allowing them to also continue to move. Note, however, that the design must ensure that deadlocks are not possible in the escape channel. As we discussed earlier, routing restrictions (e.g., dimension-ordered, turn restriction, up*/down*) can achieve that.

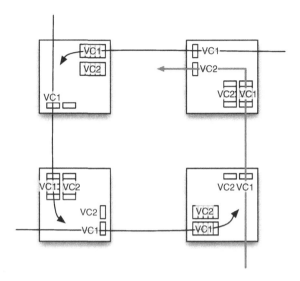

Figure 11.15: An illustration of using virtual channels to resolve a deadlock.

■ *Did you know?*

Besides deadlocks, network architects must also worry about livelocks. It is possible that some packets lose out many times resulting in a delay, possibly indefinitely. One particular case is when a data reply packet loses out to coherence request packets, resulting in it being delayed for a long time. Without the data reply reaching the requester, the outstanding coherence transaction corresponding to the data cannot be closed. Other requests to the same block address will keep getting negative acknowledged and retried. The retried requests may keep on flooding the buffer resources, not allowing the data reply packet to go through. To avoid such a situation, a router may distinguish packet types and enforce a minimum guarantee for a buffer space for each packet type. This can be achieved by providing different virtual channels for different packet types.

11.4 Router Architecture

So far, we have assumed that given a packet, a router will correctly send the packet to the next channel. But exactly what components are inside a router? Figure 11.16 shows the architecture of a router.

The figure shows an example router with a degree of 5, having five input ports and five output ports, connected to five input and output physical channels. Any of the five input channels should be able to send a packet to any of the five output channels. The *switch* provides the interconnectivity between input and output channels to enable that. A switch may be implemented as a *crossbar* or other designs. The box that connects an input channel to the switch (labeled as Box A) may have different designs as shown in the figure.

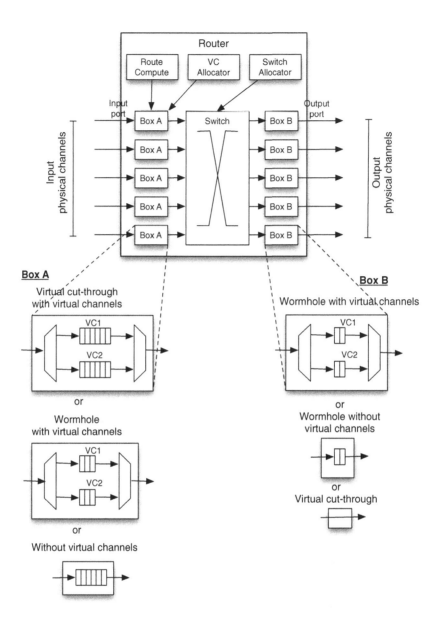

Figure 11.16: Router architecture.

Starting from the simplest (bottom diagram), Box A may simply contain a queue to buffer flits or packets that come from the respective channel. The queue may be a first-in-first-out (FIFO) queue or a different design. A FIFO queue is simple to design but incurs a risk of *head blocking*, where if the flit at the head of the queue blocks, e.g., unable to reserve the output channel, all other flits behind it are also blocked, even when they want to go to a different output channel. A non-FIFO queue may allow flits to be serviced out of order, at the expense of more complex design, and higher latency and power consumption. If there are virtual channels, then instead of a single queue, we may have two or more queues, as shown in the second diagram from the bottom. In the diagram, a packet's header flit contains the information of which channel the packet should be transmitted in. Based on that information, the flit goes to one of the virtual channels (the figure shows two virtual channels VC1 or VC2). Compared to a single channel, multiple virtual channels does not necessarily increase the buffer size. The buffer size is strongly affected by the available bandwidth per channel. Since two virtual channels will share a single physical channel, they may be designed to handle half the bandwidth, and hence need approximately only half of the single channel's queue size. When virtual cut-through routing is used, the flow control requires the buffer to be able to accommodate an entire packet, and thus the buffers need to be larger in size, as shown in the top diagram of Box A.

Moving on to the output channel, let us examine the design of Box B. With cut-through routing, it is guaranteed that the downstream router has sufficient buffer space for an entire packet. Thus, flits of a packet can flow through directly to the output channel, knowing that they are guaranteed to be accepted in the input channel of the downstream router. This is shown in the bottom diagram for Box B. With wormhole routing, flow control is performed flit by flit, thus we may have to have flit buffer at the output channel to keep a few flits temporarily buffered before the downstream router signals availability of buffer space for the flits (middle diagram). With virtual channels, the buffer space needs to be replicated for each channel (top diagram).

When a flit arrives at a router, it goes through several processing steps before it can be sent out from the router's output port. It has to be buffered at the input channel and its header decoded. Its output channel has to be computed. Then, resources at the output must be allocated, for example the buffer space for the flit or packet at the downstream router must be able to accept it. It has to ensure that the switch is available to transmit the flit to the output channel (against competing input channels that want to send flits to the output channel). Finally, it has to transmit the flit. These steps are typically designed into the micro architecture of the router's pipeline. They are:

- Decode and Compute (DC). In this step, the header flit is decoded to discover the input channel and destination. The flit is then buffered at the correct input virtual channel. The destination may be used to compute the output port, based on arithmetic calculation or based on a look up of the routing table.

- Virtual-Channel Allocation (VA): based on the output port computed in the previous step, a request for an output virtual channel is made, and a global virtual channel arbitration decides whether the requested output virtual channel is available (can be allocated) or not.

- Switch Allocation (SA): based on the output port, the global switch allocator allocates the switch to connect the input channel and output port (where the output virtual channel is connected).

- Switch Traversal (ST): transmit the flit is transmitted through the switch to the output virtual channel.

The header flit of a packet has to go through all the steps above. However, body flits will use the same output virtual channel, hence they only need to go through the last two steps: switch allocation and traversal. The tail flit releases all the resources that were allocated for the packet. Each virtual channel has a finite state machine that keeps track of the state of the channel, whether it is doing routing, allocating output virtual channel, etc.

The steps above allow the router to be pipelined. Canonically, the steps contribute to four pipeline stages. In an actual implementation, the stages may be combined, split, or new stages added. However, some stages are difficult or expensive to split. For example, virtual channel allocator involves a lot of wires connecting input channels to output channels. Splitting it into multiple pipeline stages requires the insertion of a large number of latches, which introduces additional complexity. Figure 11.17 illustrates a canonical router pipeline. Part (a) of the figure shows an example of the timing in which a four-flit packet is processed in the router pipeline. The head flit goes through all four pipeline stages, while the body flits and tail flit follow behind in a pipelined manner. The entire packet is processed in a total of 7 clock cycles; without pipelining, it would take about twice as long.

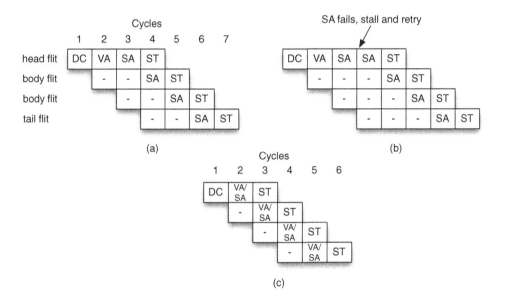

Figure 11.17: Canonical router pipeline without stall (a), with a stall (b), and speculative router pipeline (c).

As with processor pipeline, structural hazards can occur and affect different pipeline stages. For example, the virtual channel allocation may suffer from structural hazard when there is no buffer space available at the output channel. A switch allocation may fail when the switch arbitration logic decides to grant access to the output channel to a competing input channel. When structural hazard is encountered, stalls are introduced in the pipeline. Figure 11.17(b) shows a one-cycle stall due to a failed switch allocation affecting the head flit.

It is also possible to perform virtual channel allocation and switch allocation in parallel. This reduces the packet processing by one clock cycle (Figure 11.17(c)). However, the switch allocation becomes speculative, i.e., switch may be allocated but not used if the virtual channel allocation fails. The head flit is said to be a speculative flit, while the body flits are non-speculative flits.

The cost of a router is a significant fraction of the total cost of an interconnection network. First, buffers take up a lot of die area and consume a lot of power because there are many of them. The die area overhead is equivalent to the number of ports multiplied by the number of virtual channels multiplied by the depth of each buffer. Secondly, in order to connect any input port to any output port directly, a crossbar switch is often used. A crossbar switch is expensive when the number of ports is high. In order to connect n input ports to n output ports, the complexity of a crossbar is $\Theta(n^2)$. While the crossbar can be made cheaper by replacing it with a multistage network, the latency increases.

Recall that from performance and scalability perspectives, it was clear that a high dimensional network is preferred compared to a low dimensional network. However, the cost of routers is the major impediment to adopting a high dimensional network. Increasing the degree (radix) of a router increases the complexity of the control logic for arbitrating and allocating the virtual channels and the switch, and increases the complexity of the switch quadratically.

Interestingly, the cost of links and buffers does not necessarily increase with the higher dimension. While the number of links is higher for a high dimensional network compared to a low dimensional network, the links can be made narrower such that the number of wires is constant (hence the total cost for links can also be made constant). A narrower link also implies a lower link bandwidth, which requires shallower channel buffers. Thus, while the number of buffers increases linearly with the degree of the routers, the total buffer size can be made constant since each buffer becomes smaller.

Overall, in order to allow multiprocessor systems to scale, some of the main challenges in the router architecture is how to keep the cost and latency of the control logic and switches of a router in high dimensional networks.

11.5 Case Study: Alpha 21364 Network Architecture

The Alpha 21364 is a multiprocessor system consisting of single-core nodes, produced to market in the early 2000s. It connects 128 nodes with a 2-dimensional torus network topology. Each node has a single processor, main memory, two memory controllers, and is attached to a router. A torus provides a lower network diameter and higher bisection bandwidth compared to a single-dimensional topologies such as a ring. While three or higher dimensional topologies may provide an even lower diameter and higher bisection bandwidth, a torus router is simpler and cheaper as it has a smaller radix. For a system up to 128 nodes, a torus seems to be a reasonable choice.

A phit and a flit are both 39 bit in size, consisting of 32 bits of data and 7-bit of error correcting code (ECC). A message has a variable number of flits depending on the packet class. A memory read/write request packet contains a block address and has a size of 3 flits. A data response packet class contains a 64-byte data block and takes up 18-19 flits. Other classes include forward class (3 flits), non-data response class (2-3 flits), read I/O class (3 flits), write I/O class (19 flits), and special class (1-3 flits). Each router has 7 ports, consisting of four ports (north, east, south, and west) to connect with other routers in the torus, 1 local port connecting to the local cache, 2 ports to connect to two memory controllers, and 1 port to connect to the I/O. The total aggregate bandwidth of the seven ports is 22.4 GB/sec.

Each physical channel has 19 virtual channels. The virtual channels are used in the following way. First, each packet class is assigned its own virtual channel. This avoids different packet types from interfering or blocking one another, for example when request packets blocking a response packet for a long period of time. The system uses virtual cut-through routing, hence each virtual channel has a buffer space sufficient to hold one entire packet. Since different virtual channels are used for different packet classes, and packet classes differ in sizes, the buffer space differs across virtual channels.

To provide path diversity, the system uses minimal adaptive routing, where a router chooses one of two ports to forward a packet depending on various considerations such as congestion status of different ports. Only ports that will result in reducing the Manhattan distance to the destination can be selected, hence, for any router, there are only at most two ports that satisfy that. In order to spread out traffic, when the two ports are equally non-congested, the port along the same dimension is selected for the next hop. Figure 11.18(a) illustrates all valid paths going from one node to another. From node S to R, there are 4 valid paths that are minimal, and in each path, every hop taken reduces the Manhattan distance between S and R.

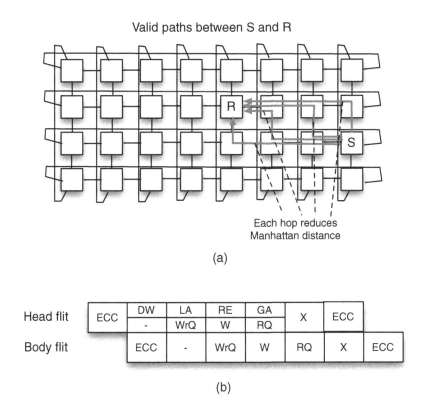

Figure 11.18: Alpha 21364's adaptive routing (a) and router pipeline (b).

With the adaptive routing, since there are no turn restrictions, there is no guarantee that deadlock cannot occur. To resolve deadlocks, two additional virtual channels are provided as escape channels. The escape channels have to ensure deadlock freedom, and thus are used in the following way. All nodes are enumerated $1, 2, 3, \ldots, N$ as their IDs. If the source's ID is lower than the destination's ID, then one of the escape channels is used. If the source's ID is higher than the destination's ID, then the other escape channel is used. Each of the six packet classes has an adaptive plus two escape virtual channels. Only the special packet class uses one virtual channel. Thus, in total there are $6 \times 3 + 1 = 19$ virtual channels.

The router is aggressively clocked at the same clock frequency as the processor (1.2 GHz). This allows deep pipelining in the router. The router has 7 pipeline stages for a flit, as shown in Figure 11.18(b) illustrates the seven stages. There are an additional six cycles for synchronization delay, pad receiver, and driver delay, hence the total router and link delay is 7+6=13 cycles, or 10.8ns. The router pipeline is illustrated in Figure 11.18(b). The head flit goes through two pipelines: the scheduling pipeline (upper) and data pipeline (lower). Body flits only go through the data pipeline. The first pipeline stage (ECC) computes error correction code of the flit and compares it with the received error correction code. The ECC detects up to 2-bit and corrects 1-bit transmission error. In a rare case when there are a larger number of errors, recovery mode is activated. In the scheduling pipeline, the head flit is decoded and table entry written (DW). Then, local arbitration is performed (LA), entry table is read (RE), and global arbitration is performed (GA). Switch traversal is performed next (X), with a new ECC generated to match the new header content (ECC). In the data scheduling pipeline, the flit is written to the input buffer (WrQ), one cycle of wait (W), and it is read out from the input buffer (RQ).

The header of a packet has 16 bits, and fits entirely in the head flit. The header consists of 1-bit east vs. west direction + 1-bit north vs. south direction, 8-bit destination coordinate (4-bit each dimension), one bit indicating if the packet can use the adaptive channel, one bit to indicate if the packet is an I/O packet, and two bits to encode virtual channel number, and two reserve bits.

Arbitration is performed in two pipeline stages: local arbitration arbitrates among competing input virtual channels for access to the switch input port, global arbitration arbitrates among competing input ports for access to the output port. The arbitration enforces fairness by using least-recently-selected (LRS) scheme for both global and local arbitration. It also uses a policy that prioritizes the data response packet class over request packet class.

11.6 Multicore Design Issues

So far we have discussed the interconnect network in general. We have not distinguished a network that was used for interconnecting multiple chips in a shared memory server, or a network that was used for interconnecting cores in a single chip. The latter can be referred to as a network on chip (NoC) architecture. While inter-chip network and NoC face similar design issues with regard to network topology, routing, deadlock, and router architecture, there are multicore-specific design characteristics that are unique to NoC. We will discuss such issues in this section.

One characteristic unique to NoC is with regard to wiring. Wiring is constrained to several (e.g., two) upper metal layers that are available for the interconnect. These metal layers are shared with power and clock distribution network. The metal layers require wiring to be laid out horizontally, or vertically when wires connect with logic in the layer below. Wires need to be short in order for them to exhibit low resistance capacitance (RC) product low, enabling low delay and power consumption. Wires also should not be laid out in such a way that they render the die area below unusable. For example, a long wire that requires a repeater in the logic layer below cannot be laid out on top of dense logic, such as the core and its L1 caches. This makes it more challenging to lay out global interconnect wires. A consequence of the wiring constraints above is that some topologies are easier to implement than others. For example, a 2D mesh topology will have shorter links than a 2D torus topology, even with folding. Furthermore, a high-dimensional topology may be attractive to use in a general interconnection network due to its low diameter and high bisection bandwidth, but may be costly to implement in an NoC. For example, a 3D mesh requires physically longer links connecting even for nodes that are topologically adjacent.

Let us look into 3D mesh in a greater detail. The advantage of low diameter and average distance over a 2D mesh is substantial when the number of nodes is high. Thus, at some high node count, it may become more attractive over 2D mesh despite its long-wire links. How a 3D mesh is mapped into a planar layout is an important determinant of how long the links are going to be. Figure 11.19 shows 3D mesh in an NoC: logical topology (left diagram), less efficient layout showing wires that span half the length of the chip (middle diagram), and more efficient layout showing wires that span at most two adjacent nodes (right diagram).

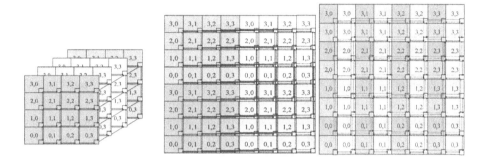

Figure 11.19: 3D mesh in an NoC: logical topology (left), less efficient layout (middle), and more efficient layout (right). Source: [31].

Another characteristic unique to an NoC is the link delay compared to router delay. In an inter-chip interconnect, the link delay is significant compared to router delay. However, in an NoC, the link delay may be small relative to the router delay. For example the Alpha 21364 example from the previous discussion, the link delay is 6 clock cycles while the router delay is 7 clock cycles. In an NoC, it is possible to have a much shorter link delay, such as one or two clock cycles. Thus, it becomes more important to design a low latency and highly-pipelined router in an NoC.

Finally, with regard to power consumption, an NoC competes for the chip power budget with other components such as the cores or caches, making it important to choose low power NoC design. In recent studies, when all cores are 100% utilized, the NoC in Intel SCC, Sun Niagara, Intel 80-core chip, and MIT RAW chip consume 10%, 17%, 28%, and 36% of the total chip power, respectively. These fractions increase when some cores enter low-power modes. In many implementations, even though some nodes are idle and are powered down, NoC resources must be kept powered to provide connectivity. This makes it more challenging to reduce the power consumption of the NoC. As the core count increases, communication bandwidth between the cores likely grows quadratically, causing the share of power consumption of the NoC to be an increasing fraction of the overall chip power consumption.

Figure 11.20 shows an estimated comparison of power consumption of various NoC topologies. The figure only shows the power consumed by the crossbar switch and links. Overall, the figure shows that a higher dimension topology incurs more power consumption. Thus, a higher dimension topology, even though it provides lower diameter and average distance and higher bisection bandwidth, it also suffers from higher power consumption.

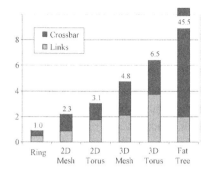

Figure 11.20: Estimated power consumption for various NoC topologies. Source: [31].

11.6.1 Contemporary Design Issues

Irregular topology. In some cases, multicore chip may integrate heterogeneous core, heterogeneous caches, and various IP blocks such as accelerators. Such a design results in a heterogeneous communication bandwidth demand. For example, a high-performance core likely needs to be fed data at a faster rate than an energy-efficient core. Such a core can benefit from higher bandwidth topology connecting it to memory controllers. Such different requirements may require the network on chip to be irregular, in terms of topology, router design, and routing algorithms. This makes design of NoC more challenging.

Quality of service. Another issue that has been researched actively recently is quality of service (QoS). The need for QoS increases as the multicore increases in diversity, in terms of applications or virtual machines that are co-scheduled on the single multicore chip, and the components integrated in the multicore chip. For example, display controllers may have specific bandwidth requirements in order to ensure glitch-free display. Such differences in bandwidth requirements may be encoded in classes of service. For example, one class of service may be designated for bandwidth-sensitive applications or IP blocks. Another class of service may be designated for bandwidth-flexible applications or IP blocks. Packets may be tagged based on their respective classes of service. The classes of service may be assigned to different virtual channels. With such an approach, when packets with different classes of service arrive at a router and compete for access to the same output port, the QoS policy can be implemented in the virtual channel allocator and switch allocator. These allocators may implement a priority-based arbitration to favor a higher class of service over a lower class of service.

Power management. Power management techniques for NoC can be divided into techniques to reduce static or dynamic power consumption. To reduce static power consumption, one possible technique is to power gate ports and links in response to bursts and dips in network traffic. Such a technique must be balanced against the risk of packets suffering from significant delay as components take time to be powered on again. To reduce dynamic power consumption, one possible technique is to employ dynamic voltage scaling, where voltage is lowered on routers or links when bandwidth utilization of the routers or links is low.

Another technique is referred to *router parking* [52], where routers connected to sleeping cores are also power gated. This requires traffic to be rerouted to alternative paths with active routers. This requires adaptive routing. Router parking must still provide connectivity, thus constraints must be placed so that the network does not become disconnected. In addition, the change in network topology due to power gating of new routers must be designed carefully so that no deadlocks are introduced.

Circuit switching. In circuit switching, connection between a sender and receiver is reserved prior to data being sent over the connection. Once the connection set up has completed, messages can travel very efficiently, with minimum amount of buffering, and with very little router delay as no arbitration for router resources is needed. Circuit switching suffers from low bandwidth utilization and high connection set up delay. However, it becomes more attractive in several situations: high router delay, high hop count, and larger packets. As multicore starts to integrate accelerators, many accelerators work not on a single cache block at a time, but more typically on a few kilobytes of data at once. At some point, circuit switching becomes a more energy efficient alternative than packet switching. Future routers may be designed to handle both circuit switching and packet switching connections simultaneously [32, 57].

11.7 Exercises

Worked Problems

1. **Network topology metrics**. Suppose we have 6 nodes that are connected through a mesh as shown in this figure.

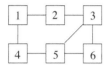

   (a) Compute the diameter and the average distance of the network.

   (b) Compute the bisection bandwidth of the network.

   Answer:

   (a) The diameter is the maximum distance in the network. The distance between node 1 and node 6, denoted by $d(1,6)$ is one of the largest. Hence, the network diameter is three. To compute the average distance, we need to list all pairs of nodes and their distances, and take their average. The pairs and their distances are:
   d(1,2) = 1, d(1,3) = 2, d(1,4) = 1, d(1,5) = 2, d(1,6) = 3,
   d(2,3) = 1, d(2,4) = 2, d(2,5) = 2, d(2,6) = 2,
   d(3,4) = 2, d(3,5) = 1, d(3,6) = 1,
   d(4,5) = 1, d(4,6) = 2,
   d(5,6) = 1
   The sum of all distances is 24, and the number of pairs is $\binom{6}{2} = 15$, hence, the average distance is $\frac{24}{15} = 1.6$.

   (b) We can partition the network in several ways, and the bisection bandwidth is the minimum number of links that need to be cut to create the two equal partitions. In this case, since there are six nodes, we need to partition them into three nodes each. If we partition them into (1, 2, 3) and (4, 5, 6), we need to cut three links. If we partition them into (1, 2, 4) and (3, 5, 6), we need to cut two links. Therefore, the bisection bandwidth is two times the link bandwidth.

2. **Routing latency**. Suppose that a multiprocessor system is interconnected using 500-MHz links that are 1 byte wide. We want to measure the maximum latency to transmit a packet between a pair of nodes. Assume that the packet size is 100 byte, and the time spent to route a packet in a router is 8 clock cycles. Compute the following latencies:

   (a) 16, 64, 256, and 1024-processor systems with 2-D mesh interconnection network topology, using store-and-forward routing.

   (b) 16, 64, 256, and 1024-processor systems with 2-D mesh interconnection network topology, using cut-through routing.

   (c) 16, 64, 256, and 1024-processor systems with hypercube interconnection network topology, using store-and-forward routing.

(d) 16, 64, 256, and 1024-processor systems with hypercube interconnection network topology, using cut-through routing.

(e) 16, 64, 256, and 1024-processor systems with butterfly interconnection network topology, using store-and-forward routing.

(f) 16, 64, 256, and 1024-processor systems with butterfly interconnection network topology, using cut-through routing.

Answer: 500 MHz link, 1 byte wide, 100-byte packet size, 8-cycle routing delay

The maximum distance (diameter):

Topology	Formula	p=16	p=64	p=256	p=1024
2D mesh	$2(\sqrt{p}-1)$	6	14	30	62
Hypercube	$log_2\ p$	4	6	8	10
Butterfly	$log_2\ p$	4	6	8	10

The packet routing delay for store and forward routing: $T_{sf} = h(\frac{n}{b}+\Delta)$, while routing delay for cut through routing: $T_{ct} = \frac{n}{b}+h\Delta$, where h is the network hop distance, Δ is the routing delay, n is the packet size, and b is the bandwidth.

Since $\Delta = 8$ cycles, and $\frac{n}{b} = \frac{100}{1} = 100$ cycles, then:

Topology	16	64	256	1024
2D mesh, s&f	648	1512	3240	6696
2D mesh, ct	148	212	340	596
Hypercube, s&f	432	648	864	1080
Hypercube, ct	132	148	164	180
Butterfly, s&f	432	648	864	1080
Butterfly, ct	132	148	164	180

3. **Interconnection network characteristics**. Compute the (i) switch degree, (ii) network diameter, (iii) number of links, and (iv) bisection bandwidth of:

(a) Ring network, where the numbers of nodes are 16, 64, and 256.

(b) 2D-mesh, where the numbers of nodes are 16, 64, and 256.

(c) Butterfly, where the numbers of nodes are 16, 64, and 256.

(d) Hypercube, where the numbers of nodes are 16, 64, and 256.

(e) Fat tree, where the numbers of nodes are 16, 64, and 256.

Answer:

Topology	Diameter	Bisection BW	#Links	Degree
Ring 16	8	2	16	2
Ring 64	32	2	64	2
Ring 256	128	2	256	2
2-D Mesh 16	6	4	32	4
2-D Mesh 64	14	8	128	4
2-D Mesh 256	30	16	512	4

Hypercube 16	4	8	8	8
Hypercube 64	6	32	12	12
Hypercube 256	8	128	16	16
Binary Fat Tree 16	8	8	30	3
Binary Fat Tree 64	12	32	126	3
Binary Fat Tree 256	16	128	510	3
Butterfly 16	4	8	128	4
Butterfly 64	6	32	768	4
Butterfly 256	8	128	4096	4

4. **Routing**. In the following network, find which paths/routes are allowed under minimal routing, X-Y dimension-ordered routing, west-first routing, north-last routing, and negative-first routing.

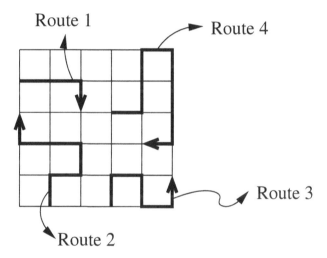

Route 1, Route 4, Route 3, Route 2

Answer:

Allowed in routing?	Route 1	Route 2	Route 3	Route 4
Minimum routing	Yes	No	No	No
X-Y dimension-ordered	Yes	No	No	No
West-First	Yes	No	Yes	No
North-Last	Yes	No	No	No
Negative-First	No	No	No	No

Homework Problems

1. **Routing latency**. Suppose that a multiprocessor system is interconnected using 100-MHz links that are 1 byte wide. We want to measure the maximum latency to transmit a packet between a pair of nodes. Assume that the packet size is 1 Kbyte, and the time spent to route a packet in a router is 20 clock cycles. Compute the following latencies:

(a) 16, 64, 256, and 1024-processor systems with 2-D mesh interconnection network topology, using store-and-forward routing.

(b) 16, 64, 256, and 1024-processor systems with 2-D mesh interconnection network topology, using cut-through routing.

(c) 16, 64, 256, and 1024-processor systems with hypercube interconnection network topology, using store-and-forward routing.

(d) 16, 64, 256, and 1024-processor systems with hypercube interconnection network topology, using cut-through routing.

(e) 16, 64, 256, and 1024-processor systems with butterfly interconnection network topology, using store-and-forward routing.

(f) 16, 64, 256, and 1024-processor systems with butterfly interconnection network topology, using cut-through routing.

2. **Topology characteristics**. For the following network, compute the diameter, average distance, and bisection bandwidth (as a multiple of link bandwidth L). Assume that each link is bidirectional.

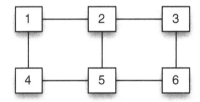

3. **Routing**. For the network below, find all valid minimal paths for sending a packet from node 4 to node 3 with (a) X-Y dimension-ordered routing, (b) west first routing, and (c) north-last routing.

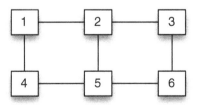

4. **Up*/Down* routing.** For network below, (a) construct up*/down* routing tree with arrows showing up directions assuming node 5 is the root of the tree, and (b) show valid paths for sending a packet from node 1 to node 6, including non-minimal paths.

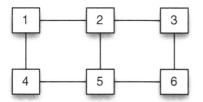

5. **Hypercube topology characteristics**.

For a d-dimensional hypercube with $p = 2^d$ number of nodes, prove that:

   (a) Its diameter is log_2p.

   (b) Its bisection bandwidth is $\frac{p}{2}$.

   (c) Its total number of links (assuming bidirectional links) $\frac{p}{2} \times log_2p$. (Hint: one helpful approach is to think of how many ways you can cut the network into two partitions with a $(d-1)$-dimensional plane, and how many links are removed by the plane).

   (d) Its router degree is log_2p.

6. **k-ary d-mesh topology characteristics**.

For a d-dimensional hypercube with $p = 2^d$ number of nodes, prove that:

   (a) Its diameter is $d(k-1)$.

   (b) Its bisection bandwidth is k^{d-1}.

   (c) Its total number of links (assuming bidirectional links) $dk^{d-1}(k-1)$. (Hint: this problem is intellectually satisfying for those who are math-inclined. A useful tool to derive this is to use induction. Start by expressing the number of links for a given number of nodes p as a function of the number of links for $\frac{p}{k}$ nodes on a directly smaller dimension. Once you have this function, you can unroll it and express the unrolled function directly as a function of d and k. Enjoy.)

   (d) Its router degree is $2d$.

Chapter 12

SIMT Architecture

Contributed by: Huiyang Zhou

Contents

Recently, single-instruction multiple-thread (SIMT) architecture has been emerging as a promising approach to achieving high throughput computing with high energy efficiency. The most well-known SIMT processors are state-of-the-art graphics processor units (GPUs). The innovations of SIMT architecture come from both the hardware architecture and software sides:

- On the software side, the SIMT programming models, such as CUDA and OpenCL, enable data parallelism to be expressed as task-level parallelism. Application developers compose scalar programs to capture task-level parallelism, which tends to be much friendlier than classical vector processing in exposing data-level parallelism.

- On the hardware architecture side, SIMT architecture provides an elegant way to convert scalar instructions into vector-style single-instruction multiple-data (SIMD) processing to achieve energy efficiency. Meanwhile, it leverages fine-grain multithreading to hide instruction execution latencies to achieve high computational throughput.

In this chapter, we use a top-down approach to describe SIMT architecture. We first present the SIMT programming model. Next, we discuss how SIMT workloads are mapped to SIMT processors. Then, we dive into the microarchitecture of SIMT processors. During our discussion, we will borrow the terminology from both CUDA and OpenCL. Our description of SIMT architecture is for a generic SIMT processor rather than focusing on a particular GPU product.

12.1   SIMT Programming Model

The SIMT programming model enables data parallelism to be expressed as task-level parallelism. It follows the single-program multiple-thread paradigm, meaning that all threads share the same program. An application developer writes the scalar code, which is often referred to as kernel functions. All threads, also called *work items*, execute the same kernel functions and each thread uses its unique thread identifiers to determine the data to be operated upon.

Code 12.1 shows an SIMT code example, which implements a vector-add operation. Each thread computes one element in the sum vector.

Code 12.1 The SIMT code for the vectoradd operation.
```
1 kernel vec_add(float * A, float *B, float *S) {
2     //tid is the thread identifier int tid = ...;
3     S[tid] = A[tid] + B[tid];
4 }
```

For the SIMT kernel in Code 12.1, the length of the vectors is not explicitly specified in the kernel code. It can be set as the number of threads through kernel invocation. To explicitly use the vector length, the kernel code can be changed to Code 12.2.

Code 12.2 The SIMT code for the vector-add operation with explicit control of the vector length N.
```
1 kernel vec_add(float * A, float *B, float *S, int N) {
2     //tid is the thread identifier int tid = ...;
3     if(tid < N)
4         S[tid] = A[tid] + B[tid];
5 }
```

SIMT threads are organized in a hierarchy. A kernel is invoked as a grid of *thread blocks*, which are also referred to as *workgroups* or cooperative thread arrays (CTAs). A thread block in turn contains multiple threads. The unique feature of a thread block is that the threads in the same thread block are able to communicate and/or synchronize with each other efficiently through special hardware support called shared memory. Thread blocks in a thread grid and threads in a thread block can be organized in multiple dimensions. The purpose is to facilitate mapping thread identifiers to data items in application domains. Typically, the number of threads in a thread block is limited by hardware.

For the vector add example, we can use the following thread organization. Each thread block contains 128 threads and these threads are put in one dimension. The number of thread blocks is set as (N % TBsize) ?   (N/128) :   (N+128)/128, where TBsize is the thread block size, 128 in this case. And all these thread blocks are put in one dimension as well. Using the CUDA convention, the SIMT thread hierarchy is described in Code 12.3 and used in the kernel invocation function.

Code 12.3 Thread organization and kernel invocation for the vector-add operation.

```
1 dim3 threadBlockDim(256, 1);
2 int numBlocks = (N%TBsize)? (N/128) : (N+128)/128; // (N+TBsize-1)/TBsize;
3 dim3 threadGridDim(numBlocks, 1);
4 vec_add <<<threadGridDim, threadBlockDim>>>(A, B, S, N);
```

Typically, one can develop SIMT kernels in two ways. The first is to start from the algorithm-level description. One thread can carry out the computation for one or more elements in the result or is responsible for one or more input elements. In our vector-add example, one thread computes one sum in the output vector. The second way is to start from existing sequential code. Parallellizable loops with high loop counts are identified first. Then, one thread is assigned for one loop iteration. In other words, the loop iterator is replaced with the thread identifier.

For example, the sequential code of matrix multiplication is presented in Code 12.4. Both two outermost loops are parallelizable as there is no loop carried dependence. To achieve high thread-level parallelism, we choose to parallelize both outermost loops. It is also equivalent to assign one thread to compute one element in the product matrix. Since the data in this example are laid out in two-dimensional matrices, we organize the threads and the thread blocks in two dimensions. The kernel code and the thread hierarchy used in kernel invocation are shown in Code 12.5.

Code 12.4 The sequential code of matrix multiplication.

```
1 void matrixMul()    //matrix multiplication C = A * B
2 {
3     for(int i = 0; i < N; i++)
4         for(int j = 0; j < N; j++)
5         {
6             float sum = 0;
7             for(int k = 0; k < N; k++)
8                 sum += A[i][k] * B[k][j]
9             C[i][j] = sum;
10        }
11 }
```

Code 12.5 The kernel code and the thread organization for matrix multiplication.

```
1 void matrixMulKernel()    //Kernel code for matrix multiplication C = A * B
2 {
3     //tidx is the thread identifier along the X direction
4     //tidy is the thread identifier along the Y direction
5     int tidx = ...;   int tidy = ...;
6                 float sum = 0;
7     for(int k = 0; k < N; k++)
8         sum += A[tidy][k] * B[k][tidx]
9     C[tidy][tidx] = sum;
10 }
11 dim3 threadBlockDim (BLOCK_SIZE, BLOCK_SIZE);
12 dim3 threadGridDim(B.width / dimBlock.x, A.height / dimBlock.y);
13 matrixMulKernel<<threadGridDim, threadBlockDim>>(A, B, C);
```

From the code examples above, we can see that the SIMT programming model enables programmers to express data parallelism as task-level parallelism using scalar code. This greatly simplifies the programming effort. Consider the matrix multiplication example, it would be non-trivial to explicitly exploit data-level parallelism using classical vector-style programming.

12.2   Mapping SIMT Workloads to SIMT Cores

In typical SIMT architecture, there are multiple SIMT cores on a chip. Such an SIMT core is referred to as a *streaming* multiprocessor (SM) using the CUDA terminology and a *compute unit* using the OpenCL terminology.

An SIMT kernel is invoked as a grid of thread blocks (TBs). With the thread grid information, the workload dispatcher forwards the TBs to SIMT cores, as shown in Figure 12.1. Each SIMT core checks its available resource, including the register file, scratchpad memory (aka shared memory), number of threads, number of TBs, etc., to see whether it can accommodate one more TB. If so, the workload dispatcher assigns a TB to the SIMT core. When a TB finishes execution on an SIMT core, all its occupied resources are released and a new TB can be dispatched.

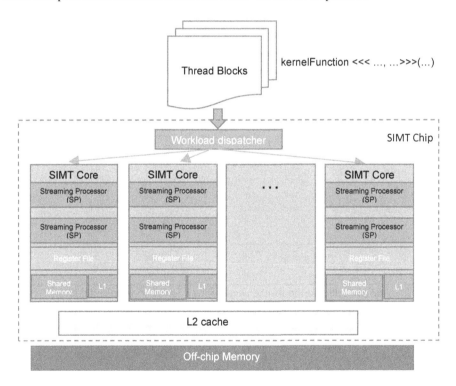

Figure 12.1: Dispatching SIMT workloads to SIMT cores.

Besides such TB-level workload dispatching, fine-grain resource management has also been introduced to utilize the resources more efficiently [65]. In either case, all the threads in a TB are executed on the same SIMT core to support synchronization among them and one SIMT core can accommodate one or more TBs.

12.3 SIMT Core Architecture

SIMT architecture uses scalar instruction-set architecture (ISA) and vectorizes scalar instructions at runtime. To hide instruction execution latency, fine-grain multithreading is employed to support massive numbers of threads to run concurrently. In a sense, SIMT architecture can be viewed as an integration of hardware-based vectorization and fine-grain multi-threading.

12.3.1 Scalar ISA

Each thread in the SIMT execution model contains a sequence of scalar instructions, identical to sequential programs running on a CPU. Recently, both AMD and Nvidia GPUs adopt RISC-style instruction set architecture (ISA). For example, the Nvidia GPU assembly code of the vector-add kernel is shown in Code 12.6.

Code 12.6 The vector-add kernel in assembly.

```
 1 PC          Binary encoding             Assembly                        Comments
 2 /*0000*/    /*0x1100e804       */       MOV32 R1, g [0x4];              /*base */
 3 /*0004*/    /*0x1100ea08       */       MOV32 R2, g [0x5];              /*base */
 4 /*0008*/    /*0x6004000500000003*/      IMAD32I.U16 R1, R0L, 0x4, R1;   /*index*/
 5 /*0010*/    /*0x6004000900000003*/      IMAD32I.U16 R2, R0L, 0x4, R2;   /*index*/
 6 /*0018*/    /*0xd00e020d80c00780*/      GLD.U32 R3, global14 [R1];      /*load */
 7 /*0020*/    /*0xd00e040980c00780*/      GLD.U32 R2, global14 [R2];      /*load */
 8 /*0028*/    /*0x1100ec04       */       MOV32 R1, g [0x6];              /*base */
 9 /*002c*/    /*0xb0020608       */       FADD32 R2, R3, R2;              /*add  */
10 /*0030*/    /*0x6004000500000003*/      IMAD32I.U16 R1, R0L, 0x4, R1;   /*index*/
11 /*0038*/    /*0xd00e0209a0c00781*/      GST.U32 global14 [R1], R2;      /*store*/
```

From Code 12.6, it can be seen that the instructions are very similar to typical CPU scalar code. In fact, among different types of instructions, control flow processing instructions are most different from regular scalar instructions due to vectorization or SIMD-style execution, which we will discuss in more detail later on.

12.3.2 SIMDization/Vectorization: Warp Formation

In a TB, threads are organized based on the TB configuration. After a TB is dispatched to an SIMT core, the SIMT core groups multiple threads with adjacent thread IDs in the same TB together to form the basic unit for execution. This basic unit of execution is referred to as a *warp* using the Nvidia terminology and a wavefront using the AMD terminology. A warp contains 32 threads with consecutive thread IDs. Figure 12.2 shows examples for warp formation when the 256 threads in a TB are organized as one dimension (256x1) or two dimensions (16x16).

All threads in a warp are executed in a lockstep manner. In other words, all threads in a warp share a single program counter (PC). This way, one scalar instruction will be executed upon multiple threads, which in turn specify multiple data using their thread IDs. This process can be viewed as hardware-based implicit SIMDization or vectorization as it does not need programmers to explicitly specify vectors.

Each thread has its own scalar registers. The aggregated registers for a warp of threads are equivalent to vector registers. Scalar instructions operating on the scalar registers of each thread

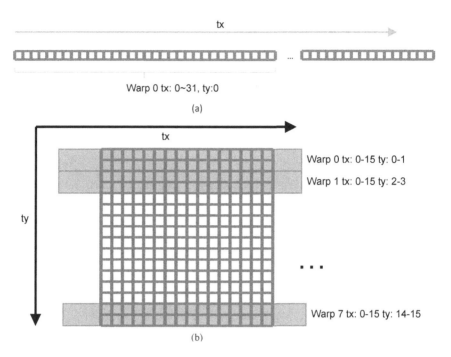

Figure 12.2: Warp formation. (a) Warps in a 1D thread block, (b) warps in a 2D thread block of the size 16x16. tx and ty are the thread ID along the X and Y directions, respectively.

in a warp essentially become vector operations. For example, the instruction FADD32 R4, R3, R2 *defines scalar operation* R4 = R3 + R2. Each thread has its own R2, R3, R4, etc. When it is executed for a warp of threads, it performs R4.0 = R3.0 + R2.0; R4.1 = R3.1 + R2.1; , R4.n = R3.n + R2.n; where Ri.k means the register Ri of thread k and the warp size is (n+1). Figure 12.3 illustrates such execution. As it can be seen, when operated upon a warp of threads, the scalar instruction FADD32 R2, R3, R2 becomes equivalent to the vector operation FADD32 VR2, VR3, VR2 where VR2, NR3, and VR4 are vector registers, and the vector length is the warp size.

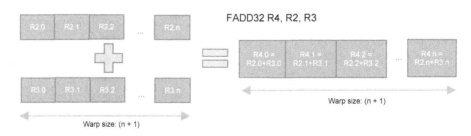

Figure 12.3: SIMD execution using scalar instructions.

Warp-based vectorization offers flexibility on how data items are vectorized. Using the matrix multiplication kernel in Code 12.5 as an example. When the TB configuration is 32x8, one warp contains 32 threads in the same row. In this case, warp 0 in TB 0 performs the vector computation as listed in Code 12.7:

Code 12.7 The vector operations for a warp of threads when the TB configuration is 32x8.

```
1 for(int k = 0; k < N; k++)
2         C[0][0:31] += A[0][k] * B[k][0:31];
```

In Code 12.7, both C[0][0:31] and B[k][0:31] are vectors with a length of 32. The SIMD computation of a loop iteration can be illustrated in Figure 12.4.

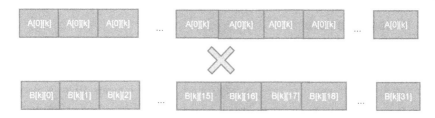

Figure 12.4: Vector operation corresponding to Code 12.7.

With the same kernel code, when the TB configuration becomes 16x16, the 32 threads in a warp span 2 consecutive rows of threads in a TB. As a result, the corresponding vector computation of warp 0 in TB 0 becomes what is listed in Code 12.8:

Code 12.8 The vector operations for a warp of threads when the TB configuration is 16x16.

```
1 for(int k = 0; k < N; k++){
2         C[0][0:15] += A[0][k] * B[k][0:15];
3         C[1][0:15] += A[1][k] * B[k][0:15];
4 }
```

The SIMD computation of a loop iteration for Code 12.8 is shown in Figure 12.5.

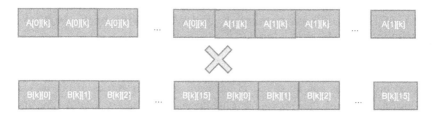

Figure 12.5: Vector operation corresponding to Code 12.8.

12.3.3 Fine-Grain Multithreading (Warp-Level Parallelism)

To hide execution latency, SIMT architecture resorts to fine-grain multi-threading or warp-level parallelism. In an SIMT core, many warps are running concurrently. After one warp issues an instruction into the pipeline, the warp scheduler is used to select a warp from all the active ones to issue an instruction in the next cycle.

Both the resource available on an SIMT core and the resource requirement of each thread (or the aggregated resource requirement of a warp/TB) determine the occupancy of the SIMT core, i.e., the number of threads/warps/TBs that can run concurrently on the SIMT core. For example, for a kernel, each thread consumes 10 registers (i.e., $10 \times 4B = 40Bytes$) and the TB dimension is 256. If the register file in an SIMT core is 64kB, the occupancy can be at most 6 ($= \frac{64kB}{256 \times 40B}$) TBs if the resource management is done at the TB granularity.

12.3.4   Microarchitecture

The microarchitecture of an SIMT core is presented in Figure 12.6. In an SIMT core, a warp scheduler selects and issues instructions from ready warps to the multiple execution pipelines, which are also referred to as streaming processors (SPs) or processing elements (PEs). A ready warp means that the next instruction from this warp has all its dependencies resolved. Each entry in the warp scheduler contains the information of a warp. Using the program counter (PC) field, it reads the instruction from the instruction cache.

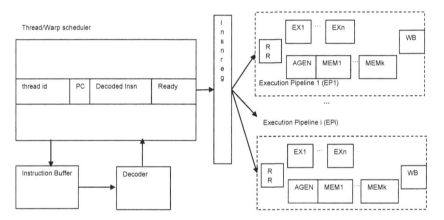

Figure 12.6: The microarchitecture of an SIMT core. RR stands for register read, EX for execution, AGEN for address generation, and WB for write back. Multiple EX or MEM stages account for multi-cycle latencies.

Decoded instructions can be stored in the warp scheduler entries or put in a separate small decoded instruction buffer. One reason for using the warp scheduler entries for decoded instructions is register renaming. As multiple warps use the same kernel function, there is a need to differentiate their operands. During decode, the TB ID, the warp ID, and the thread ID are used to generate the mapping from logical register numbers to physical register numbers for execution pipelines to read from and write to the physical register file. For example, the instruction FADD32 R2, R3, R2 may be changed to FADD32 PR12, PR13, PR12 for warp 1 and FADD32 PR32, PR33, PR32 for another warp, where PRk means the physical register k.

An issued instruction will be executed by multiple in-order execution pipelines for all the threads in the warp. Depending on the type of the instruction, it either goes through the ALU pipeline, the memory pipeline, or the special functional units. A simple way to manage the ready bits is as follows: the ready field of a warp scheduler entry is cleared when an instruction is issued from this warp; when an instruction reaches the write back stage, it uses its warp ID to locate the corresponding warp scheduler entry and set the ready bit. This way, a warp has at most one outstanding instruction in the execution pipelines.

12.3.5 Pipeline Execution

Depending on the number of execution pipelines in an SIMT core, the warp scheduler issues one instruction every few cycles. For example, if there are 8 execution pipelines in an SIMT core, for a warp size of 32, the warp scheduler issues one instruction every 4 (=32/8) cycles, as shown in Figure 12.7, where the latency of add instructions is assumed to be two cycles. From Figure 12.7, we can see that although the two instructions, $f1 = f2 + f3$ from warp 0 and $f4 = f1 + f5$ from warp 1, use the register f1, there is no dependency between them as they are from different warps. As discussed before, during the decode stage, the architectural (or logic) register f1 of warp 0 and the architectural register f1 are mapped to different physical registers based on their warp IDs.

Cycle	1	2	3	4	5	6	7	8	9	10	11	12	13	14	15	16	17	18	19	
f1=f2+f3	IF				ID				RR	EX1	EX2	WB								threads 0~7
warp 0										RR	EX1	EX2	WB							threads 8~15
											RR	EX1	EX2	WB						threads 16~23
												RR	EX1	EX2	WB					threads 24~31
f4=f1+f5			IF						ID				RR	EX1	EX2	WB				threads 0~7
warp 1														RR	EX1	EX2	WB			threads 8~15
															RR	EX1	EX2	WB		threads 16~23
																RR	EX1	EX2	WB	threads 24~31

Figure 12.7: Pipelined execution of two instructions from two different warps. There is no dependency between the two instructions although both use the register f1 since they are from different warps.

When the number of execution pipelines is increased to 16, the instruction issue rate is one instruction every 2 (=32/16) cycles. Given the instruction issue rate, the throughput of the frontend, i.e., instruction fetch (IF) and decode (ID), can also be reduced to one instruction every N (=warp size/number of execution pipelines) cycles.

Warp-level parallelism is the key to overcome pipeline hazards in SIMT cores. When a warp encounters a long latency instruction, e.g., a cache miss instruction, the warp itself will be stalled. However, as long as there are sufficient concurrently running warps, the execution pipeline will remain busy. When the cache miss is repaired, the stalled warp becomes eligible to be selected by the warp scheduler for execution.

Besides warp-level parallelism, instruction-level parallelism within a warp can also be leveraged to hide execution latency. To do so, a scoreboard is introduced for each warp to track the register dependency information. The ready bit of the warp scheduler entry is then determined based on the dependency check of the next instruction using the scoreboard. A warp is stalled only when its current instruction needs to consume some outstanding result.

Let us consider an example. Assume that two active warps running on an SIMT core with 16 execution pipelines. The kernel contains two instructions: $f1 = f3 + f2$; $f4 = f2 + f4$. The SIMT core uses a round-robin warp scheduling policy to pick the next ready warp. Assuming that the add instructions have 6-cycle latency, let us analyze how the instructions in the two warps are executed in the pipeline for the following two designs: (a) there is no scoreboard to support more than 1 outstanding instruction in the execution pipelines, and (b) there is such a scoreboard to leverage instruction-level parallelism within warps.

The pipelined execution of the instructions from the two warps are shown in Figure 12.8. As we can see from the figure, the scoreboard support for instruction-level parallelism mitigates the computational latency of the add instructions.

Cycle	1	2	3	4	5	6	7	8	9	10	11	12	13	14	15	16	17	
f1=f2+f3	IF		ID		RR	EX1	EX2	EX3	EX4	EX5	EX6	WB						threads 0~15
(warp 0)						RR	EX1	EX2	EX3	EX4	EX5	EX6	WB					threads 16~31
f1=f2+f3			IF		ID		RR	EX1	EX2	EX3	EX4	EX5	EX6	WB				threads 0~15
(warp 1)								RR	EX1	EX2	EX3	EX4	EX5	EX6	WB			threads 16~31
f4=f5+f6					IF		ID		s	s	s	s	RR	EX1	EX2	EX3	EX4	threads 0~15
(warp 0)														RR	EX1	EX2	EX3	threads 16~31
F4=f5+f6							IF		ID	s	s	s	s	s	RR	EX1	EX2	threads 0~15
(warp 1)																RR	EX1	threads 16~31

(a)

Cycle	1	2	3	4	5	6	7	8	9	10	11	12	13	14	15	16	17	
f1=f2+f3	IF		ID		RR	EX1	EX2	EX3	EX4	EX5	EX6	WB						threads 0~15
(warp 0)						RR	EX1	EX2	EX3	EX4	EX5	EX6	WB					threads 16~31
f1=f2+f3			IF		ID		RR	EX1	EX2	EX3	EX4	EX5	EX6	WB				threads 0~15
(warp 1)								RR	EX1	EX2	EX3	EX4	EX5	EX6	WB			threads 16~31
f4=f5+f6					IF		ID		RR	EX1	EX2	EX3	EX4	EX5	EX6	WB		threads 0~15
(warp 0)										RR	EX1	EX2	EX3	EX4	EX5	EX6	WB	threads 16~31
F4=f5+f6							IF		ID		RR	EX1	EX2	EX3	EX4	EX5	EX6	threads 0~15
(warp 1)												RR	EX1	EX2	EX3	EX4	EX5	threads 16~31

(b)

Figure 12.8: Pipelined execution of instructions from two warps on an SIMT core. There is no dependency between the two instructions. (a) No scoreboard to support more than one outstanding instruction from a warp. (b) More than one outstanding instruction from the same warp can be issued with the scoreboard support. "s" indicates stall.

12.3.6 Control Flow Processing

Among different types of instructions, control flow instructions are of particular interest for SIMT architecture due to branch divergence. Branch divergence happens when the threads in the same warp execute a branch instruction, which results in different branch outcomes for different threads. One such example is if (tid %2 == 0), for which the odd threads and even threads in a warp need to traverse different paths.

A typical way to handle divergent branches is to serialize each execution path through SIMD lane masking, which means that when the PC follows one execution path, only the threads actually following this path will be active and the remaining threads are disabled through predicate registers. When the path is completed, the PC will be rewound back to execute another divergent execution path. To manage the PC and the execution mask associated with different control paths, a stack structure, called SIMT stack, is introduced.

As a concrete example, we use the "IF...THEN ELSE" control structure to illustrate how a divergent branch is executed in Nvidia Fermi architecture. Each entry of the SIMT stack, called the token stack [15], contains three fields, as shown in Figure 12.9. The "active mask" field is a bit mask, showing which threads in a warp are active. The reconvergence PC is the reconvergent point of the branch. The entry type field is used to differentiate various types of control flow instructions.

Besides the token stack, each SIMT core also has special purpose registers including per warp active mask registers and per warp "active PC" registers to assist control flow processing. The former disables the threads that are inactive, and the latter is the current PC for a warp.

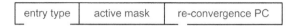

Figure 12.9: The structure of an entry in the SIMT stack.

For the "IF...THEN ELSE" code example in Figure 12.10a, the corresponding assembly code is shown in Figure 12.10b. Figure 12.10c shows how the stack content is updated. For simplicity, we use a warp size of 8. To support branch divergence, a control instruction, SSY at PC = 0x0020, is introduced in the ISA. The operand of the SSY, 0xF0, specifies a reconvergence point. When this instruction is executed, a token is pushed onto the stack. This token includes the active mask copied from the current active mask register, the reconvergence PC extracted from the SSY operand, and the entry type set as SSY.

Next, the conditional branch instruction @P0 BRA 0xb8 is executed, where P0 is a predicate register storing the branch condition. If the branch results in a divergence, i.e., the outcomes are different for the threads in the same warp, e.g., the outcome being 'taken' for the first 4 threads and 'not-taken' for the rest, i.e., the outcomes are 0xF0 for the eight threads in the warp, a token, DIV, 0xF0, 0xB8, is pushed onto the stack. The active mask is filled with the predicate register P0 (0xF0), the reconvergence PC field is filled with the branch target address (0xB8), the entry type is filled with DIV.

Then, the not-taken path is executed first by setting the active mask register as the inverse of P0 and the active PC register as branch PC + 8. Such execution continues until a stack pop operation is encountered. In the Nvidia Fermi ISA, a stack pop operation can be appended to any instruction with a .S flag rather than a specific pop instruction. In this example, the pop flag is added to the store instruction at PC = 0x00B0, marking the end of the ELSE path. The stack pop operation takes the top of the stack to set the active mask register and the active PC register. As a result, the taken path is selected and executed until another pop operation at PC = 0x00E8. At this point, the top of stack contains SSY, 0xFF, 0xF0. The pop operation again sets the active mask register and the active PC register and all the divergent threads are reconverged at the reconvergence point, 0xF0.

12.3.7 Memory Systems

In GPU programming models including CUDA and OpenCL, multiple memory spaces are supported, including global memory, local memory, constant memory, and texture memory. Global memory is accessible to all the threads in a grid. In comparison, local memory is private for each individual thread while shared memory provides a way for data communication and synchronization among the threads in a thread block. Both constant and texture memory are commonly used for read-only data (although there are ways to update texture memory) and visible to all threads in a grid. Shared memory is on-chip and located in each SIMT core. Global, local, texture, and constant memory all reside in off-chip memory. To reduce access latencies, on-chip caches are introduced, including read-only constant caches, texture caches, L1 D-caches, and an L2 cache. L1 D-caches are used for local and global memory data (or local memory data only). L1 D-caches are private in

```
int index = blockldx.x*blockDim.x + threadldx.x;
if (condition(index))    // Path 1: "IF...THEN"
{
    ...
}
else                     //Path 2: ELSE
{
    ...
}
d_e [index] = d_c [index] + d_d [index] ;
```

(a)

PC	Instruction	Comment
/*0000*/	MOV R1, c [0x1] [0x100];	
/*0020*/	SSY 0xf0;	SSY Instruction (**push stack**)
......	......	......
/*0090*/	@P0 BRA 0xb8;	Branch related to IF-THEN part (**push stack**)
/*0098*/	LD.E R3, [R2];	ELSE part entry
......		
/*00b0*/	ST.E.S [R6], R2;	ELSE part end. Notice ".S" flag. (**pop stack**)
/*00b8*/	LD.E R5, [R4];	IF-THEN part entry.
......		
/*00E8*/	NOP.S CC.T;	IF-THEN part end. Notice ".S" flag. (**pop stack**)
/*00F0*/	LD.E R3, [R10];	Threads synchronizes at this point.
/*00F8*/	LD.E R4, [R8];	
/*0100*/	LD.E R2, [R6];	Go till Exit
......		
/*0140*/	EXIT;	EXIT

(b)

PC	Active Mask	TOS	TOS-1	TOS-2	Comments
0x00	0xFF	Empty	Empty	Empty	
0x20	0xFF	Empty	Empty	Empty	Before SSY
0x28	0xFF	**SSY, 0xFF, 0xF0**	Empty	Empty	After SSY
......	0xF0	SSY, 0xFF, 0xF0	Empty	Empty	
0x90	0xFF	SSY, 0xFF, 0xF0	Empty	Empty	Before Branch
0x98	0x0F	**DIV, 0xF0, 0xB8**	SSY, 0xFF, 0xF0	Empty	After Branch
......	0x0F	DIV, 0xF0, 0xB8	SSY, 0xFF, 0xF0	Empty	
0xB0	0x0F	DIV, 0xF0, 0xB8	SSY, 0xFF, 0xF0	Empty	Before ST.S
0xB8	0xF0	SSY, 0xFF, 0xF0	Empty	Empty	After ST.S
......	0xF0	SSY, 0xFF, 0xF0	Empty	Empty	
0xE0	0xF0	SSY, 0xFF, 0xF0	Empty	Empty	
0xE8	0xF0	SSY, 0xFF, 0xF0	Empty	Empty	"NOP.S Instruction"
0xF0	0xFF	Empty	Empty	Empty	
0xF8	0xFF	Empty	Empty	Empty	Go Till Exit.
......					

(c)

Figure 12.10: Control flow processing. (a) The CUDA code segment of IF...THEN ELSE; (b) The assembly code of IF...THEN ELSE highlighting the stack management; (c) The contents of the token stack during execution. Convention: TOS: top of stack, TOS-1: the entry next to the top of stack.

each SIMT core and may use the same physical resource as shared memory. In this case, there are APIs to configure the capacity between the L1 D-cache and shared memory. The L2 cache is shared among all the SIMT cores and typically consists of multiple banks. There are multiple memory controllers integrated on the chip to provide high bandwidth in accessing the off-chip memory.

Among different types of memory, shared memory is explicitly managed by software. It is highly banked to achieve high throughput. For a shared memory array, its elements are distributed among multiple banks, as illustrated in Figure 12.11.

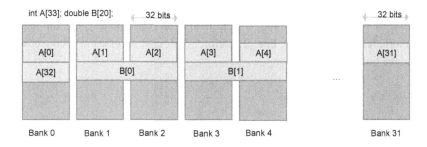

Figure 12.11: Data layout in multi-banked (32-banked) shared memory.

As shown in Figure 12.11, the width of each bank in shared memory is 32 bits. Therefore, for an integer array, each element takes one location in a bank. When the array data type is changed to double, each element spans two banks.

As each bank in shared memory has one read port and one write port, when more than one thread in a warp needs to access one bank at the same time, bank conflicts happen and such accesses have to serialized.

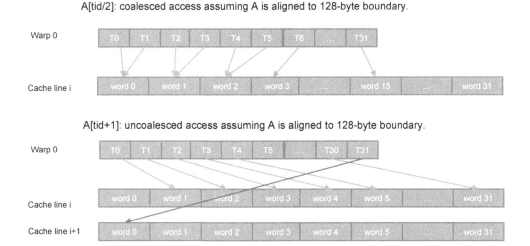

Figure 12.12: Examples of coalesced and uncoalesced memory accesses.

For global memory accesses, the key to achieve high access bandwidth is memory coalescing. When a memory access instruction is executed, each thread in the warp will generate a memory request. All these requests are checked to see whether they can be coalesced to as few cache-line accesses as possible. The cache-line granularity is used as it is the unit used in accessing the cache. For one word per thread access (e.g., the int/float data type), if all the requests of a warp can be serviced by a single cache line access, the corresponding memory access instruction satisfies the memory coalescing requirements. Otherwise, multiple sequential cache-line accesses are resulted. As an example, in Figure 12.12, we show a coalesced access `A[tid/2]` and an uncoalesced access `A[tid+1]`, which results in accessing two cache lines. For uncoalesced memory accesses, a typical code optimization strategy is to leverage shared memory to load in global memory data in the coalesced manner and then accessing the data as needed from shared memory [66].

For multiple words per thread access (e.g., double or vector data types), the required data of a warp are more than a single cache line. Therefore, coalesced accesses in such a case also result in multiple cache line accesses.

12.4 Exercises

Worked Problems

Comparison between sequential execution and SIMT execution: vector-add operation

1. Considering the following sequential code shown in Code 12.9 for the vector add operation with the vector length of 32 shown in Code 12.1.

Code 12.9 The sequential assembly code for the vectoradd operation.

```
1     MOV     r5, #0
2 L:  LOAD    f1, 0(r1)
3     LOAD    f2, 0(r2)
4     FADD    f3, f1, f2
5     STORE   f3, 0(r3)
6     ADD     r1, r1, #4
7     ADD     r2, r2, #4
8     ADD     r3, r3, #4
9     ADD     r5, r5, 1
10    BRLE    r5, 32, L  /* loop upper bound as 32 */
```

Assuming an in-order scalar processor with the following pipeline stages

```
IF ID RR EX WB
```

A variable number of EX stages represents different instruction execution latency. If FADDs have 5-cycle latency, loads/stores have 2-cycle latency, and all other instructions have 1-cycle latency, how many pipeline stalls will the data hazards in the code generate?

Answer:

In each iteration, the main data hazard is the read-after-write hazard due to the FADD instruction followed by the store instruction, which uses the result of FADD. Given the 5-cycle latency, the two instructions are executed as shown in Figure 12.13.

Cycle	1	2	3	4	5	6	7	8	9	10	11
FADD f3,f1,f2	IF	ID	RR	EX1	EX2	EX3	EX4	EX5	WB		
STORE f3, 0(r3)		IF	ID	RR	stall	stall	stall	stall	EX1	EX2	WB
ADD r1,r1, #4			IF	ID	stall	stall	stall	stall	stall	RR	EX

Figure 12.13: Pipeline stalls in one loop iteration.

As shown in Figure 12.13, there are 4 pipeline stalls each iteration. Since there is a total of 32 iterations, there are 4*32 = 128 pipeline stalls generated due to data hazards.

2. To implement the same vector-add operation in an SIMT processor, the kernel code in assembly shown in Code 12.10 can be used.

Code 12.10 The assembly code for the vectoradd kernel.

```
1   /* generate the addresses based on thread ID and the base addresses
2       of the vectors*/
3   LOAD          f1, 0(r1)
4   LOAD          f2, 0(r2)
5   FADD          f3, f1, f2
6   STORE         f3, 0(r3)
```

Assuming the same instruction execution latency as in problem 1. On an SIMT core with 1 execution pipeline and a scoreboard to support more than 1 outstanding instruction from a warp to be issued to the execution pipeline, how many pipeline stalls will the data hazards in the code generate?

Answer:

Similar to problem 1, the main data hazard in the code the FADD instruction followed by STORE. As the vector length is 32, there is 1 warp to run on the SIMT core. All 32 threads in the warp will share the single execution pipeline. As a result, the two instructions in the warp are executed as shown in Figure 12.14. From Figure 12.14, it can be seen that there are no pipeline stalls due to the data hazard. The reason is that the FADD instructions from different threads in the warp overlap with each other and when the STORE instruction is issued, the corresponding threads have already finished the FADD instruction.

Cycle	n	n+1	n+2	n+3	n+4	n+5	n+6	n+7	...	n+37	n+38	
FADD f3,f1,f2	RR	EX1	EX2	EX3	EX4	EX5	WB					Thread 0
		RR	EX1	EX2	EX3	EX4	EX5	WB				Thread 1
			...					...	...			...
				...						WB		Thread 31
STORE f3, 0(r3)								...	...	EX2	WB	Thread 0
									...	EX1	EX2	Thread 1
											...	

Figure 12.14: Pipeline stalls in the SIMT core with 1 execution pipeline.

3. For the kernel function in problem 2, assume an SIMT core with 16 execution pipelines, how many pipeline stalls will the data hazards in the code generate?

Answer:

In the SIMT core with 16 execution pipelines, for the same flow dependence due to the FADD and STORE instructions, the STORE instruction needs to be stalled for 4 cycles as shown in Figure 12.15. Compared to sequential execution in problem 1, the pipeline stalls are overlapped among all the threads in the warp, i.e., there are 4 pipeline stalls for all the 32 elements to be computed.

From the discussion in problem 1 and problem 2, we can see a key reason why SIMT/SIMD execution is much more efficient than sequential execution is that the pipeline stalls are overlapped among different data items. In a way, it is similar to unroll the sequential loop in Code 12.9 to hide instruction execution latency.

Cycle	n	n+1	n+2	n+3	n+4	n+5	n+6	n+7	n+8	n+9	
FADD f3,f1,f2	RR	EX1	EX2	EX3	EX4	EX5	WB				Threads 0~15
		RR	EX1	EX2	EX3	EX4	EX5	WB			Threads 16~31
STORE f3, 0(r3)			stall	stall	stall	stall	stall	RR	EX1	EX2	Threads 0~15
									RR	EX1	Threads 16~31

Figure 12.15: Pipeline stalls in the SIMT core with 16 execution pipelines.

Homework Problems

1. **Pipelined execution**. Assuming that four active warps running on an SIMT core with 16 execution pipelines. The kernel contains two instructions: f1 = f3 + f2; f4 = f1 + f4. The SIMT core uses a round-robin warp scheduling policy to pick next ready instruction. Assuming that the add instructions have 6-cycle latency, analyze the how the instructions in the two warps are executed in the pipeline for the following two designs: (a) there is no scoreboard to support more than one outstanding instruction in the execution pipelines (b) there is such a scoreboard.

2. **Branch divergence**. For the CUDA kernel code segment in Code 12.11, check whether it will cause branch divergence for warp 0 in thread block 0 and for warp 1 in thread block 0 assuming that each thread block contains more than 2 warps.

Code 12.11 The code segment for branch divergence checking.

```
1  gid =  threadIdx.x + blockIdx.x * blockDim.x;
2  if(gid < 8) //the branch of interest
3  {
4      //taken path
5  }
6  else
7  {
8      //not taken path
9  }
```

3. **Memory coalescing**. For the CUDA kernel code segment in Code 12.12, check whether the global memory accesses satisfy the memory coalescing requirements.

Code 12.12 The code segment for branch divergence checking.

```
1  // A is a 2D integer array in global memory with the size of 1024x1024
2  gid =  threadIdx.x + blockIdx.x * blockDim.x;
3  for(i = 0; i < N; i++)
4      sum += A[gid][i];  // A[gid][i] is the global mem access of interest
```

4. **Sequential vs. SIMT execution**. Consider the "worked problems" and their solutions.

   (a) Assume there is no scoreboard to support more than one instruction from the same warp to be issued to the execution pipeline, repeat the worked problem 2.

   (b) Change the loop bound to 64 (i.e., there are two warps to run) and repeat the worked problem 3.

(c) Besides pipeline stalls due to data hazards that are discussed in the worked problem, are there any other factors contributing to the different performance between the sequential code and SIMT code?

Chapter 13

Ask the Experts

Josep Torrellas on Parallel Multicore Architectures

Josep Torrellas is a Professor at the Departments of Computer Science and (by courtesy) Electrical and Computer Engineering at the University of Illinois at Urbana-Champaign (UIUC). He is the Director of the Center for Programmable Extreme Scale Computing, and past Director of the Illinois-Intel Parallelism Center (I2PC). He is a Fellow of IEEE (2004) and ACM (2010). He received the 2015 IEEE Computer Society Technical Achievement Award, for "Pioneering contributions to shared-memory multiprocessor architectures and thread-level speculation", and the ICCD High-Impact Paper Award for "One of the 5 most cited papers in the first 30 years of ICCD". He has served as the Chair of the IEEE Technical Committee on Computer Architecture (TCCA) (2005-2010) and as a Council Member of CRA's Computing Community Consortium (CCC) (2011-2014). He was a Willett Faculty Scholar at UIUC (2002-2009).

Torrellas' research interests are shared-memory parallel computer architecture, energy-efficient architectures, hardware reliability, and software dependability. He has published over 200 publications and received 12 Best Paper awards. In the early nineties, Torrellas was involved in the Stanford DASH and Illinois Cedar experimental multiprocessor projects. Later, he lead the Illinois Aggressive Cache Only Memory Architecture (I-ACOMA) project, which was one of the Ten Point-Design Studies funded by the federal government to accelerate the arrival of a petascale machine. He lead the DARPA-funded M3T Polymorphic Computer Architecture, and co-directed the NSF-funded FlexRAM Intelligent Memory project. He was one of the PIs in the DARPA-funded IBM PERCS multiprocessor project. As part of the Illinois-Intel Parallelism Center, he lead the design of The Bulk Multicore Architecture for parallel programming productivity. He was also a co-PI of the DARPA-funded Intel Runnemede multiprocessor, developed under the Ubiquitous High Performance Computing program, to build an extreme-scale multiprocessor designed from the ground up for energy efficiency.

Torrellas has served in the organization of numerous professional conferences and workshops. Recent major service includes Program Chair of PACT 2014, ISCA 2012, HPCA 2005, IEEE-Micro

Top Picks 2005, and SC 2007. As of 2015, he has graduated 35 Ph.D. students, who are now leaders in academia and industry.

Interview

[Yan Solihin] Josep, could you describe your experience in researching and developing support for effective parallel execution of programs on multicore architectures?

[Josep Torrellas] I have been performing research in the area of shared-memory multiprocessor architectures for over 25 years now. I have worked on cache coherence protocols, memory consistency support, prefetching, thread level-speculation, low-power design, and hardware and software reliability.

I started back in the late 80's by looking at the behavior of shared data in the directory-based protocol of the Stanford DASH multiprocessor. I then worked to characterize the performance of the Illinois Cedar multiprocessor. Later on, I contributed to the design of shared-memory multiprocessors with thread-level speculation (TLS). I showed the broad use of speculative threading mechanisms in parallel computer architecture, including in speculative synchronization, program debugging, and low-overhead program monitoring. I also showed that speculative threading is a primitive for high-performance and low-complexity sequential consistency (SC) enforcement.

In the 90's, I worked on the Illinois Aggressive Cache Only Memory Architecture (I-ACOMA) design. I contributed with several NUMA machine organizations, coherence protocols, and prefetching schemes. A couple of significant contributions are embedded-ring snoopy cache-coherence protocols and the ReVive incremental, in-memory multiprocessor checkpointing. We also released the widely used SESC simulator of multiprocessor architectures.

In the 00's, I worked on the Bulk multicore architecture, as part of the Intel Center for Parallelism. This was a novel architecture designed for parallel programming productivity. As part of this effort, I worked with Intel researchers, and we built an x86-compatible hardware prototype for record-and-replay of parallel programs.

Also, during this time, I became interested in process variation and energy-efficient multiprocessor design. As part of an effort on extreme scale computing, we developed the VARIUS-NTV models of process variation, and multiple techniques to mitigate and tolerate process variation. This work culminated in the design of an extreme-scale manycore with Intel researchers called Runnemede.

[YS] How have parallel architectures, including multicores, evolved in the last 20-30 years?

[JT] I finished my Ph.D. in the early 90's. At that time, there was a lot of excitement about cache-coherent shared-memory multiprocessors — especially, scalable ones. I did my Ph.D. thesis in the context of the Stanford DASH multiprocessor, and then joined a team that evaluated the Illinois Cedar multiprocessor at the University of Illinois, Urbana-Champaign. These two experimental machines, and the research groups that developed them, introduced many research ideas.

At that time, development groups in companies were very interested in these ideas. They would invite researchers to discuss the latest results. There were several new products in the market.

Later, in the late 90's and early 00's, there was a progressive disenchantment with multiprocessors. Superscalar uniprocessors kept improving in every generation, and multiprocessor design teams had trouble keeping up with the changes. Every new uniprocessor generation required a major redesign of the multiprocessor. A bit later, simultaneous multithreaded (SMT) processors appeared, which further pushed the performance of uniprocessors. In all of these times, I kept working on multiprocessors.

Finally, around the mid 00's, multicores appeared, driven by energy and power concerns. They have been central to computer architecture since. Many of the topics that were studied one or two decades earlier were reconsidered with different constraints. Now, parallel architectures in the form of multicores or manycores are very popular. However, the design issues that are being discussed are more incremental than before. The field is much more mature.

[YS] Q: In your view, how much effort programmers can be and should be expected to expend writing parallel programs?

[JT] Several years ago, when multicores were about to become ubiquitous, I thought that all programmers would have to program in parallel. However, it has later become clear to me that many programmers are insulated from concerns about parallelism. They program user interfaces or a variety of layers in large projects. Only those programmers who program the core parallel algorithms, including the parallel libraries, require knowledge of parallelism. They are often experienced programmers (although not always). These programmers should spend a lot of effort to design high-performing, bug-free parallel codes.

It is for these programmers that computer architects need to work hard. Computer architects need to provide the hardware support necessary to make life for these programmers easy. Specifically, architects need to provide cache coherence support, efficient synchronization, transparent caching and prefetching, and intuitive memory consistency models.

[YS] What are the key hardware techniques that have worked well in extracting or managing thread-level parallelism?

[JT] The key hardware techniques that have worked well in managing thread-level parallelism include cache coherence, memory consistency support, and synchronization. These techniques have been designed to interface well with both the memory hierarchy and the core of processors. Hardware transactional memory may end-up also being a useful support for parallelism, but it is a bit early to tell at this point.

On the other hand, it has been a disappointment to see that hardware support to parallelize codes has not succeeded. There was a lot of effort in the 00's to design structures to speculatively parallelize codes with potential dependences. This effort included techniques to monitor for dependence violations at run time, buffering multiple versions of the same data in caches, and squash and restart when a dependence was violated. None of this is currently in use, although it has inspired transactional memory. I hope that it will be used one day.

[YS] What are the limitations of current cache coherence protocols in multicore architectures?

[JT] Over the years, the academic community has come up with many improvements for cache coherence protocols. They include novel ways to make them scalable to large numbers of cores.

They also include novel designs to make them more economical in terms of time, space, or energy.

The main problem has been that multiprocessor companies have been constrained by legacy. The cache coherence protocol is a complex hardware module, whose design involves careful crafting of state machines and detailed analysis of timing issues. In addition, it interacts with multiple other parts of the machine, including the caches, processor load-store unit, and bus or network modules. As a result, it takes many person-years to debug a cache coherence protocol. When companies have implemented a protocol that works, they are very reluctant to change it in any way.

Currently, each company has a few cache coherence protocol designs that have been shown to work correctly. The full details of these designs are rarely revealed to people outside of the company. In addition, they may not be fully documented even inside of the company. In practice, these protocols are likely to be more complicated than needed, with states that were added to optimize certain conditions that may not be relevant anymore. These states may in fact be slowing down the operation of the common case.

The bottom line is that these protocols are suboptimal in performance, energy, complexity, and scalability. However, it is very unclear what researchers can do to change this status-quo.

[YS] Can you describe your research on bulk coherence? What problems does it attack and what unique characteristics it has?

[JT] Bulk coherence [1] is an effort to design a cache coherence protocol from new principles, in order to enable a more programmable environment. In addition, it also improves performance, and does not increase hardware complexity.

Bulk coherence provides to the software high-performance sequential memory consistency, which improves programmability. In addition, bulk coherence provides support for several novel hardware primitives. These primitives can be used to build a sophisticated program development-and-debugging environment, including low-overhead data-race detection, deterministic replay of parallel programs, and high-speed disambiguation of sets of addresses. The primitives have an overhead low enough to always be on during production runs.

The key idea in bulk coherence is twofold: first, the hardware automatically executes all software as a series of dynamically-created atomic blocks of thousands of dynamic instructions called *chunks*. Chunk execution is invisible to the software and, therefore, puts no restriction on the programming language or model. Second, bulk coherence introduces the use of "hardware address signatures" to operate on groups of addresses. Signatures are a low-overhead mechanism to ensure atomic and isolated execution of chunks, and help provide high-performance sequential memory consistency.

Bulk coherence enables higher performance because the processor hardware is free to aggressively reorder and overlap the memory accesses of a program within chunks without risk of breaking their expected behavior in a multiprocessor environment. Moreover, the compiler can create the chunks, and then further improve performance by heavily optimizing the instructions within each chunk.

Finally, the bulk multicore organization decreases hardware design complexity because memory-consistency enforcement is largely decoupled from processor structures. In a conventional processor

---

[1] J.Torrellas, L.Ceze, J.Tuck, C.Cascaval, P.Montesinos, W.Ahn, and M.Prvulovic. The Bulk Multicore Architecture for Improved Programmability. CACM, December 2009.

that issues memory accesses out of order, supporting sequential consistency requires intrusive processor modifications.

[YS] What are the key challenges in the future in architecture support for effective parallel execution that still need to be addressed?

[JT] Fortunately, there is no shortage of challenges in architectural support for effective parallel execution. The first and most important one is that, as multiprocessor designers are more and more concerned with energy efficiency and low power, there will be pressure to ignore programmability issues. An example of this trend is the emergence of heterogeneity. Another example is the emergence of 1,000-core manycore designs that may not be cache-coherent. The challenge in this area is to design low-overhead, energy-efficient primitives for programmability that are compatible with an energy-first philosophy.

Another challenge is how to support effective Quality of Service (QoS). In the future, we will have large manycores with hundreds or a thousand cores. They will be running many applications which will compete for resources. Effective QoS requires novel hardware support.

Another important challenge is the emergence of a new breed of dynamic languages called scripting languages. Programmers like these languages because they allow quick prototyping. However, compilers find these languages hard to manage because there is little static information. Consequently, there is a lot of work that the compilers need to do at runtime, which slows down execution. This is a great opportunity for hardware support.

Hardware support for synchronization and fences needs to be redesigned. Existing hardware is not designed for the large manycores that we expect to see in the next few years. Existing hardware is too costly and unscalable.

Finally, the emergence of security and privacy concerns presents a major challenge to hardware designers. It is a totally open problem to identify the most cost-effective hardware primitives that we need to add to uniprocessors and multiprocessors to ensure security and privacy.

[YS] Josep, I appreciate your time and insights in this interview. Thank you.

Li-Shiuan Peh on Network-on-Chip Design

Li-Shiuan Peh is Professor of Electrical Engineering and Computer Science at MIT and has been on the faculty of MIT since 2009. Previously, she was on the faculty of Princeton University from 2002. She graduated with a Ph.D. in Computer Science from Stanford University in 2001, and a B.S. in Computer Science from the National University of Singapore in 1995. Her research focuses on networked computing, in many-core chips as well as mobile wireless systems. She was awarded the MICRO Hall of Fame Award in 2011, ACM Distinguished Scientist Award in 2011, CRA Anita Borg Early Career Award in 2007, Sloan Research Fellowship in 2006, and the NSF CAREER Award in 2003. She is a PI of the Future Urban Mobility (FM) and Low Energy Electronics Systems (LEES) research centers, part of the Singapore-MIT Alliance of Research & Technology (SMART), and Associate Director of SMART since 2015.

[Yan Solihin] Li-Shiuan, can you tell us briefly about your background?

[Li-Shiuan Peh] I have been a professor since 2002. First I was at Princeton for about 8 years, then in 2008 I moved over to MIT, and I have been at MIT since then. My area of research is in networks in general, and mostly in on-die networks, in computer architecture and many-core chips, and also recently branching into networked computing in mobile systems.

[YS] Can you comment on the changes of the design of the interconnection network over the past few decades?

[LSP] Interconnection networks are networks connecting components within the system. Decades ago, the systems that required that much scale were mostly supercomputers. Over the years, we moved from supercomputers such as Cray that had a sophisticated network within the system, to clusters of workstations, such as Infiniband-like interconnects, to in the last 10-15 years with on-die network connecting components within a die. So the design has changed over the years, largely driven by the differences in the design constraints in these diverse systems. For supercomputers, we basically don't have much emphasis on cost, the system is huge, and there is an emphasis on performance, so the performance was the driving goal for the interconnection network design in that era. And then we moved to the cluster of workstations era such as Infiniband, Gigabit Ethernet, Myrinet. There, cost was an issue, and there was a demand for flexibility and extensibility of the network, so you see a lot more research into how we can make the network reconfigurable, to irregular topologies while allowing routing, deadlock-free routing, etc. And then as we went to the on-die network domain research in the last 15-20 years or so, the design became focused on chip design constraints. In addition to performance, [the design also focuses on] power, area, and complexity.

[YS] With transistor scaling, we are going to have more and more cores on the die, what factors should designers be concerned about when designing the network-on-chip (NoC)?

[LSP] I will divide it into the domains of servers, where the multicore design largely relies on an in-house IP, versus MPSoC area where IP blocks may be coming from different parties. These two domains are slowly merging, but the difference is how much of an interface you need to adhere to. In terms of the constraints that come to play, power and area are the biggest concerns, and probably timing, too. Performance in the past in supercomputers was more of network level performance, e.g., how many hops you need to go through, how much bandwidth, and path diversity. In NoC, you need to add timing to the performance angle because now timing is much tighter, trying to make sure that the NoC logic and pipeline do not become the constraint to the chip clock. As the complexity of NoC increases, in order to handle the higher bandwidth, there is also the constraint of ensuring the timing is comparable to the processor clock.

[YS] You mentioned about the increased of concern in power consumption. Can you elaborate?

[LSP] The key is within the die, the network is replacing what previously was handled by wires or buses. As a result, in the power budget of the multicore chip, for the global network, not counting the clock, people want to keep the NoC power within 10-20% of the chip power budget. That becomes an issue when you start expanding buses to manycores, basically the power goes up, and delay becomes an issue, too. The same trends affect crossbars. So NoC was motivated by the need to increase bandwidth but at a manageable power. But if we implement NoC the old way, borrowing from interconnection networks in supercomputers, it can consume significant power as well. If we look at several prior [manycore] chips that have been fabricated, they have been able to keep it to within 10-20% of chip power. The power of NoC comes from several sources. We've done work in the past in this. Basically a lot of it is from buffering. There are buffering, wires, and logic. For wiring, since the chip has to be wired regardless, you're comparing it with just dedicated wires, so NoC helps in interconnect wiring. Instead of relying on long wires, you can now share the wires, and they tend to be short. Logic and buffering are what you add to allow traffic to share these wires. In general, logic has been scaling smoothly. Logic has been scaling very well with Moore's law, so you don't get that much contribution to power. When we did our modeling, the key logic components such as the arbitration logic did not contribute much to power consumption. So ultimately I think it still boils down to storage, the buffering. So as we share the wires, try to push bandwidth to the wires, we need to have enough data, so any time something needs it, so you don't leave wires unused. If you look at the high bandwidth NoC that has been developed, for instance the Intel NoC prototypes, they have a lot of buffering, because many virtual channels require buffers, and that allows them to push it up to very high bandwidth. Otherwise, you will have low utilization of wires. So the buffering pushes up power consumption and area. In the last decade, substantial NoC research has targeted high bandwidth and low latency, more efficiently using buffers, so that the power and area overheads remain low.

[YS] Can you comment about timing issues being tighter compared to the general interconnect?

[LSP] In the old interconnect design, bandwidth was more of an issue. Supercomputers were already crossing many boards and chassis, so the time for crossing I/O pads and chips was already significant, adding a couple of pipeline stages to this [latency] is not a big deal. You have routers with more than 10 pipeline stages, and that was fine. But once you move to on die, the NoC connects caches, so you are comparing [the NoC latency] with cache access, for example the L2 [cache]. So you may have the L2 that is accessed in 5-10 clock cycles, depending on its size. Now that every hop that you go through the network becomes part of the critical path of the cache, so that adds to the memory access latency. So as a result, latency is more critical for the on-die network. There has been a lot of work in how you cannot just improve the latency in terms of cycle for going through these routers, but also ensuring that the clock cycle is what you can handle. So the number of pipeline stages should be reduced, but on top of that, the timing of your design should not be the one constraining the processor clock frequency. Of course there's also trade off [between timing] with power.

[YS] There's also another dimension which is reliability. As transistors become smaller, failure rates increase, we see increased soft errors in logic as well as caches. How does this affect NoC design?

[LSP] There has been quite a bit of research into NoC reliability. In terms of storage, people have tackled it by having redundancy in the buffering and CRC check just like typical checking errors in caches. And then for logic there is redundancy, for example relying on majority vote for arbitration. For links, they are pushing into network level retries and retransmissions. The issue there is the impact of missing packets on the overall system. Unlike other networks, the NoC is very integrated with the rest of the chip. For example in a shared memory chip, missing a certain type of messages causes problems with the cache coherence protocols, resulting in actual errors affecting programs. The ability to highlight which messages we can afford to lose versus which we cannot, and how to be able to roll back these changes along the way. Reliability becomes tougher to address in the NoC because of the issue of power. As we drive down power, we also drive down voltages. For example, for signaling in links, the more you drive down voltages, the higher bit error rate you get. So it boils down to how much do you trade off power saving versus error rates. Area is also becoming so tight, yet typical redundancy requires more area, adding two of it, three of it such as TMR [triple modular redundancy]. But that becomes tricky in NoC as we have tighter power and area constraints.

[YS] What do you think about some of the techniques that may be important in addressing these challenges in the future?

[LSP] I can plug some of what my group has done. We have been working in on-die networks since my PhD a long time ago. In terms of trying to ensure you get the performance in terms of bandwidth and latency but not trade off power, we have proposed different approaches shortcutting the router pipeline in order for you to still have the latency yet still share the wires. Our recent work includes SMART, single cycle multi-hop asynchronous traversal. The gist of it is that you have a couple of wires which allow you to set repeaters at each of these hops. Instead of having to stop at every router, which is the default in the past, we have repeaters. Each of these repeaters can be set dynamically one cycle in advance so that we can share these links in advance without actually stopping. What SMART allows is single cycle traversal across a large distance. We have shown 11-13 mm traversal within 1ns with 1GHz timing. This addresses performance issues of timing and latency while still allowing pushing the bandwidth of the interconnect, reducing idle cycles. Back to the power issue, what we have been researching on is how we can do that with limited buffers.

The intuition is basically that when traffic goes through, they don't have to stop, you actually save a lot of buffering while allowing high amount of traffic, similar to the transportation network (I like to use transportation network to illustrate interconnection network). So the technique that we have been looking into can maximize many of the metrics at the same time. Once you reduce buffers, you also reduce area, which simultaneously improve area and power, while still giving you performance in latency and bandwidth.

[YS] How do you deal with arbitration of traffic that share the NoC in that situation?

[LSP] All the complexity comes about from arbitrating, so the arbitration is not just between traffic coming in from my neighbors in the same cycle, but also from ones anywhere from how far I can fly. Now I have a lot more things that can come in. So you design multi-level arbitration. What it leverages is that logic is cheap as we go with Moore's law. No matter how we increase the sophistication of logic and arbitration, they are still a small percentage of the area, but the key is not to stretch the critical path. In our paper we study the layout of the wire. If it were just wires, we can actually push it all the way to 16mm in one cycle. But now you have to add muxes so that you have the ability to switch. Once you add those, it went down to 13mm. How far can you get in one ns, because you have to add more fan outs and muxes. And then you add arbitration, that cuts it down to 11mm. What we have recently done, we have taped this chip out with 64 routers in the NoC with 32nm. We have not done measurements yet. There has not been much fabrication, but I think chip prototyping really helps to establish the practicality of architectural ideas, and is needed to really push the NoC out to industry. There has to be a lot more demonstration of this to help industry appreciate academia's architecture ideas.

[YS] The idea reminds me of an article by Borkar and Chien where they argued using circuit switching instead of packet switching. Can you comment on that?

[LSP] Circuit switching involves setting up wires and dedicating these wires to the transmission, so typically circuit switching gives good bandwidth for that flow. Packet switching breaks down a message into smaller chunks, and then you reserve them on the fly. For circuit switching the issue is always how much you share the bandwidth, because first there is a long latency for setting up since you have go across the chip doing that, so basically it is a latency problem. If you have enough things to send then it produces high bandwidth, otherwise, it produces low bandwidth. The benefit of circuit switching is power. Once you go you don't have to wait, and you don't need buffers. Once you reserve, the latency is also guaranteed. There has been a lot of hybrid [of packet and circuit switching] along the way. SMART is basically an on-the-fly circuit switching, because there is no buffer and no stopping. It is a hybrid because you don't reserve the connection because any time someone comes in you have to contend for the channel with him. So it allows you to have most of the time as good latency as circuit switching but allows you to share the bandwidth. That has also been the focus of other research. The old circuit switching does not cut it. This points to the need to design NoC architectures that reap the benefits of circuit switching.

[YS] How do you think the design of the on-die network needs to change in the future?

[LSP] In the context of shared memory systems, regardless of the domain such as servers, laptops, embedded MPSoCs, etc., NoCs need to evolve from being just a communication fabric. Packet switching NoCs in general do not provide ordering or guarantee a certain level of service. So you have many virtual channels for different message classes, which allows you to have ordering between the requests and responses. The NoC itself is trying to meet point-to-point ordering and that adds to the overheads because every virtual network requires buffering, and as I mentioned buffering is in the critical path. We have looked how NoC can handle ordering as well. We have done several works in trying to implement cache coherence in the NoC. We have fabricated 36-core SCORPIO chip that was just published last year where we tried to demonstrate NoC is the most efficient place to handle ordering rather than right now which typically does ordering at the end point such as at the directory or at the cache controller. What we show is since the network sees all the traffic we can actually order some of that within the NoC at the interface. And that will help to address having packet switching within the shared memory system and especially as we get to MPSoC where interface is critical. Here, we cannot change the IP blocks but they require ordering in order to scale. The IP blocks assume they are connected to a bus, putting them in NoC challenges the functionality of these IP blocks. In our MIT SCORPIO chip, the main motivation is to show that we could actually build a NoC with good power, area, performance, and adheres to industry-standard ARM ACE protocol. We got PowerPC cores from Freescale that are complete black boxes that interface with ARM bus protocol, and we plug in a NoC that mimics the ordering within the NoC that connects to memory controllers from Cadence and cache controllers, and we do not change the controllers and that's the key. Hence in addition to performance, power, and area, I think we also have to handle compatibility and extensibility. With that, ordering is one of the key practical issues, since we don't want to custom design or redesign our IP blocks.

[YS] What do you think about emerging technologies such as 3D chips and optical interconnects?

[LSP] I haven't worked on 3D NoC, but I know there are many projects working on it. The key to what 3D would do is to put even more pressure on the NoC. The NoC has to supply a lot of bandwidth, and it has to be fast. The kind of saving grace right now is that a lot of the bottleneck is the off-die interface. The memory controllers struggle to supply enough data, so we can build a NoC that does not need to deal with a lot of bandwidth because not much data is coming in yet. The latency of the NoC is not that critical yet, since it still requires 100 cycles to go to the DRAM and back, so the pressure of bandwidth and performance has been relieved by the off die bottleneck. But with 3D, you solve the off die constraints, so you push the constraints to on die. Now we can provide a lot of data very quickly to hundreds of cores. NoC research has to show it can support that. Today we see research assuming only 2-4 memory controllers. Technically on die we have a lot of wires, so bandwidth on die should be very high. So if you want to scale to hundreds of cores, you have to have the NoC that can deliver that amount of bandwidth without violating the timing, power, and area constraints. Thus, I see 3D as really giving a kick to how much NoC research needs to push the state-of-the-art.

In photonics, there has been a lot of progress in the last 5-10 years. The number one thing is that photonics needs to work hand in hand with electronics research, and we see more of that in the last couple of years. I've been involved in several photonics projects trying to understand the trade offs in photonics design. The two communities need to come together because there are trade offs. For example, we can design the photonics to be low power using light sources with very low loss, but pushing complexity to the electronics because the interface to NoC in the multicore system is electronics. So there are issues that electronics has to address and a lot of it shows up at the photonics world, for example being able to disambiguate. We can trade off how good the photo-detector is, but that leads to a lot more noise for the electronic receiver to deal with so that 1s and 0s can be detected correctly. So the question is whether we boost the electronics side so that we better detect signal on the photonics side, or if we boost the photonics devices instead so we can use simpler receiver circuitry. This is the trade off that photonics and electronics researchers have to work together on. My group has done a bit of such opto-electronic modeling, with a tool called DSENT. For photonics to beat copper, we have to model a state-of-the-art electronic baseline. We collaborate with photonics and device researchers to look at the O2E [optical to electrical] interface.

We have to keep pushing the limit on the electronics side and determine when photonics can beat it. Ultimately it comes down to fundamental physics, photonics is distance oblivious in terms of latency, as opposed to electronics.

[YS] Li-Shiuan, I appreciate your time and insights in this interview. Thank you.

Youfeng Wu on Compilation for Parallel Multicore Architectures

Youfeng Wu is a principal scientist at Intel Corporation. He received his B.S. degree in Computer Science from Fudan University, Shanghai, China in 1982, and received his M.S. and Ph.D. degrees in Computer Science from Oregon State University in 1984 and 1988, respectively. Before he joined Intel in 1995, Youfeng worked for Sequent Computer Systems, Inc. for about 7 years. His current research interests include problem solving environments for high performance computing, persistent memory programming, binary translation, dynamic optimizations, and software/hardware collaborative techniques to enhance future generations of Intel processors. He was awarded the MICRO Hall of Fame award in 2012. He has served as a program committee member for PLDI, PACT, CGO, among others, and is currently the program co-chair for CGO '16. He holds more than 50 patents and has more than 60 publications.

[Yan Solihin] Youfeng, could you share your background with readers?

[Youfeng Wu] I have been a compiler developer, researcher, research manager, and the director of the Programming Systems Lab at Intel Labs. My professional career has been mainly in the areas of compiler optimization, binary translation, parallelism, performance and power efficiency, etc. Initially I worked on compilers for shared memory multiprocessors at Sequent Computer Systems. Of course during the early years most of the parallelism was multitasking. We didn't start by parallelizing single applications, rather we had multiple programs running in parallel with memory sharing among them implemented via manual efforts, typically targeted database transaction processing. At that time, the compiler's job was mainly to support manual parallelization. Manual parallelization was enabled by extensions to C/Fortran languages, with keywords such as shared, private, volatile, and directives for parallel constructs. Over time, we moved into auto-parallelization. The auto-parallelization tool we used was from KAI. It was a parallel pre-processor; given an application, the tool can generate parallel C/Fortran code, use OpenMP-like pragmas, such as parallel for, parallel doacross, and other directives. The major task from the compiler point of view is to map parallel directives to multiple processes, generate thread safe code for each process, and invoke runtime primitives for thread/process management, synchronization, memory sharing, etc. The KAI tool often wasn't able to find good parallelism, so people eventually had to implement parallelization manually.

Later, I joined Intel. Intel made a major shift from a powerful single core processor to simpler multicore. At that time people really worried whether we would have enough parallelism in applications to take advantage of multicore. In our research lab, we studied representative workloads, investigated their scalability, what kind of runtime management was required in order to achieve scalability, whether the scalability was strong or weak, and how compilers could parallelize these applications.

Even though many applications have inherent parallelism, they can't be auto-parallelized. The reason is quite interesting. Many real world applications, for example data mining applications, have plenty of parallelism, but they are difficult to parallelize automatically because of data and control dependency. It is also very hard to manage load balancing and locality automatically, so you need some help from parallelization experts.

We also attempted speculative parallelization. Automatic parallelization can only parallelize operations that are independent. With speculative parallelization, even when operations have dependencies, the compiler may still try to parallelize them. For general purpose applications, dependencies are not very clear to the compiler. The simple case is loop iterations. There are possible dependencies among them, and the compiler is uncertain how frequently they happen or if they will happen at all. In this case, the compiler can parallelize the loop speculatively. Meanwhile, you need a little bit of hardware support to detect the dependence if it happens at run time, and maintain speculative states and roll back in case the speculation is wrong. We spent quite some time in this research. But the results aren't quite good yet. One reason is the overhead, and the hardware support is not really there. For example, Intel only recently released hardware transactional memory support. Furthermore, even hardware transactional memory is not enough to support speculative parallelization efficiently. There is also the glass-jaw issue: when speculation is wrong, speculative parallelization may sometimes significantly degrade the performance.

[YS] Is the source of overheads coming more from the rollback, maintaining speculative states, or conflict detection?

[YFW] All three are important overheads. The first overhead is that you have to detect conflicts. Conflict detection overhead depends on the mechanism that is used. For example, if you have transactional memory, you have to have significant hardware support. Basically you need to detect any conflicts between threads. If you do it in software, you have to keep track of which memory locations you read or write, and which ones are changed by other threads. So conflict detection itself is complicated. Once you have conflict detected, you need to roll back, and roll back overhead can be quite high, but only occurs when a conflict happens. The third overhead is the speculative states. Until the speculative execution is confirmed to be valid, its result cannot be committed. During commit time, the speculative states need to be made globally visible. There is also the issue that in many programs, the parallel section is not big, in which case the overhead becomes important.

[YS] On the issue of granularity, there is a trade off, where if the speculative parallel region or transaction size is small, then the parallelization benefit may not be very high, but if the region is too large, buffering speculative states may be expensive or difficult. What's your thought about how the compiler can help?

[YFW] Transactional memory alone is not enough to do speculative parallelization. For example when you do speculative parallelization across loop iterations, the loop iterations need to complete in the original iteration order, while transactional memory does not provide ordering between threads. Either software or hardware extensions would be needed to allow some variables not to be tracked for conflicts, and enable synchronization by specifying order between iterations. Usually the speculative buffer is limited in size, and it is difficult for the compiler alone to decide the best granularity because it only has static information. For example, if we use an eight-way cache to buffer speculative state, and if nine speculative stores go to the same cache set, then there is going to be a cache overflow. The compiler does not know which stores go to different cache sets. So typically it's a trial and error process. You try to parallelize a certain region, and if there are many rollbacks, then you reduce the granularity. Static compilers may use profile information to help make decisions based on how frequent rollbacks are. We may also use a dynamic compiler, which at runtime will profile and decide parallel regions dynamically. We also proposed a "conditional commit" mechanism to manage the granularity of speculative regions dynamically, where hardware provides indications about the fullness of speculative resource, and software checks the indication to adapt optimizations and parallelization strategy.

Recently we have been looking at a higher level, as traditional compilers find it difficult to parallelize applications. One approach is to use domain-specific languages. You can think of a certain domain. For example, think of a graph traversal application. The application is difficult to parallelize automatically in languages like C and C++ because of the pointer chasing nature of the algorithm. If the compiler knows that the code is a breadth-first search, etc., the applications can be parallelized and executed in parallel. So a special domain specific program for graph traversal [in a DSL] can specify things like: here's a list of nodes, this is the operation on each node, the order of the nodes can be processed in breadth-first traversal, etc., then the compiler will have a much easier job to create a parallel version of the application. People who are familiar with graph algorithms know traversal well, and they can write their program using the DSL easily, so, the productivity benefit is there. The idea is related to parallel patterns. If you can write your code in certain patterns, then the compiler can parallelize them much more easily. Right now this is an area of active research. There are DSLs for graph analysis, image processing, and many others.

DSL can be embedded in a host language, such as Python, Scala, etc. So you may have a host language that supports multiple different domain extensions or patterns. As long as applications use a domain extension, they can be parallelized more. People can use the host language for anything else. That's a trend we have been studying. We may call it a problem solving environment. Within the environment, you can provide enough facilities so users can write programs easily and get parallel performance out of it via the compiler, runtime, and library.

[YS] What's your view of who the primary users of DSL are: the application programmers or library programmers?

[YFW] That's a very good question. We would need both to achieve good performance. Just using libraries alone – I don't think it is enough. DSL would enable domain programmers to provide algorithm level insights from domain knowledge, and compilers can either map it to libraries, if found, or generate target code. Some people have proposed doing everything with libraries, but that is hard for certain applications. For example, many applications involve computation with various Stencil patterns. It is hard to develop a generic and efficient library to support all the possible Stencil patterns. There is also the issue of library composition. You call one library and call the next library. How do you make sure the parallelism and locality between these two libraries are consistent? It's not easy because the library developer may not be able to anticipate all the usages. One library does not know how the data will be used by the next library. So it's hard to compose a parallel application from independent libraries. Solving this issue would need both domain knowledge in application and implementation knowledge in libraries so the compiler can help achieve the best performance. The domain knowledge would provide data access shapes and flow. The library developer would provide description about its implementation effects on data to library calls. So the compiler can coordinate domain level data flow among the library modules. With the DSL, the compiler can decide whether to parallelize code or call a parallel library. Parallelism can be contributed at the DSL source level by domain experts, at compile time by the compiler, and by calling into the library, which has parallel implementation.

[YS] In the past, the goal of the compiler was to generate machine instructions, it seems now it is moving to a higher level and the goal is to generate library calls that are optimum for the specific problem at hand.

[YFW] That's one way to look at it. Conceptually, the compiler can target at much higher abstraction by generating calls to libraries instead of generating individual instructions. On the other hand, there will always be some code that won't map to a library easily and has to be directly generated in parallel code. The compiler will try to map a parallel application to libraries as much as it can and parallelize the rest. Domain specific knowledge is needed to parallelize the application and select the proper libraries. Furthermore, most applications would need to invoke multiple libraries and compose the libraries to achieve optimum performance. This can be challenging.

[YS] In what way is the compilation of parallel programs different in multicore compared to traditional parallel systems such as SMP (symmetric multi-processor) or NUMA?

[YFW] Multicore is similar to SMP but on a single chip. It is a shared memory machine, but the cores also share the cache memory. That's a major difference. With traditional shared memory multiprocessors you mainly worry about memory sharing and coherence, but now in a multicore, for 4 cores they share the L2 cache, for 16 cores they also share the L3 cache. So now data sharing and synchronization are much cheaper and faster. It can give you much better performance by sharing data among cores in the same chip. But that causes new problems, as the caches are small and organized hierarchically. When you have a large system, you may have 4 cores sharing L2, 16 cores sharing the L3 cache, but for 32 cores they still have shared memory. Then locality and process migration becomes relatively more expensive. The users or compiler's runtime system, such as the thread scheduler, needs to know the locality of the data and allocate data in the shared cache so that they do not cross caches or nodes in order to minimize overheads.

[YS] In the multicore chip, what key parallel execution decisions should be relegated to software vs. hardware?

[YFW] From software point of view, they make two key high-level decisions. One is the data placement decision, another is the thread assignment decision – in which core a computation should be assigned and in which cache data should be placed. Those two decisions have to match. If they mismatch, you may see performance degradation. The compiler also needs to analyze the communication pattern between threads. That affects the runtime decision to minimize data movement. Hardware usually manages lower level decisions, e.g., cache replacement, coherence, etc. Software and hardware may coordinate in achieving better multicore resource management decisions, e.g., for power efficiency and energy saving.

[YS] Recently the emphasis of architecture design is on energy and power efficiency. Should a compiler be concerned about specific power efficiency issues, or should it consider them in the context of parallelization and parallel performance?

[YFW] We can look at the question from a different angle: why did we go to multicore design? One of the reasons we went to multicore is power. Power saving comes directly from the multicore paradigm. With multicore you can have a much higher throughput compared to a single core with the same power envelope. That was the original hypothesis that has been proven to be true. From that point of view, when the compiler tries to run parallel tasks, it automatically tries to save power, because we already try to distribute tasks to multiple cores which is more power efficient. However, multicore executions may involve duplication and communication overhead, so power management is still important. There are two areas that are important. One is should you run on fewer cores or on more cores? There is a trade off. If you find a region of code that has limited parallelism and would run faster on a few cores, even at higher power, versus using many cores, it may come out ahead in total energy.

The second area is related to heterogeneous cores. Accelerators are most power efficient for a certain task, the question is which task should run in there? Can you find the tasks to run on those accelerators? For example, you can think of GPU as an accelerator for graphics workloads. You can also run more general purpose applications on GPU. If you run some applications that do not fit well with GPU, the power efficiency could be worse. For any accelerators, if you don't put the right code to run on it, the power performance will be worse than if you ran on the other cores. Task scheduling for heterogeneous systems is challenging especially if you want to get good power performance benefit for general applications.

[YS] What are some of the promising techniques or important trends or challenges that compiler and runtime system designers have to consider in the future?

[YFW] A promising direction would be the co-design of language, compiler, library, and runtime, and for either general purpose or specific domains. In such a co-designed problem solving environment, applications can be developed productively, at different performance levels, tailored to users' expertise, whether you can do it fully automatically or you need users' help to get parallel performance. If we want to do it automatically, which means the language needs to be cleaned up so that we do not have too many dependencies, compared to languages like C or C++. If we do it semi-automatically, then the challenge is how we can add just enough language extensions to provide users with hints of what operations or regions can be run in parallel. Compilers can deduce the rest of the dependencies that will not occur, so the user won't have to do all the work. For example, an extension may be language support for users to specify parallel hints, and compilers may use those hints to parallelize. And the third dimension is what we discussed earlier about DSL. We need to provide certain DSL that is easy to use by domain experts. They know domain, but they do not want to deal with parallelization details. We may consider semi-automatic be an intermediate step because it is one that can be adopted in existing languages, such as C/C++ and Java. For best productivity and performance, probably DSL is needed.

[YS] Anything else you want to add?

[YFW] One new area is what would be the compiler's role in the cloud? Initially we focused on multicore CPU, which is a single node, but now more and more tasks run in the cloud. You don't know where your tasks will run. The issue with parallelization is not for an SMP anymore, but in distributed systems–how can we achieve parallelism, load balancing, quality of service, etc., in the cloud are very interesting issues. MapReduce and Hadoop are examples of cloud-based distributed programming systems, although they mainly target embarrassingly parallel problems. Another area is that when you have multiple tasks running on the system, the execution is much more complicated, so, the issue is how to make sure the programs run reliably. The compiler can help make debugging parallel programs easier. Traditionally people didn't worry much about it. But concurrent bugs take a lot of time to identify and fix. This prevents parallelism from being adopted in certain areas. If debugging takes a lot of time, people may not use parallelism and just run programs sequentially.

[YS] Youfeng, I appreciate your time and insights in this interview. Thank you.

Paolo Faraboschi on Future Memory and Storage Architectures of Datacentric Systems

Paolo is an HP Fellow in HP Labs, Systems Research lab. He joined HP in 1994 and worked in HP Labs Cambridge (MA) until 2003, where he was the principal archiect of a family of embedded VLIW cores (the Lx/ST200). He then started the HP Labs Barcelona research office in 2004, and led the group's research in system-level modeling and simulation until 2009. From 2010 to 2013, he worked on low-power specialized servers, first in research and then transfering the technology into real products as part of the Moonshot team. He moved to Palo Alto (CA) in 2014 to lead the architecture effort of The Machine project.

Paolo published over 70 technical papers, co-authored 28 granted patents, and the book *"Embedded Computing, a VLIW approach to architecture, compiler and tools"* In 2014, he became an IEEE Fellow for *"contributions to embedded processor architecture and SoC technology"* He received my PhD in Electrical Engineering and Computer Science from the University of Genoa (Italy) in 1993.

[Yan Solihin] Paolo, can you tell us your background: your prior and current research?

[Paolo Faraboschi] My research area is at the intersection of computing architecture, hardware and system software. In the last two decades, I've worked on four main technology areas: memory-centric computing (The Machine project), System-on-Chip (SoC) for hyperscale servers (the Moonshot project), modeling tools for large-scale computing systems (the COTSon simulator), and embedded VLIW (Very Long Instruction Word) processors and compilers (the Lx/ST200 project).

The work on SoC for servers (2009-2014) has been a core element of Moonshot by exploring the customization and specialization angle, and opened up the server market to a much larger variety of semiconductor players, including ARM vendors. The work on simulation (2004-2008) produced the COTSon simulation framework, developed in collaboration with AMD, which was widely used it in HP Labs for datacenter research, was open-sourced, and is currently used by several academic research projects. The work on embedded VLIWs (1994-2003) produced the Lx/ST200 family of embedded cores which was licensed to STMicroelectronics, found its way into HP printers and scanners, and shipped in hundreds of millions of video and audio consumer SoCs.

During my HP career, I've also had the opportunity to expand my research interests to other areas. For example, in 2003, I led a team developing a distributed processing system for content understanding (a precursor of today's unstructured data analytics) which was used to recapture the entire content (80 years) of "Time" magazine.

I am currently working on The Machine project at HP Labs, researching novel ways in which we can build memory-driven computing systems. Our objective is to break from the traditional CPU-centric organization and move towards a data-centric architecture that will provide significant advantages for big data applications.

[YS] Can you comment on why today we have deep memory hierarchy, from registers, various levels of caches, main memory, and storage system?

[PF] Deep memory hierarchies are all about hiding latency and saving energy by exploiting locality. CPUs have been getting faster and faster, up until ten years ago (around 2005), and then parallel, with multi- and many-core architecture organizations. However, the latency of DRAM and rotating media - the two pillars of the memory and storage hierarchy - has fundamentally remained constant. In terms of a load-to-use latency, DRAM connected through the DDRx protocol is more or less 100ns away, or about 200-300 core cycles, with a 2-3GHz clock. We should also remember that because precharge and activate are the energy hogs in accessing DRAM, row locality also significantly helps saving energy. Programmers and compilers have a really hard time scheduling useful work to hide hundreds of cycles of latency, so caches and deep hierarchies come to the rescue. Caches have been very effective when programs exhibit spatial and temporal locality, which has historically been true. Of course, having more threads does help diffuse this problem, but the increasing cost of tracking outstanding requests in the CPUs means you can't play this game arbitrarily.

The situation is very similar, at a different time scale, for storage. Fundamentally, a rotating disk is a device that operates at millisecond scale. That is millions of CPU cycles away. So, for all practical purposes, a programmer cannot possibly imagine scheduling work to hide disk latency. Compared to DRAM, disk latency is another four orders of magnitude slower. That is why operating systems have traditionally used DRAM to buffer (cache) disk accesses. Technologies like Flash, which operate at tens of microseconds latency, have recently appeared to partially close the gap, but not enough to justify removing the intermediate buffers.

If we look at enterprise-class storage systems, the situation is even more complex. They internally include a memory hierarchy similar to what is in a computing system. Storage systems, such as an enterprise drive arrays, aim at providing performance, uncompromised durability and rich features, while optimizing cost. They include a complex collection of SRAM and DRAM buffers, flash accelerators, and disk backing stores hidden behind a block, file, or object interface.

All this buffering and caching comes with increased performance uncertainty (when access patterns are not predictable), and additional burden on the programmer to optimize the data layout for locality. The result is that a large fraction of time is spent moving data up and down the memory/storage hierarchy, and wasting a lot of energy and bandwidth while doing so.

Clearly, this situation is not ideal, even though it has served us well for several decades on regular workloads exhibiting spatial and temporal locality. As we move into a big data world dominated by unstructured rich media information that needs to be analyzed and correlated, a deep memory hierarchy starts to become a performance liability, and a noticeable source of energy inefficiency. For example, several recent studies have shown that large last-level CPU caches are not as efficient for cloud workloads, and that there are better ways to build computing and memory hierarchies for the big data world.

[YS] Why do we distinguish memory versus storage? Will we continue to see them as separate, merged, continuing to coexist with perhaps an additional hybrid between them?

[PF] Historically, programmers have been trained to think about two completely separate data representations for the ephemeral working set of an application and its persistence state. The two representations are normally handled by separate program phases, have different fault domains, governance, serviceability, and sharing properties. So, the ephemeral state is usually allocated in volatile memory, and the persistent state goes to nonvolatile storage. If you think about it, this is primarily due to an "historical accident" caused by the fact that the dominant memory technology - DRAM - is volatile. Note that older main memory technologies, like core memory, were actually persistent, so had they become successful, maybe we'd be in a completely different situation today. Even if the memory technology were nonvolatile, compute-centric systems treat it as volatile, for example because they wipe it clean after a reboot, do not preserve enough information that lets you recover state across application or operating system crashes. Memory today is also "captive" to the CPU: it can only be accessed through the CPU and lives in the same single point of failure fault domain. On the other hand, storage must guarantee persistence and data availability, so it has to offer redundancy (e.g., RAID), serviceability (e.g., hot-swapping of media), multiple path, and rich data services (for scrubbing, auditing, consistency checks, mirroring, versioning, logging, etc.)

Because fast DRAM memory is volatile, programmers need to worry about periodically copying the program state to persistent media, so that important data is not lost in the presence of hardware or software failures, including application or operating system crashes. Unfortunately, in-memory representations tend to be non-portable. For example, they use application-specific virtual address pointers to link complex data structures, but these are only valid within an individual execution context. Making data persistent in a nonvolatile storage involves serializing and de-serializing the in-memory representation to a format that can be later recovered (or shared with other) by another process, or an entirely different computing system. This is where file systems, databases or object stores come into play, as they provide a standardized interface to convert in-memory representation to a persistent state. For example, in enterprise applications, it is common to push the persistent state to a database which is usually configured and managed for high availability and scalability. This way, the programmer of the business logic of the application doesn't need to worry about data integrity or application crashes, as long as the state is regularly made persistent to the database. Similarly, high-performance computing applications periodically checkpoint the relevant state explicitly to files (the so-called "defensive I/O" so that in case of a crash the state of the distributed application can be restored to the latest checkpoint. Of course, logging is an alternative to checkpointing, but similar considerations apply.

In general, even after half a century of programming, the situation has not fundamentally changed: in-memory and in-storage representations are different, and converting from one to the other requires an expensive serialization and de-serialization step. This is clearly suboptimal, especially when the memory technology is instantaneously nonvolatile and byte addressable, and every memory access could be made persistent to nonvolatile media with no involvement of a separate I/O operation. However, memory being *persistent* does not imply that the memory state is *consistent*, and that it can, for example, be interpreted correctly after an application or hardware crash. In order to do that, the programmer (or runtime) needs to run additional bookkeeping, to ensure that enough metadata is preserved to be able to recover a consistent state of memory after a failure.

From the point of view of software, the distinction between memory and storage is fairly clear, so there's an argument that they will remain separate and coexist for a long time. However, performance considerations and new technologies conspire to blur them. An example is the *memcached* layer that has appeared to improve the scalability of databases in large web services, and can be considered an example of hybrid system. *Memcached* only caches and replicates information that already is in the database, so strictly speaking it is a volatile layer. However, if the *memcached* layer is down, data becomes unavailable to the vast majority of clients because of the database limited scalability, so for all practical purposes the system is not operable. So, programmers need to be aware of the caching layer and plan accordingly.

[YS] What are some of the technical and business challenges in scaling current memory and storage technologies?

[PF] If we take a step back, it's pretty clear that memory and storage are foundational technologies that shape the entire IT industry, including hardware, software, and services. In 2013, memory and storage components represented about $100B of industry spend. Today, we are seeing the emergence of multiple customer-driven and technology-driven tectonic shifts.

After 50 years of dominance, DRAM memory is at an inflection point, having to reconcile the need of providing performance and capacity in the face of stagnant devices and a consolidating business environment. In simple terms, the technology challenges facing DRAM come from the shrinking process geometries that reduce the amount of electrical charge we can store in a memory cell, no matter how creative we can be in the manufacturing process of building deeper and deeper *trench capacitors*. On the business side, the number of DRAM manufacturers has been steadily decreasing. In 1985 there were over 20 manufacturers, and there are practically only 3 today. Manufacturers respond to market forces, and the dominance of mobile devices is causing a massive R&D investment shift towards low-power memory (such as LPDDR) and away from high-end systems.

Laws of physics dictate some of the other challenges of high-performance memory systems: it is impossible to provide high bandwidth, low latency and large capacity at the same time. So, when latency and bandwidth are important, memory systems are fragmenting towards a multiple-tier organization: a performance tier (small, parallel, and tightly co-packaged with compute) and a capacity tier (large, serially attached, and possibly shared). Avoiding to over complicate the programming model is the other challenge. NUMA is already bad enough in multi-socket systems today, and very few programmers know how to manage data locality beyond simple inner loops and array tiles. When dealing with new big data workload patterns that are much less well behaved, dealing with multiple-tier memory systems is an even harder challenge.

Storage is all about providing data availability, but it's difficult to generalize: different computing domains have a completely different view of storage and its challenges.

In battery-powered systems, making data persistent to local storage is a fundamental requirement. Would you ever buy a laptop, tablet or phone that lost its data when it run out of power? This may be partially changing with ubiquitous connectivity where state is persistent directly to the cloud, but local storage is still required to store at least the operating system and occasional offline data. The challenges here are speed and persistence at low power, and this is probably where new NVM will first appear.

Traditional enterprise storage systems focus on data availability, governance and rich services. The cost of losing, or not being able to access, business critical data is enormous, so enterprise storage systems aim at increasing the MTTF (mean time to failure) through redundancy, and decreasing the MTTR (mean time to recovery) through replication, backups, and disaster recovery setup. Providing performance and rich features at reasonable cost are the challenges.

Finally, hyperscale storage has emerged as an alternative to traditional systems. In large scale-out infrastructure with hundreds of thousands of servers, it is possible to build high availability services by replicating data on commodity storage blocks. While the MTTF of each individual system can be low, one can achieve the desired availability with a software layer that sprinkles enough copies around. In this environment, cost and energy efficiency are the key challenges.

[YS] What Non-Volatile Memory technologies are promising? What benefits can they provide compared to traditional memory systems?

[PF] First and foremost, *necessity is the mother of invention*: the key reason why all memory manufacturers are investing in NVM technologies is because DRAM and Flash are no longer scaling with process geometries. Many, including myself, believe that the transition beyond DRAM and Flash is inevitable. How long this transition will take is much less certain; we are definitely talking about several years of coexistence, and different transition rates depending on usage models, packaging options, and where the cost/benefit tradeoffs lie in the different memory markets. In other words, the single most important benefit that new memory technologies bring to the table is that they scale better than DRAM and Flash with smaller process geometries. However, this benefit will not materialize overnight, and that is one of the core business challenges and a good example of Christensen's "*Innovator's dilemma*" at work. Ultimately, the R&D investment pool to develop new memory technologies is finite, and shrinking in a consolidating market. While the combined features of new technologies remain inferior to the incumbents (DRAM and NAND Flash), it is difficult for a manufacturer to massively shift investments to the new process.

In terms of contenders, I think that we are pretty much down to three: STT-RAM (Spin-Transfer Torque), PCM (Phase-Change Memory), and Memristor. STT-RAM utilizes the spin-alignment of electrons to define its state through a Magnetic-Tunnel Junction (MTJ). STT-RAM is very fast and shows essentially unlimited *endurance* [the number of times a memory cell can be programmed reliably], but has relatively short *data retention* [the length of time correct data is retained by a memory cell reliably] and low density. A PCM memory cell consists of a chalcogenide material between two electrodes, which changes phase (crystalline or amorphous) to define its state with different resistance. PCM is moderately fast and dense, but requires high write energy, shows resistance drift that limits the endurance, and poses significant challenges in the Silicon manufacturing process. Memristors are Resistive RAM (ReRAM) devices that operate through the movement of positively charged oxygen ions within a metal-oxide junction. Memristors show very long stability and write endurance, are very fast and dense (also because they can be layered on the same device, effectively approaching an F^2 density, the best one can achieve with single-level cells in a process with feature size F) and improve their behavior as the device shrinks in size. While the jury is still out on the winning technology, I believe that Memristors show a very strong combination of fundamental properties that cover a very large range of uses and domains.

Interestingly enough, the nonvolatile property of new memory technologies is, to a certain extent, a secondary benefit, which not all markets value equally. As we already discussed, the mobile market is likely to be very interested in fast NVM before everyone else, even at a lower density, because of the potential energy savings coming from reduced traffic when the main memory can be treated as persistent, and the reduced refresh energy compared to DRAM. The server and hyperscale markets, however, can use other mechanisms to achieve durability at scale, so NVM adoption could be delayed until some of the other characteristics (density, cost per bit, or energy per bit) significantly surpass existing alternatives. Energy efficiency, especially compared to DRAM, could be the most interesting short term benefit, especially as an ever increasing share of web content is stored in the caching layer.

Finally, it's worth mentioning that some of these new NVM technologies also show promise to combine compute and memory in the same device. For example, researchers have shown that Memristors can store information and at the same time perform computation that could be used to implement neural networks. While this work is still in the realm of basic research today, it is important to overcome the traditional compute/memory barriers and truly point towards a data-centric model in the future.

[YS] With faster NVM integrated into the memory, in what way the memory will the architecture need to change?

[PF] The first component of the memory architecture that needs to change is the memory controller. Since around 2005, memory controllers have been integrated with mainstream microprocessors, to reduce the latency and take advantage of higher SoC integration. However, this has caused significant stagnation in the evolution of memory protocols (it took eight years to develop the DDR4 standard!), and has been a barrier to the independent evolution of memory and compute. I believe it is essential to rethink this relationship, if we want to accelerate the adoption of new NVM technologies. For example, we could split the work involved in issuing a memory operation in the high-level transaction protocol (residing with the processor) and the media-specific operations (residing with the memory). The CPU-side controller could concentrate in adding value where it matters (such as caching, pipelining, prefetching, or QoS). The media-side controller could deal with the media specific dependences (such as timing, addressing, buffer optimizations, or error handling). Assuming the intermediate protocol becomes a standard, the two individual systems (CPU and memory) could evolve independently at their own pace.

Another aspect that needs to change is the way in which programmers can communicate their intention of making data persistent to the processors through the instruction set. One of the challenges of a deeply stratified memory hierarchy is that programmers need to explicitly set consistency points to ensure that a cached change of a memory location reaches the appropriate visibility point for all the observers. Today, the cache coherence protocol comes to the rescue, and as long as programs correctly specify point-of-coherence barriers, hardware can protect the programmer from the vast majority of the data races. However, as NVM appears in the memory system, the instruction set needs to provide additional mechanism for the program to communicate that a memory change needs to be made persistent to the device itself, and ensure that it was written correctly. CPU vendors have recently started to acknowledge this need by adding operations that guarantee that a memory change has reached the *point of persistence*. Together with efficient cache flushing mechanisms, programs will issue these new operations when the memory state needs to be made durable. I believe this is a first step, and more research work will be needed to fully capture and optimized all the possible scenarios, including how to deal with consistence, and most importantly, failures.

As we converge storage and memory in a single NVM tier, we do need to pay attention to the properties that storage systems require today, such as sharing, high-availability, redundancy, resilience, serviceability, rich services. Memory today is captive to the CPU, in the sense that it lives in the same fault domain, and is not accessible if the CPU is down or the OS is stuck. This scenario would be unacceptable for a storage system. If we want to treat an NVM component as a truly converged memory/storage devices, we need to come up with an architecture that enables these properties. For example, we have to add resilience support (such as RAID or erasure codes).

We have to be able to service memory by hot-swapping a defective (or worn out) module without the system going down. We also have to provide alternative paths to memory that can work even in presence of a faulty processor. There are very disruptive changes to the memory architecture that involve changing the protocol beyond DDR4, the physical connection beyond DIMMs, and the logical connection beyond direct-attached architectures. I believe this is going to be a very fertile area for research in the next several years, until some standard emerges.

Finally, if we look a bit further out into a memory-centric future, we can also anticipate that traditional memory management functionality may move from the processor-centric node OS into memory-side controllers, accelerators and more novel distributed computational elements to form scale-out services. These services may include allocation, deallocation, protection, translation, scrubbing, error handling and recovery, data management.

[YS] With faster NVM integrated into the storage system, in what way will the file system need to change?

[PF] File systems have historically been optimized for rotating media, which are millisecond-scale devices. So, they include several levels of caching, buffering and metadata handling that adds up to tens of microseconds of latency. While this is perfectly fine for a device that responds with a 100x longer latency, it is clearly unacceptable for memory-speed NVM. Several research efforts in industry and academia are already tackling this problem, by removing the intermediate buffering layers, and going directly to NVM media after a thin layer implementing a high level interface.

The second area that will need a second look is the POSIX interface. While new systems have moved beyond POSIX completely by adopting object-based interfaces, many important applications – the most obvious one being Linux itself – deeply rely on a POSIX file system. With NVM in the memory system, we will have to rethink which of the POSIX interfaces we want to preserve. Ideally, what we want for best performance are a few highly optimized operations: for example open, memory map, and close. Other interfaces, for example those that are non-commutative, create several performance headaches, and it would be great to deprecate them. However, legacy applications will require a more extended subset, while still eliminating the DRAM buffer cache, and preserving atomicity and ordering properties.

[YS] What programming models, and relatedly persistence and failure models, may be needed if we want to take advantage of byte addressable fast NVM?

[PF] The answer to this question goes back to the consistent/persistent issue mentioned before. If we want persistent memory to be consistent, especially in the presence of failures, we must enforce a transactional, all-or-nothing update model of NVM-resident state. In order to achieve this, I can think of two complementary approaches.

Programs can be written without being aware of NVM, and let a middleware abstraction (such as a file system, object store, database or transparent checkpointing) take care of handling NVM. This encapsulates the durability and fault handling concerns, and as long as we assume the availability of an NVM-optimized set of libraries, we can easily port legacy programs, or write new program using familiar legacy APIs.

However, this leaves a lot of performance on the table and I expect that over time programs will become cognizant of the existence of fast byte addressable NVM directly. To exploit the persistence properties of NVM, programs written for NVM will have to borrow transactional concepts from databases. For example, recent research has shown that we can extend locking primitives with durability semantics, at least for data-race free program (for example, written using C++11 semantics), and automatically maintain a globally consistent state even in the presence of failures. In simple terms, a program can be written to use persistent regions addressed through a root pointer, and *failure atomic sections*, where updates to a persistent regions are guaranteed to be atomic and recoverable through a combination of compiler and runtime support.

In the last five years, we have seen a proliferation of research efforts addressing these, and more, challenges of programming for NVM. I believe this is just the beginning: the tectonic shifts in the memory system will bring changes of such a magnitude, and over a short period of time, that will fundamentally reshape the IT industry as we know it.

[YS] Paolo, I appreciate your time and insights in this interview. Thank you.

[PF] By the way, I would like to thank my colleagues Al Davis and Rob Schreiber for providing deep and useful feedback.

Bibliography

[1] N.R. Adiga, et al. An Overview of the BlueGene/L Supercomputer. *Proceedings of the Conference on High Performance Networking and Computing*, 2002.

[2] H. Al-Zoubi, A. Milenkovic, and M. Milenkovic. Performance Evaluation of Cache Replacement Policies for the SPEC CPU2000 Benchmark Suite. In *Proc. of the 42nd ACM Southeast Conference*, April 2004.

[3] G.S. Almasi and A. Gottlieb. *Highly Parallel Computing*. Benjamin-Cummings, Redwood City, CA, 1989.

[4] AMD. AMD Opteron Processor for Servers and Workstations. *http://www.amd.com/us-en/Processors/ ProductInformation/0,,30_8796_8804,00.html*, 2005.

[5] AMD. Advanced Synchronization Facility - Proposed Architectural Specification. *http://developer.amd.com/wordpress/media/2013/09/45432-ASF_Spec_2.1.pdf*, Publication 45432(Revision 2.1), 2009.

[6] B.M. Beckmann, M.R. Marty, and D.A. Wood. ASR:Adaptive Selective Replication for CMP Caches. In *Proc. of the International Symposium on Microarchitecture*, 2006.

[7] L.A. Belady. A study of replacement algorithms for a virtual-storage computer. *IBM Systems Journal*, 5:2, 1966.

[8] S. Borkar, R. Cohn, G. Cox, and T. Gross. Supporting systolic and memory communication in iwarp. *ACM SIGARCH Computer Architecture News*, 18(3a):70–81, 1990.

[9] Jason F. Cantin, James E. Smith, Mikko H. Lipasti, Andreas Moshovos, and Babak Falsafi. Coarse-grain coherence tracking: RegionScout and region coherence arrays. *IEEE Micro*, pages 70–79, January 2006.

[10] C. Cascaval, L. DeRose, D.A. Padua, and D.A. Reed. Compile-Time Based Performance Prediction. *Lecture Notes in Computer Science: Languages and Compilers for Parallel Computing*, 1863(2000):365–379, 2000.

[11] J. Chang and G.S. Sohi. Cooperative caching for chip multiprocessors. In *Proc. of the 33rd International Symposium on Computer Architecture*, pages 264–276, 2006.

[12] M. Chaudhuri and M. Heinrich. The Impact of Negative Acknowledgments in Shared Memory Scientific Applications. *IEEE Transactions on Parallel and Distributed Systems*, 15(2), 2004.

[13] T.F. Chen and J.L. Baer. Reducing Memory Latency via Non-Blocking and Prefetching Cache. In *Proc. of the 5th International Conference on Architectural Support for Programming Languages and Operating Systems*, pages 51–61, October 1992.

[14] S. Cho and L. Jin. Managing Distributed, Shared L2 Caches through OS-Level Page Allocation. In *Proc. of the 39th Annual IEEE/ACM International Symposium on Microarchitecture*, pages 455–468, 2006.

[15] B.W. Coon, J.E. Lindholm, P.C. Mills, and J.R. Nickolls. Processing an indirect branch instruction in a simd architecture, 2010. US Patent 7,761,697.

[16] A. Danowitz et al. CPU DB Database. *http://cpudb.stanford.edu/*, 2013.

[17] A. Danowitz, K. Kelley, J. Mao, J.P. Stevenson, and M. Horowitz. CPU DB: Recording Microprocessor History. *Communications of the ACM*, 55(4), 2012.

[18] M.J. Flynn. A taxonomy for computer architectures. *IEEE Transactions on Computers*, C-21(9):948–60, Sept 1972.

[19] K. Gharachorloo, M. Sharma, S. Steely, and S.V. Doren. Architecture and design of alphaserver gs320. In *Proc. of the International Conference on Architectural Support for Programming Languages and Operating Systems*, 2000.

[20] F. Guo and Y. Solihin. An Analytical Model for Cache Replacement Policy Performance. In *Proc. of ACM SIGMETRICS/Performance 2006 Joint International Conference on Measurement and Modeling of Computer System*, 2006.

[21] Daniel Hackenberg, Daniel Molka, and Wolfgang E. Nagel. Comparing cache architectures and coherency protocols on x86-64 multicore smp systems. In *International Symposium on Microarchitecture*, 2009.

[22] A. Hartstein, V. Srinivasan, T.R. Puzak, and P.G. Emma. On the Nature of Cache Miss Behavior: Is It $\sqrt{2}$? *The Journal of Instruction-Level Parallelism*, 10, 2008.

[23] Allan Hartstein and Thomas R. Puzak. The optimum pipeline depth for a microprocessor. In *ISCA*, pages 7–13, 2002.

[24] J.L. Hennessy and D.A. Patterson. *Computer Architecture: A Quantitative Approach*. Morgan-Kaufmann Publishers, Inc., 3rd edition, 2003.

[25] G. Hinton, D. Sager, M. Upton, D. Boggs, D. Carmean, A. Kyker, and P. Roussel. The Microarchitecture of the Pentium 4 Processor. *Intel Technology Journal*, First Quarter, 2001.

[26] Hypertransport Consortium. Hypertransport I/O Technology Comparison with Traditional and Emerging I/O Technologies. *White Paper*, June 2004.

[27] IBM. IBM Power4 System Architecture White Paper. http://www-1.ibm.com/servers/eserver/pseries/hardware/ whitepapers/power4.html, 2002.

[28] ITRS. International Technology Roadmap for Semiconductors: 2005 Edition, Assembly and Packaging. *http://www.itrs.net/Links/2005ITRS/AP2005.pdf*, 2005.

[29] J. Dongarra. The LINPACK Benchmark: an Explanation. *Lecture Notes in Computer Science*, 297, 1987.

[30] Aamer Jaleel, Eric Borch, Malini Bhandaru, Simon C. Steely Jr., and Joel S. Emer. Achieving non-inclusive cache performance with inclusive caches: Temporal locality aware (tla) cache management policies. In *MICRO*, 2010.

[31] D.N. Jayasimha, B. Zafar, and Y. Hoskote. On-Chip Interconnection Networks: Why They are Different and How to Compare Them. *Platform Architecture Research, Intel Corporation*, 2006.

[32] Natalie D. Enright Jerger, Li-Shiuan Peh, and Mikko H. Lipasti. Circuit-switched coherence. In *Proceedings of the Second ACM/IEEE International Symposium on Networks-on-Chip*, NOCS '08, pages 193–202, 2008.

[33] N. Jouppi. Improving Direct-Mapped Cache Performance by the Addition of a Small Fully-Associative Cache and Prefetch Buffers. In *Proc. of the 17th International Symposium on Computer Architecture*, pages 364–373, May 1990.

[34] M. Kharbutli, K. Irwin, Y. Solihin, and J. Lee. Using Prime Numbers for Cache Indexing to Eliminate Conflict Misses. In *Proc of the International Symposium on High-Performance Computer Architecture*, 2004.

[35] C. Kim, D. Burger, and S.W. Keckler. Wire-Delay Dominated On-Chip Caches. In *Proc. of the International Conference on Architectural Support for Programming Languages and Operating Systems*, 2002.

[36] R. Kumar, V. Zyuban, and D.M. Tullsen. Interconnection in Multi-Core Architectures: Understanding Mechanisms, Overheads, and Scaling. In *Proc. of the International Symposium on Computer Architecture*, 2005.

[37] L. Lamport. How to Make Multiprocessor Computer that Correctly Executes Multiprocess Programs. *IEEE Transactions on Computers*, C-29(9):690–691, 1979.

[38] J. Laudon and D. Lenoski. The SGI Origin: a ccNUMA highly scalable server. In *Proceedings of the International Symposium on Computer Architecture*, 1997.

[39] F. Liu, F. Guo, S. Kim, A. Eker, and Y. Solihin. Characterization and Modeling of the Behavior of Context Switch Misses. In *Proc. of the International Conference on Parallel Architectures and Compilation Techniques*, 2008.

[40] M.K. Martin, M.D. Hill, and D.A. Wood. Token Coherence: Decoupling Performance and Correctness. In *Proc. of the International Symposium on Computer Architecture*, 2003.

[41] M.R. Marty and M.D. Hill. Virtual Hierarchies to Support Server Consolidation. In *Proc. of the International Symposium on Computer Architecture*, 2007.

[42] R. L. Mattson, J. Gecsei, D. Slutz, and I. Traiger. Evaluation Techniques for Storage Hierarchies. *IBM Systems Journal*, 9(2), 1970.

[43] E. McCreight. The Dragon Computer System: an Early Overview. *Technical Report, Xerox Corporation*, 1984.

[44] S. Palacharla, N.P. Jouppi, and J.E. Smith. Quantifying the Complexity of Superscalar Processors. *University of Wisconsin Technical Report*, (1328), 1996.

[45] S. Palacharla and R. Kessler. Evaluating Stream Buffers as a Secondary Cache Replacement. In *Proc. of the 21st International Symposium on Computer Architecture*, pages 24–33, April 1994.

[46] M.S. Papamarcos and J.H. Patel. A low overhead coherence solution for multiprocessors with private cache memories. In *Proc. of the International Symposium on Computer Architecture*, pages 348–454, 1984.

[47] Fabrizio Petrini, Darren J. Kerbyson, and Scott Pakin. The case of the missing supercomputer performance: Achieving optimal performance on the 8,192 processors of asci q. In *Proceedings of the 2003 ACM/IEEE Conference on Supercomputing*, SC '03, New York, NY, USA, 2003. ACM.

[48] M.K. Qureshi. Adaptive spill-receive for robust high-performance caching in cmps. In *Proceedings of the 15th International Symposium on High Performance Computer Architecture*, pages 45–54, Feb. 2009.

[49] B. Rogers, A. Krishna, G. Bell, K. Vu, X. Jiang, and Y. Solihin. Scaling the bandwidth wall: Challenges in and avenues for cmp scaling. In *Proc. of International Symposium on Computer Architecture*, 2009.

[50] Valentina Salapura, Matthias Blumrich, and Alan Gara. Design and Implementation of the Blue Gene/P Snoop Filter. In *Proc. of the International Symposium on High-Performance Computer Architecture*, 2008.

[51] A. Samih, A. Krishna, and Y. Solihin. Evaluating Placement Policies for Managing Capacity Sharing in CMP Architectures with Private Caches. *ACM Transactions on Architecture and Code Optimization*, 2011.

[52] Ahmad Samih, Ren Wang, Anil Krishna, Christian Maciocco, Charlie Tai, and Yan Solihin. Energy-efficient interconnect via router parking. In *Proceedings of the 2013 IEEE 19th International Symposium on High Performance Computer Architecture (HPCA)*, HPCA '13, pages 508–519, Washington, DC, USA, 2013. IEEE Computer Society.

[53] B. Sinharoy, R. Kalla, W.J. Starke, H.Q. Le, R. Cargnoni, J.A. Van Norstrand, B.J. Ronchetti, J. Stuecheli, J. Leenstra, G.L. Guthrie, D.Q. Nguyen, B. Blaner, C.F. Marino, E. Retter, and P. Williams. Ibm power7 multicore server processor. *IBM J. Res. Dev.*, 55(3):191–219, May 2011.

[54] Y. Solihin. Cache coherence directory in multi-processor architectures. *US Patent Application 20140082297*, 2012.

[55] Y. Solihin. Multi-granular cache coherence. *WO Patent Application WO/2014/065802*, 2012.

[56] Y. Solihin. Aggregating cache eviction notifications to a directory. *US Patent Application 20140229680*, 2013.

[57] Y. Solihin. Hybrid routers in multicore architectures. *US Patent application US 14/005,520*, 2013.

[58] Y. Solihin. Multi-core processor cache coherence for reduced off-chip traffic. *US Patent 8,615,633*, 2013.

[59] Y. Solihin. Virtual cache directory in multi-processor architectures. *US Patent Application 20140223104*, 2013.

[60] K. Strauss, X. Shen, and J. Torrellas. UncoRq: Unconstrained Snoop Request Delivery in Embedded-Ring Multiprocessors. In *Proc. of the International Symposium on Microarchitecture*, 2007.

[61] G.E. Suh, S. Devadas, and L. Rudolph. A New Memory Monitoring Scheme for Memory-Aware Scheduling and Partitioning. In *Proc. of International Symposium on High Performance Computer Architecture*, pages 117–128, 2002.

[62] A.S. Tanenbaum. *Modern Operating Systems*. Prentice Hall, 1992.

[63] Michael B. Taylor. Is dark silicon useful? Harnessing the four horsemen of the coming dark silicon apocalypse. In *Design Automation Conference*, 2012.

[64] Devesh Tiwari and Yan Solihin. Modeling and analyzing key performance factors of shared memory mapreduce. In *IPDPS*, pages 1306–1317, 2012.

[65] Ping Xiang, Yi Yang, and Huiyang Zhou. Warp-level divergence in gpus: Characterization, impact, and mitigation. In *20th IEEE International Symposium on High Performance Computer Architecture, HPCA 2014, Orlando, FL, USA, February 15-19, 2014*, pages 284–295. IEEE Computer Society, 2014.

[66] Yi Yang, Ping Xiang, Jingfei Kong, and Huiyang Zhou. A GPGPU compiler for memory optimization and parallelism management. In Benjamin G. Zorn and Alexander Aiken, editors, *Proceedings of the 2010 ACM SIGPLAN Conference on Programming Language Design and Implementation, PLDI 2010, Toronto, Ontario, Canada, June 5-10, 2010*, pages 86–97. ACM, 2010.

[67] M. Zhang and K. Asanovic. Victim Replicatoin: Maximizing Capacity while Hiding Wire Delay in Tiled Chip Multiprocessors. In *Proc. of the International Symposium on Computer Architecture*, 2005.

Index

United States

r Publisher Services